GLOBAL LABOUR FLEXIBIL.

Global Labour Flexibility

Seeking Distributive Justice

Guy Standing

First published in Great Britain 1999 by
MACMILLAN PRESS LTD
Houndmills, Basingstoke, Hampshire RG21 6XS and London
Companies and representatives throughout the world

A catalogue record for this book is available from the British Library.

ISBN 0–333–77314–4 hardcover
ISBN 0–333–77652–6 paperback

First published in the United States of America 1999 by
ST. MARTIN'S PRESS, INC.,
Scholarly and Reference Division,
175 Fifth Avenue, New York, N.Y. 10010

ISBN 0–312–22525–3

Library of Congress Cataloging-in-Publication Data
Standing, Guy.
Global labour flexibility : seeking distributive justice / Guy
Standing.
   p.   cm.
Includes bibliographical references and index.
ISBN 0–312–22525–3 (cloth)
1. Quality of work life.   2. Industrial relations.   3. Foreign
trade and employment.   4. Labor.   5. Distributive justice.
I. Title.
HD6955.S783   1999
331.25—dc21   99–21891
                                                          CIP

© International Labour Organization 1999

This book is printed on paper suitable for recycling and made from fully managed and
sustained forest sources.

10   9   8   7   6   5   4   3   2   1
08   07   06   05   04   03   02   01   00   99

Printed and bound in Great Britain by Antony Rowe Ltd, Chippenham, Wiltshire

Contents

List of Figures

List of Tables

Preface

A preface should titillate without giving too much away. With a long book, the first task is rather daunting, the second in principle rather less so. This book is an attempt to develop a perspective for a work-based strategy for distributive justice, recognising that globalisation, technological change and the growth of flexible labour markets around the world have fundamentally changed the feasible institutional structures.

The book consists of five parts. In principle, each could be read in isolation from the others; readers may have an interest in one set of issues and not others. Underlying the analysis and set of policy proposals is a Polanyian framework, inspired by Karl Polanyi's *The Great Transformation*, and while working on it I actually used as a 'working title' for the book *The Second Transformation*, which I would not dare use for what is a modest effort by comparison with a great work by that great scholar. Nevertheless, that title would capture the essence of the theme. Slightly modifying Polanyi's terminology for our purposes, in the development of capitalism since the eighteenth century there has been a series of eras of economic upheavals in which the economy has been disembedded from society and in which old forms of distribution have been disrupted, while new forms of labour have emerged in a period of pressure on many groups to be 'flexible'. These changes intensify inequalities and insecurity, until they threaten the system's sustainability, at which point the state acts to re-embed the economy in society through new redistributive mechanisms suited to the new forms of production and labour arrangements. In the twentieth century, the post-1945 era is described in this book as the *era of statutory regulation*, which was a period of relative stability and advancing security, whereas the post-1975 period is described as the *era of market regulation*, in which economic upheaval and growing flexibility have been the primary characteristics. The challenge now is to find a synthesis in which institutions and policies combine the positive elements of these two eras, adhering to the principles of distributive justice, dynamic efficiency and deliberative democracy.

There will be readers who object that too much is compressed into a single framework, not giving due recognition to the varieties of socio-economic arrangements that undoubtedly exist. For some purposes, I would agree. However, we need an international *framework* for moving the debate on distributive justice and work policy forward. Others have made attempts to do this, and it is hoped that the contributions and views are fully and fairly recognised in the text and footnotes. Two other points should be made defensively. Although many of the data cited and the references relate to industrialised countries, the focus is global, and many of the points are relevant for industrialising economies. In the post-war era, two development models were preferred to developing countries for governments to follow as a long-term goal. In the 1980s and 1990s a single model has been proferred. Now, around the world, there are hybrids of all three, with soul-searching by policymakers on which directions to follow. In this sense, we do indeed live in interesting times, in which everywhere we should have many more questions than we have definitive answers. In the international arena, debate must be encouraged, recognising that we are in an era of experimentation and uncertainty. Those who stifle debate are usually those who fear debate. Views must be developed and subject to scrutiny through public exposure and subsequent reflection. Received wisdom must not be regarded as sacrosanct. As the great historian R.H. Tawney noted, *'The certainties of one age are the problems of the next.'*

The plan of the book is as follows:

Part I is conceptual, and is unlikely to be of interest to those concerned with policy; chapter 2 could be omitted without affecting the flow of the argument, bearing in mind the need to recognise the importance of different forms of labour regulation and control.

Part II is about the growth of labour flexibility in the latter part of the twentieth century and the factors that contributed to that development. Those familiar with the forms of flexibility may wish to skip chapter 4, although it is hoped that this succeeds in synthesising the international trends, bringing together many data as well as developing a conceptual perspective on flexibility.

Part III is about forms of labour-related security and insecurity. Chapters 5 through 8 present the stylised outcomes associated with globalising, flexible labour markets. They should set the agenda for policy strategies. Some parts of these chapters are longer than a general reader would wish because some of the stylised facts have been matters of analytical controversy among economists and statisticians. This particularly concerns the vexed and relatively well-researched issue of *employment insecurity*.

Following those chapters, Part IV considers several policies that have been proposed in the 1990s by libertarians and the 'new paternalists'. Finally, Part V presents an alternative strategy for pursuing distributive justice and dynamic efficiency, based on combining occupational security, voice regulation and deliberative democracy. Chapter 11 hinges on the preceding Parts, and recognises the need to combine flexibility with security, and dynamic efficiency with justice.

Note

Italics are used for emphasis of key concepts. Words in quotation marks are those subject to debate or several interpretations.

Acknowledgements

This book has had a long gestation, and has benefited from comments, assistance or insights from many people, who have helped in one way or another, often in conversations and seminars. Thanks are due to Sam Aaronowitch, Richard Anker, Angela Brown, Sarah Cierans, Louise Corselli, Colin Crouch, Zsuzsa Ferge, Katherine McFate, Gloria Moreno, Mario Nuti, Claus Offe, Ilona Ostner, Philippe Van Parijs, Samir Radwan, Derek Robinson, Zafeer Shaheed, Ajit Singh, Stephen Smith, Walter van Trier, Frances Williams, Laci Zsoldos and Kati Zsoldos. Special gratitude is due to Laci. I would also like to record thanks to colleagues with whom I worked on what resulted in the book on welfare states in transition around the world, edited by Gosta Esping-Andersen, which we presented at an event held within the ambit of the World Summit for Social Development in Copenhagen in March 1995. While I have a different perspective from Gosta's, his earlier book was immensely influential in setting the terms of the debate in the 1990s, and it was a pleasure to work with him and the others. I would also like to thank the many friends and colleagues in BIEN; the ideas and energy that have come from the eight Congresses held so far and the numerous meetings in between have been enriching. Of course, none of those mentioned are responsible for the conclusions or recommendations.

Finally, there is an anonymous acknowledgement and a personal one, both highly relevant to the underlying themes of the book. It is hard not to share the sense of joy of the man, apparently with plenty of work to do, who told Charles Handy, 'I'm pleased to say that I'm unemployable now.' It stimulated me to recall the remark an unemployed Jamaican had made to me in the slums of Kingston some years ago, which has lingered in the memory. 'Man,' he said, 'I want a work, not a job.' I will always regret not having asked him to explain, just to see if it meant what I think it should have meant!

A special thanks to Graeme, who throughout the period in which this book was written, made the self-interested complaint, 'All you do is work.' As a nine-year-old he could scarcely appreciate that, as implied in chapter 6, excessive labour is a response to insecurity as well as a source of it. Now that the book is done, perhaps there will be more time for the *contemplation* that we all too easily neglect, at our cost. The occupational security that the book seeks to promote cannot come without it.

For F, let me count the ways?

Part I

Conceptualising Global Labour

The labour of our body and the work of our hands
John Locke

1 Of Work, Labour and Employment

1.1 INTRODUCTION

People wish to work, yet almost everywhere they have to labour. The allusion to Rousseau's famous aphorism is deliberate. When did the need to labour become the duty to labour? When did the rights of labour become the right to labour? It is a peculiar aspect of the many debates on 'labour' at the end of the twentieth century that while there is a clamour for policies to increase the opportunity to labour (captured in the general desire to reduce unemployment) there is also a clamour (sometimes coming from the same group advocating the former view) to the effect that more people should be obliged to labour, as part of their obligations as citizens. These inherent paradoxes are easily overlooked.

1.2 CONCEPTS OF WORK AND LABOUR

We have made a mess of 'work' since we made an ideal of labour. So much has this been the case in the twentieth century that work that is not labour is not counted. Distinctions should be made between work, labour and employment. To the casual reader, such distinctions are likely to be regarded as pedantic and semantic, inherently uninteresting for anybody interested in social and economic policy. It is therefore worth emphasising that the following analysis is based on these distinctions.

In this book, work is defined as rounded activity combining creative, conceptual and analytical thinking and use of manual aptitudes – the *vita activa* of human existence. There is an eminently respectable set of reasons for not placing either work or labour as the *primary* human activity, and for reserving primacy for *reflection* or *contemplation*. Hannah Arendt argued cogently and persuasively that this was the case (Arendt, 1957). Yet contemplation is part of great work, implicit in creativity. As Cato put it all those centuries ago, in describing man in action, 'Never is he more active than when he does nothing.' Contemplation gives a balance to the functions of work, strengthening and developing human personality, as well as fulfilling more immediate needs.

Work involves an individual element and a social element, an interaction with objects – raw materials, tools, 'inputs', etc. – and an interaction with people and institutions. The degree of creativity in work may be small or at a level of 'genius'. Work may or may not produce 'goods' or 'services', or objects of 'use value', although one could define it as 'productive work' if the intention were to produce such an outcome. Each of the words in inverted commas raise important semantic and philosophical issues, which will not be discussed for the moment.

The notion of work encompasses four meanings. Work is an activity, a series of linked actions. It is also a conscious use of effort, mental and physical, to achieve some typically pre-determined objective. A 'piece of work' is also the outcome of some activity, that is, it is an inactive object. And we also refer to an artistic achievement as a 'great work'.

The notion of *labour* is quite different. Not all work is labour and not all labour is work. The word 'labour' is derived from the Latin (*laborem*) implying toil, distress and trouble. *Laborare* meant to do heavy, onerous activity, and early medieval use of *labeur* was associated with agricultural activity, typically with the plough. The French word *travailler* is derived from the Latin *tripatiare*, meaning to torture with a nasty instrument. And the Greek word for labour, *ponos*, signified pain and effort, and has a similar etymological root to the word for poverty, *penia*. All these early derivations convey a negative view of labour.

Labour is arduous – perhaps *alienated work* – and epistemologically it conveys a sense of 'pain' – *animal laborans*. We may define labour as activity done under some duress, and some sense of *control* by others or by institutions or by technology, or more likely by a combination of all three. 'Go into the fields and labour' is an exhortation based on necessity. The seasons call, the wheat is golden and ready. Similarly, 'factory labour' is determined activity, where 'determined' signifies the philosophical sense of constrained and controlled.

For the International Labour Organisation, in its Constitution and Philadelphia Declaration of 1944: 'Labour is not a commodity.' (ILO, 1982, p. 23)

This is awkward, since what presumably was meant is that workers should not be subject to 'market forces' in the same way as oranges and lemons, and that they should have rights, forms of security and forms of social protection. In the language of that era, labour should be 'de-commodified'. In this regard, the sentence seems to mix up several notions of 'labour'. For economists, labour is that which is expended in production. In neo-classical economics, it is a 'factor of production', whereas in Marxian terms labour is that which produces, or is intended to produce, *surplus value*, or *surplus product*, or product for appropriation. Frederick Engels distinguished between work and labour, the former creating use value, the latter creating value (see his footnote in Marx, 1976, Vol.1, p.138). But in any case labour as an activity must be distinguished from *labour power*, which is the individual capacity for labour, the bundle of competencies, knowledge and physical attributes of any individual. If a craftsman makes a chair for himself from wood that he cuts from the commons, he combines a creative activity with autonomous use of energy and dexterity to yield 'use value'. If a furniture factory hires a carpenter it hires labour power – the capacity to labour – and the worker then provides labour under some sort of control. Neo-classical economists treat labour as a factor of production like 'capital', the quantity and quality determined in the act of hiring. But it is the worker who is hired. The amount of effort, time, energy, skill, creativity and so on that the worker provides in the job will vary, just as will the extent of *exploitation*.

The notion of labour leads to consideration of the 'duty to labour' and the peculiar juxtaposition of the terms 'right to labour' and 'right of labour'. The first is a social relationship, historically rooted, reflecting a reciprocity, an obligation in return for something. The 'right to labour' is a contradiction in terms, stemming from mixing the concepts of work and labour, since the 'right to work' (considered shortly) is usually treated as synonymous with it. One can argue that the right to indulge in creative activity is a human right, but the right to labour, meaning somebody having the right to work in onerous conditions is, other than trivially, intuitively absurd.

Finally, as far as labour is concerned, there is the notion of the 'right of labour', which may strike the reader as meaningless but which is recognisable as 'the rights of labour', a rallying cry for many decades for the working class and trade unions. The term suddenly has an historical ring to it, whereas only a few years ago it conveyed a sense of identity, struggle and a vision of social progress.

What are the rights of labour? The basic answer is that they are the standard claims of social reciprocity for the reality of *being* labour, of workers as wage labourers. They are scarcely radical, since they do not envisage ending the labouring condition or the social relations that produce it. They conjure up images of a 'fair day's pay for a fair day's labour', and the expectation of discretionary allowances and tolerances in the face of normal *contingency risk* over the life cycle. The rights of labour are not definable outside their historical context, and reflect acquired habits and aspirations based on experience. For instance, once the rights of labour might have included the 'ten hour day' and 'Sunday for recreation'. Elsewhere they might have included an 'eight hour day' and the acquired 'right' to sick leave, to holidays and to access to a community school for the workers' children. All these have historical images, yet such 'rights' exist in all forms of labouring community. Any abrogation of habitual 'rights' may lead to retaliation in all sorts of little ways that impose costs on employers and the authorities behind them. They are normative rights, in the sense used by T.H. Marshall (1950) in his celebrated essay on the evolution of civil rights.

Labour and work are thus terms that should be kept distinct. The etymology of key words can assist in identifying aspects of reality on which analysis should concentrate. It was mainly in the eighteenth and nineteenth centuries that work was perceived in a distinctively positive manner. David Hume was one of the first to consider that 'labour' distinguished man from animals. Others followed in a similar vein. The shift in thinking was marked by *paternalistic* interpretations of technological progress and the growth of the technical and social divisions of labour, and by the grumbling discontent of the incipient working class and its intellectual representatives. The tensions between work and labour evolved. The distinction initially associated with Aristotle between work as *thinking* and work as *production* was developed by Enlightenment artists and poets, and then by critics such as

Thomas Carlyle and John Ruskin. In doing so, they went beyond the Puritan work ethic propounded by Martin Luther and later linked by Max Weber to the development of capitalism, and which has been so influential on twentieth century labour economics and its basis in utilitarianism.

It was scarcely surprising that the romanticism of the early nineteenth century generated one line of thinking. Observers such as Carlyle saw *all* work as ennobling. Faced with such exaggeration, Ruskin was more profound, and is worth quoting at length, perhaps because the points are taken for granted and thus not incorporated enough in current thinking:

> Observe, you are put to a stern choice in this matter. You must either make a tool of the creature, or a man of him. You cannot make both. Men were not intended to work with the accuracy of tools, to be precise and perfect in all their actions. If you will have that precision out of them, and make their fingers measure degrees like cog-wheels, and their arms strike curves like compasses, you must inhumanise them. All the energy of their spirits must be given to make cogs and compasses of themselves ... On the other hand, if you will make a man of the working creature, you cannot make a tool. Let him but begin to imagine, to think, to try to do anything worth doing; and the engine-turned precision is lost at once. Out come all his roughness, all his dullness, all his incapability; shame upon shame, failure upon failure, pause after pause: but out comes the whole majesty of him also ... (Ruskin, 1894)

This appreciation was coupled with a recognition that *manual* and *mental* work should be seen as an integrated whole, and that by the artificial separation, 'the mass of society is made up of morbid thinkers, and miserable workers'. Elsewhere, he made the point more poetically: 'Fine art is that in which the hand, the head, and the heart of man go together' (Ruskin, 1865, lecture ii).

Marx, in his 1844 Political and Economic Manuscripts, wrestled with similar themes from an Hegelian perspective, through considering work as man's 'human essence' and depicting the division of labour as a process of *alienation*. Whereas Rousseau had seen alienation in terms of man's estrangement from his primitive nature ('Man is born free and is everywhere in chains'), the young Marx depicted alienation as *estrangement* from man's nature. The theory of alienation starts from the presumption that an unalienated existence is *feasible* and can be depicted as a process of becoming – or as a series of trends by which a person's creative capacities are developed. There are four forms of alienation (Meszaros, 1970; Ollman, 1976). A worker is estranged from her work as life activity, doing it mainly through coercion, as a means of obtaining subsistence. The worker is estranged from the product of her work, having little or no control over its design, on how it is made or its subsequent use. She is estranged from other workers through competition, class tensions and the technical and social divisions of labour. And he or she is estranged from nature, seeing it as something to be used, yet cut off from transforming nature as a means of developing his or her own human nature.

The theory of alienation is pertinent because it highlights *some* critical aspects of work, in reality and in its potential. Only by having an image of what is *desirable* and *feasible* can we hope to identify elements of the 'labour process' that are objectively criticisable. Labour that is, involuntarily, narrowly *specialised*, or that uses only a narrow range of physical or mental attributes, or that restricts the development or renewal of physical, intellectual or psychological capacities, is a denial of 'human essence'. A critic might retort that composing music and inventing mathematical theorems are both narrowly specialised and use a narrow range of mental attributes. In a sense, this is true. But if someone were forced, by circumstance or pressure, to do either to the exclusion of other activities, creative capacity would be stunted, and there would be a tendency for one-dimensional development of personality, or physical or emotional capacities.

Attempts have been made to make use of forms of alienation to derive analytical categories based on socio-economic relations and behavioural patterns (e.g., Schacht, 1981). For our purposes, alienation is manifest in loss of *control* and loss of *autonomy* in working. But alienation is also involved for those whose existence and status depend on their control of others' labour and product. Thus, Aristotle differentiated the despot from the free man, the despot definitionally being unfree.

Alienation is crucial to the distinction between labour and work, between the negative and positive roots of words conventionally treated as synonymous. The ancient Greeks made the distinction, regarding the former as fit only for slaves and animals. To labour meant to be enslaved by necessity, and labour done out of necessity is demeaning (Arendt, 1957, pp. 79–84). Dichotomous distinctions have been made ever since, notably with 'productive' and 'unproductive', 'skilled' and 'unskilled', and 'manual' versus 'intellectual' labour. One term has been negative, the other positive. For Marx, labour belongs to the 'realm of necessity' and reflects coercion; the realm of liberty starts where labour stops. But this does not imply a goal of idleness; rather it would allow people to pursue work to an increasing extent.

Many social reformers have been concerned to reduce the need for labour, or to remove the conditions producing it, while fostering conditions for the pursuit of work as creative activity. There is a respectable tradition to the effect that the pursuit of *leisure* as 'free time' in which to consume more goods and services, more intensively and less efficiently, derives from alienated labour, in which various controls operate to direct or to restrict the type and intensity of working activity. The disquiet has crossed the political spectrum (Linder, 1970; Gorz, 1983).

Thus, work may be a human need, an aspect of 'human development', requiring both action and creativity. As Bronowski (1973, p. 116) summarised human progress, echoing Engels and Locke,

> The hand is the cutting edge of the mind. Civilisation is not a collection of finished artefacts, it is the elaboration of processes. In the end, the march of man is the

refinement of the hand in action. The most powerful drive in the ascent of man is his pleasure in his own skill.

The combination of features is crucial. To satisfy human need, work as creative activity should involve application of time, energy, effort and mental prowess. The image conveyed by William Morris, in *Useful Work versus Useless Toil*, has lost none of its appeal:

> A man at work is exercising the energies of his mind and soul as well as of his body. Memory and imagination help him as he works. Not only his own thoughts, but the thoughts of the men of past ages guide his hands; and, as a part of the human race, he creates. If we work thus we shall be men, and our days will be happy and eventful.

This theme has been reiterated by John Rawls as 'the Aristotelian Principle':

> ... other things equal, human beings enjoy the exercise of their realised capacities (the trained abilities), and this enjoyment increases the more the capacity is realised, or the greater its complexity. (Rawls, 1973, p. 426)

For work in its positive sense, the worker should be involved in both the conception and production aspects. We will come back to the notions of *control, status* and *security*. However, thinking along the lines of a dichotomy of work and labour should lead to the view that work should be assessed in terms of five elements. Work as 'human development need' should:

1. Ensure secure subsistence, on an improving basis.
2. Ensure that work activity does not needlessly jeopardise intellectual, physical or psychological health, and that some groups do not have the power or right to impair the health of others.
3. Foster and allow individual creativity in the social production process.
4. Be 'compatible' with workers' competencies, while allowing the development of potential competencies, implying as with the preceding condition that the individual has autonomy over decisions on what, with what and how to produce, and for what use and purpose.
5. Facilitate real 'leisure', which is not the same as 'free time' but which is both a complement to, and an extension of, productive, creative activity.
6. Foster self-respect.

These descriptions of desirable attributes of work can be interpreted in various ways. We merely reiterate that work as creativity should be distinguished from onerous, alienating labour. As such, the nature of any work should be assessed in terms of the extent to which it is self-directed, purposeful activity that allows the individual opportunity to develop intellectual and physical competencies, as an individual and as a human being in a set of communities and social relationships.

1.3 REFLECTING ON EMPLOYMENT

What of the notion of *employment*? In the course of the twentieth century this word has become a loose cannon, along with its much-used opposite 'unemployment'. When did employment become so precious? In the nineteenth century, to be 'in employment' was a term, if not of abuse, at least of regret. It was a term showing that one belonged to a *dependent* status. Employment is a profoundly class-based term. It became important as the middle class became a large part of the population. In a feudal system or in any peasant-based society, the term is almost meaningless. In the early phases of industrialisation, the working class had labour, only wanting employment when having nothing else to which to turn. Only the 'labour aristocracy' had *occupation*, a notion to which we will return. The *bourgeoisie* had 'capital', the *petit bourgeoisie* had their shops and their trades.

As industrialisation proceeded, and the social and detailed division of labour progressed, notably with the emergence of many more service jobs, the notion of *employment* was left uncomfortably straddling a wide variety of work trajectories. It is quintessentially a twentieth-century notion, which crystallised in the 1930s. Although population censuses had been conducted for several centuries, it was only in the 1930s that formal attempts were made to conceptualise and measure the level of employment, and with it the level and rate of unemployment.

This means that society has only felt the need to know about employment for about two-thirds of a century, whereas for many earlier centuries people did not appreciate the need. The point is not trivial, because employment became a defining 'need' of what might be described as **the century of the labouring man**. Industrial capitalism sucked in *labour*, and during the twentieth century for one reason or another became organised in ways that put a premium on labour *stability*. For the working class, labour *evolved* into employment. Of course, for a minority it had done so for several generations, but in the early twentieth century the probability of prolonged employment grew. This went with the specialisation of labour.

Employment is also used with several meanings. For many analysts, it only covers activity entailing the expectation of a wage for tasks performed. This is coupled with use of such terms as 'self-employment' or 'own-account work', defined as work for profit, income or family gain. Debates over what should count as employment have raged for over a hundred years. Alfred Marshall's celebrated point that if he hired a woman as a domestic servant national income would increase, whereas if he married her it would go down, is only one of several quandaries that have bedevilled the term. In the end, statistical practices have been based largely on convention and concern over 'unemployment', as discussed later.

Is employment a 'basic need'? It would surely not be in a society of absolute abundance, *or* in a society in which material needs were modest, *or* in one where wage labour was unimportant. Surely employment *qua* labour cannot be construed as a basic human need. Maximising employment as 'Full Employment' may have an instrumental rationale, but most economists have presumed that maximising employment is desirable in its own right. It will be a recurring theme in the following chapters that this is at best unproved, and at worst a source of injustice.

A peculiarity of employment is that it covers all forms of labour but not all forms of work. Indeed, it strangely excludes certain types of work that contribute to human welfare and development, whereas it includes activities that are unproductive or that do not contribute significantly to either. Most analysts would recognise this and then continue with their analyses as if it did not matter. A way of interpreting this schizophrenic attitude is that they feel that trying to solve the ambiguity would be too complex. Consider an example. If you do voluntary work caring for the elderly in your community, that does not count as employment. If I offer to pay you a commission to sell clothes to the elderly and you fail to sell anything, you are likely to be counted as employed.

Popular defences of the desirability of *employment* cite some of the following:

(1) Employment is a form of social participation.
(2) Employment contributes to social integration.
(3) Employment enables individuals to be integrated into society, and is increasingly important because traditional institutions, such as the church and family, are being eroded as social institutions.
(4) Employment is economically necessary to sustain the welfare state.

It is not clear that employment is the optimum way to achieve social participation or necessarily a way to achieve social integration. It is not difficult to imagine types of employment that would reduce an individual's prospect of desirable social participation or integration. As for economic necessity, this cannot apply if governments choose to operate with high unemployment. And why should paid employment be so much more desirable than other forms of work, such as domestic work, childcare or community work done on a voluntary or personal basis?

It may be worth reflecting on the use of the terms work, labour and employment in international statements and conventions. In the relevant passage from the UN Declaration of Human Rights cited in the next section, one notices that the right to work slips into language of 'employment' and 'unemployment'. All the key words raise questions about definition and realism. Consider too Article 6 of the *International Covenant on Economic, Social and Cultural Rights*, the first article dealing with specific rights:

1. The States Parties to the present Covenant recognize the right to work, which includes the right of everyone to the opportunity to gain his living by work which he freely chooses or accepts, and will take appropriate steps to safeguard this right.
2. The steps to be taken by a State Party to the present Covenant to achieve the full realisation of this right shall include technical and vocational guidance and training programmes, policies and techniques to achieve steady economic, social

and cultural development and full and productive employment under conditions safeguarding fundamental political and economic freedoms to the individual.

The Constitution of the ILO states that one of the Organisation's purposes is to promote policies to achieve

(a) full employment and the raising of standards of living;
(b) the employment of workers in the occupations in which they can have the satisfaction of giving the fullest measure of their skill and attainments and make their greatest contribution to the common well-being;
(c) the provision, as a means to the attainment of this end and under adequate guarantees for all concerned, of facilities for training and the transfer of labour, including migration for employment and settlement.

These are worthy sentiments, yet they reflect the mood of an era when trade-offs in labour markets were not fully understood. It seems from this and related documents that 'the right to work' is interpreted as 'opportunities for employment', or 'productive employment'. The right to work could be interpreted to mean that there must be both opportunities and no barriers to obtaining those opportunities. This seems the essence of the ILO's *Employment Policy Convention No.122* of 1964, a very wide-ranging Convention, which went on to define the objectives of active policy:

The said policy shall aim at ensuring that
(a) there is work for all who are available for and seeking work;
(b) such work is as productive as possible;
(c) there is freedom of choice of employment.

It is significant that this Convention came into existence at the height of faith in 'Full Employment', Keynesian macro-economics and the 'welfare state'. It states that countries ratifying it should pursue an 'active policy' to achieve 'full, productive and freely chosen employment'. If one is rigorous, one must admit that the Convention is hard to apply or to define consistently. In the 1960s, a European country operating with 10 per cent unemployment would have been regarded as failing to satisfy the *Convention;* in the 1990s, such a judgment would be less likely, and this would not be a matter of cynicism or 'real politics'. Although the Convention has value in setting standards for evaluation, all the words in inverted commas can be interpreted with some latitude and without doing injustice to the stated objectives.

1.4 THE 'RIGHT TO WORK'

Everyone has the right to work, to free choice of employment, to just and favourable conditions of work and to protection against unemployment.
Universal Declaration of Human Rights, Article 23, paragraph 1

The problematic character of that resounding acclamation in 1948 is such that one could be confident that it would scarcely be put forward 50 years later. It brings us back to the 'right to work', which has always been a source of ambiguity and political nervousness. The term is traced to Charles Fourier in the early eighteenth century, derived from the French Declaration of the Rights of Man and of the Citizen of 1789. Fourier fumed that 'politics extol the rights of man and do not guarantee the prime and only useful right, the right to work'. De Tocqueville in 1848 perceptively saw the implications of granting the right, rehearsing themes that have echoed throughout the succeeding century and a half:

> To grant every man in particular the general, absolute and incontrovertible right to work necessarily leads to one of the following consequences: Either the State will undertake to give to all workers applying to it the employment they lack, and will then gradually be drawn into industry, to become the industrial entrepreneur that is omnipresent, the only one that cannot refuse work and the one that will normally have to dictate the least task; it will inevitably be led to become the principal, and soon, as it were, the sole industrial entrepreneur ... Now that is communism.
>
> If, on the contrary, the State wishes ... to provide employment to all the workers who seek it, not from its own hands and by its own resources, but to see to it that they always find work with private employers, it will inevitably be led to try to regulate industry ... It will have to ensure that there is no unemployment, which means that it will have to see that workers are so distributed that they do not compete with each other, that it will have to regulate wages, slow down production at one time and speed it up at another, in a word, that it will have to become the great and only organiser of labour ... What do we see? Socialism.

This concern about the potential implications has bedevilled the debate ever since. But there has always been philosophical and political dispute whether the 'right to work' *is* a right. Thus, at the height of the French debate in the mid-nineteenth century, a scarcely noticed Karl Marx was writing dismissively that under capitalism the right to work was 'an absurdity, a miserable pious wish'.

In the twentieth century, the international debate on the right to work has been shaped by, inter alia, *paternalism*, the Great Depression, the emergence of Keynesianism and, in paradoxical ways, by the existence of communist states.

There has always been a strong paternalistic element in the promotion of the right to employment or work. It could be observed, for example, in the Speenhamland system in England (1785–1834), in the Declaration of the Rights of Man, in the Prussian Civil Code of 1794, and in successive episodes during the nineteenth and twentieth centuries. The state's obligation to create labour for its poor has been a continuing theme, derived from a mix of political conscience, paternalism, fear and desire for control. Putting the poor in labour, usually for as little as the state could pay as possible, has been a way of achieving several social and economic objectives. It has been a way of disciplining the poor, as well as others whose potentially wayward behaviour might lead them to fall into similar circumstances. The right to labour reached one of its cruellest nadirs in the late nineteenth century and early twentieth century when it was used to justify the onerous conditions of the 'work house' in Britain, when only the most desperate and destitute accepted the employment offered by the state. In the twentieth century, communist and fascist states found comparable ways of transforming the right to work into the obligation to labour.

There has been a more benign side to this. Liberals have consistently presented the right to employment as a human right with liberating properties. A powerful influence has been the Roman Catholic church, the leadership of which has dealt with it in several encyclicals, which have coincided with socio-political crises. The famous *Rerum Novarum* (The Condition of Labour) was written in 1891 when there was an economic crisis and a growing socialist challenge in western Europe. The Pope, Leo XIII, was a progressive paternalist, supporting the rights of workers, albeit cautiously. This theme has continued in Catholic pronouncements. Thus, Pope Pius XII claimed in 1941, in the midst of the Second World War, that labour was a right and a duty of every human being. In 1963, Pope John XXIII asserted that employment was a natural right in his *Pacem in Terris*, and in 1981 Pope John Paul II issued the *Laborem Exercens* (Performing Work) encyclical reiterating the right. His document ten years later, *Centesimus Annus* (The Hundredth Year), was more circumspect, though issued to celebrate the centenary of *Rerum Novarum*. It supported labour market policies, but undercut the right to work by concluding that 'the state could not directly ensure the right to work of all its citizens unless it controlled every aspect of economic life and restricted the free initiative of individuals'(1991, p.19).

Meanwhile, constitutions of communist states guaranteed the right to employment, and their policies amounted to the view that if citizens did not labour they were 'parasitic' (a widely-used term), since the status of unemployment was abolished. Some other states plunged in this direction, and a key point in the twentieth-century debates has been the implicit view that the right is a *state-guaranteed* right to employment, implying an obligation on the state that could not be binding. From an individual's point of view, whatever the right amounts to, it could not be enforceable. In what way, then, is it a right?

Besides the mix of morality and paternalism, the political demand for the right to work was strengthened by the Great Depression. It was given substance by the Keynesian revolution in economics, a message of which seemed to be that the state could ensure that everybody who wanted a job could have one. The Second World War boosted this perspective; the returning combatants did not want to go back to the 'dole queue'.

Since then, difficulties of giving substance to the right to work have shaped international positions. The right was asserted in the UN's Universal Declaration of Human Rights of 1948, the Organisation of American States' Declaration of Rights and Duties of Man of 1948, the Council of Europe's European Social Charter of

1961, the International Covenant on Economic, Social and Cultural Rights of 1966, and the Organisation of African Unity's African (Banjul) Charter on Human and People's Rights of 1981. In the middle came the ILO's *Employment Convention* No.122, which, although not asserting the right to work, was in the same tradition. As the 1983 International Labour Conference's Employment Committee stated,

> The promotion of full, productive and freely chosen employment provided for in the Employment Policy Convention and Recommendation, 1964, should be regarded as the means of achieving in practice the realisation of the right to work. (ILO, 1983)

In spite of the Declaration of Human Rights and its successors, few western industrialised countries have entrenched the right to work in their constitutions, exceptions being Portugal and Spain (Mayer, 1985). Where the right has been asserted it has been matched by an article asserting the duty or obligation to work as well. The regimes most forceful in promoting the right to employment were the communist bloc.

What have been the intellectual defences of the right to work? Siegel identifies the *natural rights* perspective, the *legal positivist* case, and (it seems) the *human development right* perspective (Siegel, 1994, pp. 76–90). All have had their critics. The natural rights case has been the one most associated with Roman Catholicism, although some philosophers have made a defence along those lines as well (Nickel, 1978–79). Siegel concluded that the natural rights case is strong because of the 'identity' and 'reputation' of its supporters. This is scarcely adequate. The legal positivists' case seems to rest on the fact that a body of international Covenants and Declarations exist, to which lawyers can refer. What this body amounts to is hard to determine, but the direction seems to be towards the right to fair and equal treatment with respect to employment, to equal protection and non-discrimination, rather than the right to employment *per se*. They have dealt mostly with issues of *security*, to be discussed later. The legal positivists have had little chance to draw on national legislation in recent years, because few countries have legalised anything like a right to employment.

This leaves the development rights' theorists, who have many issues to resolve before they make a strong case. It is here where the slippage between work, labour, job and employment has been crucial. Philosophers have argued that there is a 'human right to self-respect' (Bay, 1982). But while the absence of work may undermine 'self-respect', it is another matter to deduce that this means everybody should have the right to a job. One supporter of the right to work drew on Rawls' *Theory of Justice*, which emphasised self-respect and minimal standards while giving priority to liberty, and took the argument to its logical conclusion:

> The justification for a universal right to employment would lie, in this view, in the fact that because of class interests and various group prejudices any non-universal distribution of employment opportunities will be unfair to the

disadvantaged classes and minorities. Hence the only fair distribution available is one that guarantees each person a job. (Nickel, 1978–79, p. 161)

One would have to go further than that, since not every job is equally attractive or 'fair'. And use of the word 'available' merely highlights that in reality no such option arises. What type of 'job' would be 'guaranteed', and with what income? And what if a person refused the kind guarantee?

Suppose full-time jobs were scarce, so that the demand exceeded supply. Suppose such jobs had value for those holding them and those wanting them. Suppose one added that everybody had an equal right to a job. Then, suppose you were working 60 hours a week baking and selling bread, and as a result I could not bake or sell any. One option would be to insist that you work only 30 hours a week, to enable me to do the same. This response, widely canvassed in one form or another, prompts unease, not just for economic reasons but because it interferes with liberty. Another response is to suggest that in such circumstances, full-time jobs should be taxed to provide compensation to those who do not have them, as a matter of social justice (van Parijs, 1995). A likely reaction to this is that justice would be ensured without that, since everyone is free to compete for the scarce jobs. But this is not true, since people have different endowments. A second retort is that, as long as market rigidities were removed, imbalance would be corrected through declines in the wage until the market cleared. But this may be prevented by a floor to the wage defining 'subsistence' or 'efficiency'. If the market cannot clear or if the government is compelled to operate with high unemployment, then a job scarcity tax has more appeal. However, taxing jobs as a distributive device in the interest of responding to an initial injustice would be counter-productive, if the tax further reduced the supply of the scarce asset (jobs), especially if it offended the Rawlsian Difference Principle by hitting the worst off. To avoid this pitfall, and the vicious circle of consequences that flows from the reasoning, one could consider compensating those without the scarce asset. This paragraph may seem esoteric. For present purposes, suffice it to note that those who feel there is a right to work should have an ethically acceptable and feasible response to the scarcity of jobs, if they equate jobs with work.

Another dilemma arises from the difficulty of defining the right to work. Do I, as someone ignorant of the skills, have the same right to be a surgeon as someone who has passed exams in surgery? This would offend common sense. Do I have the same right to work in IBM as someone already employed there? What we mean, minimally, is that everybody *should* have an *equal opportunity* to learn the skills required and the meaning of equal opportunity should extend to access to real opportunities.

Because of the ethical and other difficulties with the notion of the right to work, it has become common to define the right in indirect terms, i.e., that this right means that there should be no barriers, legal or institutional, blocking people from applying for and obtaining paid forms of employment, as there were in the past (Held, 1991, p. 21).

In his classic definition of civil rights, delivered in lectures in 1949, T.H. Marshall stated that 'in the economic field the basic civil right is the right to work', but he then qualified this by stating that this entails 'the right to follow the occupation of one's own choice in the place of one's choice, subject only to the legitimate demands for preliminary technical training' (Marshall, 1973, p. 75). He too saw the right to work as a notion derived from the seventeenth century when guilds, local regulations and apprenticeship systems restricted access to certain occupations. Actually, Marshall then argued there was an *obligation* to work, a classic slip into labourism.

This sense of the right to work is, therefore, a negative right. Some social thinkers have gone further, and have claimed that there is no such right at all. For Ralf Dahrendorf (1988, p. 148), there cannot be a right to work because 'no judge can force employers to hire unemployed people'. More than that, there surely cannot be a right to do something unless there is a corresponding right *not* to do it. As he argued,

> In terms of liberty, it is more important to establish a right not to work, so that governments cannot force people into a dependency [from] which they want to escape.[1]

Dahrendorf was concerned with citizenship rights, and he differentiated between these, which are unconditional, and matters belonging to private contracts:

> Citizenship is a social contract, generally valid for all members; work is a private contract ... when the general rights of citizenship are made dependent on people entering into private relations of employment, these lose their private and fundamentally voluntary character. (Dahrendorf, 1988, p. 33)

Dahrendorf argued that this then became a form of 'forced labour'. He followed Marshall in believing that citizenship does entail 'general obligations'. To be a good citizen may mean providing 'community service'. This raises ethical problems, which are left aside for the moment. One may also reflect, in passing, that most commentators have asserted the right to work without making any attempt to define what they mean or to justify the assertion.

One could go back to the start, accepting it as the negative right, in the sense that social and economic policy cannot be justifiable if it *deliberately restricts any individual's opportunity to choose work relative to others' opportunity*. This is stated in this manner to preclude the situation in which a government operates a macro-economic policy that knowingly raises unemployment. The implications are profound for evaluating the social and labour market policy used by governments in recent years.

The right to work should be analogous to other 'rights', *if* it is a right. Consider the right to vote in a democracy. To most people, such a right would allow that not only do you have a right to vote for whom you wish but that if you do not like the available options, you can exercise the right *not* to vote. Similarly, one would say that it is a funny sort of right if one had to vote and if there were only one candidate, especially if his dastardly deeds were well known to you. If one were to apply this reasoning consistently to liberty, there must be a meaningful substantive *choice*. Rights to do something can only exist if there is the right not to do it. Oddly enough, while politicians and analysts speak a great deal about the right to work, they are loath to admit the right not to work, and in practice much has been done to emphasise the *obligation* to labour, notably in social security systems. Indeed, whereas in modern societies there is a right to vote and not an obligation, with work there is no practical right but there is an obligation to labour. This asymmetry should cause more unease than it appears to do.

As strange is the obligation placed on the unemployed to take jobs when there is high unemployment, i.e., when under the 'musical chairs' principle' x per cent of the people must fail. An obligation that cannot be met by everybody, even if they wished to satisfy it, is manifestly unjust. Some defenders of the right to work have argued in favour of the *obligation* to take employment because they believe this is essential in order to oblige governments to be concerned about employment in general. This is surely far-fetched.

Another difficulty is that most employment involves labour where a private 'bargain' is made between people in unequal power relations. To put it in basics: what sort of right is it to be able to doff your cap and say, 'Sir'? No assessment of protective regulations can overcome such situations, although they may ameliorate them.

The failure to differentiate between labour and work is matched by the failure to differentiate them in statements about the right to work. What is so laudable in creating circumstances in which a man will work in a sewage plant for 20 years or risk life and limb crawling along a rock face? Such examples return us to the positive notion of work and developments in the twentieth century. Why should we wish to maximise labour? Surely, a vision of humanity has been to escape from labour. There have been many distinguished advocates of this. Among those have been Paul Lafargue, Marx's son-in-law, whose book *The Right to Laziness* was kept out of debates within the labour movement because of its emphasis on liberty. In the twentieth century, Bertrand Russell's *In Praise of Idleness* and Ivan Illich's *The Right to Useful Unemployment* and other writings have been in that tradition.

Another strand in thinking about the right to work is the line on social inclusion. Consider the following confident statement, from a respected social scientist, echoing many comparable statements:

It is by having paid work (more particularly, work for a wage) that we belong to the public sphere, acquiring a social existence and a social identity (that is, a 'profession') and are part of a network of relations and exchanges in which we are measured against other people and are granted certain rights over them in exchange for the duties we have towards them. (Gorz, 1983, p. 13)

If this were true, it implies that someone who is 'self-employed' or doing voluntary or domestic work is less in the 'social sphere' and has a diminished social existence and identity compared with a wage labourer in a factory or on a construction site. It implies that everybody paid a wage has a 'profession'. It means that a woman working as a maid acquires rights over other people.

These are not minor points. Wage labour should not be idealised. Most people in wage employment, one dares to suggest, would be inclined to think that they would be able to 'belong to the public sphere' more effectively outside their wage job. Imagine the woman hunched over the lathe, the man chiselling away at the rock face deep underground, and wonder at the idealisation of employment. This is not the same as saying that work could not be a means of enriching one's social existence or that it cannot be a means of defining oneself. But idealising wage labour is dubious because it leads to a distorted policy perspective.

Now consider the oft-stated claim that there is *an obligation to work*, or a duty to do so. Leaving aside views associated with Catholicism, let us just recall the main arguments, drawing on the 'working perspectives' programme of the Netherlands Scientific Council for Government Policy. There seem to be four main contentions:

(1) Paid employment enables people to enter social networks and thereby contribute to the integration of society. If people are not in jobs, other institutions would be required to generate social integration. Since other institutions for achieving social integration have been declining (family, church, etc.), employment is increasingly important for social integration.

This prompts several questions. Is integration actually desirable or meaningful? Is it feasible through paid employment? If certain institutions are becoming less capable of integrating people into normal roles in society, does it follow that jobs should be held responsible for fulfilling this function? Does it mean that employment would be better than other alternatives for 'social integration'? If those institutions are failing, does that mean there should be a duty to join churches or form families, at the pain of condemnation or sanctions if one did not?

These questions have not been answered satisfactorily. The social integration imperative looks suspiciously like a justification for control. As Dahrendorf (1988, p. 144) put it,

> Worried neo-conservatives join forces with bewildered socialists in extolling the virtues of hard work when neither have enough employment to offer to all. They are really talking about social and political control, for which no other mechanism than the discipline of employment has been found.

This may be a polemical way of posing the issue. However, the unresolved questions surely undermine the claim that desire for social integration implies a duty to take paid jobs.

(2) High labour force participation is necessary as the economic condition for a sustainable welfare state. Without that, society would not be able to afford the social rights offered by the welfare state.

This prompts two responses. Even if one accepted that a high participation rate were desirable, there is no reason for regarding that as justification for imposing an obligation on individuals to raise it. Second, if there were high unemployment, a high participation rate would probably raise the unemployment rate or be unnecessary unless it also generated higher economic growth and raised employment.

(3) An individual has an obligation to work to match the state's obligation to provide conditions for such work, through training facilities, childcare, etc.

This contention raises questions about the meaning of obligation. It is unclear why the state has such an obligation. One may suppose that it is because it should enhance *rights*. But in this case, it would be to promote equal opportunities, and there is no justification for converting opportunities into obligations. Moreover, if the state has such an obligation, it is far from clear that it is honoured.

(4) An individual has the duty to take employment because of what Marshall (1973) stated was 'the general obligation to live the life of a good citizen, giving such service as one can to promote the welfare of the community'.

This is related to the first contention. It prompts the same questions. It can also be criticised for assuming that wage employment is the only means of promoting welfare. Community service and forms of unpaid work may do that just as well, while there can be no presumption that all wage employment does promote social welfare.

We will return to the issue of obligation to work in chapter 10, in discussing the powerful trend to *workfare*. For the present, the conclusion is that neither the right nor the obligation to work is easily demonstrated.

1.5 THE DIVISION OF LABOUR

Another conceptually important term is *the division of labour*. It can be misleading, although analytically it is an essential concept. It takes two forms, both of which have existed throughout history.

First, there is the *social division of labour*, which is the process by which certain groups select, or are selected for, some activities while others are excluded. For example, in feudal and caste-based societies the social division of labour has usually been a rigid, ascriptive process. Age, sex, race, caste, religion, language, even wealth – all have been used to obtain social divisions of labour. The resultant labour force stratification has accentuated alienation, and produced and encouraged oppression and various forms of exploitation.

Second, there is the *detailed division of labour*. This is technological, even if at least partly social in origin or in intent. Adam Smith's pin-making is the classic image, but the basis is the breakdown of tasks, crystallised in the 'separation of conception from execution' (Braverman, 1974). The principles of Taylorism, and followers such as Bedaux, merely reveal the pernicious alienation that can be involved in the progressive detailed division of labour. As Frederick Taylor put his influential views succinctly:

> The managers assume the burden of gathering together all of the traditional knowledge which in the past has been possessed by the workmen and then of classifying, tabulating and reducing this knowledge, to rules, laws and formulae ... All possible brainwork should be removed from the shop and centred in the planning or lay-out department. (Taylor, 1911, p. 111)

The ideas of Taylorism (not particularly novel even in 1911) have continued to influence labour processes into the 1990s, and have persisted in such devices as training schemes designed to provide 'minimal modules of employable skills'. Extending the detailed division of labour is linked in part to technological innovation. As the refinement occurs, it tends to reduce the creative aspects of work, but for that reason it also contains tendencies that threaten the stability of the labour process, typically necessitating more complex control mechanisms, considered later.

In sum, the detailed division of labour is concerned with the distribution of tasks across jobs, whereas the social division of labour is concerned with the distribution of groups of people across groups of jobs.

1.6 OCCUPATION AND JOB

> *The character of men depends more on their occupation than on any teaching we can give them.*
> John Ruskin, 1880

> ... *though the broad plan of classification remains much the same, huge trans-positions of numbers have been made from one class to another: the domestic class in one census includes the larger part of the population and in the next is reduced by more than half: 350,000 persons in England alone (consisting of the wives and other relatives of farmers, etc.) are taken from the agricultural class of one census and placed in the unoccupied class of another: the partially occupied wives are in no two successive censuses classed alike ...*
> Charles Booth, 1886

A feature of almost all labour analysis and statistical presentations of the 'labour process' is use of the term *occupation*. Whether valid or not, the observed distribution of 'occupations' is taken as a guide to the productive structure, as a measure of the division of labour, the 'class structure', and the distribution of 'skills'. At the micro-level, occupational status might be interpreted as a proxy measure of the degree of *control* exercised by an individual over aspects of work, the degree of an individual's subordination, and so on. Many labour analysts conflate occupation with 'skill' and divide the workforce into 'unskilled', 'semi-skilled' and 'skilled'. It is often convenient to do so, but in many respects it is inappropriate. Before considering the notion of 'skill', we need to clarify the notions of 'occupation' and 'job'.

An occupation is commonly defined as a set of related activities learned or refined through a *career*. The set of tasks may be small; the learning career may be short or long. Yet an occupation has always implied a niche in the production process. It cannot be coincidence that the etymologically earlier meaning of 'occupation' in the English language is in connection with taking possession of a piece of territory.

A *job* is a much humbler word, conveying a set of tasks that might or might not be combined into an occupation. Often, it has had a pejorative meaning attached to it, implying a lack of permanency, a lack of accumulated wisdom and skill. Usually, it conveys a task or period of employment of short duration. For example, 'job work' is another term for 'piece work'. A job is what one does, an occupation is what one is. Therein lies one conceptual ambiguity.

By contrast, an occupation conveys impressions of *status* as well as complexity of work activities. As Raymond Williams noted (1976, p. 45),

> Career now implies continuity if not necessarily promotion or advancement, yet the distinction between a career and a job only partly depends on this and is associated also with class distinctions between different kinds of work.

One may still think of an occupation as a *calling*. The term stems from a social division of labour in which the detailed division of labour was relatively undeveloped, when *apprentices* were introduced to the *mystery of the craft*. In intention at least, occupation refers to the positive sense of work, as creative activity, the combination of intellectual and manual activities – conception and execution – in the context of progressive refinement of individual competencies.

In considering the ideas of occupation and job, note that *there is no statistical representation of the occupational distribution of the population in any country*. National statistics giving the 'occupational distribution' of employment actually give the 'job distribution' of employment.[2] Thus, a person who perceives his occupation as being a gardener who is currently working as a postman is classified as a postman. Someone may have a doctorate in economics, but if working as a secretary is counted under 'secretarial'. Suppose medical doctors were paid low wages, as a result of which many took up higher-paying labouring jobs. Vacancy rates might suggest that there is a 'shortage' of doctors and – if unemployment was high – 'structural unemployment'. All they really show is that there are vacancies, which may be due to doctors preferring other jobs or that there are insufficient doctors. We may know something about the distribution of jobs, but not about the occupational structure or capacities of the population.

Having made the distinction between occupations and jobs, one can postulate a basic hypothesis underlying much of the following analysis. This is that the development of the detailed division of labour has undermined the basis of occupation over an increasing range of employment, and created conditions in which an increasing proportion of people are in *jobs*.

Whenever an occupation is created it represents an extension of the detailed division of labour. In antiquity, a person could be a carpenter and farmer, a blacksmith and fisherman. Such occupational multiplicity is still common in agrarian and industrialising economies. Using conventional statistics to allocate a person to one 'occupation' is an artificial representation of the detailed division of labour.

With industrialisation, occupations in the early sense of crafts typically have been chipped away, resulting in a greater focus on *hierarchy* in forms of employment. In the refinement of classification systems during the twentieth century, this emphasis has been strengthened. This is nicely illustrated by the British Classification of Occupations and Directory of Occupational Titles:

> The broad structure of the classification is based on the organisational pattern of many large manufacturing companies with top or general management at the beginning, followed by professional and related specialist occupations *supporting top management* and frequently found in headquarters offices, and then by technical, scientific and other specialist occupations engaged in background work. These are followed by line management and the production and service occupations *under their control.*[3]

The language indicates the priority given to elements of hierarchy and control in the taxonomic procedure. The implied structure would have been in sharp contrast with the more horizontal patterning of occupations that prevailed when the detailed division of labour was less extended.

Here is not the place to discuss occupational classification procedures, and indeed the ILO undertook a revision of the International Standard Classification of Occupations (ISCO) in 1988. Nevertheless, it is instructive to dwell on several features of ISCO. As designed in 1958, revised in 1968, and again in 1988, a difficulty is that ISCO was intended to fit several uses, the main ones being:

(1) a basis for the design of occupational job-placement services;
(2) a guide to vocational training curricula, and for vocational guidance;
(3) a model to promote the international comparability of labour statistics;
(4) a basis for identifying socio-economic groups;
(5) a basis for 'manpower planning' (sic);
(6) a basis for monitoring available 'skills';

(7) a source of analytical categories for examining the determinants of many behavioural and cultural phenomena;

(8) for use in collective bargaining.

The difficulties of relating any classification to these multiple uses stem from the haziness of the notion of occupation. The original principle is that the classification is based on 'type of work performed'. But that replaces one vagueness by another. It is scarcely surprising that classification schemas blossomed into awesomely complicated exercises. The US Dictionary of Occupational Titles (DOT) identified over 20,000 'occupations' in its 1977 edition, while the Canadians had over 6,000 titles in their Canadian Classification and Dictionary of Occupations (CCDO). Changes in nomenclature in the US Current Population Survey in the 1980s enlarged the number of categories. Did that indicate a growing detailed division of labour? The old 'professional and technical' grouping was split into two, as were the 'administrators', with 'administrative support' being downgraded to join 'clerical'(Bregger, 1982).

Such disaggregation has been continuing for a long time. Yet most labour market, economic and sociological analyses have utilised aggregates of eight or nine major categories, and at the highest level of aggregation ISCO has always been criticised for being too heterogeneous for analysis and insufficiently differentiated in terms of 'skill'.

While hierarchy has been a feature in conventional classifications, other criteria have included (i) kind of main activity, (ii) type of material used, (iii) equipment used, (iv) services rendered, (v) level of authority, (vi) skill, (vii) employment status, and (viii) qualifications. A complex French classification schema used skill, authority level, employment status, and socio-economic status (INSEE, 1982). Most systems have used something like those criteria. But a common view is that occupations should be classified on the basis of the amount of 'skill' normally involved, and that this should be given priority. This was the view underlying the revision of ISCO in 1988, by which 'occupations are identified, defined and grouped mainly on the basis of the similarity of skills required to fulfil the jobs' tasks and duties' (Hoffmann et al., 1995, p. 3). The difficulty is that the widely-used notion of skill is one of the vaguest work notions of all.

1.7 THE NOTION OF SKILL

In normal parlance, a skill implies a combination of creative, technical and manual abilities. It implies a learning process, with training and experience. One imagines that a more skilled worker would do more complex tasks than others, and require longer, higher-level training and greater experience. But what type of training? Is there a strict correspondence between training or formal qualifications and skill level of a 'job'? Is learning time more important in ranking skills than the 'knowledge base'? Should a distinction be drawn between a 'skilled job' and a 'skilled worker'? These are some of the questions that should bedevil analysis. Part of the problem stems from the fact that in the literature three notions of skill have co-existed.

(i) Skill as Technique

The most common meaning assumes that skill reflects *objective* characteristics of work, involving a combination of general and specific knowledge, where the latter is obtained through training and work experience. Georges Friedman (1961, pp. 85–8) elaborated the approach by dividing workers into 'specialists' and 'specialised'. The former receive technical training in a recognised profession or trade, do work that is not routinised, and feel 'involved' in their work; 'specialised' workers are 'semi-skilled', receive general training, do routinised work, and are cut off from the design process. One analyst suggested an additional distinction, between *discretionary* ('diffusely defined') and *prescribed* work ('specifically defined'), and emphasised the 'task range' required to define skill (Jaques, 1961).

Some have traced an historical process by which the craftsman has given way to the 'specialised worker', and have claimed that the evolution of industrial work could be defined as the passage from a system of skills to a technical system of work. The craftsman possesses *autonomy*, and is directly involved in the production. By contrast, modern production is mainly 'a system of indirect labour', whereby most workers do not manufacture. As Touraine (1972) described the industrial worker,

> He superintends, he records, he controls. His job can no longer be defined as a certain relationship between man and materials, tools and machines, but rather by a certain role in the total production picture. In a system dominated by technology most aspects of skills are now absorbed into the social aspects. The rhythm and character of the work is no longer determined by the nature of the product manufactured, or the machine utilised, or by the character of human effort, but by the way in which the work is organised.

It has also been observed that the characteristics of the labour force influence the structure of jobs. There is unlikely to be a close relationship between worker competencies and statistically-designed occupational categories. Most occupational statistics are used to give the impression that they mirror the distribution of *available* and *utilised* skills, and used as evidence of a need for 'vocational training'. But to the extent that jobs are socially structured, such impressions are misleading.

The ISCO 1988 is supposed to identify occupations on the basis of 'similarity of skills required to fulfil the jobs, tasks and duties' (Hoffmann et al., 1995, p. 3). Apparently, this similarity relates both to 'skill level' (range and complexity of tasks, where 'complexity has priority over the range') and 'skill specialisation' (type of knowledge, tools and equipment used, materials used, nature of goods and services produced). Drawing from this, classification systems have tended to define skill by the schooling and training 'new entrants into the occupations are typically expected to have'. This is ambiguous. Employers may screen by stipulating that applicants should have some level of schooling or a training certificate. But this may be a low-cost selection criterion or be used as an indicator of behavioural traits rather than a guide to the requirements of the job.

In turn, a job may be classified as skilled *because* the person has a certain level of schooling, not because of the tasks he is expected to perform. It is intriguing that the ISCO defined skill level in terms of tasks and then decided that the levels should be given 'operational definitions' in terms of formal education (ILO, 1988, p. 2). Thus, one could obtain a peculiar outcome that a general rise in educational attainment would appear to lead to a withering away of 'unskilled' jobs (or occupations) if all employers used educational attainment as a screening device in their recruitment. Given the claims that low-skilled jobs are dwindling in industrialised economies, this statistical treatment of skill should be reconsidered.

(ii) Skill as Autonomy

A second notion of skill is 'job autonomy' (Littler, 1982, p. 8). Some analysts have dismissed the first approach to skill as 'technicist', two arguing that it 'neglects the social and political (in the sense of "power") aspects of skill' and that 'a relatively skilled position was one of *trust*, where the worker was granted a sphere of competence within which decisions, whether routine or complex, could be taken by the worker himself ... It is social, not technical. The centre of the technique is not complexity, but autonomy and freedom' (Blackburn and Mann, 1979, pp. 291–2). This perspective links skills to the issue of *control*, and indirectly to issues of alienation. As such, it defines skill in a way that may not be consistent with technical competence.

(iii) Skill as Status

A third notion of skill portrays it as primarily a matter of 'social status'. An extreme version would assert that many jobs are regarded as skilled regardless of technical content and that customs and barriers to entry preserve an artificial hierarchy of perceived skills. A mild variant would claim that 'jobs' involving high status were preserved for privileged groups and classified as skilled for managerial purposes. In either case, status factors may be complemented by the establishment of a ritual of 'training' – with limited access – that bears little relation to the complexity of the job. A weak version would accept that there is some skill content in the sense of the first notion of skill, but that much of the perceived skill is outdated, illusory or unnecessary.

According to an advocate of this perspective, workers are regarded as skilled 'according to whether or not entry to the occupation is deliberately restricted and not in the first place according to the nature of the occupation itself' (Turner, 1962, p.184). This has a bearing on ideas of labour control and to *exploitation*, for it implies that some individuals receive a wage increment that does not reflect any difference in training costs or relative scarcity of supply.

So, the three notions of skill mean that we should use the word cautiously. In a sense, most workers could be described as 'skilled', in that they are likely to have *some* technical competence, even if most are in 'unskilled jobs'. Whereas the status and autonomy aspects of skill have a bearing on the social division of labour, the objective characteristics of jobs reflect the detailed division of labour. To reiterate, an occupation is what someone is becoming, a job is what someone is doing.

This brings us back to jobs. How should we differentiate between types of job, analytically, statistically and morally? One may classify them in terms of the three aspects of skill. The proposal is that jobs can be conceptualised in terms of *breadth*, *progressiveness* and *control status*. The latter refers to the sense of autonomy.

A job may be described as relatively *broad* or *narrow* by the range and complexity of the tasks required of the worker (Scoville, 1969). Breadth does have some resemblance to the notion of skill as technical competence. But some highly 'skilled' jobs are narrow in job content, while some broad jobs, combining a wide range of tasks, are not 'skilled' in that conventional sense.

One might define task breadth by reference to the 'worker functions' (dealing with 'data', 'people' and 'things') devised for the US DOT, or to some other similar system. However one proceeds, and although one need not make a judgment on the desirability of a broad or narrow job, a very narrow, specialised activity suggests some of the pejorative aspects of labour.

A job can also be regarded as relatively *progressive* or *static*. A progressive job is one in which a person has scope for developing and refining technical skills, in which there is some autonomy and discretion over conception and performance of tasks. A static job is one in which there is little or no scope for 'upward mobility', in that the tasks, responsibilities, breadth and position in the job hierarchy are largely determined at the time of entry, or shortly afterwards. A static job may be more 'skilled' than some progressive jobs, but provide less scope for on-the-job skill acquisition or for increasing the breadth of responsibilities, control over the production or movement up the job ladder. In static jobs, there is only a low private return to on-the-job continuity, where 'return' signifies rising productivity. There may even be a negative return, in that the monotony could induce shirking, etc. For employers, the costs of labour turnover would be much lower than for progressive jobs, other things equal.

Progressive jobs require and induce greater *commitment* from workers, and for this reason employers are likely to redistribute incomes in favour of those in relatively progressive jobs, to secure their commitment to the firm. Progressive jobs retain more of a 'craft ethic', whereas static and narrow jobs typically induce an 'instrumentality ethic', that is, encourage a more alienated feeling by which work is done for income alone. Workers in progressive jobs perceive themselves as having higher social status, accentuating the belief in their own 'skilled' status.

The conceptualisation of jobs into static and progressive may be useful in explaining social divisions of labour, with groups expected to have greater labour force commitment and to yield employers a higher rate of return to training and on-the-job work experience being slotted into the progressive jobs. Those put into static jobs could be expected to develop the behavioural traits alleged to be a justification for putting them in such jobs, and this could help perpetuate a social division of labour.

The more jobs are static and narrow, the more Ruskin's claim cited earlier becomes tenuous. Whether skills defined in the technical sense grow, there is a deskilling in terms of occupation. With this in mind, there is some appeal in Illich's albeit-exaggerated claim:

> In an industrial society, individuals are trained for extreme specialisation. They are rendered impotent to shape or to satisfy their own needs. (Illich, 1980, p. 60)

Such statements, tantalisingly obscure, contain a germ of truth. They usefully point us back to the nature of work and the positive connotation that reference to skill usually conveys.

1.8 THE NOTION OF LABOUR MARKET

This book is in part an attempt to come to grips with a much used but rarely defined term – the 'labour market'. What is a Good Labour Market, or a bad one? Although the term has become a euphemism and is in such wide use that there is no prospect of removing it, even if we had a wish to do so, it is useful to recognise its limitations. If one goes to a market to buy lemons, the commodity is green or yellow, large or small, fresh or dry. The price is fixed, either *ex ante* before the purchaser arrives or in the course of haggling. The lemon has no say in the process, and once bought is cut into pieces and squeezed. The problem for the lemon is that it cannot protest at the price or the cutting, and once cut from the tree cannot do anything to improve itself. It is an object pure and simple.

A 'labour market' surely has none of the attributes of a lemon market. *First*, it is not clear what is 'sold'. Except in a slave labour market, it is not the person being sold (or what Marxists call the 'labour power'). Perhaps then it is the *capacity to labour*. This too is uncertain, because nobody in their proper mind would voluntarily surrender their capacity to learn or decide on how much effort to expend, and nobody except in familial or personal relationships voluntarily would devote unlimited time to the service of somebody else. An answer is that there is an explicit contract and an implicit contract (or series of them). Yet this terminology imparts an ambiguity in any labour market transaction. The notion of 'contract' implies a legality, and consequential validity, and a non-contested, non-coercive character to many relations that scarcely deserve to be construed in that way. In deference to that ambiguity, we may use the term 'bargain', recognising that this too is less than precise. The explicit bargain is always complemented by implicit bargains.

Second, unlike the case of the lemon there is not a single bargain but a constant renewing of bargains from the outset, making the labour relationship in effect a continuing transaction. Neither the employer nor the worker in the most common labour market bargain realise fully what they are letting themselves in for when they reach their first 'formal' bargain. As recognised in a neglected seminal paper by Herbert Simon (1951), the labour contract of conventional economic theory is incomplete; if work intensity and effort are indeterminate, so is the wage. The formal bargain may specify the number of hours of work per week, the wage rate, the length of time employed in the job and sundry entitlements. But that would still leave out the implicit parts. These include the *effort bargain*, which may be short term or variable, and will depend on more than the wage rate. They also include implied norms of behaviour on the part of both employer and worker, including due process, expected continuity of the labour relationship and the modes of social interaction.

In this respect, it is common to express labour relations in terms of the so-called *principal–agent* model. The principal is the party to a contractual relationship who seeks the performance of a service, while the agent is the party contracting to perform the service. If contracts are not fully enforceable, or if the parties do not have equal and full information, outcomes will probably be inefficient. This has led to a literature on solving 'optimal contracts', whereby outcomes are subject to two constraints:

(1) the *participation constraint*, which requires that the optimal contract should be such that the agent finds it in his or her interest to accept the role of agent, and

(2) the *incentive compatibility constraint*, which requires that the agent should accept actions generating the optimum outcomes as in his interest to perform, and which if ignored leads to 'rent seeking'.

There are several difficulties with this approach as applied to the labour market. It focuses only on outcomes, usually income or product, and not on the value of processes and interactions of institutional arrangements, such as participatory or creative engagement. It presumes that motivation is purely based on gains, notably financial, rather than wider forms, such as 'social responsibility'. It presumes that motivations are given at the outset and remain the same, rather than evolve as shaped by institutional and power arrangements. And it focuses on formal contractual obligations whereas informal interactions and *trust* are crucial parts of labour relationships. Thus, the principal–agent model has inherent limitations for labour market analysis.

Third, labour market relationships are about more than effort or the conventionally recognised or norm-based application of effort and skill. It is about reciprocal *obligations* and *entitlements*. These are rarely fixed and are historically and culturally determined. Economic anthropologists such as Manning Nash and Marshall Sahlins developed ideas of structured and balanced reciprocity, and we should take due account of these.

Fourth, the labour market is also about *control* and *status*. Both of these have economic, social, political and psychological elements. The notion of control is complex, and is critical for understanding labour market transactions. The elements include the degree or extent of control, the forms of control, control by whom, control over what. These are elaborated in the next chapter.

Fifth, the initial bargain does not presuppose any definitive relationship of 'skill' development and application. The notion of *skill* is rarely subject to analytical scrutiny by labour economists. Often one hears that there is 'a shortage of skilled labour', or that 'skill bottlenecks are creating structural unemployment, and impeding economic growth'. This too will be considered later.

Sixth, the labour market is an allocative process involving inter-temporal presumptions that can never be certain, and that are often not understood by either the employer or the worker. For example, you may hire me as a 'gardener' telling me that I have to begin by mowing the grass. I may presume that mowing the grass is only part of my job, while you decide that it should be almost the entire job. The issue is further complicated because either party may change their mind. If I believe that mowing the grass is merely the path to becoming a professional gardener, my effort bargain may change once I find out that it is actually a dead end.

Seventh, the formal or initial labour bargain rarely specifies the mix of incentives and sanctions to be used to shape the effort bargain. If one looks at different countries, industries, eras and occupations, one finds that relative reliance on incentives and sanctions varies enormously. There is a distinguished literature on the forms of discipline used to forge the *proletariat* in the course of the industrial revolution. Use of the clock, fear, intimidation and so on were complemented by petty incentives associated with social status. Yet at all times the mix of financial, status and other incentives to achieve greater exertion of mental and manual labour, and the mix of sanctions, has been variable and a matter of social bargaining.

Eighth, a labour market is a social, public sphere. It is a place of social interaction and is thereby a primary means of socialisation, for better or for worse. If one privatises the labour market by some means, one tends to isolate individuals, and this could accentuate social inequality and induce disruptive reactions. This theme was captured in Karl Polyani's *The Great Transformation*, in which he depicted the labour market as linking family life to the economy, and laid stress on the 'embeddedness' of different institutions and the emergence of 'the system of self-regulating markets'.

In sum, the labour market is *not* like other markets and it is futile to think that it is appropriate to try to make it more like a commodity market. Trying to achieve that has nevertheless been a theme of the literature on labour market flexibility.

1.9 THE *VITA ACTIVA*

In arguing the necessity of differentiating between work, labour and employment, and in raising familiar doubts about the prolonged debate on the supposed right to work, we are arguing that if, in the realm of work, there is any objective worthy of calling a right it is the *right to occupation*, where the promotion of the positive side of work is identified as the desirable goal of public policy.

Neither work nor labour is absolutely desirable. In her classic and erudite book, *The Human Condition*, Hannah Arendt traced the development of thinking about human activity since antiquity, suggesting that *reflection* was the primary human condition. This is more than the term leisure conveys, let alone consumption. It means having the space and freedom to avoid the excesses of human self-centredness, and the stress that comes from the acquisitive spirit *and* the ethics of labour. It is the recognition that reflecting on what *is*, rather than what one could do to transform raw materials into output or to make money, provides a context for developing a sense of social responsibility and social solidarity. Labouring and productive activity in general diminish the space for contemplation. That space also facilitates the pursuit of occupation in the fullest, creative sense.

Since occupation can be distinguished from job, and is linked to the gradual refinement of skill in the sense of creativity, competence and human capacities, one also needs to be clear about such commonplace terms as division of labour, exploitation and skill itself. Occupation is about relationships as well as human capabilities and it is about how one relates to the world around us, and to those over whom one may have some control and to those who possess such control over us. Occupation is about freedom to be creative, but it is also about such messy aspects of labour markets as power, resistance to oppression and exploitation, and control.

In that context, it is important to highlight the essential fuzziness of the notion of the labour market, which is the institutional framework by which jobs are allocated, exploitation is achieved or combated, and controls and resistance take shape.

2 Status, Control and Regulation

2.1 INTRODUCTION

All economists learn some labour economics, and the tools acquired as students shape the way they think about labour markets for the rest of their lives. At the micro-level, the worker supplies labour for a wage and the demand and supply curves cross. Although students are sent to classes in anthropology, sociology and history to learn about class and social relationships, the model of demand and supply remains the main way of looking at labour markets, with refinements such as reference to 'principals' and 'agents' or 'institutional obstacles'. There are no peasants in the textbooks or in international labour statistics.

The conventional approach does have analytical power. This chapter does not try to summarise that approach – numerous textbooks do that and little else.[1] Rather it is an attempt to develop a framework appropriate for analysing global labour market flexibility, hinging on the concepts of *control* and *security*. A neo-classical economist might at the end feel that he could fit all the concerns into models developed in labour economics. But would the concerns arise? Emphasis on control and on the responses and compromises show how labour markets differ decisively from other markets.

The conventional approach cuts off questions, notably about labour market *structures* and labour relations. Theoretical perspectives determine the questions asked in empirical research, by including certain questions and ruling out others, and by determining what are legitimate answers to scientific enquiry. No set of concepts is right in an absolute sense. Conceptual categories are as good as the empirical richness of the questions they raise, illuminate or help to answer.

The more work resembles labour, the less the labour market will conform to the image of neo-classical economic theory, for the less the 'employer' is likely to rely on 'incentives' and the more likely to rely on forms of control, if only because the incentives would have to be greater to secure the same effort. The relevance of a focus on control is that security, freedom and social justice depend on people having adequate autonomy. Before austerely developing the concepts that underlie much of the remainder of this book it might be useful to reflect on a widely used term.

2.2 THE LABOUR FORCE HISTORICALLY

For mainstream labour statisticians, since the 1930s and abandonment of the 'gainful worker' approach, the labour force is the 'economically active population', which covers those doing or seeking (or in some variants wanting) income-earning activities. For economists and employers, the labour force is that proportion of the population that is supplying labour. In popular language, the labour force is the employed, those actually labouring, excluding those wishing to do so, who are unemployed.

Often the meanings of the term are conflated, so one has to work out what is intended. A landlord may be included in the first labour force, if he does 'economic activity' collecting his rents, but should not be included in the second notion, and is unlikely to be part of the available labour supply.

With the first meaning, ambiguities arise from the notions of 'economic' and 'active', and whereas labour supply is a *flow* it is transformed into a *stock* in both notions of the labour force. Statisticians treat the labour force as a stock, but in making refinements over the years have introduced criteria that relate more to labour supply, that is, a flow of labour that should presumably be considered in terms of an opportunity income. This applies, for instance, to inclusion of people who declare themselves 'available for work', when it is not clear what this work would be.

The second notion of labour force has a longer tradition. The Physiocrats, early demographers such as Gregory King and classical political economists all had conceptualisations closer to it than to the labour force approach now used by statisticians across the world. In different ways, they distinguished the 'productive labour' force from the 'non-productive'. For the Physiocrats, only agricultural producers were productive, whereas for political economists adhering to the labour theory of value, productive labour is that intending to yield a surplus for capital accumulation. Some twentieth-century extensions of the productive–unproductive distinction have attempted to separate 'reproductive labour', that is, work done to reproduce labour power, which may generate surplus for accumulation. This approach has had minority appeal in recent years.

The 'gainful worker' approach was also closer to the second notion of labour force than to the labour statisticians' current approach, since it tried to measure those in specified work statuses. This was used in censuses and surveys in the nineteenth and early twentieth centuries until displaced by the labour force approach.

The first notion of labour force was a child of Keynesian economics, and the concern to measure unemployment. It makes no distinction between productive and unproductive labour, it excludes some activities because they do not generate an income, and it excludes some income-earning activities on an arbitrary, moralistic basis. It is 'sexist'. It excludes housework, done mainly by women. This has been widely criticised and poorly rationalised over the years. But what is the basis for excluding a prostitute or gangster from the labour force? The *formal* definitions of economic activity cannot be used to justify such exclusions.

Figure 2.1 presents a version of the labour force approach. The terms in capital letters are not usual features of labour force statistics. The main point is to recall the way of thinking and the edifice involved. Thus, the approach begins by dividing

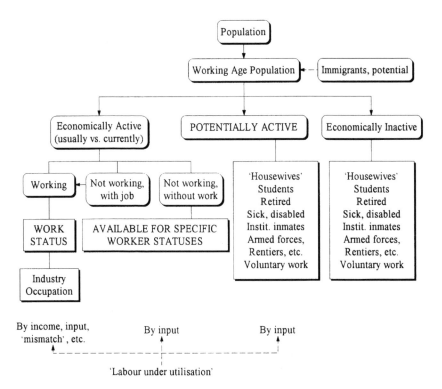

Figure 2.1 Modified labor force approach (abbreviated)

the population into the adult 'working age' population and the remainder; this is a matter of convention. Then the working age population is divided into 'active' and 'inactive', though many of the inactive are 'discouraged' or 'potential' labour force participants. Then the active are divided into employed and unemployed, and the 'employed' into self-employed, employers, wage workers and unpaid (family) workers. One might suppose that the unemployed should be divided into groups according to availability for specific work statuses, but the work status categories are over-simplifications.

The difficulties are partly 'aggregative', partly conceptual. Taking the 'population at risk' as the point of departure, at each stage of the disaggregation arbitrary decisions must be made to complement conceptual decisions. Thus, a proportion of the 'population at risk' is excluded from 'working age population' but is 'economically active' in reality. To give just one example: The conventional retirement age in some countries is 60; those employed above that age are counted as employed, but if they lose their job and search for another, they may be excluded from the unemployment count *and* labour force.

Some of the economically active, such as many migrants, will not be included in the population at risk. Some with a labour status but not working may be included as employed (such as those on 'lay-off'), others excluded. Then, there are problems of category 'priority', with multiple statuses and so on. Should someone cleaning shoes for two hours a week and searching for employment for 38 hours be called employed or unemployed? Normally, he would be classified as employed. This is a statistical convenience, no more.

The fact is that it is an *ad hoc* edifice, however neat its formal presentation. In its defence, it gives an image of reality that is useful for policymaking and for those who wish to give a broad-brush picture of the labour process. However, its deficiencies are substantial for analysing labour in low-income countries, for flexible labour systems and for social structures that do not correspond to the model of society that prevailed in industrialised countries in the mid-twentieth century. It is reasonable only for societies based on male full-time industrial wage labour. That is why the 'gainful worker' approach prevailed before the mid-twentieth century, based on occupational status and social class.

In many countries, including those classified as state socialist (or communist) and developing countries, some economists have claimed that there is no labour market. Yet almost all countries have been collecting supposedly internationally comparable labour statistics. In numerous reports and books, the percentage employment rate in a central African country, for example, is presented alongside, or a few pages from, the percentage employment rate in the USA or Germany. The unemployment rate is shown to be lower in a country in the Middle East than in France, lower in Ukraine than in neighbouring Hungary. Most economists and commentators seem content with such data. They convey an image, and if there is unease about international comparability, it is usually reserved for concern over measurement differences. Some observers have criticised the applicability of the concepts, but usually these criticisms have been relegated to footnotes to show that the points are noted. Then everyone goes on much as before.

The statistical representation of labour and work needs to be overhauled. If *occupation* and *flexible lifestyles* are to become the focus of concern, a synthesis of the gainful worker and labour force approaches is needed. Just as the former was disembedded from the twentieth-century concern for the labouring man, so the labour force approach is disembedded from a society in which informal work, multiple statuses, occupational diversity and flexible lifestyles predominate.

2.3 THE ESSENCE OF CONTROL

The term 'labour process' has come in for heavy use in recent years. It consists of relations underlying the production process and those covered by the 'work process', a term roughly covering the 'internal labour market' of the firm. Abstractly, the production process encompasses relations of producers to the work process and relations between producers and non-producers, the latter being those who have acquired control over part of the production. The key verbs in the semantics of labour are 'exchange', 'oblige', 'exploit', 'bargain' and 'control'. For present purposes, primacy lies with *control*. However, exploitation should not be neglected, defined not in the neo-classical sense of being paid less than one's marginal product, or in the Marxian sense of surplus product or labour, but in the philosophical sense of 'taking unfair advantage of someone's labour'. The relevance for our later proposals is that some critics of social protection for the poor and those not labouring have contended that giving protection is a form of exploitation because it involves giving income or support without a balanced obligation, making it 'unfair'. This influential claim rests on an implicit judgment that other economic relationships, particularly those involving labour, do involve a non-exploitative balanced reciprocity.

Intellectually, concern over control has a long pedigree. Thomas Hobbes' *Leviathan* rationalised authoritarian power as the outcome of the insecurities and brutishness of the 'state of nature', so that individuals surrendered rights and freedom in return for authoritarian protection. The debate over control, the role of the state and liberty has gone on ever since.

Control does not correspond to ownership. Owning implies a range of social rights – claims, privileges, powers, immunities – and does not necessarily imply power to control production. Indeed, some economists have equated dispersion of legal ownership in corporate production with concentration of economic ownership. Similarly, *possession*, as the capacity to put means of production to work, whether directly or in a managerial sense, is not the same as economic ownership, which is a productive relation that does not imply control over actual production.

The idea of control is linked to the philosophical concept of *determination*, the setting of limits (to an object of knowledge or range of behaviour) and the exertion of pressure, inducing a constrained range of reactions rather than a prefigured pattern of behaviour. Control may be used to compel someone to do something, to raise the costs of doing or not doing something, to prevent someone from doing something that he might prefer to do, or to excommunicate someone for doing something. Complementing these, there are six possible objectives of attempted subjection:

(1) to induce a sense of *inevitability*, that the control is 'natural';
(2) to induce behaviour to *accommodate* to a situation perceived as unjust;
(3) to induce a sense of *representation*, or ideological domination to the extent that the person under control believes that the situation is just;
(4) to induce *deference*, acquiescent behaviour induced by the belief that the controllers possess superior qualities;
(5) to induce *fear*, of sanctions or of possible alternatives, in spite of a belief in the feasible desirable alternatives;
(6) to induce *resignation*, a belief that all available alternatives would be worse.

Control also implies *hierarchy* and the imposition of obligations, whether or not there are reciprocal entitlements. The notion of 'hierarchy' is linked to 'the new institutional economics', and to Williamson's distinction between 'markets' and 'hierarchies' (Williamson, 1975; Williamson and Ouchi, 1981). This has been fruitful, with its notions of transaction costs, opportunism and malfeasance. But in depicting institutional arrangements as 'bounded rationality', whereby firms exist as governance structures to overcome complexity, ambiguity and contingencies, and by dichotomising markets and firms in a static way, the approach 'undersocialises' and neglects the fluidity of institutional arrangements in the face of relations of control, resistance and compromise (Granovetter, 1985).

Control is distinct from *authority*, which derives from moral legitimacy, inducing obedience based on more than fear or coercion. *Coercion* is a form of control, but one does not obtain authority from coercion, only acquiescence, flight or rebellion. Authority compels respect. *Markets* are a form of control over human behaviour, but not authority. *'Custom'* is also a form of control, and it may be a form of legitimacy. The outcome of market controls may be 'morally offensive', whereas customs may derive from mutual agreement without any group having control.

In production, people have control over – or are under the control of – something. Nobody has total control, and it is hard to envisage anybody under the total control of others. Where people fit in the spectrum matters for several reasons. Control limits freedom, determines personal and communal *security,* induces a consciousness of opportunities and shapes behavioural adaptation. The most effective control, from the controller's viewpoint, is that which induces the controlled to believe they have a *duty* to perform tasks they would not contemplate in other circumstances.

Elsewhere, an attempt is made to disaggregate the elements of labour subject to control, and to produce a classification of labour statuses based on forms of control. While no labour relationship is *free* in giving complete autonomy, the objective of social policy should be to enhance autonomy – real freedom – and to reduce the range and intensity of controls. Two forms of control deserve more emphasis. *Paternalistic control* involves notions of *reciprocity* and *protection*. With any paternalism, a reciprocity of welfare for labour is determined by the controller, and this discretion represents insecurity for the worker. *Occupational control* is rarely identified in labour analysis. Yet control over its own tasks is a defining characteristic of occupations. This covers the control of *access, performance, work content, evaluation* and *protection*. Medieval guilds achieved this, and modern occupational associations have done much the same (Simpson, 1985; Derber, 1982). Other forms of control are more hierarchical, and in all cases induce some form of *resistance*, involving some form of *exit* or *voice*.

Distributive justice should be concerned with relations of control and with the extent of *security* in which people work and live. Historically, economies and societies have evolved through struggles over control systems and degree of security. Thus, to give an example relevant to labour market relations at the end of the twentieth century, consider the Luddites, the name given to those who smashed machines at the end of the first decade of the nineteenth century. Their actions are usually interpreted as a misguided protest against the substitution of machines for labour and 'technological unemployment'. Yet actually they were protesting against the rupture of their established way of labour, the underlying social relations and the distributive outcomes that had been accepted as legitimate. The factory regime involved a different 'social contract', with new hierarchical relations of control. Theirs was a protest against the insecurity and controls they had not hitherto experienced.

2.4 CONCEPTUALISING SECURITY

It may be that cattle must be driven by fear. Men can and should be led by hope.
William Beveridge, 1944

Self-control cannot be divorced from the need for security, defined as a sense of well-being, of being in control over one's development and activities, and a sense of sustainable self-respect. Etymologically, in the English language security has been used in a pejorative sense, as a culpable absence of anxiety, or a carelessness. But more often it has had positive connotations. The main meanings are (i) freedom from care, anxiety or apprehension, (ii) a condition of being protected from, or not exposed to, danger, (iii) freedom from doubt, a sense of confidence and assurance, and (iv) a condition of being securely fixed, a stability. Insecurity might be defined as a state of *anxiety*, which Kierkegaard defined as a 'feeling that has no definite object', a universal emotion that is nevertheless individually definable.

Although human beings require and want basic security, there is a tension in the idea, since too much security may induce passivity and indolence – the super rich tend to have supine offspring. However, too little security can induce anomie, moral collapse, retributive action against the privileged and others, and a wretched, short life. What is required is basic security, without which creative, risk-taking behaviour is likely to be beyond the imagination. There are other distinctions. One scholar has differentiated between *essential insecurity*, such as the anxiety that most parents feel for their children, and *existential insecurity*, that due to external events and pressures.

One should also distinguish between *collective security (societal and community)*, *corporate* (or *enterprise*) *security*, and *individual security*. Collective security reflects the human need to identify with (or belong to) particular social groups, usually to exert control over the behaviour of others or to limit their control. This may be an identification with a class, occupational group, or local community. One should not narrow it to identification with only one group, for security comes from multiple forms of identity. For our purposes, the focus is on individual security with respect to work and labour, although collective security is considered later.

Economic and social security is a reflection of material circumstances and a state of mind mostly derived from real circumstances. Security is a human need, more fundamental than such notions as the supposed right to employment, for example. Economic insecurity is a sense of *relative deprivation*, relative to one's perceived needs, the income of one's social peer group, and so on. It is also linked to a sense of *opportunity* and a sense of *balanced reciprocity*, in that if one follows certain rules of conduct one can expect certain entitlements that provide security.

Above all, security is based on *self-control*, and reasonable security is a necessary condition for real freedom and autonomy. Insecurity is a form of injustice and a source of it. The distribution of security, just as much as the distribution of income, is thus an ethical issue. One might define a just society as one that maximises sustainable basic security for all, with the Rawlsian caveat that priority should be given to improvement of the position of the worst off.

We deal with seven elements of security in later chapters. For present purposes, security involves good opportunity to obtain desirable and desired outcomes (including a broadening *range* of opportunities), absence of *stress*, and modest uncertainty about potential outcomes. Sources of insecurity include the following:

- absence or reduction of control over aspects of work;
- absence or reduced probability of upward mobility in status or income;
- necessity for increased effort for any given income;
- increased risk of an adverse outcome;
- increased uncertainty about outcomes;
- fear that one could not do anything to rectify an adverse development.

Possible effects of insecurity include the following:

- sense of oppression and exploitation;
- demoralisation, anomie;
- demotivation, non-co-operation;
- ill-health, stress;
- absenteeism;
- quits, high turnover;
- sabotage.

Consider a few examples. If labour required more intensity of effort, the resultant insecurity could be debilitating and make working relationships more fragile and thus prone to undermine a sense of balanced reciprocity and *loyalty*, which underlies a relationship perceived as non-exploitative and just. Insecurity would grow if an individual lost control over aspects of the work process. If one feared one's skills were becoming obsolescent, the skill's perceived value would be reduced, even if the actual wage had not changed. If there were a decline in the probability of experiencing rising income or status, there is likely to be a *demoralisation effect*, leading to *non-application* of existing skills, and a *demotivation effect*, i.e., the *non-maintenance* of existing skills. If insecurity disrupted mental calm, it could induce mental and physical *ill-health*.

Insecurity would be intensified if the uncertainty of outcome from work increased, or if the predictability of outcomes of working diminished, or if the variability increased. Insecurity would also be intensified if risk increased, i.e., if the probability of an adverse outcome increased or if the potential cost of an adverse outcome increased. Insecurity would also grow if it appeared that if something went wrong one could not do much to rectify the situation or gain compensation. For instance, if one had a full-time job and written assurance of three months notice in case of termination of employment, that would provide some employment security. But it would be much reduced if one knew that at the end of the notice there would be no prospect of another source of income. It would also be reduced if there were no practical possibility of obtaining redress if the promise was unilaterally abrogated.

An aspect of insecurity and the accompanying stress is that it may *reveal* itself in ways that do not appear to support it. For example, fear of job loss induces stress, which may induce absenteeism, premature retirement or high labour turnover. Leaving one's job 'voluntarily' might seem a strange response to fear of job loss, yet physical and emotional adaptation to insecurity might explain the reaction. Perversely, insecurity might induce one to hold on to one's job, giving the impression that security had increased.

Above all, work security is the perception that one has adequate freedom in which to exercise occupation. As such, it is related to *control* and to *autonomy*. If a person is subject to controls that restrict opportunities, or that limit options, work-related security will diminish.

2.5 FORMS OF LABOUR REGULATION

Regulation extends and restricts freedom; only the balance of the freedoms that are lost and won are significant.

Karl Polanyi, 1944, p. 254

Labour regulations are forms of control. Yet there is an ambiguity about them that derives from what are often conflicting objectives. Controls reflect power, and power produces insecurity among those subjected to it and put at a disadvantage by its existence and use. Often, regulations have been a means of correcting for unequal power, although many have been used to enhance the advantage of some groups or to produce more stable labour supply. Some regulations have been intended to promote productivity, some to reduce exploitation and insecurity.

There is no such thing as an unregulated or 'deregulated' labour market. No society could exist without modes of regulation and a regulatory framework, and one of the stupidest terms that came into popularity in the 1980s and 1990s was 'deregulation'. Labour market regulations exist for several reasons, the most well-known being protection of groups against insecurity, oppression and exploitation. Another objective of some regulations is productive efficiency enhancement.

Abstractly, regulations are mechanisms or institutional processes that limit 'freedoms' of certain individuals or groups, in the interest of enhancing one or more forms of 'security' for others. At the macro-economic level, the regulatory system can be described as the mechanisms and institutions intended to preserve the *functional stability* of the productive and distribution system in the interest of sustainable economic growth.

Regulations also *determine* the *legitimacy* of processes and distribution of assets of those participating in them, where 'assets' include tangible and intangible means and outcomes of production. Regulations may also be a means of moderating the inequalities and imbalances that arise in labour systems. They are a method for embedding the economy in society. Regulations are also potentially the means of reducing *transaction costs*. Thus, they should be designed so as to reduce worker, job-seeker and managerial *opportunism*. Among managerial forms of opportunism is the control of information, the interaction with a limited circle of contacts, and retention of the capacity to take decisions (Smith, 1991). Among workers' opportunism is the capacity to vary the effort bargain, to resort to petty sabotage, and to resort to pilfering. The existence of opportunism as an integral part of labour markets implies a need for regulations to *legitimise* and to *monitor* behaviour, to *impose sanctions* if abuses or opportunism occur and are detected, and to alter costs and benefits of specific actions.

Libertarians and supply-side economists usually describe regulations as 'interventions'. According to the Chicago school of law and economics, guided by the notion of Pareto optimality and libertarianism, regulations are justifiable only if they both promote economic growth and involve welfare gain for some people while not harming anybody else. This perspective has been used to justify calls for 'deregulation'. However, regulations are not merely protective in character, and there seems no justification for applying a growth constraint rule.

Besides what Freud called 'cultural regulations', there are three modes of labour regulation, and within each there are several forms of regulation. Each has advantages and disadvantages. For each, there may be *implicit* erosion and *explicit* erosion, the first arising from more people drifting into statuses where they are not covered by a particular regulation, the second occurring by means of legislative or administrative reform.

(i) Statutory Regulation

Statutory regulations are what many regard as the only regulations. These are rules, procedures and institutions established by laws or decrees designed to set parameters of acceptable behaviour. They may be *pro-collective* or *pro-individualistic*, in that laws may give incentives to collective institutions or may set out to limit or control them. In labour market terms, statutory regulations come in five forms:

- *Protective regulations*   rules and procedures to protect workers, and/or to prevent those in strong positions from abusing those in weak positions;
- *Fiscal regulations*   taxes and subsidies to encourage certain forms of activity and/or discourage other forms;
- *Repressive regulations*   rules and mechanisms to prevent something that the state, or a dominant interest, does not wish to occur;
- *Promotional regulations*   rules and mechanisms (other than taxes) designed to promote certain developments;
- *Facilitating regulations*   rules and procedures that permit activities to take place, if there is a desire to do so.

The potential advantages of statutory regulations are that they are, in principle, *predictable, transparent* and *equitable*. Transparency helps structure labour bargains, since those entering labour relationships have reasonable information on the basis of the bargain. An advantage is that statutory regulations provide clear *monitoring* mechanisms. They have been justified as a corrective for *market failure*, notably that due to a lack of information among workers or employers. They may discourage short-term profit maximisation, but longer-term dynamic efficiency. There are clearly trade-offs in forms of efficiency (Kuttner, 1997). But regulations may also overcome discrimination that would not disappear otherwise.

The potential disadvantages of statutory regulations are a tendency to *rigidity*, in that no law or regulation can cover every contingency; a tendency to excessive *legalism*, which may intensify insecurities of those incapable of operating in that sphere; *complexity*, because of the numerous situations that have to be covered in any regulatory framework; and *bureaucracy*, which comes from having to operate any such system. Statutory regulations also create *moral hazards*. For example, it is sometimes reasoned that safety laws and compensation make people more careless than they would otherwise be. Statutory regulations are also inherently *paternalistic,* sometimes offering politicians and bureaucrats the means of exerting control over citizens. This is why libertarians argue that state intervention encourages individualism and actually discourages voluntary co-operation (Murray, 1997).

One must not presume that statutory regulations have a redistributive effect, even if that is the intended objective. Often they may help one vulnerable group relative to another. Regulations may also sanction or reinforce forms of discrimination and injustice. This applies to statutory quotas for the disabled, for instance.

A system that relies mainly on statutory regulations will be inclined to generate *opportunism*, particularly if the labour system is diversified and flexible. Opportunism may breed disrespect and undermine the system's legitimacy, encouraging avoidance and evasion, with tacit connivance from others in the system, perhaps including those with responsibility to operate it. The onus on statutory regulations is the capacity of the legal and administrative apparatus to operate them efficiently and equitably.

(ii) Market Regulation

Market regulation is where the authorities seek to maximise reliance on market forces and use legislation and other regulatory instruments to achieve that. Those who have advocated 'deregulation' have actually been advocating regulations to weaken protective regulations, restrict collective institutions and strengthen pro-individualistic regulations. Advocates of market regulations, from Freidrich Hayek onwards, have wanted legislative measures used to regulate the labour market. Market regulation increases *market dependency*, whereas statutory regulation decreases market dependency, through reducing the insecurity associated with labour force participation.

The advantages of market regulation are that it encourages and rewards risk taking, involves less costly administration than statutory protective regulations, fosters an atmosphere of entrepreneurship in which the 'animal spirits' can pursue economic opportunities, and is likely to lower transaction costs of most economic activities.

Market regulation has disadvantages. It encourages short-termism, since there is no pressure to be locked into stable labour relationships. It allows decision-makers to avoid responsibility for externalities such as environmental damage and unemployment. For these reasons, a preference has existed for government interventions, including public investment in infrastructure, to overcome market failure. Pro-individualistic and pro-market regulations tend to be inegalitarian, since they allow power and control to grind out unequal rewards. And market regulation tends to permit *opportunism*, which comes from the modest monitoring capacity.

Those claiming that they advocate 'deregulation' usually support market regulation and more often than not favour a mixture of *repressive* and *fiscal* regulations, with some *promotional* regulations, while vigorously opposing protective, pro-collective regulations and institutions.

(iii) Voice Regulation

This derives from Albert Hirschman, who memorably contrasted Exit and Voice options to social dilemmas. Voice regulation implies that labour relations, practices and changes are managed through bargaining between representatives of potentially conflicting interests, which to be effective should embrace those on the margins of society as well as established interests. There is insignificant voice regulation where a powerful firm confronts an insecure worker, or where a landlord confronts a bonded labourer.

Those who favour voice regulation recognise that labour embodies conflict of interest. The best response is to legitimise and institutionalise those conflicts that, if managed properly, have positive outcomes in terms of distributive justice. To be effective, institutions of voice regulation must be inclusive in character and the bargaining environment must be balanced. Being balanced requires mutual strength, not the strong confronting the weak, or the fearful confronting each other. Mutual weakness is only trivially balanced, and the voice content would be shrill and desperate. To be effective as instruments of distributive justice and as instruments of *dynamic efficiency* agencies of voice regulation must be able to ensure that all bargainers have sustainable strength. The agents must believe that they will have to deal with each other again and again. There must be **the shadow of the future** lingering over their deliberations.

In terms of a firm and the labour market, bargaining with the future in mind should induce pressure for dynamic efficiency, in which, for example, desirable restructuring results in, or is intended to produce, shared losses and gains. Voice regulation means a greater likelihood that exploitation and sub-standard practices would induce retribution and sabotage, lowering efficiency. It should mean that it would be harder for controllers to ignore grievances among the controlled, and it should mean that grievances could be managed, innovation encouraged and reciprocities established and maintained. For these outcomes, representatives must be well informed and have an interest in making the process efficient *and* equitable. Therein lies the challenge for any structure of voice regulation.

Voice regulation has three potential disadvantages. It is *time consuming*, since it involves explicit bargaining. For their own legitimacy both parties may find it necessary to take postures, demonstrate disagreement and prolong negotiations. Against that, both parties may adapt to the expected positions of the other, and thus become less opportunistic. Second, there is a tendency for co-ordination failure, where lack of information, different information or some other factor leads to a breakdown in communication. Lack of shared and accurate information can create tensions. Finally, voice regulation may intensify labour market inequalities and insecurity if the institutions exclude the interests of more vulnerable groups.

The potential advantages of voice regulation are considerable. It can reduce both the excesses of market forces and the rigidities of statutory regulation. At the firm level, it can encourage dynamic efficiency and restructuring. It can incorporate the interests of all 'stakeholders', and it can reduce exploitation of vulnerable groups, thereby deterring low effort bargains, sabotage, exit through quitting and other forms of worker retribution. And it can prevent unilateral control by management from distorting the choice of technique away from provision of firm-specific training. In sum, voice regulation can provide monitoring so as to reduce opportunism.

The necessary conditions for success with voice regulation are the sharing of accurate and relevant information, without which co-ordination failure is almost certain to occur, and the recognition by all sides of the shadow of the future, the recognition that the bargainers will be facing each other over a prolonged period. The mechanisms must be inclusive of not just the strong but all those on the margins, and the powers of the negotiating parties must be approximately balanced and strong.

Thus, the onus on voice regulation comes down to the question: is the institutional bargaining and decision-making sufficiently representative and responsive?

2.6 CONCLUSION: CONTROL, FREEDOM AND SECURITY

Neo-classical economics assumes that legal and statutory regulations can enforce complete contracts costlessly, and that labour contracts are complete, which means that, as Paul Samuelson (1957, p. 894) so memorably put it, 'In the competitive model it makes no difference whether capital hires labour or the other way round.' Complete contracts do not require controls. Labour relations are not complete contracts.

The loss or surrender of self-control over work is what makes *labour* the reality for most labour force participants. This surrender is at the heart of the social malaise, the unhappiness of humanity. The surrender is never total, and from time to time even the most subordinated worker will rebel, so that his spirit sparkles for a brief moment. But the norm is that labour control induces a profound insecurity, which is very unequally distributed in society. In the twenty-first century freeing the worker from labour control will be one of the great challenges.

Control is the antonym of *trust*. All forms of control run against the grain of the human spirit. Where relations of trust are replaced by control mechanisms those subject to them will harbour thoughts of opportunism to evade them, or rebellion to overthrow them, the theme of Barrington Moore's wonderful book on injustice (1978). This reaction in turn has costs for individuals and for society. Only if labour evolved into co-operative work, so that conflicts of interest were not of primary importance, would there be the *self-control* required of a good society.

Control is also the negation of freedom. The control may be minor or almost total, but it always compromises freedom of choice, freedom of action and freedom to work. If one accepts that the controls are extensive, then they surely compromise decisions based on the expression of *preferences*. If there is no equal opportunity and if some people are under the control of others, it is dubious to treat preferences as representing the real interests of people, because as Elster (1979) and others have noted, cognitive dissonance shapes preferences. The peasant, serf, bonded labourer or wage worker forms preferences based on his or her human condition. Freed from a particular control, a person develops different tastes, values and orientations to work. Seen in this light, the validity of preferences and the value of social involvement depend on maximising individual *self*-control and security, without which cognitive dissonance will be involved.

Labour control induces passivity. It breeds passive jobholders, people who know what to do but not what or how to think. As Hannah Arendt (1957, p. 324) so memorably put the outcome, it is 'far easier to act under a tyranny than it is to think'.

Control and security should be part of social justice. There has been a rich debate since the early 1970s on what constitutes distributive justice. All modern theories of justice begin with the premise that everyone should be treated as equal in some respect. We may end with the assertion, developed in chapter 11, that the Good Society should be one in which freedom, security and self-control would be equalised as far as possible. How to pursue distributive justice with flexible labour markets and globalisation is the subject of the final section of this book.

Part II

The Sirens of Flexibility

It is not fashionable to talk about flexibility,
and yet this is an answer to all our problems.
Serge Dassault, Chairman, Dassault Aviation, 1998

Part II examines the factors that have led to the growth of more flexible labour markets and the forms of flexibility that have developed. An underlying hypothesis is that economies, or productive systems, evolve through eras of security and stability into eras of insecurity and flexibility, which create conditions and socio-economic pressures that could induce a new era of security. The years from 1945 to about 1975 should be characterised as an era of security and stability, or the *era of statutory regulation*, whereas from the mid-1970s until the late 1990s there was an *era of market regulation*, in which greater insecurity came with the pursuit of flexibility.

3 The Pursuit of Flexibility

Everything is in flux
Herakleitos

1.1 INTRODUCTION

The notion of 'labour market flexibility' has been a key euphemism of the last quarter of the twentieth century. It is not a neutral term; it is a euphemism for more than could be conveyed by any definition. Yet it prompts an image. Who could be against being 'flexible' or in favour of being 'inflexible'? Often, the term 'rigid' has been used interchangeably with 'inflexible'. Even more dubious uses of the term have been common. In many international reports and statements by public figures, calls for flexibility have been little more than ill-designed masks for proposals to lower wages or worker protection.

One claim or presumption of those who advocate more flexibility is that regulations, legislation, institutions and conventions apparently designed to protect workers and their families are often counter-productive, primarily because they raise unemployment. It is this that has given the topic of flexibility such a high profile.

The most common interpretation of flexibility is the extent and speed of adaptation to market shocks, the suggestion being that institutional and behavioural rigidities in labour markets and enterprises slow price and quantity adjustments. A difficulty is that numerous reports and articles have called simply for *more* flexibility. Yet surely one could have too much of a good thing. After all, a highly flexible system is also an unstable one, since it is sensitive to shocks that may be short-lived or random. Just as a car goes faster with brakes, and electricity needs some resistance, so any social system needs some inertia to give it stability.

There is another way of looking at the issue. Systems and relations of production evolve through eras of flexibility until the prevailing procedures and regulations become rigid and over-complex. Historically, all labour systems have evolved through flexible and more 'rigid' (or stable) phases, the rigid collapsing into more flexible forms, and flexible practices stabilising through the establishment and legitimation of norms and regulations, until these have fettered the development of production. Consider slavery. Initially, it was a highly flexible system of production, with slave-owners having little difficulty in replacing tired, old, recalcitrant, injured or dead slaves. Subsequently, the slave mode of production became rigid in the face of a shortage of slaves, and the periodic need to quell unrest; the rigidity restricted productivity growth and raised costs of control. The system was undermined by the limitations of a rigid labour control system.

Similarly, feudalism evolved through its flexible, 'free' phase, when peasants typically provided labour or produce-rent semi-voluntarily in return for protection from landlords. Over time the system became more rigid, as serfs were 'tied to the soil'. Mobility was curtailed, and economic surplus was extracted by increasingly onerous forms of rent, coercion, taxes and supplementary payments. Although feudal relationships have persisted in some parts of the world, the system collapsed primarily because its rigidities prevented the development of productive forces. Feudalism has typically given way to phases of 'free labour', when flexible labour systems have characterised both agrarian and industrial expansion. These have included migratory labour, labour circulation, putting out systems, outwork, gangwork, sub-contracting, and use of other forms of casual labour, easily hired and fired, easily replaced (Standing, 1981).

In the industrialisation of western Europe, the early phase was flexible in just those respects, during which time a surplus population was generated (if not unemployed, at least impoverished), which gradually instilled a sense of discipline and 'labouring ethic' among the nascent working class (Thompson, 1963; Dobb, 1946). During the nineteenth century the flexible phase started to give way to forms of rigidity, as trade unions and political organisations began to struggle for protective measures, limits on working time, regulations on unsafe working conditions, minimum wages and the like. This process was helped by paternalistic employers keen to provide security and benefits for workers so as to raise productivity, morale and acceptance of the increasing intensity and skill-content of labour. A period of flexibility has usually given way to one of stability when a coalition of well-established employers has seen the virtue and economic appeal of stability, security and social fairness.

It was a seminal contribution of Karl Polanyi to recognise a failing of mainstream Marxism, which foresaw a sharpening of class antagonisms as capitalism developed until the 'proletariat had nothing to lose but his chains'. Polanyi's 'double movement' recognised that as market forces were developed in a period of market expansion the state would respond by ushering in a period of protective regulation to moderate the resultant tensions, by offering social progress and security for the working class. Thus the social dislocation that was a feature of the transformation of the market system in the early nineteenth century precipitated institutional action to provide protection against impersonal market forces, to re-embed the economy in society. As Polanyi put it, 'Society protected itself against the perils inherent in a self-regulating market economy' (Polanyi, 1944, p. 76). Every period of economic reconstruction, associated with major technological change and the renewed pursuit of flexibility, has eventually induced a counter-movement to provide new systems of social protection compatible with the new structures and processes. Some historical eras seem to produce a stagnation or reversal in social progress – of growing inequalities – whereas others see a strong forward march. Every period of social *progress* has been based on specific institutions and commitments to some mechanisms of redistributive justice. In the era of statutory regulation, the objective was to redistribute income and welfare to the 'working class', broadly defined to include manual and non-manual workers. As Polanyi recognised, and as Offe reiterated (1984, p. 263), welfare was not a late part of capitalism, but a pre-condition for the commodification of labour.

3.2 THE ERA OF STATUTORY REGULATION: PURSUIT OF SECURITY

The twentieth century has been the century of the labouring man. From the earliest years, his needs and contribution to economic expansion became the primary impetus to social and labour market policy. The century began with a clamour for the *rights of labour*. For a brief period, there was a conflict among those leading the clamour, between those who saw freedom *from* labour as the objective and those who saw securing better labouring conditions as the goal. The latter view prevailed. The time was propitious for concessions, yet the social and economic instability bred caution. The savagery of the First World War and the Bolshevik Revolution of 1917 made ruling elites everywhere uncomfortable, ushering in a period of instability that culminated in the Second World War, after which the rights of the labouring man were legitimised more than ever.

Subordinated to the dictates of mass production and large-scale organisations, worker stability was regarded as the desirable norm for industrial society. In industrialised countries, a more 'rigid' or stable phase of production and distribution came to fruition in the period after the Second World War, with the extension of various forms of welfare state capitalism. By that time, globally there was a competition between two dominant models of long-term development, both of which had an objective of what many authors have called the *decommodification of labour*. Part of this meant consciously making the labour market less like other markets and thus deliberately less *flexible*.

Although there were several variants, the two models in competition were *welfare state capitalism* and *state socialism*. Although there were crucial differences, these had much in common. On their own terms, initially they were successful. Yet ultimately both have been rejected, one decisively, one by stealth as its adherents slip away. The authoritarianism and lack of freedom in the state socialism model were always its fatal flaws, making comparisons with welfare state capitalism unfair. Nevertheless, there were common developmental goals that in one form or another were exported to developing countries.

These two models of desirable society were based on the interests of the *labouring man*, and the pursuit of his basic needs and aspirations. Everywhere people were to be made more like the norm of the labouring man. For communist society, success was measured by the fact that almost everybody was labouring, with those not doing so condemned as parasitic. All men and women were expected to labour for as long as possible, in full-time wage labour. In welfare state capitalism too,

Full Employment was put on a pedestal, and social success was measured by the number of men in full-time labour.

This characterisation is made polemically to emphasise several points. First, the two dominant models were oriented to the role of labouring *man*. Second, means and ends were mixed up. Third, women's social progress was implicitly measured by how far they were becoming like labouring man. Fourth, both models gave pride of place to the promotion of individual and collective labour *security*.

One cannot envisage autonomy and freedom unless there is adequate security in the work process. One can interpret social and labour market policy during much of the twentieth century in terms of the pursuit of different forms of labour security. The great advance in most respects came in the 1950s and 1960s, although the roots of many developments came much earlier.

A way of looking at the two models is to see them as alternative systems for achieving progress on **seven forms of security**, leaving aside the issue of national security, which could be described as an eighth form shaping socio-economic developments. The labour market developments can be characterised as the steady extension of labour *rights* and *entitlements*, which may be captured conceptually by seven forms of security:

- *Labour market security* – adequate employment opportunities, through state-guaranteed full employment;
- *Employment security* – protection against arbitrary dismissal, regulations on hiring and firing, imposition of costs on employers, etc.;
- *Job security* – a niche designated as an occupation or 'career', plus tolerance of demarcation practices, barriers to skill dilution, craft boundaries, job qualifications, restrictive practices, craft unions, etc.;
- *Work security* – protection against accidents and illness at work, through safety and health regulations, limits on working time, unsociable hours, night work for women, etc.;
- *Skill reproduction security* – widespread opportunities to gain and retain skills, through apprenticeships, employment training, etc.;
- *Income security* – protection of income through minimum wage machinery, wage indexation, comprehensive social security, progressive taxation, etc.;
- *Representation security* – protection of collective voice in the labour market, through independent trade unions and employer associations incorporated economically and politically into the state, with the right to strike, etc.

The seven forms of security are considered in later chapters.[1] It is argued that primacy should be given to income security and representation security, because they are essential for ensuring other forms of security. We also surmise that the appropriate policies for attaining improvements in any form of security will vary according to the *character* of the labour market and the employment structure.

In the middle part of the century, the two models offered alternative visions of success and alternative forms of paternalistic labour control. These visions were put on offer to intellectuals, politicians, military men, religious circles and ideologues in 'developing countries'.

In state socialism, the state offered everybody security defined in terms of satisfaction of needs set by the centralised government, the party and their organs. If people conformed, they would receive an income, housing, schooling, a job, healthcare and recreation. Because the system lacked the reckless energy of capitalism, the goods and services produced were limited and the security was always of a low level. But there was security.

With the Leninist model, decommodification involved a low money wage with employment-based benefits assuming a growing share of remuneration and every adult in full-time employment. Redistribution was expected to come from low wage differentials and universal access to social services. Although there was a labour market, in that labour turnover was extensive and wage differentials were significant, the model did not involve a flexible labour market in any sense of the term. For better or worse, it was a model for stability, security and full employment.

The model of *welfare state capitalism* crystallised in the mid-twentieth century, although it took shape in the previous three decades and has had several variants. It should be differentiated from 'welfare capitalism', which is the term used to describe the paternalistic character of corporations in the USA during the early part of the century and which collapsed in the aftermath of the Crash of 1929. The term welfare state seems to have dated from 1951, and symbolised a central role of the state. In welfare state capitalism, there was an underlying historical compromise, made explicit in the Swedish model in the famous agreement of 1938 between employers and unions, and less explicitly in other countries, often through neo-corporatist bargaining. The compromise legitimised the managerial right to manage in return for a distributional consensus that there would be redistribution of income *from* growth, so that there was expected to be a gradual reduction in socio-economic inequality. The private ownership of capital was preserved beyond a few 'commanding heights' of the economy or spheres regarded as 'natural monopoly'.

At the heart of welfare state capitalism was an orientation to improve *distributive justice* through the labour market, oriented around the seven forms of security backed by regulations and institutions oriented to the perceived needs of the labouring man. In the aftermath of the Depression and the Second World War, the international community of policymakers from the victorious countries of North America and western Europe recognised the dangers of socio-economic inequality, and the global economic pressures tending to increase it, by largely taking labour rights out of international competition. Franklin Roosevelt among many recognised that the welfare state was a means of protecting capital from its own excesses, against the tendency for exploitation to grow, in part through the threat of shifting investment to where labour rights and standards were undeveloped or minimal.

The managerial right to manage legitimised variants of Taylorism, in which there was mass production, a hierarchical job structure and a highly developed technical division of labour. There was no desire for flexibility in this respect, either by managements or unions. Skills as job titles became symbols of status and security. Another feature was so-called *Fordism*, a term that originated with Antonio Gramsci and came to have a sizable progeny (e.g., Boyer, 1988; 1991). Essentially, economic growth was based on mass consumption by the working class, which through boosting the demand for goods created a virtuous circle with employment generation. In a sense, capital's tendency to increase profits at the expense of labour was constrained by the implicit and always fragile distributional consensus, and it was this that underpinned the macro-economic stability that prevailed in the era.

The dominant economic strategy was Keynesianism, by which macro-economic policy was expected to ensure so-called Full Employment, micro-economic policy to control inflationary pressures and promote efficiency, through regulations, anti-monopoly measures and institutions, and incomes policy. The Swedish model was a variant of what prevailed elsewhere. Under that, macro-economic policy was intended to achieve less than Full Employment, in order to contain inflationary pressures, while 'active labour market policy' was expected to fulfil a counter-cyclical function, where 'active' meant counter-cyclical and where it was used to lessen inflationary pressures and assist labour mobility (Standing, 1988). Several variants can be identified, as discussed elsewhere (Standing, 1991a). In all variants, the labour market was underpinned by the welfare state, based on social insurance and the premise that state transfers would be required primarily to cover 'temporary interruptions of earning power', including frictional unemployment, ill-health, and a short period of retirement. Since Richard Titmuss first began to differentiate societies, several variants of welfare state have been identified, producing a rich literature (see, for instance, Esping-Andersen, 1990; Castles and Mitchell, 1992; Jeffreys, 1995; Leibfried, 1993).

The labour market presumed by most post-war policymakers was one based on the vast majority of the *men* being in secure, full-time wage employment, with women being 'economically inactive' or in jobs as 'secondary' workers. It may never have been like that – in the sense that many women were in the labour market continuously – but that was the dominant image and the basis of the labour system (Lewis, 1992; Sainsbury, 1994).

Within employment and the labour market, the growing forms of labour control were bureaucratic and paternalistic. Indeed, the paternalistic ethos of the welfare state was recognised by some of its outstanding analysts. Thus, whereas in western Europe governments were expected to take over the role of social protector, US firms were expected to reward worker *loyalty* with security. Sumner Slichter, a founder-figure of modern industrial relations, saw the dangers of paternalism at an early stage, commenting:

> But is there no need among wage earners for more initiative and enterprise, for more mental independence, and for more disposition to rely on co-operative self-help than modern personnel practice is disposed to encourage? Is it not, in general, desirable that men be encouraged to manage their own affairs rather

than that they be deliberately and skilfully discouraged from making that attempt? And if much paternalism is inevitable, would it not be more satisfactory, from the standpoint of the community that it be paternalism of the government rather than paternalism of the employers? (Slichter, 1929)

He was describing what has been called welfare capitalism, when the big enterprises that were coming to dominate twentieth-century industrialised economies began to provide fringe benefits, job careers for loyal workers and company unions. Slichter's secondary wish was close to being realised in the post-war realities of western Europe and North America, when many forms of paternalistic labour control were taken over or extended by the state, with various forms of security and compensation made dependent on the performance of labour. Building that edifice began before the war. In the USA, the transition was manifested in the *Wagner Act* of 1935, the *Social Security Act*, the *Fair Labour Standards Act*, and measures to legitimise and regulate collective bargaining. The Wagner Act in particular legitimised statutory and limited voice regulation for the succeeding period. In 1948, Slichter, then President of the US Industrial Relations Research Association (IRRA), described the USA, approvingly, as 'a labouristic state'. There and elsewhere, the post-war period saw the state alter the balance of control, facilitating conflict resolution through legislation and institutions, obliging employers and unions to make concessions, integrating adversarialism while preserving control over labour and preserving labour as the legitimised way of existence.

It was as if the middle years of the century integrated Taylorism into the mainstream of society, by modifying its excesses and extending bureaucratic labour controls. In government institutions, which led the way, and in large corporations, this was epitomised by the proliferation of personnel jobs, associated with the growth of personnel departments, which internalised welfare worker functions. This was encouraged by governments and statutory regulations (Baron, Dobbins and Jennings, 1986).

From 1945 to the mid-1970s could be characterised as the *era of statutory regulation*. It deserves to be called that rather than the Golden Age or one of 'social consensus', because it was based on an inequitable and unsustainable international division of labour, and because there was much social strife led by workers wanting progress to continue or be speeded up. There was a spurt in economic growth in the post-war period, once stability had been restored, but it was a period of tension, in which employers typically made concessions to workers, and in which distributional conflict was extended to other forms of conflict in Asia, Africa and Latin America.

Social and distributional progress was led by western Europe, and reformers in much of the world, including so-called developing countries, typically looked there for guidance for policy initiatives. The welfare state and the march towards some notion of equality were seen as the main goals. The major labour market achievements were the steady extension of labour *rights* and *security*. Although the pace and progress varied from country to country, there was progress in most respects, and there was the presumption that the progress in countries taking the lead would be spread to other countries.[2] There was a gradual extension of government commitment to labour standards and statutory, protective regulations, although on most major issues few countries committed themselves to the type of standards illustrated in Table 3.1, as measured by ratification of ILO Conventions. Even at the end of the period relatively few countries had ratified them.

Table 3.1 Percentage of ILO member states having ratified selected ILO Conventions, 1995

Convention on	No.	1995
Reduction of hours of work	47	7%
Freedom of association and protection of the right to organise	87	62%
Application of the principles of the right to organise and to bargain collectively	98	68%
Employment Policy	122	46%
Employment Policy	132	11%
Minimum age for admission to employment	138	25%
Organisation of rural workers and their role in economic and social development	141	19%
Vocational guidance and vocational training in the development of human resources	142	30%
Occupational safety and health and the working environment	155	13%
Termination of employment on the initiative of the employer	158	12%
Occupational health services	161	7%
Safety and health in construction	167	6%

In the industrialised countries at least, a feature of the era was the presumption of a closed economy and something close to *stability*, in which the industrial structure was expected to change slowly and predictably, which provided the basis for the extension of security. There was the perception of labour market security through Full Employment, and the mix of protective statutory and voice regulations gave the era a powerful impetus in favour of other forms of security for a growing proportion of the population.

There was also the presumption that the 'advanced' economies were mainly trading with countries with similar levels of labour rights or were exporting manufacturing goods and financial services to countries that were exporting primary products, often in 'unequal exchange'. This was a crucial feature of the system, for it meant that labour rights in any one country were not perceived as onerous costs or 'burdens on business' affecting their competitiveness with other firms elsewhere.

The era was also one in which the *social wage* rose by more than money incomes, in that the institutionalised rights had monetary value and in that the state provided a growing array of social transfers financed from contributions and taxation, with direct tax expected to bear the brunt of the cost. There were also price and subsidies to consumer goods, which were common in industrialising economies. A consequence of all this was that – perhaps with one or two exceptions, including France where there was relatively little income distribution in what some have dubbed *le trente glorieuses* – economic inequality declined more than income inequality, although both declined by more than wealth inequality. Golden Age it certainly was not. Yet there were achievements that should not be forgotten, including economic growth rates above the long-run trend over the past one hundred years, open unemployment rates in most of western Europe of 1–2 per cent, historically low poverty rates and a presumption that a 'working-class' voice was ensured. Although many bridled at the pace of it, few doubted that the forward march of the working class was merely a matter of time.

Labour market relations were governed mainly by *statutory pro-collective regulations*, backed by voice regulation through unions and employer organisations incorporated into many areas of governance, most notably through tripartism and incomes policy. *Neo-corporatism* was the popular term. Not only was centralised or sectoral collective bargaining favoured and trade union confederations and employer organisations regarded as legitimate parts of governance, but statutory regulations promoted collective institutions and procedures. In state socialism, statutory regulations were taken to extremes in complex labour codes while unions were incorporated into the state as managerial organs of the Party. In developing countries, efforts were made to promote collective interests and neo-corporatist mechanisms. There was a presumption that statutory regulations would extend security and reduce labour market inequalities.

In sum, the post-war era was one in which individual security was extended, in which the social income rose and in which distributive justice was extended to groups hitherto marginalised or excluded from the labour process. In recalling that period, an intriguing paradox is that while it was a pro-collective era, many western industrialised countries elected right-of-centre governments, as if those were expected to limit the extent of the social revolution. Paradox or not, the situation was not to last.

3.3 THE ERA OF MARKET REGULATION: PURSUIT OF FLEXIBILITY

We are not in the days of redistribution. The important thing in order to survive in this world, whether as an individual, enterprise or country, is to be more competitive than one's neighbour.

Helmut Maucher, Chief Executive, Nestle[3]

A series of changes in the 1970s and 1980s undermined the era of statutory regulation. For state socialism, the failure was due to two fatal flaws – lack of economic dynamism and lack of freedom. Security without freedom breeds stagnation because motivation is denied. Freedom without security breeds opportunism and leads to a Hobbesian world of chaos where success is measured by the successful in their own image, and where they define security. In the 1980s, those who rejected the state that offered them security saw the denial of freedom as anathema, and were so oppressed that they scarcely valued the security enough to struggle for it. Not many at that time saw that freedom without security has its own horrors, a lesson to be relearned in the 1990s.

For welfare state capitalism, the strains began to show in the late 1960s, and grew stronger during the 1970s. Whereas the early part of the era was characterised by flexibility and economic and social progress, in which changes were mostly negotiable, as regulations, welfare arrangements and corporatist mechanisms became more embracive, they became more attuned to the preservation of stability than to the promotion of economic restructuring. The labour market became increasingly 'rigid'. This did not matter much if the presumption of a closed economy could be maintained, or if trade in manufactured goods was taking place between countries with similar labour rights. By the 1970s these could no longer be taken for granted. In some developing countries massive changes were taking place, and these were coming to influence what happened in the industrialised countries. Led by Japan, the international division of labour began to change.

The intellectual climate mirrored economic changes, and has profoundly influenced the character of policies that have spread across the world in the 1990s. The agenda was set by critiques of the developmental objectives pursued in the post-war era. The grumbling began in the 1960s and eroded its legitimacy through the 1970s. This took various forms. In developing countries, there were critiques of the presumptions of 'trickle down' and redistribution from growth. There was recognition that the agenda of labour security was one for strengthening the position of privileged 'insiders'. Terms such as 'labouring aristocracy' became common. There was an attempt to articulate a *basic needs approach* to development, focusing on measuring success by reference to access by the poor to food, shelter and schooling. There was the romanticising of the *informal sector*, as a vehicle for labour absorption and means of redistribution. These were the defensive reactions of those in the social democratic tradition. Without pleasure, one suspects that the whole approach was suffused with sentimental populism.

In any case, a different critique, coming from a long intellectual tradition, was to emerge into intellectual hegemony in the 1980s and 1990s. Its adherents claimed that much of what had passed for success in the previous era was actually failure, and was preventing success in the future. The liberals preached heresy in the 1970s, and were mocked as intellectual oddities. By the end of the decade they were strutting like peacocks. In most of the 1980s and 1990s they had the field almost entirely for themselves.

There were always problems with an agenda of success based on extension of labour security. Unless conditions are appropriate, labour security can induce passivity and 'dependency'. This is particularly likely when opportunities and incentives to achieve independent competences and standards of living are restricted, and is even more so when security is used as a means of social control. This was the corrosive reality in state socialism. But even in welfare state capitalism, and in its pale shadows in some middle-income countries, in the 1970s critics started to depict sources of security as sources of 'rigidity'. In the 1980s, the tired old leadership of the Soviet Union epitomised the sterility of state socialism. In western Europe, as well as in North America, the *language* was captured by the neo-liberals. There was the delightful image of 'Eurosclerosis' – conjuring up an image of an elderly man suffering from a tightening of the arteries, a stiffening of the sinews and a failure to summon up the blood.

The debate on the merits of security was not helped by the visionless defensiveness of those opposing the neo-liberal onslaught. Besides the contradictory character of security, both of the post-war development models failed in part because they could not handle or tolerate behavioural diversity.[4] Based on the enthronement of labouring man they were ill-equipped for managing society increasingly not based on the working class or on the expected growth of the working class to be the core of society.

A weakness of both was the nature of the State. In communism, the state could control, in the sense that it could limit autonomy and block initiative. But it did so by removing incentives for any behaviour other than passivity and opportunism, by preventing flexibility and by causing productivity to stagnate. In welfare state capitalism, the state proved unable to provide the combination of labour market and income security in an open economy in the context of globalisation.

Many factors undermined the era of statutory regulation, some of which are amenable to empirical analysis, some of which will remain a matter of debate. For our purposes, we can identify ten changes that have shaped the character of labour markets and that policy options for the early part of the twenty-first century.

(i) Macro-economic Instability

For welfare state capitalism, the first failing to assume crisis proportions was macro-economic policy. Inflationary pressures built up, the perception spread that the state's capacity to achieve redistributive objectives was ineffectual, and the welfare system of regulation ran up against a series of crises – a fiscal crisis, a demographic crisis, social equity and unemployment trap crises, an efficiency crisis and a moral-political crisis. Those issues will be considered later.

The capacity of the welfare system was eroded, so that the legitimacy of its objectives and the procedures and institutions for achieving them were undermined among important groups and institutions. It is difficult to overemphasise the significance of this erosion, which occurred in the 1980s, although the wounds were inflicted in the 1970s when progressive reform still seemed possible. The defeat of the Swedish 'wage earner funds' could be regarded as a defining moment, when redistributive objectives were whittled down into a petty gesture. The economic instability not only legitimised deflationary macro-economic policy but checked the redistributive zeal of the post-war period.

(ii) Libertarianism and Security

Social thinking about security has fluctuated through human history. Economics, or political economy, has evolved through eras in which leading figures have seen security as desirable or undesirable. In the eighteenth century Adam Smith was on the side of the security optimists. Thus, he and Condorcet advocated high wages and security as the way of raising the wealth of nations. Thomas Malthus represented the opposing doctrine of insecurity and fear as the necessary conditions for inducing productive (rather than reproductive) activity. The conflicting attitudes to security have continued ever since. In the 1920s, Alfred Pigou and the Chicago economists represented the market regulationists, which before the 1980s was the last time insecurity and low wages were seen as appropriate. In the 1930s, Keynes, the Fabians, the New Deal, Beveridge and followers successfully launched an era of social and economic security. This was matched by the Swedish and other social democratic economists, most notably in the work of the principal architects of the Swedish Model, Gosta Rehn and Rudolph Meidner.

The conventional wisdom of the 1950s and 1960s was that security was a social right and was compatible with economic growth, and that if a policy did not enhance security it was unjustifiable. The 1970s saw a resurgence of the ethics of insecurity and inequality, initially tentative and defensive in tone, then increasingly strident.

In the 1980s, under the rubric of libertarianism, those favouring the cold bath approach were back in ascendancy, and it is no coincidence that in the latest era of insecurity no fewer than eight Nobel Prizes have been awarded to economists from the University of Chicago, where what is often called the Chicago school of law and economics depicted regulations as impediments to growth. From Chile to the UK to Russia, taking in much of Africa, Asia and Latin America, the supply-siders have been enjoying their time in the sunlight. In the 1980s and 1990s, security has been derided as the source of 'rigidity' and 'dependency', while protective regulations have been regarded as supportable if and only if they demonstrably foster economic growth. Epitomising this mood, in the USA social policy debate came to be dominated by writers such as Lawrence Mead and Charles Murray, who represented the latest in a long line of advocates of insecurity as the stick of necessity. Libertarians and supply-side economics set the agenda and tone, came up with the best phrases, images and euphemisms, and dominated international discussion throughout the 1980s and 1990s.

The supply-side economic doctrine is merely the latest variant of the way of thinking that has ebbed and flowed since the beginning of capitalism; the belief that individual security hinders economic growth, that public institutions impede market clearing, and that inequality acts as the motivational force for accumulation.

In the late 1990s, as insecurity has intensified and become more widespread, the tide of debate began to turn, and one can anticipate a move back in the direction of policies to promote greater security. The evidence suggests that at the turn of the century a new crisis of insecurity is emerging. But for most of the last quarter of the twentieth century the libertarian views that gave credibility to policies intensifying insecurity were in the ascendancy.

(iii) Supply-side Economics

The increasing difficulty of redistributing income and extending forms of labour security within industrialised countries, and the inflationary pressures there, coincided with an international shift of economic dynamism, and precipitated the widespread adoption of 'supply-side economics' that has swept the world, beginning in the late 1970s in the UK and USA, being adopted by stages within western Europe and exported to Latin America, Africa and most recently South Asia in the name of 'structural adjustment'. Its biggest triumph was to come in the early 1990s, when Russia and other parts of the former eastern bloc adopted the same prescription under the name of 'shock therapy'.

Much attention has been given to the oil price shock of 1973, and the second one some years later, and the associated collapse of the Bretton Woods fixed exchange rate regime. These were undoubtedly important, yet they were crises waiting to happen. They coincided with the intellectual loss of faith in Keynesianism. In economics, a revolution took place in the 1970s mainly through rational expectations theory. This led through monetarism to *supply-side economics*. Critics contended that the Keynesian targeting was inherently inflationary, since if governments promised to achieve, and to *maintain,* Full Employment and low inflation, that implied they would accommodate wage rises by lowering interest rates. Once workers and unions realised that, they would push up wages further and thus boost inflation. So, if government used active macro-economic policy it would be inflationary, periodically running into *credibility crises*, particularly bearing in mind the influence of political elections, since pump-priming expansionary policy would be anticipated before a general election.

The new orthodoxy reversed the targeting of policy instruments. Macro-economic policy was to be used to control inflation, notably through changes in money supply and public expenditure cuts, while micro-economic policy was expected to *influence* but not determine levels of employment and unemployment, by establishing 'free' labour markets and providing conditions for employment generation. The goal of Full Employment was abandoned as impractical, although if institutional and regulatory rigidities were removed, then a lower level of unemployment could be achieved. The credibility thesis was taken one step further. According to anti-Keynesian critics, democratic governments would always be inflationary in their operation of macro-economic policy because they would wish to boost the economy by cutting interest rates in the year or two before elections.

Since then, governments have been persuaded to transfer monetary policy to independent central banks, which being unelected are expected to take a longer-term view and be more consistently dis-inflationary than workers, voters and politicians. By mid-1997, when the new UK government made its unprompted decision to transfer control of monetary policy to the Bank of England, all G7 countries had taken this step, and a growing number of other countries had done so or were planning to do so.

The rationale for an independent central bank is that it would operate a monetary policy to lower inflation, and that this would boost economic growth, in part because it would induce workers to accept lower wage increases *more quickly* because they would believe in the credibility of the central bank. The evidence that this is correct is far from clear. Although the causation is questionable, there has been a correlation between degree of central bank independence and inflation. But there has been no correlation between central bank independence and economic growth. Worse, several studies have demonstrated that reducing inflation below about 8 per cent does not improve long-term economic growth and that the recessionary cost of reducing inflation has been higher under independent central banks (e.g., Debelle and Fischer, 1994). Although there will be a protracted debate on issues of duration of policy, and so on, economic policymaking has entered an era of central bank independence and abdication of governmental control of monetary policy, without which Full Employment is hard to envisage other than by means of micro-economic policy.

Thus emerged the notion of a *natural* rate of unemployment and the sister concept of a 'non-accelerating inflation rate of unemployment' (NAIRU), supposedly ground out by prevailing institutions and labour market structures. The view evolved that labour market rigidities raised the natural rate by checking the flexibility of response by workers and employers to changes in aggregate demand. This led to the view that the solution to unemployment was removal of institutional measures and statutory regulations.

(iv) Globalisation

> *The capacity of the state to look after the welfare of its citizens has been severely impaired by the globalisation of the capitalist system, which allows capital to escape taxation much more easily than labour. Capital will tend to avoid countries where employment is heavily taxed or heavily protected, leading to a rise in unemployment.*
>
> George Soros[5]

From the 1970s onwards, a factor undermining the era of statutory regulation was the changing international division of labour, or what was in the late 1990s to be called *globalisation*. Globalisation is not something that suddenly happened. It is almost as if a threshold was reached in which long-term trends became sufficiently strong as to induce a profound change in perceptions of policy options. This began with the increasingly open nature of industrialised economies, with the rising contribution of exports to industrial growth (Figure 3.1). International trade in manufacturing goods has grown relative to production for national consumption, and has been attributed in part to the decline of barriers to trade and to the decline in costs of transport and communication (Krugman, 1995).

The growth in manufacturing trade also reflected the industrial emergence of Japan, followed by the rise of the Newly Industrialising Countries (NICs) of east Asia, along with import-substituting and export-led industrialisation elsewhere. However, its sustained growth has been primarily due to the plunging fall in communications costs, the growth of multinationals and the liberalisation measures of the Uruguay Round, backed by a global multilateral institution to regulate free trade, the World Trade Organisation, and the emergence of regional trading blocs.

A key factor in the NICs was that these economies had fewer labour rights and costs than those that had spread in industrialised welfare states. The industrialisation that has occurred in many parts of the world over the past quarter of a century has been assisted in part by lower labour costs and the more flexible labour supply there, which reflect the relative lack of protective regulations, weak systems of collective bargaining and lack of working-class traditions and expectations. Much has been made of 'north–south' differentials in skills, wages, productivity and so on. However, perhaps the biggest difference between the newly industrialising and

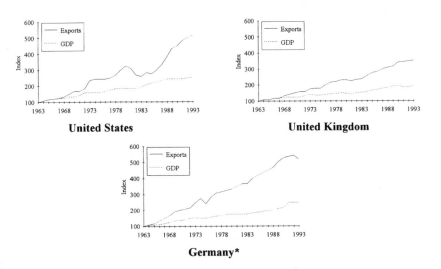

Figure 3.1 Exports and GDP, selected industrialised countries, 1963–93 (exports and GDP index 1963 = 100)

Note: * Western Germany prior to 1991.
Source: Datastream, IMF.

the industrialised economies in the 1970s and 1980s was that differences in labour costs were greater than any differences in productivity, particularly as some of the former were able to mould disciplined (often largely female) and flexible labour forces.

For countries in which capitalism was being established, the rights of labour were impediments to 'progress', and nationalistic elites became unenamoured by the appeal of the social democratic or state socialism models that in their different ways made the rights of the labouring man the yardstick of success. In all rapidly industrialising economies of the era, the state imposed extensive regulatory and more direct controls on workers, often including restrictive legislation banning unions in export processing zones (or everywhere) and freeing employers in export industries from limits on working time, wages or benefits.

Some analysts have questioned the existence of globalisation (Hirst and Thompson, 1996). Others have claimed that the industrialisation in emerging economies has not had much effect on labour markets in industrialised economies, citing the low share of manufactured imports from such countries into western Europe and North America. This neglects the effect on the *structure* of production (Wood, 1994). It is also hard to gauge the effect of the *potential* inflow on the behaviour of employers, governments and workers in the industrialised economies, while the reports of firms shifting their production to industrialising countries have been so numerous that it is scarcely credible that there has been no effect. And the NICs' emergence and accelerating industrialisation elsewhere destroyed the presumption of a closed economy, so crucial to the viability of the welfare state capitalism model.

Increasingly, production is being organised on a global scale, with multinational enterprises and international capital being major engines of economic growth and determinants of economic, social and labour market policy. This means that there is a *long-term* trend towards a single, borderless economy, which is being cemented by the trade liberalisation and the dismantling of tariff and non-tariff trade barriers under the aegis of the Uruguay Round and the World Trade Organisation (WTO).

With globalisation, there is increasing reason to dispense with the oft-used dualism between *tradables* and *non-tradables*, or with the presumption that it is only about tradables, which has been taken to mean manufacturing. Since the 1980s services have also become subject to international mobility, with a shifting and volatile international division of labour reflecting the information technology revolution, the development of off-shore information processing and the shift of jobs to developing and industrialised economies according to shifts in relative costs and the availability of suitable labour (Posthuma, 1995; Pearson and Mitter, 1993; Keen, 1991). Globalisation does not require labour to become much more mobile, since multinationals can shift the distribution of their employment relatively easily, with little cost.

Yet a crucial aspect of globalisation is that capital mobility has become extremely volatile, as well as extremely large. Capital flows from industrialised countries accelerated in the 1980s. Foreign direct investment has been growing faster than international trade. Direct investment by rich countries in poorer countries tripled between 1990 and 1996, and private capital flows rose by nearly a third (*Wall Street Journal*, 13 March, 1997). National production systems are increasingly determined by foreign developments, and links between firms and parts of multinational enterprises are increasing.

Although currency trading has also multiplied, portfolio capital mobility accelerated even more sharply in the 1990s than other forms of capital mobility (Figure 3.2). Cross-border share dealing has grown ten times as fast as national incomes (*The Economist*, 18 October, 1997, p. 29). It is the extraordinary increase of financial capital mobility that has marked out the period of globalisation, and this has intensified the volatility and uncertainty with which firms, governments and workers have had to contend. Commentators have claimed this has merely returned the situation to what it was at the end of the nineteenth century. But the relevant comparison is with the mid-twentieth century when welfare states were established. At that time trade and capital flows were modest, regulated by the Bretton Woods system. That has changed, and potential mobility is greater still. It would surely be hard to reverse globalisation, unlike the situation in the early twentieth century. For instance, the 'Tobin tax' – a proposal to tax foreign exchange transactions intended to 'throw sand in the wheels of international finance', to reduce volatility and profitability of speculative activity – would probably be ineffectual simply because of the sophistication of technology and financial mechanisms. What has been done in Chile, imposing a reserve requirement on all short-term capital

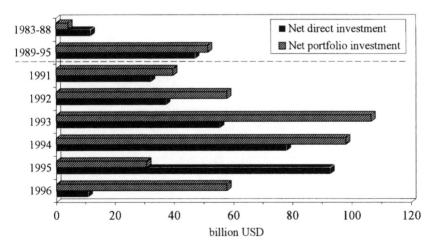

Figure 3.2 Net direct investment and net portfolio investment to developing, 'transition' and newly industrialised economies, 1983–96

Source: IMF, World Economic Outlook, October 1997, p. 29, Table 7.

inflows, effectively taxing short-maturing loans, might have some short-term effect, but is scarcely likely to alter the underlying dynamics.

Increased *capital mobility* reflects the integration and sophistication of capital markets. This means that with *relatively* fixed exchange rates, national monetary policy independence is eroded. If monetary policy is used to influence national aggregate demand, then the credibility of the national exchange rate is threatened. This constrains use of expansionary monetary policy. Financial market liberalisation imparts a deflationary macro-economic policy stance in many countries, thereby reducing the scope for macro-economic policy to stimulate aggregate demand to raise employment.

In the 1990s, financial markets have been disembedded from national economies, existing in their own global space. It started in the 1960s with the Eurodollar market, grew with the international debt crisis, the development of offshore banking centres and rapidly expanding government borrowing, and then flourished in the 1990s with what some have called 'derivatives capitalism' or 'casino capitalism'. Meanwhile, and significantly for proposals in chapter 11, the ratio of equity to company debt has risen around the world. Instead of borrowing, firms are turning more to share issues, which are acquired by affluent individuals, workers in employee-ownership schemes (ESOPs) and powerful 'blocholders' (pension funds, banks, insurance companies, etc.). The latter's ability to transact shares has strengthened short-termism in economic decision-making and created the grounds for instability, as witnessed in east Asia in 1997. If markets perceive that variable costs are rising, a flight of financial capital could precipitate a crisis. There might be nothing wrong with the economic fundamentals, but the disembedded financial markets have made real economies dependent on injudicious statements, poorly timed speeches, strikes or simply speculative gambles. Unless financial capital is re-embedded in the real economy, the instability will cause untold misery for millions. There is need for less flexibility, not more.

There is an international convergence of monetary policy, with the spread of 'independent' central banks oriented to the control of inflation. There is also convergence of fiscal policy, with fiscal 'restraint' being the orthodox view and with reduced public expenditure being justified as reducing inflation. The perception is that if any country attempted to operate a more active (counter-cyclical or progressive) fiscal or monetary policy, the capital and foreign exchange markets would force it to abandon the idea. Imports are responsive to changes in domestic demand, putting strong limits on fiscal policy (Franzmeyer, Lidlar and Trabold, 1996, p. 40). And independent monetary and fiscal policy is constrained by the interdependence of interest rates, as well as exchange rates.

Globalisation reduces national autonomy in macro-economic policy. Thus with monetary or fiscal policy, if a country moves out of line with its neighbours or other countries with which it is in competition for foreign capital or trade, it may experience a destabilising capital outflow or loss of exports. Moreover, if politicians, employers and unions believe that the government has less room to manoeuvre, they will act more prudently. Among other implications, this loss and perceived loss of national autonomy has meant that governments have operated less expansionary policy and have downgraded employment policy in their priorities, leaving it mainly to micro-economic measures.

Whether in response or as part of the process, the strengthening of 'continental' blocs has been a feature of recent years. Monetary union in western Europe is an aspect of globalisation. The Maastricht Treaty set out to achieve monetary union by 1999, and by stipulating fiscal 'convergence criteria' – i.e., that to qualify, countries must have a budget deficit of less than 3 per cent of GDP or have accumulated national debts less than 60 per cent of GNP – western Europe entered a more deflationary phase. European monetary union will prevent individual countries from public borrowing above a low level, and will be run by a democratically unaccountable European Central Bank. And a single currency will require flexible labour and capital markets, to even out economic fluctuations.

Reducing budget deficits will be difficult because pushing up interest rates to maintain exchange rate parities will be deflationary, squeezing tax revenue, necessitating more government borrowing, which will push up interest rates, because governments will have to sell bonds. The only way that the adverse effect on unemployment could be checked in such circumstances would be through rising inter-state transfers, so that low-unemployment countries subsidise the unemployed in high-unemployment countries.

Continental blocs – EU, NAFTA, ASEAN, and so on – may limit autonomy in social, employment and labour market policy. Fear of 'social dumping' reflects the fear of a competitive debasement of pay and working conditions. Recognition of this may strengthen efforts to obtain international regulations. For instance, a strike by lorry drivers in late 1996 made the French government more concerned to see a statutory harmonisation of working conditions within the EU. This may materialise. Critics have warned that this would encourage a shift of production to where such regulations did not apply, abroad or into informal transactions that bypassed them.

There is also a view that labour market policy should be co-ordinated internationally and not be left to national governments (e.g., IMF, September 1997). However, although intended to enhance skills, 'employability' and employment, such co-ordination could actually restrict such policy, because of internationally determined public expenditure constraints and pressure from governments disinclined to boost labour market policy.

Globalisation threatens the feasibility of a redistributive welfare state. This is because redistribution to some extent must involve progressive taxation and solidaristic contributions in which the more affluent pay to support those unable to support themselves and to prevent the disadvantaged and dispossessed from disrupting the peace of the affluent. In the aftermath of the Depression and Second World War, the international community recognised the dangers of inequality, and the global pressures increasing it, by taking labour rights largely out of international competition. Franklin Roosevelt among others recognised that the welfare state was a means of protecting capital from its excesses, against a tendency for exploitation to grow, through shifting investment to where labour rights and standards were undeveloped. The IMF and World Bank were set up to *regulate* capitalism, to prevent and reduce inequalities, while the GATT was intended to strengthen provisions to protect workers from 'unfair trade'. Yet in the 1980s and 1990s, the international financial agencies were in the forefront of efforts to 'de-regulate' economies.

Globalisation has intensified pressure on governments to scale back on labour rights and welfare, because these are presentable as costs eroding a country's capacity to compete in tradables and as encouraging portfolio and direct foreign investment to shift to where such costs and *prospective* costs are lower. The danger of beggar-my-neighbour whittling away labour rights may extend to measures to promote employment. The debate of the late 1990s on international labour standards is about an attempt to check this process. The international community is far from realising a consensus on the desirability, let alone feasibility, of an international regulatory regime.

Industrial growth in the NICs and in other low-income countries has been accompanied by a shift from non-wage to wage forms of labour, along with urbanisation and agricultural commercialisation, all of which have been converting large numbers of rural 'under-employed' into a readily available (flexible) labour supply. Traditional social rigidities have been giving way, while manufacturing and other firms have been able to take advantage of labour market insecurity to impose controls in employment relations. Given the labour surplus, there has also been ample scope to resort to informal labour arrangements. In the 1980s and 1990s, policies to increase flexibility in industrialising economies crystallised in 'structural adjustment strategies', which the IMF, World Bank and others persuaded numerous governments to adopt, in part due to the debt crisis.

Thus, pressures on labour systems in industrialised countries came in part from the changing international division of labour and the character of labour systems in industrialising countries, and whereas examples of policies of welfare state capitalism had been transferred to industrialising countries in the 1950s, 1960s and 1970s, those countries have been under pressure to weaken those policies. As examples of policies that have been transformed from 'good' to supposedly 'bad', governments all over the world were long encouraged to operate a statutory minimum wage and centralised, tripartite collective bargaining. In the 1980s and 1990s, that was far from being the case.

Growing industrialisation in developing economies surely has had some effect on the 'de-industrialisation' in northern America and western Europe. Although there is debate on the extent of the effect, one study concluded that one-third of de-industrialisation could be attributed to trade with developing countries (Saeger, 1995). There has been substantial restructuring, and import penetration and loss of potential export markets have contributed to the decimation of manufacturing and mining sectors, notably labour intensive industries such as shipbuilding, steelmaking, machine engineering and textiles and garments. Some maintained output while becoming more capital intensive, others shifted from mass to niche production. For a while, in the 1960s and 1970s, the impact on unemployment was limited by expansionary macro-economic policy and public sector jobs. This was not to last.

The notion of 'de-industrialisation' began life as a critique of the failure of the British economy to generate productive employment and economic growth in the 1970s, and gained strength in the 1980s as one explanation for mass unemployment in western Europe, when alarm arose over the erosion of manufacturing jobs. Recently, the hypothesis has been integrated with an earlier thesis, associated with Colin Clark and Simon Kuznets, to the effect that the sectoral share of employment shifts roughly as in Figure 3.3. This is consistent with three long-term trends – a

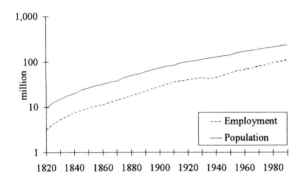

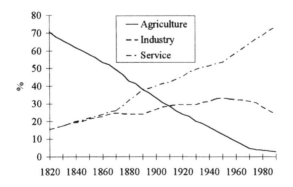

Figure 3.3 US employment growth, population growth and sectoral employment shares, 1820–1990

Source: Maddison, 1995.

changing international division of labour, technological change involving capital–labour substitution and rising productivity in manufacturing, and a shift in consumption towards 'services'. Trends they may be, but globalisation could influence the dynamics, since comparative advantage considerations might lock economies into a production structure that corresponded less and less to its pattern of consumption. In any case, sectoral shifts in production and employment need a better term than 'de-industrialisation'.

Whatever one calls it, there are implications for the labour market, including the character of employment in industrialised economies, the distribution of labour statuses, the pattern of labour insecurity and the forms of institutional, collective and individual bargaining. A vast amount of controverial research is in progress on these issues.

The view that globalisation involves a shift of employment from industrialised to industrialising economies has been challenged on the grounds that the latter still do not have a large share of global manufacturing exports, and so have not had much effect on industrialised country labour markets. This view has been supported by the IMF, although not much evidence has been provided (IMF, April 1997). Governments are urged to make their production and labour market systems more competitive to maintain growth in the more open global economy, yet at the same time it is argued that globalisation has little or only beneficial effect. Although UNCTAD have been more critical, most international organisations have been keen to emphasise the benefits of integration (World Bank, 1995a; ILO, 1995a; OECD, 1994; IMF September 1997; UNCTAD, 1995b). Although it would be hard to be sure with available statistics, one way by which it has had an effect is through multi-nationals being able to use so-called 'whip-saw' bargaining, threatening to close plants in specific countries and transferring production elsewhere unless wage and other concessions are made by unions.

It is claimed that imports from industrialising countries have not had much impact on manufacturing employment in industrialised economies because the trade balance in manufactured goods has hardly changed, the increased imports from low-wage countries being matched by increased exports from industrialised countries. However, if the labour intensity of imports from developing countries is greater than that of exports from industrialised countries – as is the case – an erosion of manufacturing jobs is likely from an increased level of manufacturing trade, even though the balance in value terms is preserved. The same applies for the 'skill' mix, so that increased trade could displace less skilled manufacturing jobs in industrialised economies.

Globalisation is also linked to changes in the level and incidence of tax. Because capital has been more mobile than labour, this has been one reason for a shift of tax from capital to labour (Tanzi, 1995). As *The Economist* put it with character-istic bluntness,

Certainly it makes sense these days for revenue-seeking governments to shift the pattern of taxation. The basic principle of efficient 'fiscal ranching' is obvious: tax immobile factors of production more heavily than mobile ones. That means going easy on taxing the rich; given sufficient reason, they can get away more readily than the less rich. Also, where possible, tax the income generated by 'sunk' capital, but offer tax breaks for new investment, so as to attract footloose financial capital. More broadly, since capital of all kinds is more mobile than labour, shift the overall balance of taxation so that it weighs more heavily on workers and less on owners of capital ... By and large this has been happening, though some governments have shown more imagination than others. (20 September 1997, p. 20)

This has eroded an instrument for redistribution, one for maintaining high aggregate demand that underpinned welfare states. Almost throughout the world, tax on capital has been lightened, notably through the reduction of corporation tax rates, which have tended to become similar across industrialised countries, and by changes in the basis of assessment. For instance, as shown in Figure 3.4, the shift of tax from profits to wages has been a strong trend since the early 1980s in Germany (west), the Netherlands and the UK (Franzmeyer, Lindlar and Trabold, 1996).

Just as the changing level and incidence of taxation have been rationalised by the claim that capital is harder to tax and that higher-income groups can avoid or evade high taxes as a result of globalisation, so an irony is that in the era of market regulation, when the removal of subsidies for workers and consumers has been justified on the grounds of needing to remove market distortions, so national and local governments have been increasing their subsidies to capital by leaps and bounds, ostensibly on the grounds of attracting capital and direct investment that would otherwise go elsewhere.

Subsidies to capital have become rather generous. UNCTAD (1995a) concluded that governments would overbid to attract foreign capital, which would lead to more going to countries that could afford to provide subsidies and to excessive subsidies to capital in general. The desire of governments to create jobs has led to some costly exercises. UNCTAD found that to attract Mercedes-Benz to set up a plant in Alabama in 1993 the US State provided the firm with a subsidy that worked out to be $168,000 per job created, and the French authorities gave a subsidy to the firm to set up a Swatchmobile plant in Lorraine in 1995 that came to $57,000 per job created. Such huge subsidies have proliferated.

Paradoxically, local government *subsidiarity* has intensified globalisation, by increasing competitive auctioneering to give subsidies to capital. Regional development authorities in the UK, for instance, have competed to subsidise foreign firms. The Korean electronics company Lucky Goldstar received a subsidy worth £30,000 a job for its £1.7 billion semi-conductor plant in Wales, to create 6,100 jobs (*Observer*, 23 November 1997). Between 1987 and 1997, £1.4 billion in regional aid was given to foreign firms, excluding the provision of land at low cost,

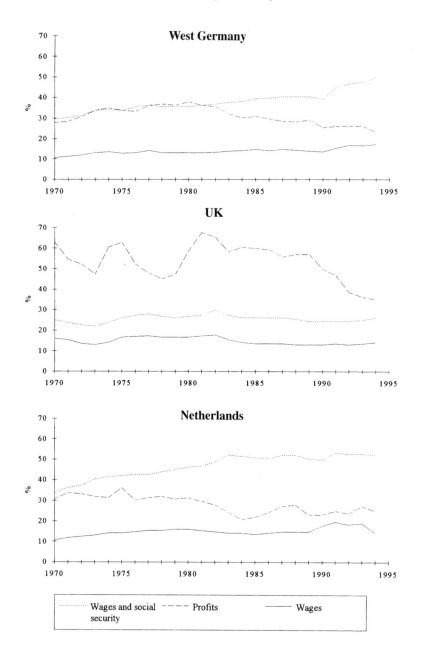

Figure 3.4 Trends in income taxation and social security contributions in selected OECD countries, 1970–94 *(per cent of the respective factor income)*

Sources: OECD, *Revenue Statistics of OECD Member Countries, National Accounts.*

subsidised utilities and other benefits, such as infrastructural investment in new roads. Much the same has happened in Germany. In 1997 the government offered Volkswagen DM780 million (£260 million) to construct two plants to create jobs for 2,300 workers in eastern Germany. Perhaps such subsidies are justified. But it is strange that one criticism levelled at consumer and worker subsidies built up in the era of statutory regulation was that they *distorted* market mechanisms. It is unclear why the argument could not be applied to other forms of subsidy.

Subsidies in general are inequitable and inefficient. If the same amount of money were handed to firms through lower corporation tax, there would be fewer objections on the grounds of substitution effects, deadweight effects and administrative costs. Or it could be given in lower taxes for workers or in other transfers. *Whatever the argument for or against subsidies, globalisation has involved a redistributive shift in the form of subsidies.*

Paradoxically too, while inducing desires for international co-ordination of economic and social policy, globalisation has contributed to the *decentralisation* of responsibility for social and labour policy within countries. In attempting to cut central government expenditure and public deficits, more responsibility has been delegated to local authorities. The most conspicuous case is the USA, with its 1996 welfare reform based in part on block grants to States. There and elsewhere, local authorities will be less capable of resisting pressure to provide subsidies to foreign capital, to exert investment-friendly controls over labour rights, and so on.

Finally, the *idea* of globalisation is partly ideological, linked to economic liberalisation, demands for *more* labour market flexibility, governmental support for large-scale business ventures and redesign of social policy. It has helped to set an agenda and way of thinking, and reflects the increasing impact of distant institutions and regulations on individual behavioural options. It may involve a shake-out of institutions, involving new forms of socio-economic fragmentation. Globalisation has ruptured the embeddedness of the economy in society, and in de-socialising economic processes has reduced societal control over capital, encouraging opportunism and incipient malfeasance.

In sum, 'globalisation' is associated with economic integration and a shift in the bargaining strengths of capital and 'society'. For a while, the rhetoric engendered a belief that the world had entered a period of more rapid economic growth, into what the UN Secretary General, Kofi Annan, in 1997 called 'a new golden age'. Global growth rates appear to have picked up. The upturn has been attributed to the expansion of economic 'freedom' and property rights, coupled with a rise in trade and private investment. Whether all this has had beneficial effects on labour markets and social well-being is another matter.

(v) Privatisation

Globalisation has been associated with a convergence of view among mainstream economists and politicians on the desirability of reducing public expenditure and privatising both economic activities and social policy to a greater extent. Pressure to cut the public budget deficit is a global reality, the ostensible rationale being that this is needed to reduce inflationary pressure, to 'crowd in' private investment, to reduce bureaucratic inefficiency and transaction costs, and to improve the attractiveness of the economy for international capital. The argument is made in many countries that, if the national budget deficit is greater than the international average, international portfolio investment managers will treat it as a signal of potential economic instability and accordingly divert capital elsewhere. *Actual* capital flows would not be necessary to show that the pressures were operating.

During the 1960s and 1970s governments acted as guarantors of Full Employment by becoming the employer of last resort, implicitly downgrading administrative or economic efficiency. The expansion of the public sector was the primary means of boosting employment generally, and this applied to many industrialising and low-income economies.

In the 1970s, and then more stridently in the 1980s and 1990s, critics of public provision and state control of a wide range of goods and services began to win the arguments and win over the mainstream of economists and politicians. Initially, the key argument was the critics' claim that using the public sector as an automatic stabiliser to absorb labour was at the expense of steadily worsening inflation, which fed on the expectation that governments would adopt whatever monetary and fiscal policy stance was needed to prevent unemployment deviating far from some customary 'Full Employment' level. The critique was to extend to many other issues.

Defenders of the public sector as employer of last resort, as well as a redistributive device, were losing partly because their constituency was shrinking. We come back to the peculiar evolution of attitudes to public provision. For the moment, we may merely note that the pressures that led to privatisation of economic activity and social policy were fundamental to the erosion of the era of statutory regulation and to pursuit of labour flexibility. Even defenders of the old era seemed to admit that the public sector was saturated, and instances of inefficiency and administrative distance from consumers were used to weaken the legitimacy of the public sector.

A consequence of privatisation has been that major sectors have ceased to give maximisation of employment – and stability of employment – the priority it received in the previous era. To give just one example from many, British Steel (privatised) produced the same amount in 1997 as in 1987, but with a quarter of the workforce. It had responded to global competition by cutting costs and investing abroad, whereas a nationalised undertaking would have done neither.

In brief, privatisation has been a global phenomenon in the 1990s. It has been driven by ideology, by powerful interests – notably international financial intermediaries and corporations wanting to take over the provision of goods, utilities and services – by efficiency arguments and by the pressures emanating from globalisation that are making governments feel that they must cut the size of the public sector. And, as discussed later, it has extended to the privatisation of social policy.

(vi) Market regulations

Another key change in the 1970s and 1980s was the attitude to regulations, including labour market relations. The rational expectations and supply-side economic revolution transformed the mainstream perspective. The political debate was won by presenting it simplistically as 'deregulation', when in fact it was a matter of displacing some regulations by others. The initial claims were twofold. First, regulations held up the natural rate of unemployment and the NAIRU. Second, according to the Chicago school of law and economics, statutory or institutional regulations can be justified only if they promote, or do not impede, economic growth. If they do not do that, they are impediments to efficiency, and therefore, because efficiency and growth are equated with improvements in social welfare, most regulations are suspect. This perspective was to become pervasively influential.

Nobody should be misled into thinking that the resultant rolling back of protective and pro-collective regulations constitutes 'deregulation'. What supply-siders have promoted is *pro-individualistic regulations* (or anti-collective regulations) and greater use of *fiscal* and *promotional regulations*, intended to prevent or discourage people from making particular choices and to encourage, facilitate or promote other types of behaviour. There has been *explicit* and *implicit* erosion of pro-collective regulations, but numerous regulations have been introduced to 'distort' the market, by means of fiscal incentives for certain types of activities, subsidies and so on. Later chapters consider ways this has been put into effect, along with the social and economic consequences.

The mid-1970s began what can be called the *era of market regulation*. An important part of the agenda amounted to a strategy for changing the boundaries of control over labour relations. In that context, it is worth recalling the revealing statement by one of the fathers of the economic orthodoxy of the last quarter of the twentieth century, the Nobel Prize-winning Frederick Hayek:

> The successful use of competition as the principle of social organisation precludes certain types of coercive interference with economic life, but it admits of others which sometimes may very considerably assist its work and even requires certain kinds of government action. (Hayek, 1944, p. 27)

Apparently, the road to freedom requires a little coercion. One could give numerous examples from recent developments, where flexibility has meant control exercised through regulations and government action. Two will suffice to indicate how industrial growth has been assisted by changes in the regulatory system. A classic case where the supply-side school were enabled to apply their approach was Chile, highly relevant in the late 1990s because it has been hailed as an exemplary case of 'comprehensive' market reform. Under Allende, the *Labour Law* established a centralised system of collective bargaining and labour rights, and provided protective regulations on employment security and income security. Following the coup in 1973, the Pinochet military regime introduced repressive regulations, not deregulation. Collective bargaining was eliminated, as were union activities, and no employment security was allowed. Under the 1979 *Plan Laboral*, *decentralised* (plant-level) wage bargaining was made obligatory, while public workers were banned from striking. To call such measures deregulation would be a misuse of language. They have been called that. And there have been powerful pressures to see Chile's institutional and regulatory reforms replicated elsewhere.

Another instance where regulations were used to achieve what should be called *subordinated flexibility* is the Republic of Korea, a good example of a changing mix of types of regulation, as well as a country long held out as an exemplary instance of export-led industrialisation. For many years in the early phase of its industrial growth, it relied on paternalistic and repressive labour regulations. The latter included police enforcement of factory discipline in the 1940s and 1950s, the disbanding of independent unions in 1961, the 'temporary' law of 1970 – which lasted until May 1986 – restricting labour rights in foreign-owned firms, and the 1971 *Law Concerning Special Measures for Safeguarding National Security*, which *inter alia* banned all collective action and extended compulsory arbitration to all industries (West, 1987). When the IMF pushed for a stabilisation programme in the early 1970s and urged wage restraint, the Government backed up its previous interventions with *paternalistic* regulatory measures, including company-specific welfare with the avowed intention of strengthening worker commitment to firms, measures to ensure that company unions prevailed over independent unions, the Factory Saemaul (New Community) Movement by which work teams were created to reduce costs and improve productivity (Quality Control, Zero Defect, etc.), and a campaign promoting 'enterprise as family', which in practice meant workers providing more labour through unpaid overtime, longer working hours, abolition of summer holidays and so on.

In these stark instances, regulatory reforms have been intended to restrict voice regulation and collective action, decentralise labour relations and wage bargaining and promote subordinated flexibility. Governments elsewhere have been shifting their regulatory system in a similar direction, although often sanctioned or quasi-legitimised by democratic procedures and often involving relatively little coercion. Nevertheless, a feature of the era, in which labour market flexibility has been pursued globally, has been a global campaign to reorient labour regulations.

(vii) The Technological Revolution

In eroding the era of statutory regulation, one cannot leave out the impact of the *technological revolution* that has swept the world since the 1970s, primarily automation, information technology and robotics, or what has been called the new 'heartland technology' because of the widespread application and potential. Globalisation and the global phase of flexible labour markets cannot be assessed adequately without taking the ramifications of technological change into account.

Four features of *informatics* are crucial. First, it has given managements many more options in their organisation of production, in terms of technological options and alternative forms of work organisation, and by making it easier to shift production from one site to another or to combine different parts of production in different sites. It has facilitated managerial flexibility, allowing faster and more adjustments. Second, it has facilitated the enormous growth in capital mobility that has occurred in the past two decades, particularly portfolio capital. Communication speeds have accelerated, but in production too, technological change has been transmitted more rapidly than when the main heartland technological innovations were based on large-scale plant, heavy machinery and heavy raw materials. Third, it has enabled large firms not only to decentralise production and advance the detailed division of labour but have greater cost control. If a least-cost way of production is not accepted in one area, or if a subsidy is not provided, workers, governments and local managements know there is a more credible threat that at least part of the production (or anticipated expansion) could be shifted elsewhere before they could do anything about it. The uncertainty is a source of power and control.

A fourth feature of the technological revolution is conjunctural. Globalisation and the international redivision of labour have been associated with something like a *Kondratieff long wave*. The idea of a long wave is that development has involved a long era of economic dynamism followed by a prolonged downturn, which eventually gives way to a new era of sustained growth. Each wave has involved phases of technological innovation followed by one of 'technological stalemate', in which process innovations have predominated over product innovations.[6] This was roughly what was happening in the latter stages of the era of statutory regulation. Once a clustering of product and capital innovations occurs, a new global upswing starts. In the 1970s, the informatics technology marked out a new upturn. And as in previous long-wave upswings, the economic centre of dynamism shifted globally. In the previous upswing, the shift was from the UK (and western Europe, notably Germany) to the USA. In the 1980s, it was a shift from the USA (and to some extent western Europe) to Japan and the Pacific Basin (Freeman, 1987). Many factors played a part in the industrial growth and receptiveness to technology and forms of work organisation of those economies – land reform, mass mobilisation of 'cheap' female labour, Confucianism, individualistic wages, the existence of a pool of easily disciplined and exploitable workers, foreign direct investment, an interventionist state prepared to assist in the accumulation process, and author- itarianism thinly veiled as paternalism.

Whatever the factors, the impetus for use of new technology and forms of work organisation has stemmed from that region since the 1980s. Those who argue that globalisation has had little effect on labour markets in industrialised countries usually focus on trade, neglecting demonstration effects of organisational and technological change. This does not mean that what becomes accepted in one part of the world spreads to other parts in identical forms. Hybrid forms of technological adaptation and work organisation may emerge that take account of preceding institutional structures, or bargaining strengths of conflicting groups. Whatever the outcomes, the forces of globalisation cannot be measured simply in terms of trade or investment flows.

(viii) The Fiscal 'Crisis'

Another factor undermining welfare state capitalism has been the weakening *link* between economic growth, incomes and employment in industrialised countries. As the era of statutory regulation ran into difficulties in the 1970s, employment expansion had to come increasingly from the public sector and from services generally. This meant that fiscal policy had to play an increasing role, as a counter-cyclical instrument and as a progressive policy, through financing more public sector employment and through enabling more people to purchase non-tradable services. However, the perceived and actual capacity for fiscal policy to play this dual role diminished, in large part because the distributional consensus had cracked and because of the gathering forces of globalisation, in which international capital mobility became not only much greater but potentially greater still. A co-ordination failure also emerged, for in a globalising economy it appeared no longer in the immediate interest of many corporations to ensure high levels of aggregate demand in the particular economies in which they are producing. What matters are the costs of production and distribution, including fiscal costs.

As a result there has been a shift in the incidence as well as in rates of direct taxation, away from capital and onto labour. In part, this has reflected the changing balance of power of capital and labour and the greater mobility of capital relative to labour. A paradox is that while one objective of cutting corporation tax has been to attract foreign investment and retain national direct investment, so as to boost employment, the shift of tax incidence has made it more expensive to employ labour. This has increased pressure to increase labour flexibility so as to reduce the costs of labour.

A factor in the contextual explanation of the new phase of global labour flexibility is the *fiscal crisis* – particularly but not only in industrialised welfare state capitalist countries – which has accompanied globalisation, mass unemployment and the growth of flexible labour relations itself. Since the mid-1970s, when the first oil-price recession hit the industrialised economies, public budgetary balances have deteriorated substantially in those countries. Initially they did not cause public indebtedness because of economic growth, but in the 1980s debt service costs increased sharply. It is widely recognised that the resulting levels of public debt were unsustainable, and that it would take many years of balanced primary budgets to reduce the net debt position to tolerable levels (Franzmeyer, Lindlar and Trabold, 1996).

In the 1970s and 1980s, there was a spate of literature on the fiscal crisis of the state. In the 1990s, this merged with the supply-side debate on the desirability of reducing public spending and taxation and the drive to *privatisation*. Ironically, while supply-side economists and their political representatives have been in the ascendancy, the share of GDP attributed to government spending has *risen* almost everywhere (Table 3.2).[7]

Nevertheless, governments have been attempting to reduce the size in a period of powerful pressures to increase it. Among these have been public sector debt interest, which in industrialised countries has been the item of public spending that has grown most rapidly, and transfers and subsidies, which have remained by far the largest component, accounting for over 15 per cent of GDP in industrialised countries in 1960 and over 22 per cent in 1990.

Table 3.2 Government spending as percentage of GDP, industrialised countries

	1870	1913	1920	1937	1960	1980	1990	1996
Austria	–	–	14.7	15.2	35.7	48.1	48.6	51.7
Belgium	–	–	–	21.8	30.3	58.6	54.8	54.3
Canada	–	–	13.3	18.6	28.6	38.8	46.0	44.7
France	12.6	17.0	27.6	29.0	34.6	46.1	49.8	54.5
Germany	10.0	14.8	25.0	42.4	32.4	47.9	45.1	49.0
Italy	11.9	11.1	22.5	24.5	30.1	41.9	53.2	52.9
Japan	8.8	8.3	14.8	25.4	17.5	32.0	31.7	36.2
Netherlands	9.1	9.0	13.5	19.0	33.7	55.2	54.0	49.9
Norway	3.7	8.3	13.7	–	29.9	37.5	53.8	45.5
Spain	–	8.3	9.3	18.4	18.8	32.2	42.0	43.3
Sweden	5.7	6.3	8.1	10.4	31.0	60.1	59.1	64.7
Switzerland	–	2.7	4.6	6.1	17.2	32.8	33.5	37.6
UK	9.4	12.7	26.2	30.0	32.2	43.0	39.9	41.9
US	3.9	1.8	7.0	8.6	27.0	31.8	33.3	33.3
Average	8.3	9.1	15.4	18.3*	28.5	43.3	46.1	47.1
Australia	–	–	–	–	21.2	31.6	34.7	36.6
Ireland	–	–	–	–	28.0	48.9	41.2	37.6
New Zealand	–	–	–	–	26.9	38.1	41.3	47.1
Average	–	–	–	–	25.4	39.5	39.1	40.4
Total average	8.3	9.1	15.4	20.7	27.9	42.6	44.8	45.9

Note: * Average without Germany, Japan and Spain undergoing war or war preparations at this time.
Source: IMF.

Treating transfers as government spending is problematical, since it is passing income from one group of citizens to another. Nevertheless there has been disquiet about the aggregate trend. An aspect of globalisation is that the *demonstrated willingness* of governments to cut public spending and public sector debt has almost become a litmus test of credibility for international portfolio managers, so that there has been increasing pressure on governments to reduce the role of fiscal policy to underpin the labour market. Arguments about 'crowding out' private investment have been coupled with arguments that the public sector is less efficient than private business.

The so-called *transfer state* has been condemned as inimical to economic growth and flexibility. But, as shown in later chapters, efforts to shrink it have both contributed to some forms of flexibility and hindered the growth of others. The transfer state that grew up in the era of statutory regulation was intended for a stable society based on the labouring man, not for the flexible worker.

(ix) Mass Unemployment

Another factor behind global labour flexibility has been the growth and persistence of *mass unemployment*. The causes are numerous, and much disputed. Advocates of more flexibility have constantly claimed that a lack of it causes unemployment. Consider a quotation from the OECD *Observer* in March 1984 when the debate was at its zenith, and when the OECD were leading the advocates of greater flexibility:

> The greater the flexibility of the labour market, the lower the economic costs of adjustment: there will be less unemployment and less loss of output. Standard microeconomic theory postulates that, in a perfectly free labour market, wages and employment adjust to rectify imbalances between supply and demand.

The paradox is that whereas commentators have claimed that a lack of flexibility has caused the rise and persistence of unemployment, the unemployment has contributed to the flexibility, directly and indirectly, partly because it has weakened workers' bargaining position. Unemployment itself represents a form of flexibility; mobility from one area to another, or from one type of job to another, is scarcely needed if there are ample workers available in all areas. However, persistently high unemployment strengthens employers' bargaining position and enables them to take advantage of workers' fear of unemployment and poverty to introduce labour and product innovations. It also creates a political climate in which legislation to increase employer control and lessen worker protection can be enacted without too much opposition from unions, and in which individual firms are confident enough to use existing laws and regulations to induce changes in work practices or concessions on employment or income security.[8] Globalisation increases the demonstration effects of such concessions, for countries in which the social climate did not change have felt under pressure to move in the same direction to 'remain competitive', by adopting similar approaches in the interest of 'harmonisation'.

(x) Feminisation

In the 1960s, women's labour force participation began to rise across the world, and was to change the presumptions underlying the welfare state everywhere. The rise has been global, has accelerated, and has been cause and consequence of the growth of flexible labour markets (Standing, 1989a). The typical pattern has been for female participation and employment to rise, and male to fall (Table 3.3). Yet as women have become more regular labour force participants, so the unreal *universalism* of social protection systems has been exposed, because, as chapter 8 shows, women have not been entitled to many social benefits, and because feminisation has contributed to the erosion of non-wage forms of income as well as to forms of labour flexibility. The changing role of women is perhaps the most important factor in changing the social policy agenda at the end of the century of the labouring man.

Table 3.3 Trends in adult activity rates* between 1975 and 1995, by percentage of countries with each type of change, total and by gender

Gender	Type of change	Developing countries	Developed countries
Women	Increased	74	70
	Decreased	17	15
	No change	9	15
	Total	100	100
Men	Increased	26	5
	Decreased	66	95
	No change	9	0
	Total	100	100
Total	Increased	52	35
	Decreased	40	45
	Compensated**	3	20
	No change	6	0
	Total	100	100

Notes: *For national definitions of activity rates, refer to the ILO Yearbook of Labour Statistics. For a critique of the concept, see Standing (1981). Figures are rounded.
**Activity rates of men and women changed in the opposite directions, involving a fall in male and a rise in female activity rates, so that they approximately offset each other.

3.4 CONCLUSIONS

Ultimately, labour flexibility is about control. You wish to be flexible on your terms; you want me to be flexible on your terms; and vice versa. When someone calls on workers or on employers to be flexible, it usually means he wants them to make concessions. Besides the growing recognition of women as workers, the greatest change that took place in the late 1970s and early 1980s was that *fear changed sides*. In the post-war era, employers were inclined to make concessions to worker demands and were committed to the distributional consensus, that with economic growth more income would be transferred to lower-income groups, so reducing inequality.

In the era of market regulation, that consensus was jettisoned. As emphasised in later chapters, concessions have been made by workers, such that growth in income inequality has exceeded the measured growth in some countries and has meant that the stability in income distribution recorded in others masks a growth of inequality. The unemployment has been instrumental in the pursuit of flexibility, the redistribution of economic power and control, and the renewed insecurity that facilitated reorganisation of the labour market. In the transformation of social and labour relations, unemployment has been a messy midwife.

4 The Renewed Growth of Labour Flexibility

Rank Xerox announced that it would cut its workforce by 10 per cent to improve productivity. Its stock rose by 7 per cent on the day of the announcement.

4.1 INTRODUCTION

There is an extensive literature and ample evidence that more flexible economic, labour and social relationships have been emerging at a rapid rate across the world, undermining the institutions and regulatory framework of welfare state capitalism. Yet economists and international organisations have proclaimed that unemployment, low growth and inflationary pressures are due to labour market inflexibility and other forms of inflexibility. Little attention has been given to this paradox.

One might reconcile the views by suggesting that the *need* for flexibility has increased *faster* than its growth, or that reforms and structural and behavioural changes have not been *comprehensive* and sufficiently *systemic*. There has been comment along these lines, notably in the International Monetary Fund's *World Economic Outlook* of 1997. But the evidence to support this has not been presented.

This chapter considers the forms of flexibility that have grown in the last quarter of the twentieth century, in order to assess the labour market and distributional implications.

4.2 PRODUCTION OR ORGANISATIONAL FLEXIBILITY

Underlying both welfare state capitalism and state socialism was a presumption that production consisted predominantly of large, stable organisations and enterprises. In the state socialism model, these became huge, cumbersome giants spreading over whole towns. Early twentieth century industrial capitalism also had this at its core, with hierarchical enterprises and Tayloristic systems of mass production, involving paternalistic controls and the expectation that large enterprises would suck in an 'informal' economy of small-scale businesses. The mid-twentieth century saw the apogee of this model. Although there were partial exceptions, such as the *Mittelstand* network of small and medium-sized manufacturing firms in western Germany, large scale was expected to become the norm. Economies of scale were presumed, and this was one justification for *nationalisation* of production.

Since the 1970s, after a period in which mergers were a reaction to increased instability, large-scale mass production has gone into decline. However, paradoxically, large-scale *enterprises* have spread to control much of the global economy, epitomised by the growth of multinationals and household-name products known throughout the world. Yet a message has been that decentralisation is essential for dynamic efficiency, and that the future will be characterised by small scale production and 'flexible specialisation' (Piore and Sabel, 1984). Some have attributed the success of Silicon Valley to the high failure rate among firms, calling it 'flexible recycling'. Commentators have suggested that small firms could thrive in the globalising economy through collaboration, and some have explored the Marshallian concept of industrial districts, identifying regions where clusters of small-scale flexible firms co-exist in collaborative competition and partnership. Others conclude that small firms cannot be expected to flourish in the globalising economy, or that they are an illusion, or part of a passing phase of adjustment. There is an exciting literature on enterprise *networking* and *global commodity chains* that highlights the diversity of production systems (for a review, see Palpacuer and Parisotto, 1998).

The death of Fordism is exaggerated. Mass production still accounts for a substantial part of industrial employment around the world, large bureaucratic enterprises are still found everywhere, and small firms find it difficult to move into the international economy. Nevertheless, there has been global 'downsizing' and 'outsourcing' associated with a splintering of production and distribution processes, and a trend for medium and large firms to *contract out their employment function.*

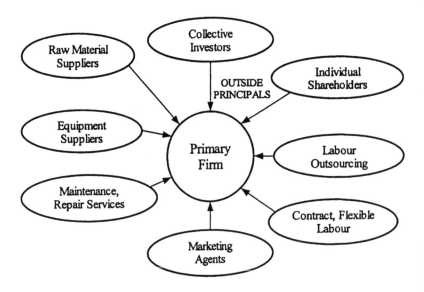

Figure 4.1 Stylised production chains

Concentration of capital has increased while the centralisation of labour has decreased. Many multinational enterprises and established national enterprises have extended their division of labour by linking activities between firms and by outsourcing or selling off activities previously done in-house to firms dependent on them. The notion of 'production chains' has become popular, in which a string of firms are linked in producing a complex product, as illustrated schematically in Figure 4.1. Dominant firms can download risk and uncertainty, retaining flexibility to alter production in the face of fluctuations in market demand or unanticipated technological options.

Globalisation and the technological revolution have been primary factors in this trend. Globalisation implies greater *uncertainty*, while the technological changes have made more organisational options feasible. That is the context for assessing the issues of firm size and organisational flexibility.

What determines and limits firm size? One factor is the diminishing returns to management, a point first emphasised by Frank Knight in 1921, elaborated in a classic paper by Ronald Coarse and incorporated into transaction cost economics. The key issue is *uncertainty – primary* (random events), *secondary* (due to ineffective communication), and *behavioural* (due to opportunism and unique actions that do not have a probability distribution). Uncertainty increases with size and complexity of organisation. As size increases, organisational control problems multiply and bounds of cognitive competence are reached. Increasing the size of firm also increases the layers of control needed, because to be effective any manager can only deal directly with a limited number of subordinates (Williamson, 1985, p. 134). There is also the impairment of incentives that comes with distance from positions of control and management, from centres of knowledge and influence, and from market signals.

Large bureaucratic enterprises are inherently inefficient. There is a trade-off between economies of scale – coupled with the quasi-monopolistic position of most such enterprises – and high transaction and other costs that characterise bureaucratic organisations. Williamson referred to 'control loss' as limiting firm size in a market economy. But a bureaucratic organisation does not suffer the consequences because inefficiency is unpunished (Williamson, 1967). Pursuit of efficiency is diluted by the multiplication of internal, 'political' objectives. As anybody who has worked in a bureaucracy knows, quality and quantity of output are not primary motivating factors. The notion of a *soft budget constraint*, cited so often with respect to state socialist enterprises, scarcely captures the inadequacies of bureaucratic organisations. Politics typically prevail over performance, making the internal labour market inefficient. And 'managerial' positions multiply because achieving management status is a primary motivational mechanism.

The *propensity to manage* represents the propensity of insiders to use resources of the organisation to pursue sub-goals that do not benefit it or the 'market' it is supposedly serving. Procedures become ends in themselves and individual output becomes only one, often minor, criterion of performance and reward. Lack of linkage between productivity and income or position also means that the *monitoring, control* function becomes a heavy cost. For these reasons, the larger and longer-established the bureaucratic organisation, the higher the ratio of co-ordinators (managers) to output producers is likely to be.

The relevance of this is that globalisation and technological changes have encouraged a reduction in optimal size of firm (not enterprise). In the globalising economy, the spheres of uncertainty have been increasing, as has the extent of uncertainty. The greater focus on competitiveness means that costs and hard budget constraints become more critical for organisational survival and growth. The uncertainty, volatility and competition have put pressure on managements to cut all costs, including the semi-hidden costs of co-ordination and control.

Globalisation and the technological revolution have weakened the tendency of the 1970s for enterprises to expand through the acquisition of firms and mergers across different types of firm. Difficulties of control and co-ordination costs were too large, given growing uncertainty and the need for adjustment. The idea of *strategic alliances* between corporations was strengthened, and analysts have even questioned whether the concept of an enterprise is appropriate any more (Dunning, 1993; Mansell, 1994). This may be going too far, yet the drift is towards flexible structures, with firms more loosely linked, for strategic reasons.

Critical analysis by economists and management theorists of public sector and other bureaucratic enterprises has drawn attention to their inherently political character and resultant systematic inefficiency. This has helped to justify *privatisation*, has encouraged owners and managers to break up large enterprises, to out-source, and so on. For those that have remained large bureaucracies, it has become evident that, to become competitive, delegation to semi-autonomous units is required to give more scope to entrepreneurship and intrapreneurship. Many large enterprises have also tried to overcome the inefficiency of bureaucracy by shifting to *performance-related pay* and *team-based performance targets*. But the tendency for co-option by managements and the scope for opportunism raise the costs of such devices and necessitate new layers of monitoring and control mechanisms. The long-term future of large bureaucracies is questionable.

In pursuit of organisational flexibility, governments have promoted small firms, often supported by corporate interests. Competition between large and small firms is limited, often because they operate in segmented markets. Many small firms provide large firms with cheap inputs and services, in which the larger do not have expertise or capacity. Through sub-contracting, large firms save on labour and other costs, evading laws, taxes, regulations, and so on. Sub-contracting also increases a large enterprise's market flexibility. Governments want to conserve small firms because of political and labour market advantages, possibly including employment generation in the expectation that small firms are labour intensive and reduce social protection costs. Small firms are also thought to provide cheap wage goods and services, in effect reducing the cost of reproducing labour power. Finally, small firms can function as a labour reserve for larger units.

If there is to be more organisational flexibility and a splintering of large bureaucratic control systems, it is important to reflect on what large firms provide workers that small firms cannot or typically do not. They provide *constrained security*, and cushion some insiders from competitive pressures, while imposing their norms of behaviour and bounded rationality. The *job structures* and types of *skill* emphasised in such organisations tend to be distorted relative to the image of skill suggested in chapter 1. Yet although large firms and bureaucracies have been the main means of ensuring employment in the twentieth century, they and the 'company man' they have favoured seem destined to shrink, both in number and size.[1] While it would be an exaggeration to expect the new notion of 'virtual company' to sweep all other forms of organisation aside, there is no doubt that there is an ongoing growth in small companies in which many services are contracted out, allowing a few core staff to run the business (Ettighoffer, 1992). There are expectations that groups of small firms will link up through 'telepartnerships' (European Commission, 1994b).

So, global concentration of capital has been coupled with deconcentration of production, increasing organisational flexibility. A by-product is that the scope for bypassing statutory and some other regulations is growing, as is the ability of firms and individuals to detach themselves from mainstream systems of social protection. Since the scope for 'black' and 'grey' economic activity is greater, the scope for concealing income and employment is also greater.

4.3 WAGE SYSTEM FLEXIBILITY: GLOBALISATION OF SOCIAL INCOME

Across the world, during the last quarter of the twentieth century an extraordinary amount of attention has been devoted to the need for wage flexibility. High, persistent unemployment has been attributed to a lack of it. In many cases the claim has appeared almost tautological, since the existence of high unemployment has been taken as evidence that there must be a lack of wage flexibility. Low economic growth has also been attributed to wage inflexibility. In sum, the orthodox position has been that real wage flexibility is essential for low unemployment, stable and high economic growth, low inflation and successful structural adjustment.

It has also been a constant refrain that wage differentials must be wide and flexible, and that measures to hold up real wages or to reduce wage inequality amount to *market distortions*, which impede economic efficiency, impede labour mobility, and harm the employment prospects of the 'low productivity', 'unskilled' groups. In short, if market clearing wages were allowed, unemployment above the 'natural' level (defined by frictional and structural factors) would be short-lived. This reasoning has been applied to all types of economy. A common feature of the analysis has been the presumption of labour market *dualism*, in which 'formal sector' wages have been held up by statutory minimum wages and other 'price distorting' mechanisms, notably unions and statutory obligations on employers (Fisher, 1984; Lal, 1985; Edwards, 1988). Although the dualism has been more prominent in analyses of industrialising economies and debates on structural adjustment, this reasoning has also been applied to industrialised economies (e.g., Burda and Sachs, 1987).

The prescriptions derived from this have been to 'deregulate' the formal sector, reduce 'non-wage labour costs', decentralise wage bargaining to the individual worker–employer level if possible, or to the individual plant or firm as the next best alternative, and remove or erode minimum wage machinery, so that labour costs fall and the quasi-voluntarily unemployed will filter into available informal sector jobs or find jobs in the more informalised formal sector. Stylised models formulated around the World Bank were influential in formalising this perspective (e.g., Lopez and Riveros, 1989; Edwards, 1988). And the policy proposals have been influential components of structural adjustment and shock therapy strategies of the 1990s.

This is a long way from the approach to wages that predominated in the middle decades of the twentieth century. Then, mainstream policy objectives amounted to labour decommodification through measures to reduce the role and variability of wages. The ILO's Philadelphia Declaration symbolised this approach. If 'labour is not a commodity', then the wage could not be a price in the normal sense of the term. One cannot realistically interpret policy developments in the post-war era of statutory regulation without recognising the centrality of this objective in that period.

Bearing this in mind, and to appreciate subsequent developments in the context of globalisation and labour market flexibility, consider the notion of the wage at an abstract level. Conceptually, the wage is part of any individual's **social income**. To survive, any person has five possible sources or forms of income, in money or in kind. Many people have access to merely one or two sources, while a minority in any society have access to all five. Bearing in mind that individual items might not apply, these elements can be portrayed in a straightforward identity:

$$SI = W + CB + EB + SB + PB$$

where SI is the individual's social income, W is the money wage, CB is the value of benefits or support provided by the family, kin or the local community, EB is the amount of benefits provided by the enterprise in which the person is working, SB is the value of state benefits provided, in terms of insurance or other transfers, including subsidies paid directly or through firms, and PB is private income benefits, gained through investment, including private social protection.

We may disaggregate the elements as follows:

$$SI = (W_b + W_f) + (FT + LT) + (NWB + IB) + (C + IS + D) + PB$$

where W_b is the base or fixed wage, W_f is the flexible part of the wage (bonuses, etc.), FT are family transfers, LT are local community transfers, including any income from charity, non-governmental organisations, etc., NWB are non-wage benefits provided by firms to their workers, IB are contingency, insurance-type benefits provided by firms to their workers, C are universal state benefits (citizenship rights), IS are insurance-based income transfers from the state in case of contingency needs, and D are discretionary, means-tested transfers from the state.

By depicting an individual's income in this way, one can assess the full value of individual components and the roles they play in the labour process. Thus, the subjective value of the money wage could be said to rise if, in the event of the current activity ending, the probability of obtaining a similar level of income fell.

The two identities for SI are abstractions, and would be hard to translate into empirical form. However, we hypothesise that certain patterns prevail in different parts of the world, that there are trends in the relative distribution of the components, and that both the distribution within the total and the trends in the distribution of the components within countries are related to globalisation.

The flexibility of the remuneration system will reflect the structure of the social income. Thus, in most cases, if the money wage were a large share of total income, that would imply more potential flexibility than if enterprise benefits were relatively large. Flexibility might also be greater if the sum of W and EB was a low share of SI, leaving CB and SB to bear the brunt of the cost to employers, or if EB and SB were reduced, or if W_f was high relative to W_b, or if W_b were set for shorter periods, and so on. What is most important for assessing wage flexibility and the impact of changes in real wages is the *structure* of the social income. As a consequence, wage flexibility may be greater or less than indicated by changes in money wages. With that in mind, consider a developmental objective of the two dominant models of the post-war era.

In both of those models, there was a process of 'labour decommodification'. In state socialism, a long-term, Leninist objective was a 'withering of the wage', so that in the Soviet Union and countries under its influence the money wage comprised a declining and ultimately low proportion of a worker's social income. As such, the wage itself was unable to play an incentive function. Although tariff-based wage differentials always existed, the wage was not intended to be flexible in the sense of responding to market pressures, and was set administratively. It became an impediment to productivity because it was low and because increments were correspondingly small. Neither the wage nor the differentials were related to labour skill or input. It is incorrect to think that there were no differentials, or that there was wage 'levelling'. Rather than absent, wage differentials were distorted, in favour of manual 'materially productive' labour. Before and in the period of *perestroika*, reforms of the wage tariff system did try to make it more flexible and efficiency-oriented, as in the case of the 'Unified Staff Table' system introduced in Bulgaria in 1979. But the points and tariff scale were status-oriented and not closely related to actual work contributions or skills.

Coupled with low and rigid wages was what might be called *administrative welfare*, or what was known as *sotskultbyt* in the Soviet system.[2] Underpinned by the state, and managed by unions on behalf of the Party, enterprise-based benefits comprised a high and rising share of total income. The extensive benefits were distributed in paternalistic ways, used as a form of labour control and did not have legally enforceable claims attached to them. Thus, the security they provided was always conditional and discretionary, reducing their value to the worker, and inducing the providers to be unconcerned about their quality or efficiency with which they were provided. The EB were intended to ensure subservience to authority, particular skills, adequate effort, loyalty to the regime, a willingness to co-operate and compliance with rules, regulations and the authority chain. They were oriented to induce everybody to prepare for and participate in state-based economic activity. A sort of social contract involved enterprise-based income security in return for lifelong, passive labour. The EB-oriented remuneration system also had a redistributive function, since it involved 'redistributive privileges' for valued workers and employees, through the allocation of subsidised goods and services.

Complementing the high EB, the system of community and kinship support was eroded by what could charitably be called state paternalism, even though an informal, secondary economy evolved to complement people for low state-derived incomes. The system was unsustainable because it eroded the *incentive* function of the money wage, lowering productivity and ultimately undermining welfare as well because it resulted in squalid inefficiency, petty opportunism and the neglect and decay of facilities. Given the imbalance between incentives and security, the formula could not last. The low wages and assured benefits gave security, provided there was a lumpenised willingness to labour in return. But it bred a peculiar passivity epitomised by the cynicism of the oft-quoted adage, 'They pretend to pay us, we pretend to work.' It was achieved through a bureaucratic control system, and the workers responded with the most sullen resistance possible. In the end, they were paid their efficiency wage, and the income security disappeared into nothingness.

The welfare state capitalism model was also oriented to 'labour decommodification', which amounted to a reduction of wage flexibility, at least at the individual level.[3] Although there were differences between social democratic and conservative welfare systems, in western Europe there was a steady expansion in the share of total compensation coming from state benefits. Enterprise benefits also expanded in scope and value, whereas informal community transfers were relatively low. This model was sustainable as long as trade and investment allocations were largely between countries with similar labour rights and forms of wage supplements. In the USA, a *residual* welfare state meant that private benefits and enterprise-based occupational welfare comprised greater shares of total income and compensated for lower state benefits, although these too expanded in the post-war era.

The welfare state model has had several variants. At one end of the spectrum are what Richard Titmuss called *residual welfare states*, or what Esping-Andersen called *liberal regimes* (Titmuss, 1963; Esping-Andersen, 1990). In countries with this system, most notably the USA, occupational welfare or enterprise benefits always comprised a relatively high share of social income, while universal state benefits and insurance-based benefits have been modest or low. In countries with a *redistributive welfare state,* the pattern has depended on whether the system corresponded to Esping-Andersen's *social democratic* or *conservative regime.*

In the social democratic case, there have been high state benefits (SB), with a tendency for C (universal state benefits and citizenship rights) to be high and rising. The conservative regime could be sub-divided into those with a Catholic tradition and those with a Confucian tradition (i.e., Japan) (Esping-Andersen, 1997). In both cases enterprise benefits (EB) have been dualistic in character, with privileged occupational groups (consisting predominantly of male workers) having high levels, others low. In both cases, although in different form, CB have been relatively high, because the role of the supportive family has been emphasised. In the Catholic model, IS (insurance-based benefits) have been high; in the Confucian model, IS have been rising. Finally, C has been low in both variants.

Before considering recent changes, consider the stylised patterns of social income that predominated in the post-war era in different parts of the world. Because data are lacking to map social income, one cannot give estimates. However, based on descriptive material (and, for what it is worth, personal experience of working in different parts of the world), one may 'guesstimate' the median distribution (or relative weight) of the components in different regions relative to others. The main point is to capture the essence of the process, and for illustrative purposes we may use just three levels – high, medium, low. For each region, one component was relatively high. We surmise that in Africa wages may have accounted for a higher share of social income than they did in other regions; this does not, of course, mean that W in Africa were high by the standards of other regions.

Thus, *relative to other regions as a proportion of total personal income*, the values of the components of social income as expressed in the first identity were as follows:

	W	EB	SB	PB	CB
Africa	High	Low	Low	Low	High
Western Europe	Medium	Medium	High	Medium	Low
Eastern Europe	Low	High	Low	Low	Low
North America	Medium	Medium	Low	High	Low
South Asia	Low	Medium	Low	Low	Medium
South-East Asia	Low	Medium	Low	Low	High

Although there were variations within those regions, what distinguishes most of them is that one source of non-wage benefit comprised a high share of social income. It also highlights the sources of poverty and income insecurity. For example, one can see that one factor in the poverty (and low productivity) of workers in Africa has been the low capacity of rural and urban communities to supplement money wages, in the absence of other sources of income, even though the need for the income has been high. Traditionally, migratory labourers have been expected to send back remittances from their wage income to their rural community, with relatively little flowing in the opposite direction.

This contrasts with the typical pattern that prevailed in South-East Asia and some other rapidly industrialising economies, and it is that which has surely influenced the changes in the structure of social incomes globally in the recent era. In large parts of South-East Asia, the payment of low money wages in emerging industries and commercial agriculture was made feasible by the community and kinship transfers to wage workers. Most production workers could be paid an 'individual wage' rather than a 'family wage', but had *sufficient* income security. Whether working in quasi-peasant agriculture or in informal, peri-urban economic activities, relatives of wage workers (and often the workers themselves) were able to supplement the low money wage with other income. Among the sources of their social income have been *remittances*. There is a rich theoretical and empirical literature on remittances, most focusing on the flow from workers to their rural communities. Often neglected is that there has been substantial *rural-to-urban remittances*, which in the phase of the region's 'take off' into rapid industrialisation and export expansion, made it possible for factories and other firms to pay low money wages, without that involving low and stagnant labour efficiency, and gave the economies a competitive edge when technological and capital mobility rose in the 1980s.

We may surmise that globalisation and associated shifts in economic and social policy have precipitated a restructuring of the social income in much of the world. The stylised trends are not identical, largely because the typical 'initial' patterns were quite different in the various regions and because pressures have come mainly from the economies in which the remuneration system was initially relatively flexible. However, there seem to be several common trends, notably a relative decline in the share of state benefits in social income and a relative (and absolute) growth in private benefits gained by those able to save or in positions where companies feel inclined to subsidise them (blurring the distinction between private and enterprise benefits).

Overall, one could hypothesise that the median changes taking place in the various regions are as follows, where a plus sign implies a rise in the *relative* contribution to total individual income, a minus sign implies the opposite. Where both a plus and a minus sign are given, one surmises that part of the growth of income differentiation is due to a shift in one direction for some groups and in the opposite direction for others.

	W	EB	B	PB	CB
Africa	–/+	–/+	–	0	0
Western Europe	+/–	+/–	–	+	+
Eastern Europe	+	–	+/–	+	+
North America	+/–	+/–	–	+	+
South Asia	0	?	–	+?	0
South-East Asia	+	+	0	+	–

As a result of global pressures on labour costs in industrialised countries, many workers have seen an erosion in state transfers and enterprise benefits, resulting in a shift to the money wage coupled with an expectation that more benefits would be acquired privately. To compensate for the erosion of state benefits, and in order to retain potentially mobile groups of key staff, enterprise benefits could be expected to have risen for some groups (managerial staff, professionals, etc.) while they have been eroded for others as a way of reducing labour costs and as a way of making the remuneration system more flexible.

An international convergence is likely. Successfully industrialising countries have absorbed more workers into regular wage labour and other forms of labour associated with industrial firms. Historically, as this happens, the share of community income support drops, while the money wage becomes more important. In the era in which the welfare state was held out as the development model to copy, this would have been complemented by a growth of state benefits. However, in the 1980s and 1990s that was no longer regarded as the trend to follow. Meanwhile, in industrialised countries there has been greater reliance on informal networks and family work as a means of 'social protection'. But it is harder for industrialised societies to recreate (or create) informal kinship and community support systems than it is to fade them out in industrialising economies.

The relevance of this perspective is that it points to a process whereby wage flexibility and income insecurity have been growing with globalisation. The absolute and relative growth of state and enterprise benefits in the post-war era, particularly in industrialised countries and in state socialist countries, increased income security because it made personal and family welfare less dependent on the intrinsically more insecure money wage. If people lose state and enterprise benefits, or lose the prospect of obtaining them should they need them, they have to fall back more on money wages and informal support systems, or/and expect an effective cut in their living standards.

The most common trend may be the renewed *monetisation* of incomes. For many groups, this may not match the increased need for money wages, because of the loss of other forms of income. The most obvious case of this is that because of the growth of single person households and because women have been drawn into the labour market, domestic work has tended to decline to the extent that time available has been reduced. This has tended to increase the need for money income.

If the two models that dominated the post-war era involved a steady movement away from the money wage to other forms of remuneration, globalisation and labour market flexibility have induced a shift back to the money wage and have also induced pressures to increase informal and community-based support, in part because the wage has commonly become more of an individual wage rather than a family wage.

The state socialist model had low W relative to EB, but a high W_b (fixed wage) to W_f (flexible wage). Trends in the 1990s in the countries moving away from that model have meant that the ratio of W to EB has risen and the ratio of W_f to W_b

has risen, so that there has been an enormous growth in W_f that has come as a result of a shift away from EB. For instance, basic wages in Russia accounted for about one-quarter of production worker earnings by the mid-1990s, by when the average value of enterprise benefits were shrinking fast (Clarke, 1996, p. 17; Standing, 1996a, ch. 5).

Enterprise benefits have had several motives, depending on their instigators. To the extent that they have been employer-determined, they have been a reflection of paternalistic control, or they have been introduced because of the 'merit good' view that the individual worker would not value the goods or services as much as they are worth either for the individual or for the firm or for the community, or they have been introduced because collective provision is less costly and/or more beneficial than individual provision (because of externalities).

If enterprise benefits are government 'mandated', the reason could be because the costs of such provision are lower if the whole community provide them. This could arise, for example, if employers were not paying health insurance for their workers. If those workers were not covered, the cost to society might be that general taxpayers would have to assist through paying higher taxes to cover public assistance. Or the reason could be that the benefits were more than realised by any individual employer or worker, as with healthcare generally. Or the reason could be that mandated benefits would counter adverse selectivity, i.e., if an individual firm offered benefits for specified groups (e.g., sickness coverage for technicians or for permanent employees) that would attract more from that group to the firm.

The pressures that have changed the structure of the social income in industrialised countries come in part from wage policy in the rapidly industrialising economies. It would be a misuse of language to describe the policies there over the past few decades as promotion of a free labour market in which wages were allowed to adjust to market forces. Countries that have emerged as NICs have used *wage repression*, not free labour markets. For instance, for many years in Singapore the government placed restrictions on the provision of enterprise benefits, union leaders were jailed, strikes were outlawed, and the government-dominated National Wages Council and the National Trades Union Congress held down wages (Deyo, 1987). In the early 1980s, wage repression was reversed briefly 'to restore wages to market levels', the intention being to induce restructuring away from labour intensive production, which further demonstrated that industrialisation had not been based on free labour markets. The government acted to 'distort' the price of labour by lowering the social wage, through providing housing subsidies, schooling and healthcare for industrial workers (Lim, 1989).

In the Republic of Korea, the authorities long controlled union activity and pressured employers to prevent wage rises, directly and through the banks (You, 1988). In Taiwan, the Union Act restricted workers' bargaining rights when unionisation was made mandatory and when strikes for wage rises were banned. In Malaysia and elsewhere, wages and labour costs were controlled in export processing zones, and independent unions were curtailed. In short, wage repression has been an integral part of successful industrialisation, not avoidance of 'price distortions'. This was precisely what happened in European industrialisation.

In both industrialising and industrialised economies, in the era of market regulation not only have there been numerous ways by which wages have been repressed rather than left to the 'free market', notably in the context of structural adjustment programmes, but supposedly in the interest of 'pricing workers into work', economists have advocated wage subsidies, 'two-tier' wage structures, and other contrived interventions to influence wage rates. By contrast, minimum wage regulation and collective bargaining have been criticised as creating wage inflexibility.

There is evidence that wage flexibility has increased in industrialised countries in the 1990s, and this has been mirrored or exceeded in industrialising and so-called transition economies. Interpretation of the trends at the level of the firm might be assisted by considering the remuneration system as depicted in Figure 4.2. For instance, the system would be prone to inflexibility if the fixed wage was a large part of the total remuneration. As discussed in chapter 8, there is ample evidence that the fixed wage has been shrinking in relative terms, that bonuses and profit-

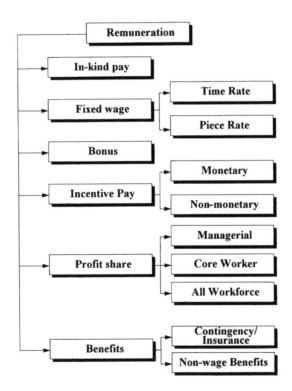

Figure 4.2 The enterprise wage flexibility loop

sharing pay have increased, and that for production workers there has been a shift
from non-wage forms of remuneration to money wages.

Another source of wage flexibility reviewed there is the erosion of minimum
wages, which are harder to apply in more flexible labour markets. But governments
across the world have let the value of a minimum wage fall relative to average wages
and to subsistence, or have abolished or weakened regulatory machinery, often under
the influence of international organisations critical of minimum wages in general.

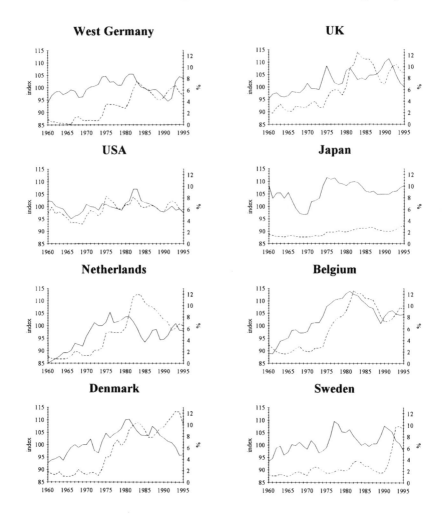

Figure 4.3 Adjusted wage share in selected OECD countries, 1960–95 *(1970–72=100, wage
share is continuous line, left scale; unemployment with dashed line,right scale)*

Sources: OECD, *National Accounts, Main Economic Indicators.*

At the macro-economic level, a sign of wage flexibility is that the wage share of GDP has fallen in many industrialised economies. After rising in the 1960s and 1970s, during the crisis years, when the distributional consensus cracked, high unemployment and imposition of supply-side economic policy reversed the trend, so that by the mid-1990s the wage share of GDP, on average, was back to what it had been at the beginning of the 1970s (Figure 4.3). To that extent, industrialised economies had demonstrated considerable macro-level wage flexibility.

Another sign of wage flexibility is that wage differentials have widened in many countries. This is covered in chapter 7, so we merely note that the growth of wage and income differentiation has been a feature of the era of market regulation. Another feature is that collective bargaining has commonly turned into *concession bargaining*, with unions at national, sectoral or enterprise level committing themselves and their members to wage restraint or real wage cuts in return for commitments by employers to create jobs or to maintain some of the jobs under threat. This is a different social consensus from the one that prevailed in the preceding era. For instance, in the case of the metalworkers in Germany, the union *IGMetall* in 1995 began lobbying for a deal involving wage restraint and lower starting wages in return for a promise by employers to create 300,000 jobs between 1995 and 1998 (*European Industrial Relations Review*, July 1995, p. 13). This proposed package represents a changing role for unions, and a redistributive policy effectively disadvantaging younger workers relative to older workers. The employers rejected the proposal, responding with one to reduce the cut in jobs and increase employment security in return for wage restraint and acceptance by the union of more flexible work practices. An agreement along these lines was reached in the textile industry. In other sectors, concession bargaining has been shifted to the level of the plant, with the objectives of controlling costs and increasing working practice flexibility (*International Herald Tribune*, 28 March 1996).

The most pervasive means by which wage flexibility has been increasing is through decentralisation and *individualisation* of wage determination. This has been intensified by the growth of organisational flexibility, by diversification of 'skills', the erosion of unions, workers' loss of bargaining strength, and the drift to pro-individualistic labour regulations, or erosion of pro-collective regulations.

4.4 LABOUR COST FLEXIBILITY

Globalisation has increased the perceived significance of all forms of costs of production, because the growing integration of economies means that production and capital could shift more easily to where production and distribution costs are lower. Although labour costs may not be as important as implied by the amount of debate devoted to them, they surely influence the international division of labour.

Labour costs cover wage and 'non-wage labour costs'. How such costs are conceptualised depends on the purpose of the analysis, and it is important to bear in mind that the notion of costs for economists is broader than for accountants. A common procedure is to divide them into *fixed* and *variable* costs, or *employee-related* and *hour-related* costs. For analysing labour flexibility, one should consider a more disaggregated approach that links costs to the division of labour, control mechanisms and forms of flexibility.

As an approximation, we can identify ten categories of indirect, variable labour costs. Many have one or more functions for employers, so that incurring them has benefits. They vary in significance depending on job structure, extent and 'strength' of labour regulations, composition of the labour force, technology, and so on. The costs are the following, in no order of implied scale:

(a) Overhead costs. These refer to fringe benefits, such as occupational pensions and subsidised health services, which are part of the compensation for individual workers. Not all groups are entitled to such benefits or have need for them. Overhead costs may not vary with wage rates, although some may vary according to grade of worker, length of service, age or other characteristic.

(b) Fiscal costs. These are costs that firms and/or workers are obliged to pay to the government, including payroll taxes, such as employer and employee social security contributions. The employer part probably accounts for the largest part of conventional 'non-wage labour costs'. In the mid-1980s, the OECD estimated that in some countries, social security contributions accounted for more than half of non-wage labour costs, which they defined more narrowly than is proposed here (OECD, 1986). Note that fiscal costs could rise as a share of labour costs even if the wage system was growing more flexible. In industrialised countries they have varied considerably as a share of labour costs and in most countries have risen (Table 4.1).

(c) Training costs. These are related to the division of labour, character of jobs and orientation of the firm, and are not just to do with imparting 'skills'. Of course, different types of training involve different types of cost and benefit. Costs include direct expenditure on training, output loss if on-the-job training is conducted by other workers, and efficiency recovery costs (i.e., the post-training costs incurred until the trainee achieves the productivity of an experienced worker).

(d) Co-ordination costs. These are the costs of administering, supervising and controlling the workforce. They include remuneration of supervisors, welfare services provided as a means of maintaining the workforce, and costs of control systems. The range and extent of co-ordination costs will reflect the job structure, division of labour and complexity of statutory and voice regulations.

(e) Protection costs. These arise from statutory or other arrangements to give workers protection from injury, health hazards, psychological stress and employment insecurity. Although firms may find ways of avoiding some of them, protection

costs are a function of type of product, technology, job structure and workforce composition, as well as the 'strictness' and application of statutory regulations. Apart from general protection costs, selective costs arise from arrangements required or desired to shield some groups from certain tasks or strains, such as those with physical impairments, young workers, or the elderly. If regulations were introduced or more tightly applied, such costs may induce discrimination against such groups.

Table 4.1 Non-wage labour costs as share of total labour costs, 1985–95[a]
(Percentages)

	1985	1990	1995	Percentage point change over past	
				5 years	10 years
Austria	18.4	18.3	18.9	0.6	0.5
Belgium	23.1	25.9	26.3	0.4	3.2
Canada	10.7	11.1	13.7	2.6	3.0
Finland	18.4	20.4	22.4	2.0	4.0
France	27.9	27.9	28.2	0.3	0.3
Germany[b]	18.8	18.8	19.6	0.8	0.8
Italy	26.8	28.7	29.9	1.2	3.1
Japan	13.0	14.6	14.2	–0.4	1.2
Norway	16.4	16.9	16.2	–0.7	–0.2
Sweden	26.5	27.2	26.4	–0.8	0.0
Switzerland	13.1	13.1	14.1	1.0	1.1
United Kingdom	13.5	11.9	12.6	0.7	–0.8
United States	17.7	17.8	18.7	0.9	1.0

[a] Data derived from national accounts estimates of labour costs for the whole economy. Wage costs refer to all wages and salaries, non-wage labour costs refer to employer social security contributions.
[b] Data refer to western Germany only.
Source: OECD, *National Accounts 1983–95*, Vol. 2; *Employment Outlook* (Paris, OECD, 1997).

(f) Labour turnover costs.   These cover recruitment costs (adverts, interview time, travelling expenses, initial bonuses, induction, etc.) and dismissal costs (notice, severance pay, etc.), and may include loss of profits due to having unfilled vacancies, inexperienced workers in jobs, or diversion of workers to other jobs. Turnover costs will reflect the type of job and job structure, and may be small, as where productivity declines after a short period due to the monotony or intensity of the tasks, or where seniority pay systems are in effect.

(g) Motivation costs.   These would be hard to quantify, although they are real. A motivation cost arises if the job structure is such that workers are unmotivated. An example is where prospects for job and income advancement are minimal, as

might be the case if the firm's workforce was shrinking. Another is where the detailed division of labour is developed, as in Tayloristic systems of work organisation.

(h) Productivity costs. All job structures and workforce compositions have benefits and costs, and the costs include productivity losses due to some groups being relatively unproductive. The cost is the lost potential implied by retention of such workers, and if that is greater than the expected cost of replacing them, they may be displaced. However, other factors may prevent the firm from doing so or make it not wish to do so, perhaps because of anticipated *motivation* costs, or the effect on morale of other workers. Examples of productivity costs are where firms retain full-time workers where part-time working could permit greater labour intensity and where some groups have to take time between tasks, the time representing an avoidable cost.

(i) Adaptability costs. These relate to adjustment and change. Some groups may be as productive as others but be less adaptable, perhaps taking longer to adjust or being less willing to do so because of a greater feeling of *status frustration* if actual or perceived 'deskilling' is involved. If so, a firm's adjustment to demand shifts, or to product or process innovations, may be more costly than if the workforce were composed of more adaptable workers.

(j) Bureaucratic behaviour costs. In large organisations with internal labour markets, promotions and job structures will reflect more than productivity and dynamic efficiency considerations. The costs of bureaucratic behaviour will be greater in service-oriented, office-based organisations than where tangible products and identifiable revenues are involved. Bureaucracies induce political behaviour that detracts from efficiency. The costs include *clique-scheming* costs. Those wanting to climb in the firm will do favours for those above, alongside or below themselves to create a network of mutually-supportive clientage that has nothing to do with productivity. The resultant costs will be endemic in large organisations. Strategic opportunism may induce complex monitoring procedures, which spreads costs of bureaucratic behaviour into larger co-ordination costs.

Although this classification is broader than the usual notion of non-wage labour costs, even on a narrow definition there is evidence that, at least in industrialised countries, they have been substantial and in recent years have risen faster than wages. Globalisation and pursuit of labour flexibility have provoked extensive debate on how to reduce such costs and on their effects. Fiscal costs have been cut – or their rise slowed – by a shift in the revenue for social protection expenditure from social security contributions to general taxation, and by firms turning to types of labour that do not involve such payments or the entitlements acquired by full-time regular workers. Firms have been lowering the EB part of the social income.

Protection costs have been the most controversial, the main claim being that employment protection regulations lower employment and raise unemployment. Numerous reports and papers have made this claim since the 1980s. Other forms of regulation have attracted similar claims, with similar calls for measures to make the labour market more flexible so as to reduce costs for firms. These are considered in later chapters. However, most costs have benefits as well, for the firm, the workers or both.

4.5 EMPLOYMENT (NUMERICAL) FLEXIBILITY

Since the early 1970s, there has been a global growth in employment or 'numerical' flexibility. As firms have tried to become more 'competitive', they have wanted to be able to alter employment with minimal constraints, quickly and with little cost. Employment flexibility reflects the ability of firms to hire and dismiss workers easily and at low cost, and would grow if any of the following conditions held:

- legislative change weakened employment protection (explicit derogation);
- employment shifted to labour statuses with less employment protection (implicit derogation);
- the distribution of employment shifted to *sectors* with more workers in statuses with little employment protection;
- a shift to *firms* that have high shares of flexiworkers;
- a change in collective agreements to give more employment flexibility ('concession bargains');
- a shift to non-profit and voluntary organisations.

In the post-war era, it was almost taken for granted that an 'easy hire, easy fire' regime was unacceptable and that slowing employment fluctuations had macro-economic advantages, being a counter-cyclical stabiliser. While individual firms might benefit from being able to off-load labour costs quickly and at low cost, the benefits of some inertia included the inducement to employment planning by firms, inducing them to take a longer-term perspective and regard labour as a 'quasi-fixed factor of production' involving investment in on-the-job training, and so on.

The era of market regulation has seen a shift in attitude. Globalisation has made it harder for individual firms to handle uncertainty and risk, and has increased pressure on them to reduce costs. And higher unemployment has made it easier for firms to turn to sources of labour other than regular full-time wage employment.

To explore employment flexibility, consider the stylised enterprise labour market shown in Figure 4.4. A firm can hire regular, full-time workers, which is still the prevailing image of the norm. Or it can turn to forms of non-regular worker. A popular model in the 1980s postulated that in the pursuit of flexibility, firms were creating dualistic structures consisting of core and periphery workforces (Atkinson, 1985; 1989). This oversimplified the process, as did other 'dual labour market'

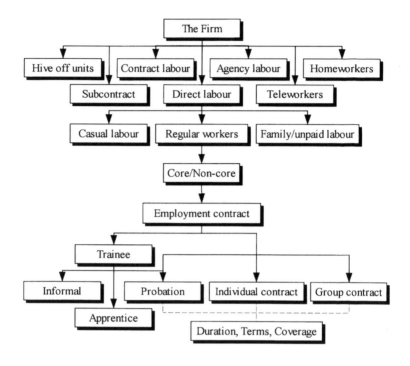

Figure 4.4 The firm's employment function

theories popular at the time (Rosenberg, 1989). Different forms of employment flexibility reflect different cost and control considerations. What is remarkable is the proliferation in forms of labour relationship, which cannot be captured in any simple model of a firm's labour market. Besides diversity, the global trend seems to be towards distancing the producer firm from long-term commitments to workers. This does not apply to all groups, for the capitalised value of some firms may depend on the accumulated competencies, experience and contacts of an inner core of employees. However, anecdotal evidence suggests that the relative size of such core groups is shrinking, and that this is a global trend.

To appreciate the global character of employment flexibility it may be useful to distinguish between forms of flexible labour found in industrialising economies and those that have been spreading in industrialised economies and in industrial enclaves of other countries.

(i) Industrialising Economies

It is often assumed that the labour process in low-income economies is inherently flexible, due to the undeveloped character and ineffectual application of statutory regulations, and the absence of voice regulation and employment protection. The reality is more complex. Not only are many features of pre-industrial societies 'rigidities' by any sense of the term – caste barriers, feudal and 'patronage' relations of production, religious dictates, and so on – but some regulations have been designed to create forms of *subordinated flexibility*, as in the numerous Export Processing Zones dotted around the world.

Perhaps the main feature of a flexible labour process is the growth in the number of workers in dual or multiple labour statuses, at any one time or in some alternating sequence. Instead of landlords confronting peasants, or firms hiring full-time wage workers, or plantations having a bonded or paternalistically-dependent permanent workforce, more workers become part-peasant, part-wage labourer, or part-time 'own account' producer and part-time estate worker or miner, or whatever. The main reason, as ethnographic and economic analyses have testified, is that labour costs are reduced because a paltry wage is subsidised by other work. This duality is an important aspect of wage flexibility and globalisation.

A difficulty in appreciating the significance of these flexible forms of labour relationship is that the statistics needed to analyse such phenomena are not available, partly because the concepts used for census and labour force surveys have been designed for single, 'rigid' labour status categories. The following seem to be the main flexible labour statuses in industrialising economies:

(a) Migratory labourers. These are the classic floating labour reserve, often taking a regular route, either moving seasonally to do harvest labour in one place, construction labour in another, petty services in another, and so on. 'Tramping' as a way of social existence is perhaps the ultimate form of labour flexibility.

(b) Labour circulants. These differ from migratory labourers in that they have a fixed point of residence, are likely to do different types of work when away than when at 'home', and may have more income security since they or their immediate family may combine small-scale peasant-type farming with seasonal or longer-term wage labour. Circulants have been widely used as cheap labour, because they are paid on the supposition that they are subsidised by their own domestic production or by work of their kin. However, although use of circulants has allowed employers to cut wages and avoid overhead and other labour costs, circulation has been an unstable form of flexibility, because the process erodes the productive capacity of the 'informal' supplementary activity in their base area.

(c) Labour contract workers. Although these overlap with the preceding categories, their distinctive characteristic is that they are dependent on 'middlemen' or 'agents', who hire out workers to employers, often in labour gangs. Commonly, there has been a debt bondage relation between sub-contractors and workers, which leads to exploitative labour and subordinated flexibility, with workers deployed when and where needed and for wages that fluctuate daily or even hourly. For the

ultimate employers, the advantages are that indirect labour costs are minimal, because payment to middlemen covers *co-ordination costs*, usually at the expense of the workers' wages. Classic examples of such flexible arrangements are the *boias frias* in Brazil and the *enganche* system in Peru. There have been many others throughout history (Egger and Poschen, 1997).

(d) Outworkers. These have featured in early phases of industrialisation, and consist of those on standby for daily wage labour or piece work. They cover *contract* and *casual labour*. For employers, such labour potentially has advantages and disadvantages. Mostly, indirect labour costs are avoided, flexibility is assured by the fact that labour is paid for only when needed, the payment system can be flexible, and low rates of pay are usual for such isolated and unprotected workers. Mostly, the workers are easily 'disowned' and lack the collective voice to resist onerous working conditions. Thus, outworkers represent a flexible and risk-reducing form of labour, particularly in times of industrial or economic restructuring. But some costs restrict the use of such workers, including loss of control over quality, quantity and type of production, and loss of economies of scale that could arise if production were concentrated in one place or if the workforce were bound to longer-term employment.

In the early phases of industrialisation, outworking has been a wretched experience for those involved. The insecurity is considerable, and usually the only insurance against impoverishment is complementary labour activities. Outworkers also face high 'technological risk', since they typically have to develop skills, without employers having to incur training costs, and have to possess petty equipment, which can easily be made obsolete.

(e) Sub-contractors. Often, these are really indirect workers, concealed as such to avoid coverage by regulations or social security contributions, or to make an undertaking look smaller so as to fall beneath some regulatory threshold.[4] Sub-contracting takes many forms, some involving workers in relatively autonomous units, others merely surviving by combining labour statuses.

(f) Employed labour reserves. To compensate for uncertain or fluctuating demand, absenteeism, sickness among workers or labour turnover, many firms in industrialising economies have operated with a labour reserve, retained on or around the premises but only paid when required to fill in for other workers. Perhaps paid a small retainer, they usually have to be available at almost any time. They exist as a visible threat to those in jobs, and usually exist because of labour surplus conditions. The extent of the use of such labour is unknown, although there is ample historical and anecdotal evidence of the substantial role they can play. A famous case is the *badli* system in Bombay, where they may have accounted for about 20 per cent of the 'employed' workforce in the textile industry.

Although there have been other flexible labour forms in industrialising countries, these six forms cover the main sources of employment flexibility. Usually it has been easy for firms to resort to such labour, and this is why one should be wary about claims about the impact of protective regulations, since in most cases these would apply only to regular wage labour, if at all.

(ii) Emerging Forms of Employment Flexibility

The distinction between forms of employment flexibility found in industrialising economies and those found in industrialised contexts is arbitrary, since most are found under different guises in all types of economy. A key point is that those in full-time regular wage employment are in a shrinking minority, and most of the following are spreading, although the order in which they are presented does not signify that the numbers are greatest in those mentioned first.

(a) Casual and temporary workers

It was long presumed that casual labour was a feature of early industrialisation and rural economies. Since the 1970s, there has been a resurgence in industrialised economies. A distinction is useful between *temporaries*, who have a contract, usually for a fixed term or on a rolling basis, and *casual labour*, those hired without employment security, typically paid on a piece-rate basis or for the specific hours for which they are hired. But the notion of temporaries has been blurred by the creation of *permanent temporaries*, workers expected to stay with a firm for many years but who lack the benefits and entitlements of regular or 'permanent' employees.

For firms, the advantages of casual and temporary labour usually include lower wages, lower and fewer benefits, lack of entitlements and rights in the firm and, most fundamentally, lack of employment security, making them easily removed without cost. There may also be a *behavioural advantage*, in that temporaries might be motivated by a desire to shift to a regular contract and so provide a higher effort bargain.

For firms, the disadvantages have been that use of temporary labour may be divisive and be resented by regular workers and unions, which successfully fought for decasualisation in the early part of the twentieth century. Temporaries also do not justify firm-specific training. And presuming that individual productivity rises with familiarity on the job, and that there are costs of recruitment as well as retrenchment, additional costs of using temporaries may be considerable. The *behavioural disadvantage* of casual labour is that the workers will lack a reason for loyalty to the firm, leading to lower effort, lower output and neglect of materials and equipment.

The costs of temporary labour may be declining and the benefits increasing, due to more market and technological uncertainty. Where competitive pressures are growing, firms see casual labour as a means of reducing costs at short notice. Higher unemployment expands the pool of available labour, reducing turnover costs. For more jobs, the main competencies required may be general rather than firm-specific, making it less costly to replace workers. And if statutory and voice regulations are deemed 'strict' (using the OECD's loaded term) or potentially costly, firms may use more casual labour.

It is usually presumed that casual or temporary labour has no advantages for workers. However, if income is secure, or if the job is combined with another activity, the temporary character of the employment may be welcome, and may give the person a sense of 'freedom'. Lack of pressure to show loyalty to a firm may be liberating and may even prevent the individual becoming dependent on the labouring relationship. The significance of this would depend on the person's competence and support network.

Growth of temporary and casual employment in western Europe and North America has been remarkable. In the USA, the number of workers recognised as temporary almost trebled between 1980 and 1988 to over a million (Belous, 1989; Samuelson, 1989; Bureau of National Affairs, 1986). In Canada, employment contracts of under six months rose by nearly 2 per cent a year between 1978 and 1988 (Economic Council of Canada, 1990). 'De-industrialisation' has contributed to this. Many workers made redundant in manufacturing have ended up in temporary jobs elsewhere. In France, a well-documented instance was the industrial district of Lorraine, hit by the decline in the iron and steel industry, where the number of temporary 'interim companies' increased by over 50 per cent between 1984 and 1988 and where fixed-term contracts increased from 58 per cent of all jobs in 1983 to 70 per cent in 1989 (Villeval, 1990, p. 5).

Casualisation has also been stimulated by regulatory reforms. In some places, it has been facilitated by the legal system. It has been claimed, for instance, that it grew faster in the UK than in continental Europe because in the former common law allowed a slide into casualisation, whereas elsewhere legislative changes were required (Hakim, 1990). Nevertheless, in the UK in the 1980s and 1990s legislation accelerated the process, most notably in the docks. However, temporary employment *appears* limited in the UK. In 1995, only 7 per cent (1.5 million) of the employed were classified in temporary jobs; about 40 per cent of temporaries said they had a temporary contract because they could not find a permanent one. But the difference in employment security between those in nominally permanent posts and those in temporary jobs is less than in some countries, since employment protection for newly hired workers has been cut.

Legislative changes in France, Germany, Spain and elsewhere have encouraged the trend to greater use of temporary labour. A justification was that this would promote employment and lower unemployment, because it would make it less costly for employers to hire and fire workers. This view persisted even though there was no evidence that more employment flexibility had that effect (Nerb, 1986). For example, in Germany legislated erosion of employment protection and the consequent growth of fixed-term contracts had no effect on the *level* of employment (Buechtemann, 1989).

Some contend that the growth of temporary employment actually reflects *inflexible* labour markets, because protective regulations force firms to turn to temporary workers. However, the extent of *temporary* or *casual employment* is usually regarded as an indicator of employment flexibility, since it implies that firms can change employment quickly and relatively cheaply, usually because they do not have to pay compensation for terminating contracts. In any case, temporary employment has grown in many guises in most countries.

This has applied to eastern Europe, as brought out in our enterprise labour flexibility surveys in such countries as Albania, Bulgaria, Russia and Ukraine, and it has been *increasing* in industrial and other firms in developing countries, as shown by our comparable surveys in such countries as Chile, India, Malaysia, the Philippines and South Africa (e.g., Deshpande et al., 1998, ch. 3). In short, contrary to the model of labour markets long expected to become the global norm, the current era has seen a regrowth of casualisation.

(b) Consultants.   This is a relatively small but significant form of flexible employment. They include self-employed individuals with a niche skill, including management consulting, and in general deserve to be identified as a distinct group because they are not like most other forms of 'self-employment'. They typically have individualised contracts tailored to the needs of the firm and their capacities. They are typically operating outside the mainstream regulatory system, so their employment is not impeded by it. On the contrary, if statutory or voice regulations were onerous, firms would turn over more activities to a broadening range of 'consultants'.

For firms, their main advantage is that specialisation is such that there would be a high fixed cost if they were employed on a continuous basis when demand for their services would only justify occasional input. Rank Xerox was an early leader in this practice, for this reason (Child, 1984). Firms save on the high costs of salaries paid for non-productive time arising from full-time employment of such specialists.

(c) Sub-contractors.   Large corporations have 'out-sourced' more activities to small-scale, semi-independent businesses. These may be family firms or even individuals, who do not work for the enterprises directly for a wage but who are in a *dependent* relation to one or several large enterprises, typically paid on a piece-rate or job-work basis. Statistical and anecdotal evidence suggest that this type of employment relationship has been growing quite rapidly, in private and public sectors. By the late 1990s, it accounted for a substantial part of the labour force – and conventional statutory regulations scarcely apply to them. Since much of the shift to sub-contracting has involved out-sourcing of service functions from manufacturing and other industrial sectors, it has inflated the statistical growth

of service employment and encouraged the growth of small firms providing specialist services.

(d) Agency workers.   These may become the major form of employment for a wide array of jobs. Increasingly, firms are *contracting out the employment function* by turning to private employment agencies. In the 1980s, several governments eased legislation restricting such employment, including France and Germany. In West Germany, temporary work agencies trebled between 1982 and 1987, while the share of employment mediated through agencies rose sharply, as it did in France, the UK and elsewhere (*European Industrial Relations Review*, 1989). The same trend occurred in North America. In Canada, the number employed by temporary work agencies tripled in the 1980s (Economic Council of Canada, 1990). Most were women. The main reason workers went to agencies was that they could not find regular full-time jobs; a 1988 survey found that this applied to 41 per cent of all those doing such work.

The growth of temporary labour agencies has been quietly transforming the labour markets of industrialised economies. Already by the late 1980s there was an International Confederation of Temporary Work Firms, and the decision of the European Court of Justice in March 1990 to allow Spanish and Portuguese firms to transfer their temporaries to other parts of Europe opened the door to a new form of employment flexibility. In western Europe, the rate of increase of agency labour has been impressive. Thus, 3.5 per cent of all workers in the Netherlands in 1996 were hired through temping agencies, and the temping market grew by 24 per cent in that year alone.[5] Outside Europe expansion has been equally if not more impressive. By the late 1990s, Manpower Inc. was the largest private employer in the USA, with 2,400 offices around the world. Its Chief Executive, Mitchell Fromstein, was on the White House panel on welfare reform, and Manpower had moved into the business of placement of welfare recipients. Its European business expanded by about a quarter in 1997 alone, helped by legalisation of temporary employment agencies in Italy, the removal of some restrictions on temporary work in Germany and growth of temporary employment in Spain since the market was opened to temporary agencies in 1995.

Agency workers cover the full range of skills in terms of technical competencies. Indeed, in the USA Manpower's technical and professional placements grew by 40 per cent in 1996, making that the fastest growing part of its placements (*International Herald Tribune*, 31 January 1997). The country's largest agency specialising in scientists reported that its placement growth has been about 25 per cent a year for some years. By 1996, one in every six temporary workers in the USA were professional and technical workers. The image of 'temps' needs to be revised.

For firms, the main advantages of out-sourcing are that it reduces supervisory and co-ordination costs and allows lower wages and benefits. In the USA, for instance, temporary scientists are paid a flat weekly fee, enabling firms to avoid disability insurance, fringe benefits and other overhead costs, while the worker is paid about 60 per cent of the fee by the agency, usually plus some benefits. A Canadian survey found that workers hired through temporary agencies earned less than others and had minimal fringe benefits (Economic Council of Canada, 1990). In the case of technicians, agencies have also been acting like an apprenticeship mechanism, giving technically qualified workers opportunity to gain work experience before they are assimilated into regular employment.

For firms, the potential disadvantages are similar to those for temporary workers. In addition, since many hired out by temporary labour agencies are on longer-term retainer contracts with the agencies themselves not only is there a 'disciplinary' intermediary inclined to enforce a higher effort bargain but the tendency of a temporary worker to leave the job may be reduced, while leaving the agency with the responsibility of providing replacement labour.

(e) Homeworkers. These operate from their home as dependent workers. Although they have always existed, conventional statistics rarely identify them. They are often mixed up with 'self-employed' or 'own account' workers, suggesting an independence that they do not possess. Such workers are highly exploitable, are paid low wages, have no union protection or coverage by protective regulations, and are easily pushed into economic inactivity. Common in industrialising economies, they have been expanding elsewhere. In 1995, in the 15 EU member countries over 12 per cent of the employed usually or sometimes worked from home, with over 21 per cent in Ireland and 27 per cent in the UK (Eurostat, 1996, Table 63). In four countries one in ten labour force participants *usually* worked from home.

The advantage for firms is that there are few overhead costs. The traditional disadvantage of lack of control over quality and duration and intensity of labour has been increasingly overcome by information technology, by which work can be monitored more easily and cheaply, and controlled from a central office without the need for managerial intermediaries.

(f) Teleworkers. These are another rapidly growing flexible employment relationship. They work primarily through the use of computers and other advanced information technology. Although many work from their home, and therefore could be said to belong to the category of homeworkers, it is useful to keep them as a distinct category because they have greater control over their skills, means of production and labour. They overlap with consultants, some of whom are 'white-collar homeworkers'. Teleworkers often network, and there has been a growing practice of teleworkers going to work in groups in their local vicinity and communicating with the firm's premises elsewhere. So, although the isolation of individuals is often considerable, countervailing trends may operate in some places.

Huws (1994) has differentiated between five types of teleworking:

(1) home-based teleworking, which covers (a) part-home based, part-employer premises, (b) full-time home-based teleworking for a single employer, and (c) freelance home-based teleworking;

(2) mobile teleworking;
(3) intra-firm teleworking;
(4) inter-firm teleworking, or out-sourced back-office functions, whether carried
     out in telecottages or telecentres or through commercial sub-contractors;
(5) distributed team working.

Teleworking involves using telecoms and computer technology while working wholly or mainly outside an office or factory. It has been spreading rapidly, although estimates vary widely and statistics on the labour status are undeveloped. In the mid-1980s, studies in the USA gave estimates of business-related homeworking, many working part time, which ranged from 15 to 23 million people (Pratt and Davies, 1985). In 1994, a study estimated that there were seven million people working as *mobile teleworkers* in the USA, and forecast that this group would grow to an extraordinary 25 million by the year 2000 (Illingsworth, 1994). For the UK, a study based on the 1991 Population Census estimated that 1.2 million people worked mainly at home, of whom 264,000 were employers and managers, 68,000 professionals, 133,000 intermediate non-manual workers, and 102,000 junior non-manual workers, suggesting that nearly half were 'white-collar' teleworkers (Felstead and Jewson, 1995). Another study estimated that the growth had been substantial over the previous decade, although it warned about the precise meaning of the available data (Gillespie, Richardson and Cornford, 1995). A comparative survey of firms in five European countries in 1993 found that 7.4 per cent of British firms were using teleworkers, 7 per cent of French firms, 4.8 per cent of German firms, 3.6 per cent of Spanish and 2.2 per cent of Italian firms (TELDET, 1994). Subsequent surveys in the UK found that many more firms were turning to the use of homeworkers, and teleworkers in particular (Huws, 1996, p. 22).

Teleworking has grown because of the falling cost of telecommunications, lower installation charges for network facilities, faster modems that are reducing operating costs, falling computer and software costs, the spread of the internet and intranets (corporate internets), the perceived need to improve office productivity, the growth of global organisations and the rise of the 'virtual company' (Pagoda Associates, 1997). It has been predicted that by early in the next century many corporations will use their offices primarily to provide corporate identity and social interaction, and that after a period of working individually teleworkers will be brought together in *telecottages*, which have been spreading. The notion of telecottage is one of a host of new key words of labour.

For firms, the advantages of teleworking include higher productivity, because interruptions take the time of the worker rather than the time of the firm's office. The increases in productivity have been considerable (Huws, 1996, p. 60). There is also considerable saving in travel time and cost, and offices within a firm can be shared by workers who only come into them irregularly. Apparently, some larger firms have saved considerably. For instance, UNISYS, a US computer company, introduced a Virtual Private Network by which 800 of its UK workers could work from home, enabling the firm to cut its offices by 70 per cent and convert office blocks into Business Centres where workers could go occasionally.[6] A further saving comes from lower wage rates, often because teleworkers work outside big cities, where wages are higher. Costs are also lower because less supervisory or management labour is required. In the UK, a survey of telework managers found that three out of ten reported that teleworking had enabled them to reduce costs, nearly half of them said it had increased the firm's flexibility, and about a quarter said it had increased productivity, solved travel problems and resulted in savings in office space (Huws, 1993, p. 48). Against these advantages, although there was no evidence of lack of loyalty or reliability, over a third reported management problems and difficulties arising from the workers' social isolation.

The main constraint to an even more rapid growth of telework is the employers' difficulty in maintaining control. As one long-term observer, Jack Nilles, put it, without giving evidence:

> The primary concern of almost every executive is the fear of loss of control over the teleworkers. But given proper training, particularly of the managers, together with some selection of the teleworkers, this fear is unfounded. (*Financial Times*, 8 January 1997)

The control mechanisms used in teleworking are diffuse, with the tendency being project-to-project relations rather than a single contract. In some cases, there are additional costs for the firm, if it has to equip the workers, provide training or provide administrative and maintenance support. However, control over the means of production may be released to the workers, giving them responsibility for maintenance, repairs and replacements. The firm thereby passes on the risk and reduces costs.

(g)   *Part-time workers.* Although part-timers are more often recognised in labour statistics than any of the preceding categories, the usual definitions are arbitrary. The standard practice is to define as a part-timer anybody who *usually* works less than 30 hours a week in paid employment. Someone who has a job for 5 hours a week is as much a part-timer as someone who has one for 28 hours, while someone who has one for 32 hours is a full-timer. The difference between the first two is much greater than the difference between the latter two. In some countries, the threshold for defining full-time employment is 35 hours a week, and with shrinking standard workweeks this could soon lead to the majority being classified as part time.

In flexible labour markets, the distinction between part time and full time is dubious. But focusing on working time variation is important in part because part-time employment builds flexibility into the labour market, increasing the ability of firms to adjust labour input to short-term variations in demand.

Part-time workers cover several types of situation. Besides the distinction between those in part-time jobs 'voluntarily' and those in them 'involuntarily', it is useful to distinguish between three types of part-time working:

(1) *short-time workers*, that is, those required to work on a part-time basis because of fluctuating production, perhaps expected to bear the brunt of cutbacks in production due to plant breakdown, repairs, shortage of raw materials, and so on;

(2) *shift workers,* those working relatively short workweeks because of shift systems and/or because the firm recognises that the high intensity or character of the job reduces productivity after a short period.

(3) *split-job workers*, those sharing a job, typically by consent, on an equal-work, equal-income basis, a practice that in some countries has been encouraged by government subsidies to cover additional indirect costs that such jobsplitting involves.

In industrialised economies, part-time employment has spread considerably since the 1970s. The potential advantages to firms are that the wage and many indirect labour costs are often lower and that longer-term employment planning can be made without the cost of either having too many full-time employed on the books or having to pay dismissal or recruitment costs incurred by altering the level of full-time employment. Another factor is that in many countries, statutory protective regulations have not applied to part-time workers or have not applied to the same extent as for full-time employees. With part-time workers it is easier for firms to obtain additional labour, often by paying undeclared wages or bonuses that can be lower because they are not subject to tax or social security contributions.

(h) Concealed workers.   These comprise a rapidly growing form of flexible labour. These are employed informally in the 'grey' or 'black' economy, often illegally. Reasons include tax evasion and avoidance, and a desire to avoid bureaucratic paperwork. In industrialised economies, estimates of the number vary from about 2 per cent of the working population to over 15 per cent. For obvious reasons, nobody knows. Policymakers are ambivalent about labour of this sort. Those wanting erosion of protective regulations, less state intervention, lower taxes and so on have regarded such opportunistic initiatives as evidence that market activity is being stifled. Even though they also advocate law abidance, their ambivalence has helped legitimise such practices, encouraging the growth. Opportunism is a form of flexibility.

For firms, the disadvantage represented by the possible cost of being apprehended is weighed against the cost advantage of avoiding insurance or pension contributions, being able to avoid costs of dismissal, and so on. Where the tax wedge is a high proportion of compensation, the incentive for the firm and worker to collude becomes substantial. Thus, if the wage is $100, the tax and contribution $50, it would pay the firm to 'split the difference'. Would the worker be inclined to report such a practice, equally opportunistically?

Among reasons for worker connivance are that he would be breaking the law as well, so that once a bargain had been struck the employer would have assurance that the worker would regard it in his interest to keep quiet. For the worker, accepting an illegal payment would be attractive if (i) there were few alternative income-earning opportunities, (ii) the tax wedge to be shared was large, (iii) the tax burden was mainly on 'labour', (iv) prospective state benefits derived from the contributions were small or uncertain, (v) the type of work was off the firm's premises, and (vi) many others were believed to be indulging in the practice. All of these conditions have grown in the current era. The growth of flexible employment, including teleworking, has helped. One study concluded that in two counties in the west of England, teleworking was twice as common as reported, mainly due to the black economy (Smith, 1995). So, perversely, making state benefits 'ungenerous' and harder to obtain – as shown later – may drive more employment 'underground'.

The labour statuses identified in this section do not cover all forms of employment flexibility. For instance, there have been reports of a growing practice of lending or leasing workers in surplus to other companies, as in Michigan, where firms have attempted to keep skilled workers while reducing labour costs through lending surplus workers to other firms on a short-term basis.

Changes in the use of the various categories of flexible labour will reflect the changing relative costs and benefits of each category. For firms, regular workers would be most valued if the jobs in the firms are progressive in character and if the labour market is tight. To obtain and retain such workers, firms will be prepared to pay some non-wage labour costs. But to the extent that the jobs become more static and the labour market slack, such costs will be regarded as costs or rigidities inhibiting employment. In the latter circumstances, employers will have reasons for substituting flexible forms of labour for quasi-permanent workers.

For firms, the advantages of employment flexibility include the ability to reduce fixed labour costs. Thus, firms are contracting out maintenance work rather than have a pool of skilled workers on standby, encouraged by technological changes such as self-diagnostic machines that warn engineers of likely faults. Technological flexibility has induced labour flexibility. But cost reduction is surely the main advantage of such flexibility. There are also disadvantages for employers. A workforce that knows it is regarded as dispensable may have less loyalty to the company. This may induce an *opportunistic* reaction by workers, reducing their effort bargain, leading to neglect of plant, machinery or raw materials, and to pilfering and sabotage. These reactions might be overcome by changes in the wage system. But the lack of loyalty could be relatively unimportant for the firm.

For workers, the advantages of employment flexibility depend on the income support provided and access to skills and mechanisms for retaining skills. Employment flexibility usually means insecurity. It usually increases the cost and difficulty of making financial commitments, raises the income required to secure a given level of living, since additional saving is needed to cover for the uncertainty, and may threaten the value of pension schemes, which are determined by duration of employment and final salaries, which often rise with duration of employment.

Finally, there is the debate on the impact of *labour regulations* on employment flexibility. The typical firm has a wide range of potential employment strategies. It can respond to a regulation by altering its technology, cut employment, shift the structure of employment, bypass or evade the regulation, hive off part of its production, change its recruitment policy to make the regulation less relevant, or take some other measure. There is no reason to *presume* that a regulation will have any specific effect.

The impact on labour market outcomes is equally unclear a priori. There have been numerous claims that western European labour regulations raise the natural rate of unemployment. A well-known approach is that developed by the OECD in its 'strictness of regulation' index for the 1994 *Jobs Study*. The European Commission also produced a report in 1996, purporting to show an inverse correlation between an index of regulations and employment across 14 of the EU countries, and between termination costs (in terms of salary months) and employment. But this proved so controversial within the Commission that it was cut from the report because of methodological criticisms. As one official stated, 'There is no evidence that low dismissal costs help job creation' (*Financial Times*, 8 November 1996).

Employment protection regulations, such as layoff procedures and severance pay, may reduce gross job generation and destruction (Bertola, 1990; Burgess, 1994). But the net effect on unemployment is unclear, since they reduce the number becoming unemployed but may increase the average duration (Lazear, 1990; Boeri, 1997). They may *reduce* unemployment by inducing firms to be more careful in their screening and recruitment practices, so reducing mismatch labour turnover, and by facilitating job-to-job mobility. So, it cannot be presumed that protective regulations raise unemployment and impede employment flexibility.

4.6 WORK PROCESS (FUNCTIONAL) FLEXIBILITY

The image of 'functional' flexibility is that of work organisation being adaptable to technological innovation and market fluctuations. This covers working time, job mobility and flexibility, and work organisation. In the era of market regulation, managers have sought all sorts of ways of achieving functional flexibility, due to increased emphasis on competitiveness and responsiveness, the information revolution and the shift from mass production. Managements have been under more pressure to utilise capacity optimally and to minimise costs, which has given impetus to measures to alter working time practices.

Functional flexibility has been a means of increasing managerial control. For example, in the British mining industry in the 1980s new flexible working practices restricted mineworkers' traditional forms of work autonomy (Heycock, 1989). The flexibility reflected the increased capacity for technical control through use of electronics. In that and many cases, functional flexibility has come through a concession bargain, in which in return for a wage increase or benefit, unions accept practices that increase labour intensity.

Functional flexibility is linked to external flexibility, and has been facilitated by forms of non-regular labour. Thus, growth of *teamworking* has been linked to *teleworking*, enabling fluid networks to be set up with teleworkers as members of temporary groupings for projects (Huws, 1996). This is limited by the persistence of hierarchical management structures (Maier et al., 1995; Korte et al., 1988). Nevertheless, the *language of work* is being transformed as new forms of technological co-ordination coexist with new forms of employment relationship.

Working time flexibility has been another aspect of functional flexibility pursued in recent years. It has taken many novel forms. Various euphemisms have sprung up; two in Germany are 'chronological denormalisation' and 'chronological discontinuity'. Demands that workers should accept almost complete working time flexibility have been growing in many countries. A method has been to oblige workers to agree to a total number of working hours in a given period, perhaps a month or year. Working time flexibility could involve use of part-time workers, ending of standard hours of work, acceptance of more hours of work, more overtime, shiftwork, agreement to work on weekends (or during periods usually regarded as leisure in the country concerned), flexitime (agreement to work as and when required up to a limit, within terms of a group or individual contract), staggered working times (agreement to work in certain blocks of time), 'working time corridors' (agreement to work within a range of working hours depending on management, as in the German chemical industry), and 'job-sharing'. Another form of flexibility is a negotiated arrangement whereby working time is reduced temporarily so as to secure the jobs of workers under threat of redundancy (the so-called 'Volkswagen time model').[7]

Germany has been a leader in this sphere. Of the various forms of working time flexibility, 'flexitime' has become common in all sectors there, 'shift working' has remained concentrated in manufacturing, and 'staggered working hours' has become most pronounced in services. By the mid-1990s, 24 per cent of all employment contracts in nearly every sector involved flexitime, with the figure rising to nearly 57 per cent in public services (Bellmann et al., 1996, p. 20). More than three-quarters of German firms were using flexible working time practices of some kind.

In the EU, *shiftworking* remains the main way of 'decoupling working time and operating hours' in manufacturing (European Commission, 1995, p. 25). This is a relatively rigid form of working time flexibility, since it allows for little variation (Brewster et al., 1994, p. 182). By contrast, shiftworking has been greater in the economies of East Asia than in industrialised economies. For instance, in the Malaysian Enterprise Labour Flexibility Survey of over 3,000 manufacturing plants, we found many firms operating three-shift days, and some were operating four. In a similar survey in the Philippines we found two or three shifts to be common. By contrast, the norm in Germany and other European economies in the mid-1990s was a one-shift arrangement, with two shifts being the most common if shiftworking was involved; a major reason for low shifts has been the predominance of small firms (Bellmann et al., 1996, p. 28).

Weekend working has become more common, although national patterns vary. For instance, Table 4.2 suggests that in Belgium and Germany a growing proportion of those in the labour force work on Saturdays and Sundays or at nights. The picture is less clear for France, although a substantial minority work outside the regular workweek. Saturday working has become the most common deviation from the 'standard employment relationship' in western Europe, although Sunday working has also been increasing. Both have been encouraged by relaxations of statutory regulations restricting weekend working.

Overtime might be expected to decline if working time flexibility grew, because of the cost of overtime wage rates. Overtime actually lacks flexibility because it tends to be built into normal working time, yielding a predictable income, so that a change in the amount of overtime may induce high *motivation costs*. Overtime may become outmoded, as may such time-honoured notions as 'unsocial hours'. Annual hours systems and flexitime can give firms greater flexibility and lower labour costs, particularly *productivity costs*. In some countries overtime may persist, because there are fewer statutory restrictions than on some other forms of working time flexibility, as in Germany. However, many firms can increase employment flexibility through using part-timers, outworkers and so on, rather than rely on extensive overtime. Overtime can be expected to decline as other forms of flexibility increase.

Differentiating firms' flexibility strategy on the basis of numerical and functional flexibility and internal and external orientation, a German survey found that firms were resorting most to internal numerical flexibility, adjusting overtime, short-time working and shifts, advancing or postponing holidays, and making internal transfers of workers (Bellmann et al., 1996, pp. 38–9). But they were also increasing numerical flexibility, using fixed-term contracts, sub-contracting and temporaries. In the UK, *variable working hours* has been the form of flexibility that has grown most. Between 1984 and 1994, while temporary and part-time employment increased modestly, the percentage of the employed with varying hours increased from 31.3 per cent to 56.3 per cent, with overtime being the most common form by which hours varied (Casey et al., 1997). Internal flexibility had become extensive. There and elsewhere, concepts such as *zero hours contracts* have been introduced, in which the worker is not guaranteed work but is formally employed. One flexible form of labour, which has caused Swiss trade unions concern, is 'on-call work', whereby workers have to be on stand-by to go to a job and are only paid for hours

worked. There are no hard statistics, because it is not legal, but unions believe it
is widespread and growing (Ulmann, 1997, p. 11).

Table 4.2 Usually working on Saturdays and Sundays,
European Community, 1992–96

	Saturdays		Sundays	
	1992	1996	1992	1996
Austria	n.a.	25.1	n.a.	14.3
Belgium	16.8	18.5	8.6	9.6
W.Germany	21.1	n.a.	10	n.a.
E.Germany	17.3	n.a.	9.8	n.a.
Denmark	26.1	25.9	19.4	19
Spain	39.5	38.2	14.1	15.6
Finland	n.a.	29.1	n.a.	20.4
France	26.2	24.2	8.8	8.3
Greece	41.8	43.4	13.8	14.1
Ireland	32	n.a.	18.4	n.a.
Italy	39.4	41.2	7.8	8
Luxembourg	18.2	20	8.5	7.9
Netherlands	26.5	27.3	14	14.7
Portugal	28.1	32.6	12.3	13.7
Sweden	n.a.	18.6	n.a.	16.2
UK	24.2	24.3	11.5	12.5

Working time flexibility is linked to wage flexibility, and has been accentuated
through *concession bargaining*. Among the changes affecting wage flexibility is
the emergence of *working time accounts*, in which workers receive additional income
or time off later based on building up individual 'credits'. This practice has
coincided with a lengthening of reference periods for calculating wages.
Individualisation of working time arrangements has also been associated with
individualisation of wage determination.

So, working time flexibility has become greater, bringing advantages for firms.
It could bring advantages for workers, but not if it implies more insecurity of one
type or another, the issue considered in later chapters.

4.7 JOB STRUCTURE FLEXIBILITY

The evolution of job structures is part of labour market flexibility. The following
presents a stylised interpretation of the evolution of job structures, to indicate
tendencies that have implications for labour market and social policy.

Consider the traditional *craft* form of manufacturing, regarded as typical of pre-
industrial societies and small-scale crafts surviving in industrialised economies,
which could apply to a small-scale manufacturer, an independent farmer, restaurateur

or profession. The main job could be described as *progressive* and *broad*, in that a person entering the firm could expect to improve skills, status and income, learning a broader range of skills. Typically, an apprentice would enter the bottom rung and learn a wide range of tasks as he progressess, learning the *mysteries of the craft* as he did so. Usually, what Kerr (1954) called the *port of entry* would be at the lowest level, although auxiliary 'unskilled' workers might be appended to craftworkers.

Figure 4.5 depicts the *craft job structure*. Typically, work tasks are learned on the job, the main port of entry is at the bottom, and the job is progressive, in that skill is a function of experience in the job and firm, and is broad. Probability of advancement is high once the apprenticeship has been served successfully. This is indicated by dotted lines to suggest separate job grades or statuses. The number of grades is small, so that control mechanisms are direct and personal. The key form of flexibility is *work task flexibility*, since those who become craftsmen are usually capable of performing the various aspects of the production. Wage flexibility may be high, since piece-rate wages are often linked to the firm's performance.

In most respects, the craft job structure involves low indirect labour costs, which has given it an historical flexibility. Because of the small-scale nature of production and integrated character of jobs, *co-ordination costs* are usually low, while *motivation* and *productivity costs* are minimal because of the progressive nature of jobs and the ladder of job (and occupational) mobility, while *adaptability costs* are low because of the stable (or slowly changing) technological basis of small-scale production. *Training costs* may become a source of strain because of the progressive nature of jobs, requiring training and long-term retention of craftsmen. That may induce high *overhead costs*, incurred to discourage turnover by workers with firm-specific knowledge and experience, and to raise the potential costs to other firms tempted to poach trained workers.

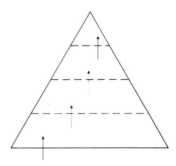

Figure 4.5 Craft job structure (closed system)

Note: Although the pyramid is drawn only schematically, the width of each rung is drawn to suggest the relative number in each job grade.

For craft-based firms, statutory regulations and a social security system would imply high *fiscal* and *overhead costs*, because the unit cost of provision would be high, with bureaucatic procedures and so on, and because labour productivity tends to be lower in such firms. If they rise, the most likely reaction is to 'informalise' the firm out of official existence, disappearing into concealed employment.

Although the craft model has persisted, historically it evolved into what may be called the *Taylorist job structure*, after its pioneering propagandist. This became the dominant model during the first two-thirds of the twentieth century, and was admired and copied by Lenin in the establishment of the state socialist model of labour control.

The growth of the factory system with its economies of scale, and the adoption of 'Fordism' and Tayloristic control techniques involving highly developed technical divisions of labour, transformed job structures and made them internally less flexible. This is illustrated schematically in Figure 4.6, with the suggestion being that there was a tendency to move from systems such as illustrated on the left to the rigid phase on the right. The triangular shape is for convenience only; the largest number of workers might be 'higher up', and there might be large categories of jobs interspersed by smaller strata. Dotted lines indicate a high probability of upward mobility by those in the lower category, hard horizontal lines indicate low probability of moving from the lower to a higher job category.

In the more flexible phase of the Taylorist job structure, there are ports of entry for the main job strata and a possibility for internal mobility, within broad bands of related jobs. In the more rigid phase, close to the model envisaged by Taylor himself, there may be more ports of entry but greater job segmentation and stratification, with more jobs being *static* – in that skill acquisition is restricted (deliberately) and on-the-job advancement limited – and *narrow*, in that the degree of specialisation is greater than in craft jobs or in the flexible phase.

The critical distinction is the separation of *conception* and *execution* in the classification of jobs, making knowledge of the whole production process virtually

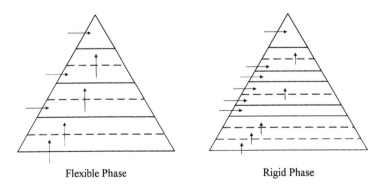

Flexible Phase   Rigid Phase

Figure 4.6 Open, integrated job structure (Taylorist system)

impossible (Braverman, 1974, p. 114). Also, because on-the-job skill acquisition is limited, in the rigid phase *labour turnover costs* tend to be lower, making resort by the firm to the external labour market greater than in the flexible phase. This has implications for the type of worker desired by the firm and for the type of payment system. For instance, it may mean that older workers would be recruited for non-manual jobs, whereas for many manual jobs young workers would be hired, because their high turnover would not matter much to the firm. But given the need for co-ordination, the highly developed technical division of labour would require substantial *supervisory* strata, such as foremen, supervisors and middle management. Their existence is part of the costs of a rigid job structure. The number of intermediary control personnel grew remorselessly when Taylorism and Fordism were at their height, and the number of workers allocated fully to the task of controlling production workers grew sharply as a proportion of all wage and salary earners (Weisskopf et al., 1983).

Because of its rigidity (desired by managers), *co-ordination costs* tend to be high, epitomised by the proliferation of middle-management jobs and by the need for them to be well paid so that, as controllers, they identify with the company rather than the workforce. *Overhead costs* may also be high, although that depends on the degree of paternalism exercised by management. Overhead costs are borne partly because they can reduce motivation costs that arise from the rigid job structure, consisting as it does of a stratified workforce with few prospects of upward job mobility.

With narrow, static jobs predominating, *training* and *turnover costs* tend to be low. The breakdown of craft jobs into detail labour tends to reduce wages by reducing the workers' bargaining strength, a point not lost on Taylor, who established 'scientific management' at a time of rising worker militancy. *Adaptability costs* are small, since workers are not required to change jobs except across a narrow range. *Productivity costs* are at least predictable, so that they can be controlled. Large-scale firms would also find it hard to avoid *protection* and *fiscal costs*, unless the state was lax or corrupt. Thus, with Taylorist structures firms come to cavil at indirect labour costs.

The Taylorist job model has evolved into two variants. One can be described as the *fragmented job structure*, typically found in large corporations and bureaucracies in the latter part of the twentieth century, in which the technical division of labour has gone to the point where the firm itself is fragmenting into separate units, with little horizontal mobility across units and only modest upward mobility within them. Figure 4.7 presents a stylised version, drawn to show just two fragments. There are numerous job categories, and given the pronounced technical division of labour (job demarcation) opportunities for promotion are often contrived, for motivational reasons. The appearance of mobility is largely unrelated to technical skill acquisition.

This structure tends to be rigid because it is hierarchical, while control operated from the top is hard to sustain without the inefficiency that comes with high *co-*

ordination costs. Administrative control replaces executive control. Work rules are formalised and centralised, leaving little discretion to the layers of intermediary controllers. Centralised control is exercised over job categorisation, promotion procedures, discipline, wage scales, grading and definitions of responsibilities, obligations and entitlements. The existence of job ladders and the workforce stratification mean that the firm can avoid the *appearance* of strong sanctions against workers, the sanctions being depersonalised by enterprise rules and procedures.

With the prevalence of static jobs, bureaucratic principles of grading and 'incentives' produce internal mobility that is not a function of technical ability. Social attributes replace technical skills in promotions, which constitute the essence of bureaucratic control. Scope for *patron–client* behaviour and opportunism is enormous, with lower graded workers showing deference to superiors as the means of advancing. *Inefficiency is embedded in such structures, as are self-reproducing rigidities.* Motivation has to be contrived through the prospect of upward mobility and then maintained through rigid work rules and job demarcations. A combination of static jobs and seniority entitlements mean that when employment in the firm is stagnant or declining, the number in jobs without prospect of advancement increases to the point of impairing productivity. *Co-ordination, productivity* and *motivational costs* mount. As 'careerless jobs' abound in such job structures, employers, unions and workers all have a short-term interest in the multiplication of income-differentiated job titles, to increase the appearance of internal mobility. One example may epitomise the outcome: in the 1970s, Polaroid had over 2,000 job classifications for just over 6,000 hourly-paid workers. Such a structure increases the cost of adaptation and adjustment to process innovations, since workers will resist job belittlement or disappearance of job titles to which status, income and mobility potential were attached.

As the fragmented structure is an extension of the Taylorist model, indirect labour costs are similar, and some may be greater. Wage costs tend to be rigid, because bureaucratic control requires security of employment and job tenure for most of the workforce if it is to be effective. *Co-ordination costs* are sure to be high, and

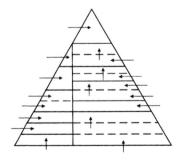

Figure 4.7 Open, fragmented job structure

because of the fragmented character of the organisation – with few units being responsible for their own or the firm's productivity, and with little opportunity for demonstrable efficiency – *motivation* and *productivity costs* may be substantial. *It is an inflexible and inefficient system of job arrangements.*

Given the rigidities and inefficiencies of the bureaucratic enterprise, it is giving way to what may be called a *federal job structure*, as well as to more radical notions, such as what is known as the *virtual organisation* or *virtual firm*. The federal structure is more flexible than preceding job structures, although it too is based on a well-developed technical division of labour and a high ratio of static to progressive jobs. The organisational integration of the firm is loosened, as illustrated schematically in Figure 4.8, so that there is either a core to which a set of satellite units are almost umbilically tied or a core that shrinks to little more than a co-ordinating unit. An archetypal 21st corporation may be ABB, which in 1998 had 1,300 companies and 5,000 profit centres, run by a head office in Zurich of 135 people. It employed 215,000 people, 82,000 in developing countries.

In such a system, most units are flexible, periodically dissolving and being reformed. There is scope for 'intrapreneurship'. In some cases, the core enterprise may cease to be a large-scale employer. It may split off activities, to separate companies or sub-contract. This characteristic phenomenon of the late twentieth century creates new layers of 'employers' and 'self-employed', who come to bear much of the *uncertainty* and *risk* of production, while the core enterprise is able to dispense with many of its middle management and supervisory workers. An instance was Goodyear, a corporation that globally shed a third of its managerial personnel in ten years.

Among the changes is an erosion in status-based distinctions between 'white-collar' and 'blue-collar' workers. Traditionally, the former were expected to identify with management, being responsible for controlling and directing production, and to exhibit *loyalty* to their firms, whereas blue-collar workers had to be induced to provide effort. This dichotomy has been breaking down (Price, 1993). Even so, statutory distinctions between types of worker have persisted, as one review of 19 countries demonstrated (*European Industrial Relations Review*, December 1995). In the late 1990s there were still differential regulations on notice periods, unfair dismissals, termination payments, pay systems, holiday entitlements, working time, sick pay and probationary periods. The job structure and status stratification are accentuated by statutory regulations. In some EU countries, such as Austria, Belgium, Denmark and Greece, laws and regulations have protected white-collar workers, while for manual workers similar issues are left to collective bargaining. This does not mean that job hierarchies have not been flattened or fragmented as the federal job structure has evolved, merely that regulations have hindered the process.

For firms, the federal job structure is suited to periods of unstable economic growth and to the uncertainty of globalisation, acute market competition and rapid technological change. In some respects, the evolving model is a marriage of the

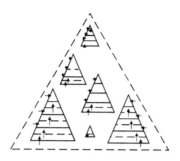

Figure 4.8 Federal job structure

job structure models described earlier, in that the restructuring involves a shift from a bureaucratic structure to one consisting of 'companies within companies', some of which have craft-like job structures, some retaining Taylorist principles.

New product and process innovations made feasible by information technology increase the range of organisational choice and managerial options. The actual shape of the organisation will depend also on the bargaining power of different interest groups, including workers and other *stakeholders*, and the range of indirect labour costs. *The system is inherently flexible and the owners and managers of firms will want to operate in a flexible environment.*

The rapidity of technological change and its international diffusion have reduced the role of mass production, on which Taylorism was based. Smaller batch production has become more economic because of machine and system flexibility, associated with a proliferation of computer-based systems of control, such as CAD (computer-automated design), CAM (computer-automated manufacturing) and CIM (computer-integrated manufacturing). These reduce co-ordination costs, making federal job structures more feasible. Commentators have depicted the demise of large corporate head offices, and reflecting the changes a host of new terms has emerged, such as *distance working, re-engineering, teleworking* and *virtual organisations* – where groups or individuals are scattered, linked by information technology, rather than concentrated in one workplace – and *intrapreneurship*, where units within firms are organisationally and spatially separated, flourishing or declining according to the success of the product or functions for which they are responsible. The division of labour has become more complex, with 'teams' of workers with multiple skills being established, rather than a technical division of labour based on complementary discrete skills (e.g., Gillespie and Li, 1994). There may be three trends in 'craft flexibility'. Either a *core skill* remains, with some familiarity with other skills, or *dual skill* emerges, consisting of proficiency in two sets of tasks, or workers develop *multi-skills*, consisting of familiarity with a wider range of technical competencies (Connock, 1985).

124   *The Sirens of Flexibility*

These developments are facilitated by the enhanced managerial control that can be exercised through the technology, in which the 'network firm' can combine decentralisation of functions with enhanced centralisation of co-ordination (Antonelli, 1988). Meanwhile, bureaucratic enterprises and organisations always resist cost-induced pressures to delegate, decentralise and promote intrapreneurship. In doing so, their capacity to compete with emerging firms and consultancies has been eroded, and the quality of their products and service has declined, as has their dynamic efficiency. In response, some public sector bureaucracies have been reformed to move them in the direction of federal job structures and systems, and in doing so they have promoted, for better or worse, labour market flexibility.

A correlate of federal job structures is business *specialisation*, with more companies evolving into firms concentrating on specific products, markets or services. Whether autonomous or dependent on a parent corporation as sub-contractors, their evolution implies more enterprise flexibility. Reflecting the growing incidence of such firms – rising and falling with fashion, technological change or as new products or processes take over – labour turnover in federal job structures is likely to be high, and thus employment security is likely to fall.

Federal job structures can be expected to have more ports of entry, with mostly static jobs (although many may be broader than in Taylorist job structures), which should raise inter-firm or inter-unit mobility. Although it may be offset by forms of intrapreneurship, internal mobility may be limited by the fragmented character of the organisation and limited opportunity for workers in one satellite to learn the skills in another or to acquire the contacts or status needed to broaden their jobs.

The federal job structure enables a core firm to reduce indirect labour costs. Previously, high *co-ordination costs* would have been an impediment to decentralised systems. But these are reduced by information technology, which lowers co-ordination, overhead, protection and labour turnover costs, allowing use of sub-contractors, outsourcing and other flexible labour arrangements. Training costs may also be minor if more workers can be obtained from the external labour market. Motivation costs should be less than in Taylorist or fragmented structures, if only because membership of a small, self-contained unit is likely to induce what Wright Mills called the *craft ethic*, leading to a higher effort bargain.

Unless the vast management literature and anecdotal evidence is deceiving us, federal job structures have spread globally since the 1970s, bringing with them more enterprise system flexibility and accentuating various forms of labour flexibility. They produce more economic dynamism, but – as should become clear in later chapters – they also bring into question many of the social and labour market policies built up in the post-war era of statutory regulation.

4.8 CONCLUDING REMARKS

In the era of market regulation and globalisation, there has been a trend away from large enterprises and stable workforces characterised by Tayloristic job structures, bureaucratic controls, fixed wage rates and enterprise benefits intended to encourage stable, committed and predictable labour. The trend has been towards flexible production, within firms and through federal structures of large corporations, towards flexible forms of employment and payment systems. Almost as important as the actual trends is that workers, employers, unions and governments *believe* that the trends in those directions are strong.

Flexibility has spread in developing countries, transitional economies (with their own brand of euphemisms, such as 'unpaid leave') and industrialised countries. Symbolic of the global appeal of 'flexibility', President Jiang Zemin opened China's 15th Communist Party Congress in September 1997 by urging workers to be more flexible, coupling his remarks with a description of the planned shift in social protection from enterprise-based cradle-to-grave child care, housing, health insurance and related services to a social security system. He was reflecting the perceived incompatibility of old systems of social protection and labour regulation with the dictates of flexibility. He was also responding to what had become a global trend, the inability to maintain the redistributive strategy of state socialism or welfare state capitalism, a theme taken up in the remainder of this book.

Although some economists believe little has changed in labour markets in the past half century, it is hard to take this view seriously. The consequences of the changes are considered in later chapters. But it is worth citing the opinion of the Executive Vice-President in charge of international operations of *Manpower Incorporated*, the temporary staffing company:

> The perception is that Europe is changing very slowly. But the market is changing faster than the laws are. Things are changing faster on the street than most people realise. It is true in France. It is true in Spain. It is true in Italy.[8]

Manpower employs hundreds of thousands of temporary and part-time workers. In Europe, where it has been expanding, other agencies have also been taking over more of the employment function. The era of market regulation has been an era of labour flexibility. There has been a shift to pro-individualistic regulations and away from pro-collective regulations. There has been *explicit* erosion of protective regulations, due to legislative changes, and *implicit* erosion, due to the shift from regular full-time wage and salaried employment.

Although there is inadequate statistical evidence, ample anecdotal evidence suggests that there is a trend from Taylorist and bureaucratic job structures to federal job structures and enterprise system flexibility. There is also a proliferation in flexible labour statuses and working arrangements not covered by conventional labour force statistics. To some extent – and one predicts that this will become more pervasive – there has been a *contractualisation of employment*, with more individualised contracts specifying functions and obligations. Firms are increasing their control by *contracting out their employment function*, making intermediaries responsible, whether they be labour contractors, sub-contracting firms, private employment agencies or public welfare agencies. Governments have created the space for various forms of flexibility, by controlling unions, eroding protective regulations and introducing legislation and regulations to promote flexibility. And they have extended a form of control suited to the era of market regulation – *auditing* (Power, 1997). Its intrusiveness does not overcome the challenge of trust; just like any other form of control, it induces resistance and opportunism, but it is a form of regulation.

While there is pervasive evidence of extensive flexibility, a powerful international lobby advocates even more flexibility as a means of lowering unemployment, raising economic growth, improving incomes and reducing inequality. But even the OECD (1996) – long a leading advocate of measures to boost flexibility in western Europe – concluded in 1996 that it increased inequality, recognising that flexible labour markets in the USA, UK and New Zealand explained why inequality had risen more in those countries than in continental western Europe. It noted that about a quarter of the employed in the USA were in low-paid jobs compared with 6 per cent in Finland. That did not reflect differences in skill, because fewer workers with secondary schooling in western Europe were in low-paid jobs than in the USA. It reflected a differential propensity to generate low-paying jobs.

Another finding of recent research is that the inverse wage–employment trade-off is weak. Although there were declines in the relative wages of unskilled in the USA in the 1980s and little decline in continental western Europe, the declines in the employment rates of the unskilled were similar (Card et al., 1996). In other words, wage flexibility did not explain the differential employment of the unskilled.

There is an awkward question to be answered by advocates of more labour market flexibility as the route to unemployment reduction. After a decade and a half of numerous measures to make labour markets more flexible, and in the wake of an enormous growth of flexible labour practices, in the late 1990s governments were still being urged to increase flexibility to lower unemployment. For example, the European Union's industrial directorate produced a contentious report in late 1996 urging precisely this route.[9] The IMF's *World Economic Outlook* also recommended that in 1997. Sceptics were entitled to ask why unemployment was higher at the end of a prolonged period of growing flexibility, if flexibility was supposed to lower it.

That issue comprises part of the next chapter. A crucial point is that the labour force has become a more elastic concept, with many people moving in and out of it, and altering the extent of their participation as opportunities and needs arise. This is not just a feature of industrialised economies, since it is characteristic of industrialising countries with large informal economies. Flexibility undermines the validity of the conventional division of the working-age population into employed, unemployed and economically inactive. At the end of the century, labour analysis and policymaking are hampered by the increasingly inappropriate character of official labour statistics.

A new era has arrived. Flexible labour markets are the reality, and policies should respond to that reality. The economic flexibility embraces organisational forms (enterprise, production and distribution chains, etc.), labour relations (decentralisation, contractualisation, etc.) and socio-economic relations (family forms, social networks, etc.). New technological and managerial controls have been transforming relationships between market mechanisms and society. History teaches us that such upheavals make old systems of social protection and economic redistribution ineffectual or even counter-productive, losing legitimacy as part of the system of social governance. History also teaches us that periods of flexibility induce the state to turn to new forms of protective regulation to overcome new or more virulent forms of insecurity that come with any great transformation.

Part III

The Rocks of Insecurity

5 The Crumbling of Labour Market Security

5.1 INTRODUCTION

Labour market security arises from the availability of employment opportunities for everybody wanting employment. One might define it practically as (i) a high level of *opportunities* for 'freely chosen', productive, adequately paid employment, (ii) low unemployment, (iii) a short average duration of unemployment, and (iv) a low probability of being unemployed at all stages of working-age life cycles. Since the 1970s, in much of the world there has been a deterioration in all these indicators, although the deterioration has taken different forms in different countries.

The post-war era was one based on the extension of labour market security through so-called Full Employment. This was the cornerstone of both development models, and was a defining characteristic of the post-war era. Both postulated the *objective* and *attainability* of Full Employment. It was a euphemism of the era.

In state socialism, Full Employment was attained by obliging almost every adult to labour, albeit for low wages, mostly in low-productivity jobs, scarcely freely chosen. In welfare state capitalism, Full Employment was underpinned by the optimistic belief that stimulating aggregate demand could ensure a high level of employment consistent with minimal 'involuntary' unemployment. Keynes' *General Theory*, published in 1936, had a profound impact on several generations of economists, politicians and civil servants. The full force of its message that Full Employment could be attained coincided with the euphoria associated with the end of the Second World War and the establishment of the United Nations.

Epitomising this, numerous pronouncements were made on the guarantee of Full Employment. Franklyn Roosevelt promised that this would be the case in the USA in the post-war period, and his Secretary of Labour came before the ILO's Philadelphia Conference in 1944 to pronounce a similar message. The British established the welfare state explicitly based on the notion of Full Employment; Sweden constructed the Swedish Model in which counter-cyclical labour market policy ('active') was expected to maintain Full Employment.

Keynes defined Full Employment as the level of employment at which there was no involuntary unemployment, begging the question of how to define voluntary and involuntary unemployment. Beveridge (1944, p. 18) defined Full Employment as the situation in which there were 'more vacant jobs than unemployed men' and where there were 'jobs at fair wages of such a kind, and so located that the unemployed men could reasonably be expected to take them'. Beveridge believed that, due to job-changing associated with 'frictional' unemployment, Full

Employment meant an unemployment rate of 3 per cent, and that 'this margin would consist of a shifting body of short-term unemployed who could be maintained without hardship by unemployment insurance' (p. 128).

Beveridge's image was sexist, and only if one accepts the validity of the image could one conclude that countries succeeded in the post-war period in attaining Full Employment. Thus, in a defence of Full Employment, Eddy Lee commented, 'This commitment to full employment was successfully translated into reality in the immediate post-war decades' (Lee, 1997, p. 35). However, with the exception of very small countries and periods of war, no industrialised economy has had very low unemployment coupled with high levels of employment of both men *and* women. One might cite Sweden, but the relative success there was achieved only by placing many unemployed in special schemes. In short, *when advocates call for a 'return' to Full Employment they are calling for a return to something that has never existed.*

Nevertheless, Full Employment was a great progressive idea in the century of the labouring man. It would not have been appropriate for an agrarian economy, or in a feudal or slave society, where there has also been rather full employment, except for landlords, slaveowners and the 'idle rich', whose non-employment has never excited enough attention. In the middle of the twentieth century, it was progressive because it offered a redistributive vision in industrial society based on regular, full-time wage labour providing 'family wages'. In such circumstances, raising employment could be expected to reduce poverty, raise national income, strengthen socio-economic integration and be fiscally beneficial. The post-1945 era not only seemed to offer this fortuitous combination of circumstances, but involved an historically unprecedented 'catch-up' period of sustained economic growth.

The notion of Full Employment, for all its conceptual and definitional ambivalence and sexist origins, was progressive by the standards of earlier eras, and was progressive for a brief moment of optimism in economics and politics when permanent Full Employment seemed both feasible and desirable. In over 2,000 years of recorded human history, this view predominated among politicians, economists and other social thinkers for a twinkle of about 30 years.

What transpired was progress. In western industrialised economies, in the 1950s and 1960s Full Employment meant the almost full employment of *men*, with measured unemployment rates of up to 3 per cent (or 4.5 per cent in the USA). The 'Full Employment' was a particular way of obtaining a low level of recorded unemployment. In industrialised economies, for a short period, regular reasonably well-paid, reasonably productive, full-time manufacturing and service employment *were* the predominant economic features, while the female labour force participation rate was quite low, with women characterised as, and usually treated as, 'secondary' workers. Often, women's unemployment was simply not measured or the definition of unemployment was such that when not employed they (and some men) disappeared into a vague category of 'discouraged workers', a subject of voluminous research and puzzlement. Even if one wished to reproduce such circumstances, they will not reappear (and nor should they).

The situation became tenuous in the early 1970s, before the first oil shock, which merely precipitated an upheaval in economic policymaking. Once women began to assert their demand for equal economic status, Full Employment became a mirage. Even the famed Swedish Model only managed to sustain the image by putting more people into so-called active labour market schemes. It was the end of an era.

5.2 MODERN LABOUR MARKET INSECURITY

There are many reasons for the growth of labour market insecurity in the last quarter of the twentieth century. The simplest index of this is the unemployment rate, and although an inadequate index, for reasons discussed shortly, this has attracted an enormous amount of attention. The main hypotheses have been that the changing international division of labour has shifted investment and employment to industrialising economies, that there has been low aggregate demand due to deflationary macro-economic policy, that welfare state capitalism has produced rigid labour markets (lack of labour market flexibility), that there has been inadequate investment in skills (structural unemployment), and that 'insider' power has prevented wages from adjusting to clear the market.

Among a broad cross-section of economists, there is something approaching a consensus that the *causes* of the growth in unemployment include deflationary monetary and fiscal policy and structural factors, and that the determinants of the *growth* in unemployment should be differentiated from the causes of its *persistence*. This has generated a literature on *hysteresis* explanations. Rather than try to summarise the debates (reviewed in ILO, 1997a), it may suffice to highlight a few points reflecting the changed perspective to labour market security.

Besides the changing position of women, the low open unemployment rates of the 1950s and 1960s were based on historically high rates of economic growth in industrialised countries, which were well above their long-term levels. This is important, because when advocates of a return to Full Employment call for higher rates of economic growth it must be recognised that the 1950s and 1960s were special, and that the lower rates of economic growth in the 1970s, 1980s and 1990s are close to the norm for the one hundred years before 1950 (Singh, 1995).

One must recall why Full Employment was lost or abandoned in both post-war models. In state socialism, Full Employment was preserved through low wages, stagnant productivity and authoritarian labour control. It had no future, and was swept aside. In welfare state capitalism, the supply-side economics revolution of the 1970s and 1980s effectively removed government use of macro-economic policy to boost employment, for reasons mentioned in chapter 3.

Since the 1970s most economists and policymakers have been convinced that an economy *needs* to operate with some involuntary unemployment. There is the view that there is a 'natural rate of unemployment', which reflects 'voluntary' behaviour and structural factors and which was originally defined by Milton Friedman as the steady-state value in the absence of economic shocks. A variant of the natural rate thesis is that there is a 'non-accelerating rate of inflation rate of unemployment' (NAIRU), above which inflation would accelerate.[1] The consensus among mainstream economists is that there is some validity in this genre of concepts, even though the notion of a 'natural' rate is not regarded by many economists as valid. There is no need to review the Phillips curve literature here; many others have done so (for a punchy critique, see Eisner, 1995, pp. 169–94). Suffice it to note that recent evidence suggests that there is a short-run non-linear trade-off between unemployment and inflation and that pushing unemployment below the NAIRU generates more inflation than the same amount of unemployment above it lowers inflation (Clark and Laxton, 1997). This has been regarded as a reason for erring on the side of keeping unemployment above the estimated NAIRU.

A version of this reasoning is the 'shirking model' of wage determination. This assumes that workers need to be induced to work by decent wages, but to prevent wages rising there must be *sufficient unemployment to make workers insecure* and to act as a 'worker disciplining device' (Shapiro and Stiglitz, 1984). This reasoning has a long history, and has been behind the fluctuating attitude to security for workers. The idea of keeping unemployment high to make workers sufficiently insecure may appall many people. But the awkward implication is that either we deny the validity of the behavioural reasoning, or accept some level of unemployment required to curtail workers' bargaining power to socially acceptable levels, or demonstrate that the bargaining power would not lead to rising inflation.

If one accepts that there are structural, or 'supply side', determinants of unemployment, one should ask whether it is more desirable to change those structural factors to reduce unemployment *or* to preserve them and adjust social policy to the higher unemployment. *A priori*, it is not clear that the welfare or ethical benefits of lowering the NAIRU, perhaps by cutting unemployment benefits, would be preferable to maintaining the institutional structures and level of social protection. This is an argument for being more eclectic about the desirability of pursuing Full Employment.

5.3 MEASURING LABOUR MARKET INSECURITY

The simplest index of labour market security is the unemployment rate. By this measure, globally there has been a considerable decline in labour market security in the past two decades. But the measure is inadequate, particularly in flexible labour markets, as well as in economies where wage labour is relatively uncommon.

Unemployment is a social construct, hinging on conceptual, statistical and administrative decisions that make the recorded unemployment rate a somewhat arbitrary indicator of labour underutilisation and labour market insecurity. In many countries, anybody working for *one hour* or more for income, profit or family gain is counted as employed, and employment status is given priority over unemployment or inactivity status. These definitions and the prioritising depress the unemployment rate and inflate the labour force participation rate. For example, if you sell tomatoes for three hours in a market on a Saturday morning and spend 30 hours during the week looking for a paid job, you would be counted as employed, not unemployed. In many countries, only those satisfying the four conditions of being without paid work, wanting paid employment, being available for it almost immediately and seeking it in a recent short period by active means are counted as unemployed. Some have become even more restrictive. In the UK, for example, the authorities in the 1980s and early 1990s redefined unemployment so that only those claiming and receiving unemployment benefits counted. The change led to a sharp drop in measured unemployment. In other countries experiencing persistently high unemployment, political decisions have also been taken to change the basis of the figures.

In many countries, some of those who would call themselves unemployed have been placed in 'active' measures or 'special schemes' and classified as either employed or out of the workforce, even though they have evidently wanted employment and have not been in employment. In some cases, supply-side measures have transformed unemployment status into inactivity status, as in the case of early retirement or disability status, or where as a result of a tightening of administrative rules and procedures some are disqualified from unemployment status or induced by benefit rule changes to drop out of the labour force.

With these caveats, globally unemployment has grown enormously since the 1970s. In eastern Europe, it has risen from a fictitious zero to well over 10 per cent, in reality if not in the official statistics. Indeed, the vast area designated as 'eastern Europe and the former Soviet Union' became suddenly a region of mass unemployment. In the wake of market reforms, national output slumped by over 50 per cent in much of the region. Although the extent of unemployment has been ridiculously concealed, it may have become the region of highest unemployment in the world. A *mafiosation* of the labour market has come too.

The picture in developing countries is also complicated. In the world's largest country, China, which has adhered to a state socialism model, the official unemployment rate is about 3 per cent, but millions of workers have been on 'lay-off', and the Government has estimated that including them would raise the rate to 7.5 per cent (*Financial Times*, 8 December 1997). In Africa and Latin America, and increasingly South Asia, unemployment has risen with urbanisation, the spread of wage labour, and adoption of 'structural adjustment programmes'. With the exception of Bolivia, unemployment rose steadily in Latin American countries in the 1990s, even though GDP growth rates improved (Weeks, 1998). Until 1997, only the Pacific Basin countries had kept unemployment low, with a few exceptions, such as the Philippines, which adopted structural adjustment programmes and had lower economic growth. Although the image is that the era of market regulation has coincided with the *global* growth of *unemployment,* the Pacific Basin is the one area where there have been tight labour markets, with low unemployment and widespread concern about 'labour shortage'. Until the crisis of 1997–98, much of the region had experienced extensive restructuring and urbanisation without mass unemployment.

In the USA, the rise in open unemployment has been contained, in part because of the low level and short duration of benefits, and the difficulty of obtaining them. Another industrialised country where unemployment has been kept low is Japan, but there the unemployment rate is a questionable measure of labour market insecurity since recessions have been marked by a withdrawal of women from the labour force and an involuntary adjustment in working hours by the employed. In the recession starting in 1991, which reached its bottom in 1996, average working time dropped from 2,050 hours a year to about 1,900 (Inoue and Suzuki, 1998). The modest rise in unemployment during the prolonged recession of the early 1990s was attributed to the flexible internal labour market within Japanese firms, employment adjustment subsidies and the 'shunto' wage bargaining process. So, although underemployment grew, the worsening of visible labour market insecurity was checked.

In the 1990s, unemployment in western Europe has attracted most attention. From the 1950s until the 1970s, there was a debate among economists on why US unemployment was persistently higher than western European levels. In the 1980s and 1990s, while labour market insecurity has grown in much of the world, the relative lack of institutional and statutory protective regulations allowed the US labour market to create millions of low-wage jobs with only slightly higher unemployment. In western Europe, unemployment multiplied. For more than a decade, the average rate has been in double digits, led by Spain in which a nominally 'socialist' government presided over an unemployment rate of 22 per cent. In 1996, the EU average was about 11 per cent, and was forecast to remain above 10 per cent (European Commission, February 1997).

Not only have definitions of unemployment been made more restrictive, but modest reductions in the level have mostly reflected the impact of special measures or changes in labour supply. For example, the UK's labour force participation rate fell, which according to the Bank of England explained the fall in open unemployment in the mid-1990s, while in many parts of Europe more workers have been maintained in jobs by subsidies, as in the case of short-time working, which has increased in such countries as Austria, Belgium, France, Germany, Italy, Portugal and Spain (Mosley and Kruppe, 1996). In the Netherlands, about 800,000 have been put on disability benefit and a similar number on sick leave. Thus some of the unemployed have been classified elsewhere.

Many analysts have attributed Europe's chronic unemployment to the slow pace of job creation. However, although the rate of employment growth has slowed since the mid-1970s, it had been slow for a long period (Table 5.1). *The slow pace of job creation in western Europe is something that has continued for the past 40 years.* An important change in the 1980s was that the working-age population continued to rise while job creation slowed further. In many countries, the share of the working-age population in employment declined in the 1990s, but the level was not conspicuously better in the USA or Japan than in several European countries (Table 5.2).

Table 5.1 Employment, working-age population and per capita employment, USA and western Europe, 1960–95 *(average annual growth rates)*

	Employment Change		Working-Age Population Growth		Per Capita Employment Change	
	1960–73	1974–95	1960–73	1974–95	1960–73	1974–95
USA	2.0	1.8	1.7	1.1	0.3	0.7
EC-12*	0.3	0.2	0.6	0.6	–0.3	–0.4
Former EFTA	0.5	0.3	0.7	0.5	–0.1	–0.2

	Labour Force Change		Participation Rate			MLFPR*		FLFPR*	
	1960–73	1974–95	1960	1973	1995	1973	1993	1973	1993
USA	1.9	1.8	64.5	66.6	77.5	86.2	84.9	51.1	69.1
EC-12	0.3	0.7	67.5	65.5	65.7	88.8	77.6	44.9	55.5
Former EFTA	0.5	0.6	73.8	72.4	74.0	88.2	82.6	56.1	66.2

Source: ILO and OECD. The EC-12 data exclude the Lander of the former GDR.
Note:*MLFPR and FLFPR, adult male and female labour force participation rates, respectively.

While job creation has long been slow in most industrialised countries, the rate of employment growth in the newly industrialising countries has been impressive (Table 5.3). What has been even more impressive is the prolonged period of very rapid economic growth. Indeed, the elasticities of employment growth have actually been lower than in western Europe. What this suggests is that in the 1990s countries have had to experience very high rates of economic growth for a sustained period in order to generate substantial employment growth. Such sustained economic growth has never been experienced by European countries.

So, the stylised trends are that western and eastern Europe are suffering from chronically high unemployment and slow employment growth, while economic dynamism and employment growth has shifted to South East Asia. The image of *global unemployment* is correct if one takes a purely global perspective. But regional differences reflect the changing international division of labour, suggesting that globalisation is producing geographical divergences and disparities as well as some forms of economic convergence.

Table 5.2 Per cent of working-age population in employment, 1990–95 *(percent of population aged 15–64)*

Country	1990	1995	Annual change	Rank order of change
Austria	65.5	68.7	0.64	1
Belgium	57.1	55.7	−0.28	11
Denmark	77.1	73.4	−0.74	13
Finland	74.1	61.3	−2.56	18
France	60.6	59.5	−0.22	10
Germany*	64.8	65.1	0.06	7
Greece	55.0	54.2	−0.16	9
Ireland	52.4	55.0	0.52	2
Italy	55.7	52.1	−0.72	12
Netherlands	61.7	64.3	0.52	2
Norway	73.9	74.0	0.02	8
Portugal	72.0	65.7	−1.26	16
Spain	49.9	45.9	−0.80	14
Sweden	80.9	71.1	−1.96	17
Switzerland	77.6	79.2	0.32	4
UK	71.8	67.8	−0.80	14
Japan	72.6	74.1	0.30	5
USA	73.0	73.5	0.10	6

Note: *The 1990 figure is for the former western Federal Republic; that for 1995 is for united Germany.
Source: OECD *Employment Outlook*, July 1996 (Paris, OECD, 1996)

The European experience is actually worse than it appears. The conventional notion of unemployment as a measure of labour security is most appropriate in an industrial society where the labour force consists of a simple division of those in full-time employment and those in full-time 'open' unemployment. In such circumstances, the unemployment rate is a reasonable proxy for labour slack. This is surely no longer the case in Europe. Involuntarily working for a few hours a week is a form of labour market insecurity.

Regular full-time employment has ceased to be the overwhelming norm. Conventional employment aggregates treat part-time and full-time jobs as identical. Suppose large numbers are in 'involuntary' part-time employment. If so, one should not treat that as the same as if most part-timers wanted part-time employment. Another change taking place in the European labour market is increased *labour force flexibility*, whereby people move in and out of the labour force, not just between full-time employment and full-time unemployment. Given the growing diversity of employment statuses and the tightening of conditionality for access to benefits, many in part-time employment may leave the labour force if they lose a job, waiting for an economic upturn before returning. Finally, many of the unemployed become 'discouraged job-seekers', dropping out of the 'active' labour force but wanting and remaining available for employment.

Table 5.3 GDP and employment growth, selected countries,1974–95
(average annual growth rates)

	GDP	Employment
USA	2.4	1.8
EC-12	2.2	0.2
Former EFTA	1.9	0.3
Japan	3.3	0.9
Brazil (1976–90)	2.8	3.6
Chile (1975–94)	5.4	3.3
India (1975–89)	4.9	2.0
Pakistan (1975–92)	6.3	2.4
Hong Kong (1979–93)	7.0	2.3
Indonesia (1976–92)	6.3	1.8
Korea, Rep. (1975–93)	8.6	2.7
Malaysia (1980–90)	6.0	3.4
Singapore (1979–93)	7.5	3.6
Thailand (1975–91)	7.9	3.4

Source: ILO.

These issues have long teased labour economists and statisticians. The following proposes an alternative approach. As it is a measure developed to correspond to available data, it is not conceptually ideal, although it does capture some crucial aspects of the increasing diversity and flexibility of labour statuses.

For reasons of data availability and because the debate on labour market insecurity has been concentrated there, the following focuses on western Europe. For EU countries, thanks to the standardised Labour Force Survey overseen by EUROSTAT, we may estimate an *index of labour slack*, which is a proxy measure of labour market insecurity.

We start by distinguishing between those employed full time (E_{FT}) and those employed part time (E_{PT}), with the latter sub-divided into those working part time 'voluntarily' or because of personal constraints (E_{PTV}) and those working part time 'involuntarily', wanting and available for full-time employment (E_{PTI}). Those working part time voluntarily are treated as half in employment and half outside the labour force. Ignored is the possibility that if labour demand picked up some part-timers might develop a preference for full-time employment. Those working part time 'involuntarily' can be treated as half in employment and half in unemployment. It is assumed that part-timers work on average for half as long as full-time workers. So, total part-time employment is:

$$E_{PT} = E_{PTI} + E_{PTV} \qquad (1)$$

Next, to adjust the unemployed in a symmetrical manner, we divide the 'actively unemployed' into those without paid employment seeking full-time employment (U_{FT}) and those seeking only part-time employment (U_{PT}), so that:

$$U = U_{FT} + U_{PT} \qquad (2)$$

Assuming that those seeking part-time jobs are half in the labour force as unemployed and half outside it, we may convert the simple unemployment rate into a figure for a *full-time equivalent open unemployment rate*, as follows:

$$U_{FTE} = \frac{\left(U_{FT} + 0.5U_{PT} + 0.5E_{PTI}\right)}{\left(E_{FT} + E_{PTI} + 0.5E_{PTV} + U_{FT} + 0.5U_{PT}\right)} 100 \qquad (3)$$

Note that U_{FTE} need not be higher than the conventional unemployment rate, if a disproportionately large number of the unemployed are seeking part-time jobs. In fact, the data indicate that the adjusted unemployment rates have been higher than the standard unemployment rates for all countries. The difference is most substantial for Sweden, where part-time employment has long been widespread. For 1995, Sweden had a lower unemployment rate than Germany or Greece, but had a higher adjusted rate than either.

Next, an adjustment should be made to include those who are unemployed but do not satisfy one conventional criterion, that is, they indicate that they want and are available for employment but had not sought employment in the reference week because of discouragement. One should not exclude this group. The ratio of passive to active unemployment is unlikely to be constant, and if that is the case the open unemployment rate will not be a stable proxy for overall unemployment. If there is high unemployment, the ratio of passive to active is likely to rise, and if policies reduce the incentive to register at employment exchanges, because unemployment benefits are cut or because of higher long-term unemployment, then the ratio is also likely to rise.

These *passive unemployed* should also be divided into those wanting full-time jobs (U_{PFT}) and those wanting part-time jobs (U_{PPT}). Unfortunately, the Eurostat data do not identify what length of workweek the passive unemployed want. So, we assume that the proportions of the passive unemployed wanting full-time and part-time jobs are the same as reported by the active unemployed.

Adding the passive unemployed gives us an adjusted full-time equivalent unemployment rate, U_{FTE}:

$$U_{FTE} = \frac{\left(U_{FT} + 0.5U_{PT} + U_{PFT} + 0.5U_{PPT} + 0.5E_{PTI}\right)}{\left(E_{FT} + E_{PTI} + 0.5E_{PTV} + U_{FT} + 0.5U_{PT} + U_{PFT} + 0.5U_{PPT}\right)} 100 \qquad (4)$$

This is significantly higher than the standard unemployment rate for most EU countries, and the country ranking of labour market performance is also affected by the adjustments. In particular, in full-time equivalent terms the Netherlands has had a worse record of labour market insecurity than Germany, Portugal and Greece, whereas on the standard unemployment rate basis the ranking was the other way round.

The next stage is to take account of the fact that at any time a proportion of those in employment are on lay-off or are not working for *economic reasons*. These are called 'employed without work' (NW). Depending on the character of the labour market and the regulations, this category may be small or substantial. Whatever the number, as part of the unused labour force they should be taken into account.

Finally, there are those on 'short time' (ST), that is, working actual hours shorter than their normal or contractual hours for economic reasons beyond their immediate control. To make NW and ST comparable to the preceding aggregates, we convert each into full-time equivalent numbers. For non-working employed, the number is adjusted by multiplying the number of workers in the category by what they report as their average usual hours (H_{UNW}) divided by the usual hours of all the employed (H_{UST}). For the short-time employed, the absolute number is converted into a full-time equivalent number by multiplying the number of workers in that situation by the ratio of the difference between their 'usual' hours (H_{US}) and their 'actual' hours of work (H_{ACT}) in the past week divided by their usual hours (H_{US}). These give:

$$NW_{FTE} = NW \frac{H_{UNW}}{H_{UST}} \tag{5}$$

$$ST_{FTE} = ST \frac{H_{US} - H_{ACT}}{H_{US}} \tag{6}$$

So, by adding the NW_{FTE} and ST_{FTE} to the denominator, the *index of labour slack* is defined as follows:

$$LS = \frac{\left(U_{FT} + 0.5U_{PT} + U_{PFT} + 0.5U_{PPT} + 0.5E_{PTI} + NW_{FTE} + ST_{FTE}\right)}{\left(E_{FT} + E_{PTI} + 0.5E_{PTV} + U_{FT} + 0.5U_{PT} + U_{PFT} + 0.5U_{PPT}\right)} 100 \tag{7}$$

Drawing on data from the annual Labour Force Survey conducted in EU member countries, the figures for the standard unemployment rate and an estimate of labour slack for western European countries for the period 1985–95 are shown in Figure 5.1. Although not all of the countries are covered for all years, because several were not in the EC until recently, the standard unemployment figures show how persistent the high levels have been. However, labour slack has been consistently higher, often substantially so. We cannot measure labour slack in all the countries for every year, either because they were not in a survey round or because some figures were not collected. For those with data, in most countries labour slack has been very high for more than a decade, only being usually below 10 per cent for Luxembourg and Portugal.

For EU countries, we can measure the ratio of labour slack to unemployment since 1985. The data show that unemployment has been much lower, has not been a stable proxy for labour slack and in several countries, most notably the Netherlands, has fallen relative to labour slack. Overall, the latter has risen. For all countries with data, in 1995 the aggregate EU labour slack rate was 27 per cent higher than the standard unemployment rate.

By way of comparison, note that labour slack in the USA has also been much higher than the unemployment rate (Table 5.4). This is measured slightly differently from the labour slack rate for the European Union, but in the late 1990s taking account of discouraged jobseekers and involuntary part-time workers meant that labour slack was almost double the observed rate of unemployment.

Table 5.4 US labour market indicators, August 1996–July 1997

	Employment–Population Ratio	Unemployment	Under-employment
All	63.6	5.2	9.7
Male	71.2	5.1	9.1
Less than High School	48.3	11.1	19.3
High School	73.4	5.5	9.7
White	72.3	4.0	7.3
Black	61.1	10.8	17.3
Female	56.6	5.3	10.4
Less than High School	29.8	13.4	24.0
High School	55.4	5.6	11.3
White	57.7	3.9	8.2
Black	55.2	10.3	17.8

Source: US Bureau of Labor Statistics.

Second, there has been a change in the trend. In the 1980s, there was a slight tendency for the ratio of labour slack to unemployment to rise (six countries experienced a rise, four a fall); in the 1990s, the ratio has tended to fall (six falling, three rising). This may reflect a change in firm behaviour. In the 1980s, and beforehand, the responsiveness of firms to falls in demand was slow, and there was a tendency to hold on to surplus workers, presumably in the hope or expectation that demand would pick up again fairly quickly. However, in recent years firms have become more flexible in their responses, or have found it easier or more beneficial to operate with a narrower margin of surplus labour. In other words, it may be that greater employment and labour market flexibility have reduced labour hoarding. Another factor may have been an increase in labour force flexibility, so that people move between labour force and non-labour force statuses with more alacrity.

Third, the rise in total employment has been modest since 1985. If one takes countries for which EUROSTAT data were available for 1985 and 1995, employment rose by approximately ten million (making rough adjustments for the inclusion of east Germany). For the same countries over the period, employment in full-time equivalent numbers rose by much less (Figure 5.2). The 1995 full-time equivalent employment level in the UK was only 2.4 per cent higher than in 1985, and in Belgium it was only 4.1 per cent higher. Most conspicuously, employment in full-time equivalent terms *fell* in Italy between 1985 and 1995, although in terms of the standard figures employment was static.

These figures suggest that labour market insecurity, as measured by the high levels of labour slack and the slow growth in employment, has been substantial for a long time. Table 5.5 summarises the pattern across EU member countries in 1995.

Table 5.5 Employment, unemployment and labour slack,
European Community, 1996 *(in thousands)*

Country	E	ΔE	E_{FTE}	ΔE_{FTE}	U	U_{FTE}	LS
Austria	3,617	–1.6%	n.a.	n.a.	5.3%	6.7%	n.a.
Belgium	3,791	–0.1%	3,574	–0.2%	9.5%	13.7%	14.0%
Germany	30,868	6.2%	28,504	6.7%	7.6%	9.8%	9.9%
Denmark	2,623	0.8%	2,402	1.4%	6.7%	8.5%	8.8%
Spain	12,342	2.6%	11,879	2.4%	22.2%	23.6%	23.6%
Finland	2,064	2.4%	1,982	2.5%	14.1%	16.9%	17.3%
France	22,195	0.6%	21,040	0.5%	12.3%	14.8%	15.0%
Greece	3,868	1.3%	3,767	1.2%	9.7%	10.9%	12.1%
Ireland*	1,262	4.6%	1,198	4.2%	12.0%	14.1%	14.5%
Italy	20,014	0.4%	19,521	0.3%	11.9%	17.1%	17.3%
Luxembourg	165	2.0%	160	2.2%	3.3%	3.6%	3.6%
Netherlands	6,932	2.2%	6,236	2.2%	6.4%	9.4%	9.5%
Portugal	4,431	0.3%	4,298	0.0%	6.2%	7.2%	7.3%
Sweden	3,988	–3.5%	3,678	–3.0%	9.1%	12.2%	12.5%
UK	26,177	0.9%	23,294	0.6%	8.1%	10.1%	10.3%

Note:
E	= Total employment
ΔE	= Percentage annual employment growth
E_{FTE}	= Total employment, full-time equivalent
ΔE_{FTE}	= Percentage annual growth in employment, full-time equivalent
U	= Traditional unemployment
U_{ADJ}	= Adjusted unemployment
U_{FTE}	= Unemployment, full-time equivalent
LS	= Labour slack
*1995	

Figure 5.1 Indicators of labour market insecurity (unemployment and labour slack), European Community, 1983–97

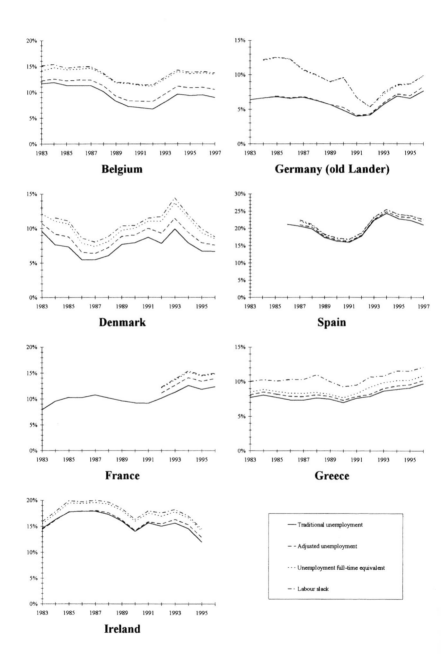

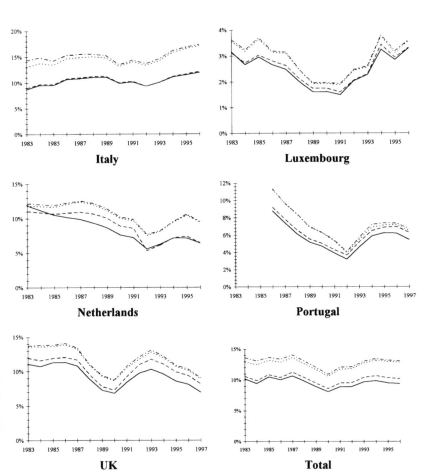

Italy

Luxembourg

Netherlands

Portugal

UK

Total

Source: Eurostat LFS data.

A critical aspect of labour market insecurity is the relationship between economic growth and employment. If labour market flexibility has increased, and employment flexibility in particular, fluctuations in employment should have become more sensitive to changes in the rate of economic growth.

The traditional Keynesian view is that if governments raise aggregate demand employment growth will follow, and so in a recession, raising public expenditure or manipulating fiscal and monetary policy would push the economy back to Full Employment. Monetarists and the 'New Classical' school typically respond that this would stimulate inflationary pressure. Monetarists agree that fiscal policy can influence short-run demand and thus employment, but contend that this will be undermined in the longer term by 'crowding out' effects on private investment. Most would accept that higher rates of economic growth raise employment. A question is whether the strength of any relationship has changed.

Recent analysis has suggested the following stylised facts:

- Economic growth has a positive impact on employment, but in most indus-trialised countries low employment growth has occurred over the long term regardless of economic growth, suggesting the impact of differences in productivity growth and other factors (Layard et al., 1991);
- The positive relationship between growth in GDP and employment change has not weakened since the early 1970s (Boltho and Glyn, 1995; ILO, 1997a).

To assess this latter conclusion and the interpretation of the results, consider the regression function tested to support it:

(8) $D.\%Emp_t = a + b\ D.GDP_t$

where the dependent variable is the percentage change in employment in period t (the year) and the independent variable is the economic growth rate. The authors tested this relationship (admitting that it was a simple way of doing so) with pooled cross-section and time-series annual data from all but four of the OECD member countries over the period 1973–93, testing the relationship for the periods 1973–79, 1975–82, 1979–90 and 1982–93. They took three alternative measures of the dependent variable – average annual growth rate of total employment, average annual growth rate of private sector employment, average annual growth rate of total hours worked.

What they found was that the elasticities with respect to growth declined for all three measures between the earlier period (measured as either 1973–79 or 1975–82) and 1979–90. The coefficients were statistically significant in the first periods and tiny and insignificant in the latter period. The authors did not dwell on that, describing it as 'perturbing'. When the period tested was extended to cover the years 1982–93, the coefficient for total employment became large and statistically significant. They then reported on the relationship between *changes* in average annual growth rates of GDP and changes in the employment growth rate in two periods, concluding that 'jobless growth' could be rejected.

Finally, they examined the relationship between change in GDP and change in their three employment measures for three recessions separately (mid-1970s (1973–76)), early 1980s (1979–82, for most countries) and early 1990s (1990–93, for most countries), concluding that the short-run responses had increased.

One should distinguish between *short-run* and *long-run elasticities of employment with respect to GDP*. The implicit assumption of Boltho and Glyn's model is that the effect of GDP on employment takes place fully in the same year. Although this may be so, it is more likely that a pick-up in economic growth has a lagged effect on employment. One can distinguish between the *speed* and the *extent* of the response. This could be tested by postulating the following equation:

(9) $d.\%Emp_t = a + b \, D.GDP_t + b \, D.GDP_{t-1}$

Suppose that part of the impact takes place within the first year and part in the second and that the total effect is 1 per cent, with 0.5 per cent in each year. If the flexibility of the labour market improves, so that the *speed* of response increases one might find that the first year response increases relative to the second, so that testing for a change in the total effect by a one-period model would be invalid. Interestingly, Boltho and Glyn cited the OECD (1992, p. 15) as suggesting that the short-run elasticity had increased:

> part of the explanation for rapidly rising unemployment may be not only the severity of the slowdown in economic activity but also a somewhat faster employment response to fluctuations in demand.

Accordingly, we test for the relationship with current and lagged GDP growth rates as independent variables. We could also add as a control variable the percentage of total output accounted for by services, on the grounds that measured productivity is lower in services and thus the employment elasticity could be expected to be greater than in other sectors of the economy.

Another point about their study is that by testing for fairly long sub-periods they implicitly assumed a symmetrical relationship through cycles of upturns and recessions. This is reasonable enough. However, an average coefficient could come from (i) a positive effect on employment due to a rise in the GDP growth rate *equal* to the negative effect of a fall in the growth rate, or (ii) a positive effect of a rise that is *greater than* the negative effect of a fall, or (iii) a positive effect of a rise that is *smaller than* the negative effect of a fall.

We hypothesise that the third possibility is correct and that the elasticity of employment decline in recessions has increased since the 1970s. Accordingly we should test for the relationship separately in periods of recession and in periods of upturn. This is prompted by the fact that Boltho and Glyn rescued their hypothesis of *no change* in the job-generating capacity of economic growth by adding the recession period of 1991–93, and by the fact that whereas their estimated elasticities

Figure 5.2 Total employment and in full-time equivalent, European Community, 1983–97

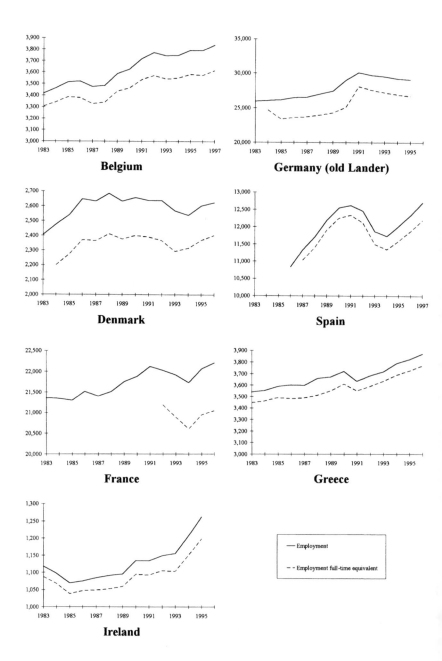

Belgium

Germany (old Lander)

Denmark

Spain

France

Greece

Ireland

Employment

- - Employment full-time equivalent

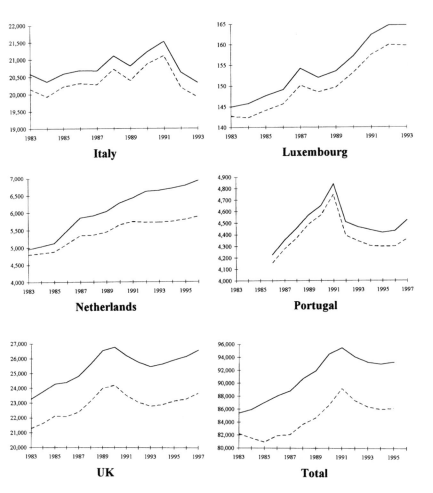

Source: Eurostat LFS data.

were negligible and statistically insignificant in the recessions of the mid-1970s and early 1980s, the reaction to the later recession was strong and statistically significant.

The authors added an interesting hypothesis – consistent with their support of the proposition that the effect of growth on employment has not fallen – that this reaction suggests that employment would increase at an earlier stage of the upswing. However, they did not test this suggestion and apparently did not examine the relationship between growth and employment changes in three successive *upturns*.

Accordingly, we could test both their one-period and our two-period version for their three recessionary periods and for the intervening non-recessionary periods (1977–78, 1983–89). Or we could test to determine whether there are differences in recessions and upturns by identifying specific years as recessionary if they have rates of growth of GDP below, say, 1 per cent.

To complicate matters, since the 1970s most industrialised countries have tried to increase the 'employment intensity of growth', through use of wage or employment subsidies, weakening of protective labour regulations, the greater use of special measures to absorb some of the unemployed into jobs or training and the erosion of unemployment benefits, through tighter conditionality and lower income replacement rates, which are supposed to induce more unemployed to take low-paid jobs, etc. The numbers of people covered by these measures have been growing in both recessions and upturns, although not always at the same rate. Thus, there has been increasing resort to demand-side measures (subsidies, job creation schemes, etc.) and supply-side measures (reducing employment protection, etc.), so that labour market and employment flexibility should have increased.

Table 5.6 Regression coefficients of impact of GDP growth on employment growth, industrialised countries, 1971–96 *(coefficients for growth of GDP in current year and for growth of GDP one year previously)*

	All		Booms		Recessions	
	(1)	(2)	(1)	(2)	(1)	(2)
1971–79	0.19***	0.17***	0.19***	0.14***	0.01	0.03
		0.15***		0.14***		0.21
1980–89	0.41***	0.32***	0.44[3]	0.31***	0.46***	0.46***
		0.25***		0.29***		0.05
1990–96	0.69***	0.57***	0.83	0.74***	0.54***	0.48***
		0.36***		0.36***		0.50***
R^2	0.38	0.46	0.33	0.37	0.16	0.55

Note: Three asterisks signify that the coefficient was statistically significant at the 1% level; two asterisks, 5% level; one asterisk, 10% level. This applies to all subsequent tables. The R^2 is for the last regression.

Using data for all industrialised countries for the period 1971–96, Table 5.6 reports the regression coefficients for the impact on employment change of changes in GDP. The results are not quite comparable with those of Boltho and Glyn because more countries and more years are included. The results are given for three periods – 1971–79, 1980–89 and 1990–96. The coefficients suggest that the positive correlation between changes in GDP and employment *increased* steadily over the three periods.

Another way of expressing this change is that if the same correlation had held in the 1990s as in the 1970s the observed employment growth would have been a third of what it was. The table also suggests that in years of relatively rapid economic growth the employment elasticity was consistently higher.

The relationships are also tested for western European countries and for other OECD countries separately. Table 5.7 suggests that in the 1970s and 1980s the direct relationship was stronger outside Europe, but that between 1990 and 1996 it was significantly stronger in Europe. It also shows that for both groups of countries the elasticity increased steadily over the quarter of a century.

Table 5.7 Impact of growth of GDP on employment growth, Europe and other OECD countries, 1971–96 *(regression coefficients)*

| | 1971–79 | | 1980–89 | | 1990–96 | |
	Europe ΔE	Non-Europe ΔE	Europe ΔE	Non-Europe ΔE	Europe ΔE	Non-Europe ΔE
Constant	0.154	1.025	−0.255	−0.043	−1.086	0.108
ΔGDP$_t$	0.177***	0.244***	0.379***	0.493***	0.72***	0.54***
R^2	0.12	0.27	0.28	0.37	0.39	0.42

We also test the relationship for European Union countries, for the period 1985–95 for those countries applying the EUROSTAT Labour Force Survey. The results are given in Table 5.8. They show that, within the EU, economic growth has been positively associated with growth in employment and growth in employment in full-time equivalent terms. They also suggest that GDP growth explains only a small part of the variance in employment growth, and that economic growth has to be well over 1 per cent just to stop employment falling.

Table 5.9 gives the results for 1985–90 and 1990–95 separately, suggesting that whereas there was no single-period relationship in the former years, and only a lagged effect, there was a surprisingly strong direct and immediate relationship in the 1990s. One way of interpreting this is that *employment flexibility with respect to economic growth has grown.*

The relationship between GDP and employment is by no means the same as that between GDP and unemployment or *labour slack*. Intriguingly, Boltho and Glyn did not examine the latter, claiming that factors other than GDP growth affect 'registered unemployment'. While reference to registered unemployment seems unnecessary, the same argument could be applied to the relationship between GDP and employment.

Table 5.8 Regression coefficients of impact of GDP growth on employment and full-time equivalent employment, European Union, 1985–95

| | 1985–1995 | | | |
	ΔE	ΔE_{FTE}	ΔE	ΔE_{FTE}
ΔGDP_t	0.67***	0.69***	0.57***	0.6***
ΔGDP_{t-1}			0.22	0.23*
Constant	–0.79	–1.07	–1.14	–1.42
R^2	0.26	0.29	0.27	0.3

In any case, using the national Labour Force Surveys, we can examine the correlation between economic growth and open unemployment in the European Union member countries for the years for which we have comparable data. The measure of unemployment is as close as possible to a 'standardised' measure, and this can be regressed on economic growth as was done for employment, using a mixed cross-section and time-series regression.

Table 5.9 Impact of growth of GDP on growth rate of employment, European Union, 1985–95

| | 1985–90 | | 1990–95 | |
	ΔE	ΔE_{FTE}	ΔE	ΔE_{FTE}
Constant	1.395	1.12	–1.496	–1.768
ΔGDP_t	0.028	0.053	0.992***	1.018***
R^2	0.01	0.01	0.44	0.45
Constant	0.728	0.366	–1.702	–1.958
ΔGDP_t	–0.088	–0.079	0.927***	0.958***
ΔGDP_{t-1}	0.322	0.364	0.147	0.136
R^2	0.1	0.17	0.45	0.46

The percentage labour slack rate is regressed on growth in GDP and the result compared with that obtained for unemployment in the years for which all data for calculation of labour slack were collected. Table 5.10 shows that economic growth has been associated with a decline in unemployment and a smaller decline in labour slack. What is more interesting is that the equations suggest that there has to be an economic growth rate of over 2.5 per cent to prevent unemployment from rising and nearly 3 per cent to prevent labour slack from rising. When the relationships are tested for 1985–90 and 1990–95 separately, it appears that the impact of growth on unemployment *diminished* in the 1990s, even though the positive impact on employment seems to have increased. This implies that labour supply has become more elastic, or that there has been *an increase in labour force flexibility*. If the elasticity of labour supply with respect to economic growth has increased, or if more people can and do move between employment and outside the labour force, then the character of unemployment changes, becoming more of a 'pool' rather than a transitional status of a 'temporary interruption of earning power' as envisaged by Beveridge.

Table 5.10 Impact of growth of GDP on growth rate of unemployment and labour slack, European Union, 1985–95 *(regression coefficients)*

| | 1985–90 | | 1990–95 | |
	ΔU	ΔLS	ΔU	ΔLS
Constant	3.638	3.197	6.47	6.012
ΔGDP$_t$	−2.405***	−2.298***	−1.553**	−1.327**
R^2	0.32	0.34	0.07	0.05
Constant	7.453	6.664	7.329	6.657
ΔGDP$_t$	−1.738***	−1.692***	−1.285*	−1.126
ΔGDP$_{t-1}$	−1.842***	−1.674***	−0.611	−0.461
R^2	0.43	0.45	0.06	0.04

In sum, economic growth has continued to be associated with employment creation and with cuts in unemployment, but the respective impact is increasingly dissimilar. Economic growth does create jobs. Nevertheless, with both sets of data, the estimated effects of GDP growth on employment (and unemployment) suggest that to make a substantial difference there would have to be a long and sustained period of high rates of economic growth. Is that feasible or likely? It seems not. Even the European Commission concluded in 1995 that with feasible economic growth in the coming years unemployment would only drop by two percentage points from 11 per cent (*Financial Times*, 15 May 1995).

Although macro-economic policy may be able to raise economic growth rates, globalisation and other developments have restricted the capacity of most governments to do so. This particularly applies to fiscal policy (Leibfritz, 1994). Fiscal policy may have become more uniform across countries, inducing a decline in the variability of output, employment and most policy variables, the apparent exception being public expenditure (Boltho and Glyn, 1995, pp. 459–61).

The opportunity to raise economic growth through internationally co-ordinated action by a group of countries may have also declined, although more research on this issue is needed. That aside, sustainably high rates of economic growth are surely only feasible if balance of payments constraints do not emerge. This means that exports (tradables) must grow, which means that 'competitiveness' and productivity must improve. However, in industrialised countries the traditional positive relationship between productivity growth and employment growth, shown in a classic study by Salter (1960) covering the period 1924–60, has ceased to apply, and may have become an *inverse* relationship (Applebaum and Schettkat, 1995). To re-examine this, we regressed national productivity growth rates on employment growth and also found a weak *inverse* relationship (Figure 5.3), which became stronger when we added the growth rate of GDP. Even more notably, in the 1990s the inverse relationship between productivity growth and employment became much stronger (Figure 5.4).

If there is an inverse relationship, it represents a barrier to the use of higher economic growth rates as the means of substantially boosting employment. Although some economists (including the chairman of the US Federal Reserve) have questioned the productivity statistics, believing that productivity is underestimated in services, it is notable that the USA has had a combination of relatively poor productivity growth (averaging less than 1 per cent per year in the 1990s), a burgeoning balance of payments deficit and a relatively rapid growth of employment.

In short, raising economic growth rates substantially by demand management policies is probably not feasible, even if it were desirable (which should not be taken for granted). There is no evidence of 'jobless growth'. It has been more like an expansion of 'growthless jobs', in that, despite low rates of economic growth, employment has expanded. It would be an exaggeration to suggest that jobs are withering away in Europe, although it might be the case that more are being created for the sake of 'job creation' and that more *partial* jobs are being substituted for more desired types of employment. Meanwhile, there has been a simultaneous increase in employment and unemployment. An example is Austria between 1970 and 1996. However, as elsewhere, in Austria, the average expected number of years of employed working life has fallen; it was 44 years in 1970, and 36 years in 1990. This is a remarkably large decline. Although such changes may reflect a desire to remain outside employment for longer, they may reflect what might be called *longitudinal* labour market insecurity. In other words, the expected number of years in employment has declined. This has implications for income security, particularly in the light of the more years of employment required to obtain entitlement to full pensions.

Earlier it was emphasised that employment growth in European industrialised countries has been low for over 40 years. Much is made of the 'jobs miracle' of the USA in recent years. In that regard, it is worth noting that in relative terms the US experience has not been that impressive, and that as a result of changes the percentage of the adult population in employment has been similar to some European countries and that some European countries have experienced a faster rise in recent years, as observed earlier (Table 5.2). What is also notable is that the ratio has fallen in two countries commonly cited as successful in terms of employment generation or unemployment reduction, namely the Netherlands and the UK.

Besides the changes in employment, unemployment and labour slack, other developments have indicated an erosion of labour market security. For instance, a feature of the post-war era was that it was the growth in *public sector jobs* that

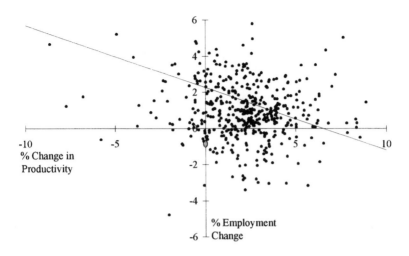

Figure 5.3 Relationship between employment change and change in productivity, 1971–89, European Community *(scatterplot of observations and regression line)*

Notes: $R^2 = 0.11$, F = 4.68, n = 456

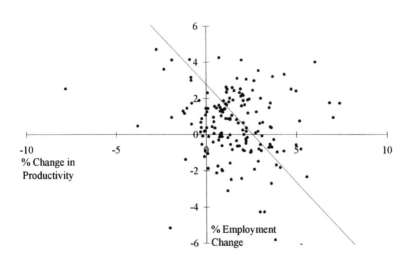

Figure 5.4 Relationship between employment change and change in productivity, 1990–96, European Community *(scatterplot of observations and regression line)*

Notes: $R^2 = 0.46$, F = 54.63, n = 168

ensured high labour market security. Between 1970 and 1994 the number of private sector jobs in the European Union actually declined, and the net increase in total jobs was due to a modest rise in public sector jobs. This might suggest that it is when there is a higher rate of economic growth that governments have been in a position to expand public investment, expenditure and employment.

Labour market security is fundamentally a distributional issue. It was often said of Margaret Thatcher's strategy that as long as about 40 per cent of society were not losing, in terms of income and security, the liberal market policies would not result in unsustainable erosion of popular support. There is a difference between situations in which *most* people feel threatened by labour market insecurity and situations in which many see little change in their prospects, or even improvement, while a minority experience greater insecurity. If the insecurity faced by all groups were approximately equal, the political pressures to ensure adequate compensation would be strong. Conversely, if only a minority experienced extreme insecurity, the majority might be relatively indifferent, and as a result compensation might be reduced.

With more flexible labour markets, it appears that labour market insecurity has spread, even though it has remained much greater for some groups than for others. This can be seen by considering the main contours of differentiation – demographic, geographical and occupational.

First, however, while insecurity has been increasing for most groups in European labour markets, the severity of the insecurity is reflected in the rise in *long-term unemployment*. It is estimated that over 40 per cent of the unemployed in western Europe have been out of employment for more than a year, compared with 11 per cent in the USA. Part of the difference may reflect statistical differences, but if the probability of prolonged unemployment on becoming unemployed is high, the insecurity associated with the threat of unemployment is intensified. It is phenomena such as this that may explain why a large proportion of the population continues to express anxiety about the labour market even when recorded unemployment falls.

It seems that the extent of long-term unemployment is primarily a reflection of the total unemployment rate, and that at least in western Europe this relationship has not changed, contrary to many assertions. Regressing the percentage share of unemployed in long-term unemployment (12 months or more) on the unemployment rate of the preceding year and a time trend dummy for two recent periods, it appears that the long-term share rises with total unemployment and that, although the sign of the coefficient on the time trend changes from negative to positive, neither coefficient is statistically significant (Table 5.11). This is important, because some economists have suggested that policies should concentrate on the long-term unemployed and that the long-term unemployment is indicative of rising structural unemployment.

If one takes the percentage of unemployed who are in long-term unemployment as one indicator of labour market insecurity, coupled with the unemployment rate and the overall rate of labour force participation, then one could estimate another variant of a *labour market insecurity index:*

$$LMI1 = \frac{1}{600}\left[3(100 - \text{UNEMP}) + 2(100 - \text{LTUNEMP}) + \text{LFPART}\right]$$

where UNEMP is the unemployment rate, LTUNEMP is the percentage of unemployed in long-term unemployment, and LFPART is the adult labour force participation rate. An alternative (LMS2) is to replace the unemployment rate with the labour slack rate, as measured earlier. The resultant index is estimated so as to give a value of between 0 and 1. Table 5.12 shows that, according to this, labour market insecurity has grown in most industrialised countries, and Table 5.13 gives a sample of results for industrialised countries using the OECD standardised unemployment rates in place of labour slack rates. Figure 5.5 shows that the labour market insecurity index has hovered at a high level for many years in countries with supposedly improving labour market situations.

Table 5.11 Regression of impact of unemployment on per cent in long-term unemployment, European Union Countries, 1983–1996 (regression coefficients)

	1983–96	1983–90	1990–96
U_{t-1}	0.590***	0.636***	0.562***
T	−0.007	−0.058	0.024
Constant	−0.806	−0.368	−1.283
R^2	0.842	0.836	0.847

Note: The dependent variable is the percentage share of total unemployment out of employment for more than a year, the independent variables are the unemployment rate lagged by one year and a linear dummy variable with a value of 1 for 1983. Replacing T by the growth rate of GDP had little effect, and the coefficients on DGDP were statistically insignificant.

Table 5.12 Labour market insecurity index (LMI-3), 1983–96 *(using labour slack)*

Country	1983	1996
Belgium	0.35	0.34
Denmark	0.22[b]	0.17
France	0.24[e]	0.26
Germany	0.23[a]	0.26[f]
Greece	0.27[d]	0.29[f]
Ireland	0.24	0.34[f]
Italy	0.28	0.37
Netherlands	0.28	0.27
Portugal	0.29[c]	0.27
Spain	0.39[d]	0.37
UK	0.24	0.23

Notes: [a]1984, [b]1985, [c]1986, [d]1987, [e]1992, [f]1995
Source: Eurostat Labour Force Survey data.

Another feature of the labour market insecurity in Europe is the *geographical disparity* in unemployment. Research has shown that within the European Union there has been no convergence in regional unemployment rates over two decades of European unification (Baddeley et al., 1997). This may reflect growing difficulty in rectifying labour market insecurity, because the disparities have persisted in spite of numerous policies trying to reduce them. If the disparity has been exacerbated by economic integration, it may grow more with the increased integration through the EMU.

Table 5.13 Labour market insecurity index#2 (LMI), 1990–96
(using standardized unemployment rates)

Country	1990	1996
Australia	0.15	0.18
Belgium	0.33	0.31
France	0.23	0.25
Germany	0.23	0.25*
Japan	0.12	0.12
Netherlands	0.27	0.26
Sweden	0.05	0.15
UK	0.19	0.22
US	0.09	0.10

Note: * Data for Germany are for 1995.
Source: Eurostat and OECD data.

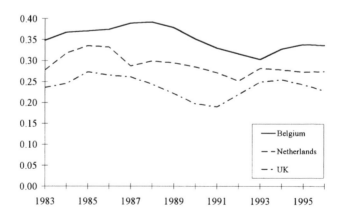

Figure 5.5 Labour market insecurity index#3 (LMI3), 1983–96 (using labour slack)

Source: Eurostat LFS data.

As for demographic disparities, three major changes have taken place in most labour markets since the demise of the era of statutory regulation. *Youth* unemployment rates have risen to very high levels, and have risen relative to other demographic groups. In Spain, for example, in 1996 almost half of those aged under 24 in the labour force were unemployed; in France and Italy, the figure was over one in every four. In eastern Europe, by the mid-1990s youth unemployment rates were comparable to those in western Europe. In many countries labour market measures to compensate and assist teenagers have shifted labour market insecurity onto the age group 20–24, so spreading the insecurity up the age spectrum. Even so, for the EU overall, youth unemployment and labour slack both rose in the 1990s, until falling in 1997 (Figure 5.6). A variation was the Netherlands, where youth labour slack rose while unemployment fell and then stabilised (Figure 5.7).

Second, *older workers* (45+) have been marginalised in the labour market, and since the 1980s have had greater difficulty in holding jobs until the normal age of retirement. Much of their unemployment has been disguised through early retirement, which has been widespread in eastern as well as western Europe, and in many other parts of the world. In western Europe, the difference between their unemployment rate and overall labour slack widened in the 1990s (Figure 5.6). And, even though there was a growth in the older working-age population, between 1983 and 1996, the number of employed older workers actually declined.

Third, *male unemployment* has risen relative to female almost everywhere. Suffice it to state that as far as the most visible aspect of labour market insecurity is concerned there has been a trend towards 'equality'. Although the overall European level of labour slack remained higher for women (at least until 1997), since the 1980s there has been a convergence in both unemployment and labour slack (Figure 5.8).

Meanwhile, the ratio of unemployment of so-called 'unskilled' workers to the rate for 'skilled' workers has been high, and has attracted much comment. Surprisingly, the ratio has been relatively high in the USA (Table 5.14), which is not easily reconciled with the image of a highly flexible labour market in which relative wages adjust to counter shifts in demand and supply of skill categories of worker.

In sum, in the post-war era labour market security existed primarily for men, and the appearance of satisfactory security was achieved through relatively low employment rates because women were largely a labour reserve. In the 1980s and 1990s, labour market insecurity has grown almost everywhere, and has *grown* most for young and older men. In some countries, the deterioration has been less than elsewhere, in some it has *appeared* to be less than elsewhere, but in some cases this has been partly because labour market insecurity has taken a less visible form than open unemployment. Thus, recently open unemployment has been relatively low in the Netherlands because the employment rate has been rather low, at 62 per cent of the working-age population, and because of rising involuntary part-time employment.

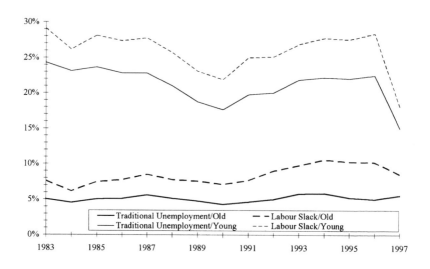

Figure 5.6 Unemployment and labour slack for old and young workers, European Community, 1983–96

Source: Eurostat LFS data.

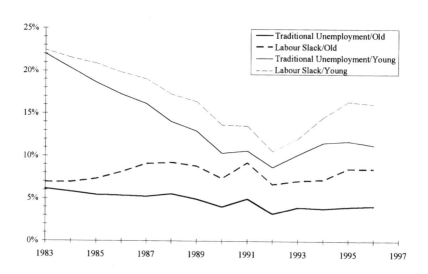

Figure 5.7 Unemployment and labour slack for old and young workers, Netherlands, 1983–96

Source: Eurostat LFS data.

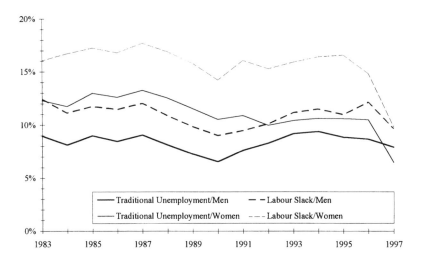

Figure 5.8 Unemployment and labour slack for men and women, European Community, 1983–96

Source: Eurostat LFS data.

Finally, there is the changing institutional arrangements for reducing labour market insecurity. Intermediary mechanisms influence the level, the forms and the incidence of labour market insecurity. For example, by tightening the conditions for entitlement to unemployment benefits, governments induce some of the unemployed to drop out of the labour force. This may induce a behavioural adaptation by some of the unemployed, so that some people cease to perceive themselves as unemployed even in the passive sense of discouraged workers. Similarly, an extensive system of visible, high-quality public employment exchanges will reduce the transaction costs of being unemployed. Whether they will have a net negative or positive effect on open unemployment will depend on whether they reduce the duration of unemployment and the ratio of job vacancies to unemployed by more than they encourage people on the margins of the labour force to participate in it.

Turning over public employment exchange functions to private agencies may alter the incidence of unemployment and induce some to become passively unemployed. Similarly, if a government changes policy to oblige the unemployed to take designated jobs or training places the effect on labour market insecurity cannot be predicted a priori, since some of the unemployed could withdraw from the labour market into passive unemployment rather than take one of the available options.

Given that all these trends exist in industrialised countries in the 1990s – tighter conditions for unemployment benefits, a shift to private employment services, and welfare-to-work obligations – they have surely intensified labour market insecurity.

Table 5.14 Relative unemployment rates, selected industrialised countries, 1983–95[1]

Group unemp-loyment rate:	Youth[2]		Women		Unskilled[3] (U)	High-skilled[4] (H)	Ratio U/H
Year:	1983	1995	1983	1995	1992	1992	1992
Large Countries							
Germany[5]	11.0	8.5	8.8	9.8	8.9	3.7	2.41
UK	19.7[a]	15.5	11.5	4.3	12.3	3.6	3.42
Japan	4.5	6.1	2.6	3.2	–	–	
USA	17.2	12.1	9.2	5.6	13.5	2.9	4.66
Small Countries							
Netherlands	24.9	13.1	12.9	7.1[b]	8.0	3.9	2.05
Belgium	23.9	21.5	17.8	10.8[b]	13.0	2.2	5.91
Denmark	18.9	9.9	10.4	11.1[b]	15.6	4.8	3.25
Sweden	8.0	15.4	3.6	6.9	4.6	2.0	2.30
Average	16.0	12.8	9.6	7.4	10.8	3.3	3.27
Variation coeff.[6]	0.43	0.35	0.48	0.38	0.33	0.28	

Notes: 1. Standardised OECD data except for Denmark, Netherlands.
2. Unemployed aged 15 to 24 in per cent of the labour force in the respective age group.
3. Unemployed with primary or lower secondary schooling as per cent of population aged 25 to 64.
4. Unemployed with university degree as per cent of population aged 25–64.
5. West Germany before 1991; data on discouraged workers not available.
6. Standard deviation divided by the mean.
a 1984 b 1993

Sources: OECD, *Education at a Glance 1995*, *Employment Outlook 1995*, *Labour Force Statistics*, *Quarterly Labour Force Statistics*, calculations by the DIW.

In sum, after more than a decade of decline, there is no sign that labour market security is improving, or that policies are likely to have success in making that happen. Realities can defeat statistical presentation too. In the USA, economists and politicians have presented the low official unemployment as indicative of a tight labour market and near Full Employment. Yet opinion polls have found that, when asked to estimate the level of unemployment, people on average gave a rate much higher than the official figure. Whether this reflects differences in what people perceive as unemployment or the fact that many people fear the threat of unemployment is hard to determine. Yet it is surely one indicator of pervasive labour market insecurity.

5.4 LABOUR MARKET INSECURITY IN 'TRANSITIONAL' ECONOMIES

The state socialism model provided Full Employment based on low wages, stagnant productivity and early age for pension receipt coupled with high rates of employment among the pensioner population, because of low pensions and dependence on enterprises for benefits and services. In most economies operating some version of that model, primary employment was coupled with secondary, informal activity.

From the late 1980s onwards, that model came apart. Initially, employment declined because with high rates of labour turnover, vacancies dried up in state enterprises. Then there was a phase in which there were some redundancies, mostly consisting of individuals and small groups of workers. Then there was a period of mass redundancies and bankruptcies. In the 1990s, the budgetary sector (public services) was squeezed for funds, and in some cases employment was cut less than proportionately, so average wages fell and wage arrears became endemic.

Nevertheless, in no country was employment maintained at levels reached in the 1980s. In most countries, labour market insecurity rose through cuts in employment that showed up in an extraordinary rise in open and concealed unemployment, declines in labour force participation among both men and women, a resort to early retirement schemes, a huge cut in the employment of disabled workers, and a cruel phenomenon of 'unpaid administrative leave', documented in the ILO's Enterprise Labour Flexibility Surveys in Albania, Armenia, Bulgaria, China, Georgia, Russia and Ukraine. In the two large countries of Russia and Ukraine, this has been so substantial that it has distorted the unemployment count in two ways, by overestimating employment and by preventing workers who were really unemployed from appearing in the unemployment count. Another factor was that, as shown in chapter 7, the low probability of obtaining benefits, and the low value of the benefits if they were to obtain them, discouraged the unemployed from registering and thus being counted. There was also the disappearance of hundreds of thousands of workers with disabilities, who lost their jobs in the 1990s without appearing in the statistical count of unemployment (Chikanova and Smirnov, 1993).

The rise in labour market insecurity in Russia has also been partially disguised by the cruellest means possible. Not only have a rising proportion of those becoming unemployed drifted into crime or prison, but a substantial number have disappeared altogether because they have died. Between 1987 and 1995, male life expectancy at birth declined by eight years to merely 58, with a rise in the mortality rate of 87 per cent for men aged 40 to 49 between 1990 and 1994 alone (Standing, 1998). There has also been an enormous increase in morbidity and disability, reducing the readily available labour supply.

Across central and eastern Europe and the former Soviet Union, the 1990s saw the emergence of mass unemployment, made worse by the lack of understanding of the phenomenon, the lack of institutions to deal with the traumas, and the lack of social networks, including those needed to provide community benefits that comprise part of the social income. In most ex-state socialism countries, registered unemployment rates rose sharply in the 1990s but unemployment as measured in labour force surveys rose much more. Many workers simply dropped out of the labour force altogether.

With the exception of a few regions that will become growth poles, high unemployment and labour market insecurity will surely continue to characterise most economies evolving from state socialism. Shock therapy increased that by more than was necessary. Unemployment has been concealed, by inadequate and inappropriate statistics, and by reduced eligibility for benefits and lower income–replacement ratios and shorter duration of benefits. Although in some countries women have been more marginalised, groups hardest hit have been the disabled, minorities and older men.

One unique state socialism model country evolving along distinctive lines is China. There labour market insecurity could become globally significant early in the twenty-first century. As noted earlier, China has had official unemployment of 3 per cent, but with millions of workers on 'lay-off', the Government estimated that the real rate was 7.5 per cent. Taking account of labour slack, the figure could be much higher. With unemployment benefits below the subsistence wage, social tensions could become considerable. At the end of 1996, there were 3.5 million unemployed, 9 million workers temporarily laid off and 11 million nominally employed with wage arrears. The World Bank believes that unemployment was even higher than these figures imply. A World Bank survey in 1997 of five large cities estimated that open unemployment and redundant state enterprise workers accounted for 13 per cent of the labour force. Government estimates concluded that 15–20 per cent of state enterprise workers could be released without affecting output.

There has been extensive *ria gang,* that is workers being off-post, on lay off, retaining employment but with minimal income and no work. These could be called the workless employed. Semi-official estimates put the number at 20 million workers and 5 million government employees. If these were added to the registered unemployed, unemployment would have been at least 15 per cent in 1995. Meanwhile, the informal economy has spread, with incomes not being declared because of fear of losing subsistence wages and welfare benefits from former employers. This unemployment trap boosts the grey and black economy, lowering tax revenue and inducing inefficient opportunism.

So, in transitional economies labour market insecurity has taken forms not easily captured by Keynesian labour force statistics. The statistical tools are inadequate, and it is likely that the policies that would be appropriate for dealing with the flexible patterns of disemployment would differ from those devised for labour markets as envisaged in the early part of the twentieth century.

5.5 CONCLUDING POINTS

Throughout the world, the era of market regulation has coincided with erosion of labour market security. Unemployment is higher than in the previous era, but with growing employment and labour force flexibility, the unemployment rate understates the insecurity and labour slack. In the late 1990s, some prominent economists have concluded that because of greater *employment insecurity,* the NAIRU has come down, implying in their judgment that the economy could operate at a lower rate of unemployment without igniting accelerating inflation. Perhaps unemployment has become a less appropriate proxy for the underlying theoretical relationship. Bearing in mind that unemployment understates labour slack (S) by more than in the past, perhaps they should think in terms of a NAIRS, rather than a NAIRU.

Labour market insecurity was conceded by adoption of supply-side economics, and in no country adhering to conventional economic strategy is there commitment to minimising unemployment. Most governments facing high unemployment would like to see it reduced. But they see some involuntary unemployment as functional. In that context, a government sees a situation where 1 in 20 workers are unemployed as a success, and possibly as too much of a success.

In industrialised economies, the image of Full Employment has surely faded. If one recalls the clarity of the post-war commitments, one can appreciate the change of perspective in the provision added to the Dutch Constitution in 1983: *'The promotion of sufficient employment is an object of care of the state.'* While calls are still made for a 'return' to Full Employment, pervasive labour market insecurity is the context in which social and labour policy will have to be refashioned.

Much of the debate since the early 1980s has been couched in terms of the alleged deficiencies of western European labour markets compared with the supposedly more flexible US economy. One paradox is this. For nearly two decades economists have been urging European Union governments to make their labour markets more flexible as the means of reducing unemployment. In many ways they have done so. Yet at the end of the period, unemployment is higher than at the outset, and labour slack is much higher. To escape from this paradox, the IMF (September 1997) have suggested that labour market reforms must be 'comprehensive' and that they take time to work, citing the UK and the Netherlands as examples. However, neither of these countries has done conspicuously better than average in terms of full-time equivalent unemployment, employment or labour slack.

Labour market security has never been strong in the sense of freely chosen productive employment opportunities for all. There has been something like full employment in agrarian economies, where notions of employment and unemployment are misleading. Labour market security was promoted as the source of distributive justice in the twentieth century, through Full Employment. If an economy is an industrial one in which about half of the working-age population is expected to take full-time jobs paying a family wage or social income, and if this is called full employment, then that is a laudable objective, if the employment is freely chosen and productive. If those premises do not apply, or if they are rejected for their perceived unfairness, what is left? Should jobs be shared? Should artificial jobs be created, perhaps by public bodies? Should wages and social incomes be lowered to clear the labour market? Should those who do not obtain good jobs be obliged to take bad or unproductive jobs or jobs paying much less than those in good jobs are receiving? These have been key questions of the last quarter of the century of the labouring man. We come back to them in the final part of the book.

With more flexible labour markets and more heterogeneous forms of labour and employment, the unemployment rate is an inadequate index of labour market insecurity, seriously underestimating the depth of insecurity that has accompanied the era of market regulation. No doubt it could be reduced, but if this means reducing other forms of security, critical decisions have to be made about priorities. It is by no means clear that labour market security is the key to a good society of the future.

6 Insecurity in Employment

6.1 INTRODUCTION

Although labour market security was given high priority in the post-war era, other forms of security were also part of the fabric of social and labour policy. The norm in both welfare state capitalism and state socialism was that there would be a steady growth in employment security, and there was the presumption that this was desirable on welfare and economic grounds. Job security, work security, skill reproduction security and representation security were also seen as legitimate concerns to be extended by statutory and institutional means.

This chapter considers how these have evolved in the era of market regulation, when all forms of security were given less emphasis in policymaking. The most relevant concern is whether more flexible labour markets have had implications for the extent of security and whether or not conventional policies have had beneficial effects.

6.2 EMPLOYMENT INSECURITY

Employment security was part of the agenda for the labouring man. It meant protection against arbitrary dismissal from employment, the imposition of costs on employers (or on the state) for abrogating that right and for making workers redundant, and the provision of benefits for workers losing jobs. The image of society as consisting of everybody in secure, stable employment has been an appealing one over the past 50 years. But throughout the twentieth century the offer of such security has also been a form of control and stratification. It has been a benefit for which there have always been underlying or explicit reciprocities. It was a *sine qua non* of the communist system, conditional on passive labour. It has also been a functional part of the welfare state, since the edifice of social insurance rested on people being in stable full-time employment for most of the time, paying their contributions or having them paid for them. If large numbers of people, for whatever reason, move in and out of employment, that erodes the contributions and entitlements basis of the welfare state.

For much of the century, the notion of employment security was spread to developing economies where it was incongruous. Thus in India, for example, some groups of male workers, in the main, attained employment security, notably in the public sector and in large factories. This also became common in urban areas of Africa, Latin America and elsewhere. But the vast majority of men and women were not in that position. Should one measure success in terms of the proportion of workers with employment security? Probably not. As the century of the labouring man comes to an end, employment security has been slipping down the agenda of social objectives. Once it ceases to be an explicit objective, it may be appreciated that it has been a restraint on constructive thinking about the future of other forms of security.

Protection against arbitrary dismissal from employment or sudden loss of employment has traditionally been strengthened by regulations on hiring and firing practices, collective agreements and legal procedures establishing fair and due process, and by the imposition of costs on firms for abrogating this acquired right and on employers wishing to cut employment without notice.

Employment security has a *subjective* and an *objective* reality. It may reflect a mood, or set of fears, and it can reflect characteristics of employment. Thus, an 'objective' indicator of employment security is the proportion of the employed with stable or regular contracts of employment; a 'subjective' indicator is the reported expression of belief that employment continuity is assured.

Superficially, the evidence on subjective perceptions is strong. In industrialised countries, whether the reality has reflected it, there has been a growth in the public perception of insecurity. For instance, a survey of newspapers found that the number of stories referring to employment security rose in various countries over the period of 1982 to 1996 (OECD, 1997b, pp. 130–1). This could mean that there is a greater fear of losing employment, or it could mean that the ideological debate has changed, so that more commentators are questioning the desirability of employment security.

More substantively, workers in various countries have reported that employment security is among the most important aspects of a job, with one survey suggesting that in a sample of nine countries on average it was the most important factor in their considerations (International Survey Research, 1995). Perceived employment insecurity is not merely a function of unemployment. Proportionately more workers have reported 'unfavourable' levels of employment security in Japan, France, the UK and the USA than elsewhere (OECD, 1997b, p. 130). The attitudinal questions used to devise such rankings are rather soft, but they have been applied fairly consistently across countries. Japan has had the highest incidence of perceived insecurity, which is ironic given the image of its 'lifetime employment' system and relatively low unemployment. One reason may be that the cost of employment loss to the worker has been relatively high in Japan because of the prevalence of seniority pay systems (Aoki, 1988, p. 59). Someone who has been with a firm for some years would lose a great deal if he lost the job and had to start in another firm.

Employment insecurity is partly a perception of risk. Thus in the USA, although unemployment has been low by European standards, and although there has been job growth, it was estimated that between the 1980s and mid-1990s nearly three-quarters of all households had 'a close encounter' with layoffs. The threat to employment, with all the trauma and income difficulties, would have acted as a source of insecurity for those not directly involved. Moreover, if the threat were spread to most groups, as may have been the case, it would result in more generalised insecurity. By the 1990s, downsizing was affecting high-paid professionals as well as others, whereas in the past it mainly affected manual workers (Manufacturing Institute, 1996).

Internationally, in terms of the *incidence* of perceived insecurity, surveys suggest there is little difference between men and women. This might reflect a tendency for more women to *expect* less security. It is also apparent that there is no simple relationship between schooling and perceived employment security. Unlike other countries surveyed, in Austria, Denmark, France, Italy and the UK those with higher education have been more likely to report that their employment is insecure, even though workers in manual jobs have been more likely to report insecurity (OECD, 1997b, p. 133). Except in Sweden, those working in public administration have been less likely to report employment insecurity, suggesting that privatisation would increase it.

Perceived employment security is the aspect of jobs that deteriorated most in the 1990s, according to surveys from seven western European countries (International Survey Research, 1995). It has also apparently deteriorated in the USA, where a survey by Princeton Survey Research Associates in July 1997 found that, despite what most observers regarded as the tightest labour market in 25 years, 70 per cent of respondents said they had less employment security than 20 or 30 years earlier. The British Household Panel and Social Attitudes Surveys suggested that such insecurity jumped in 1992, and continued to rise in the following three years (Spencer, 1996). The OECD (1997b, p. 134) was convinced that perceived employment insecurity had spread in the 1990s in all OECD countries for which data were available.

This may be true. However, the evidence should prompt caution. A rise in feelings of insecurity could stem from a rise in expectations about one's job or labour market experience. If one felt that, because of high unemployment, having any income-earning job was fortunate, one might be less inclined to report the insecurity, whereas if job prospects were improving one might resent not having greater employment security, through not having a long-term contract, for instance. Or an expression of employment insecurity could stem from increased concern about *income* security, whether one were employed or not. If one felt that loss of employment would no longer be followed by assured benefits, or if there were a low probability of obtaining another job, the sense of employment security might fall. It is essential, for analytical and policy reasons, to differentiate between employment security and income security.

Another possibility is that the sentiments are misinterpreted. Expressions of concern about anticipated retention of employment should not be interpreted automatically as feelings of employment insecurity. One might expect to lose a job and not feel insecure about it, or conversely feel insecure about employment even though actually there was little prospect of losing it. It is puzzling that, according to survey data, more people report that they are 'satisfied' with their employment security than report that they have secure employment. A clue to the dynamics comes from the International Survey Research data on worker attitudes in various countries. In almost every country, the proportion of workers expressing satisfaction with employment security was greater than the proportion believing their employment was assured. But the differences were much greater in some countries than in others. In Spain, in 1996 only 21 per cent of workers said they were sure of their employment, whereas 60 per cent said they were satisfied with their employment security; in Mexico, the respective figures were 25 per cent and 67 per cent. In both countries, objective employment security was probably much less than in, say, Sweden where the respective figures on assurance and satisfaction were 39 per cent and 43 per cent, or in Japan where they were 37 per cent and 44 per cent.

These differentials suggest that subjective security reflects expectations linked to labour market and income security. For example, if someone has a one-year contract and realises that unemployment is 20 per cent or that half the labour force is in poverty, he is more likely to be 'satisfied' with his employment security than is someone with a similar contract who sees that most workers are employed or have longer contracts.

An intriguing result from time-series data in Germany is that more people have reported feeling employment insecurity than have reported being worried about it (OECD, 1997b, p. 136). Although this applied to both men and women, the relative lack of concern has been much greater for women. The percentage worried was roughly the same in 1995 as in 1985, but the percentage reporting that they thought there was a chance of losing employment over the next two years was 18 percentage points higher.

So, one should be cautious about attributing too much significance to the subjective indicators of employment insecurity. This is not to suggest that they are unimportant, merely that they are likely to mean a mix of several phenomena. The responses to attitudinal questions do not necessarily point to a widespread loss of employment security or an increasing desire to improve it *per se*.

What about the objective aspects of employment security? A range of indicators could be taken, including *behavioural* indicators (such as labour turnover rates), *contractual* indicators (such as the percentage of workers in regular employment) and *governance* indicators (such as the existence of employment protection legislation and regulations, and the percentage of workers covered by collective agreements providing employment protection).

According to these various indicators, employment security was probably at its greatest in a few industrialised economies in the middle part of the twentieth century. Even then, the image of long-term assured employment with one firm or organisation was for a minority – typically men in full-time 'skilled' jobs.

There are two ways by which employment security has been reduced – *explicit disentitlement* through legislative reforms, and *implicit disentitlement*, associated with a shift of people into statuses and situations in which there has been less protection.

Explicit disentitlement has primarily affected industrialised countries, because regulations and institutional safeguards were most developed there. Since the 1980s, when criticism of protective regulations became so influential, reducing employment protection has become a policy objective. The language of analysis also changed, and became loaded. If one says that employment security means protection from arbitrary dismissal, one is likely to support measures to strengthen employment security. But in the 1980s and 1990s, the tendency has been to present such measures as interfering with 'employers' freedom to dismiss workers' (OECD, 1994a, p. 69).

For instance, in western Europe there have been numerous reforms to roll back protective employment regulations (Saint-Paul, 1996). There and elsewhere, among the explicit measures creating more employment insecurity are:

- Regulations barring certain groups from employment protection, or allowing employers to hire them without giving them such protection. This has been common for young workers, as in Spain.
- Regulations limiting compensation for those laid off.
- Regulations lengthening the period of employment required before protection is provided and regulations reducing the number of weeks of notice required before retrenchment.[1]
- Regulations increasing the conditions required of workers to enable them to have employment protection.
- Tripartite or bipartite national agreements to reduce employment protection and compensation for dismissal in return for something else. Such 'concession bargaining' was a feature of collective agreements in the USA in the 1980s and spread in Europe, a prominent case being the agreement between employers and unions in Spain in April 1997.

There has also been *implicit disentitlement* to employment security associated with the drift to more flexible labour relationships. Globally, there has been a trend towards more insecure, irregular forms of employment, typically involving lower wages, less representation security and fewer social entitlements. More firms have been turning away from reliance wholly or largely on full-time workers to temporary workers, part-time workers, contract labour and out-workers, and have been sub-contracting or using other forms of 'outsourcing'.

This has long been prevalent in East Asian economies, and was one reason for their low social wage, and a contributing factor to their economic dynamism.[2] In recent years, a trend in that direction has become widespread in Europe and other industrialised labour markets. Although some economists and international reports have questioned the trend, Table 6.1 shows how extensive these forms of employment have become. Although data are missing for some countries, and although adding the individual categories is not entirely valid, the final two columns suggest that in most countries about a third of all workers are in non-regular, non-full-time employment. In Spain it may be over half, in Japan and the UK over two in every five. The low figure for temporary employment in the UK reflects the fact that many workers in their first two years have no employment security, and are thus 'temporary' in all but name. The strongest *relative* shift to temporary employment has been in Scandinavia, though there has also been a rise in France, Germany and the UK, and elsewhere. In the 1990s, over three-quarters of those on short-term contracts in EU countries were in full-time employment (Eurostat, 1995, p. 106).

The data in Table 6.1 omit some forms of flexible labour, such as wage-based homeworking and 'networking', in which most workers labour for piece rates without entitlement to social benefits (e.g., Dallago, 1990). There is also anecdotal and case-study evidence that *open-ended employment contracts* have become rarer, implying that employment insecurity and flexibility have increased by more than implied by the statistics on non-regular forms of economic activity. Meanwhile,

Table 6.1 Non-regular forms of employment, selected countries, 1973–96

	Self-Emp. as % of non-agr. emp.		Part time as % of total emp.		Temporary as % of total emp.		Total% Non-Reg.***	
	1973	1996	1973	1996	1973	1996	1973	1996
USA	6.7	8.7[a]	15.6	18.6[a]	n.a.	2.2[b]	(22.3)	(29.5)
Canada	6.2	10.5[a]	9.7	18.6[a]	7.5	8.8[b]	23.4	(37.9)
Australia	9.5	15.6[a]	11.9	24.8[a]	15.6***	23.5[b]	(37.0)	(63.9)
Japan	14.0	12.3[a]	13.9	20.1[a]	10.3	10.3[b]	38.2*	(42.7)
Belgium	11.2	15.4	3.8	11.0	5.4	5.9	20.4*	32.4
France	11.4	11.3	5.9	10.1	3.3	12.6	20.6*	34.0
Germany	9.1	9.6	10.1	15.1	9.9	11.2	29.1*	35.6
Italy	23.1	24.8	6.4	4.5	6.6	7.5	36.1*	36.7
Spain	16.3	21.5	n.a.	7.4	15.6**	33.6	(31.9)	62.5
UK	7.3	12.6	16.0	21.7	5.5	7.1	28.8*	41.3

Source: ILO and OECD.

Note: * This is based on the presumption for illustrative purposes that the 1983 figure for temporary held for 1973, so almost certainly giving an overestimate for 1973.

** For Spain, data for 1987; for Australia, 1984.

*** It is presumed that the part-time category refers to the per cent of regular wage and salaried employment. Many temporary workers would also be part-timers.

Those countries without estimates for temporary employment in one year (or in the case of Spain, part-time employment in 1973) are in parentheses. The data for Germany for 1993 refer to the whole of Germany. In most countries, the percentage in temporary employment refers to the share of paid employees only; in Belgium the share is lowered by being expressed as a share of all those working, including the self-employed.

[a] 1995, [b] 1994

Table 6.2 Per cent temporary employment, by age and gender, industrialised countries, 1983–94

	Total		Men		Women		Aged 16–19 yrs		Aged 20–24 yrs		Aged 25 yrs	
	1983	1994	1983	1994	1983	1994	1983	1994	1983	1994	1983	1994
Australia[1]	15.6	23.5	9.0	17.9	26.2	30.6	29.8	58.7	14.0	26.1	14.0	19.5
Belgium	5.4	5.1	3.8	3.5	8.5	7.5	29.2	38.6	12.9	16.0	3.2	3.6
Canada[2]	7.5	8.8	6.9	9.2	8.2	8.5	13.6	16.7	–	–	6.0	7.3
Denmark	12.5	12.0	12.2	11.1	12.7	12.9	40.1	28.6	25.7	33.1	6.6	7.6
Finland[3]	11.3	13.5	9.3	12.3	13.3	14.7	–	–	–	–	–	–
France	3.3	11.0	3.3	9.7	3.4	12.4	36.5	80.8	5.9	35.0	1.4	7.6
Germany[4]	10.0	10.3	9.0	9.8	11.5	11.0	62.3	74.0	16.9	23.2	3.5	5.9
Greece[5]	16.2	10.3	16.6	10.2	15.4	10.5	33.8	29.6	25.9	20.3	14.0	8.8
Ireland	6.1	9.4	4.7	7.4	8.8	12.1	18.4	32.8	7.2	14.3	3.9	6.8
Italy	6.6	7.3	5.2	6.1	9.4	9.3	15.1	24.0	10.2	14.5	5.6	5.9
Japan[6]	10.3	10.4	5.3	5.4	19.5	18.3	17.0	31.7	8.5	11.8	10.2	9.4
Luxembourg	3.2	2.9	2.2	2.0	5.5	4.4	17.1	28.5	3.5	7.0	1.6	1.7
Netherlands	5.8	10.9	4.1	7.9	9.3	15.0	19.0	40.5	9.9	20.7	4.3	7.4
Portugal[7]	14.4	9.4	13.5	8.5	15.9	10.5	39.8	27.2	28.3	22.7	9.3	6.4
Spain[8]	15.6	33.7	14.4	31.4	18.4	37.9	48.2	87.5	31.6	70.6	11.0	26.5
Sweden	12.0	13.5	9.7	12.3	13.9	14.6	57.0	61.1	26.5	39.5	6.9	9.6
UK	5.5	6.5	4.2	5.5	7.3	7.5	20.4	15.7	5.7	10.1	3.9	5.4
USA[9]	–	2.2	–	2.0	–	2.4	–	8.1	–	5.1	–	1.4

Notes:
1 1984 and 1994. The age group is 15–19.
2 1989 and 1994. The age group is 15–24.
3 1982 and 1993.
4 1984 and 1994. Data refer to western Germany prior to 1992.
5 Due to a definitional change in 1992, the data are not strictly comparable with 1983.
6 The age group is 15 to 19. Data by age refer to non-agricultural industries only.
7 1986 and 1994. Due to definitional change in 1992, the data are not strictly comparable with 1986.
8 1987 and 1994.
9 February 1995.
– Data not available.

173

the part-time share of employment has been rising in every industrialised country for which there are data (OECD, 1995a, p. 17). In the UK, the official Social Trends publication reported that the number of men working part time more than doubled between 1984 and 1997, to 1.3 million, while the number of women part-timers rose from 4.4 to 5.4 million. It also showed there had been a marked rise in temporaries.

Interpreting data on non-regular forms of employment is difficult because of the widely reported use of classifications by firms themselves as a means of putting workers in more insecure positions and as a means of increasing employment flexibility. For instance, over 40 per cent of all workers in Japan are in non-regular forms of employment. A survey suggested that just over one in every four of those in wage employment in a cross-section of industries were in such statuses (Table 6.3). However, many so-called 'part-time' workers actually work full time and are only classified as part-timers so as to be paid less and be denied employment rights (Takahashi, 1997, p. 61). Flexibility for firms comes at the expense of workers' security – and statistical misclassification.

Beyond such difficulties in the data, flexibility has made the old norm of employment security a minority phenomenon. To give an example: in Canada, only about one in three workers have a regular full-time job (Figure 6.1). Flexible 'atypical' employment has become the norm, and the shift to such arrangements has been due primarily to employer preferences, not those of workers (Lipsett and Ressor, 1997).

All these figures imply growing employment insecurity, since in most countries workers in 'non-standard' forms of employment are not covered by employment protection, or are not covered to the same extent as those in regular, full-time jobs. Few have access to enterprise-based, or even state, benefits, and even where legislation has provided for equal treatment for part-timers, it is doubtful whether the reality is equal treatment, if only because they are relatively unlikely to build up the continuity of employment that provides enhanced benefits.

The growth of *employment flexibility* implies that the labour market is spreading employment insecurity, through forms of casualisation. A prominent case of an *explicit* policy to weaken protection is Spain, where the perception of high non-wage labour costs for full-time regular workers led the government in 1980 to permit part-time contracts with less employment protection, resulting in a growing dualism in employment security, as well as a tendency for youth to be laid off first because they were concentrated in unprotected contracts.

Less appreciated as a means of extending employment insecurity has been the 'active' labour market policy of 'guaranteeing' the long-term unemployed *temporary* jobs, as in the Australian Government's *Jobs Compact* programme of 1994–96, for example. There has been extensive debate about the substitution effects of such schemes, but little analysis of their impact on the character of employment security. They help to legitimise temporary employment arrangements.

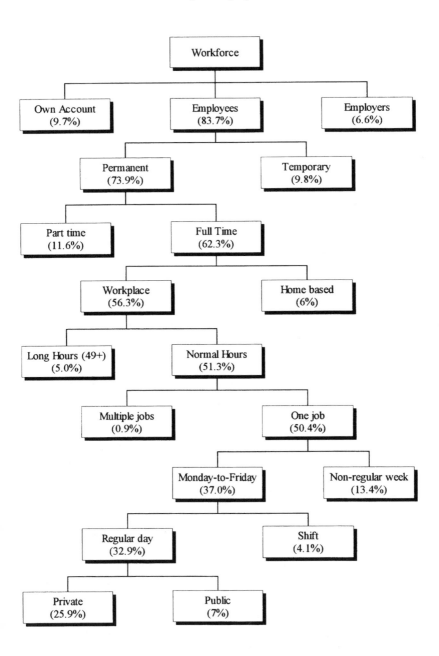

Figure 6.1 Distribution of Canadian employment, by work status, 1995

Source: Human Resources Development Canada, *1995 Survey of Work Arrangements*

The Rocks of Insecurity

Table 6.3 Percentage of non-regular workers, by industry and gender,
Japan, 1994 *(percentage of employment)*

	Total	Transferred Worker	Agency Worker	Part-time Worker	Temp. and Day Worker	Others
Industries covered	22.8	1.4	0.7	13.7	4.4	2.7
Mining	9.2	2.0	0.2	1.5	3.0	2.4
Construction	22.5	1.1	0.4	1.3	16.3	3.4
Manufacturing	15.9	1.1	0.5	10.8	2.3	1.2
Electricity, gas, energy and water	9.2	1.5	0.2	1.4	1.2	4.9
Transport and communication	10.0	1.5	0.5	3.2	2.6	2.1
Wholesale, retail trade, catering	35.7	1.1	0.6	28.5	2.6	3.0
Finance and insurance	12.3	0.8	3.6	3.4	0.6	3.9
Real estate	18.2	4.7	0.6	8.8	1.1	3.0
Services	25.9	2.0	0.8	13.6	5.4	4.1
Men	13.1	1.9	0.4	4.4	3.9	2.4
Women	38.6	0.5	1.2	28.6	5.1	3.2

Source: Japanese Ministry of Labour, *General Survey on Diversified Types of Employment* (Tokyo,1994).

As with labour market security, employment security is both a general and a distributional issue. In the post-war era, it was concentrated among male full-time workers, with women given scant attention. Latterly, employers wanting more employment flexibility have turned more to women, and as female employment has grown, there has been a partial convergence in experience of insecurity. For instance, in the UK, between mid-1993 and mid-1996, women gained 85,000 full-time jobs, while men gained 42,000; by contrast, men took 70,000 part-time jobs, whereas women took 69,000. Usually part-time jobs have less employment security.

So, the spread of more flexible forms of labour has, almost definitionally, increased employment insecurity. Another standard indicator of employment security is average *duration of employment*. This is not ideal, since short duration could reflect voluntary mobility or the ability of firms to make workers redundant at will. Nevertheless, many believe that long duration indicates employment security.

Two measures of duration are the *median average duration of employment* and the *percentage with short-term employment tenures*. These vary considerably across the world. The trouble with the former is that most data refer to incomplete spells of employment, and the average is likely to drop if employment is growing and if a rising proportion of the employed are older workers. So increasing average tenure could simply reflect a slowdown in employment growth.

For what the data are worth, among industrialised countries the mean average is relatively low in Australia, the USA and the UK and is still relatively high in eastern Europe. But in most countries the average has been modest, while the trends are unclear. Table 6.4 shows mean averages in a few industrialised countries for the early 1990s. According to assessments by the OECD, in 1995, the average rose in Finland, France, Japan and the USA, and fell in Germany (for men, although it rose marginally for women), Spain and the UK (for men, although it was up for women). One would expect that in a period of stagnant employment, the average (incomplete) duration would rise. So, any fall might be interpreted as indicating an increase in employment insecurity. As it is, between 1985 and 1995 average tenure rose in 7 out of the 10 industrialised countries for which data are available, was unchanged in the USA, and fell in the UK and Spain.[3]

Table 6.4 Average employment tenure, industrialised countries, 1995 *(in years)*

Countries	Mean	Median[a]	Countries	Mean	Median[a]
Australia[b]	6.4	3.4	Japan[e]	11.3	8.3
Austria	10.0	6.9	Korea[f]	8.7	2.5
Belgium	11.2	8.4	Luxembourg	10.2	7.2
Canada	7.9	5.9	Netherlands	8.7	5.5
Czech Republic	9.0	2.0	Poland	17.5	17.0
Denmark	7.9	4.4	Portugal	11.0	7.7
Finland	10.5	7.8	Spain	8.9	4.6
France	10.7	7.7	Sweden	10.5	7.8
Germany	9.7	10.7	Switzerland	9.0	6.0
Greece	9.9	7.5	United Kingdom	7.8	5.0
Ireland	8.7	5.3	United States[b, i]	7.4	4.2
Italy	11.6	8.9			
			Unweighted average	9.8	6.7
			Standard deviation	2.2	3.1
			Coefficient of variation (%)	22.0	46.0

Note: [a] The median is calculated by taking the tenure class into which the middle observation falls and assuming that observations are evenly distributed by tenure within this class.[b] 1996.[c] 6 months or less; 7–12 months; 1–5 years; 5 years or less; 6–10 years; 11–20 years; over 20 years.[e] Less than year; 1–2 years; 3–4 years; 0–4 years; 5–9 years; 10–14 years; 15–19 years; 20 years or more.[f] 1992.[g] 1 to under 3 years; 3 to under 5 years.[h] Under 1 year.[i] Under 6 months; 6–12 months; 13 months to 23 months; 2 years to under 5 years; under 5 years; 5 years to under 10 years; 10 years to under 15 years; 15 years to under 20 years; 20 years or more.

Sources: Data for Austria, Belgium, Denmark, Finland, France, Germany, Greece, Ireland, Italy, Luxembourg, the Netherlands, Portugal, Spain, Sweden and the United Kingdom come from unpublished data provided by *Eurostat* on the basis of the European Community Labour Force Survey. For data for Australia, Canada, the Czech Republic, Japan, Korea, Poland, Switzerland and the United States, see Annex 5.A, OECD, *Employment Outlook* (Paris, OECD, July 1997), p. 138.

If one focuses on the share of workers in short-term employment, a very high share of employment in the USA has consisted of workers in jobs for less than a year (Table 6.5). By contrast, only 9.8 per cent of workers were in that situation in Japan, where employment has continued to be characterised as having a relatively high proportion of workers in long-tenure employment and a relatively high average tenure. However, both the proportion in long-term employment and the average tenure are much less than conveyed by those depicting Japanese employment as consisting of 'life-time' employment. Such security seems largely reserved for 'white-collar' employees of large firms (Table 6.6).

Table 6.5 Employment tenure, industrialised countries, c.1992

Country	Average stay in a specific employment in years	% in a specific employment for less than one year
Austria	–	13.8
Finland	9.0	11.9
France	10.1	15.7
Germany*	10.4	12.8
Netherlands	7.0	24.0
Norway	9.4	14.9
Spain	9.8	23.9
Switzerland	8.8	17.6
UK	7.9	18.6
Japan	10.9	9.8
USA	6.7	28.8

Source: OECD, *Employment Outlook, 1993* (Paris, OECD, 1993).
Note: * Unified Germany

Table 6.6 Per cent of employed men with specified tenure, by size of enterprise and educational background, Japan, 1994

Size of firm (employees):	1000+	100–999	10–99
% with upper secondary school having 25+ years of tenure	82.3	48.7	22.8
% with college or university having 20+ years of tenure	91.4	74.1	44.9

Source: Ministry of Labour, *Basic Survey on Wage Structure* (Tokyo, 1994).

In some countries, the *median* tenure has been falling. Again, this is a distributional issue, and growth of employment insecurity may be concealed by the differential experience of men and women. For example, according to the UK's Employment Policy Institute, in the UK between 1986 and 1996 the average duration of a job for women rose by eight months, while for men it fell by eight months. To interpret those data as implying there had been no change would be wrong. Since men still comprised a majority, the net change was downward.

Short-term employment is also cited as an indicator of employment insecurity. This encompasses those in short-term contracts, those with contracts without employment protection, and high turnover among the employed. One could have a large number in temporary jobs but with low turnover, or vice versa. But turnover statistics are as difficult to interpret as tenure statistics. One indicator used is the 'five year retention rate', i.e., the percentage of workers in the same employment five years later. Among industrialised countries with data, this has been highest in Japan (over 60 per cent) and lowest in Australia (about 40 per cent). Between 1985–90 and 1990–95, it rose in Australia and Canada, but fell in Finland, France, Germany, Japan, Spain and (probably) the USA. The OECD (1997b) concluded that 'the overall picture is of fairly stable average tenure and retention rates'. However, the declines were more significant than any rises. The big decline in the retention rate in the USA occurred in the mid-1980s, which was followed by a modest fall in the early 1990s. The decline in the retention rate in Spain was probably the greatest, although the fall in France and Germany scarcely warranted the term 'stable'.

Some other puzzling developments emerge from available data. In a few countries, such as France, newly recruited workers have experienced a declining retention rate whereas those in employment for five years or more have experienced a rising retention rate. The opposite has been the case in Japan. France has emerged as the most dualistic labour market in terms of retention, in which the retention rate of newly recruited workers is the lowest and those of longer-term employed the highest.

In most countries, *manual workers* have had lower retention rates than others, but in some there has been little difference (e.g., Canada), while in Germany 'white collar' workers have experienced rising retention rates at the same time as 'blue collar' workers have experienced a sharp decline. In the USA, those in lower-wage jobs experienced a decline in retention, or employment stability, while those in white-collar jobs may have experienced increased stability (Diebold et al., 1997).

Women have experienced increasing retention rates in Australia, Canada, Germany, Japan and the UK, but have experienced declines in Finland, France, Spain and the USA. Men's retention rates have risen in Australia and Canada but have fallen in other countries. *Young workers* have not experienced any notable change. Workers with more *schooling* have usually had higher retention rates, but there is insufficient evidence to identify a general trend.[4] One is not sure what it would mean if there were. In short, the retention rate is not a good indicator of employment security. In a period of growing insecurity, fear could induce more people to hold on to jobs, whereas in a time of improving security they might be more prepared to take risks.

Short-term employment turnover is another indicator of employment security. One analysis proposed the following measure of short-term turnover:

$$[(E_{1<3} - E_{3-6})/ E_{1<3})\ 100\ ]$$

where $E_{1<3}$ is the number of workers who have been currently employed for less than three months, and E_{3-6} is the number employed for between three and six months (Gregg and Wadsworth, 1995). The OECD (1997a) regarded this as an indicator of employment security. However, the ratio will depend on the hiring rate. If this rises in one quarter relative to the previous quarter, the measured turnover rate will go down, other things equal. This means the ratio would be misleading, since one would expect a rise in the hiring rate to increase the sense of employment security. The suggestion is that the ratio represents a measure of 'unsuccessful matching' of workers and jobs, and that this is high in many countries. The term 'unsuccessful' implies an inefficient hiring (and firing?) process. But it might be the reverse, since a flexible labour market might reallocate workers to where there is demand for their labour. Workers hired for the harvest are hired for a short period; their departure at the end of the season is scarcely indicative of mismatch. Workers hired as guides or cooks for the tourist season are hardly mismatched if they return to studying when the sun loses its strength.

Another indicator of employment security is the *rate of employment loss*. This has attracted much comment and analysis in the USA, where the rate long followed a cyclical pattern of rising in recessions and falling in expansions. However, the data suggest that in the 1990s, during a sustained upturn and tightening labour market, the rate of employment loss did not decline and may have increased (Farber, 1997; 1998). It increased most for older, more experienced workers (Neumark et al., 1998). The greater employment loss implies an increase in employment insecurity. And, given the changes in the design of the CPS used to measure job loss, the rate may have been underestimated in the later period.[5]

Among the reasons for a rising employment loss rate may be the impact of actual and prospective imports. Research suggests that because wages have been less flexible than employment (the elasticity of industrial wages with respect to import prices being less than the employment elasticity), a trade shock causes industrial adjustment primarily through employment (Revenga, 1992; Kletzer, 1998). Since globalisation has increased trade, this could have increased the employment loss rate.

Another indicator of employment insecurity is the proportion of the employed who are searching for another job because they believe their employment is at risk. There has been a rise in the share of the employed looking for alternative employment. This may indeed reflect growing risk of employment loss, possibly because of reduced employment protection or because wage and employment flexibility have increased, such that it has become easier, less costly and more beneficial for firms to displace higher-paid, longer-duration workers, or threaten them with displacement.

The trouble is that job searching by the employed could reflect either *employment* or *job* insecurity, or the interpretation of the reasons could be misleading. It is not clear that job searching would increase if employment insecurity increased, particularly if there were a *generalised* increase in employment insecurity, perhaps due to a legislative change or a change of government. Another interpretation of the rise in the employed's job searching propensity could be the realisation that if they became unemployed they would face more income insecurity.

This section has concentrated on subjective and objective trends in employment security in 'western' industrialised countries. Stronger declines surely characterise the chaotic labour markets of eastern and central Europe, as a result of casualisation, out-sourcing and an extraordinary growth of informal activities, often undertaken to avoid tax and social security contributions, as well as the economic depression, enterprise restructuring and privatisation. In industrialising countries, it has always been pervasive, made the more so by the spread of informalisation and flexible employment relations in the industrial and public and private service sectors of the economy. In Bombay, we found that firms were increasing employment insecurity by *increasing* their use of informal labour (Deshpande et al., 1998). We found similar trends in modern firms in the Philippines and Malaysia. In the era of statutory regulation it was presumed that the long-term trend would be towards the pattern of employment security found in industrialised economies. That has been arrested in many countries, often involving *explicit disentitlement* policies introduced as part of structural adjustment programmes, involving a weakening of employment protection regulations. For instance, as part of its IMF-inspired Economic Structural Adjustment Programme (1990), the Government of Zimbabwe abandoned procedures to limit and regulate retrenchments. The previous regulations were described by a World Bank study as 'among the most onerous prescribed anywhere'(Fallon and Lucas, 1993, p. 242). That was harsh since, although the law required employers to apply to a tripartite Retrenchment Committee if they wished to make redundancies, about 38 per cent of all such applications were approved, and on average the process took three months from application to decision (Shadur, 1994, p. 152).

Employment security is almost definitionally less in *informal activities*. There has been much romanticising of the 'informal sector', a term to be avoided.[6] However, if there is shift of employment from large-scale public and private enterprises to small private firms and own-account activities, employment insecurity is almost certain to increase. This is an instance of *implicit* erosion of security, in that it arises from structural changes rather than from changes in labour regulations, although the latter may also exist. The growth of informal activity represents more insecurity not just for those working informally but for others in mainstream employment. It is hard to demand employment security when a growing number of others do not have it.

One problem with tracing employment security is that most available data are methodologically questionable. For instance, *security* could decline even if employment stability or average employment tenure did not. This could arise if employment contracts were shortened or made more insecure or more vague, or if the probability of employment termination due to lay-offs, plant closure, dismissal or contract termination rose relative to the more voluntary reasons for departure from employment. The latter has occurred in the USA (see, e.g., Boisjoly et al., 1994; Farber, 1996). The increase in involuntary employment separation has been particularly marked for older and more-tenured workers (Polsky, 1996). The trend underlines the point that we should be cautious about treating employment duration figures as indicative of employment security.

There are also methodological reasons for supposing that employment insecurity has increased more than it seems. For instance, surveys may treat agency or contingency workers inappropriately. Suppose someone is allocated to temporary jobs through an employment agency, a growing practice. The person may be classified as having a high degree of employment insecurity or the reverse, depending on whether the situation is interpreted, by the person or the questionnaire, as employment with the agency. If one is interested in the character of the labour market, treating the 'permanent temporary' or 'flexiworker' as having employment security would be misleading. And even if the worker had an arrangement with the employment agency, that should scarcely count as employment security in the proper sense of the term.

Another problem concerns the notion of *continuity* of employment. A person may do a seasonal job for a firm then have a break for lack of work, then return. If asked how long he has been with the firm, he may say some years, but in reality he has been in and out of employment. This is relevant for assessing US data, because the questionnaires used to monitor employment security dropped the word 'continuously' in 1995. This gave an upward bias to employment tenure.

Decentralisation of employment and wage bargaining may also have accentuated perceived and actual employment insecurity. It may not be coincidence that workers in countries with decentralised bargaining systems are more likely to report employment insecurity (OECD, 1997b, p. 150). A lack of national or sectoral labour market anchors may increase feelings of insecurity, which may not be connected with actual employment security. Decentralised systems also allow local firms to operate practices that suit their needs and local labour market realities, rather than according to national (or international) norms.

Labour market and income insecurity could induce employment insecurity in several ways. Three relevant trends have emerged:

- in industrialised countries, at least, employment separation has been increasingly likely to lead to joblessness;
- for those who become jobless, employment separation has been associated with increasing duration of joblessness;
- for those who find a job, employment separation is increasingly likely to be followed by a job with a lower income. One reason may be that entry-level

wages have fallen relative to average wages, as in the UK. (Gregg and Wadsworth, 1996)

All of these reflect labour market and income insecurity, even though employment insecurity may be a symptom of them. The questions they prompt are: if policymakers wish to reduce worker insecurity, should they focus on improving employment security *directly*? Or should they try to improve it *indirectly* by tackling its causes? Or should they tackle the insecurity by trying to lower the costs of such insecurity? Or should they not be bothered unduly?

Employment security is being abandoned in many spheres. A survey by the US Conference Board (1997) of US and European firms found that two-thirds had abandoned an explicit or implicit bargain with employees by which they had guaranteed employment in return for loyalty, and a further quarter reported that such a bargain had never been part of their labour relations. Only 6 per cent of all firms were operating the paternalistic relationship. In the 1980s, according to the report, managers and employees commonly denied that employment security was being undermined, and this had led to a lack of trust when downsizing and other changes proved the implicit bargain was false. Now they more freely admit that they do not provide such security.

In sum, the objective of employment security has receded, both in terms of the extent of security deemed appropriate by policymakers and the proportion of the workers expecting to have it. Reasons include fears associated with unemployment and labour market insecurity, the reduced prospects of re-employment for those losing employment, knowledge that more people have such insecurity because of their labour status, informalisation of economic activity, explicit erosion of protective regulations and greater income insecurity due to the lower probability of acquiring an equivalent replacement income, whether in employment or from income transfers. With respect to that, workers in countries with relatively high unemployment benefits have been less inclined to report employment insecurity.

Should employment security be strengthened? The arguments for and against it can be summarised as follows. For employers, offering employment security has been a means of securing workers' loyalty, a high effort bargain, and a willingness to accept *job insecurity* (considered in the next section). *It has been a mechanism of labour control.* On the negative side, it is more costly to reduce employment if workers must be given notice and compensation for abrogation of employment commitments.

For society, one rationale for employment security is that firms making workers redundant impose costs on the community, and in *effect* raise taxes for other firms and workers if the state provides unemployment benefits. This is a reason for mandatory plant-closing notification by firms, and is why it is a mistake to concentrate just on the needs of firms or workers, which is after all a reason for statutory regulations.

For workers, on the positive side, it has a welfare value in a context of labour market and income insecurity. On the negative side, it can induce *employment dependency*, or passivity and lack of mobility, a sense of being held to jobs that are deskilling or failing to offer the opportunity to develop skills and occupational achievement. *Employment security is a polarising labour market variable.* Many workers have very short-term jobs and some long-term jobs, so that the average looks reasonably long. But the benefits of the long tenure detaches the privileged from the larger number of short-tenure workers. The debate on the increase of employment insecurity can be exaggerated. Employment security has never been strong for the majority. This must be so because most firms have shorter 'lives' than the expected working life of the typical worker. It may not be coincidental that the debate became topical when the public sector started to downsize, when large firms became more like others in their employment policies, and when more people were being put on short employment contracts, though they might stay in the same employment for longer.

For workers, employment security is surely an instrumental objective, in that most want it for what is associated with it, and would probably be prepared to lower it, or even dispense with it altogether, if they had income security and other forms of security. If a flexible labour market is essential economically, and if employment protection is an impediment to flexibility, then as long as other forms of security are provided, employment security is surely a tradable right.

6.3 JOB INSECURITY

Job security is often mixed up with employment security, but one could have one without the other. Job security arises from the existence of institutions, regulations and practices that enable people to obtain and retain a niche and to pursue an occupation or 'career'. In the post-war era, this meant acceptance and legitimation of practices of job demarcation, erection of barriers to skill dilution, craft boundaries, codes of job qualifications, restrictive practices, and entrenchment of some craft unions. Job security can be interpreted as a system of defence against the development of the technical division of labour, often through measures preserving a specific social division of labour, or segmentation process.

In the craft model of work, privileged groups had control over their jobs, and employers (if they were not the craftsmen themselves) were under pressure to abide by time-honoured structures and division of tasks. In the industrial model, employers typically gained control over job descriptions and the technical division of labour. This reached its apogee in the Tayloristic job structures that spread around the world in the twentieth century. However, trade union and social democratic strategy was to defend job barriers, so entrenching job descriptions, demarcation procedures and so on. This became a rigidity, and in the 1980s and 1990s firms and sympathetic governments have wished to dismantle job boundaries, while unions have often lacked the power to prevent them. Functional flexibility represents a form of job insecurity.

A refrain in the 1980s and 1990s has been that workers must be more flexible in terms of skill and expect to change tasks more often. The image of 'flexible specialisation' may appeal to those who anticipate a working life of variety and autonomy. But for many people skill flexibility offers the prospect of job insecurity, necessitating the repeated learning of 'new tricks' or the prospect of failing to remain in the economic mainsteam. It is not frequent career changes that beckon but frequent job changes; a career remains the prerogative of an elite.

By the end of the 1980s, according to the US Department of Labour, the average worker could expect to hold five jobs over his working life in two or three different occupational areas (Kleiman, 1990). More educated workers could expect more changes than other groups. One unidentified researcher concluded,

> The career-oriented college graduate today will hold 10 to 12 jobs in more than one industry before retiring. The normal stay of a graduate in one company will average around three or four years. One in five persons now changes jobs every year; one in ten changes careers.

Although this mixes employment and job security, if such mobility involves a steady expansion of knowledge and valued experience, well and good. If it involves a turbulent search for a sense of personal stability, the portents are less enticing. Another study concluded that career advancement had become less predictable, compensation increases less routine, and insecure jobs more common (Doeringer et al., 1991). By the late 1980s, one-third of all male manufacturing workers were ending their 'career jobs' by the age of 55, leaving them to rely on 'bridging jobs' – involving substantial cuts in earnings – before moving into retirement. Collective bargaining has not helped. According to a report by the AFL-CIO in 1993, 99 per cent of union contracts contain a 'management rights' clause that reserves the right of management to make organisation change. And technological change is not a mandatory subject of collective bargaining under US labour law.

With less job and career stability, firms may turn more to workers with different behavioural characteristics than if they wanted employment stability. This may alter the patterning of labour market advantage, perhaps contributing to feminisation and the marginalisation of older workers. In recruiting, firms increasingly screen on the basis of adaptability, communication and inter-personal skills (see, e.g., Economic Council of Canada, 1993). One feature is that there is a polarisation, with more workers having partial skills. In Canada, for instance, although so-called skilled jobs comprised 77 per cent of employment growth in the mid-1980s compared with a third in the earlier period, the skill distribution of employment became more polarised, the suggestion being that in services there are fewer 'intermediate skills' than in manufacturing.

For much of the twentieth century, job security and employment security, rather than occupational security, were defended. A feature of Tayloristic and bureaucratic control systems was that workers in effect conceded occupational security in return for employment security. Then unions defended job boundaries, but did so mainly for traditional manual jobs. As large firms and organisations set patterns, notions of skill and job became more nebulous.

Large organisations and bureaucratic control systems deskill many jobs and members of many firms, because people are assimilated into the culture of the organisation and adapt to the administrative appeal of organisational mobility. Perversely, employment security may lead to *career deskilling*. This happens to some occupations more than to others. Engineers apparently are prone to *upgrading-deskilling* through moving into management or administrative positions, and losing touch with their specialist skills. One should not focus exclusively on the Tayloristic mechanisms of deskilling. Organisational upward mobility – often with the objective of giving individuals an organisational career and to create organisational skills – is perhaps a major source of deskilling. It is an end-of-century norm for employees in mid-career to confess to having been deskilled through their job. This is not just because of the pace of knowledge and technological change, but because many have to perform a growing range of administrative tasks that prevent or discourage them from using the technical skills by which they define themselves. Deskilling-by-promotion should receive more attention, and when considering 'structural unemployment' one should also consider 'structural mal-employment'.

The drift from regular, full-time employment has also weakened job security. Part-timers are often 'dead-ended' in jobs, with little access to training or promotion, unlikely to gain the skills or credentials needed to advance in an occupation. Job insecurity also implies more labour market risk and uncertainty, with more scope to fall out of the economic mainstream. A society in which most obtain a niche at an early age and remain in one until retirement requires and generates a different network of social support from one in which changes in jobs and labour force status are a recurring, uncertain part of lifetime activity.

6.4 WORK INSECURITY

This refers to secure and reasonably safe working conditions, encompassing safety and health and the working environment. In the post-war era, it meant statutory protection of health and safety in the workplace, coupled with strong voice regulation in large firms, with the onus of proof of safety placed on employers. The state was expected to play a role in ensuring access to medical services and in regulating working relations so that workers had protection against risk of injury and illness and against risk of not receiving treatment. In most economies, trade unions played an important role in regulating working conditions, and it is a feature of large-scale stable enterprises that formal procedures and mechanisms can exist to monitor practices and impose sanctions on firms that do not provide work security.

Since then, there has been *implicit* and *explicit* erosion of work security. It would be wrong to claim that the record has been entirely negative, since there seems to have been an international trend to lower levels of accidents and occupational diseases.The number injured in work-related accidents per 100,000 insured or employed has declined in the 1990s in the EU, and has fallen in central Europe (WHO, 1996). But the latter reflects the slump in industrial production and shift from heavy industry into services. To some extent, declines elsewhere have been due to industrial and technological change, rather than to changes in work security. And there has been growth of new types of adverse symptoms.

In some countries, there has been explicit erosion of work security because of cuts in statutory forms of regulation and the shift to 'self regulation'. Implicit erosion has arisen because of the spread of forms of labour traditionally less protected or less easily protected. Establishing adequate procedures in small firms is relatively hard, and ensuring that contract workers and other out-workers have adequate safety and access to mechanisms to limit work insecurity is harder than for those in regular wage labour.

With more flexible production, with numerous smaller firms, with lower levels of trade unionism and with an ethos regarding statutory regulations as labour costs, the pressure on firms to provide work security has been reduced. Most worrying has been the virtual collapse of safety and health committees in many factories in countries of the former Soviet Union, as we observed in several enterprise surveys.

In general, with more labour market insecurity and non-regular labour, the threat to occupational safety and health may rise because safeguards do not cover some categories and because their weak bargaining position induces them to accept more onerous or risky work. A WHO report (1990) concluded that as a result of flex-ibilisation of labour contracts there had been a substantial increase in work-related accidents, most notably among the self-employed in the construction industry.

Shadow work, or undeclared employment, definitionally entails lack of entitlement to health or disability insurance, and has also been associated with more exposure to toxic substances and related dangers. In the USA and elsewhere, part-time workers are also less likely to be covered by health insurance than full-time workers (US General Accounting Office, 1991, Appendix III). Teleworking also brings work security risks. Among these are onerous conditions imposed in offshore information processing in developing countries, where jobs have involved long unsocial hours, health hazards and low wages (Soares, 1991; Huws, 1996). In general, there is mounting evidence that teleworking brings stress and insecurity because of the social isolation of the work.

Work security could also be expected to accompany erosion of representation security. In the UK, the TUC has reported that injury rates are twice as high in firms where there is no union–employer safety committee as where there is one (MacErlean, 1998). In the USA, work-related fatalities have been much higher in 'right-to-work' states, where unions have been prevented from pressing collective safety demands as effectively as in other states (AFL-CIO, 1989). The problem extends to the basic right to go to the toilet, which many workers do not have, and which can cause illness and penalties. A toilet break is not a general right under Federal law or under the law of most states. Firms often argue that giving such a right would encourage shirking and loss of managerial control. Over 40 per cent of collective agreements did not include a right to a rest period, and in non-union plants the pattern was worse (Linder and Nygaard, 1998).

In industrialised countries, another cause of increasing work insecurity is the pressure to find alternative ways of funding healthcare. Expenditure on health services has risen to over 8 per cent of GDP on average, double what it was in 1960 (OECD, March 1995, p. 49). This has led to reforms to shift part of the cost from employers and the state to workers. This has been a particularly powerful trend in eastern Europe.

Explicit erosion of work security may have been increased by reforms to make working time more flexible and to weaken protective regulations. This has meant that firms have been able to adjust working time to suit their needs, rather than the workers' desire for a stable or predictable schedule. More workers are obliged to work long shifts or 'unsocial hours', causing physical and medical problems. Japan may have led the way in this, where *workaholism* has been a spreading phenomenon. There is even an illness known as *karoshi*, death from overwork, which in recent years may have claimed 10,000 lives a year.[7] In Europe, and probably elsewhere, a new sickness has mocked the jobholder society – *presenteeism*, instead of *absenteeism*. Insurance companies, doctors and others are reporting that workers are doggedly turning up to their job even if unfit or ill, for fear of losing their job. As a consequence more people with minor illnesses are becoming seriously ill, and then needing *longer* to recuperate or are losing their jobs. Little research seems to have been done on this, which reflects a bias of the age. But in Switzerland, it has been reported that *presenteeism* has been associated with a decline in the number of spells of absenteeism but, according to health insurance companies, the average duration of sick leave has increased (*L'Hebdo*, 1998).

One indicator of overwork is the proportion of workers with long workweeks. The average can be misleading. In industrialised countries, there has been some polarisation, with a growth of part-time working coupled with a growth in the number working long hours. In the UK, according to the official *Social Trends*, in 1996 full-time workers had longer average workweeks than in 1986, and men's average workweek was 45.8 hours compared with 44.5 in April 1978. On average, women in full-time jobs had experienced an increase from 37.5 to 40.6 hours. High-status, high-income groups experienced the greatest increase. In 1996, the longest *average* workweeks were those of full-time managers and administrators (48.4 hours), the lowest those of clerical and secretarial workers (41.8 hours). In 1995, 61 per cent of workers said they worked at least some time on Saturdays and 41 per cent did so on Sundays. That is not unusual. In western Europe, as shown in chapter 4, working in jobs on Saturdays and Sundays and at night became more common in the 1990s.

Work insecurity may have grown for 'white-collar' employees, who are expected to work long workweeks and in many cases *must* do so to keep up with competitor workers, and remain attractive enough to retain their 'employability' with their employers, merely to maintain adequate knowledge. A US survey found that nine out of every ten top managers worked more than 10 hours a day, 18 per cent worked 12 or more hours, and over nine in every ten did some work at the weekend as well (Kantor, 1989, p. 268). Non-managerial 'white collar' employees in the 1990s were working the equivalent of four weeks a year more than their equivalents in 1970, reflecting what Juliet Schor (1991) has called 'a shrinkage of leisure'. Ironically, increased *labour intensity* has coincided with high unemployment and a spread of part-time jobs. Stemming from this is *burn out*, the inability of those working with great intensity to sustain the pace after a few years.

Stress-related illnesses have increased. There is ample evidence that much of it is real, but part of the reason is that more have been recognised and legitimated as illnesses, with more being covered by medical insurance, and recognised by healthcare providers, firms, and insurance companies and by workers themselves. Some have become sources of profits for insurance companies, and to some extent have become sources of moral hazard, inducing people to classify themselves as sufferers.

In the USA, a survey by Princeton Research Associates in July 1997 found that 73 per cent of workers said they experienced more stress at work than they had 20 years earlier, and 59 per cent said that they had to work harder. In the UK, a survey by the Institute of Management found that 77 per cent of managers considered the amount of time they had to devote to their job was stressful and were worried about the impact on their family. It has been estimated that stress-related illness and absenteeism cost 10 per cent of GDP in the UK, 2.5 per cent in Denmark and 10 per cent in Norway; and that about half of the working days lost to absenteeism in the USA are stress-related (Cooper et al., 1996). According to a survey by the Massachusetts Institute of Technology cited by Handy (1998, p. 18), labour-related depression cost the US economy $47 billion a year. Among occupational psychologists, there is a consensus that the primary cause of stress in work is lack of control over one's situation. An atmosphere of insecurity induces stress that feeds back into labour costs, and distorts rational pursuit of occupation.

Work insecurity may be linked to employment and job security in complex ways. If workers feel 'overskilled' for their jobs, or frustrated by the control structure, they may develop a sense of inequity and react with disruptive performance or show psychological distress and lower tolerance of other stressors. Similarly, workers of all types may suffer from 'golden handcuffs' due to employment security, in which fear of changing jobs results in a self-imposed limitation on pursuit of a 'career' or occupation, creating years of stress. Flexiworkers may also suffer from career stress.

Work insecurity overlaps with income insecurity. For example, a declining proportion of US workers have been covered by employer health plans (Committee for Economic Development, 1996). Losing a job in such circumstances becomes disastrous, for the person and his or her family, especially if falling ill while in a job results in a rundown of savings or an accumulation of debt incurred to meet medical bills. In the UK, firms apparently have responded to pressure to cut non-wage labour costs by selecting for redundancy workers with poor sick records (*Observer*, 8 June 1997).

A survey of civil service workers in the UK found that those in low-grade positions with little control over responsibilities had a 50 per cent higher probability of developing symptoms of heart disease than those in higher-level jobs with greater autonomy.[8] The conclusion was that boring and repetitive jobs induced heart disease. This prompts questions about the advisability of pursuing labour market security through low-level jobs. It also prompts the view that greater personal control, and worker-determined flexibility, would improve health status and that the unequal situation of people in terms of jobs contributes to broader forms of social injustice.

So powerful is the labouring ethic that loss of employment becomes psychologically unbearable. Every recession induces a sharp rise in suicides, usually concentrated among those with relatively high incomes, wealth and status. In Japan during the recession of 1997 suicides rose by 16 per cent. The link between job stress and suicides has been taken to extremes in the former Soviet Union, where suicides among young men almost doubled in the 1990s, largely attributable to the stress of adjusting to new forms of employment (Standing, 1998).

In modern industrialised economies, it is almost as if the labouring ethic has imprisoned or drugged people. The job becomes a commitment, while home is a distraction to be avoided as much as possible, a place where 'chores' (work) must be done as quickly as possible (Hochschild, 1997). Work at home has become perceived as constraining labour in the job, rather than part of leisure. The result is that families try to 'outsource' family work, such as childcare, housework and gardening. Parenthood-outsourcing is a reflection of labour market flexibility.

Stress and self-destruction are consequences of giving labour excessive priority, coupled with the market regulation that removes vital checks on self-exploitation as well as other forms of pressure on individuals to labour. So, while some forms of work security may be improving, in some parts of the world at least, 'modern' forms of work insecurity may be an ultimate reflection on the century of the labouring man. Humanity will have to reduce the pressure.

6.5 LABOUR/SKILL REPRODUCTION INSECURITY

Workers of the world compete!
            Percy Barnevik[9]

Labour reproduction security covers basic rights to form families, access to primary and secondary schooling, access to basic health services, and provision of training opportunities to develop skills required in order to become good labourers. For welfare and economic reasons, in the post-war era, progress in this was considerable, although there were negative features, including the different treatment accorded to young men and women, and a tendency to forget differences between education and schooling, and between craftsmanship and training. In English, schooling has two meanings, one associated with learning and the acquisition of knowledge, the other with discipline. One schools a horse. In the nineteenth century, mass schooling was perceived by ruling elites as a disciplining device, and in many places this view has persisted through the twentieth century.

For the most part we need to go to institutions to learn. But indicators such as years of schooling or 'functional literacy' should be regarded with caution. The glorification of schooling is a twentieth-century fetish: if one fails in life it is because one has not had sufficient schooling. Yet perhaps it is intellectual arrogance for middle-class observers to deplore working-class drop-outs from school. That commonly stems from poverty, but it may, just may, be a sign of human development, rejecting an unpleasant and unuseful reality. Similarly, statistics on schooling attendance can be misleading. For instance, in parts of South Africa blacks have more years of schooling than other groups, but this is because they have to resit exams because of inadequate attendance.

Although this may seem a digression, the commitment to extend labour reproduction security was part of the development models in the era of statutory regulation. In welfare state capitalism, schooling was conceived primarily as a *public good*, in that although the private return to schooling and training was substantial, its appeal was that it contributed to the culture and civilisation of society and to social cohesion. This attitude has changed under the influence of supply-side economics and the pressures of globalisation. Increasingly, schooling is regarded as little more than an investment, and policymakers are encouraged to think there can be 'over-investment' as well as 'under-investment' in education. Schooling that does not generate a rate of return is regarded as dispensable, a target for public spending cuts. Similarly, while privatisation of schooling has been advocated partly on grounds of quality – the view being that better quality derives from any service that is paid for rather than provided free – it is also advocated as a means of cutting public spending, to enable governments to cut taxes. Public schooling costs about 5 per cent of GDP in the USA and western Europe (*Economist*, 20 September 1997, p. 50).The resurgence of market principles means that schooling is assessed increasingly by its labour market consequences. Symbolising the change in values, whereas in the 1960s the UK government established the Open University to enable adults to acquire degrees on subjects that interested them, to broaden intellectual horizons, as a social good, in the 1990s, the government was establishing the University for Industry, to provide marketable skills for jobholders.

Skill reproduction security has never been strong in the sense that it has been experienced by a majority of the labour force, since it has been selective and linked to the social and technical divisions of labour in society. For an individual, it can be defined as a situation in which competences can be developed, applied and refined. This form of security includes more than skill development and skill reproduction. It also includes the existence of facilities for childcare and education and for parents to be able to combine other forms of work with childcare.

In the welfare state model, the definition of labour reproduction security that best describes the ethos of the era was the state's commitment to underwrite the costs of schooling and skill development, and to raise the social productivity of the workforce and potential workforce through subsidised schooling, pre-employment and on-the-job training, subsidised health facilities, and so on.

The state socialist model was designed to achieve a comprehensive form of labour reproduction security, primarily through enterprises and organisations of employment, the locus of the 'social construction of labour power' (Szalkowski and Olbrycht, 1992). Social policies were intended for the development and maintenance of labour power. Thus, family policy was pro-natalist, enabling women to have children while remaining formally employed, maintaining high levels of labour force participation even though many were on prolonged maternity leave at any time. Indeed, the reproduction of labour power and not labour performance was the decisive objective of wage policy and social policy (Potucek, 1992, p. 2).The state provided free healthcare, schooling and training, subsidised housing to help in the reproduction and stabilisation of labour power, while extensive childcare services were intended to free women to labour and to obtain control of the socialisation of children.

The collapse of state socialism has led to a withering of many of those functions. They had many faults, not least in limiting choice and in quality and flexibility. However, the erosion has not been matched by the transfer of effective responsibility to local or national public authorities. The costs of schooling and training have risen, and the provision of facilities has shrunk, leading to a rationing in favour of those from affluent backgrounds (Cusan and Motivans, 1998). In some countries, educational expenditure rose as a share of GDP, but this was because GDP fell sharply. In most, real expenditure fell. Because fewer have been able to go into higher education, the supply of qualified people is falling, raising the relative wages of the 'skilled'. Apart from that, insecurity in eastern Europe has been intensified by some of the same factors affecting skill security in industrialised economies in which more flexible, informal forms of activity have been spreading.

In the USA, the Labor Secretary's Commission on Achieving Necessary Skills (SCANS) concluded in 1991 that more than half of all those leaving school lacked the skills needed to obtain productive employment. Their disadvantage is compounded by the fact that few firms have provided vocational training. Most expenditure on training has been on employees with college education, and most training has been provided by a small handful of large companies. According to the National Center on Education and the Economy, 0.5 per cent of firms accounted for more than 90 per cent of all training expenditure.

For industrial workers, a traditional form of skill security was access to *apprenticeship*. In most of the world, this has always been reserved for a minority of privileged young men. In a few countries, it became more than that. And in the post-war era the institutionalisation of apprenticeship in countries such as Austria, Denmark and (west) Germany kept the youth unemployment rate down relative to adults and relative to youth rates in other countries. However, a means by which skill reproduction security has declined has been through the global decline of apprenticeship. Apprenticeships in the USA and the UK have practically disappeared, and have declined in many other countries, such as Australia, Denmark, France and Ireland. Even in Germany, famed for its commitment to apprenticeships, a survey in 1996 found that only a third of firms were training any apprentices (Upchurch, 1997, p. 200). Among the many developing countries exhibiting decline in recent years are South Africa and Zimbabwe (Standing et al., 1996; Knight, 1996a, b). Apprenticeship scarcely goes with flexiworking, and represents a fixed cost in economies facing more uncertainty and fluctuations in demand due to globalisation and technological change.

In many countries, there has also been declining in-firm training. Nowhere has this been more so than in eastern Europe. Since the 1980s, old-style enterprise-based training has declined sharply in countries of the former Soviet Union, as recorded in our enterprise surveys. In parts of western Europe as well, training by firms has not been extensive. In the UK, firms have long spent only about 1 per cent of their payroll on training (Training Agency, 1989). One factor eroding on-the-job training is employment flexibility. For instance, with teleworking the absence of a group of experienced workers alongside teleworkers deprives recruits of potential mentors. Teleworkers may easily lose touch with technical, product and organisational changes, and find their skills becoming obsolete, as well as *thinking* they are becoming obsolete.

Sweden, with its school-based vocational orientation, and Germany, with its 'dual system' based on apprenticeship, may provide more skill reproduction security than elsewhere. However, the German system has displayed signs of fragmentation, with a shrinking core being provided with technical skills, and *de facto* non-application of collective agreements, particularly in eastern Germany. Decentralisation and the role of multinationals may have irrevocably disrupted the Swedish system as well (Crouch and Traxler, 1995). Wherever flexiworking is growing the structures necessary for skill acquisition and application are likely to shrink, threatening to push more people into a whirlwind of short-term jobs and short-term training, with little security to encourage skill refinement. And if job-changing and career-changing become more common, young workers will be increasingly disinclined to invest in any one 'skill'.

In the 1980s and 1990s there was increasing expenditure on – and faith in – *labour market training* as a means of reducing unemployment, increasing *employability*, reducing income transfers and upgrading skills. The evidence is strong that this has not had any of these effects to a substantial extent. For some people, refusing to participate in a labour market training scheme is rational, since it may narrow their options. For example, if an unemployed university graduate were offered training as a plumber, he would risk being categorised – or stigmatised – as a plumber thereafter, lowering the type of job and income to which he would have access. With unemployment benefit schemes increasingly stipulating that a person must accept any 'suitable job' or face disentitlement, taking a labour market training place could result in 'deskilling' in terms of subsequent opportunities.

Finally, there is the subjective *perception* of skill insecurity. Because both firms and politicians have an interest in proclaiming that workers lack skills, rather than admit that they are not creating adequate opportunities, more people will feel inadequate. If unemployment, low productivity and 'uncompetitiveness' are blamed on lack of skills, and if managerial responsibility for stagnant company profits is shifted onto workers' alleged lack of skills, is it not likely that their sense of skill security will be undermined?

In the USA, in 1997 when there was a tight labour market, the chairman of the Federal Reserve, Alan Greenspan, attributed low inflationary pressure to pervasive employment insecurity, which he attributed to workers' fears that their skills had become inadequate, making them believe that they would not be able to obtain other employment if they lost their jobs. So, employment insecurity may disguise a more profound skill insecurity. People fear losing a niche and a capacity to function in work.

Skill reproduction security arises from the opportunity to acquire and to retain viable skills. What people want, what they need and what is available must be in reasonable balance. In that regard, it is ironic that with schooling more widespread than at any time in history there is a constant refrain almost everywhere that there is a 'skills shortage' and that workers are ill-equipped. Perhaps there is accelerating obsolescence in technical skills, widening inequalities and leaving those with modest skills and capacity for retraining at a distinct disadvantage.

6.6 REPRESENTATION INSECURITY

Bargaining now is impossible for any task that can be exported. This now is universally true. This transformation in the condition of labour in the advanced countries, as well as in the developing world, is permanent. Nothing currently envisaged can restore the European or American worker's lost job security ... Nowhere in the public debate have I seen this really addressed.[10]

Women together are strong!
If I were together, would I be strong?
                              Anon (a woman)

Representation security comes from the existence of organisations able to defend the interests of those in vulnerable positions, giving those subject to controls a collective voice to bargain with controllers. It depends on strong voice for those in and potentially in the labour market. There is no reason for that to depend on trade unions, but during the twentieth century it has been presumed that unions can 'voice regulate' labour relations. As noted in chapter 2, unions have always had a dualistic character, being a means of resistance to control – improving the security of their members – and being a means of managing labour.

In the historical development of capitalism, the predominant forms of representation, and their range and success, have changed. In the nineteenth century, *craft unions* evolved from guilds, reflecting the separation of owners and workers. This represented a decline of *artisanal security*, and proletarianisation, with craft unions being defensive associations of working men intent on preserving some control over their skill, work organisation, wage rates and social status. In many places, they operated to limit and control the quantity and quality of labour supply.

The early part of the twentieth century saw a shift to *industrial unions* and sectoral (or centralised) collective bargaining. This represented a loss of worker control over occupations. Industrial unions evolved within mass production and Tayloristic work organisation, which was a concerted managerial effort to turn working-class occupations into jobs. Although the institutions and processes varied from country to country, the character of representation shifted to the labourist priorities, of raising the social wage, giving members improved income security, employment security, job security as stability, and work security through protection of working conditions. Mostly, unions went along with Tayloristic job structures and often became defenders of them through demarcation agreements and the like.

For most of the twentieth century trade unions, and unionism as a movement, were in the vanguard of social progress, an instrument for the pursuit of distributive justice in terms of advancing the interests of the labouring man. In the post-war era, unions were integrated into the state in distinctive ways in the two development models, and this has shaped the evolution of labour representation security in the era of market regulation. Although reviewed in greater detail elsewhere (ILO, 1997b), it might be useful to trace recent trends in each type of economy and society.

(i) From State Socialism[11]

Representation security in state socialism was more formal than substantive, in that the extremely high rates of unionisation were offset by the fact that the unions were little more than organs of the Party and agents of management, mainly concerned with matters of labour discipline and the dispensation of enterprise benefits and services to workers and their families.

The collapse of state socialism in eastern Europe induced a deep erosion in unionisation there, coupled with a fragmentation of unions, new and old. Unions and employer organisations often had unclear organisational boundaries, and demarcation lines between policy concerns were contested and hazy. They had to struggle to maintain morale and credibility in the context of declining (and often passive) membership and unsettled bargaining routines. Among the worst aspects for the development of voice regulation have been cleavages between local, regional and national bodies, and hazy lines of organisation on sectoral or occupational lines.

At national level, through nominally tripartite bodies, *voice regulation* was promoted in many countries, an exception being the Czech Republic. Much of that amounted to ineffectual formalism as well, since the representative character of employer and trade union associations on tripartite bodies was often dubious, while the information at their disposal was often scanty and unreliable, and the capacity to make and implement decisions was often minimal. Typically, decisions were taken by officials from several government ministries and were pushed through the tripartite bodies or introduced without reference to them.

Representation insecurity has become pervasive, reflected in sharply declining unionisation. If one puts aside the few countries where the old union structure has been preserved because the character of the state has hardly changed, then with fragmentation and a *reformed* old union structure retaining a central role, de-unionisation has reflected the following:

- real decline caused by anti-union stance of enterprises;
- real decline due to the emergence of new private firms in which union representation has not been possible due to size or employer resistance;
- real decline caused by the withdrawal from unions of 'passive' members;
- real decline caused by withdrawal of working members due to the unpopularity of unions because of past associations;
- real decline due to the growth of categories of workers with a low propensity to join unions, such as higher-status, higher-income workers and migrants;
- real decline caused by the erosion of enterprise benefits, for which unions had been responsible and which gave workers an incentive to join unions;
- real decline due to the rising cost of union dues, both absolutely and relative to the income needs of workers;
- real decline caused by workers feeling less inclined to join unions because employers bypass them in decisions on wages, working conditions and other matters;
- real decline caused by the existence of alternative structures, such as company unions or their equivalent, or enterprise boards that seem to offer a workers' voice in enterprise affairs;
- real decline caused by the much higher levels of unemployment;
- real decline because of inter-union rivalry, sometimes fomented by outside critics of 'old' unions;
- real decline because unions are seen to represent the losers in a time of stagflation;
- artificial decline, caused by more realistic estimates of union membership and by more monitoring of membership numbers.

It would be hard to estimate which factors have been most important, although privatisation has surely played a prominent part. In Russia, unionisation in privatised firms is much lower (Standing, 1996a, ch. 9). This was also true in Ukraine and Bulgaria. Given their role in supervising enterprise benefits, unions have suffered in two respects from the decline in the range and value of those benefits, being resented by workers as possibly responsible for the decline and being less attractive because the declining function of allocating benefits has eliminated the main appeal of membership.

Unions have also failed to attract younger workers, which is why a rising proportion of union members have been old, with an increasing number being economically inactive (Tapiola, 1995). This erodes the strength of unions as bargainers.

Although the tale of deunionisation in former state socialism countries is worrying for those who believe that unions are required for representation security, several positive points should be noted. The very high unionisation was artificial, and undermined the *legitimacy* of unions, which is a prerequisite for strong voice. More significantly still, the erosion has created pressure on those who recognise the need for collective voice to seek alternative institutions more appropriate for the emerging flexible labour markets. For the meantime though, there is little representation security in these countries, and little prospect that the vacuum will be filled in the near future.

(ii) From Welfare State Capitalism

In welfare state capitalism, representation security was seen as requiring independent trade unions, with a high degree of unionisation and the state-guaranteed right to strike as a means of limiting the control of capital and of ensuring that income security. This was coupled with the desired existence of employer associations representing mainstream capital, able to negotiate on its behalf, to make concessions and negotiate compromises. Mainstream unions and employer bodies were expected to be incorporated economically and politically into the state.

The assumptions and requirements in this respect began to fade in the 1960s and 1970s. In industrialised countries, the forward march of labour coincided with a fattening of the working-class stomach and growing socio-economic mobility. While attesting to the success of the extension of rights of security, these eroded collective working-class strength. It was always too fanciful to speak of the end of the working class, as Andre Gorz put it, but surely not wrong to depict a dwindling of its size, power and cohesion, as well as a process of class fragmentation that eroded representation security (Gorz, 1983). Whether the view was fair or correct, unions and their political allies seemed to become atavistic, and looking back to the 1970s and 1980s, that must be the biggest 'failure' for those who value distributive justice.

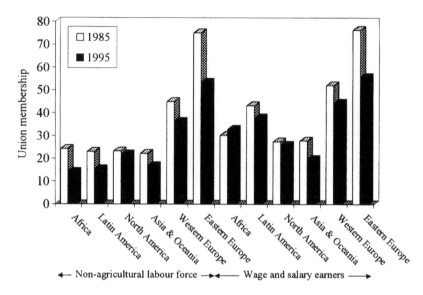

Figure 6.2 Trade union density, by sector, 1985–95 *(unweighted average of union membership percentages of individual countries, years 1985 and 1995 or closest)*

Source: ILO.

Whether or not those social forces could have done anything to arrest the erosion of security is moot, since one may guess that the game was up, and that those bulwarks of the conservative working class were institutionally incapable of responding positively to the currents that were sweeping them aside. This is not a criticism, merely a recognition that all institutions belong to historical eras. In any case, by the 1990s it was too late to arrest the trends.

De-unionisation has been extensive in all parts of the world, except Africa (Figures 6.2 and 6.3). And, even where high rates of unionisation have persisted, the strength and effectiveness of union activity has often been reduced. Although it was always quite low, could anyone in the post-war era have predicted that less than 10 per cent of the French labour force would belong to trade unions by the 1990s?

In the USA, private sector unionisation has declined to about 11 per cent. In the UK, by 1997 union membership as a percentage of the labour force (31 per cent) was the lowest for over 60 years. There were 7.2 million members, compared with nearly 9 million in 1989. Supporters took comfort from the fact that the rate of decline had fallen from 3 per cent a year in the 1980s to 1 per cent in 1996. In many other countries unionisation has also fallen. And in some cases the effective decline may have been much greater than the recorded decline, since an increasing proportion of union membership has consisted of retired workers, as in Italy, or non-employed members, so that actual bargaining strength in the workplace is overstated.

Briefly, the main reasons for the global decline in unionisation have been the following, again in no implied order of significance:

- Labour market insecurity has eroded membership. This has been direct, through fewer workers being employed, and indirect, through making it easier for employers to resist or derecognise unions and through making it harder for workers to organise or have the confidence to do so.
- External flexibility has made an increasing proportion of jobs less unionisable. There is extensive evidence that temporary, part-time and other non-regular workers are less likely to be in unions (Applebaum and Gregory, 1988). Unions have found it hard to organise flexiworkers, notably teleworkers, other home workers, and temporary and casual labour, as well as those having an intermediary labour status, neither wage labour nor employer but regarding themselves as 'self-employed' even if they hire themselves out from job to job as consultants or contract workers. Reasons include the organisational difficulty of reaching and retaining such workers, the tendency for them not to identify with unions, the difficulty of integrating flexiworkers into union structures, and the legal ambiguity over the position of contingent workers, which has inhibited them from joining unions. This has caused friction in the USA. As an AFL-CIO report (1985, p. 4) concluded, 'Working people not classified as "employees" in the labor law are subject to open reprisal for seeking to join a union and have no legal right of recourse.'

  Just as most of these forms of employment are costly to organise, most of those in such jobs seem ambivalent about the advantages of unionisation. Among the difficulties is that for them union involvement may have a substantial cost, through increasing the probability of being dismissed and of not being rehired. This has been a barrier to unionisation in developing countries with inherently flexible labour systems (Streefkerk, 1985, p. 243). One countervailing tendency might be that as various forms of insecurity spread up the 'skill' spectrum, workers may find greater appeal in unions. To some extent, as temporary agency work has extended to technically skilled groups in the USA, more regular workers threatened by displacement have joined unions, including scientists.

- The changing composition of the labour force and the increased labour force flexibility have tended to lower unionisation, since intermittent and marginal labour force participants are less inclined to join or stay in unions. Even though women have become less marginal, their unionisation has remained lower than for men. Thus, in the USA although women's unionisation has not fallen by as much as men's, their level has remained much lower (National Displaced Homeworkers' Network, 1991).

- In many countries, an increasing proportion of jobs have been in small-scale units and in firms that have a short life. These are less unionisable. Decentralisation, whether through the splintering of firms or through sub-contracting, makes organisation and retention harder. And the growth of such decentralised structures makes pattern-setting bargaining harder as well, with different terms and conditions between units and with non-union plants or units weakening the bargaining power in the organised plants (Windmuller et al., 1987).
- Many governments have taken advantage of the weakness of unions to tighten regulations over union activities, making the benefits of unionisation more unpredictable, recognition harder and derecognition easier, and limiting the right to strike. Anti-union legislation, such as that introduced by the British government, may have played a smaller role than some commentators suggest, having reflected the weakness of unions and their declining public image as much as having been a cause of their decline (Brown et al., 1997). However, there can be little doubt that it has been an influence.
- Statutory regulation has helped retain relatively high unionisation in some countries, notably where unions have retained a role in providing social protection. In Germany, representation security has been retained to some extent because under *co-determination* worker representatives are on supervisory boards of large and medium-sized firms, and in the coal and steel

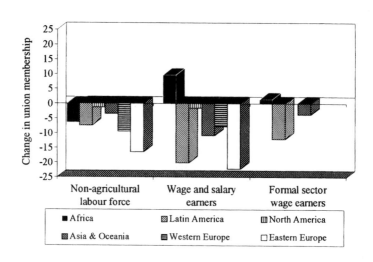

Figure 6.3 Change in trade union density, by sector, 1985-95 *(unweighted average of change in union membership percentage points of individual countries, period 1985 to 1995 or closest)*

Source: World Labour Report, 1997-98, pp. 239–40.

industry workers nominate personnel directors. According to the president of Germany's largest employer federation, the *Gesamtmetall*, some personnel directors need union backing to keep their jobs, and unions insist that they be union members as a precondition for a collective agreement (*Financial Times*, 21 August 1996).

- The historical image of unions has impeded their appeal to growing groups in the labour force, whether it be more educated workers, more individualistic workers, women or minorities, even though there is ample evidence that unions often benefit some of those groups more than male manual workers. There has been concern over the representative character of unions, which is not necessarily due to the intentions or values of unionists themselves. In most countries women and immigrants have been persistently underrepresented, as in the Netherlands (Visser, 1991). This means that there has been a growing divergence between the image, or perceived voice, of unions and the composition of the labour force. Unions have been criticised for protecting 'insiders' at the expense of 'outsiders', such as women, young labour force entrants, migrants, and ethnic minorities. The criticism is probably unfair, since their 'sword of justice' effect in this regard has been well documented (Freeman and Medoff, 1984; and for an empirical study in a developing country, Standing, 1992). Nevertheless, the impression that unions represent the values and aspirations of labouring man is ingrained in the public mind.

- Employer and managerial attitudes to unions have changed. In the period of industrialisation, employers commonly created communities or estates on which the bulk of the workforce lived. This paternalism produced a controlled workforce, but also tended to create a sense of identity and solidarity. The growth of more flexible production systems, and mass transport, has encouraged large-scale firms to dispense with this tactic. A classic case was the UK mining industry. In the 1980s, as part of a managerial onslaught, British Coal did not build new estates to accompany its new pits, but rather dispersed miners over surrounding villages (Tomaney and Winterton, 1990). This weakened the sense of solidarity and representation among mineworkers.

- More generally, many firms have been emboldened by the weakness of their institutional adversaries to restrict the capacity of union bargaining or to bypass unions altogether. This has been encouraged by the tendency to move away from group contracts to individual employment contracts.

- As unions have evolved from craft to industrial to *general unions*, they may have become more distanced from the interests and self-image of potential members. Increasingly workers do not identify with a particular 'sector', industry or even a recognised craft. Sectoralism as a principle of industrial relations and representation has been eroded, even though in some countries there have been attempts to strengthen sectoralism, as in Canada, South Africa and Zimbabwe.

- Independent unions have been threatened by the efforts of firms and governments to set up company-based alternatives. These have long been regarded as 'pet' unions easily coopted by management, if not part of the managerial control system. Enterprise unionism has been pushed by some governments, and has spread because of the influence of Japanese labour practices, particularly to industrialising economies such as the Republic of Korea, Malaysia and Chile. Where they were long regarded with hostility by traditional unions, they have spread because of union weakness, and in part because managements have seen them as useful as part of the labour control system and as conducive to work process flexibility.
- Unions have been less capable of exerting pressure through traditional mechanisms. Strikes are less succcessful in globally integrated production systems. If the union prevails, the firm's competitiveness is weakened, leading to job losses, or to job transfers within a geographically diversified enterprise, or to bankruptcy.
- Unions have lost credibility and *legitimacy*, partly as a result of the incessant ideological attack on them. One distinguished labour historian has written that 'the dissolution of the labour movement is ... the counter-revolution of our time' (Phelps-Brown, 1990). He predicted that by the end of the century private-sector unionised plants would be a rarity in the UK, confined to the north of the country, because workers did not identify with them. In the USA, an opinion poll conducted when unionisation was at its lowest for generations found that 40 per cent of the public believed unions had too much power and only 22 per cent thought they did not have enough. Even more alarmingly, 50 per cent believed that private-sector workers should not have the right to strike without the risk of losing their jobs. The negative consciousness among workers has eroded worker representation. Most worrying about the survey of opinions carried out for the Dunlop Commission in 1994 was that, faced with a hypothetical choice between a strong organisation that would face managerial opposition and a weak one that would co-operate with management, workers chose the latter by three to one.
- While more corporations are becoming internationally mobile, with the capacity to shift production at the margin with ease, unions have been unable to develop equivalent capacity. International unionism has been financially weak. For instance, the ICFTU receives 1 per cent of the income of member organisations willing and able to pay, whereas by contrast Amnesty International receives 30 per cent of the income of its national affiliates. With limited financial strength, the ICFTU is limited.

    Another feature is that globalisation has altered institutional rights. Regional integration agreements have given formal rights to capital but not corresponding rights to labour – giving, for example, guaranteed freedom of movement of capital but not the guaranteed right to strike. This and other

instances have been noted for the NAFTA and MERCOSUR arrangements
for Latin America (Weeks, 1998).

• There has been a strong international trend to decentralisation of collective
  bargaining, to plant or company level (Figure 6.4), and this has made it easier
  for firms to erode and bypass unions and move to individualised contracts.

Unionism, in sum, is in trouble. It might be that other forms of representation
have been taking the place of more traditional forms of trade union. *Works councils*
have been one mechanism, which in one form or another are compatible with
unionisation or could exist without unions. They have been well-established in
continental western Europe, and workers elect representatives to works councils
in Belgium, Denmark, France, Germany, the Netherlands and Spain. However, they
are not necessarily a force for co-determination. They benefit insiders over excluded
groups. Since they exist mainly in larger companies, voice regulation is stronger
in those firms, and since they are more common in firms with predominantly male
workers, it gives men stronger voice potential than women. For example, in the
Netherlands, 83 per cent of all works council members have been men (Leisink
and Beukema, 1993). Thus, voice regulation may not be egalitarian in its effect.
And workers not in regular employment have no participation rights, since in
countries such as the Netherlands short-term, part-time and trainee workers do not
have voting rights. Similarly, there is often little contact between works councils
and trade unions, while managements often bypass works councils, with impunity.
In the UK, only about one-fifth of workers have access to a works council or similar

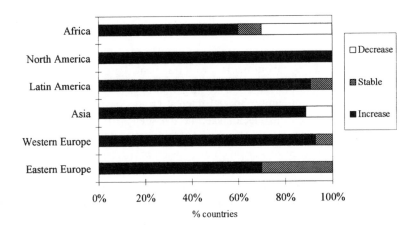

Figure 6.4 Trends in company/plant-level collective bargaining from mid-1980s to mid-1990s,
by regions of the world

Source: ILO.

structure, and most believe that they have little or no influence (Gallie et al., 1998).

Works councils may also have strengthened workplace segmentation, the representatives being more concerned to defend the interests of core insiders than other groups. Works councils seem better tuned to stable industrial structures based on mass production than to flexible labour markets in which small firms and flexible forms of employment relation are growing. They do not promise a community voice.

Representation security in terms of consultation and negotiation with workers is not extensive even in western Europe. A survey in 1996 found that 48 per cent of UK firms gave no worker representation in decision-making and in the Netherlands the figure was even higher (57 per cent). Only 16 per cent of French firms involved workers in negotiations or decision-making on work organisation, and only 18 per cent of UK firms did so. Paradoxically, firms that did consult workers were more likely to report cost reductions and had better performance in terms of output, quality and absenteeism, and were more likely to have cut employment (EPOC, 1997).

Other developments that seem to offer forms of representation security are team-based production and what have been called *'employee involvement programs'* (EIPs) in the USA. The former seems to bypass unions altogether, and leaves workers without effective voice. EIPs are associated with non-union firms, and their principal drawback is that they are voice mechanisms that 'leave hierarchical power relations unchanged'(Jacoby, 1995, p. 388). Management set up channels for workers to express concern over labour matters, but there is evidence that employee complaints fail to protect workers in non-union plants (Heckscher, 1996; Lewin and Peterson, 1988). At least by themselves, EIPs do not offer the prospect of strong representation security.

Since representation security is derived from a sense of community among workers, in a globalising labour market, with fragmented groups with dissimilar interests and patterns of labour force participation, traditional unions do not seem to offer a sense of community. Special interest groups have proliferated, and competition between them has undermined collective strength. For reasons discussed in chapter 11, this could change. However, by the late 1990s it had not done so.

Many commentators have welcomed the erosion of representation security as a reflection of individualisation and flexibility. However, without strong voice regulation, other forms of security will be fragile. Besides more income insecurity for many groups, even potentially advantageous changes in work organisation can be undermined. In the USA, for instance, workers in 'high performance' work settings reported higher levels of job-related stress than other workers (Berg et al., 1996). It turns out that the absence of a strong independent voice representing workers collectively means that there is no check on excessive labour. This suggests that, unless worker voice is strengthened, participatory labour, 'teamworking', so-called self-directed teams, delegation of responsibility and so on may merely increase labour insecurity.

The time has come to rethink the institutional basis of representation. What constitutes a *legitimate* voice? What form of voice would be most effective in labour market terms? These are awkward questions, which many would prefer were not asked. Unless they are answered, this form of insecurity will persist. How to revive representation security must be a fundamental part of a strategy to strengthen distributive justice and a work-based society.

6.7 CONCLUDING POINTS

The certainties of one age are the problems of the next.
Richard Tawney, 1938

Under the impact of globalisation (or its perceived or prospective impact), the desire to increase 'national competitiveness' and the adoption of supply-side economics and libertarian ethics, in the 1980s and 1990s governments have overseen the growth and *legitimation* of various forms of insecurity in the name of flexibility. There have been trade-offs. In many European countries, for instance, labour market security was allowed to deteriorate while employment and work security were protected to some extent. Then, as if to rectify the imbalance, erosion of other forms of security has been presented as necessary to improve labour market security.

Globalisation makes it hard for governments to manipulate macro-economic policy to boost economic growth and thereby absorb more labour. Firms feel that they must reduce overheads in order to become or remain 'competitive' with foreign firms. So politicians and firms claim they need to reduce fiscal and labour costs, particularly indirect labour costs associated with employment, job and work security (as well as income security as discussed in the next chapter). This opens up an image of a beggar-my-neighbour process by which governments and firms try to attract foreign capital (or retain their own) by offering the most attractive package – subsidies, low direct costs, assurance of flexibility, assurance of free and costless exit if desired, etc. Any reform strategy should probably begin by accepting this as reality and then seek ways that would induce greater dynamic efficiency, reasonable labour flexibility and sufficient security. How this might evolve is considered in chapter 11.

For most people, all forms of labour-related security are desirable. Usually, primacy has been given to labour market security in the name of Full Employment. In many countries, the pressure in the 1980s and 1990s has been to put more people in jobs or quasi-jobs. Is such an emphasis detrimental to other forms of security?

It is possible that it weakens skill reproduction security, part of which comes from work that is not recognised as work, in and around the home? Women (and men) looking after their children are pressured to take jobs and are threatened with income insecurity if they do not do so. If this reduces fiscal outlays, that may appear to be cost effective. If personal and community welfare are considered, the costs and benefits become less clear.

The various forms of insecurity interact. Employment insecurity intensifies income insecurity, as does any erosion in labour representation security. As a result, one could not draw an optimistic conclusion from finding that one form of security has not apparently diminished if there is evidence that other forms have increased.

There is a trade-off between forms of labour security. The twentieth-century bias has been towards the most labourist forms, which had the effect of hindering the development of occupational security. For example, consider the changing forms of representation security. Craft and industrial unions had a role in controlling labour supply and skill reproduction security through their involvement in apprenticeships. This gave workers some defensive control over skill dilution and the incomes they could command, through limiting the number of apprentices and content of apprenticeship. This was a feature of printing in the USA, for instance. In the 1970s and 1980s, the union conceded job control in return for employment security, signing automation agreements, gaining lifetime employment guarantees and buy-out packages for their members in return for giving up occupational control (Cornfield, 1997, p. 35). This is a case of concession bargaining giving subordinated functional flexibility or gaining some employment security for some *currently* employed at the cost of loss of job security for current and future workers – ultimately at the cost of eroding representation, skill reproduction and income security as well. In general, the decline of representation security leaves job security in tatters.

Managerial control over occupation can soon lead to deskilling. With weakened worker voice, technological change, globalisation and both recessions and booms offer firms opportunities to assert administrative control over occupational control, intensifying job insecurity in particular. *Technological change* may offer a means of deskilling, as with the printers in the 1970s. *Booms* raise profits, which enable firms to offer income to workers in return for increased managerial control over job content, while the firm or industry makes longer-term efficiency gains in return for short-term gains by workers, who gain income at the expense of the job control for their younger colleagues or those who enter skill-diluted jobs. *Recessions* facilitate skill dilution because workers are fearful and vulnerable to making job content concessions in return for preservation of their jobs or maintenance of the value of their wages. Finally, globalisation operates as a threat to obtain job content concessions.

Reconsidering employment security is crucial. Those wishing to reduce employment protection in the name of flexibilising the labour market and increasing the employment intensity of economic growth should recognise that, unless there are countervailing measures, employment insecurity may erode the incentive for workers to invest in skill, much of which is job-specific and enterprise-specific, and they are likely to lower their effort bargain, in part because of lower morale (e.g., Burchell, 1993). Those experiencing employment insecurity are more likely to experience stress and depression. However, if that reflects income insecurity, then perhaps employment security is exchangeable for other factors conducive to income security and the pursuit of occupation. Strong employment security can itself be a source of stress.

There are many unanswered questions. Are firms jettisoning employment security because they have less need for worker loyalty or because the cost of compensating for loyalty is excessive when they need to alter employment levels and structures quickly? Or do they not need loyalty because they have more options should workers leave or should they suddenly need more of certain types of worker?

A growing number of flexiworkers and consultants are surviving in employment insecurity, and more firms are giving workers a non-wage benefit in terms of training and advisory services to prepare them for employment mobility and job mobility. Firms are trading employment security for 'employability' and portability. One wonders how many firms are doing what IBM has been doing, operating *Career Fitness Centres*, with counsellors drawing up action plans to help individuals develop a sense of control over their careers. Motorola and Intel in the USA and Unipart in the UK, among others, have set up their own 'universities'. Does this imply growth of skill reproduction security or increased control over skill content and options?

The employment *contract* is changing for different groups in different ways. Technical, professional and skilled workers – 'proficians'— are increasingly unlikely to be able to rely on the *paternalism* of the core labour relationship regarded as the norm during the twentieth century – 'service' and 'loyalty' given in return for lifetime employment security as long as the firm survived. It is not yet replaced by a norm of a high effort bargain in return for an assurance that the firm would help develop *employability*, if needed. But this looks like a leading contender for the norm of the early part of the twenty-first century. It will not come as an act of benevolence. It will come only if the voice of workers is strong enough and if the potential consequences of not doing it are high enough to deter rejection of this compromise bargain. One cost that firms will wish to avoid is opportunistic loyalty on the part of workers, through low effort while moonlighting on other jobs, premature departure from the firm when it suits the worker, and so on.

This and the preceding chapter prompt the question: to improve distributive justice, should one focus on labour market and employment security, or on phenomena that induce *feelings* of employment and labour market insecurity? The proposed answer, discussed in the final chapter, is that these forms of security should be regarded as instrumental rather than fundamental. If employment flexibility is required, and if this implies employment insecurity, then the task should be to find ways of making the costs acceptable to all.

7 Income Insecurity in Employment and Unemployment

7.1 INTRODUCTION

Income security may be defined as the reasonable assurance of an income corresponding to the individual's perceived needs, expectations and aspirations. This is the most basic form of security, if one is concerned with survival and freedom. Income security covers both *adequacy* and *assurance* of income.

In the post-war era, income security was pursued primarily in the interests of the labouring man and the industrial working class. For those labouring, there was the promise of *minimum wages*. In welfare states, for men in the labour market there was the promise of social protection through social insurance to cover periods of 'temporary interruption of earnings power'. This was held out as the path for developing countries to take. There was a commitment to freedom of contract (thus an attack on such feudalistic practices as bonded labour, artificial sharecropping and slavery). In state socialism, as unemployment was banned as parasitic there was no need for unemployment benefits. 'Cradle-to-grave' benefits were organised through the labouring collective.In both models, there was also rhetorical commitment to the reduction of discrimination on grounds of gender, race and so on.

There was a general commitment to reduce income and wealth inequality. Everywhere the norm was to expect inequality to fall with economic growth, although development economists agonised over whether inequality was needed to boost accumulation, as implied by standard growth models.

Looking back to the era, there were improvements in income security, notably within welfare states but also in the large part of the world adhering to state socialism. Although it was not a Golden Age, much of the world saw progress. Unfortunately, it was unsustainable because the models of the labouring man were neither sustainable nor deserving of being sustained.

7.2 CONCEPTUALISING INCOME SECURITY

Income security is as complex a concept as poverty or deprivation. One might measure it by associations. One might surmise that it is greater the higher a person's income relative to perceived and anticipated needs, and greater the stronger the assurance that the income will continue. It may also be greater if the income corresponds to that received by one's peer group, if there is an *expectation* that future income will exceed current income, if alternative income opportunities are similar, and if one's current income is as high or higher than one's past income. So, the idea of income security is complex, which does not invalidate it.

Consider a few situations. In a society in which there is a right to free primary and secondary schooling and health services the income likely to provide security will be relatively low because their cost would be covered if one were in employment and the cost of job loss would be lower because the benefit would be available regardless of job status. Whittling away those rights would diminish income security. Another situation is where a person experiences a decline in income. If 'subsistence' income were $100 a month and actual income fell to $75, income security would be reduced because consumption and saving were oriented to the higher level, there would be fear that it would drop further, and there would be a sense of status deterioration. This has been particularly relevant in eastern Europe in the 1990s.

If labour market security deteriorated, the employed's income security would fall, in that unless the labour market was totally segmented the greater risk of income loss would make it desirable to increase the savings rate. Similarly, if entitlement to unemployment benefits were restricted, the income security of the employed and unemployed would fall. Income security does not depend just on own income or on degree of assured income. It could deteriorate even though income or probability of employment loss did not change.

Inequality affects income security directly and indirectly via *relative deprivation*. For instance, if inequality increased, the opportunity to move from a lower-income status to a higher-income status would *probably* fall. If so, envy or frustration would be intensified, or a feeling of income adequacy would be weakened because consumption levels of higher-income groups would be distanced from those feasible with the median income. Similarly, if one could progress to a higher level, someone receiving a low income would find it more 'secure' as well as adequate. This is relevant for apprentices and trainees in 'professions', paid a pittance for several years on the expectation that they would gain later. If the probability of achieving the skilled grade and higher income were reduced, the trainee's income security would fall.

Income security is linked to household and labour market structures. Household and kinship structures affect income security by the extent to which they offer support and balanced reciprocity. However, if labour markets were highly individualised and fragmented, there would not be strong social solidarity or reciprocity, because the privileged would conclude they would not need others' support, while those wishing to support those in need would be unable to do so.

Consider a three-generation family. It provides income security to its members for love and other reasons, its members expecting to give when they can and to receive when they need. It depends on balanced reciprocity. Typically, the middle generation support the oldest, because of past receipt of support and to preserve a system that will benefit them when they become elderly. Similar reciprocities take place with the youngest generation. This has characterised most societies.

However, this balanced reciprocity has been eroded during the twentieth century. Leaving aside pension developments, longer life expectancy of the elderly and the increased burden on younger family members have made it harder to maintain a balanced reciprocity and have reduced the income security of older generations. This is compounded by competition for funds from the young. If familial transfers to the elderly fall to a trickle their income insecurity is intensified, but the middle generation's income security is not necessarily increased, because although the net income of 'prime age' adults will have risen, norms of inter-generational behaviour will have been transformed. Something like this has been happening in industrialised countries.

Two behavioural changes have been occurring. The young's 'dependency' on parents has grown because of longer schooling and the required financial and service support, *and* because in many economies probability of post-school unemployment or a period of low or precarious income has risen for any level of schooling completed. If probability of state support for schooling and post-school unemployment declines, the income security of both parents and youths will fall further. And while user payments have risen, the prospect of *either* the capacity of younger cohorts to provide transfers subsequently to parents *or* the desire to do so will fall.

Flexible labour markets erode the balanced reciprocity of inter-generational transfers, thus eroding family-based income security. A related factor is growth of single-person and single-adult-with-children households, a trend attributable in part to feminisation of the labour market, making it more feasible for women to escape from economic dependency when faced with unhappy relationships, and reflecting the shift from family to individual wages. Another is the trend to means-tested social security, in which the partner's income threatens entitlement to social assistance. In short, household individualisation increases income insecurity.

Recall the concept of a **social income**. Any person may receive income from money wages, enterprise benefits, state benefits, private welfare benefits, and community benefits. In each component, questions of adequacy and of assurance arise. Thus, the subjective value of the money wage would fall if, in the event of a current activity ending, the probability of obtaining a similar income fell.

In the post-war era, income security was a primary objective of both development models. In state socialism, 'labour decommodification' meant that enterprise-based benefits (EB) comprised a high and rising share of total compensation. The security was conditional and discretionary, reducing its value to the worker, but there was a sort of bargain – income security in return for passive labour. The EB-oriented system had a distributive function, since it involved 'redistributive privileges' for valued employees, in subsidised goods and services. It could not last, since there was an imbalance between incentives and security due to the low money wage.

In contrast, welfare state capitalism gave income security by raising state benefits. Although welfare systems varied, in western Europe there was a steady expansion in the share of compensation coming from state benefits. EB also expanded, while community transfers played a minor role. This was sustainable as long as trade and investment allocations were largely between countries with similar labour rights and forms of wage supplements. The growth of state and enterprise benefits in the post-war era increased income security by making personal and family welfare less dependent on intrinsically insecure money wages. If people lose such benefits, or the prospect of obtaining them should they need them, they must fall back on money wages and informal support systems, or/and expect a cut in their living standards.

The major trend may be renewed monetisation of income. For many, this may not match the increased need for money wages, because of loss of other forms of imputed income. The most obvious case in industrialised countries is the contribution of *domestic work*, which because of the growth of single-person households and because women have been drawn into the labour market, has tended to decline, in that time available has been reduced. This has increased the need for money income.

If the two models that dominated the post-war era involved a movement to non-wage forms of remuneration, globalisation and labour market flexibility have induced a shift back to the money wage and induced pressure to increase informal and community-based support. The changing composition of social income, changing household and family structures and more individualistic behavioural norms have combined to increase income insecurity.

7.3 INDICATORS OF OVERALL INCOME INSECURITY

One could measure income insecurity in several ways. Risk of poverty is one way. Standard proxies are the percentage of the population with incomes below a 'poverty line' and the 'poverty income gap', the amount that would have to be transferred to the poor to bring all of them up to the poverty line. Usually, the poverty line is differentiated by group, so that it is set at a higher level for working-age adults than for children, for example. No definition could be entirely 'objective', and in many countries may be 'massaged' by zealous officials, particularly where state administration is not transparent.

Whatever the definition, the picture is that in spite of economic growth, poverty in many countries rose in the 1980s and 1990s. In the USA, the poorest decile experienced a drop in real incomes of 11 per cent between 1973 and 1992 (Finance and Development, 1995). In 1995, 13.8 per cent of the population were classified as poor, and the median real income was below its 1989 level. In western Europe, as measured by the Luxembourg Income Survey and other data, poverty rates have risen in the past two decades (see, e.g., McFate et al., 1995). By 1993 (the latest year for which there were comparable data in 1998), the overall poverty rate in EU countries was 17 per cent, defined by the share of households having an income less than half the average in their country.[1] According to Eurostat data, about 52 million people were in poverty, up from about 44 million in 1989. In eastern Europe, the extent and depth of poverty rose extraordinarily in the 1990s, producing levels far higher than in other industrialised countries (UNDP, 1997, ch. 4).

Poverty has also affected more groups than used to be the case, and has affected many more of those in employment, reflecting the growth of precarious, low-paid jobs. These have been called the 'new poor', in that for many years the poor were mostly outside employment. While unemployment is associated with poverty, jobs do not necessarily prevent it. In the EU, in 1993 one-third of the poor were living in households in which at least one person was employed, one-third were retired, 19 per cent were inactive. Only 13.8 per cent were unemployed. Yet the most dramatic growth of the new poor has occurred in eastern Europe, accompanying a huge growth of 'old poor'.

Income insecurity is also related to *income inequality*. Most people measure their income security by a sense of *relative deprivation*. They may relate their income to a previous level, to some notion of what is fair or feasible for someone in their circumstances (as in Russia, to what is regarded as *normalmo*), to those higher up the income distribution, or to a combination of these. The links are complex, but a highly unequal society surely excites widespread feelings of relative deprivation.

Inequality has grown in many countries in recent years. In the USA, whereas economic growth was associated with reductions in inequality in the 1950s and 1960s, it was associated with widening inequality in the 1980s and 1990s. In the UK, inequality grew through the 1980s and 1990s, reversing all the redistribution achieved during the twentieth century. In other countries too, inequality has increased, notably in Germany, the Netherlands and Sweden (Atkinson, 1996). Inequality increased in 20 of the 21 OECD countries for which data are available (OECD, 1997a, Annex 1). Although lack of up-to-date data makes it hard to be sure, in the late 1990s the trend showed no sign of being arrested, let alone reversed. As elaborated later, there are reasons for believing that *income* distribution data underestimate *social income* inequality, and do so by an increasing amount.

In eastern Europe, the collapse of state socialism precipitated a sharp increase in inequality, so that by the mid-1990s some of the countries had the dubious distinction of having income distributions that were among the most unequal in the world, even though the collapse of fiscal and other regulatory mechanisms coupled with hasty privatisation programmes had surely resulted in more inequality than the available data suggest (Vericik, 1996).

In sum, poverty and inequality have increased even in industrialised countries, creating a basis for pervasive income insecurity. In that context, the remainder of the chapter considers the changing situation of the employed and unemployed.

7.5 INCOME SECURITY OF THE EMPLOYED

Income security in both post-war models was largely dependent on labour. The link was strong in state socialism, which provided security through a highly regulated wage system based on a minimum tariff wage and the presumption that all adults were in full-time employment receiving a wage covering individual needs. Their children's needs were covered by free schooling, healthcare and childcare, coupled with family benefits and subsidised food and other basic goods. The security was conditional on the willingness to prepare for and participate in continuous labour. Those not in labour were regarded as 'parasitic', and undeserving of income security.

In welfare state capitalism, income security was pursued through linked measures for the employed, unemployed and economically inactive, with the presumption that the nuclear family was the societal norm. The thrust of policy was that income security should be linked to labour, although the state managed to justify tolerance of a privileged elite excluded from this necessity, by virtue of inherited wealth or other good fortune. For the remainder, income security was related to labour, or for those experiencing an 'interruption of earning power', a willingness to labour.

In the heyday of welfare state capitalism, income security involved a majority of those in the labour market being in regular, full-time employment. For those at the bottom, a *statutory minimum wage* or some equivalent mechanism, such as the UK's Wage Councils, offered protection and was usually adjusted periodically to keep pace with average incomes. In industrialised economies, *most* employment consisted of full-time jobs in registered firms or state enterprises, and there was a reasonable assurance of continuous employment. Beyond the security provided by a minimum wage, wage determination was largely left to collective bargaining at the plant, sectoral and national levels. Not only was a large share of the working population covered, but the presumption was that coverage was extended beyond the bargaining unit, formally as in sectoral agreements in Germany or informally because employers moved wages into line with negotiated wages, for ease of administration and to forestall unionisation.

A trend towards centralised bargaining, epitomised by the resort by many governments to *statutory incomes policy*, was associated with a narrowing of wage differentials. This was a union objective, accepted by governments and by many employers as a long-term tendency. There was widespread admiration for the Swedish *solidaristic wage policy*, which regarded compression of wage differentials as not just a social objective but a means of economic adjustment, encouraging a shift of labour from low-productivity to high-productivity sectors.

Low wage differentials translated into modest income differentiation as a result of progressive income tax, subsidies on consumer goods accounting for a high share of the budget of low-income workers, and universal state benefits that had a higher relative value for the low-paid. The cost of employment loss was no greater for a low-paid worker than for a salaried 'white-collar' employee. Both could expect a redundancy payment (or at least the probability of receiving one was little different), both could expect to find another job reasonably easily, and both could expect that their future income would be similar to what they had been receiving.

Since the 1970s, in many countries the post-war trends have been reversed, leading to greater *differentiation* in income security. At the bottom, the spread of non-standard forms of employment has eroded coverage by minimum wages. To imagine that informal arrangements between sub-contractors and home-workers could be covered by minimum wages is fanciful; there are numerous ways by which firms could circumvent regulations and reasons for workers grudgingly or unknowingly to accept the situation without protest. The same has surely been true for non-wage benefits.

In many countries wage determination has been decentralised. In some, this has been government policy, as well as an employer objective, as in the Netherlands since the mid-1980s. Decentralisation there and elsewhere has tended to widen wage differentials. These have been converted into greater income differentiation, because whereas there has been pressure to convert enterprise benefits for ordinary workers into monetary payments, so as to increase wage flexibility, a growing share of remuneration for higher-income, higher-status workers has come in the form of bonuses, fringe benefits and personalised insurance benefits. One way of interpreting this is that wages have been supplemented by additional benefits to enable firms to increase the incentive function of wages for those employees from whom they want loyalty. This has been encouraged because of social security contributions levied on money incomes. By increasing monetisation of remuneration of manual workers the effective contribution rate rose, whereas shifting from salary to non-monetary remuneration for 'white-collar' and other privileged workers diminishes their effective contribution rate. Taken together, monetisation for ordinary workers and demonetisation for higher-income groups has surely increased income inequality.

There has also been a shift in the incidence of the costs of social protection. A larger share of contributions has been borne by workers, and there has been a greater growth in the costs for lower-paid than for higher-paid workers. Healthcare is a case in point. Many governments have shifted part of the cost from the state to firms, making firms bear more of the cost of employees' sick leave or healthcare, and for their part employers have become more inclined to require workers to bear a part of the costs, in some cases not paying them for days off or not paying them for initial days off. In the case of pensions, more workers have had to pay higher contributions or have been put into labour statuses that exclude them from entitlement or that give them lower entitlements. There has also been a tendency for the workers' contribution to state or private pension funds to rise relative to the employers' share, and relative to the government's share where relevant.

Another trend, with implications for income security and distribution not yet built into statistical measures of inequality, is the growth in the average *duration of employment required to secure entitlement to social transfers*. In effect, this amounts to a reduction in the state benefit share of social income, to which we will return.

(i) The Minimum Wage

The statutory *minimum wage* has historically been an instrument of income security, especially in industrialised economies. It was the rallying cry of organised labour at the end of the nineteenth century, and has been its rallying cry for much of the twentieth century. It is about time that its moral appeal were separated from the pragmatic consideration whether in globally flexible labour markets, it has much effect one way or the other.

Criticism of minimum wages was muted in the era of statutory regulation, when measures to give minimal income protection were regarded as a sign of social decency. In the 1970s, critics gained confidence, and were given legitimacy by the veiled or open hostility to minimum wages shown by such organisations as the World Bank, OECD and IMF. Whatever the arguments for or against a minimum wage, there has been an international decline in coverage and in levels of income provided, while some governments have opted for *multiple-tier minimum wages*, which have undermined one of its principles, that of promoting social solidarity. Most EU countries still have a minimum wage, although their value varies enormously, and neither Ireland nor the UK (as of early 1998) had one. In some countries, regulations have set differentiated minimum wages, rather than one for all workers. For instance, although it is one of the few countries where the minimum wage has risen slightly relative to the average wage, Japan moved to a regionally decentralised system in 1968, and over the years has made it variable by sector as well (Suzuki, 1995). New Zealand followed other countries in introducing a lower minimum for youths. Each time a system moves away from a single value it moves away from the objective of providing general income protection.

Typical of trends, in Portugal the minimum wage fell from 56 per cent of average non-agricultural earnings in 1985 to less than 46 per cent in 1993, and for unskilled workers the fall was even greater (ILO, August 1997, p. 2). In the Netherlands, the minimum wage also fell relative to the average, and lower minima for youths were adopted in 1974, being very low for teenagers and rising by steps up to the adult rate applicable at age 23. In the USA, the upgrading in 1996 merely returned the level to close to what it had been many years earlier. It was still a low percentage of average wages by international standards.

In some countries, successive governments have taken contrasting views to the notion of a minimum wage. Thus, in the 1980s the British Government abolished the Wages Councils that had set sectoral minima. In 1997, committed to reduce the prevalence of low pay, the new Government set out to introduce a national minimum wage, and in 1998 the Low Pay Commission set the scene for a new national minimum wage. Critics expressed concern that it would affect wage differentials, cause job losses if set above £3.50 an hour and adversely affect wage negotiations. Advocates claimed it would set standards of acceptable pay and reduce poverty, although the IMF concluded that the actual level proposed would have little impact on poverty. If workers under the age of 26 are exempted, any effect will be limited.

In eastern Europe in the 1990s, the statutory minimum wage was still the base of the wage tariff system and determinant of state transfers. As such, it has had disastrous effects (Standing and Vaughan-Whitehead, 1995). In Russia and in most of the region the minimum was allowed to drop to a small fraction of the average wage (Figure 7.1) and to a small fraction of official poverty lines.

Because of pressure to cut public spending and budget deficits, governments were put under pressure to hold down the monetary and real value of the minimum wage. This led to some strange outcomes, as when the IMF's Managing Director, Michel Camdessus, stated that the IMF would block a loan to Russia if it went ahead with a proposal to double the minimum wage. The rise would have set the minimum at about 20 per cent of the income required for bare survival. Similar situations have arisen elsewhere. Clearly, the link should be cut between the minimum wage and state benefits, such as unemployment and family benefits. By

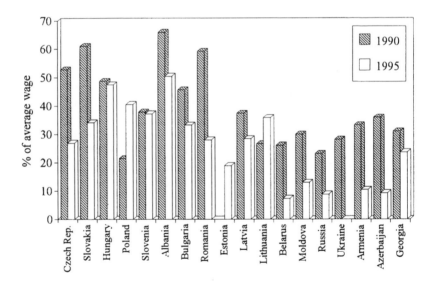

Figure 7.1 Minimum wage/average wage ratio in central and eastern Europe, 1990–95

Source: *Children at Risk in Central and Eastern Europe: Perils and Promises*, UNICEF, Economies in Transition Studies, Regional Monitoring Report No. 4, p. 141.
Note: Figures for the Czech Republic and Latvia are from 1991 (instead of 1990) and figures for Albania and Armenia are from 1994 (instead of 1995).

the mid-1990s, the minimum wage had become a source of destitution rather than of income security.

In developing countries, the trend towards statutory minimum wages characteristic of the era of statutory regulation has been reversed. For instance, in Zimbabwe, the minimum wage introduced in 1980 was abandoned in 1990 under the IMF-led Structural Adjustment Programme, even though evidence had shown that it had no effect on average wages in industry and had been applied with diminishing effectiveness (Knight, 1996a). In Brazil, the value of the minimum wage in absolute terms and relative to average wages declined in the 1990s to about half what it had been in 1980 (Ramos, 1997). In Mexico, the minimum wage has fallen sharply relative to the average wage. In Uruguay, by December 1994 the national minimum wage was one-third of what it had been in 1969, and was below the poverty line (Melgar and Guinovart, 1997). In Mauritius, minimum wages were kept low as part of the industrialisation programme, and kept particularly low in the export processing zone (Ramsamy, 1997). In the Republic of Korea, where the minimum wage has fallen relative to the average, as in many other countries, there has been a differential between the minimum wages of adults and youths (Won, 1997).

Other countries have had similar records, of declining value of the minimum wage and different minima for identifiable groups. The minimum wage has ceased to be a practical vehicle for obtaining income security for the low paid, even if it were applied strictly according to the law, which in informal, flexible forms of labour would be unlikely.

(ii) Flexible Pay and Low-paid Employment

In market-based economies, workers' main source of income is the money wage. This imparts security if it is adequate, stable, predictable and perceived as 'just'. The push for wage flexibility has meant that the relatively fixed part of the wage is likely to have declined, increasing income *uncertainty* and lowering the perceived value of any level of wage. The wage is relatively fixed if a base is established by statutory regulation or if collective bargains set minimum and actual wage rates. As discussed in chapter 4, the international trend has been from *fixed wages* to flexible forms of remuneration such as bonuses, profit shares and incentive payments. This, almost definitionally, increases income insecurity.

The assurance of the wage depends partly on the strength and form of labour regulation. Under both post-war models, statutory and voice regulations made the contractual wage reasonably secure. In the 1980s and 1990s, several factors have weakened this. There has been a decline in the incidence of group contracts, coupled with individualisation of employment relations and decentralisation of collective bargaining. These create more scope for non-payment of contracted wages, since monitoring mechanisms are weaker, and the risk of action for an aggrieved worker is greater without collective or statutory back-up.

The most bizarre developments have been in eastern Europe, where there has been widespread non-payment of contracted wages. In Russia and Ukraine, among other places, a feature of recorded wages in the 1990s has been that official statistics have given the average *contractual wage*, which has greatly exceeded the actual wage, because often it has not been paid in full or has been paid long after it is supposed to be paid, which in an inflationary environment implies that the real wage is less than it seems. The ability to alter the timing of payments lowers the wage and increases income insecurity. One may guess that the ability of firms in any flexible labour market to alter the timing and form of remuneration imparts greater insecurity to workers.

This has been accentuated by the trend towards individualisation of wage determination, and more diversity of wage-setting formula, because of the uncertainty about whether they will be paid in full and because any individual worker will feel less able to obtain redress, or be able to afford to seek it. This applies even if contract enforcement law is extended, as is likely as labour individualisation spreads.

In the post-war era, the public sector tended to be a wage leader, and public sector employees had strong income security. In the 1980s and 1990s, this changed in numerous countries, and not just in industrialised economies. In developing countries, structural adjustment programmes targeted the public sector for spending cuts and for real wages cuts, rather than cuts in total employment. In some African countries, for example, the decline has been extraordinary. In 1991, the public sector average wage in Zambia was less than one-quarter of what it was in 1975, and in Zimbabwe the decline was nearly as large (Colclough, 1998). Elsewhere the decline has been sharp as well, as in Argentina, where the fall was even greater than in most African countries. There has also been a shift towards more flexible forms of wage remuneration, such as 'performance-related pay'. Wage differentials have shrunk in the public sector in many countries, implying that income security for higher-level groups has deteriorated even more than for others. The mix of falling wages and compressed wage differentials has adversely affected public sector productivity and morale.

However, the most conspicuous aspect of growing income insecurity is the growth of low-wage employment. An extensive literature has documented the growth of low-wage jobs in the USA as part of the 'jobs miracle'. Low-paid part-time jobs have been expanding disproportionately in Europe as well. Indeed, in industrialised countries poverty has been linked to labour force participation much more than used to be the case. For a growing number of people, taking a job has not enabled them to achieve an adequate or reliable income.

In industrialising economies as well, achieving downward wage flexibility has been part of structural adjustment programmes, as in Zimbabwe in 1990–93, when real wages on average fell by 36 per cent (Knight, 1996a). In practically every adjustment programme, measures have been introduced to reduce statutory protection of wages.

There has also been a trend to pay youths lower wages than adults, and for the differential to grow. This has been linked to greater use of probationary employment and the lower wages that this involves. *Multiple-tier wage* systems have spread in many economies *and* become an objective of governments and employers, and even tacitly of many unions. Youths are often paid lower minimum wages, recruits are being put on to probationary wage rates more often, and policies are being proposed by which newly recruited workers would be paid less than existing workers, as was proposed for South Africa by the IMF and powerful national bodies.

Temporaries and casual workers are usually paid lower wages than regular workers, which has been a primary reason for firms using such workers more. Outworkers paid on a piece-rate basis are usually not provided with benefits or entitlement to social protection. This practice has spread in eastern Europe. Table 7.1 shows that in Russia and Ukraine, most industrial firms admitted paying lower wages to temporaries and part-time workers. This has also been found in comparable surveys in Latin America, India, South Africa and South East Asia. So, the growth of external flexibility has increased income insecurity through lowering wages, by making wage flexibility greater than suggested by data on full-time regular employment, and by making others fearful that this would be their fate as well.

Table 7.1 Percentage of firms paying lower wage rates to part-time workers, compared to regular full-time workers, manufacturing, Russian Federation, 1996 and Ukraine, 1995

	Russia	Ukraine
Metals	20.0	100.0
Engineering	40.0	88.5
Chemicals	40.0	76.0
Wood and paper	34.8	79.2
Construction mat.	47.6	87.5
Light industry	38.3	89.7
Food processing	37.8	80.3

Source: ILO Enterprise Labour Flexibility Surveys (RLFS6, n = 223 and ULFS2, n = 317).

Wage flexibility and income insecurity have also increased through transformation of *concession bargaining*. In the era of statutory regulation, bargaining usually involved wage increases coupled with improvements of working conditions, strengthening most forms of security. Since the 1980s, it is workers who have usually made concessions, in enterprise and plant-level bargains and in national-level concession bargaining, as epitomised by the famous Wassenaar Agreement in the Netherlands in 1982, when the unions agreed to freeze wages and the government agreed to cut payroll taxes (subsidising capital) in return for a commitment by employers to hire workers. *The essence of concession bargains has been that one or more forms of security have been weakened in return for retention of another.*

Commonly, income security has been sacrificed for retention of employment security for some groups of workers.

(iii) Wage Differentials

Flexibilisation of payment systems, decentralisation of wage determination, de-unionisation and the erosion of protective statutory regulations have allowed a regrowth of wage differentials in the era of market regulation. In some countries, these have widened very considerably. For instance, wage inequality has widened in the UK such that the gaps between the top decile and the median wage and those earning low wages are similar to what they were in the late nineteenth century (Dickens, 1997). The widening of differentials has been attributed in part to the shift to performance-related pay (Rajan et al., 1997). In Canada, worker earnings polarised in the 1980s; the gini coefficient rose to 0.42, and the size of the middle-income group (with earnings between 25 per cent of the median on either side) shrunk while the number in the upper and lower income groups rose about equally (Economic Council of Canada, 1993, p. 14). In the USA, the wages of the 'unskilled' have fallen steadily relative to average wages, and in 1996 were only about 9 per cent of the median (Phelps, 1997, p. 3). It is strange that the USA, reputed to have a highly flexible labour market, has one of the widest wage differentials in the world when it has one of the highest ratios of unskilled-to-skilled unemployment.

Germany was the only industrialised country in which the low-paid's relative wage did not deteriorate in the 1980s, which has been attributed to near-universal secondary schooling (Nickell, 1995). However, in the 1990s differentials seem to have widened. Differentials between skill, sector and educational categories have also widened in industrialising economies. In Latin America, where income inequality rose considerably in the 1980s and 1990s, wage differentials according to skill have grown particularly sharply. A similar pattern has occurred in the Middle East and North Africa, while wage differentials have grown in other developing countries, if less acutely (World Bank, 1995b, p. 120).

Wider wage differentials intensify the income insecurity of those earning low wages, especially if there is little prospect of upward mobility. We may surmise that such mobility is at least no greater than in the era of statutory regulation when differentials were lower and shrinking. If so, that is intensifying income insecurity for those employed near the bottom of the income distribution, who will be concentrated among those with 'flexible employment'.

Many economists believe that globalisation is widening wage differentials between the 'skilled' and 'unskilled'. The size of the effect is a matter of controversy. Minford, for instance, estimated that the unskilled's wages in industrialised countries would fall by 2 per cent a year, whereas Wood estimated that the effect was much greater (Wood, 1994). In the USA, the consensus seems to be that increased trade with developing countries has increased differentials (Lawrence, 1996; Borjas and Ramey, 1993). New technology may have had a greater impact (Bound and Johnson, 1992).

Some economists have concluded that it is hard to separate the effects of trade and technology.[2] One view is that the internationalisation of production, through multinationals and the type of production chains suggested in chapter 4, has resulted in relatively low-skilled production jobs being 'outsourced' to lower-wage developing countries, while non-production jobs have grown inside the country (Berman et al., 1992). It seems also that pressure on wages has been greater at the lower end of the labour market, for the less skilled, while international competition has lowered wages in monopolistic sectors and in sectors where unions bargained to obtain relatively high wages for workers with low skills, although the strength of this has been challenged (Lawrence, 1996, p. 9). In the USA, economic growth has also been associated with *falls* in wages of the lower-paid and increased rates of growth of income of the most highly-paid groups. Thus, there was a 13 per cent drop in real weekly earnings of non-supervisory and production workers between 1979 and 1995, despite a 21 per cent improvement in labour productivity, according to AFL-CIO estimates.

There is a tantalisingly undeveloped link between globalisation of capital markets and low-skilled employment. If globalisation raises long-term interest rates because of more uncertainty, the expected return to training investment declines, or the cost of on-the-job training rises, which must deter investment in such training, particularly for those for whom the returns would be modest in any case. Rising interest rates would also lower the wage at which firms would wish to recruit, since the investment outlay required would yield a lower expected return because it would need to be discounted by the higher interest rate (Phelps, 1997, p. 186). This effect on differentials and training would not necessarily emerge as an outcome of globalisation.

Wage differentials may also have widened because of the emergence of *regional economic blocs*. According to the gravity model of trade theory, trade between two countries or regions is proportional to the product of their GDPs divided by the distance between them raised to a power of approximately 0.6 (Leamer, 1996). Establishing a regional bloc shrinks the effective distance between economies and strengthens the impact on labour demand and wages (including relative wages within a national labour market). Thus, having low-wage neighbouring countries means that labour demand is made more elastic and wages are more likely to fall.

The main conclusion is that regulatory mechanisms have not prevented the growth of wage inequality. In many countries, real wages at the lower end of the labour market have fallen, and this has intensified income insecurity.

(iv) Cost of Employment Loss

Another reason for growing income insecurity in industrialised economies has been the greater adverse *income consequence* of loss of employment, due to lower benefits, lower duration of benefits, greater conditionality for access to benefits, lower probability of returning to an income-earning activity and lower probability that the income from any such activity would equal or exceed income from current employment. As the OECD recognised – reflecting an outcome of policies that it had recommended for its member countries – in industrialised economies the expected income loss from employment separation has increased (OECD, 1997b, p. 129).

For an individual worker, the potential cost of loss of employment, following the OECD, may be portrayed as follows:

$$C = s(V_j - rV_N - (1 - r) V_{ij})$$

where C is the cost of loss of employment, s is the probability of the current employment ending, V_j is the value of current employment, V_N is the expected value of a new job, V_{ij} is the expected value of being without a job, and r is the probability of finding a new job.

There are reasons for concluding that for the median jobholder the cost of employment loss has risen. If employment security has fallen, s will have increased, thereby raising C. If labour market insecurity has increased, r will have fallen, further raising C. And V_N will have fallen relative to V_j, since it has been established empirically that a person losing a job is on average increasingly likely only to find a subsequent job with a lower income (OECD, 1997b, p. 149).

In sum, the income insecurity of the median employed is likely to have increased because employment is more likely to end at any time, the chance of finding a comparable job has fallen, and the income is likely to be less than in the current job. Thus, one factor in the increased income insecurity in the USA has been that whereas most of those laid off in the early 1970s found jobs paying as well as those they had left, in 1996 only just over a third did so.[3] As we will see, the difficulty of securing an adequate income is compounded by the decline in V_{ij}.

(v) Non-wage Benefits

For the employed, social income consists of wages complemented by enterprise benefits, state transfers, community networks, kin transfers, and assistance from non-government organisations. In the current era, in industrialised countries at least, income security has become more differentiated because state benefits have stagnated or been cut, enterprise benefits have grown for privileged groups and shrunk for others, income from capital (private benefits) has grown for those with high earnings, and workers have been obliged to rely more on support from relatives, voluntary organisations and community groups. There has been more need for 'balanced reciprocity', in which people provide informal services and assistance to others as a form of insurance for which they expect support if they should need it. The difficulty is that this is not secure, to materialise or to match the value required or expected.

The welfare state presumed there would be mechanisms to ensure a worker received a family wage. Labour market security helped, enabling workers to

Table 7.2 Job-related employee benefits, by work arrangement,
Canada, 1995 *(percentage of employees entitled to benefit)*

	Pension Plan Other than CPP/QPP	Health Plan Other than Provincial Health Care	Dental Plan	Paid Sick Leave	Paid Vacation Leave
Full-time	58.4	68.1	63.4	65.7	81.9
Part-time	18.7	17.8	15.9	17.8	29.9
Permanent	55.5	64.4	60.0	62.2	78.5
Temporary	19.9	19.3	16.5	19.3	28.4
Firm Size < 20	12.8	22.1	19.7	29.2	55.3
Firm Size > 500	74.6	77.2	73.8	72.9	81.3
Union	81.1	82.8	75.9	77.0	84.2
Non-Union	33.0	44.4	41.9	44.8	65.3

Note: With respect to paid vacation, respondents were asked, 'Through his/her employer, is [the person] entitled to paid vacation leave?', and were expected to answer yes if they were allowed paid time off work, and 'no' if they were paid 4 per cent of their salary as 'vacation pay' but were not entitled to take vacation time off.
Source: HRDC, based on the 1995 Survey of Work Arrangements, Statistics Canada.

command adequate wages. Income risk was covered by occupational welfare, through enterprise benefits and entitlements. But these have been a *differentiating* part of remuneration in western Europe and North America. Employment flexibility has been associated with fragmentation in access to enterprise benefits. For example, in Canada, temporaries, part-time workers, those working in small firms and in non-union firms have a lower probability of access to such benefits than others (Table 7.2). In the USA, part-time, self-employed and 'contingent workers' receive lower and fewer fringe benefits than regular workers (Table 7.3). Such benefits were extensive in long-established firms, differentiating their income from others, by providing family-friendly benefits, such as health insurance, pension, life insurance, vacation leave, sick leave, parental and maternity leave, childcare benefits, parenting workshops or counselling, and company picnics (Osterman, 1995). Between 1982 and 1996, high-income earners on average gained in enterprise benefits, while the low-paid lost them. While all groups tended to lose enterprise-provided health insurance, the loss was much greater for low-wage workers. Firms have been differentiating their workforces through such benefits, as the US Bureau of Labor Statistics has found. And in some cases the insecurity is intensified because it is the lower-paid who have greatest need for the benefits, as in the case of on-the-job injuries, which are more common among the low-paid.

In eastern Europe, enterprise benefits have been withering, and access has been polarised, as shown by the Russian Enterprise Labour Flexibility Survey (Table 7.4). Growth of external flexibility has also been associated with differential access to benefits, as in Russia and Ukraine (Table 7.5). Privatisation has also been associated with a cut in benefits, as our enterprise surveys have shown in Albania,

Armenia, Georgia, Russia and Ukraine. And the trend towards smaller firms is also associated with erosion, since for all forms of benefit the probability that a worker has entitlement is much lower in small-scale firms.

Table 7.3 Wages and benefits, by contingent work status, USA, 1996

Percentage Receiving	Non-Standard Workers*	Regular Full-time Workers
	Men	
High wages**	22.1%	21.8%
Poverty-level wages	33.4%	17.7%
Fringe benefits	16.0%	80.1%
	Women	
High wages**	17.4%	23.0%
Poverty-level wages	52.3%	27.6%
Fringe benefits	22.8%	79.9%

Note: * Including part-time, self-employed, and independent contracting.
** Top 20 per cent of wage distribution
Source: Economic Policy Institute, Women's Research and Education Institute, *Business Week*, September 15, 1997.

Table 7.4 Percentage of manufacturing firms providing benefits for regular workers, by type of benefit, Russian Federation, 1991 and 1996

Benefit	1991	1996
Paid vacation	100.0	100.0
Rest houses	80.9	42.4
Sickness benefit	96.8	93.7
Subsidised rent	29.1	12.0
Subsidies for kindergartens	58.0	32.3
Bonuses	94.9	65.8
Profit sharing	76.4	59.5
Retiring assistance	28.5	69.6
Supplementary pension	5.1	5.7
Possibility for training	32.9	68.4
Subsidy for canteen or benefit for meal	57.6	36.7
Subsidised consumer goods	13.3	5.1

Source: ILO Russian Labour Flexibility Survey (merged RLFS1 and RLFS6, n = 158).

In developing countries, firms have also turned to external flexibility as a means of cutting overhead costs, and have provided temporary labour with fewer benefits, as illustrated for South Africa in Table 7.6 and as found in comparable surveys in Chile, Malaysia, Mexico and the Philippines (Table 7.7). We found this in Bombay as well (Deshpande et al., 1998).

Table 7.5 Entitlement to enterprise benefits, by labour status, selected eastern European countries, latest year available *(percentage of firms providing benefit)*

Labour Status	Russian Fed. Reg.	Temp.	Ukraine Reg.	Temp.	Albania Reg.	Temp.	Georgia Reg.	Temp.	Armenia Reg.	Temp.
Paid vacation	98.8	20.4	100.0	21.9	94.8	16.1	76.7	6.3	80.3	3.2
Additional vacation	61.2	4.4	88.3	11.5	n.a.	n.a.	10.5	3.1	27.2	1.0
Rest houses	36.4	5.9	58.6	14.8	91.6	29.9	1.9	3.1	7.7	0.8
Sickness benefit	92.0	31.1	95.2	51.2	90.1	24.7	16.9	6.3	44.3	3.8
Paid health services	41.7	7.4	29.5	12.3	n.a.	n.a.	6.4	3.2	9.7	1.2
Subsidised rent	9.2	0.0	20.4	3.5	6.1	2.7	1.7	0.0	2.4	0.4
Subsidies for kindergartens	29.3	5.0	24.9	6.7	63.1	19.3	4.7	0.0	4.2	1.0
Bonuses	63.9	17.2	84.1	45.6	34.2	9.8	9.1	3.1	19.5	1.4
Profit sharing	49.1	6.2	53.4	15.1	n.a.	n.a.	8.6	0.0	10.6	0.6
Loans	71.3	11.2	90.5	27.3	8.5	1.8	21.9	6.3	32.5	2.2
Retiring assistance	65.4	4.4	83.9	10.4	25.7	7.5	4.2	0.0	17.1	1.0
Supplementary pension	8.6	0.6	6.6	0.6	3.8	1.5	1.7	0.0	3.6	0.6
Possibility for training	65.1	9.2	69.5	14.1	16.7	4.8	19.7	9.4	7.4	0.8
Subsidised food	n.a.	n.a.	35.1	22.1	28.6	12.2	5.5	3.1	7.2	1.6
Subsidy for canteen or benefit for meal	35.5	15.1	43.3	25.5	n.a.	n.a.	6.1	6.3	5.8	1.6
Subsidised consumer goods	4.7	3.6	17.6	12.3	47.1	15.9	1.1	0.0	2.8	1.0
Transport subsidies	22.2	3.0	24.8	11.0	20.8	10.7	4.7	6.3	6.2	1.4
Unpaid shares	13.6	0.6	n.a.	n.a.	n.a.	n.a.	16.6	6.3	2.8	0.6

Source: ILO ELFS surveys (RLFS6, 1996, n = 497; ULFS2, 1994, n = 566; ALFS2, 1996, n = 346; GLFS1, 1996, n = 361; ArLFS1, 1995, n = 498).

Deunionisation has contributed to the erosion and fragmentation of enterprise benefits. Unionised firms tend to provide workers with a wider array of benefits than non-unionised firms, and firms with *independent* unions are more likely to provide benefits than firms with *company* unions. The former has been found in industrialised countries (e.g., Freeman and Medoff, 1984). Both patterns have also been found in industrialising economies, notably in East Asia, such as Malaysia and the Philippines (Standing, 1992). Similar phenomena have been occurring in transition countries. The erosion in representation security, and the shift from independent to company unions in parts of the world, have surely contributed to an erosion of entitlements and a recomposition of social incomes, with more income insecurity.

What about the changes in the role of *community benefits*, a term covering all forms of informal support in the social income? The most relevant example of how vital they are as a system of social protection is the experience in eastern Europe. In some Asian republics of the former Soviet Union, it has been observed that more Russians have been dying of hunger and related illnesses than Uzbeks or Kazakstanis, which has been attributed to the lack of extended family support networks for Russians living in those communities.

Table 7.6 Entitlement to enterprise benefits, by labour status, 1996, South Africa

Benefits	Regular workers	Temp. workers
Paid vacation	96.1	16.4
Paid sick leave	96.5	15.1
Medical aid	67.8	1.4
Medical facilities on site	53.0	33.8
Subsidised housing/ housing allowance	12.9	0.5
Childcare services	2.2	0.5
Incentive bonuses	37.6	6.8
Profit share bonus	12.5	1.4
Severance pay	77.5	8.7
Transport allowances	29.3	5.9
Occupational health service	45.0	25.9
Provident fund	85.7	8.7
Paid maternity leave	61.6	2.3
Pension	62.1	6.4
Hostel benefits	5.2	0.5

Source: SALFS2, n = 234

Table 7.7 Entitlement to enterprise benefits, by labour status, 1990, Philippines

Benefits	Regular	Temporary
Medical benefit	65.6	18.0
Empl. accident and disease	54.4	16.6
Paid leave	63.1	4.7
Sick leave	66.3	4.6
Maternity leave	48.8	5.4
Pension	14.4	0.8
Retrenchment	33.1	4.3
Loans	44.2	7.0
Transport subsidies	26.4	6.5
Accommodation allowance	16.5	3.8
Meal allowance	33.5	8.6
13th month allowance	76.0	26.4

Source: PLFS1, n = 1311

Internationally, the most intriguing indicator of the changing and increasing role of community benefits in social income is the growth in voluntary work by hundreds of thousands of *non-governmental organisations* of a non-profit-making type. Such organisations have always existed. But the expansion in their numbers and the diversity of their economic and social roles are late twentieth century phenomena. To some extent, they have been able to fill gaps left by the erosion of state benefits, adequate wages and enterprise benefits. With existing data, it would be hard to estimate how extensively they have counteracted growing income insecurity. What we do know is that millions of people are employed in socially-oriented NGOs, and that millions more work for them voluntarily without remuneration. In industrialised economies, NGOs have been providing a growing range of social benefits, such as medical care, education, training, kindergartens, cultural services and housing.

The outstanding questions relate to their potential role as societies move away from the perceived ideal of welfare state capitalism. Do informal networks allow the state to reduce its social responsibilities? Does informal support adequately substitute for cuts in state and enterprise benefits? Is it viable to place the onus of responsibility on institutions that have neither the capacity nor mandate to undertake the role of providing more elements of social income? Is there a danger that, in providing benefits to workers and their families, NGOs would become *controllers* of their behaviour, acting as intermediary for the state or firms?

Finally, there is the role of the family in providing benefits to workers as part of the social income. Globally, there may have been a decline in the strength of the family as conventionally conceived. This implies that there is less scope for the provision of benefits, although the need for income is not reduced.

7.5 INCOME SECURITY OF THE UNEMPLOYED

For the unemployed and those facing the prospect of unemployment, income security is represented primarily by the probability of receipt of unemployment benefits, of which there have been two main forms – unemployment insurance and unemployment assistance, the former supposedly determined as an employment right, the latter by perceived need. A third form is family, kinship or community transfers, on which most of the unemployed throughout history have had to rely.

Unemployment benefits have always had a double character – a mechanism of social protection and labour market regulation. They have always tended to divide the unemployed into the 'deserving' and 'undeserving'. For instance, when unemployment insurance was introduced in Great Britain in 1911 two conditions were applied, ostensibly to safeguard against abuse and to legitimise such benefits – the unemployed had to be 'available for work', and should not have left employment 'without good cause'. In every age, the 'fear of the scrounger' has been brought into the public debate of proposals for state provision of income security. This underpinned the 1834 Poor Law, which specified that the destitute could be identified by their willingness to perform unattractive labour, in the 'workhouse', in return for survival assistance. Similar debates figured in the introduction of unemployment benefit regimes in the twentieth century.

Entitlement conditions have often been tightened in recessions or prolonged periods of mass unemployment. In the UK, the contributions condition was relaxed after the First World War, because it was politically impossible to leave millions of ex-soldiers and others who had worked to support the war dependent on poor relief. But with high unemployment in 1921 the condition was inserted that a person had to be 'genuinely seeking whole-time employment', and in 1924 the condition was added that the person had to be 'making all reasonable efforts to secure employment'. After six years of arbitrary application and social suffering, the 'genuinely seeking work' test was removed. For some time afterwards, entitlement conditions were relaxed, and in the post-1945 period this corresponded to the ethos of the era and the perception that high unemployment was unlikely to come back.

In that era, unemployment benefit systems spread around the world, although they were regarded as unaffordable in many low-income countries, where they were applied to a minority, or regarded as a long-term objective. In countries adopting state socialism, the coercive character of full employment meant that nobody could be unemployed legitimately. If, by some twist of fate, they became unemployed they were classified as parasitic, so that there was no need to have income provision for unemployment. In welfare state capitalism, the presumption of Full Employment meant that benefits were only deemed necessary for 'temporary interruptions of earnings power' associated with frictional unemployment. Given the presumption of stable, full-time employment for men who had a small risk of frictional unemployment, it was presumed that unemployment benefits could be paid from social insurance contributions from employers and/or workers, leaving a small minority of unfortunate people to be assisted by other means.

When state socialism began to unravel, countries in eastern Europe and the Soviet Union, beginning with Hungary in 1986, introduced unemployment benefit schemes based on those operating in industrialised countries. The trouble was that they did so when the systems were under strain almost everywhere. In the 1980s the premises for unemployment benefits were eroded in welfare state economies, producing three crises – a *fiscal crisis*, a *moral crisis*, and a *legitimation crisis*.

The fiscal crisis was an outcome of mass unemployment and flexible forms of labour, which resulted in fewer contributions and a rising demand for benefits. This induced pressure to reduce the level and duration of benefits, raise contribution rates and tighten conditions for entitlement. The pressure intensified with the new orthodoxy of macro-economic policy, in which cutting public expenditure and deficits were seen as the means of controlling inflationary pressure and boosting growth.

The moral crisis also stems from labour market developments. Unemployment benefits were originally designed for labour markets consisting of full-time, reasonably well-paid workers, with only a small minority needing them. Because of the presumption that an individual's unemployment would be short, that average earnings were rising and that those losing jobs would be able to obtain others paying approximately the same, the benefits provided reasonable income replacement rates. In the 1980s and 1990s, none of those presumptions were justifiable. A dilemma has been to decide whether replacements rates should rise or fall.

With higher unemployment, in most countries the average duration of unemployment has increased, the number of long-term unemployed has grown, more of the unemployed have been labour force entrants, more have not built up insurance contributions because they have been in some flexible form of labour, and more have had low pre-unemployment wages. As a result, there has appeared to be high income replacement rates, not because of 'generosity of benefits', as some economists have claimed, but because of low earnings associated with part-time and casual jobs available for many of the unemployed.

The interaction of flexible labour markets and unemployment benefits has created more *unemployment traps*, whereby earnings replacement rates are close to or even above what someone could reasonably expect to obtain in a new job. A moral crisis has permeated policy discussion. Cutting replacement rates erodes the insurance principle (fictive or not, depending on the country and system). A person paying insurance contributions for many years does not have a known benefit, and could not realistically estimate a probable income. And it threatened to mean that the unemployed received less than a poverty income. Maintaining replacement rates was deemed to encourage 'voluntary unemployment', thus raising the NAIRU. Indeed, some economists have argued that *cutting* benefits would help the unemployed, because that would induce pressure to lower wages, boosting labour demand, thus absorbing the unemployed into employment.

In practice, it is virtually impossible to define voluntary unemployment without making arbitrary judgments. There is also a moral dilemma arising from erosion of the insurance principle, the poverty implications of lower replacement rates, and behavioural presumptions behind advocacy of 'reduced generosity' of unemployment benefits. The latter has been advocated by, among others, the OECD, IMF and World Bank, particularly for western Europe, and in eastern Europe. The moral crisis has been intensified because policy changes have been influenced by decisions on who is 'deserving' and who 'undeserving' of income support.

Unemployment benefits have also run into a legitimation crisis. Like many forms of income provision, their political legitimacy has depended on the perception by enough people that they might need a benefit at some time, a commitment to social solidarity, and a feeling by a majority that the benefits are not likely to penalise them (or their families or friends). If people feel they are paying taxes for the benefit of others with whom they do not identify, erosion of public legitimation is likely. If people feel that they themselves have a low probability of being unemployed, they are likely to vote for someone promising to cut benefits. If they think that even if they were to lose a job, their probability of prolonged unemployment would be low, they would be more inclined to vote for someone promising to cut the duration of benefit entitlement. Politicians are likely to think along analogous lines. There are countervailing factors, such as the threat of violence and agitation by the losers, and the unsavoury sight of wretchedly poor unemployed on the streets. But a legitimation crisis seems to have been spreading.

Across the world politicians across the ideological spectrum have followed the lead of libertarians and supply-side economists in accepting that the unemployed should receive lower benefits – to increase the incentive to take jobs and to reduce upward pressure on wages – and in claiming that the 'undeserving' should be excluded from entitlement altogether. This reflects a desire to regulate the lower end of the labour market and a realisation that the labour market does not correspond to the one presumed in the model of welfare state capitalism. Those on the political 'left' have tended to favour the preservation of benefits, justifying their support for cuts in levels and tighter conditions as necessary to retain public legitimacy for them, while the 'right' have wanted to whittle away at levels and tighten conditions for other reasons.

The fiscal, moral and legitimation crises have influenced the restructuring of unemployment benefit systems around the world in the 1980s and 1990s. To appreciate how they have been 'disembedded' from the labour market we must consider developments associated with flexibility and changes made to unemployment benefit regimes. Figure 7.2 presents a stylised picture of this process.

This presents the main routes from employment into unemployment. The standard labour market model presumes a route from full-time, regular employment into unemployment, from that to receipt of unemployment benefits, and then back into employment. Besides the fact that many people change jobs without unemployment, the standard model may account for a diminishing minority of transitions in flexible labour markets. Excluding the direct route from one employment to another, or into an on-the-job training scheme, the Figure shows eight possible exits from secure employment. The path could be direct into unemployment through redundancy or 'quitting', however 'involuntary' that might be in practice. Or the worker could go from employment into one or more intermediate statuses. If she had little employment security, a direct route into redundancy would be relatively likely. If he had little job security, he might be bumped into a lower-wage job initially or into involuntary part-time employment, or be transferred into a casualised post. In principle, the worker could object or take legal action against any of these moves. In practice, since the prospect of retaining an income would be reduced if he did object, discretion would lead him to accept a compromise if offered. The first phase might involve taking a cut in income or part-time employment paying less. This might continue for some time – unless he were reabsorbed into regular employment – until the worker quit in despair, took a moonlighting job or was made redundant.

In all these cases, entitlement to benefits might be adversely affected, *if* entitlement is conditional on past employment or on the means by which the person becomes unemployed or if the benefit level is a function of recent wages. A critical point is that if employment becomes flexible it may affect unemployment benefit entitlements, which would not be the intended result for employer or worker.

This leads to Figure 7.3, which deals with the unemployed's income security through the process of entitlement and disentitlement. Those leaving a job could enter another directly, become unemployed or leave the labour force. If becoming unemployed, they could be 'passive' (available and waiting for employment but not seeking it) or 'active' unemployed. By definition, the former do not seek unemployment benefits. Many active unemployed also do not do so, because of ignorance, fear, stigma, cost of travel to employment exchanges, or inability to go there. In some countries, these may have been the reasons for a *majority* not receiving unemployment benefits. They have been important in the ex-state socialism countries, due to the legacy of stigma associated with unemployment, lack of facilities, long distances and other obstacles to registration for claiming benefits, and low level of benefits (Standing, 1994).

Leaving non-applicants aside, the remainder enter the unemployment benefit regime, where they face obstacles or tests, which may result in disentitlement or non-receipt even if entitled. In early schemes, conditions were relatively few and use of them was variable. In the current era, in which the language of the deserving and undeserving poor has regained political legitimacy, the unemployed's income security has declined for several reasons. One should differentiate between *explicit disentitlement*, which arises from governments applying new conditions or tightening old conditions, and *implicit disentitlement*, whereby more workers find themselves

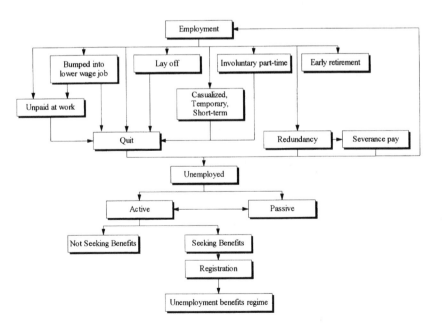

Figure 7.2 From labour surplus to labour market marginalisation

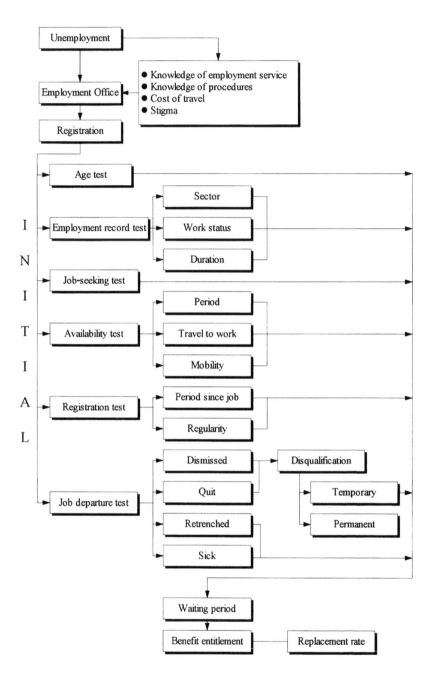

Figure 7.3 Entering the unemployment benefits regime

in statuses or with experience preventing them from gaining entitlement or giving them a lower benefit. Labour market flexibility has led to implicit disentitlement, as has growth of long-term unemployment. This can be considered by assessing the *entitlement tests* the unemployed have to pass to obtain or retain benefits.

Figure 7.3 presents the stylised initial stages in a typical unemployment benefit regime. The upper half refers to the initial application for benefits. Presuming the unemployed have made the journey successfully to the employment exchange to register (passing the *claimant registration test*), the first condition they must satisfy is the *age test*. This might seem uncontroversial, the rationale being that the person has to be in a certain age range. In practice, some countries have lowered the upper age for entitlement, and put older unemployed into early retirement or disability status.

The second condition is the *employment record test*, which means that they must have proof that they have paid insurance contributions for so many months over a certain recent period, or have had them paid for them. If the required number of months is low and if the period is long, probability of passing this test will be high.

Increasing the number of months and shortening the period during which the number must have been accumulated are ways of eroding entitlement. In some countries, certain types of employment or sectors do not count; in some, youths are excluded from entitlement because they do not have an employment record. There is no standard rule, and no rule would be any more just than any other.

There may be pragmatic fiscal reasons for specifying what counts as employment and what should be the minimum number of months of such employment. But the rule is arbitrary. All sorts of anomalies are likely. For example, someone who has worked for six months part time might qualify for benefits, while someone who has worked three months full time may not – or vice-versa. Given the rising number in temporary and part-time jobs, the condition may be responsible for growing disentitlement.

As Table 7.8 shows, even within the European Union, employment 'continuity requirements' have varied a lot (Rubery and Grimshaw, 1997). Further east, all sorts of rules have applied, often guided by foreign advisers and foreign models of unemployment benefits. In Bulgaria, it has been at least 6 in the past 12 months, in the Czech and Slovak Republics it has been at least 12 months in the past 3 years; in Poland, it has been at least 365 days in the past 18 months; in Lithuania, it has been at least 24 months in the past 3 years. So, someone in Bulgaria employed for 7 months in the past year would receive benefits while someone in the Czech Republic who worked for just as long would not. In some countries, the benefit to which a person is entitled has varied according to duration of past employment. In Latvia, for instance, entitlement to full benefit has only been achieved if the person had paid the social tax for 5 years. In Azerbaijan, full entitlement has required proof of employment for at least 10 years.

No employment record rule is fair, and any rule introduces inter-personal inequity. What is apparent is that internationally there has been a tendency to increase the required number of months in employment and to shorten the period in which those months have had to be worked, resulting in more explicit disentitlement.

The next barrier is the *job departure test*. In many countries, those who '*quit*' employment or who are dismissed for disciplinary reasons (whether proven or not) can be disqualified from entitlement to benefits, for an initial period or for the entire period of their unemployment. The rationale is that this condition discourages frivolous job leaving. In practice, it discourages labour mobility, and some have even described it as a version of workfare, in that threat of disentitlement forces workers to stay in jobs that have unsatisfactory wages, working conditions or work security.

Again, this test has been tightened, dramatically so in the UK in the 1980s. A person deemed by local officials to have left a job without good cause was initially disqualified from benefits for 6 weeks but this was lengthened to 13 weeks and then extended to 26 weeks (Byrne and Jacobs, 1988). Such changes can have impressive effects on the official unemployment rate, but intensify the unemployed's income insecurity. Most US States have disqualified those reported to have quit their past job 'without just cause' for the entire period of unemployment.

Flexible labour markets make such rules harder to apply with consistency or fairness. The procedure is subjective, because the distinction between so-called voluntary quitting and being declared redundant or laid off is not clear. Personal interpretation comes into play, as with the ending of a fixed-term contract. Many workers do not like to admit that their firm declared that they were of no use, so that the test becomes a source of embarrassment and stigma. To say, 'I left' is easier to say than 'I was pushed out.' Yet the little white lie in one direction could result in disentitlement, the little white lie in the other could result in entitlement.

The job-departure test has been a source of income insecurity in eastern Europe. Probably the worst case is where workers have been placed on unpaid 'adminis-trative leave' (a situation captured in Figure 7.2, which one might call flexibility). In Russia, Ukraine and other places, millions of workers have been trapped in an absurd situation. If they quit jobs paying little or nothing (because of 'wage arrears' or because they have been placed on leave) they would have lost entitlement to severance pay and probably to unemployment benefits, either because they could not obtain them if they 'quit' or because they could not obtain their work history book from the enterprise, required for registration at an employment exchange. It did not pay enterprises to retrench the workers because the cost of retaining them on the books was less than the cost of paying them severance pay (3 months' wages) and possibly less than the 'social cost' (loss of prestige, morale, etc.) of retrenching. Moreover, for a long time, boosting the recorded number of employees kept down the excess wage tax. So, millions who were really unemployed were trapped in non-paying, non-working employment, which neither they nor their employers – nor the government, nor their well-paid consultant advisers – had an incentive to end.

This may seem extreme and reflect a passing phase. Yet in flexible labour markets, particularly with weak representation security, the job departure test will be a source of inequity and disentitlement, with discretionary judgments being required of local bureaucracies. A tick in a box here or there could alter an applicant's entitlement, and the person might shuffle off no wiser, but poorer. Anyone who has seen the process at work or who has been involved will understand that. And a further source of income insecurity flows from this test. Once disqualified, a person is surely less likely to go back, or be able to face the process, psychologically or financially.

If the unemployed passes the employment-record and job-departure tests – which would depend on the benefit system, ethos of employment service and level of unemployment – then the *job availability test* must be passed. This may seem straightforward. It may not be. The rule may require a person to be available for a job at 24 hours' notice, a week's notice, or longer. The shorter the period the more likely disentitlement. The person may also have to give a commitment to be prepared to travel to take a job or to move to another area to do so. There has been tightening of the availability condition in some countries, and more assiduous application of it.

Assuming that the claimants pass all these tests, they are likely to face a *waiting period* before being entitled to receive unemployment benefits. This can be a week or two weeks or even longer. In some countries, the period has been lengthened.

For those who have made it so far, the regulatory control system could then lead to second-round disentitlements, presented in Figure 7.4 (although not all systems use all the tests). First, they will usually have to pass the *job-seeking test*. This is regarded as reasonable, requiring the unemployed to search 'actively' for a job in the past week or four weeks. It does raise problems. There is not much point in searching for jobs when there are none available. The rule also invites abuse, allowing employment officials to intrude into the private lives of claimants. Governments wishing to cut public spending tend to tighten such rules, demanding proof and questioning the motives of those already feeling insecure.

Having been a source of suffering in the 1920s, there was prolonged distaste for the job-seeking condition for entitlement to benefits in the UK. However, the condition was reinstated under the *Social Security Act* of 1989, when once more onus of proof was placed on claimants through the 'actively seeking work' condition, allowing local officials discretionary powers in determining entitlement. Since then, probing, follow-up interviews with officials and other devices have been deployed to check on job seeking, putting more pressure on claimants. The test has also been tightened in other countries. Australia led the way, with 'activity agreements' and Job Search Allowances, which replaced unemployment benefits in 1991.

No doubt, checking on job seeking could identify some who are not seeking, perhaps justifying the expenditure on seeking out 'undeserving' or fraudulent claimants. Whether the saving covers the cost of the extra policing is unclear. The existence of the test makes it a strange use of words to call unemployment benefits 'passive' policy. And while commentators have referred to the moral hazard of benefits in encouraging those covered by 'unemployment insurance' to become and remain unemployed, such tests raise moral hazards for officials operating them. Is not the test and the prospect of snooping on their lives likely to lead many unemployed, in a vulnerable stage of their lives, to withdraw a claim, even if fully entitled to make it?

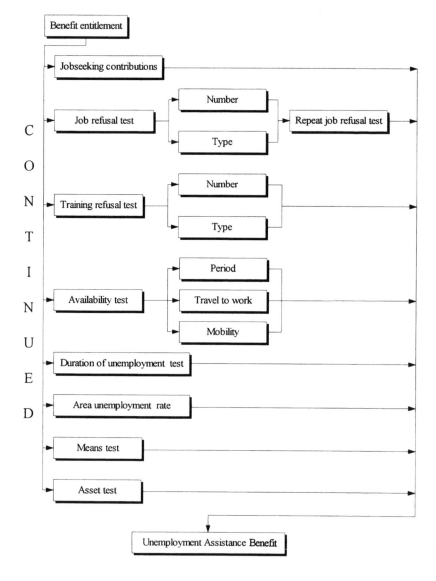

Figure 7.4 Continued entitlement in unemployment benefits regime

Next, the unemployed would probably be subject to a *job availability test*, which could cause disentitlement even if did not do so at the outset. The availability condition has always been arbitrary. In the UK, it was tightened in the 1980s, particularly in 1988 when the unemployed were required to fill in a form with 18 questions; any wrong answers resulted in suspended benefits and if the Department of Employment subsequently supported the suspension the person was declared unavailable for work and ineligible for benefits. The intentions of the tighter conditions were clear, as shown by a Departmental Circular sent to benefit managers:

> A claimant must be able to accept at once (or at 24 hours notice in certain specified circumstances) any opportunity of suitable employment.This also means not just being ready to take a job, but taking active steps to draw attention to their availability for work. A claimant must not place restrictions on the nature and conditions (such as pay, hours of work, locality, etc.) they are prepared to accept which would prevent them from having reasonable prospects of getting work.

Here is a prescription for control through insecurity, giving discretionary powers to local officials. In this instance, it seems the intentions were to enforce labour mobility, to lower reservation wages, and to deter claimants altogether.[4]

The third condition is the *job refusal test*. The unemployed are usually required to accept a job if offered by the employment exchange, and may be required to accept 'suitable employment'. This might correspond to their aspirations, their perceptions of their skills or to those as perceived by local officials. Or the rule may stipulate that the unemployed must accept any job, or that certain groups of unemployed must accept any job. The rules may be established with varying degrees of harshness. The rationale is that this demonstrates willingness to work and that unemployment is not 'voluntary'. It is not as simple as that seems. The rule invites bureaucratic, paternalistic intrusiveness, and presumes that some local official knows better than the job-seeker what is best for him or her. It also raises the problem of defining 'suitable'. The intrusiveness and arbitrariness are likely to increase if employment exchanges are under pressure to demonstrate efficiency by raising their 'placement rates'. A rush to placement may not be in the long-term interest of the unemployed.

The job refusal test has been tightened in many countries in the 1980s and 1990s. In many, refusing more than one or two job offers results in disentitlement, and even refusing a job requiring less skill than possessed by the job-seeker or paying lower wages than the person's past wage can lead to disentitlement. In the UK, where the *job-refusal test* has existed for many years, under the 1989 *Social Security Act* most unemployed, after a short period, were no longer entitled to refuse a job on the grounds that the wage was low. In Australia, entitlement rules were amended to require the unemployed to accept temporary jobs if offered. Such moves may encourage labour casualisation and undermine the person's subsequent entitlements.

A fourth condition is a *training refusal test*, which may have grown in significance. With governments giving more attention to so-called 'active' labour market policy, a person refusing a training place offered by an employment exchange may face disentitlement – or drop out of the pool of claimants before a decision is made, making it hard to attribute 'disentitlement' to this factor.

A fifth test has been the least common. In a few countries, entitlement to unemployment benefits may be determined by a *means test* or *assets test*, as in Australia since 1987. These normally apply to unemployment assistance, granted to some whose entitlement to unemployment benefits has expired or been denied.

A sixth source of disentitlement is the *unemployment duration test*. The rationale is that benefits are supposed to provide income security while a person seeks employment, and a time limit should concentrate the mind on taking a job. A drawback is that it could induce the unemployed to make poor long-term decisions, by taking unsuitable jobs from which they subsequently 'quit', so disentitling them to benefits, or by taking temporary jobs that offer no chance of building up entitlements or skills before a new spell of unemployment strikes. It cannot be *presumed* that a short duration benefit regime lowers unemployment.

In some cases, duration of entitlement has been made a function of the level of unemployment, either cyclically, as in the USA, or according to some level of unemployment in the area in which the unemployed person is residing, as in Poland. If living in an area of 'crisis-level' unemployment, the person has been entitled to 12 months of benefit; if living in an area of lower unemployment, entitlement has been for 6 months. Not only does this rule discourage mobility from high-unemployment to low-unemployment areas, but it is unfair on an inter-personal level. Why should someone in an area with 9.9 per cent unemployment receive half the benefit of someone in an area of 10.1 per cent unemployment? However pragmatic the rule, it offends any principle of distributive justice. Both persons are unemployed, and if the person in the higher unemployment area has a higher skill level, he would almost certainly have a higher probability of re-employment than the person in the other area.

There has been an international trend to reduce the duration of entitlement to unemployment benefits. The Netherlands, Switzerland and the UK were among European countries to reduce the duration in the 1990s. In the UK, it was reduced from 12 to 6 months with replacement of unemployment benefits by Jobseekers' Allowance. In Switzerland, in 1996 those aged under 50 had the maximum duration cut from 400 to 150 days, after which they had to participate in a workfare scheme.

The tendency has been most pronounced in central and eastern Europe. Initially, most countries allowed for up to 12 months, often with a declining level of benefits during the period of unemployment. Since then, the period has been shortened, often to 6 months, as in Belarus, Bulgaria, the Czech Republic, Estonia, Kyrgyzia and Lithuania, or to 9 months, as in Latvia, or to a declining level over successive months, as in Moldova and Romania. The shortening occurred as job prospects declined with rising unemployment, and as rules became more selective and complex. In Bulgaria, duration of entitlement was made dependent on age and duration of past employment. In Slovakia, if the unemployed was aged 15–29, duration of entitlement was 6 months; if aged 30–44, it was 8; if aged 45–49, it was 9 months; and if aged 50 or more it was 12 months. One may comprehend the rough logic, but it represented a rough sort of justice.

In sum, many factors make entitlement to unemployment benefits precarious. And probability of entitlement has declined. For instance, Atkinson and Mickelwright listed 27 measures that had cut benefits for the unemployed in the UK between 1979 and 1988, compared to 4 that had benefited them, and 7 that were about neutral (Atkinson and Micklewright, 1988). In the USA, for many years only a minority of the unemployed have actually received unemployment benefits (Rejda, 1994, p. 392). In the 1980s and 1990s, the average fluctuated between 30 per cent and 40 per cent. In most 'right to work' states, the figure has been lower, with states like South Dakota and Virginia having situations in which less than 20 per cent of the unemployed were receiving unemployment benefits (Shapiro and Nichols, 1991).

A study by Mathematica Policy Research (1988) of the decline in coverage of unemployment benefits in the USA concluded that the decline reflected:

- a falling proportion of the unemployed coming from the relatively well-covered manufacturing sector (accounting for 4–18 per cent of the total decline);
- regional shifts in the composition of unemployment (16 per cent);
- state programme changes (22–39 per cent), which involved:
    an increase in base period earnings requirements (8–15 per cent);
    an increase in income-based denials for benefit (10 per cent);
    other, non-monetary eligibility conditions (3–11 per cent);
- changes in Federal policy, with partial taxation of unemployment insurance benefits (11–16 per cent);
- changes in unemployment as measured by the CPS (1–12 per cent).[5]

At the end of the 1980s, obtaining entitlement became even harder in the USA. In most states, the person now must have been employed for at least 6 months in the past year to qualify for minimum benefits, with other states having a minimum duration specified in terms of a required amount of wage earnings in the year. In 1989–90, 15 states raised the base year earnings required to qualify for minimum weekly benefit, and 39 increased the level required for maximum benefit. Another trend has been stricter application of disqualification rules. A study found that of the 14.2 million 'monetarily eligible' initial claimants for unemployment insurance benefits in 1989 no less than 24.3 per cent were disqualified – 5.9 per cent for supposedly not being able to work or for not being deemed readily available for work, 6.8 per cent for leaving a job 'without good cause', 4.1 per cent for being fired for misconduct, 0.3 per cent for refusing 'suitable work', and 7.2 per cent for other reasons. Once disqualified – perhaps for 'voluntarily' quitting a job or for 'refusing' a job deemed 'suitable' – the unemployed in many states cannot receive benefits during the entire period of unemployment (Corson and Nicholson, 1989). This is a system being used as a means of labour market control and regulation, not as a means of providing income security.

Entitlement has become harder in many other countries. According to government reports (OECD, 1997c, Table 6), in the 1990s alone eligibility conditions were tightened in Austria, Canada, Denmark, Finland, France, the Netherlands, New Zealand, Norway, Spain, Sweden and the UK, while tighter job availability requirements were applied in Belgium, Canada, Denmark, Germany, Italy, the Netherlands, New Zealand, Spain, Sweden and the UK.

As for insurance benefits for those who manage to receive them, they have been eroded in terms of both levels and accessibility in most countries. In the USA, it has long been the case that only about one-third of the unemployed receive UI benefits, and a falling proportion of workers are covered by them. In the EU, similar trends have emerged since the 1970s. By the late 1980s, 30 per cent of the unemployed in Spain were receiving unemployment benefits, in France 39 per cent, in West Germany 55 per cent and in Sweden (supposedly a model of universalism) 68 per cent. By the late 1990s, only a minority of the unemployed in Europe were receiving unemployment insurance benefits, and in the EU only one-third of the unemployed received benefits or assistance (Table 7.8). Although these figures overstate receipt of unemployment benefits, taking them as upper limits, we have a clearer picture of the 'generosity of unemployment benefits'.

Table 7.9 indicates that in EU countries, where entitlement and recipient rates are higher than elsewhere, the share of the active unemployed receiving unemployment insurance or assistance benefits ranges from 83 per cent in Belgium to less than 8 per cent in Greece and Italy. In most countries, women were less likely to be receiving benefits. But these figures overstate the probability of receipt of benefits. According to EUROSTAT data, if we count all the unemployed, including those wanting but not currently seeking employment, in 1996 less than 20 per cent were receiving benefits.

In eastern Europe, the situation is more peculiar because in some countries, including the two largest, most unemployed are not registered and do not receive unemployment benefits. If registered, probability of entitlement was high in Russia. But entitlement has not necessarily meant receipt, since many *oblast* employment services have not had the funds to pay. Even if 80 per cent of the registered received benefits, since three-quarters of the unemployed were not registered, that would imply only about 20 per cent were receiving benefits. In other countries, there has been a sharp decline in the proportion receiving benefits – in Bulgaria to 23 per cent in 1996, in Latvia 47 per cent, in Poland 52 per cent, all well down from the levels in 1992.

The OECD have made a valuable effort to monitor trends in unemployment benefit replacement rates – the benefit relative to average earnings. The task is

Table 7.8 Access to unemployment benefits in EU countries, mid-1990s

	A.per cent of ILO-unemployed receiving unemployment benefits or assistance 1994		**B.** Continuity requirements for unemployment benefits	**C.** Requirements for access of part-timers to unemployment benefits	**D.** Duration of non means-tested benefits
Country	Male	Female			
	High share (%)				
SF	90.4	91.6	Low	High	Medium
B	84.0	85.8	Medium	High	Long
S	78.7	76.8[1]	Low	High	Short
DK	68.2	70.4	Low	Medium	Long
D	77.5	69.2	Low	High	Medium
	Medium share %				
FR	53.5	43.8	Medium	Low	Medium
IRL	82.0	42.9	High	High	Short
UK	71.0	36.8[2]	Medium	High	Short
NL	62.2	33.9	Medium	Low	Long
	Low share %				
E	37.4	19.2	Low	Low	Medium
L	26.6	30.7	Medium	Medium	Medium
P	25.5	23.5	High	–	Medium
GR	10.2	5.2	Low	–	Short
I	8.5	7.1	Medium[4]	–	Short
A	–	–	Medium	Low[5]	Short
EUR(12)	38.1	33.0			

Column **B**. Continuity requirements: Low – less than six months in past year or equivalent; Medium – approximately equal to six months in past year or equivalent; High – greater than six months in past year.

Column **C**. Requirements affecting part-timers' access to unemployment benefits: Low – minimum hours threshold of 12 hours or less; no requirement to be available for full-time work; Medium – minimum hours threshold more than 12 hours, less than 17; no requirement to be available for full-time work; High – minimum threshold of 17 hours or more, or minimum earnings requirement or requirement to be available for full-time work.

Column **D**. Duration of non means-tested benefits: Short – 15 months maximum or less; Medium – more than 15 months maximum but less than three years maximum; Long – more than three years maximum.

Notes: 1990; 2 Data missing for UK, so from Labour Force Survey for winter 1995–96; 3 Data missing for Luxembourg, so figures refer to 1991, based on annual census; 4 For Italy, 'ordinary unemployment benefits'. 5 In Austria, benefits are earnings related with no minimum for part-timers.

Source: EUROSTAT, *Labour Force Survey: Results 1994* (Luxembourg, 1996); Grimshaw and Rubery, 1997, Table 1, p. 296.

not easy, and neither is the task of interpreting the OECD's data base. One must distinguish between *gross* and *net* replacement, i.e., before and after tax. In some countries, there is a substantial difference. The figures also presume that all claimants receive their entitlement, which is not the case because incomplete take-up of benefits is often considerable (Atkinson and Micklewright, 1991). Unfortunately, data on take-up rates are not available. Third, *average* replacement rates over an extended period often differ from *initial* replacement rates. Some commentators exaggerate the replacement rate by giving the figure for the first month of unemployment, *after* the waiting period, which is when the rate is at its height. If someone expects to be unemployed for longer, that is not the relevant figure. Tracing trends is further complicated because of *explicit* and *implicit disentitlement*.

Table 7.9 Unemployed receiving benefits, European Community, 1992–96
(percent of active unemployed receiving)

Country	1992	1993	1994	1995	1996
Austria	n.a.	n.a.	n.a.	63.1	68.9
Belgium	83.9	83.3	84.5	81.1	82.6
W. Germany	60.2	64.6	66.0	63.2	68.0
Denmark	79.9	82.6	64.2	65.4	55.1
Spain	29.7	31.2	28.1	23.5	20.4
Finland	n.a.	n.a.	n.a.	67.6	60.4
France	45.0	45.0	46.5	43.6	43.6
Greece	7.1	6.7	7.1	8.1	5.8
Italy	4.6	6.0	7.0	5.8	5.1
Luxembourg	30.8	21.0	36.0	37.9	36.5
Netherlands	36.9	41.3	45.0	40.8	42.2
Portugal	18.7	25.9	25.3	27.9	25.5
Sweden	n.a.	n.a.	n.a.	70.3	68.7
UK	62.3	62.5	59.9	56.4	55.6
Total	41.8	43.1	42.0	40.0	39.7

Note: Calculated from data supplied by EUROSTAT.

According to OECD data, average gross replacement rates in the mid-1990s varied from less than 20 per cent in Japan, USA and the UK to 71 per cent in Denmark, although the latter was an outlier since the next highest was the Netherlands with 46 per cent (Martin, 1996). The unweighted overall average was 31 per cent, which has risen since the beginning of the 1960s. But in some countries, the rate rose, then fell or stayed about the same (Belgium, Germany, Japan, New Zealand, UK and USA), and in *most* countries the rate fell in the 1990s. There has also been a convergence in gross replacement rates.

The apparent rise may be explained in part by a tendency for tighter eligibility conditions to exclude those with low replacement rates. Another factor in the apparent rise is the fall in the earnings of those most likely to experience unemployment. So the appearance of constant or rising 'generosity' of benefits may be due to low incomes received before unemployment.

Table 7.10 OECD estimates of replacement rates of unemployment benefits, European Union, 1972–90

	1972	1980	1990
Belgium	0.83	0.73	–
Denmark	–	0.60	0.47
Germany	0.74	0.64	0.42
Spain	–	0.39	0.40
France	0.34	0.41	–
Ireland	–	0.43	0.35
Italy	0.11	0.14	0.08
Netherlands	–	0.93	0.75
Austria	0.55	0.57	0.57
Finland	0.32	0.50	0.61
Sweden	0.31	0.49	0.64
United Kingdom	0.43	0.28	0.16

Note: Calculated as the ratio of payments of unemployment insurance benefits to number of unemployed, with respect to the average gross pay of all production workers.
Source: OECD, 1993, p. 105.

Net replacement rates are higher than gross rates in most countries, and probably these are more relevant for assessing income security and behavioural responses, because they refer to what the unemployed would 'take home' relative to what those with average earnings would take. Net replacement rates in the mid-1990s varied from a low of 16 per cent in the USA and 19 per cent in Italy to a high of 81 per cent in Denmark, followed by 69 per cent in the Netherlands. The unweighted average for 18 industrialised countries was about 50 per cent.

In some countries the value of benefits has fallen because they have been linked to the declining minimum wage. This has been the case in the Netherlands, where unemployment benefit has been set at 70 per cent of the minimum wage, payable for up to six months for those without earnings-related benefits. In the UK, in the 1980s earnings-related supplements to unemployment benefits were abolished, and the new Job Seekers Allowance gives a very low replacement rate indeed.

With the possible exception of Germany, because of labour market changes and tighter conditionality, there has been a strong drift to *means-tested unemployment assistance*, which has low take-up rates and additional conditionality coming into effect at regular intervals. As with insurance benefits, the value of unemployment assistance has tended to fall, as in the Netherlands, where it has been set at 70 per cent of the minimum wage, which itself has fallen in relative terms.

In a few countries unemployment assistance has become the base of the regime. In Australia, unlike most countries, not only are most social benefits means-tested, but in 1987 unemployment benefits became assets-tested. Thus the conditional nature of support became greater, the benefits being essentially social assistance.

Means tests, assets tests and income tests may have been reasonable in the early days of the welfare state when the norm was that unemployment benefits applied mainly to married men, the presumption being that wives were not in the labour market and that youths went from school to work or into apprenticeships. The norm and presumptions were always dubious, but in recent years the use of means tests and similar devices has been increasingly onerous. To illustrate, consider a standard 'unemployment trap'. If an income test is applied on a family-unit basis, as is common, an unemployed man with an income-earning wife may be disqualified from all or part of his unemployment assistance, in some cases making it financially advantageous for the wife to become unemployed as well or leave the labour force. So, the means test could raise unemployment, although if the wife 'quit' her job she might be excluded from entitlement to unemployment benefits and perhaps not even be counted as unemployed. It was for such reasons that, controlling for other influences, in the UK wives of unemployed men have long had a lower labour force participation rate than other married women.

Much has been written on unemployment and poverty traps created by means tests. They may have contributed to the feminisation of the lower end of the labour market. Those with the right to unemployment benefits have been in a trap, since they could lose more than they would earn by taking low-paid or part-time jobs. The poor could not afford a long-term view to such jobs – by seeing them as stepping stones into higher-paying jobs – so it makes sense to take the benefits for longer. This situation became more pervasive in the 1980s and 1990s, as in the Netherlands (de Neubourg, 1990). A reason is that many flexible jobs have had lower wages than those that have been disappearing or from which the unemployed have come, a tendency associated with the 'cost of employment loss'. Many of those jobs have been taken by women not in an unemployment trap because they did not qualify for benefits.

As discussed in the next chapter, means-tested benefits have the drawback that they do not reach many of those they are supposed to reach because of low take-up rates, which have little to do with need or entitlement. However, the unemployed's dependency on social assistance has increased since the 1970s, and in many countries this source has become more important than unemployment benefits.

Unemployment traps induce behavioural and institutional reactions that compound the unemployed's insecurity. Means-tested benefits induce some to remain unemployed 'involuntarily', some to work in informal activities to evade taxes and escape being penalised by loss of benefits. They have also been a disincentive to personal saving, since that could lead them to being barred from benefits. This increases their income vulnerability. Unemployment traps also encourage officials to cut the replacement rate to increase the 'incentive' to work, so obliging the unemployed to take jobs paying much less than their previous jobs. The result is a mish-mash of controls and poverty-level benefits, intensifying the unemployed's income insecurity.

Some claim that cutting benefits would reduce 'structural unemployment' (e.g., Scarpetta, 1996, p. 63).[6] It is often asserted that 'the generosity of unemployment benefits' has contributed to high unemployment and 'welfare dependency'. The evidence on low entitlement, and low replacement rates even if entitlement is gained, makes such claims hard to accept. There can be little doubt that in many countries with unemployment benefits, the unemployed's income insecurity has been intensified in the 1980s and 1990s. In this respect, it is worth recalling a review of unemployment benefits in EU countries:

> The principal conclusion of this study is that an unemployment scheme does not necessarily affect employment decisions adversely, nor does it encourage long-term unemployment. (Christian and Velasquez, 1994, p. 37)

By way of conclusion, we may estimate the unemployed's *income security index*, or the probable income replacement rate. For this, we need three ratios – the probability of claiming, conditional on being unemployed, the probability of being entitled to and receiving benefits, and the income replacement rate. None of these is easy to measure, and the data available are not adequate. Because we do not wish to exaggerate, the assumptions made in the following tend to overstate each ratio.

For illustrative purposes, we concentrate on EU countries. It is assumed that the per cent of unemployed who were 'active', as defined in chapter 5, measures the unemployed's probability of claiming benefits. Since this may have a selectivity bias, we adjust the figure by adding half the difference between the per cent active and 100 per cent.[7] We also need the *beneficiary ratio*. We saw earlier that on average about 33 per cent of the active unemployed receive benefits, although this varies enormously, being lower for women. The third ratio is the hardest to estimate. The data available are for all unemployment benefits, including assistance, which gives an upward bias. Another problem is to decide on the duration. It is inappropriate to take the replacement rate for the first month of unemployment, or a rate expressed as an average over a five-year period of unemployment. So, we take the gross replacement rate as a percentage of average earnings for a single person and for a married man with a 'dependent wife' (sic) during the first 12 months of unemployment. The average and standard deviation for married men with 'dependent wife' are shown in Figure 7.5.

Thus, using the three ratios we can estimate the unemployed's income security index. For Belgium, for example, in the mid-1990s a married man would have had a probable replacement rate of 0.8 multiplied by 0.84 multiplied by 0.38, giving a figure of 26 per cent of average earnings. A man in Germany would have had slightly less than that. These levels are scarcely conducive to voluntary unemployment and are impoverishing.

In sum, while there has been a drift from insurance benefits to unemployment assistance, the combination of tighter conditions for entitlement and implicit disentitlement due to the trend away from regular, full-time employment means that the unemployed face increasing income insecurity. Benefits have evolved into regulatory instruments, and do not protect the unemployed from poverty. In the USA, for instance, about 20 per cent of the long-term unemployed are in poverty, and among unemployment benefit recipients who are sole earners in their families, the poverty rate has been over 40 per cent. In western Europe the trend has been in the same direction, and in eastern Europe the situation is much worse.

The tightening of conditions for entitlement to benefits raises an ethical question. Workers have directly or indirectly made contributions to unemployment *insurance* schemes under one set of conditions only to see the conditions changed and have experienced a decline in probability of entitlement in an *ex post* manner. The *insurance* character of benefits has always been precarious, but has grown more so.

When politicians and economists mention the 'generosity' of unemployment benefits they usually mean they think they should be lowered. The reality is that the income security of the unemployed, and those anticipating unemployment, has deteriorated in the last two decades. This has surely lowered subjective employment security as well as the employed's income security, and eroded representation security by making workers more fearful. Unemployment benefits may also have become a greater source of social inequality. In some countries, income replacement rates have continued to be higher for men, as Table 7.11 showed. Women in

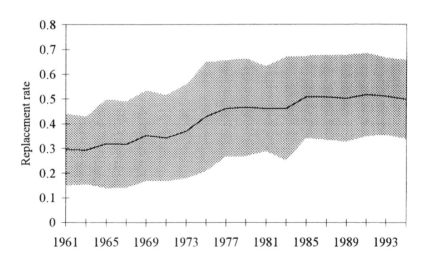

Figure 7.5 Average gross replacement rate at 100% of average earnings during first year of unemployment, with dependent wife, OECD Countries, 1961–95 *(grey area showing standard deviation in replacement rates across OECD countries)*

Source: OECD Database on Benefit Entitlements and Gross Replacement Rates, 1996

Table 7.11 Unemployment benefit replacement rate for initial period based on average gross weekly earnings of men and women full-time manual workers in manufacturing, as proportion of male average earnings, European Union countries, 1993

Country	Formula for replacement rate	Addition for dependent spouse	Threshold level	Average replacement rate for full-time manufacturing manual workers			
				Ratio of gross benefits to gross earnings for a single person		Ratio assuming men claim for a dependent spouse	
				Male	Female	Male	Female
Belgium	55%	5%	yes	0.44	0.41	0.48	0.41
Denmark	90%	no	yes	0.63	0.63	0.63	0.63
Germany[1]	60% of net earnings	no					
Greece	40%	10% of benefit	yes	0.36	0.27	0.41	0.23
Spain	70%	yes	yes	0.25	0.25	0.28	0.25
France	40.4%+1645F or 57.4%	no	yes	0.66	0.54	0.70	0.54
Ireland	IR£55.60 p. w.	IR£35.50	n/a	0.58	0.50	0.58	0.50
Italy	20%	no	no	0.21	0.21	0.33	0.21
Luxembourg	80%	no	yes	0.20	0.16	0.20	0.16
Netherlands	70%	no	yes	0.54	0.54	0.54	0.54
Austria[2]	60% of net earnings	yes[3]	yes	–	–	–	–
Portugal	65%	no	yes	0.65	0.46	0.65	0.46
Finland	Ranges from 38% to 77%[4]	no	no	0.58	0.49	0.58	0.49
Sweden	75%	no	yes	0.70	0.58	0.70	0.58
United Kingdom	UK£45.45	UK£28.05	n/a	0.15	0.15	0.25	0.15

Notes:
1. Calculation of replacement rates for married men and women is complicated by the impact of the 'joint assessment system'
2. Figures for average gross earnings for men and women were not collected; so estimates for replacement rates for 1992 are not reported.
3. A small addition up to 600 ATS per month is available as a family allowance which also covers long-term partners, children and other family members.
4. The range is based on an earnings-related formula.

Source: Grimshaw and Rubery, 1997, Table 2, p. 305.

Germany, Ireland, the Netherlands, Spain and the UK have received less than men, largely because they have been unable to build up insurance contributions and because means-tested schemes tend to adhere to the traditional 'bread-winner' model (Schmid and Reissert, 1996, pp. 246–7). Women have a lower probability of receiving unemployment benefits.

In sum, in flexible labour markets, unemployment benefits are inefficient in terms of providing income security, inequitable, increasingly intrusive and increasingly directive in regulating the lower end of the labour market. To call them 'passive' policy would be a misuse of language. Conventional benefit schemes are inappropriate for the flexible labour markets that will predominate in the twenty-first century.

7.6 CONCLUDING POINTS

Income insecurity has grown in many parts of the world. For the employed, the minimum wage has dropped, wage differentials have widened, access to enterprise benefits (or occupational welfare) has been more fragmented, and there has been a growing incidence of informal/black economy work without entitlements. For the unemployed, access to benefits has shrunk, income replacement rates have fallen and duration of entitlement has been shortened.

An apparent feature in income inequality is the growth of less-measured components of income. High-income earners receive these to a much greater extent than others, and with more flexible and decentralised labour relations, scope for concealment from tax and other state authorities is growing.

Income insecurity has also been intensified by the privatisation of infrastructural and public services. This is because the utilities' pursuit of profits leads them to charge differential prices for the affluent and for the poor. A survey in the UK in 1997 found that low-income families had to pay more than twice as much for gas as other families, 4 times as much for their telephone service, 5 times as much for home insurance and up to 24 times as much for loans. Private insurance was priced higher in poor areas, and home insurance was more costly for the unemployed. No doubt these differences reflect commercial calculations. In the post-war era, in a growing number of countries utilities were government-owned and were operated in a way that gave widespread income security and were mildly redistributional. In the era of market regulation, privatised services have become a source of growing inequality not captured by income distribution statistics. A defensive reaction would be a resort to statutory regulation, banning discrimination against people with particular labour statuses, for instance. This could reduce differential pricing. But it may be costly in terms of transaction costs, would be clumsy and would lead to commercial schemes to circumvent the regulations by more ingenious formulae. The best way to overcome these practices would be to reduce inequality and income insecurity.

Governments should be encouraged to develop indexes of income security. The statistical authorities could derive indexes to take account of situations and entitlements of different labour-related statuses. A measure might be something like the New Economy Well-Being Index (NEWBI), devised by the UK's Institute of Public Policy Research, which measures well-being as an average of real income per capita, growth in real income per capita, unemployment, percentage change in unemployment, income inequality, the inflation rate, and the base interest rate. The value of this index fell between the 1960s and 1990s (Hawkins et al., 1996). Although it has an ad hoc character, it suggests how indicators could be combined to produce an income insecurity index.

It is easy for middle-class commentators to call for more flexible labour markets when they have savings, and access to enterprise and state benefits, should they need them. But for the *flexiworker* earning two-thirds of median income, unprotected by a statutory minimum wage and with low unemployment benefits in prospect, the anxiety is not conducive to stable behaviour. It encourages opportunism, pilfering, stress and political populism. For the unemployed without benefits, income insecurity is acute. Conventional statistics do not capture the idea of income insecurity. Yet it is there, and people are telling everybody about it. We need an index that takes account of the position of different groups of employed and unemployed. If we had such an index, it would surely show a deterioration in recent years.

Economic progress also benefits from income security and reduced inequality. The supply-side view is that inequality provides incentive to risk taking, and that in the longer term higher inequality benefits society by raising average incomes. It has even been argued that Latin American economies performed worse than East Asian economies between the 1960s and 1990s because the former's greater inequality led to pressure for redistribution via government transfers, which weakened incentives to invest in 'human capital', and slowed economic growth. However, those societies did not introduce more redistributive transfer and tax policies and there is no positive link between income inequality and share of government transfers in GDP. Indeed, countries with low pre-tax inequality have high shares of transfers in GDP, whereas the USA has high pre-tax poverty and one of the lowest shares of government transfers (Benabou, 1996).

There may actually be a positive relationship between government transfers (including spending on social insurance, education and pensions) and economic growth. If so, one could conclude that income security boosts growth. There is evidence that economies characterised by lower income inequality have higher economic growth (Persson and Tabellini, 1991). An explanation is that less inequality creates more social stability and a social atmosphere conducive to savings and investment. At the very least, the evidence does not justify the argument that substantial inequality and insecurity are necessary for growth and development. This is what has been accepted implicitly by policies that promote wage flexibility, erosion of the social income and diminished transfers for the unemployed.

Growing income insecurity has been linked to globalisation, in that the tension between the market-driven income distribution (raising the share received by capital) and the promotion of social rights through the welfare state has become greater and more oriented to the former. In the post-war era, rights were strengthened and these are based on 'need', whereas the market system of distribution is based on 'labour' and the ownership of assets. The contradiction between the democratic, egalitarian principles of the welfare state and the hierarchical, inegalitarian tendencies of the economic sphere was sharpened in the 1980s and 1990s, because capital became more mobile, as did technology, skilled labour and management.

As the balance was tipping in favour of capital in terms of any social consensus on distribution, the number in 'need' was growing relative to the number contributing 'labour'. For instance, the ratio of active to inactive in the Netherlands was 12.6 in 1960, 9.9 in 1970, 4.3 in 1980 and 2.9 in 1989 (van der Veen 1993, p. 81). This further eroded income security among the majority locked out of the high-tech economy.

Globalisation has also intensified income insecurity in industrialised countries because of the *perception* and *expectation* that wages are being dragged down towards those in developing countries. One study calculated that if wages were equalised internationally by liberalisation US average wages would fall by nearly 80 per cent (Leamer, 1996). This will not happen. Yet the fact that, coincidentally or not, real wages in the USA have stagnated and skill-based wage differentials have grown since the trade share of GDP started to grow rapidly has leant credence to the sense of income insecurity.

What are the behavioural consequences of income insecurity? It may raise the *satisficing income* – the amount an individual would regard as adequate. Among the employed, it may lead to pressure to raise wages and thus be inflationary. But psychologists would probably be unhappy with this hypothesis. The insecurity might make individuals more hesitant about pushing for higher wages for fear of increasing the risk of loss of employment. There has been much satisfaction in the US financial community because of the belief, expressed by the chairman of the Federal Reserve, that increased insecurity has dampened wage pressure in spite of a tightening labour market. However, pushing for higher wages is not the only response to the need for income security. Another is to increase labour supply, by working longer, taking a secondary job or allocating more time to informal activities. This increases stress and work insecurity. Another is to reduce the effort bargain, so lowering productivity.

Income insecurity has other adverse effects. An extreme case is Russia in the 1990s, where plunging male life expectancy has been attributed in large part to the stress of adjustment and income insecurity among young and middle-aged men. In western Europe and elsewhere, increased life expectancy is also associated with reduced poverty (Wilkinson, 1996). These points may be obvious, yet concern about income insecurity has been woefully inadequate in the latter part of the twentieth century. Have social protection policies rectified the adverse trends? The next chapter considers the evidence.

8 Social Protection, Fragmentation and Detachment

8.1 INTRODUCTION

The twentieth century has been the period of history in which a part of the world achieved reasonable economic security. As long as he was prepared to labour and be loyal to factory, farm, company or organisation, the labouring man could expect benefits 'from cradle to grave' for himself and 'his' family. This was true in different ways in both state socialism and welfare state capitalism. As women were absorbed into the labour force, state transfers and services were extended, often to enable them to labour more effectively and 'equally' with men.

In welfare state capitalism, *social rights*, along the lines developed by Marshall, were extended steadily during the post-war era. As they did so, anti-discrimination measures were strengthened, notably for women, ethnic minorities, and those with disabilities. Some welfare states were more redistributive than others. Indeed, Titmuss' original distinction was between the *institutional-redistributive model* and the *residual model,* the former relying largely on universalistic access to benefits and services, the latter on selective access. The USA was regarded as the primary residual welfare state, while western European countries were in the redistributive mould.

The extension of the welfare state in the 1950s, 1960s and 1970s represented a strengthening of individual security in a welfare-regulated labour market while proceeding with 'labour decommodification'. State benefits rose as a share of social income and – although social rights, transfers and services were intended to facilitate and regulate labour – they were increasingly delinked from labour force participation. Esping-Andersen (1990) has differentiated between what he called *liberal, conservative* and *social-democratic* welfare state regimes. Three criteria were used:

- the extent to which social benefits were redistributive;
- the extent to which the state administered benefits;
- the extent to which benefits and services decommodified beneficiaries.

The liberal regime is close to Titmuss' residual welfare state, relying largely on selective targeting of state benefits, according to perceived 'needs'. The conservative regime relies largely on social 'insurance', with benefits depending on contributions, which depend on income from employment. The social-democratic regime is the

one most closely associated with the gradual extension of social 'rights', which
in turn is associated with the extension of universal social services.

One cannot assess the development of socio-economic security without
recognising the labourist basis of all existing forms of welfare state. The historical
debate over the right to work is linked to the evolution of social insurance and other
social protection policies, associated with the names of Bismarck and Beveridge.
For Bismarck, its originator, social insurance was a means of binding the working
class to the existing social order. The state granted income security if the worker
satisfied his labour obligations, although Bismarck did not provide insurance for
unemployment. For Beveridge, in his *Social Assurance and Allied Services* report
of 1942 and in *Full Employment in a Free Society* of 1944, the model of the nuclear
family, with male breadwinner and dependent wife, guided the design of labour-
based welfare. For Beveridge, women were secondary workers, and the state had
no right or duty to diminish the obligation of the husband to the wife (Glennerster
and Evans, 1994).

Welfare state capitalism was oriented to the income security of those in regular
wage labour, and extended 'exit from labour' rights. Feminist analysts have
criticised the neglect of 'exit out of family' rights (Hobson, 1990). While the
welfare state boosted the state benefit components of the social income, social policy
was intended to bolster wage labour and strengthen the conventional family. If one
is concerned with personal autonomy, one must assess the roles and effectiveness
of policies for providing income security for all groups and equal opportunity for
self-control. This makes it important to integrate thinking of social transfers and
social services.

Whether or not one could agree on a classification of countries by type of
welfare state, for more than two decades welfare policies succeeded in embedding
the economy in society, by covering standard contingency risks to a large extent.
The trouble was that the bureaucratic nature of systems of income protection
meant there was difficulty in responding to behavioural and circumstantial *diversity*.
Statutory refinements created complex edifices that were rarely transparent and
that were administratively costly, as well as prone to *moral hazards* and *adverse
selection*. Since the 1970s there has been an international trend towards a hybrid
of the conservative and liberal regimes, with re-commodification a prominent
feature. In the 1980s and 1990s, many countries moved in the direction of Titmuss'
residual welfare state, in the process, prompting questions about the legitimacy of
certain rights.

By the mid-1990s, the conventional wisdom was that industrialised countries
could not afford extensive welfare states, that benefit systems built up during the
twentieth century were 'inflexible', that they 'artificially increased unemployment',
and that there was a 'dependency culture'. Although expressed by many beforehand,
these were even the views expressed by European Union officials (*Financial
Times*, 3 December 1996). Those who had good words for the welfare state were
a dwindling minority. And in developing countries it had long been realised that

social security policies advocated in the welfare state era were inefficient and regressive, catering for privileged minorities or elites with secure incomes and formal jobs (Midgley, 1984).

As suggested earlier, the model of *social income* embodied in the core of the welfare state came under strain in the 1970s. To appreciate the current situation and to consider options for the future, we need to reflect on three types of crisis that have prompted policy trends in the 1980s and 1990s.

8.2 FISCAL, MORAL AND LEGITIMATION CRISES

In the 1970s, criticism of the panopoly of transfers and social services gathered intellectual and political support. This crystallised in the 1980s, led by the newly emboldened libertarians, who regarded welfare protection as contravening liberty. The effectiveness of the onslaught was aided by a loss of faith or defensiveness on the part of supporters of the welfare state, because they did not have convincing answers to the critics, because there was an ambivalence about the roles and effectiveness of the welfare system, and because in most countries social protection was consuming a high and growing share of national income.

A belief developed that there was a *fiscal crisis*, which spawned a substantial literature. This reflected the growth in the range of transfers and services, and in the number of people entitled to and receiving them. The welfare system had evolved on the basis of an extension of *categories* of person demanding and being granted entitlements to transfers or social services, which can be expressed as an extension of risk and need categories. It was also characterised by increasing *inclusiveness*, in that more people became part of the entitled population. For a long time it was characterised by moves to set the value of benefits according to state-determined estimates of need. This meant that a rising share of national income was devoted to social income. The word saturation crept into the debate, amidst complaints by disinterested commentators about high taxes.

The rise and persistence of unemployment compounded the pressure. It became harder to retain the contributory basis of social insurance and employment-based social protection. The share of general tax revenue allocated to welfare schemes rose in many countries, implying growing 'fiscal subsidies'. This continued into the 1990s. Reasons included unemployment and the spread of informal and part-time employment from which contributions have been less than from full-time employment and from which it has probably been easier to evade or avoid making contributions.

There has also been pressure on contribution and tax rates, since although the rising demands for transfers required higher rates, these strengthened poverty traps, inducing avoidance and evasion by encouraging workers and employers to opt for arrangements that bypassed contributory rules. High social security charges seemed to raise labour costs, encouraging labour-saving changes and a shift of labour-intensive production abroad.

The perceived fiscal crisis also seemed to reflect an insatiable demand for improvements in healthcare and a rising old-age dependency ratio, which although questionable as a generalisation contributed to extensive early retirement schemes that have compounded short-term fiscal strains (European Commission, 1994a).

Finally, in order to finance social security, higher rates of economic growth were required, which were harder to achieve in the 1980s. This has given an extra push for policies to boost growth, against pressures to limit growth in the interest of long-term social protection and environmental sustainability. One might question the economic reality of a fiscal crisis, but it existed as a political reality.

The fiscal crisis fed into a *moral crisis*. A sentiment spread that state benefits encouraged behaviour and situations they were supposed to overcome, by creating extensive *moral hazard*. Some claims by libertarian critics were fanciful and offensive, such as the well-rehearsed one that teenage girls were rushing to have babies in casual relationships so as to claim food stamps or child support. More sensibly, they may have facilitated what was happening in any case – a slow dissolution of the family type that had been the norm in industrial society. In any case, there was enough momentum for the view that 'welfare' encouraged 'scrounging', 'voluntary unemployment', 'idleness' and behaviour designed to enable them to become eligible for benefits that defenders of the welfare system were put further on the defensive.

Contributing to this defensiveness were Charles Murray's three laws of social programmes derived from his analysis of US experience between 1950 and 1980:

- *The Law of Imperfect Selection*: Any rule that defines eligibility for a social transfer irrationally excludes some people; and because of this, according to Murray, policymakers broaden target populations.
- *The Law of Unintended Rewards*: Any social transfer increases the value of being in the condition that prompted the transfer in the first place.
- *The Law of Net Harm*: The less likely that the 'unwanted behaviour' will change voluntarily, the more likely that a programme to induce change will cause net harm (Murray, 1984, pp. 212–16).

By the third rule, Murray meant that if a benefit was provided for someone in a needy position it would encourage people to move into that position or stay in it; the case of single teenage mothers has often been cited, although others have figured in the imagery. Murray belonged to a long tradition of thinkers advocating insecurity, so his conclusion was not surprising – that transfers should be cut. That aside, his perspective and that of others working in a similar vein helped to show that scarcely any social policy is *passive;* they condition individual behaviour, regulate it in some way, and intervene in economic and social relations.

While the moral crisis was shaping the policy debate, defenders of the welfare state were feeling uncomfortable because of a *legitimation crisis*, which has been unresolved for the last two decades of the twentieth century. Like the fiscal crisis, it arose in part from the fact that over the post-war period there had been a rise in the proportion of people receiving state benefits, coupled with a corresponding rise in the share of national income being devoted to social transfers. A much-discussed case was the Netherlands. In 1960, there were 1.2 million beneficiaries; by 1990, there were over 4 million; the ratio of economically active to inactive fell from 3.4 in 1960 to 1.3 in 1990; in 1960, income transfers were about 10 per cent of GDP; in 1991 they accounted for 29 per cent (Adriaansens and Dercksen, 1993, p. 194). Many other countries had moved in the same direction.

The legitimation crisis also arose from dissatisfaction with welfare policies as mechanisms of social control. There has always been a minority who have criticised state benefits as they have developed since the late nineteenth century as a system of paternalistic labour control. After all, Bismarck's original idea of social insurance was to induce loyalty to the state and stable labour by a core group of Prussian workers. Beveridge also saw insurance benefits as a means of stabilising male wage labour.

Given the labourist stance, those who felt that state benefits were part of the apparatus of regulatory control and criticised it for that were regarded as irrelevant for most of the twentieth century. Ironically, in the 1980s and 1990s, in the wake of the multiplication of selective schemes coupled with high unemployment and more flexible labour relations, libertarian and other critics have criticised the system precisely on the ground that it did not control behaviour, since it did not apply sufficient conditions on potential recipients. Faced with this, defenders were put in a quandary, since they could not easily reconcile a commitment to the steady extension of social *rights* with acceptance that the element of *control* needed to be strengthened. Many found their way to do so, either with pragmatism, along the lines that unless concessions were made the critics would be strengthened in their onslaught on the 'system', or with enthusiasm to accompany their zeal for the properties of labour.

The legitimation crisis also arose from a perception that policies were ineffectual in protecting against contingency risks or in achieving income redistribution. This may have bred disillusion and intensified feelings of deprivation (Mayntz, 1975). There is a perception that the promises of the welfare state are increasingly unfulfilled, that many schemes have intensified inequities, and that some groups receive too much or are 'undeserving'. The legitimacy crisis has been strengthened because some believe that the cost does not match the benefits, and that there is no value for money (Peillon, 1996, p. 176). Others have criticised it for being paternalistic, stifling independence from the 'nanny' state (Marsland, 1992).

Another source of disquiet is that people recognise that discrimination against those deemed undeserving is arbitrary and unfair. And there is a lack of legitimacy that comes from erosion of motivation, due to a lack of a relationship between individual performance and well-being. This sentiment is often taken to mean that only those deserving support should receive it, although it could be that the targeting causes resentment among others, encouraging them to be opportunistic and eroding the legitimacy of the regulatory system.

The legitimation crisis also reflects a perverse feature of the welfare state. The universalistic tendency of early policies coupled with the presumption that most potential recipients were in regular employment *and* the fact that regular wage labour was the route to adequate protection meant that the 'middle class' built up entitlements to a greater degree than those on the margins of society, who were not in regular wage labour, were often unemployed and were poor. The groups with more secure employment have more benefit entitlements, and these are the salaried white-collar workers, technicians, skilled manual workers and professionals.

The welfare state evolved through a middle-class and labouring-class coalition of mutual interest in a set of entitlements. In fact, the middle class tended to benefit disproportionately. Thus, in the UK in the 1980s, the wealthiest fifth of the population received 40 per cent more of public health spending than the poorest fifth; 80 per cent more of secondary education; five times more of university education; four times more in bus subsidies; seven times more in housing subsidies; ten times more in rail subsidies (Goodin and LeGrand, 1987).[1]

If governments try to redress this perverse outcome they risk further eroding the political support for social protection. If they *target* by means tests and behaviour tests, and lower universal benefits, as many have done, they risk finding that a majority of the voting population do not feel that they are beneficiaries and vote for politicians who promise tax cuts facilitated by benefit cuts.

As the demand for transfers expanded in what has been a period of structural change and economic upheaval, questions arose about the relative legitimacy of claims made on behalf of diverse groups, the level of income protection provided and the political appeal of making transfers to particular groups. The new economic policy orthodoxy compounded the crisis by stipulating that public expenditure should be cut. The *politics of income security* have since played a role in shaping the character of social protection and state benefits.

Objectively, affluent countries could provide enough income transfers so as to give everybody an adequate level of living. It might be necessary to raise taxes, slow economic growth, or pursue more progressive income redistribution, and so on. But it could be done. What makes it more likely that it will be done? It is hard to answer this without entering the realm of sociological speculation. Legitimation of social policy seems to require a popular perception that those in need or distress cannot or should not be blamed for their condition. Their *need* must be perceived as due primarily to factors beyond their control. There must also be a popular feeling that people in need should not be expected to accept their condition, quasi-religiously, as something for which there will be reciprocity later, here or in the hereafter. There should also be a popular feeling that society can *afford* to support those in distress. Undermine that feeling and you go a long way to undermining notions of social solidarity. Probability of support is also likely to be higher if a relatively large number of people think that they could suffer from a similar fate.

Finally, even more opportunistically, support for social transfers is more likely if elites and the middle class believe that if the state does not provide income support the *retributive* consequences would be costly to society and to themselves, perhaps through acts of desperation, the spread of infectious diseases, vandalism, sabotage or violence.

In the 1970s and 1980s, the combination of an increasing range of perceived needs, an increasing number of people in groups traditionally expected to receive transfers, and rising levels of social expenditure led to a perception of *saturation*.[2] A lobby created an image, by which public social policy expenditure was 'crowding out' private 'productive' activity, impeding economic growth and employment. More flexible labour markets and labour market insecurity pushed more of those with identifiable 'disadvantages' into situations where they needed income support.

An apparent unwillingness to vote for tax-rising parties – even though taxes continued to rise – coincided with the shift in economic orthodoxy, giving public expenditure cuts high priority, and justifying a drive to increase the *selectivity* of benefits and to privatise social policy. In western Europe (and in central European countries intent on joining the EU), these tendencies have been further institutionalised through the EMU agenda. Thus a new threat to social protection has been the Maastricht Treaty's rules on national debt and borrowing, since the goal of a single currency by 1999 has meant a new rationale and legitimation for public spending curbs.

In developing countries, pressure in the same direction has been couched in terms of stabilisation and *structural adjustment* policies, with the message that social expenditure must be cut. So the track leading towards comprehensive social protection provided by the state has been hastily scrubbed out.

In political democracies, the higher levels of poverty, inequality and income insecurity since the 1970s might have been expected to lead to more electoral support for redistributive policies, if only because the pivotal or swing voter is in the middle of the income distribution, and because the *median* person's income is below the mean average. In the UK, for instance, average weekly earnings in early 1995 were £337, whereas the median earner made £290. Since the median earner would expect to gain from redistribution, this might be expected to lead him to favour redistribution.

It does not *seem* to work like that. Middle-class swing voters *seem* to want the promise of tax cuts. A reason may be that pivotal *voters* have incomes above the median because the poor (often younger and less educated) are less likely to vote than others. Moreover, if inequality hits one or several groups disproportionately (the detached) the remainder may be unconcerned. One analyst speculated that it is because growing inequality has come mainly from hurting already low-income groups that there has been less support for redistributive policies in the 1980s and 1990s (Saint-Paul, 1996).

Poverty and insecurity co-exist in flexible labour markets. The impoverished suffer not just from a lack of money but from 'social exclusion' or 'social isolation'.

They lack state benefits, they lack access to public facilities, while paradoxically they become more dependent on the state, relying on bureaucratic authorities for survival. The state has been shrinking from providing the required support, even though the increasing demand or need has checked the decline in social spending.

8.3 RECOMPOSITION OF SOCIAL INCOME IN THE ERA OF MARKET REGULATION

In response to the perceived crises, the state could opt for any of the following:

- raise taxes and contributions;
- reduce the range of its commitments;
- increase selectivity and tighten conditionality;
- raise contributions for middle-income and upper-income groups;
- privatise social transfers and services;
- shift from benefits to public services;
- shift from benefits to private services;
- withdraw functions, leaving them to voluntary, non-governmental organisations, perhaps paid by those who could afford them, provided free to the homeless and so on.

Most of these have been happening. Governments have cut the value of transfers as a means of lowering labour costs. In some cases, the value fell for lower-income groups because the level has been linked to the value of the minimum wage, as with the minimum state pension in the Netherlands, set at 100 per cent of the net minimum wage for couples, 90 per cent for one-parent families and 70 per cent for those living alone. Given the decline of the minimum wage, this has intensified the income insecurity of low-income elderly people. The value of benefits has fallen drastically in eastern Europe, and one reason has been that they have been tied to the statutory minimum wage, which has been allowed to fall to dismally low levels.

Another international tendency has been to delink the real value of social benefits from real earnings, through removing indexation altogether or by indexing them to prices rather than average earnings. One way of interpreting the changing level of benefits is that an individual's income security has been made more dependent on labour market experience.

However, the major trends have been partial privatisation and increased selectivity. In short, the consequences of the perceived crises that have dogged welfare states in the last quarter of the twentieth century have been lower transfer payments, increasing selectivity, through means tests and tighter conditionality, *privatisation of welfare* through a shift to private agencies and multiple-tier pension systems, and encouragement of private *occupational welfare*, through negotiated systems of support based on firms and workers. The responses to the strains and pressures have in turn helped to erode the system's legitimacy. Let us consider the main structural trends.

8.4 THE DRIFT TO SELECTIVITY

Globally, there has been a strong shift from universal, state-based social protection to selective, targeted schemes. In state socialism, social benefits and services were mostly channelled through the enterprises and organisations of employment, were in principle universal in character and were provided to the vast majority of the population to the extent that they were in labour or had parents in labour. The collapse of that model led to a shift to one or other variants of the model of welfare state capitalism, based on social security.

The global erosion of the state socialism model has been accelerated by reforms in China. In his opening statement to China's 15th Communist Party Congress in 1997 President Jiang Zemin outlined a plan to restructure state enterprises, urged workers to be more flexible, and described the planned shift in social protection from enterprise-based cradle-to-grave childcare, housing, health insurance and related services to a social security system. In eastern Europe and countries of the former Soviet Union, in the 1990s this led to a deep erosion of enterprise and state benefits, to explicit and implicit disentitlement to benefits and to partial privatisation of social protection.

The trend in those countries has been more pronounced but similar to what has been happening in other industrialised countries and in many other countries that had moved in the direction of welfare state capitalism in the post-1945 era. The language of selectivity, targeting and social safety nets has swept the world. The trend to selectivity involves an increase in:

- 'targeting', notably by treating more finely disaggregated groups differentially;
- discretionary decision-making and action by local officials;
- reliance on means-testing, income-testing and asset-testing;
- reliance on behavioural conditionality, notably labour tests.

Selectivity raises awkward issues of equity and efficiency. In terms of equity, it is difficult to decide which groups deserve help, what priority to give each of them, and so on. There are three forms of efficiency to consider – administrative, horizontal and vertical. A policy is said to be horizontally efficient if it succeeds in reaching a high percentage of the target group; it is vertically efficient if those it reaches consist mainly of those in the target group. Policymakers concerned with curbing public expenditure will give vertical efficiency higher priority than horizontal efficiency.

The primary motivations for increased selectivity have been the desire to reduce public spending and to differentiate between those deemed to be deserving and those deemed to be undeserving of public support. The trouble is that targeted schemes are relatively complex, demanding well-established and legitimate administrative structures to be efficient in any sense. In developing and eastern European countries in the 1990s, it was almost cynical to advocate sophisticated targeting, when there would be low take up, because of a lack of institutions, lack of knowledge among potential beneficiaries, poorly trained officials, and the psychological state of both applicants and officials.

In some western European and other industrialised countries, there has been talk of 'Victorian values' and 'tough love', with supposedly 'left' and 'right' political parties wanting to link benefit entitlement more tightly to employment, or to the demonstrated willingness to labour. The libertarian or neo-liberal tendency has been to reduce replacement rates – or, in the euphemism of the era, to reduce the *generosity* of benefits – and tighten eligibility conditions. The social democratic tendency has been to maintain levels to a greater extent but to tighten conditionality, one rationalisation for the tactic being that, to maintain social support for the welfare state, a broad cross-section of society must sense that they could benefit directly.

'Targeting' has gained popularity globally, but difficulties start with identification of the target. Formulation of unambiguous groups 'needing', 'meriting' or 'deserving' assistance is always difficult, and the matching of legal and social reality will always be incomplete. The more a category is narrowly defined the greater the difficulty of maintaining an equitable boundary in a practical definition. Judgments have to be made, discretion exercised, rules and regulations written and implemented reasonably consistently and transparently. It requires a practical, efficient administrative structure, in which local officials can apply procedures properly. In practice, interest group pressure and lobbying shape the selectivity and level and assurance of transfers. A well-documented case is Food Stamps in the USA, which were preserved and expanded because they were supported by the farmers' lobby, not because they were well-targeted on the poorest. Even those became more labour-tested; in 1997, food stamps could only be received by the poor for three months in any three-year period, if the person was able-bodied without children or jobs. The entitlement period had been cut to 'encourage' people to find jobs.

Selectivity has also been intensified by the increasing complexity of rules and procedures and because the systems of social protection have tried to take account of the increasing diversity of household types and income sources. The increased use of selective conditions is likely to have intensified the income insecurity of many of those in need. The merging of service provider and regulator of individual behaviour, which has accompanied the policymaking faith in 'active' social and labour market policy, involves greater transaction costs, including costs of collecting and assessing information, costs of administration, and greater costs for the applicant/client.

Selective policy is always *discretionary*. The more 'active' the policy, the more discretionary the implementation. Social services are the most discretionary, since they allow officials to decide whom they will meet, whom they will help, what form of help to offer, what form of follow-up, what form of monitoring, and so on. Individual case treatment is often required because laws cannot be specific enough to cover all circumstances that arise. Above all, means-tested and behaviour-tested transfers allow discretionary control by local officials – in terms of interpreting, applying, monitoring and sanctioning rules and regulations – and selective oversight. The right of appeal may not always exist, and where it does may be curtailed, costly and time-consuming.

Governments often lack information with which to make equitable and efficient judgments in the design of selective schemes. Agencies requiring judgment by officials or their advisers require professional knowledge, which will be variable in quality and variably judgmental. So, targeting depending on bureaucratic judgment is inevitably discretionary. By apparent contrast, employment exchange officials in handling unemployment benefits or other conditional transfers are supposed to be guided by tight regulations and procedures. But the monitoring is doubly oriented to *dis*entitlement because both the claimant and official are subject to monitoring and because the monitoring is asymmetrical. If a claimant makes a claim that is subsequently deemed false he could face a penalty, whereas if he does not make a claim that would be valid he would not risk any sanction. If the official blocks a valid claimant, he would not be punished, whereas if he gave to someone who should not be paid under the rules he could be rebuked and penalised (in terms of promotion prospects, if nothing else).

Behavioural conditionality has been tightened in many countries. For example, rules that came into effect in the UK in October 1997 meant that claimants of Jobseekers' Allowance could have payments delayed unless they produced all documents required to support their claim. If they fail to produce them within a month, they lose entitlement until they produce them. The documents include a P45 form from their last employer, their last few pay slips, and information on their partner's earnings. Thus, another person could prevent a claimant receiving benefits. A *Social Security Bill* also proposed to restrict the period for backdated claims from three months to one month.

Selectivity is based on the dichotomy of the 'deserving' and 'undeserving poor', which elites and governments have used throughout history. The notion of undeserving will be shaped by *statistical discrimination* in the application of discretionary policy. For example, officials may have more sympathy for the elderly because they themselves have parents who are elderly, or simply because they envisage becoming elderly themselves. This may lead them to adopt less intrusive monitoring of the elderly's claims than they apply to other groups.

One should not criticise officials for inter-personal inequity in the administration of selective schemes, since complex rules may induce them to rely on procedures that, perhaps unintentionally, erect barriers to entitlement, and even to the claiming of benefits. Officials will fall back on attitudes to what they perceive as types of claimant, which may lead them to focus on ways of exerting control, by 'processing the client' – a point first made in a study of local bureaucracy (Lipsky,

1980). Their strategies will mean that the actual distribution of benefits and obligations placed on claimants will differ from those stipulated by the rules. In some cases, they may be overly strict, or tend to disentitlement, perhaps because of a stigma associated with a certain type of person; in others, they may be much 'softer'.

The 'law's delay and the insolence of office' also contribute to disentitlement. Delays in processing lead people to drift away in discouragement, and the frustrations may induce behaviour that increases the prospect of disentitlement. Relations between officials and applicants can become a barrier, made the more likely by the discretionary character of selective benefits, the rising caseload and the monitoring role officials are expected to play.

Selectivity can have other perverse effects. It creates moral hazards *and* discrimination against the group selected *and* poverty or behavioural 'traps'. One hazard is the possibility that the targeting – intended to shrink the number receiving benefit – leads to an expansion in the number of claimants in the group. That would induce public condemnation and stigmatisation of the group, leading to more surveillance and limitations on their freedoms. The circle is completed to the extent that social disapproval leads to discrimination against them, and to low take-up rates among genuinely needy people.

Much has been written about moral hazards and poverty traps. The discrimination-inducing effects of selectivity should be emphasised as well, since those selected for special treatment are in danger of being stigmatised. There are reasons for special benefits for those in disadvantaged situations. The point is not to condemn all forms of selectivity, but to suggest that selective policies cannot be evaluated satisfactorily, in prospect or practice, unless measures for dealing with moral hazards, behavioural traps and discrimination are covered as well. Selective policy may necessitate morally unacceptable or impractical supportive measures to make it efficient or equitable. Given the negligible attention this has received, abuses are likely to have gone unchecked.

Consider *disability benefits*. In the Netherlands, in the early 1990s about 14 per cent of the labour force were receiving them, which was two or three times as much as in neighbouring countries.[3] Nobody seriously imagines that disability is greater in the Netherlands than elsewhere, or that the definition of disability is substantially different. Quite simply, officials had put unemployed on disability pensions and some unemployed had opted for this. Similar patterns existed with respect to *early retirement*, used by government, unions and employers to reduce labour supply. Eventually, alarm was sufficient for policymakers to reduce the number of recipients.

Incapacity benefits are *relatively* free of moral hazard failure. But they can be used in a regulatory manner, with inequitable consequences. They may be used to push people out of the labour market into disability status so as to reduce responsibility for providing them with jobs and reducing recorded unemployment. For employers, a moral hazard is that they could dismiss the disabled rather than others on the rationalised expectation that they would receive benefits, so that the firm need not feel concern. This was actually cited by the former Dutch Prime Minister as a reason for his government having reduced the level of disability benefits in the Netherlands (*Wall Street Journal*, 16 September 1997).

Another likely consequence is that employment service facilities are not placed at the disposal of such groups, because they are treated as a matter for social protection. Therefore, incentives to enter or re-enter the labour market are reduced.

Another perverse effect of selective benefits is that the actual and presumed provision to those in need may reduce the private benefit share (CB) of social income. This has been observed in middle-income countries when state schemes have been introduced where family and community support were the traditional means of overcoming income deficiency (Cox and Jiminez, 1989). The presumption that state benefits will be paid may not be justified, but the private transfers may dry up as a result of the presumption, leaving the individual and family worse off. Perhaps this tendency is not extensive, but it deserves scrutiny in the context of growing reliance on selective benefits.

The language of deserving and undeserving reflects a feeling that society is fragmented, in which 'we' are not like 'them'. The character of social protection depends on 'the scope of moral universalism' (Offe, 1993, p. 219). The more society is fragmented, or divisible into distinctive groups, the more fragile a universalistic system. The more the activity profiles of groups differ from one another, the more fragile the support for public policy. The consequences become qualitatively distinct once differentiation becomes large enough to be one of fragmentation of lifestyles and life chances as well as of wealth and income.

If one does not expect to be in a circumstance, one may feel detached from a system of support, justify finding ways of not contributing to it, and be inclined to support more punitive systems. Offe called this the *'potential self-inclusion'* consideration. Ironically targeting may undermine public support because it implies dividing the recipient population into a greater number of groups deemed to deserve or need different amounts of support. For instance, if eligibility is tightened through more conditions the probability of satisfying all conditions for a particular classification will diminish. On the other side, the more individualised actual and expected experience of people, the less they will identify with specific groups. This is a dilemma for those supporting selectivity and tighter conditionality.

The legitimacy of universalism is also threatened if there is a popular sentiment that claimants have genuine and affordable alternatives. Thus, to give an obvious example, if a belief is fostered that the unemployed have access to jobs, with reasonable wages, etc., support for decent benefits will decline. In other words, the trend to selectivity could be reinforcing.

Selectivity goes with a trend towards *multi-tierism* in several areas of social policy, considered later. Selectivity means narrowing the targets for support while multi-tierism means narrowing the state component. Although it need not be so, selectivity has been associated with cuts in state benefits and with income-reducing restrictions, inducing a quest by those who can afford it to look for other sources of income protection. Thus, *state pensions* are being restructured in many parts of the world. There has been a tendency to raise the age of pensionable retirement, most notably in eastern Europe where the former system gave very low pensions at early ages but also elsewhere, as in Sweden (from 65 to 66), USA and Germany, and, for women, in Austria, and for public sector workers in Finland. More significantly still, the number of years of employment required to obtain a full state pension has been rising remorselessly. In 1960, for OECD countries an average contribution period of 13 years sufficed to obtain a full pension. By 1985, that had doubled (Palme, 1990, p. 53). And it has gone on rising, so that by the mid-1990s within the European Union, the number of contribution years for a full state pension ranged from 35 in Greece and Spain to 48 in Ireland. This trend accentuates inequality and worsens the income security of those in low-income jobs, the flexiworker categories.

There has been a trend to cut the state pension relative to incomes of the employed, while in some countries it has been de-linked from economic growth and earnings. In the early 1980s, the UK's state pension was indexed to price inflation rather than changes in real earnings, while incentives were given to encourage people to take out private pensions. State pensions fell from 4.8 per cent of GDP in 1981 to 3.7 per cent in 1996, in spite of an increase of over one million pensioners. On average, pensioners' real income rose, due to the spread of occupational pensions. But the state pension fell to below 20 per cent of national average earnings. In other countries too the basic state pension fell in relative terms, widening the differential between the average pension and the minimum pension (Palme, 1990, pp. 54–5). One way it did so was by increasing the number of years of employment used to calculate the pension, as in Austria, France, Portugal, Spain and the UK. Another was by applying an earnings test to determine entitlement to the basic state pension, as in Scandinavia and the Netherlands.

All these changes indicate that pensions have become increasingly labour-based rather than citizenship-based. Those without a record of prolonged regular employment have been doing worse. Given labour market flexibility, this makes the pension system more likely to contribute to socio-economic fragmentation.

Disability Benefits have also become more selective and conditional. In the UK, for instance, stricter testing of eligibility for Incapacity Benefit was justified on the grounds that it would target those genuinely incapable of work. Indicative of the diminished legitimacy of state benefits and the emphasis on cutting public expenditure, authorities have added tests of eligibility, strengthened *application* of such tests and increased the *penalties* for failing them. In 1997, the new government followed its predecessor in launching a programme of 'visits' to the homes of those claiming the maximum disability allowance. In other countries too, access has been tightened, reversing the misuse by governments in the 1980s, when some, such as the Netherlands and Spain, used disability benefits to reduce recorded unemployment.

However, the main trend has been a drift from insurance-based support to means-tested *social assistance*. Changes in policy design have pushed more people into dependency on social assistance. Poverty and income insecurity have also been responsible for increasing the numbers, and more people have been in labour statuses without entitlement to other forms of social protection. The term 'social assistance' has several meanings. One might divide social protection policies into the following:

Benefit Type		*Eligible Groups*
Universal	–	All citizens
Categorical	–	All citizens within a social category
Employment-based	–	Social/national insurance
Contributions-based	–	Social/national insurance
Means-tested:		
Poverty-tested – cash or tied	–	Safety-net for those below 'poverty line'
Income-tested – cash or tied	–	Benefits related to income over low range

In practice, many schemes are both categorical and insurance-based or means-tested, and many have behavioural tests added to obtain entitlement. The trend has been towards both means-tested and behaviour-tested benefits. Some countries have allowed recipients of social assistance to have some income from work (earnings disregards), such as Australia, New Zealand, Belgium, Germany and many US States; others have not, such as the Nordic countries, Switzerland, Japan and Austria. Most have added labour tests, although these are relaxed for some groups, such as those with disabilities and lone parents (Bradshaw et al., 1996). Many schemes have *treatment conditionality* built into them, notably in the Nordic countries, linked to their localised, discretionary character of assistance. Some countries link assistance to social 'integration' requirements, as with the Minimex in Belgium, the *Revenu Minimum d'Insertion* in France and the *Revenu Minimum Garanti* in Luxembourg. Some still rely relatively little on social assistance, but some have relied very extensively indeed, led by New Zealand and Australia, followed by Ireland, the USA and the UK. Even where it has not been the base of the system, large numbers have become dependent on means-tested benefits – 7 per cent of the population in Germany and Sweden, for instance (Gough et al., 1997, Table 2, p. 24; Salonen, 1993).

This has happened most rapidly and extensively in eastern Europe and countries of the former Soviet Union, where in the 1990s millions of people came to depend on selective, means-tested benefits (Table 8.1). Not only have the numbers risen sharply but the income to which they have been entitled has shrunk. And many of the poor have been denied entitlement, partly because it has in some cases only been granted if the person's income was below the statutory minimum wage. Since the minimum wage has been so low, many poor people have been denied entitlement.

Table 8.1 Reported number of recipients of regular and occasional social assistance, central and eastern Europe, 1990–95 *(per 10,000)*

	Regular		Occasional	
	1990	1995	1990	1995
Armenia	18.2	64.5[93]	3.4	14.9[94]
Bulgaria	934.3	998.5[94]	516.1	895.8[94]
Czech Republic	101.2	1,041.2[94]	215.5	513.0[94]
Georgia	10.8	269.7[94,b]	32.7	309.7[94]
Hungary	132.9	521.6[94]	845.7	2382.4
Latvia	77.0[92]	2,776.0[94]	406.0[92]	5,567.0
Moldova	n.a.	n.a.	600.0[93]	1,372.0
Poland	281.1	468.5[94]	571.0	769.794
Russia	991.[192,a]	n.a.	2,200.0[92,c]	n.a.
Slovakia	39.1	929.6	60.6	228.7[94]
Slovenia	52.0	172.2[94]	181.1	237.4
Ukraine	262.0[93]	353.0	93.0[92]	575.0[94]

Notes: Number in superscript indicates a source year different from the year at the top of the column; e.g., 92 indicates data from 1992 instead of 1990.
[a] Data from a survey showing that 10.2 million pensioners, 2.5 million families with children and 2 million students received additional payments from local authorities.
[b] Besides regular in-kind assistance, 29,00 people also received regular cash aid and 5,400 social pensions.
[c] Free or reduced-price meals supplied by local administrations.
Source: UNICEF, *Children at Risk in Central and Eastern Europe: Perils and Promises* (Florence, UNICEF, 1997), Tables F7 and 8, p. 152.

An albeit less dramatic rise in recipients of social assistance has occurred in most industrialised countries. In France, the number tripled between 1980 and 1992, and in most countries the share of the population dependent on selective, means-tested assistance increased, as did the share of national income devoted to social assistance (Table 8.2). In Norway and Spain, the share of GDP rose nearly fivefold. The trends continued into the 1990s. By 1995, 34 per cent of all social benefits in the UK were means-tested. Between 1974 and 1994, in the USA social assistance expenditure rose by one-third as a share of national income (Phelps, 1997, p. 2). In all welfare regimes the share of social protection expenditure devoted to means-tested selective schemes has risen.

Many studies have shown that the take-up rate for social assistance schemes is always well below 100 per cent, and in some cases as low as 20 per cent. This has been shown in even the most sophisticated and statutorily regulated countries. In Sweden, the take-up rate for *socialbidrag* (a means-tested safety-net benefit) may have been 20 per cent, and in Germany the take-up rate for *Sozialhilfe* (a similar means-tested benefit) has been estimated at between 21 per cent and 64 per cent, depending on the method of calculation (van Oorschot, 1991). In the UK, the take up of means-tested Family Income Supplement was 55 per cent (Atkinson and Hills,

1991, p. 89). In Japan, where means-tested benefits are still rare, the take up has been particularly low, about 25–30 per cent (Goodman and Peng, 1996). In eastern Europe, anecdotal evidence suggests that take-up rates have been equally low. In Poland, the number of households receiving some state benefits was less than half the number classified as having incomes below the modest poverty line.

Table 8.2 Changes in cash social assistance, industrialised countries, excluding all tied assistance, 1980–92[a]

Country	Change in of recipients as % of pop. 1980–92	Recipients as % of pop. Index 1992/1980	Change of expenditure as % of GDP: 1980–92	Expenditure as % of GDP: Index 1992/1980
Australia[b]	4.2	131	1.4	126
Austria[c]	−0.4	92	0.3	124
Belgium	1.7	189	0.2	156
Canada	4.1	170	0.9	197
Denmark	n/a	n/a	n/a	n/a
Finland	5.7	265	0.3	438
France[d]	1.5	296	0.2(0.7)	196(205)
Germany	2.9	172	0.6	160
Greece	n/a	n/a	n/a	n/a
Iceland	n/a	n/a	n/a	n/a
Ireland	3.7	142	2.2	174
Italy	1.2	135	0.4	135
Japan	−0.5	59	−0.1	60
Luxembourg	n/a	n/a	n/a	n/a
Netherlands	1.1	143	0.5	133
New Zealand	−5.7	82	4.4	151
Norway	2.5	271	0.5	486
Portugal	1.2	241	0.2	221
Spain	n/a	n/a	1.0	473
Sweden	2.7	164	0.3(0.7)	272(186)
Switzerland[f]	0.5	130	−0.1	89
Turkey	n/a	n/a	n/a	n/a
UK	6.7	177	1.2(2.1)	190(212)
USA[g]	1.0	116	0.2	115

Notes: Numbers in brackets include housing assistance for France, Sweden and UK.
[a] Increase to 1991 or 1990 where no data for 1992. [b] Social assistance data for financial years (1/7 to 30/6) related to later calendar year: e.g., 1991/92 as proportion of 1991. [c] Includes payments to residents in homes. [d] API and AAH only. [e] Social assistance data for financial years. These ran from April to March until 1990, then from July to June. Social assistance data related to earlier year until 1990 (e.g. 1988/89 as proportion of 1988) and to later year after 1990 (e.g., 1991/92 as proportion of 1992). [f] Supplementary pensions only. [g] Recipients: SSI plus AFDC only.
Source: Gough, et al., 1997, p. 27.

Low take-up rates do not mean that most of those not receiving assistance do not meet the criteria for entitlement, let alone do not 'need' the support. It simply means that they do not apply or that if they do they fail some administrative or behavioural condition, which may or may not be in their control.

Low take-up rates create moral hazards for policymakers. They could favour selective schemes because they would reduce public expenditure and allow them to assert that those not claiming benefits cannot need them (Nicholls and Zekhauser, 1982). Low take up is usually regarded as relating to means testing, but a labour test does not avoid the difficulties. In developing countries, in particular, it is often argued that a labour test is an effective form of targeting, as with rural public works, because those in need can be identified by coming forward to labour in the scheme. This is dubious. Many of the poorest will be the least able to do so, and the stigma of doing so will deter others since the act is even more clearly visible than having to go through the form filling of means testing.

Selective social assistance typically has high administrative costs. Again, in developing countries or wherever administrative systems are poorly developed, targeted schemes will entail large leakages in maladministration (Burgess and Stern, 1991, p. 64). This probably applies everywhere. For this reason, among others, many analysts favour targeting based on physical or easily recorded needs. Yet most forms of targeting run into moral hazards – they make it more likely that someone will enter the condition. This raises administrative costs on screening, monitoring and policing behaviour, which can comprise a substantial share of the expenditure. In the UK, administrative costs for means-tested Supplementary Benefit (which became Income Support) amounted to 11.3 per cent of the total spent on the benefit and 45 per cent of administrative costs of the entire social security programme, for a benefit that accounted for only 18 per cent of social security expenditure (Atkinson and Hills, 1991, p. 89). In the 1990s, fraud and administrative error cost 16 per cent of the £80 billion annual social security budget. In short, the more conditions that are attached and the more the system opts for tight monitoring, the higher the administrative expenditure. Given the desire to cut public spending, it is regrettable that a high proportion of available funds is spent in this way.

Another feature of selective, means-tested policies is that men have benefited disproportionately from rights-based entitlements (insurance) whereas women have depended more on 'client-based' means-tested transfers. Thus, 62 per cent of social assistance claimants in Germany have been women (Sainsbury, 1993; Gough et al., 1997). Typically, women do not have anything like equal access to social transfers, and feminisation of labour markets is linked to the drift to selectivity. Tightening of entitlement conditions for social assistance will affect women disproportionately.

In sum, defined as the value of all benefits provided to the out-of-work poor who satisfy the means tests and behaviour tests, social assistance has given income replacement rates varying from a high of over 80 per cent of average male earnings in Switzerland to less than 20 per cent in some US States (Gough et al., 1997, p. 32). This overstates the benefit, because of low take-up rates. The situation is surely worse in those countries emerging from state socialism. Even for industrialised countries, if one assumes a 50 per cent take-up rate, average replacement rates would vary from about 40 per cent to 10 per cent, which gives a rough order of magnitude of the limited effectiveness of social assistance and selective benefits in general. Yet the trend to selective, tested schemes has continued through the 1990s, with new euphemisms and variants, such as 'affluence tests' (excluding high income-earners from benefits), being introduced to differentiate between the deserving and undeserving. Although the variation in the design and operation of selective schemes is so great that any generalisation should be regarded as hypothesis rather than established fact, the trend to selectivity and testing surely accentuates the income insecurity of the poor and near-poor.

Not only will benefits targeted at the poor tend to stigmatise them, but the defence of such benefits will depend on the social voice of the numerically weak. It is surely no coincidence that in the USA, where social protection is divided between social security (social insurance, mainly benefiting the middle classes) and welfare (mainly means tested), in the 1980s and 1990s the value of welfare benefits declined, while the value of social security benefits was preserved (Weir et al., 1988). As Titmuss tersely concluded long ago, benefits specifically for the poor will be poor benefits.

8.5 MULTI-TIERISM AND THE PRIVATISATION OF SOCIAL POLICY

The privatisation of social policy has been following the privatisation of economic activity. This has been more advanced in some countries than in others, of course. However, the general trend is clear. It has been true of schooling, healthcare, pensions, social care and employment services. Privatisation is linked to what we might call *multi-tierism*, the differentiation of elements within specific forms of social protection, usually based on income, forms of economic participation and mode of delivery. The drift to private provision has been accelerated by the growing selectivity and conditionality of state-based social protection, the spread of more flexible forms of labour and the diminishing share of income of the affluent coming from employment.

To appreciate what has been happening, recall the notion of social income. Essentially, there has been a shift from SB to PB, and within that to PIB (private insurance). The first stages of the process involved a differentiation within state benefits (SB), with basic or flat-rate benefits being replaced by or supplemented by earnings-related elements. In the 1990s, multiple-tier benefits have gone with privatisation of benefits. One should add that not only is this a broad generalisation but dichotomising public and private can be misleading. In practice, there are gradations of private and public, since state involvement could be partial in several

ways, without the state being wholly responsible for the scheme. To illustrate the
trends, a few points on the main spheres of social policy may be useful.

Healthcare has become more diversified, with a shrinking role for public provision
and funding. Although the trend has been stronger in some countries than in others,
there has been a tendency to shift part of the funding from employers to workers
in terms of contributions, to increase user-payment for services, to differentiate
services, with payment for some and free or subsidised provision of others, and
to reduce the direct public provision of health services.

The partial privatisation of healthcare, coupled with more flexible employment,
means that *occupational welfare* is becoming a more important source of inequality.
For example, in the United States higher-earning occupational groups are more
likely to have pension and health plans with their company than those in lower-
earning jobs, women in any occupational group are less likely to have such plans,
and those in part-time jobs are substantially less likely to have a health or pension
plan (Blank, 1990, Table 4).

Schooling, particularly higher education, has shown analogous trends, so that even
when the state seems to be paying for the system, part of the costs and responsibilities have been passed to students and their families, and as a result their income
security has been eroded. These trends have been most conspicuous in ex-socialism
countries.

Pensions are where privatisation and multi-tierism has been most advanced and
most contentious, primarily old-age pensions. Multi-tierism developed early in the
process, with an international trend to a mixed contributions-and-assistance pension
structure (Overbye, 1997). Indeed, recent reforms should be seen against the
backdrop of a long trend to hybrid forms of state pensions (Table 8.3). Pension
reform has been a global phenomenon of the last few years of the twentieth
century.[4] To some extent it was precipitated by the perception of a fiscal crisis in
Pay-as-You-Go state pension systems due to ageing, although some authorities retain
belief in the long-term feasibility of PAYG insurance pensions (Cichon, 1997). That
may be the case, but it has been the *perception* of a fiscal crisis and the *image* of
impending fiscal difficulties that have induced politicians to rush to reform, adding
to the interest-based reasons for privatisation – private pensions has become big
business and pension funds have become major players in the corporate economy
globally.

Besides demographic difficulties with state pensions, funding difficulties are likely
to arise from the informalisation and labour flexibility, since these increase the
likelihood of avoidance and evasion of contributions. Attempts to raise contribution
rates merely strengthen this tendency, as was found in Poland and other ex-state
socialism countries.

Table 8.3 Paths towards mixed contributions-and-assistance pension systems in west European and Anglo-American countries

Type of scheme	Tax-financed minimum pension	Minimum plus compulsory contribution-based (dual mandatory system)	Subsidised voluntary schemes	Compulsory contribution-based
First pension scheme[a]	Australia, Canada, Denmark, Iceland, Ireland, New Zealand, Norway, Sweden, UK		Belgium, France, Italy, Spain	Austro-Hungarian Empire, Finland, Germany, Greece, Netherlands, Portugal, Switzerland, USA
Pension structure in 1996	Denmark[b], Ireland[c], New Zealand	Australia, Austria, Belgium, Canada, Finland, France, Greece, Iceland, Italy, Netherlands[d], Norway, Portugal, Spain, Sweden, Switzerland, UK, USA		Germany[e]

Note:
a   Some countries adopted a mixed approach from the beginning, as in Sweden in 1913.
b   With almost total coverage of occupational pensions and small-flat-rate contribution-based pension.
c   Minimum pension for employees is contribution-based.
d   Mandatory membership only in 62 of the 83 industry pension funds supplementing the minimum pension as from 1980.
e   With standardised social assistance. Periods of higher education and registered unemployment, as well as up to three years of child-rearing, count as contribution periods. Pension rights are split between spouses in case of divorce.

Source: Overbye, 1997, p. 108.

There has been a trend to *multi-tier pension systems*, in which the 'guaranteed' state pension is a modest amount, while a second tier consists of an individualised insurance-based pension handled by a private pension fund, and a third tier is voluntary, through personal savings, or through arrangements between a worker and an employer. In the 1990s, there has been a spread of variants of the *Chilean pension system*, and the World Bank has taken a leading role in moving systems in a multi-pillar or multi-tier direction, particularly in eastern Europe and the former Soviet Union.

One factor eroding the old system's legitimacy has been the apparently low rate of return. The PAYG basis for state pensions has been a convenient fiction, since social security is tax-based. Government spending on pensions accounts for a high share of GDP – 5 per cent in the USA and averaging nearly 8 per cent in EU countries, for instance. The taxes that are contributions for state pensions have been treated as savings or as investment for old-age support. Critics, such as Martin Feldstein, have estimated that the annual real rate of return on social security taxes in the USA had fallen to 1.5 per cent by the 1990s, compared with an average 9 per cent return on private investment (Feldstein, 1996; Feldstein and Samwick, 1996). This is an argument for shifting to private funded pensions, the claim being that as the expected rate of return on investment by pension funds is higher, pensions will be higher. Feldstein's estimates have been challenged, but a powerful body of opinion has supported moves to private funding. One claim is that if people can see that their pensions are related directly to their contributions, they will regard what they pay as saving not taxes, which will raise their incentive to work (Wolf, 1997). This is not necessarily the case, since it depends on income and substitution effects. It is more likely that the main behavioural effect of funding schemes would be to alter the timing of labour force participation and labour intensity over the life cycle, making it more likely that high-income earners work intensely in their years of highest earning capacity and retire from that employment relatively early.

The trend to funded, multi-tier pensions is sweeping criticisms aside. Several variants have been in competition, such as the Chilean and Swedish models. For our analysis, the most important part of the trend is the low base pension that is envisaged, in some countries provided by the state on a means-tested basis. Those who do not secure entitlement to the employment-based tiers will be in grave difficulty in old age.

It is unclear whether a single dominant model has been established. In Latin America, the Chilean model and Argentian and Bolivian variants are gaining ground. Although the Chilean model has been most influential, a particularly interesting model is the Bolivian 'collective capitalisation' scheme, under which shares from enterprise privatisation are used to fund two privately managed pension funds mandated to use dividends to provide small pensions for all Bolivians and to establish individual accounts for higher pensions. In South East Asia, the dominant model has consisted of pension funds controlled by governments directly, whereby mandatory schemes have shifted workers' savings into funds run by government-appointed managers. However, Hong Kong has adopted the Chilean model.

As in Latin America, after initially strengthening PAYG schemes in the early 1990s, countries in central and eastern Europe have rushed into reforms based on private funded schemes. By 1997, Hungary and Poland had passed acts to cut state pensions and establish private funded schemes coupled with encouragement of voluntary private and occupational pensions. Similar reforms were being prepared or proposed in countries such as the Czech Republic, Estonia, Kazakstan and Russia.[5] Most have moved to pension *pluralisation*, in allowing voluntary private pensions.

In Poland, in 1997 the authorities, encouraged and partially funded by the World Bank, devised a three-tier pension plan in which the first tier would be a means-tested minimum pension (Office of the Government Plenipotentiary, 1997). The second would be an obligatory plan for all the employed, in which contributions would be invested in designated private pension funds, so that the value of the pension would depend on the rate of return on investments, presumably a mix of bonds and equities. The third tier would be a voluntary plan to be worked out between employers and workers. The main difficulties with this scheme are that the basic 'guaranteed' pension would be very low, set at 28 per cent of the average wage (unguaranteed), that workers would face more income insecurity because their pensions would depend on the success of fund managers, and the value of the basic state pension would be in danger of declining since it would only be a major concern for a disadvantaged minority.

In the Hungarian pension reform, modelled on the Argentinian variant of the Chilean pension scheme, one-third of the 30.5 per cent payroll tax allocated to the National Pension Insurance Fund was allocated to private pension funds as from 1998, which is coupled with the PAYG scheme, both based on obligatory contributions. All Hungarians entering the workforce must join the private scheme, while older workers can choose between the two. Among the stated objectives was lower public spending and an enlarged private capital market, through creating a pension fund industry.

Being under less pressure (and with more political support for their established systems), western European countries have been more cautious about pension reform than Latin American and eastern European countries, although they have been moving in similar directions, or as in Germany have been trying to do so. Thus the new British government launched a major 'review' of options in mid-1997. Among the possibilities was a second-tier *stakeholder pension*. There was little doubt that the direction of reform would go towards mandated funded private schemes, especially as private pensions already account for as much as the basic state pension. Meanwhile, the Swiss have operated a variant of their own since 1985, with a 'five-level split system with two of its pillars split into smaller and uneven parts' (Vittas, 1993, p. 4). The first pillar is a PAYG basic state pension, the second a set of mandatory occupational schemes (with a reasonably high replacement rate), the third an optional, supplementary individual savings-funded scheme, with tax relief. The scheme's success depends on male full-time employment and strong norms of nuclear or extended families.

The 'Washington consensus' has been that the core of the pension should be a 'mandatory, funded, privately managed pillar (based on personal accounts or occupational plans) to handle people's savings', while the state pension should be secondary and 'modest in size, to allow ample room for other pillars' and low taxes. The third should be a voluntary personal plan 'for people who want more protection' (World Bank, 1994, p. 292). The distributional consequences would be more income insecurity for marginal groups, more income inequality in old age, and more inequality generally because those locked out of the system by their life experience would not only receive low pensions but require transfers from their families and communities.

The World Bank has shifted from presenting the public pension as the first and main pillar to presenting the private one as the first of two mandatory pillars. The ILO, initially critical of the Chilean AFP and moves away from PAYG pensions because of the insecurities involved, moved to propose a three-tier model (resisting the term pillar), consisting of a 'a flat-rate, possibly means-tested, basic pension, chiefly as an anti-poverty measure', topped up with a middle tier consisting of 'a compulsory, defined-benefit, PAYG social security scheme, perhaps providing benefits of more modest scope than would be the case if this were the only mechanism for providing for old age', supplemented by a voluntary, private tier of defined-benefit or defined-contribution schemes (ILO, 1995b, p. 68). The ILO in an effort to update its position has since prepared a review of the advantages and disadvantages of the options.

The international debate on pensions will have a bearing on the future of social policy. The important point for our analysis is that the directions of reform in the current era are individualistic and inegalitarian, leaving those outside wage employment or without access to the capital market bearing more risk and exposed to long-term income uncertainty. The new pension schemes are also a form of fiscal regulation, in that they reward those who have regular, well-remunerated employment.

Other spheres of social protection have also become more pluralistic. Multi-tierism and privatisation in *unemployment protection* has received little attention, although a private market is emerging, with high-income, securely-employed workers taking out insurance or having it taken out for them, and with core firms offering high-skilled, high-status employees and management generous redundancy benefit packages, capped by *'golden parachute'* clauses for directors and senior managers. This is part of the fragmentation of enterprise benefits. But if unemployment benefits are being cut or made harder to obtain, the availability of severance pay for privileged groups would make it less likely that they would oppose the trend. Moreover, this intensifies the inequality of income security, as does private insurance protection, since the premiums are sure to vary by probability of loss of employment and income.

Finally, *welfare delivery services* are being partially privatised. In the USA, some States have contracted out their entire system of social protection and services. Texas put out its services to tender and the final three bidders included the world's largest *defence* contractor (Lockheed Martin) as well as two other corporations with no prior involvement in welfare policy. Whatever regulations were applied, and whatever the rhetoric, such companies would act to maximise efficiency and profits, making them unlikely to concentrate on helping the most vulnerable or impoverished. Companies have been awarded contracts to place welfare recipients in jobs, and are paid according to their success in placing them. Thus, in 1997 *America Works* received $985 per person placed in a job, plus $3,855 if the person was offered a full-time job after a probationary period, and another $650 if she remained in it for some time. A danger must be that out-sourcing and such incentives will result in 'creaming', with better treatment being given to some groups and discrimination against others, which will result in private control functions, with no social accountability.

Privatisation of social policy is also *individualisation* of social protection. This is inegalitarian, definitionally removing the solidaristic element, and creating discriminatory problems. For example, those with disabilities or long-term illnesses usually cannot obtain health insurance or have to pay more for it. This also applies to those in insecure or physically risky jobs or living in areas of high joblessness.

Because of the extent of change, the UK is a useful example for evaluating the international trend. Thus, although it declined a little in the 1990s, private health insurance became widespread in the UK in the 1980s. It is spreading in other countries. Insurance companies will find ways of screening out above-average risks, refusing to insure those deemed risky, or demanding such high premia that they cannot insure themselves. Another case is private motor insurance, the cost of which is often differentiated by area of residence, type of car, occupation and personal background, with exclusion clauses, premium loadings and designated uninsurable risks. Privatisation produces fragmentation of insurance benefits and costs, facilitated by informatics, which enables companies to check up on individuals and work out probabilities of them making claims. Labour market flexibility compounds this tendency. Most worrying is that for those with low incomes, private insurance to cover gaps between short-term jobs is prohibitively expensive or unavailable. This creates a moral hazard, since coverage for such gaps would encourage them to make the spells short, to gain benefits. This would make coverage for employment insecurity more expensive and probably more condition-bound.

Privatisation of benefits can produce new poverty traps. In the UK, since the state is providing fewer or less-assured benefits, many people have been taking out loan protection insurance. But applicants for the means-tested Jobseeker's Allowance have found that payments from the insurance are counted as income, resulting in lost entitlement to the Allowance. In some cases, they have actually lost more than the value of the insurance pay-out.

A study of mortgage payment protection, and insurance for long-term incapacity and long-term care has also documented the fragmentation involved in privatisation of welfare (Burchardt and Hills, 1997). We could be seeing an *underclass of the uninsurable*.

8.6 SOCIAL SERVICES

Welfare state capitalism ushered in a substantial expansion in the state provision of social services, to some extent mapping the development of transfers (Kolberg and Uusitalo, 1992; Jamieson, 1991). Indeed, Esping-Andersen's 'North European' model was distinguished by the high priority given to universalistic social services, not monetary transfers, financed out of taxation. The availability of social services reduces an individual's dependency on private care, in the sense that he would otherwise have to pay or reciprocate for such care or would otherwise be obliged to provide care for others. Both labour market and social protection analysis have tended to omit the roles of social services.

In the era of market regulation, the trends observed in other forms of income protection have also characterised social services – selectivity, multi-tierism, individualisation and partial privatisation. Several models of state provision have emerged. One might be described as the *client model*, in which a person can obtain social services on application if satisfying basic conditions, but can obtain only the modest assistance on offer. Some commentators have described Australia and the Netherlands as operating along these lines. Another model is the *conditionality model*, where the applicant can obtain more than basic assistance if he is prepared to satisfy more conditions and go through the stigma of more bureaucratic procedures, form-filling and inspection. Some have depicted Sweden as corresponding to this. The UK went in the same direction with its Social Fund, since a shortage of finance for the Fund obliged the bureaucracy to ration by discouragement.

Perhaps the major change in social services has come with partial privatisation of services and the renewed expectation that *care* would be undertaken privately, by families or voluntary organisations. Recalling the composition of social income, social policy has changed direction by shifting part of the social income back onto the CB from SB. Thus, there has been partial reprivatisation of caring for children, elderly parents and relatives. Parental leave has been introduced or extended in some countries, as has subsidised parental care of young children. More countries are introducing conditional cash transfers for care, income-entitlement protection for those providing care and insurance for care (Daly, 1997). The state has also been providing a subsidy to encourage families and the old themselves to take responsibility for caring for elderly, chronically ill and incapacitated relatives.

In some countries, the right to care for others is recognised to the extent that entitlement to social assistance is not lost if the person is deemed to need to care for someone, as in the Netherlands until 1996, when it was curtailed to apply only to care for children under the age of five. In others, such as Denmark, caregiving has not been accepted as justification for being unavailable for paid jobs, and benefits could be lost. Thus the labour line has been strengthened in the Netherlands and has persisted in Denmark. In other countries, the right to give care is recognised by entitlement to benefit, but the amount for such 'citizen carers' is less than available for 'citizen workers'. In some countries, contribution credits for pensions and some other social benefits are granted to cover a period during which someone is deemed to be doing caring work.

Five ways of remunerating care work have been used.[6] They highlight a dilemma at the heart of restructuring of labour market relations, social protection and work. First, under various guises, *carer allowances* have been paid, as in the case of tax credits (such as the US Federal Dependent Tax Care Credit) or social security payments, as in Denmark and in the Irish Carers' Allowance introduced in 1990. This approach does not require the recipient to demonstrate that care is being given, merely that there is a need for care. As such it is nearly a citizenship-based entitlement (Ungerson, 1997, p. 367). But the assistance may be means-tested, as in the Irish scheme, or employment-related, as in Denmark. So it is not really a citizenship right.

A second form is what Ungerson calls *routed wages*, where care recipients or users are given cash or vouchers with which to pay for care. This has been a recent trend. In the USA, there is the Housebound Aid and Attendance Allowances for the care of war veterans. In Italy, there are 'companion payments', which are paid to more than a million people each year (Glendenning and McLaughlin, 1993). In France, benefits have been paid to care recipients to pay care providers, and in 1996 vouchers and tax credits were introduced for care recipients, which they are expected to use to employ personal assistants from their neighbourhood and family network (*'emplois de proximite'*) – a scheme intended not just to ensure care but to formalise grey economy work. Denmark and Austria have allowances for care recipients. In the UK, the Community Care (Direct Payments) Act of 1996 gave cash as an option rather than care services, intended to promote consumer choice and market efficiency. But unlike the others, the UK regulations forbid employment of close relatives on the ground that this would erode the emphasis on family responsibility. The country that has gone furthest in this direction is Germany, where in 1995 the 'need for care' became the first new social insurance risk category since unemployment insurance was introduced in 1927, making care insurance compulsory.

In Germany, the payment is made to the person *receiving* care. In Belgium, a 'career break' is allowed under the unemployment insurance scheme for persons wishing to *provide* care for seriously ill or elderly people. This raises a moral hazard, in that it would encourage a family to claim that a person needs care, where no such need would be discerned in the absence of a benefit. It might also absolve the state from regarding the need for care for the elderly as a priority, making it less likely that the elderly without relatives would receive good quality care. If the probability of needing state care is reduced for the median voter, he will not pressure policymakers to develop good social services for the elderly. And, if one allows career breaks for the care of the elderly, why not for other reasons?

A third form of payment is *proper wages*, which was common in Sweden and Norway, whereby informal carers have been employed by municipalities and provide care to residents requiring it. A fourth form is *symbolic payments*, small payments made to care recipients to pay for supplementary costs of living, including care. Over one million people were receiving this in the UK in the mid-1990s. These payments reduce the sense of dependence of the disabled on relatives, but it is informal, unregulated, blurring the boundary between gift and market exchange. A fifth form of payment is *paid volunteering*. This is more likely where there is no minimum wage. An intermediary, such as a voluntary organisation or local authority, contracts volunteers to provide care and pays them a symbolic payment. This may be ostensibly for expenses or be a sum that would not give the person an income above an earnings-disregard level for social security. Such practices might spread with workfare. If so, it would threaten the voluntary character of care work, eroding the 'gift relationship'.

The spread of all these forms of payment reflect what has been called the 'care deficit' in the latter part of the century, where divorces have multiplied, single parents have grown in number, elderly people are more likely to be cut off from family support systems, people are living longer, and so on. This has put conflicting pressures on the composition of the social income. The need for care has encouraged the state to shift SB (state benefits) to needs-based payments or, as in Germany, to social-insurance care benefits. But partial reprivatisation also means that CB is rising through a need for more community assistance. Although trends vary – and perhaps one should resist a desire to identify 'care regimes' – there is a pluralisation of care and multi-tier income support, involving mixes of cash payments from government, payments from charities, paid and voluntary care work, and a hidden subsidy in the form of unpaid time by carers and volunteers. Pluralisation could lead in a paternalistic direction or to greater self-control, through state withdrawal and marketisation. As discussed later, care work is a pivotal issue for the future orientation of a work-based society.

Two other aspects of social services should be noted. The desire to make social services more efficient has led to greater use of market mechanisms and has turned citizens into 'customers'. There has also been widespread contracting-out of public social services, which has become commercially big business in some countries, most notably the USA. A related tendency has been the policy of integrating public employment services with social protection functions, in one office or ministry. This is often justified on cost and efficiency grounds. However, it also risks turning social protection more into regulatory policies.

The partial privatisation of social policy has given a growing role to non-governmental voluntary organisations (NGOs). These have sprung up for many reasons, one of which is to fill gaps left by the receding role of government as provider of state benefits and services. Governments have encouraged these through subsidies and other means. The model of *civil society* this encourages is complex, since it risks turning *representative* interests into *regulatory* interests, in part through the spread of a 'contract culture', whereby charities receive money from the government in return for taking responsibility for certain tasks.

It has been claimed that NGOs have a comparative advantage in making transfers to the poor, because they have better information, more local contacts, reduce leakage in administrative costs, and are less likely to be corrupt (Besley, 1997). The evidence is mixed, since there has been a tendency for NGOs to flourish as rent-seeking devices, documented in both industrialised and developing countries, such as the Philippines (Balisacan, 1997). Nevertheless, the trend to reliance on private organisations seems an integral part of the constellation of structures in flexible economies. The challenge is to find forms of governance and regulation to enable them to play a redistributive and productive role.

8.7 DETACHMENT AND FRAGMENTATION

We are now in a position to draw together the strands of flexibility, insecurity and social policy to portray the outcome in terms of socio-economic distribution. In recent years, in contrast to neoclassical models, there have been several dualistic approaches to labour analysis – 'insiders' versus 'outsiders', 'skilled' versus 'unskilled', 'formal sector' versus 'informal sector', 'core' versus 'periphery', and so on. Although many insights can be gained from these, it seems more useful to depict the flexibility–insecurity trends as associated with socio-economic fragmentation and detachment. This is superimposed on traditional labour status categories, and individual societies will have distinctive structures depending on level of economic development and other historical factors.

What the emerging fragmentation represents is the result of tensions and developments associated with globalisation, the new technological revolution and the flexible labour market relations. The distinguishing characteristics are the relationship to the mainstream regulatory and social protection mechanisms and the bundles of forms of security possessed by some groups in society and not others. One hesitates to use class terminology. Others, recognising the fragmenting tendencies of globalisation, have tried to do so (e.g., Rodrick, 1997). Clearly, relations of production and control do play a part in distinguishing groups in society. Yet access to security and the relationship to the welfare state are also important in defining the distinctive strata. Although the fragmentation could be refined, particularly if there were appropriate data, it should be sufficient for our purposes to present a brief characterisation of the seven strata that make up the emerging structure. The seven are as follows:

(i) The Elite

In the era of globalisation and market regulation, at the top of the income spectrum is what can be called an *elite* stratum, consisting of highly mobile, extraordinarily wealthy global citizens, who escape from all regulatory systems and have no desire (or need) to have the security that could be offered by welfare states. Some have made their fortunes through a mix of brilliant hard work and positional good fortune, and through the fact that their particular technical breakthrough happened to be the one that made commercial exploitation enormously profitable.[7] At the very pinnacle, besides some laudable characters, are some multi-billionaires including a bunch of crazed individuals seeking their nth billion dollars, some of whom seem to have a propensity to fall off boats, to disappear or to end up having a spell in prison before renewing their activities. Ignoring the quaint behaviour of this section of the stratum, one may note that those in the elite have a power out of all proportion to their numbers. In 1998, Percy Barnevik, chairman of the Swedish Investor group, boasted that he owned or was a director of companies employing more than two million workers (*Observer*, 8 April 1998). That is real power.

Many in the elite encourage the erosion of redistributive entitlements for other social groups since they have no interest in them, and they are detached from regulatory frameworks, making little contribution to social protection structures (beyond the occasional noisy, glitzy philanthropic gestures) and, by being beyond them, eroding the financial basis as well as the legitimacy of welfare systems.

In 1994, Robert Reich, then US Secretary of Labour, suggested that 15 per cent of the US population were in an 'over-class', increasingly segregated from the remainder of the population, with 15 per cent belonging to a deprived 'under-class'. Squeezed between the two, in his imagery, was 'the anxious class', whose average incomes had been static for two decades. This probably puts too many dissimilar groups into single categories. The truly elite is probably less than 1 per cent of the adult population of industrialised countries. No data are available to measure them accurately, and their wealth and global character make it unlikely that this will change.

One factor in the growth of an elite detached from the mainstream has been the growth of what has been called 'winner-takes-all markets'. According to the conventional textbook model of labour markets, the existence of high incomes for a particular skill would lead to an increase of workers with those skills until the wages were brought back into line with marginal product. In the case of winner-take-all markets, a few individuals receive extremely high incomes because of their 'super-star' status. This image was initially applied to sport (Rosen, 1981), then to film stars. But it has spread to many other professions (Frank and Cook, 1995).

In such markets, the conventional labour adjustment process simply does not work. The market does not pay by any simple measure of absolute performance, but according to relative and imagined performance. The winner-takes-all market has become more significant because informational technology and globalisation have expanded the market from a local or even national one to an international or global one.

Besides those winners, some groups benefit from positional advantage. Among the *elite* are those people managing investment funds. It seems that even leading figures inside the system recognise that those who become enormously wealthy as a result of their involvement in the mutual fund business achieve this through luck more than by individual brilliance. As one prominent figure concluded, brains and skill play little part in relative performance.

The elite have also benefited from the declining incidence of tax on capital and the increasing incidence on wages. In the USA, corporate tax fell from one-third of federal revenue before the Second World War to 12 per cent in 1997, and the change has been similar in western Europe. On average, the standard rate of corporate income tax in OECD countries fell from 43 per cent in 1986 to 33 per cent in 1995. Meanwhile, marginal rates of personal income tax rose for lower-wage workers but the average top rate fell from 59 per cent in 1975 to 42 per cent in 1995 (*The Economist*, 20 September 1997).

The elite include chief executives of major corporations. In the USA, the salary of the average chief executive rose from 35 times the earnings of an average production worker in the mid-1970s to 120 times that salary in the late 1990s. Beyond that, their access to shares and hefty bonuses has been well-documented in the mass media. Like many others in the elite, their opportunities to avoid taxes (often aided by expert advice which they can easily afford) are growing as are their opportunities to increase their revenue from capital, making them increasingly detached from the income insecurity of those below them.

In some countries, the elite have benefited and swelled in number through risk-free share options, which give senior managers or directors the right to buy shares of the company in which they are working at a fixed price regardless of their value in the open market when they take up the option. So, when the financial market is buoyant, the income gain can be substantial. These come on top of annual bonuses and long-term incentive plans (L-TIPS). The link to direct contribution is tenuous. In the UK in 1997, for instance, the value of options jumped, often in companies in which profits and employment fell. The fact is that the price of shares rises for economic, international and political reasons that have nothing to do with company performance, let alone the contribution of the recipient of the risk-free options.

The ease with which the affluent can avoid taxation has been widely noted, and is an international phenomenon. Significantly, in Germany, while income from capital was rising much faster than income from labour, the Bundesbank reported that tax revenue from non-wage income declined from 41.5 billion Deutschemarks in 1992 to merely 11.6 billion in 1996, and in 1997 there was even a negative figure (Vinocur, 1997). The trends in that country have been matched elsewhere.

Coupled with the multiplication of opportunities to make money from novel forms of investment, the elite have established an aura that makes them both respected and feared by governments around the world, which of course has only further strengthened their position and offers of special privileges.

(ii) The Salariat

Below the elite in terms of income and need for security come what one might call the *salariat*, those in secure salaried employment, in 'white-collar' jobs. They have many forms of security, but their numbers are modest. The main ways by which they shape the character of labour markets is by being inclined to opt for occupational welfare and private transfers, thus making them disinclined to support the state welfare system or pro-collective institutions. An increasing proportion of their income has been coming from their investment income.

One source of the relative decline in the size of the salariat in industrialised countries, in particular, is that the shift from Taylorism in the production process has been reducing the middle layers of management and administration.

The shift from status-based salaries to performance-related pay has also eroded the income security of part of the salariat, notably in public sectors. This has been due in part to the employer and managerial desire to download risk, legitimise greater inequality and avoid tax. This may have set up contradictory tendencies. It may erode employee commitment and the much-discussed 'loyalty', and it may induce opportunistic work behaviour. Among some groups offered enticing income prospects it may produce 'burn out', due to a tendency to overwork and over-achieve. Thereby, it may induce behaviour consistent with the next stratum.

However, the salariat have contributed to the erosion of the legitimacy of welfare state capitalism by being able to turn their savings into high-return investment, aided by the higher interest rates induced by greater reliance on monetary policy, globalisation of capital markets and pressure on exchange rates. The much higher, and more assured, income from investments has reduced their dependency on labour for their income security, *and* they have been able to pass on to their children sufficient wealth to make them less dependent on labour for their income security. Indicative of this detachment, in Germany, according to the Federal Statistics Office, between 1991 and 1997 earnings from capital rose by two-fifths, four times the rise in *average* worker earnings. Stock prices had risen by 350 per cent since 1987, and by 1996 there were 4.4 million stockholders in Germany, 1.1 million more than in 1988 (Vinocur, 1997).

A lack of need for protective regulations and state transfers to cover potential contingencies makes them less inclined to support income transfers for the more vulnerable in society, helping to undermine the socio-political pressures to provide adequate benefits and leading them to put pressure on governments to 'save' public expenditure by tightening conditions for entitlement to benefits.

(iii) Proficians

Below, or alongside, the salariat in the income-security spectrum are what one might call *proficians*, consisting of those with only loose attachment to any one employer, those who combine different forms of work status or have personal bundles of skills, and those living on contracts or as 'consultants'. They possess marketable skills, and straddle the two conventional occupational classifications of 'professional and administrative' and 'technical and related' workers. As the suggested name implies, proficians often do not have a sense of career that goes with the traditional notion of 'professional' and they tend to have a bundle of technical skills that gives them the capacity to survive in what is potentially considerable labour insecurity.

Proficians have been one of the growing strata of the era. Few studies seem to have been done of the phenomenon, yet it is surely a rapidly expanding, global one. Although one cannot equate the occupational category of 'technicians' with the type of status and behaviour of what is here called profician, they are closely related. It is therefore relevant that technicians have been exhibiting a dramatic growth in absolute and relative terms. In the USA, they already comprise the largest broad category of the employed, and are expected to account for 20 per cent of the workforce by the year 2000.

Proficians often have high incomes but lower income security by comparison with the salariat above them in the hierarchy. This is because they operate mainly on the basis of individual contracts, or as partners. They would be at least partially detached from the regulatory labour market framework, since they would be detached from the social security system, if only because they would not build up adequate contribution records or be in work statuses that gain entitlements. They may receive very high incomes, avoid (*and* evade) direct taxes, and supplement their money incomes with private fringe and contingency benefits. Their work styles and occupational variability preclude membership of conventional craft or industrial trade unions, let alone company unions. They are the nomads of the modern world. When they tire, they cease to belong and drift out of the transient existence that comes with being a profician.

Whether individual proficians survive as affluent citizens will depend on their capacity to sustain the frenetic work pace, and in many cases to keep up with the modern jargon and technical wizardry. By age 40, many are likely to be 'burnt out', and move into a sedentary existence or entrepreneurial dabbling, perhaps with extensive income security provided from capital. A new vogue term is 'downshifting'. The failures are likely to drift into the fifth stratum described below.

Will the new generation of labour force entrants increasingly go straight to temporary activities as budding proficians? This is not likely, because work experience is a vital part of the skill required, and because firms are likely to resort to trainee contracts and bonded training for their technically qualified workers.

(iv) Core Workers

In terms of income and security, the fourth stratum down the income security scale consists of *core (or standard) workers*. This stratum consists loosely of the old working class, regular full-time workers, mostly male, with manual skills, adherence to trade unions and seeking the security of mainstream welfare state mechanisms. This stratum never became 'the immense majority' predicted by Marx, and is no longer 'working class' in the fourfold Marxian sense of being the producers on whom society depended, being exploited, being the majority (with families) of society, and being poor. These four characteristics were supposed to be combined with two others – having nothing to lose from overthrowing capitalism and having the ability to transform society. Critics have long held that these two characteristics have not applied. Old-style labourism and welfare capitalism were at least functional and legitimated when the first four characteristics approximately held.[8]

The core stratum constitutes the only one of the socio-economic strata with a firm attachment to the regulatory framework of the era of statutory regulation. Yet, reflecting their diminishing numerical size and the expectation that their numbers will continue to shrink, in most countries workers in this stratum have suffered a series of reverses during the era of market regulation.

They now face a problem of legitimation. They are a dwindling minority, whereas once they were a powerful vanguard of the working class. If their leaders try to draw support and union membership from the lower ranks of the salariat they tend to make further concessions to individualisation of employment relations and wage flexibility, which erode the sense of solidarity that trade unions have always espoused. If they push hard to maintain the real value of wages, and their income and employment security, they risk not only alienating the salariat (and those of their own ranks aspiring to that status) but will encourage firms to restructure in favour of outsourcing, and to shift to greater use of workers in the fifth stratum.

In industrialised economies, the core stratum has long been shrinking and has also had the 'effort bargain' redefined through changing payment mechanisms and the changing structure of the social income. From the old piece rates and then time rates, there has been a shift to performance-related, bonus-related systems, raising W_f relative to W_b.

Even here there are contradictory issues, for the more that core workers are protected by statutory regulations, the more that the cost is likely to be borne by casual workers forced to accept lower pay and worse working conditions. There may be a redistribution of wages from casual workers to core workers, but at the cost of reducing the core workers' job prospects. But increasingly, without strong representation security, core workers have been unable to defend their wages or other forms of security. Significantly, in the final decades of the century of the labouring man, in the USA, average earnings for men in working-class jobs declined in real terms, while those of women at all levels of schooling improved in real terms, as did those of men with tertiary levels of schooling. The core was going backwards.

Due to globalisation and related political developments, the tendency to shift from taxes on capital to taxes on labour has involved a greater tax burden on core workers, and because they have been shrinking in number one may surmise that the per worker burden has also tended to rise. Because there are limits to that process, governments have tended to respond by cutting expenditure. But as the incidence of tax has shifted in the last 50 years from capital to labour, this group has experienced the greatest tax increase.

Thus, while the marginal income tax rates have been cut on high incomes in many countries, in industrialised countries the marginal tax rates have risen on average for those earning the average wage, and have risen even more for those earning two-thirds of the average wage. In the G7 countries, the marginal income tax rate for a single person on average earnings was 39.7 per cent in 1978 and 41.4 per cent in 1995, for a single-earner couple with two children it rose from 36.2 per cent to 38.7 per cent. For those on 66 per cent of average earnings, the respective figures were 32.6 per cent in 1978 and 38.4 per cent in 1995 and 27.8 per cent in 1978 and 38.4 per cent in 1995. Thus tax rates had risen most for those below the average and for one-earner households.

Ironically, the rising tax rates may have reduced the regular workers' support for redistributive social policy, because they are likely to perceive themselves as paying for most of it, through supporting the unemployed and the poor.

(v) Flexiworkers

Below the core workers in terms of income security are what may be described as *flexiworkers*. These are workers who move in and out of employment, being required to 'rotate' from job to job, with skills that have to be updated periodically. They have little or no income security or employment security, little job security, and little of the other forms of security. They are the part-time workers, temporary workers, agency workers, outworkers, and so on. One may speculate that the actual number of flexiworkers is greater than conventional statistics suggest, although even those indicate that in industrialised countries, they already account for a large and growing share of the employed. As noted in chapter 4, by the mid-1990s, the largest single employer in the USA was Manpower, the private temporary employment agency. In other countries, such employment is growing very rapidly indeed.

Flexiworkers are detached, in that they have only fragile adherence to the mainstream regulatory and social security systems. Flexiworking looks likely to be the future for many people – perhaps even a majority – and one may predict that to a growing extent production enterprises will contract out their employment function. This could mean that a growing share of all workers will be employed and supplied to firms through private employment agencies. This is already happening, not just for secretaries but for a wide range of jobs.

(vi) The Unemployed

Below flexiworkers in the income hierarchy are the *unemployed*. They deserve to be treated as a distinct stratum of the labour market, because whereas a presumption of the Beveridge and Bismarkian welfare states has been that unemployment would affect only a small minority of the labour force and that the unemployment would represent a short 'temporary interruption of earning power', it is increasingly the picture that for many people a spell of unemployment can be expected to last for as long as a spell of employment. Recall that the mean average job tenure in the USA is less than seven years, which means that for many workers tenure is short. In some European countries, average employment tenure of *full-time regular workers* has been higher, but if account is taken of the growing number of part-time and temporary workers, the image of impermanency becomes more accurate.

The unemployed have been another stratum that has been growing, and as elaborated earlier, in the era of market regulation their income insecurity has worsened, through restrictions on entitlement to unemployment benefits and lower income replacement rates for such benefits. It has long been the case that only about a third of the unemployed in the USA receive unemployment benefits. Now this applies to the European Union, while elsewhere an even smaller minority of the unemployed receive unemployment benefits.

For those who do receive benefits, the amount received has been falling. It is now quite low in many countries. For example, in 1994, the average gross replacement rate before tax in the first month of unemployment for a couple without children was 57 per cent in France, 42 per cent in Germany and 26 per cent in the UK. A growing proportion of the unemployed have had to rely on means-tested social assistance and as such are detached from any sense of belonging to mainstream regulatory and social security systems.

(vii) The Detached

This leads to the seventh stratum, about which so much has been written. At the bottom of the labour market and income spectrum are those detached from it, whether by result of prolonged unemployment or through some social illness.

It could be called the *detached* stratum. The term 'underclass' has been popular, although problematic. It was first used by Gunnar Myrdal in his study of US poverty; he had in mind the victims of so-called structural and technological unemployment (Myrdal, 1964, p. 40). Wilson populised the term in his book on the black urban poor in the USA (Wilson, 1987). Frank Field, briefly a social security minister in the New Labour government, used the term to describe the poor in the

UK in the 1980s (Field, 1989). It has slipped into common usage. In class terminology, one might be inclined to use the term *lumpenproletariat*. But the image of an anomic, passive, helpless mass of unsavoury individuals sleeping in cardboard boxes in the streets of New York, London, Moscow and elsewhere is only part of the reality. It also encompasses what are sometimes called 'the dangerous classes', the rootless footsoldiers of the *mafioso* economy. Neo-liberals have branded the detached as a problem of 'dependency' on state transfers, and have wanted to use their insecurity to 'reintegrate' them into mainstream society. We return to this in the next chapter.

However, two key points for our understanding of the fragmentation of the labour market are, first, that the detached have no adherence to the regulatory and social security system and, second, that they are an incipient drag on economic growth. This is partly because they represent a threat of crudely retributive justice. Go to Moscow, Naples, Johannesburg, New York or London to see how anomic some parts of the detached can be. The labour market in criminal 'services' is thriving in the era of market regulation. Meanwhile, policing the losers in society is a costly business. But building up the capacity to police the 'undeserving poor' further erodes the security of losers and winners alike.

One group in the detached are those who have transgressed society's rules. With high unemployment and inequality, as well as socio-economic detachment that has accompanied the growth of insecurity, a remarkable number of people have been drifting into crime and out of the labour force as a result of it. Thus, 2 per cent of men in the USA are in prison; a growing number of women are too; in total about 1.5 million people are in prison, and presumably most would otherwise be in the labour force looking for jobs. It is a way of keeping the detached stratum smaller. The USA imprisons 4 times as many of its citizens as the UK, 6 times as many as other European countries and 14 times as many as Japan (Gray, 1998). But the pattern has been spreading. In the UK, for instance, in 1994–95 the prison population increased by 10,000, and in 1996 the number of men in prison was rising by 1,000 a month (*Guardian*, 5 October 1996). A perverse development in the UK was that resources for public prisons were slashed as a means of cutting public expenditure. Putting people in prison without access to training or social services will perpetuate the problem, for on coming out they will be unprepared for alternative types of activity.

The detached is the bottom of the social pile. The sevenfold characterisation is intended as a guide to differentiating trends. It is preferable to the conventional one-digit ISCO occupational classification, which is treated with notably little criticism. Intriguingly, after this chapter was drafted, a report was produced for the UK's Office for National Statistics recommending that the conventional fivefold classification of the labour force based on 'occupational groups' should be revised into eight social classes, with occupation and employment security being the primary criteria. Table 8.4 presents the pre-2001 system and the proposed classification for censuses and surveys after the year 2000, with the first column indicating the standard groups used for opinion poll purposes. What the change reflects is the proliferation of what in the USA has been called 'semi-professionals', those who have some technical qualifications and some self-control who but are not in control in the production process (Heckscher, 1996, p. 68).

Table 8.4 Labour status fragmentation, United Kingdom, 1990s

Social Class	Pre-2001	Post-2000
A/B	I: Professional	1 Professionals, employers, administrators and managers in firms with 25+ workers
	II: Managerial, technical	2 Associate professionals, employers, administrators and managers in firms with 1–24 workers, supervisors
		3 Intermediate occupations in administrative, clerical,
C1/C2	III (N): Skilled (non-manual)	sales and service work
		4 Self-employed non-professionals
	III (M): Skilled (manual)	5 Other supervisors, craft and related workers
		6 Routine occupations in
D/E	IV: Semi-skilled	manufacturing and services
		7 Elementary jobs, labourers
	V: Unskilled	8 Long-term unemployed, never worked, long-term sick

Source: D. Rose and UK Office for National Statistics.

We may see labour fragmentation as both an outcome and as part of the process of labour flexibility, in which social relations of production and distribution are visibly changing. The groups with attachment to the post-war welfare and protective regulations have been shrinking, whereas those with tenuous attachment or with active opposition to them have been expanding.

Detachment by the poor is an alienating and an anomic experience. The conditional nature of a rising proportion of state benefits has tended to accentuate detachment and make it harder for the detached to participate in society, including community services (which might even preclude the unemployed from seeking wage employment). As some observers have noted, attaching stricter conditions for entitlement to social welfare could have the opposite effect to the one intended, erecting barriers to social and economic participation, not pulling them down.

In sum, poverty that leads to social isolation and detachment in the current era has also pushed more people into dependency on 'official care', dependence on the state, on a bureaucracy that becomes increasingly intrusive because of the dictates of targeting and the pursuit of efficiency and effectiveness.

8.8 CONCLUDING POINTS

The coming political battle will be for the souls of the anxious class.
Robert Reich, US Secretary of Labour, 1994

It has been said that the essence of the class system is not that the privileged are conscious of their privileges, but that the deprived are conscious of their deprivation. Deprivation in the 1990s has been about insecurity, and it will continue to be about insecurity in the foreseeable future.

Although it has always been the case for the vast majority in developing countries, in the past decade or so, income insecurity has become pervasive in industrialised countries as well, among growing proportions of the employed, among those working at the margins of flexible labour markets, among the unemployed, and among those outside the labour force. Income insecurity is linked to the socio-economic *detachment* of people and groups from the regulatory mainstream of society.

The systems of socio-economic security built up during the middle part of the twentieth century were oriented to the needs of the labouring man and a productive system based on the labouring man and his nuclear family, safeguarded by his trade union, where the state could take responsibility for providing income security during occasional periods of temporary interruption of earning power. That framework will not be the future, and the system of social protection cannot be moulded as if it were.

Libertarians have responded by advocating selectivity, a narrowing of benefit entitlements, a cut in the 'generosity' of benefits and privatisation of social transfers and services. They want strong market regulation, with individual contracts and legal redress to uphold individual rights. For them, collective entities imply inefficiency, inter-personal inequity and 'insider–outsider' inequalities. For them too, individuals owe society obligations and responsibilities, which implies that the state should intervene to give incentives to productive activity and sanctions against those who contravene society's norms. Their real agenda is privatisation *tout court*.

The social democratic or 'labourist' response to the erosion of legitimacy of the welfare state has been defensive. They have tried to resist the decline in legitimacy by strengthening the 'productivist' or 'labourist' character of welfare. They have joined those advocating tougher conditionality in entitlement to benefits, rationalised as the means of maintaining legitimacy among middle-income groups, and they have joined those advocating less 'generosity' of benefits for those not in jobs, for cost-saving reasons, for legitimacy and to show that labouring must be regarded as the socially responsible norm. They also tend to believe that the middle classes must benefit from welfare schemes to preserve their commitment to the system.

Both political responses converge on a more selective, more conditional, more judgmental, less 'generous' and more paternalistic welfare system, without arresting the erosion in efficiency, legitimacy and protection provided by the state. There are historical parallels. Erosion of universal forms of social protection has usually come in eras of economic transformation. In the late eighteenth century, old forms of social protection guaranteeing food security for everybody were attacked by economic liberals, who asserted that poverty and insecurity were needed as incentives to labour, hunger being effective because it was 'peaceful, silent and continuous' (Polanyi, 1944, pp. 113–14). In the late twentieth century, the language may be more circumspect and genteel (although not always so). But means tests, labour tests and discretionary judgments on the deserving and undeserving are little different from their forebears.

The attempt to relegitimise social policy has been taken furthest in the USA. The 1996 welfare reform, discussed in the next chapter, disentitled many poor from benefits and strengthened workfare. But the 1996 Minimum Wage Act was supposed to help some in low-paid jobs, while health reform made health insurance portable for the employed, leaving the non-employed poor to rely on underfunded Medicaid and charity. In the same direction, the 1993 Family Law Act guaranteed time off a job to care for a sick child or dependent, and the Earned Income Tax Credit improved the income and incentives of those in low-paid jobs, implicitly redistributing from the non-employed poor to the employed. The biggest losers of all were the children of the non-employed poor. Are they deserving or undeserving?

So, as the intellectual and political debates have proceeded, policy developments have exhibited seven trends:

(1)   conditionality for entitlement to benefits and social services has been tightened and extended;
(2)   transfer payments, relative to average incomes, have tended to fall, making it harder to survive decently in the absence of labour income;
(3)   duration of many benefits has been shortened;
(4)   contributions have been raised relative to benefits;
(5)   social services have been reduced, or eroded in terms of quality, with explicit and implicit 'privatisation' of social services.
(6)   more discretion has been introduced in implementation of social protection policy.
(7)   income-insecurity inequality has tended to widen.

These have made the provision of social income more paternalistic, labourist, fragmented – conferring privileges on some, and reducing solidaristic burdens – and insecure. Globalisation and flexible labour markets increase economic uncertainty, and it was partly to limit uncertainty that welfare states were developed. Faced with greater uncertainty, the policy trends have strengthened socio-economic fragmentation and detachment. They have resurrected the distinction between the deserving and undeserving, and made it clear that the deserving are those in jobs, who may have their parental leave, enterprise benefits, health insurance, sickness pay, paid holidays, personalised pension accounts, and much else. The flexiworkers may have to do with a lesser package. The unemployed and detached are the 'undeserving'.

In a more fragmented society, what could be the leading agency to improve income security? There are four strategic options. First, some neo-Marcusians believe in a 'rainbow' option, in which minorities coalesce around a redistributive agenda. This is unlikely, because minorities have different, often conflicting interests. Second, there is 'producer politics', aimed at overcoming parasitism, rather than exploitation, by opposing non-productive advantaged groups in society. In the globalising context, such a strategy would be hard and limited. Third, there could be an attempt to recreate 'labourism', through relying on the remnants of the working class or a coalition of class interests along classical lines. That is not an option in industrialised societies. Fourth, there could be increased emphasis on needs-based welfare, coupled with a strengthening of civil society based on non-government organisations and economic democracy. We consider this in the final chapter.

Part IV

Labourist Options

Since the 1980s, many policies have emerged as prescriptions to overcome the labour market insecurity and other forms of labour insecurity that have accompanied the era of market regulation and globalisation. Many of these have been designed to restore the commitment to labour and the opportunity for labour.

The following two chapters consider three types of policy that have been advocated or tried in various parts of the world in order to achieve that goal by one means or another. These are a strengthening of a statutory minimum wage, the introduction of labour subsidies, including those oriented to job training, and variants of workfare, including schemes to strengthen labour market and job training.

9 Minimum Wages, Subsidies and Tax Credits

9.1 INTRODUCTION

In response to the insecurity of flexible labour markets, liberals and social democrats have continued to pin their hopes on measures to make wage labour more attractive and remunerative. Consistent with promoting labour, they have argued that strengthening statutory minimum wages would provide income security without harming labour market security, or have pushed for subsidies as a means of boosting the demand for labour, thus improving labour market security without harming income security – indeed, perhaps, improving income security of the 'low-skilled' as well. Or they have pushed for tax credits intending to encourage labour supply while boosting earned income security.

This chapter considers the appeal of these three responses in the context of flexible labour markets. The following chapter deals with the complementary labourist policy of workfare and its derivatives known colloquially as 'welfare-to-work'.

9.2 PROS AND CONS OF MINIMUM WAGES

Chapter 7 concluded that the coverage and protection offered by statutory minimum wages have declined during the last quarter of the twentieth century. Yet the minimum wage has continued to be regarded as a main instrument for providing income security to those in the lower end of the labour market, and has been a prominent part of the redistributive strategy throughout the twentieth century.

The question arises whether minimum wages can or should be strengthened. Internationally, there has been prolonged debate about the desirability of abolishing the statutory minimum wage. Critics usually claim that it pushes the wage above the 'market clearing' level and thus causes unemployment. More elaborate variants include a belief that they raise the whole structure of wages. One can answer these by referring to efficiency wage theory, productivity effects and lack of evidence that minimum wages do raise unemployment. In spite of claims by the OECD that minimum wages lower employment, studies in North America and western Europe (such as Katz and Krueger, 1992, and Koutsogeorgopoulou, 1994) have not shown large or consistent effects, and those pointing to the absence of an effect – as well as some suggesting a *positive* effect – were overlooked in the OECD *Jobs Study*. At best, one should be eclectic about the effects on employment and unemployment. One reason is that because employers are inclined to pay an efficiency wage, a rise in the minimum wage may not translate into an equivalent increase in the actual wage (Card and Krueger, 1995). And a rise in the minimum wage may reduce labour turnover, which in itself should reduce labour costs. Finally, there must be a strong probability that many employers could find ways round a minimum wage if it seriously affected their possibility of employing labour.

Increasingly, workers who need the sort of income protection sought through statutory minimum wages are not stuck in mills or large-scale factories. They are doing part-time work in services, in domestic or consumer services; they are homeworkers doing piece work; they are on the periphery, the 'flexiworkers' who have to spin out their working lives through odd jobs, casual labour and the like.

Statutory regulations are unsuited for those situations. The high probability that such work is in the black, shadow or informal economy – and that part of the payment is 'under the table' – means there is likely to be a fear or reticence on the part of the workers to giving information that might implicate them in illegality or expose them to retribution. The probability is high that they will not be paying employee contributions or self-employed contributions to social security, or be taking account of all their earned income in applying for means-tested benefits. The fact that in most cases were they to reveal the little income they receive would mean no difference to their entitlement does not alter the reality that the working poor lack the voice or sense of security to exercise their rights.

Yet if there is reason to regard the arguments of critics of minimum wages as unconvincing, there is also reason to doubt the strength of arguments traditionally put forward by its advocates. Let us briefly consider the arguments in favour of the minimum wage in the light of the insecurity characteristic of the 'flexible' labour markets of the 1990s.

First, traditionally it has been promoted as an instrument for preventing poverty. The trouble here is that it is increasingly inefficient, because most of the poor in modern societies are outside regular wage employment and in part because however you measure the minimum wage (hourly, weekly, monthly) the difference between money income and the level of full income required to raise a person above the poverty line has been growing. The minimum wage cannot provide low-paid workers with income security effectively, because it cannot reach most of those who need it and because the wage share of total remuneration has fallen so much.

Second, it is a mechanism for integrating the low paid into the labour force. Increasingly, collective mechanisms are bypassed by the individualisation and *contractualisation* of labour relations. Labour markets are moving from being based on collective or 'team' contracts to being based on individual contracts. If so, then however one might feel about it, one should recognise that the trend erodes the regulatory potential of statutory minimum wages.

Third, it may have a *demonstration effect* by setting decency thresholds for wages, leading employers to set higher wages even though they are under no regulatory pressure to do so. For this to be anything more than a gesture requires the minimum wage to be socially legitimised and be applicable to a sufficient number of workers who would be in poverty without it. If most workers perceive that they are not affected by the minimum wage, its demonstration effect will be minimised. How many workers would take to the barricades in defence of the minimum wage?

Fourth, a minimum wage is intended to combat *'sweating'*, i.e., limiting pressure to work excessively long in order to achieve a minimal subsistence income. But when the monthly minimum wage is set as the statutory instrument, what is to control working time, work intensity or the implicit 'contract' between employer and worker by which certain tasks must be done in addition to those covered in the formal working week? As more of the working poor are outside factory or office blocks, what is to protect them from sweating? There are many reasons deterring such workers from protesting against sweating, notably fear of dismissal, loss of income and difficulty of proving the case.

Fifth, a minimum wage may be defended as a means of *boosting productivity* and efficiency. This relates to the 'efficiency wage' hypothesis – a worker who has sufficient income to afford adequate food, clothing, etc., can work more efficiently – and to the 'effort bargain' of the employment relationship. This argument is surely correct, but probably does not go very far. A minimum wage may boost efficiency and the effort of some workers, but there are better ways of doing that, including incentive-based payment systems.

Sixth, it is believed that statutory minimum wages stimulate productivity more generally by *inducing technological change* and by inducing skill upgrading by checking resort to low-wage, cheap labour production strategies. This argument is usually overlooked by critics of the minimum wage. However, it is of diminishing importance in modern high-tech production systems, in which wage costs as a share of production costs are so low that small changes in the wage rates of the low skilled would not induce much reaction.

Seventh, defenders of minimum wages argue that they *reduce income inequality*, because they lead to a compression of wage differentials higher up the wage ladder. To the extent that they do, they may lead firms to opt for more training to raise the supply of high-skilled workers. Good, if that is empirically supported, although many neo-classical economists believe wage differentials should increase so as to assist the low skilled find employment. However, the more flexible labour relations of the 1990s erode the relevance of this argument. For many groups the wage is a diminishing part of total remuneration, and probably over a wide range of earners the ratio of non-wage to wage remuneration rises the higher the income category of employee.

Raising the minimum wage may encourage the shift towards money wages for lower-paid groups, and a cut in other forms of 'remuneration', including training. Decentralisation of wage bargaining may also mean that raising the minimum wage would have little effect on wages higher up the scale because such structures are increasingly things of the past.

Eighth, the minimum wage provides an *anchor for social transfers* and the system of social protection. This has been one of its major roles in central and eastern Europe

(Standing and Vaughan-Whitehead, 1995). The quicker the link is broken the better. With high unemployment, flexible labour markets and economic informalisation, public expenditure has been targeted for cuts everywhere. When confronted with a choice between that and protecting a minority of low-paid workers, governments can rationalise concentrating on reducing public expenditure by holding down the minimum wage as a relatively easy means of limiting public transfers, as was done in many countries of eastern Europe in the 1990s. We may deplore this, but it is an awkward political reality. The minimum wage should be set by reference to social productivity; the income level for social protection should be linked to the need to prevent poverty and social deprivation in the socio-economic conditions of the country at the time.

Ninth, there is the argument that the minimum wage is efficient because it is *administratively simple*. This simplicity is all right as long as you do not expect too much of it. Workers paid less than the minimum are supposed to be in a position to report violations. In practice, most would have neither the voice nor social strength to do so. Moreover, because of administrative difficulties, many governments have exempted some types of employment from coverage by statutory minimum wages – such as part-timers in the Netherlands, casual labour in Belgium, and those working in small-scale businesses in the USA and elsewhere. Yet those not covered comprise many of the lowest-paid groups in flexible, informal labour markets.

In sum, although the traditional arguments for a statutory minimum wage remain, they are of diminishing relevance as labour markets evolve towards a different model than when a minimum wage was the anchor of working-class aspirations in industrial society.

If one wishes to protect the low paid and working poor, and reduce exploitation in modern societies, something more radical and comprehensive than the statutory minimum wage is needed – or something to complement it to compensate for its shortcomings. The poverty and income inequality, the erosion of entitlement to income protection and the low *take up* of means-tested selective transfers have produced social detachment, anomie and social deprivation. Measures such as minimum wages were meant as instruments for integrating the vulnerable into a society of common human dignity, as instruments for citizenship and social solidarity. They do not offer that prospect now, and will not do so in the future. Given what is happening to poverty and inequality, one might conclude that with the minimum wage one is tinkering with a small part of the engine and that too much is left out of the tinkering to make it worth a lot of debate.

9.3 EMPLOYMENT SUBSIDIES

In response to persistently high unemployment, its shifting incidence and high long-term unemployment, there has been increasing advocacy by economists and others for employment and wage subsidies. Several governments have introduced employment subsidies, and subsidies have been implicit in many so-called 'active' labour market policies. However, some economists have proposed more explicit forms, and variants have been jostling for attention. In whatever guise, such subsidies are quintessentially a *labourist* response to the crisis of insecurity, being based on the premise that the problem is a low and skewed demand for labour and that the solution is a high and restructured demand for labour. In effect, the perceived problem is a lack of jobs for 'unskilled' workers and the solution is more jobs for 'unskilled' workers.

Since employment subsidies have been among the most popular labour market proposals of the 1990s they deserve extended discussion, especially as some prominent economists have advocated them. The following briefly considers the types of subsidy scheme and the potential advantages and disadvantages of them.

(i) Types of Subsidy

Labour subsidies can be divided into *wage subsidies* and *employment subsidies*. The former are payments made to low-wage workers intended to close the gap between what is or would be their market wage and some wage deemed socially acceptable. The usual objectives of wage subsidy proposals are to diminish poverty among those labouring and to increase labour supply in terms of number of workers entering the wage labour market (Palmer, 1978). Employment subsidies are wage supplements paid to employers, and consist of two types, general and selective.

A *general subsidy* would be a payment for all workers in all sectors, designed to reduce the costs of employing anyone. Selective subsidies can be sub-divided into four types. A *sectorally-targeted subsidy* is a payment for all workers employed in a specially designated sector, such as food processing, clothing or export-oriented manufacturing. A *size-targeted subsidy* is a payment for workers employed in, say, small-scale firms with fewer than 20 workers or in newly established firms. A *group-targeted subsidy* involves a payment for each worker employed coming from some pre-defined social group, defined by sex, age, race, long-term unemployment status, or whatever. Finally, a *marginal employment subsidy* is a payment for every worker added to employment within a firm after a certain date or in a pre-defined period. This final form has had most advocates, and was the model for the US New Jobs Tax Credit Programme in the late 1970s.

All forms of employment subsidy have a general objective – to stimulate employment – and usually a distinctive social or economic objective. Therefore, one must be careful to distinguish what one means when talking about employment subsidies, particularly when attempting to monitor and to evaluate the effectiveness of such schemes.

Besides being differentiated from wage subsidies by the fact that the employer receives the subsidy, employment subsidy schemes may be either *temporary,* whereby the firm or worker is given a payment covering employment in a short period, such as six months or a year, or *permanent*, whereby it is given for a prolonged period, intended to make the subsidy offer 'credible'. Of course, no government would be unwise enough to guarantee a permanent payment, but might do so for a prolonged period subject to legislative revision.

(ii) Claimed Advantages

Advocates of employment subsidies usually cite one or more advantages of employment subsidies. The standard claim is that they help to reduce unemployment and to raise employment by reducing the cost of hiring and retaining workers, by encouraging more 'labour-intensive' forms of production, by encouraging firms to expand output, and by encouraging firms to retain workers in recessions. Arthur Pigou and Nicholas Kaldor in the 1930s were among the first to argue for such subsidies, and they have had many followers (e.g., Jackman and Layard, 1986; Phelps, 1996). Empirical studies suggest that the New Jobs Tax Credit, which operated in 1977–78, and the Targeted Jobs Tax Credit Programme (TJTC), the US marginal employment subsidy scheme that operated between 1979 and 1994, did generate extra jobs (Bishop and Haveman, 1979; Mortensen, 1994). One study suggested that, based on estimates of wage supply and demand elasticities, employment would probably rise slightly, although there was substantial uncertainty about the predictions (Katz, 1996). Another suggested that firms using the TJTC may have added between 0.13 and 0.3 of a job for each job subsidised (Bishop and Montgomery, 1993).

It is conventional wisdom among neo-classical economists that there is a straightforward trade-off between the wage rate and employment, so that the main way of raising employment would be by cutting the real wage, which an employment subsidy would achieve, in principle. However, according to supporters, such a subsidy would be superior to a real wage reduction as a means of increasing employment for at least one of the following reasons:

- There might be no feasible wage rate low enough to clear the market.
- A subsidy would mean that the worker would receive an adequate wage income to maintain a socially acceptable level of living.
- A subsidy would reduce poverty more effectively than if employment were increased by a cut in wages.
- A subsidy would enable relatively low productivity, labour-intensive firms to meet minimum wage levels, helping them to promote employment legitimately.
- A subsidy could be used to enforce adherence to statutory regulations, if eligibility were made conditional on compliance with such regulations.
- A marginal employment subsidy could be targeted on groups who would face barriers to labour force integration, notably the long-term unemployed. Thus, in the Netherlands the government has provided a subsidy to firms if they

hire long-term unemployed, and it is to improve their job prospects, which has led economists to advocate marginal employment subsidies.

Another advantage claimed by proponents is that employment subsidies would reduce unemployment not only in the short run but in the longer term by enabling more people to have jobs in which to obtain and retain skills. Indeed, because the number of workers covered by a subsidy could be adjusted, an employment subsidy is often presented as a counter-cyclical stabilisation device.

These seem to be the main advantages claimed by supporters of employment subsidies, and seem to apply with equal force to universal as to selective subsidies. However, none are entirely convincing, as may become clear in considering the potential disadvantages.

(iii) Claimed Disadvantages

Against the advantages, real or imagined, there are potential disadvantages of employment and wage subsidies. The first that is likely to be raised is that of *fiscal cost*, although it is notable that advocates of employment subsidies often justify the cost on equity grounds when they would not allow any such defence of, say, a citizenship income scheme.

Although there might be savings from a reduction in other transfers, such as unemployment benefits, any ambitious employment subsidy scheme would increase public expenditure, and to that extent would tend to increase a government's budget deficit. Although they did not examine marginal employment subsidies, the OECD (1994a, ch. 6) concluded that employment subsidies were not cost effective for boosting employment. As the cost would be greater in recessions, a Keynesian or an adherent of the Rehn-Meidner Swedish model would be inclined to argue that this would be an advantage, since it would mean that the subsidy would be a counter-cyclical stabilisation device. Even so, the budgetary cost argument might raise problems of political legitimation. This is why Edmund Phelps (1997) devoted so much of his book advocating employment subsidies to what he regarded as the prospective savings from general employment subsidies. According to him, a subsidy in the USA would virtually pay for itself, because he believes (without citing evidence) that subsidies would have remarkable curative powers to reduce drug addiction, crime, illegitimacy and other social ills.

Against the claim that a marginal employment subsidy would cut unemployment by boosting employment, critics have suggested that the wage elasticity may be very low. The more inelastic the labour demand curve, the less effect any subsidy would have on employment – and as known from the minimum wage research, the elasticity for low-wage labour may be a little over 0.1. So employment growth may be modest, while wages might actually adjust upwards, so as to choke off additional demand. The cost could exceed any benefit from increased employment. This conclusion is supported by evidence that group-specific (or categorical) employment subsidies are used only by a small percentage of employers, partly because they do not wish to alter recruitment practices (Lerman, 1982). US experience has found low take-up rates and high publicity costs. There is also a suggestion that the low utilisation of the TJTC was due to the regulatory burden and the stigma associated with targeting groups perceived as welfare recipients (Burtless, 1985). Even participating firms seem to have created fewer extra jobs than implied by the number subsidised (Bishop and Montgomery, 1993). So employment subsidies are expensive. Only schemes that have been combined with subsidised training have had success in generating jobs (Katz, 1996). In such cases, one must wonder which was the main factor, and whether the job generation would be replicated on an enlarged scale.

A second potential disadvantage is that employment subsidies encourage *inefficient labour utilisation*. Managers not required to bear the full cost of labour will undervalue it. Even in the case of short-term subsidies, they will also encourage firms to retain the existing employment levels and structures because there will be less cost pressure on them to restructure. In effect, employment subsidies may tend to ossify the production and employment structure, when restructuring might well be desirable, because the past capital–labour ratio was not optimally efficient. And if the wage subsidy were given directly to the workers, the marginal income from labour would be reduced, thereby reducing the incentive to labour.

A third potential disadvantage is that both general and selective employment subsidies may have high administrative costs. Just consider a few basic questions. What counts as a 'job' for receipt of a subsidy? Phelps (1997, p. 109) argued that only full-time low-wage jobs with working weeks of 35 hours or more should be counted. This reflected his view that people should be in full-time jobs, although his reasons seemed to be speculative. But the point here is that any cut-off is arbitrary and would be hard to apply efficiently without high administration costs. And what would count as the wage? The treatment of bonuses, tips and other fringe benefits would not be easy. And how would officials process the paper work that would be involved in applying for and granting subsidy payments?

Another administrative cost would arise because different information would be required than is normally needed by tax authorities, such as data on hourly wage rates and hours worked (Haveman, 1996). How much of the allocation to the subsidy would reach the target groups? In discussions of employment subsidies, little attention is given to such transaction costs of implementation. Those are likely to be particularly high in flexible labour markets or where the regulatory system is weak or cumbersome. The US New Jobs Tax Credit had lower administrative costs than some subsidy schemes because it was operated through the tax system, but a result was that it only provided incentives for firms with positive tax liabilities.

A fourth adverse effect, of unknown proportions, is that an employment subsidy would be inflationary. Knowing that firms are receiving a subsidy, workers or unions could push up wages, knowing that the true cost to the firm would be less than it appeared. And employers might be less resistant to wage pressure for that reason.

A fifth disadvantage is that employment subsidies may be *regressive*, perversely increasing income inequality. In most cases, the subsidy involves a payment to employers, and even though this should mean that some workers would receive a wage which they would not without the subsidy, at least some of the money would go directly to the firm and to profits, and if the next disadvantage to be cited is accepted, then that would mean that a large proportion of the funds would go to established and presumably relatively affluent firms.

The subsidy would definitionally exclude the poor who were not in jobs, and would thus not benefit the poorest of all. But if the subsidy was paid to low-skilled, low-wage workers, there would also be a tendency for the wage of low-paid workers to fall because there would presumably be an increase in the labour supply of relatively low-skilled workers in response to the higher take-home pay. This is part of the classic 'Speenhamland' objection, the other being that it would allow employers to cut wages to below a subsistence or efficiency level.

Another regressive aspect could arise because many low-paid workers are 'secondary' income earners in households, and may not be among the poorer groups in society. Thus, the 'target efficiency' of a wage or employment subsidy could be lower than alternative redistributive policies. In recognising this, some economists, such as Haveman (1996, p. 39) have suggested that the subsidy could be 'made more target efficient ... by limiting eligibility for the benefit to family heads and, perhaps, gearing the size of the subsidy to the size of the worker's family'. This would surely generate opportunist reactions, and is paternalistic conceptually in focusing on differentiating 'family heads' from others, presumably designated as 'dependants'.

A further regressive tendency is that the subsidy could encourage firms to operate with a more labour-intensive, less efficient technology, and – if economic 'justice' involves income corresponding to efficiency and productivity – then a scheme that disproportionately compensated the inefficient could be construed by a libertarian as regressive. Finally in this respect, if the scheme was a marginal employment subsidy it might increase income inequality because the subsidy would be given to firms that were currently expanding. Such firms tend to pay above-average wages, because of the positive association of employment growth and wages. So, either the subsidy would go to relatively prosperous firms or to workers earning above average wages within a specific sector or other category.

A sixth potential disadvantage is that any employment subsidy would involve substantial *deadweight effects*. This is a criticism of so-called 'active' labour market policies in general. What it means is that many jobs that receive a subsidy would have been created anyhow, so that the cost of jobs actually created would be higher than the per unit subsidy would suggest. Although some studies have been challenged on methodological grounds, international evidence indicates that the deadweight effect in many schemes has been large. Thus, the Irish Employment Incentive Scheme (a marginal employment subsidy) had a 91 per cent deadweight effect, in that on average employers admitted that 68 per cent of the hires receiving a subsidy would have taken place anyhow and 23 per cent had merely been brought forward. Large deadweight effects have also been found for schemes in Australia, the Netherlands and Sweden.

Besides standard deadweight losses recognised in such studies, two others can arise. We might call one the 'auntie effect', whereby relatives and friends are added to a firm's payroll in order to increase the subsidy claim. The other might be called the 'dead souls effect', whereby included on the payroll would be those who have left the firm in unfortunate circumstances or have their names retained on it for longer than warranted. These perverse – if not illegal – forms are particularly likely in the informal labour markets that are spreading, and would be rife in industrialising economies or in eastern Europe, where monitoring and regulating economic behaviour is hard and where so many foreign economists have eagerly advocated 'active' labour market policies.

Phelps (1997, p. 115), for one, recognised this drawback, but his proposed solution would be inequitable, costly and likely to induce its own moral hazards. He advocated 'the usual stiff penalties for tax evasion' and restriction of subsidy 'eligibility to good-sized firms'. This implies that small firms should be excluded, which is not equitable, and would be likely to induce opportunistic camouflage, and exclude precisely those firms where an employment subsidy might make a difference to the number of workers hired.

A final deadweight effect would be the hardest to trace of all. Subsidies might generate jobs that would not exist otherwise, because they are not really required or have such low productivity that they would not be viable or wanted in the absence of a hefty subsidy. This might be called the *phoney jobs effect*.

Although deadweight effects may be among the strongest of the disadvantages, they are compounded by the sixth drawback, namely *substitution effects*. If a scheme were a marginal employment subsidy for all workers, there would be a tendency for jobs that are subsidised to displace those that are not, to the extent that the firms benefiting from the subsidy could undercut the competitive position of those that did not. This could produce offsetting job losses, and could even result in a net employment reduction, since marginally viable firms could go bankrupt, and since the reduced cost of labour in the expanding firms could increase the profit rate and enable them to make labour-saving innovations.

Group-specific schemes, such as subsidies for hiring youths, encourage a substitution of the groups for which there is a subsidy for those without such entitlement. That has been found in the USA (Bishop and Montgomery, 1993). The tendency might be checked in a labour market with highly flexible wages, if those pushed out of jobs lowered their reservation wage. But in that case the effectiveness of the group-specific subsidy in serving its main objective would be undermined.

If the subsidy were paid for hiring from the long-term unemployed, not only would there be inefficient hiring practices, but it would also amount to an inducement to 'discriminate' against the short-term unemployed. The hiring would be 'inefficient' in that firms would bypass those workers they would regard as relatively productive in favour of those they expected to have lower productivity. And they would also be induced to hire workers who would have a higher probability of labour turnover in the subsequent period, thereby *raising* so-called 'frictional' unemployment.

Thus, the UK *Workstart* experiment (providing a subsidy to employers if they hired workers who had been unemployed for more than two years) found that half the employers admitted that they hired long-term unemployed instead of short-term unemployed or other jobseekers as a result of the subsidy. One might defend this sort of outcome by claiming that by concentrating on the long-term unemployed the policy would prevent the growth of a group cut off from the labour market. But the existence of any sizeable substitution effect would mean that the actual effect on total unemployment would be exaggerated by any reference to claims that the subsidy had generated the number of jobs on which it was paid.

Among the paradoxes of a scheme addressed to the long-term unemployed is that it would tend to increase the duration of unemployment among those unemployed for less than the period selected as defining long-term unemployment. Thus, those unemployed for 10 months might suddenly find that they were being bypassed by those who had been out of work for 12 months. Both groups deserve and need support, but neither equity nor efficiency grounds unambiguously exist to support a scheme targeted on those unemployed for over 12 months.[1] There is little reason to think the targeting would reduce overall unemployment by very much, if at all.

Seventh, there are what might be called *opportunism effects*, or *distortion effects*. Consider subsidies paid for the initial six months of new jobs. Unless there were strict conditions on job retention for longer – which would be hard to apply and in practice probably circumvented rather easily – temporary subsidies could be expected to lead to a substitution of short-term for longer-term jobs, intensifying employment insecurity. If the subsidy were activated in a recession, it could lead to a bunching of new short-term jobs, and even postponement of job creation to wait until the scheme came into effect. If the temporary subsidy were for additional 'unskilled jobs', intended to reduce the high unemployment of 'unskilled' workers, then it could easily lead to the opportunistic reclassification of jobs and workers as 'unskilled'.

Any employment subsidy would encourage and reward opportunism since workers and employers could collude to misreport wages, hours worked and the form of remuneration, as well as shift part of the labour into concealed employment.

If the scheme consisted of *long-term subsidies*, it could lead to (a) locking-in effects, discouraging the restructuring of employment and production, and (b) workers being inclined to stay in low-productivity jobs rather than seeking alternatives that might not attract a subsidy. If there were a *sectorally targeted subsidy*, say, for export-oriented manufacturing, then if the incentive was big enough, one could envisage some artificial reclassification of firms, or a cutback in whatever production that did not, in the planner's mind, merit a subsidy. This might be called *horizontal inequity* vis-à-vis other firms unable to make similar adjustments.

There would also be a tendency for *vertical inequity*. In some countries, there have been proposals to give a labour-intensive 'sector' a subsidy to encourage a shift to more labour-intensive production. What this could mean is that some firms in a production chain would receive subsidies even though their production and market depended on other 'sectors', while others in the chain were excluded. For example, suppose food processing was labour intensive and that the authorities wished to promote it to create more jobs. Its success might actually depend on the country's or region's agriculture or on its tourism industry. Why should one element in a production chain be favoured relative to others?

Group-targeted subsidies have analogous effects. They may lead to *intra-group inequity*. Thus, if the subsidy were provided only for workers hired if they had been unemployed for a year or more, the firm would be encouraged to hire people who had been out of the workforce for more than a year and record them as 'long-term unemployed'. If an age category were selected for eligibility for a subsidy, there could be a spate of false declarations of age, or some pre-dating of recruitment. Even racial origin could be blurred if the subsidy were to be offered for the recruitment of minorities. Conversely, targeting subsidies to the disadvantaged groups could stigmatise the potential workers and discourage employers from hiring from that group, as has been found in the USA (Burtless, 1985). Group-targeted subsidies could also lead to inter-group inequity, through a false lay-off of workers from the target group to be substituted by others and then rehired as new workers.

Marginal employment subsidies could also lead to *inter-firm inequity*, with those firms that had expanded employment just before the scheme was introduced being penalised relative to those that timed their expansion to obtain the subsidy, whether intentionally or by chance. This is rarely mentioned by proponents of marginal employment subsidies, although it is an effect that is unambiguous.

9.4 WAGE SUBSIDIES AND LABOUR TAX CREDITS

Another increasingly popular policy as a pro-labour reform is earned-income tax credits, designed to alter labour incentives and offer more income security for those earning low incomes from labour. They are a subsidy to wage labour.

For a long time, relatively little attention was given to this measure. But it underpinned the US labour market in the 1980s and 1990s and may be a primary explanation of that country's greater flexibility and employment performance. The *Earned Income Tax Credit* (EITC) was enacted in 1975 as a modest measure, was expanded in 1986 and was further expanded in 1993. By the 1990s it was the largest income *assistance* programme in the USA, as well as easily the fastest growing one, providing income credit to over 13 million families in 1996.

The American scheme, at least until recently, has given the tax credit only to families with at least one child, with at least one adult in employment, with a low income from employment and with a tax return. As of 1997, the credit was provided at 36 per cent of the first part of earnings, then gradually phased out once the earned income exceeded $11,000 up to an income of $23,755 for a family with one child and $25,300 for one with two children. The credit reached a maximum of about $3,500. Total cost was estimated to be about $20 billion. A family was entitled to tax credit as soon as any member started to earn an income from employment. The EITC was paid on a family basis, because the US income tax system has used the family unit as the basis of assessment. As the amount received tapered off as the family's earnings rose, it has been essentially a family-based negative income tax.

The EITC represents a response to the fact that a great deal of so-called new poverty consists of the working poor and that many people are in 'poverty traps' that discourage them from moving from 'welfare to work'. Similar proposals were made by the government in the UK in the early 1970s and 1980s, and in 1997 were revived by the new government.

Difficulties with the EITC include the fact that the tax credit is paid at the end of the year when a family submits its tax returns, so that it may come long after it is most needed. It is also paid on a family rather than individual basis. The scheme is intended to raise incomes of the low paid and boost labour supply, provided the person is in employment. Studies show that it has raised the labour force participation rate of single mothers, but because of offsetting income and substitution effects on working time of those in employment there is some ambiguity about the effect on total hours worked. Thus, Dickert, Hauser and Scholz (1995) concluded that total hours and participation rates rose, while Eissa and Liebman (1996) found no effect on hours.

The EITC is a classic *fiscal regulation*, intended to induce more labour. As a subsidy, it clearly 'distorts' the labour market, at least facilitating low wages and encouraging downward wage flexibility. Anybody arguing that the US labour market is 'deregulated' when the EITC has been expanding so rapidly is missing the reality. Whether or not it is desirable, the fiscal regulation is also promoting the feminisation of the US labour market since it has tended to raise female labour force participation.

In Canada, the *Self-Sufficiency Project* (SSP) has been an experimental variant of the EITC, although the targeting is more specific and the labour conditionality even tighter. This is even more of a fiscal regulation of labour activity. It is an earnings supplement paid to single parents aged over 18, who had been receiving Income Assistance (IA) for at least 12 of the past 13 months, if in employment for at least 30 hours a week during the past month and if receiving at least the hourly minimum wage. The SSP supplements are half the difference between the person's gross labour earnings and a target income level, the latter being above the welfare benefit level to give a labour incentive. Other family incomes and transfers are not taken into account.

The SSP overcomes the unemployment trap and, unlike the IA which is removed once a person is employed, also weakens the poverty trap because it is withdrawn gradually, at a 50 per cent rate. The full-time employment requirement also prevents recipients from reducing working hours. Card and Robins (1996) found that the SSP has induced a substantial number of single parents to take full-time jobs.

In the UK, *Family Credit* was similar to the EITC, but was paid through the social security system. It was also paid only once a person had worked for at least 16 hours a week, at which point it was paid fully. Its value then tapered as earnings rose, although it rose if the person passed the 30 hours a week threshold, the intention being to encourage full-time employment. Figure 9.1 compares this with an EITC.

Paying the money through the tax system does have the advantage of reducing the stigma associated with receipt of 'welfare' and of making payment almost automatic, unless the family concerned does not fill in a tax return. But it would not remove all the stigma, since means-tested Housing Benefits would remain. Family Credit requires application and some means testing. An advantage of shifting to tax refunds is that it appears to reduce government spending on transfers, which as noted earlier has been a rising part of public expenditure. This has made income support look like a tax cut, assisting in the legitimation of transfers for the poor.

The British quandary in trying to move to a full tax credit system has been that since 1990 income tax has been based on individual earnings, not family income, while social assistance has been based on family income. Reformers have not liked the idea of paying tax credits to low-earning individuals in high-income families.

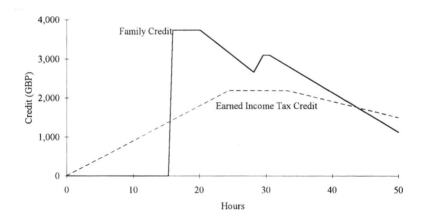

Figure 9.1 Annual amount of Family Credit and Earned Income Tax Credit a lone parent with two children would receive depending on the number of hours a week worked (£4/hour)

Source: Institute of Fiscal Studies.

Some have contemplated returning to the family-based tax system, but see that, rightly, as reintroducing a poverty trap situation for so-called secondary earners in a family; they have also recognised that a return would be administratively burdensome and costly.

Another controversial aspect is that Family Credit is paid to individuals, and in practice to women, regardless of whether it is the man, woman or both, who is the employed person. Critics of the proposal to shift to an employer-based tax credit system claim that it would involve redistribution from women to men, since the EITC is paid to the employed person, who still is more often the man. It would be regressive in that respect, although with computerisation this objection could be overcome, perhaps by arranging for half of the money to be paid to each partner.

Family Credit provides weekly income support but at a level determined for a forthcoming period of six months, even if the family's circumstances change in that time. By contrast, the EITC pays a lump sum at the end of a year. If a credit payment were to be made monthly and the tax situation adjusted at the end of the year, some would receive a welcome sum, others would find they have a large bill to pay. Again, this problem could probably be overcome by continuous assessment, or by at three monthly intervals to keep credits and rebates in reasonable balance.

Another criticism of tax credits is that, although under a pay-as-you-earn system employers could work out what should be claimed in credit by the worker, this could only be done if workers gave information on their family circumstances to the employer. The Trades Union Congress has criticised this as harmful to worker privacy.

Another criticism is that a tax credit would increase the number of people on the Inland Revenue's records, since those not paying income tax have not been included. This, it is claimed, would raise administrative costs. To this, one might suggest that any move towards an integrated system would be advantageous socially and economically in the longer term.

The main motivations for tax credits and Family Credit are that they induce people to shift from reliance on benefits, they 'make work pay' for low-earning families, and they strengthen the family unit. Either approach leaves the benefits system dualistic in character, with measures for those out of employment contrasted with measures for those in employment.

Many criticisms of employment subsidies apply with wage subsidies or earned-income tax credits. The following are the main actual or likely drawbacks:

- They raise administrative costs on income tax monitoring and evaluation, and require more information, such as data on hours worked and hourly wage rates.
- They create incentives to under-report wages and overstate hours, and thereby add moral hazards.

- They strengthen the dichotomy between those doing wage labour and those doing non-wage work.
- They reduce the expected rate of net return to low-skilled workers of investments in training, schooling and job-search, and thus actually encourage the persistence of low productivity.
- They are not well-targeted as an anti-poverty income transfer because they do not assist the poor outside wage labour and because they may well assist many families in which the low-wage worker is a supplementary income earner or in which non-wage income is a high proportion of total family income; thus, about two-thirds of the $20 billion spent on the EITC in 1996 went to families at or below poverty.
- They tend to lower the wages of low-wage workers, in that labour force entrants could accept lower wages knowing they would be topped up with the tax credit or wage subsidy.[2]
- In practice, the tax credits have been selective, giving benefits to parents of young children or to some other pre-determined group, effectively making a judgment on those deemed to be 'deserving' and on those who are less deserving when the criteria are unclear and almost inevitably unfair.
- Although offering incentives for those outside employment to take jobs, they reduce incentives to work among middle-income earners.

Most of these are major drawbacks. As with all market interventions, earned-income tax credits or wage subsidies are intended to affect market outcomes, and for many economists and others that is not a criticism. However, one must admit that they influence inter-personal differences in welfare, and advocates and critics alike should be clear about the ethical basis and bias of those outcomes.

Besides general criticisms, there should be a debate on the role of tax credits for labour – or wage subsidies – in globalisation, international trade and investment. A country providing hefty tax credits or wage subsidies clearly lowers production costs by making real wages and labour costs downwardly flexible. This may not violate World Trade Organisation rules if the subsidy is not targeted on export sectors. But there could be pressure on other countries to follow the practice, while those countries that do not do so might find labour costs putting pressure on their exchange rates.

9.5 CONCLUDING POINTS

The minimum wage, employment subsidies, wage subsidies and earned-income tax credits are all attempts to increase income security for those in low-wage labour, although the former is not intended to boost the demand for labour. As redistributive instruments they are rather blunt, particularly in flexible labour markets.

A statutory minimum wage is relatively suitable where the majority of the workforce are in regular, full-time employment, and where unions are strong. Yet what should be the minimum wage if half the workers work variable hours in a mixture of wage and own-account work, when one month you earn practically nothing on the implicit understanding that in another you will earn substantial profit-related pay? What happens to the man who helps a friend with a local business to give himself a supplementary income, and as a result the friend reduces the working hours of his assistant to the point where it falls short of the minimum wage?

One could multiply such examples. They are likely to be typical of the more flexible productive and labour market systems that are emerging all over the world. It seems unlikely that we will be still debating the merits and demerits of statutory minimum wages in ten years time. For the present, let us put them in their proper place, to protect the poor, not impoverish victims of structural adjustment.

A statutory minimum wage has appeal as a standard-setting mechanism, as a means of indicating a level of decency that employers should follow. But in a society in which there are more sources of income than a single 'family wage', more people may wish to take casual jobs paying low wages, for the sociability, or for the intrinsic worth of the work in question. This view can be overstated or misinterpreted, since there is no question that many workers paid low wages want and need higher wages. A minimum wage should be preserved, as long as not too much is expected from it and as long as it does not justify ignoring other ways of improving income security.

An employment subsidy is a labourist response to labour market and income insecurity. It does not aim to overcome poverty, but is rather an attempt to restructure the lower end of the labour market. It is a deliberate act of state intervention intended to regulate the labour market. It is also part of a panoply of subsidies provided to capital in the era of market regulation and globalisation.

Indeed, the renewed interest in employment subsidies raises questions linked to globalisation, 'unfair trade' and income inequality. Numerous countries have been competing to offer subsidies to capital to induce firms to come to their country, or to stay or expand there, offering them the prospect of cheap labour and other cost-limiting advantages. Thus, in Jamaica – to give just one of numerous possible examples – in the Montego Bay Free Trade Zone foreign companies have been drawn by cost savings of 25 per cent as a result of government subsidies, tax benefits and assured cheap labour (ILO, 1990, p. 109). If countries resort to wholesale subsidies to attract capital and boost jobs, the distributional and economic consequences could be very substantial indeed.

Although a drawback of an employment or wage subsidy is that it would subsidise inefficient labour, there are some forms of work that have a lower market value than social value, and there may be a redistributive reason for using a subsidy to promote forms of work that are desired on social grounds, such as community work, charitable work or caring activities of one kind or another.

Finally, tax credits or wage subsidies are forms of labour market regulation that are profoundly pro-labourist in intention. Although research is needed to consider their distributive effects, they encourage those on the margins of the labour market to take low-wage labour, and to that extent they surely weaken the position of those already in low-wage labour, thus lowering their opportunity wage. They are not well-targeted on the poor. They also encourage *opportunism* and are likely to be inefficient as a labour market policy. What they do is strengthen the labouring ethic. In this they are thoroughly in tune with the dominant ethos of the twentieth century.

10 The Road to 'Workfare': Alternative to Welfare or Threat to Occupation?

10.1 INTRODUCTION

The ascendancy of supply-side economics and libertarianism since the 1970s has ushered in a prolonged campaign to repeal the welfare systems of North America, western Europe and other industrialised parts of the world. In some cases, the campaign does not deserve the name of 'reform', in that it has been a concerted attempt to reduce the breadth and depth of social protection by the state. The emphasis has been on 'repealing' rather than on reforming. However, another strand of thinking has been sweeping the world, which has become a new orthodoxy. This has three variants, reflecting a search for legitimacy. The first is that 'active' labour market policy should be expanded relative to 'passive' policy. The second is that 'workfare' should replace 'welfare'. The third – and by 1998 the favourite euphemism – 'welfare-to-work' programmes should become a core of welfare systems.

Active policy derives from Swedish social democracy; workfare sprang mainly from libertarian roots and welfare-to-work from a centrist bloc of social democrats, liberals, moderate conservatives and Christian democrats. It is probably fair to say that the choice of term has reflected a difference of emphasis on *incentives* or *obligations*. Whatever the euphemism, the essence of the approach can be summarised in two imperatives – the State should place those on the margins of the labour force in jobs (or training for jobs), or induce them to take jobs, and the unemployed should be *obliged* to take and remain in such jobs. In practice, the objectives have been wider, the rationale more complex. Often, explicit objectives have been combined with others pursued through it and complementary policies, a main one being a determination to reduce childbearing by unmarried women, above all teenage women.

Workfare represents a strand of social thinking that has figured strongly for hundreds of years. It was enshrined in the English *Poor Law* of 1536 dealing with 'sturdy vagabonds'; the French *Ordannance de Moulins* of 1556 was similar. But the most famous precedent was the 1834 *Poor Law Amendment Act* in Great Britain, a 'targeted' system designed to reach only the deserving poor and the desperate poor. If a person wanted support he had to agree to work in a workhouse run by the local parish, which according to the Poor Law Commissioners was to be 'the hardest taskmaster and the worst paymaster'. The work had to be harder than that performed by independent labourers, and thus not be competitive with them. From 1834 onwards, the practice was to give 'relief' in return for labour, but because the workhouses could not deal with all those in need, the authorities also came to operate an 'outdoor labour test' as a deterrent to potential claimants, not primarily as a generator of public employment. This was modified at the end of the nineteenth century with municipal relief works, and then the *Unemployed Workmen Act* of 1905 became a precedent of another form of 'targeting', providing labour for the merit-worthy of the unemployed and not for those regarded as undeserving of assistance, those deemed to lack 'good character' and not 'honestly desirous of obtaining work'.

These two themes, of helping the *deserving* and deterring the poor from applying for benefits, have figured prominently in social reforms of the late twentieth century. Even though extensive testing for conditionality and screening have proved ineffectual labour regulations, governments have never given up the ideas that guided those early legislative initiatives. Indeed, resort to some variant of workfare has coincided historically with periods of transition, when the economic basis of society has been out of step with the regulatory devices inherited from a period of relative stability. Above all, workfare and welfare-to-work belong to the paternalist tradition, and must be assessed as the labourist solution to the crisis of insecurity. It may not be hyperbole to describe workfare as the great social experiment of the late twentieth century. Its success or failure will determine social and labour market policy in the early part of the twenty-first century.

10.2 WORKFARE SCHEMES

Although the idea has had a long history, the term workfare originated in the United States in the late 1960s, notably with the Federal *Work Incentive Programme* (WIN). The practice was partially introduced there in 1981, when Federal legislation enabled states to establish welfare-for-work programmes. By 1986, 29 states were running variants of workfare schemes for beneficiaries of the *Aid to Families with Dependent Children* programme (AFDC). In the 1988 Presidential election all the major candidates advocated a Federal workfare policy of some kind. An important move in that direction was the 1988 *Family Support Act*, designed to encourage job seeking by lone mothers.

By the mid-1990s, through a series of 'waivers' allowing them to experiment with deviations from the rules of AFDC, most states were operating some variant of workfare, often given a grand name that gave politicians credibility and made critics seem churlish.[1] The nature of the reforms was evident in the euphemisms used in the titles of experiments, such as GAIN (Greater Avenues for Independence), SWIM (Saturation Work Initiative Model), a workfare scheme in San Diego, New Chance, Wisconsin Works, Quantum Opportunities, and Express to Success.

In the 1980s and 1990s, the rhetoric surrounding workfare in the United States moved from work-for-benefits to preparation-for-self-support-while-on-benefits, to 'term limits'. By the mid-1990s, most states had developed schemes by which, if welfare recipients did not want to forfeit all or part of their welfare cheques, they had to choose between taking a stipulated non-contractual job (i.e., one without an employment contract providing normal employment protection), attending 'job-hunting classes', and returning to school or undertaking full-time training. Although the state-level schemes varied considerably in terms of perceived success, in 1990 federal welfare reform confirmed the trend towards the widespread adoption of workfare.[2]

The measures culminated in passage of the *Personal Responsibility and Work Opportunity Reconciliation Act* in August 1996. In effect, this ended the Federal commitment to provide aid to poor Americans, shifting responsibility back to the states. It also limited entitlement to welfare benefits to a maximum of five years in a lifetime, obliged recipients of welfare payments to accept designated jobs after two years, banned legal aid to legal immigrants, and cut food stamps. Henceforth, the AFDC was to be converted into a new scheme and acronym, TANF (*Temporary Assistance for Needy Families*). The Government anticipated that the reform would reduce Federal spending by $56 billion over six years.

As stated, the objectives of the radical reform were threefold – to cut public spending, reduce poverty, and alter the behaviour of the poor, notably poor women with children perceived to suffer from 'welfare dependency'. Capturing the main objective, President Bill Clinton told the National Governors' Association in July 1996:

> Anyone who can work must do so. We'll say to welfare recipients: Within two years, you will be expected to go to work and earn a paycheck, not draw a welfare check.

The Federal Government had merely built on the state initiatives over the preceding decade. Among the most interventionist states, Wisconsin introduced a *Pay for Performance Scheme* in 1994, under which welfare recipients had to choose between (i) transitional work, (ii) community service, (iii) trial jobs lasting up to three years, and (iv) subsidised private employment. Wisconsin introduced a pilot scheme, known as 'Work-not-Welfare', at the end of 1993 by which AFDC benefits were denied to those who did not accept an assigned job or enroll in a training programme. In return, the State guaranteed a cash supplement to reach the AFDC level if the wage fell below that level, and paid for full-time childcare, transport to the jobplace and job-placement assistance. This was to last for up to two years, after which there was no resumption of AFDC benefits. This has been called the 'two years and you're out' condition. Wisconsin set the precedent for the Federal reform of 1996, and leading up to that reform passed a law known as *Wisconsin Works*, or W2, in May 1996.

With workfare in Wisconsin came a complementary trend towards 'learnfare' and 'trainingfare' aimed at teenagers, whereby non-employed youth can receive income support from the state *only if* they attend school or a training course. Such a scheme was presented as a stage in the development of a 'social contract' between teenagers and society (Corbett et al., 1989).

Another aspect of the reforms has been the targeting on 'unmarried' or 'single' mothers, a group in society who has been demonised in the 1990s. The main measure directed at them has been the *Family Cap*, whereby in New Jersey, Wisconsin and some other states, an unemployed single woman conceiving a baby while receiving welfare payments cannot receive extra benefit for the child. This was the first time that the positive link between the size of benefit and number of children had been broken. Wisconsin has also operated a *Bridefare* scheme, which halved child benefit for a child born to an unmarried teenager. Finally, under the US welfare reform, unmarried teenage parents on welfare must sign a *Personal Responsibility Contract* in which they agree to stay at school or live at home.

Another feature is devolution of welfare policy to the states, primarily through 'block grants', often to counties within states. This has reduced the Federal Government's responsibility, although states were instructed to cut welfare rolls by 50 per cent between 1996 and 2002. Some central regulations have been made. Most importantly, married parents were to be allowed only two years of welfare at most, and welfare recipients were to be required to increase the weekly hours they work in jobs each year or start to lose benefits. States not meeting those targets will receive less Federal cash. Thus the devolution was scarcely delegation of responsibility, although laws in some states have been tougher than the Federal law. As of 1997, 18 states required TANF recipients to work before the two-year time limit was reached, and seven had imposed work requirements from the outset of receipt of benefits.

Workfare has been spreading in Europe, in part through the tightening of conditionality and the drift to means tests and poverty tests. The trend began in the 1980s, notably in the UK, with measures such as the *Employment Training* and *Restart* schemes, but also in the Federal Republic of Germany, with the Federal *Social Assistance Act*, in Sweden, with its Youth Teams scheme in particular, in Denmark, in Italy and elsewhere. By the late 1990s, elements of workfare were common. For instance, in the Netherlands the unemployed had their monthly benefits cut if they refused an offer of a training place considered necessary by a local authority official. In January 1998 the German Government introduced a jobs package in which local authorities were to provide jobs for some long-term unemployed receiving social security payments. If they refused a job they would have their benefits cut. This was described as a 'welfare-to-work' programme. Outside Europe, some countries have been moving in a similar direction, as in Australia where the Government announced a 'work for dole' scheme in early 1997, targeted on those aged between 18 and 24.

In the UK, in 1996 a pilot workfare scheme was tested in two areas, under which the long-term unemployed received 13 weeks of job-search training followed by 13 weeks of compulsory job experience, for which they received unemployment benefit plus £10 per week. The scheme was expanded in late 1996. The new Government announced in mid-1997 a plan to introduce a four-choice scheme for 250,000 young unemployed – (i) six-month subsidised private job, (ii) six months with a non-profit organisation, (iii) paid full-time study, (iv) a place on an environmental task force. The Chancellor also announced plans to introduce a £75-a-week tax rebate for firms hiring an adult who had been unemployed for more than two years.

The USA and UK may have gone furthest towards workfare as a pillar of social policy, but there can be no doubt that the trend is a global one. It is a *labourist* response to the crisis of labour insecurity. It is also a *paternalistic* response, which its advocates are keen to proclaim. Given its appeal and the radical implications for social and labour market policy, this chapter briefly considers the arguments that have been used to justify workfare or something like it.

10.3 THE ARGUMENTS FOR AND AGAINST WORKFARE

The following assessment should not be taken to imply any order of presumed significance, although some issues are more important than others. Although evidence comes predominantly from the United States, the discussion is intended to refer to the drift to workfare as a regulatory instrument of social and labour market policy.

(i) Social Reciprocity?

Workfare is based on a claim of *reciprocity* – the view that social rights are conditional on labour obligations. According to its advocates, rights should be matched by duties, which is the essence of citizenship. This argument has adherents on the political right and left. Thus, Gorz (1985) argued for an obligatory duty to perform a specified social service to match the right to a basic income grant from the State.

There are two counter-arguments against this position. First, the right to do something can only be a right if there is a corresponding right not to do it. Workfare threatens that principle of justice, compromising choice and freedom. The proponents' point that the right to income should be matched by the duty to labour can be seen as an unbalanced reciprocity, since the insistence on duties threatens to stigmatise prospective recipients and so encourage them to forgo their rights. Economic rights are meaningful only if individuals are able to exercise them. For those without resources, this can only be done by belonging to a group that provides the collective strength to overcome their vulnerability. Proponents of workfare link it to the notion of citizenship; but citizenship must be universal and equal. Why should the poor be forced to take directed work while the rich are not? If it is desirable to enable and empower the poor to participate as 'active citizens', that is an argument for decoupling income support from labour market activity, not for workfare.

A second counter-argument is that the presumption of *balanced reciprocity* is unfair because for those on the margins of society there are not fair opportunities or the prospect of them. Unless the state can guarantee fair and equal access to all forms of job in society, one cannot justify the claim for reciprocity. If there is less than Full Employment – even defined as a level of unemployment consistent with minimal frictional unemployment – more people would be looking for jobs than could have them. If, in other words, one accepts that there is involuntary unemployment, imposing an obligation that citizens should take jobs or lose entitlement to state transfers is unfair, because the condition for fairness of opportunity does not exist.

The dilemma of inadequate opportunity has been the primary justification for the view held by some advocates of workfare that there must be a *guarantee* of a job or its equivalent. This has been called 'fair workfare' or 'new workfare', and has been adopted by many who would not call themselves libertarians (see, e.g., Gutmann and Thompson, 1996, pp. 291–4). The proposed reciprocity upsets some libertarians, because it offers the prospect of continued *dependency* on the state. This was behind the 'two years and you're out' rule. Charles Murray put the rationale most starkly, in stating that social policy should encourage 'independence' and allow 'better people' to receive their 'merit' because 'they deserve more of society's rewards' (Murray, 1984, p. 231). Unfortunately, he continued, 'Government cannot identify the worthy, but it can protect a society in which the worthy can identify themselves.' The worthy identify themselves only if the Government does *not* guarantee jobs. Only if this condition exists will a government encourage self-sufficiency and basic liberty, enabling the most deserving, merit-worthy citizens to make most effective use of opportunities.

It is easy to caricature this line of reasoning as heartless. However, Murray concluded that it shows 'no lack of compassion' and expresses 'the principle of respect', because it conveys a message to people that they have responsibility for themselves. In our terms, they have self-control. The difficulty with this rationale for unconditional workfare is that it presumes that the conditions exist for individual responsibility and basic opportunity, ignoring discrimination, ill-luck and injustice. The notion of 'worthy' or deserving is at root just as paternalistic as any form of dependency that libertarians condemn with such gusto.

Adherents of so-called 'fair workfare' claim,

An obligation to work should be contingent on the availability of work. Furthermore, even when employment is available, children should not be penalised for their parents' unwillingness to work, and therefore family caps are not justifiable. (Gutmann and Thompson, 1996, p. 290)

While agreeing with the second assertion, and that it would be unfair to impose an obligation if there were no 'work' available, the statement still begs many questions. What sort of work? What amount of time should an individual be allowed to spend in seeking a job before having to meet the 'obligation'? One can only answer such questions arbitrarily. Gutmann and Thompson claim that 'the opportunity principle is consistent with imposing an obligation to work on able-bodied citizens' on the grounds of 'limited dependence' in which citizens are 'mutually dependent, each obligated to contribute his or her share in a fair scheme of social cooperation'. But what is a 'fair scheme'? What is the 'share' that each is obliged to contribute? Does a property speculator who receives millions of dollars contribute his 'fair share' to society? Who asks him to do so? Fair workfare seems to imply that the poor and disadvantaged should be obliged to contribute, while those born with wealth or who gain wealth by other means have no such obligation, and certainly do not have an obligation bestowed on them by somebody they do not select for the task. Decision-makers on such matters are rarely those for whom such decisions are made, and they would surely fail the Rawlsian test that, behind a veil of ignorance, they would be prepared to put themselves in their place and choose workfare.

(ii) Promoting Functional Citizenship?

Perhaps the most basic claim is that workfare increases the ability of government to improve the functioning of its citizens. One advocate of workfare argued that, 'to improve social order', government must use benefits 'to require better functioning of recipients who have difficulty coping' (Mead, 1986, p. 7). He defined functioning as the ability to discharge what he regarded as 'social obligations', such as learning, working, supporting one's family and respecting the rights of others. He claimed that US welfare programmes, notably the AFDC, meant that the recipients' 'place in American society is defined by their need and weakness, not their competence [to discharge those obligations]. This lack of accountability is among the reasons why non-work, crime, family break-up and other problems are much commoner among recipients than Americans generally.' In such circumstances, workfare would transform welfare from means-tested entitlements into reciprocal obligations between society and individuals.

Critics might retort that it is questionable whether the State should presume to turn individuals into 'functioning citizens' by obliging poorer groups to do specified activities. There is little evidence that lack of accountability is a major cause of the crime and so on, and it is by no means clear that any such relationship exists, or if it does that cause and effect are identifiable. In a breathtaking statement, Mead (1986, p. 10) asserted, 'far from blaming people if they deviate, government must persuade them to *blame themselves*'. Why should the victim of a mishap, whether by ill-luck or because he lacks the particular knack of obtaining or holding the type of job on offer, be encouraged to feel so blameworthy? Can it really be the duty of a citizen to feel personally responsible and culpable for every personal mishap? One wonders too at the desirability of benefit programmes being used to 'inculcate values'.

Mead and others have argued that a recipient of State transfers should have obligations in return. This focuses exclusively on *individual* obligations and reciprocity, neglecting *collective* aspects of reciprocity. As Katz (1989, p. 164) noted, '... obligation implies mutual responsibilities, and Mead fails to ask what we in our organized capacity as government ... owe in return'.

What are the collective social obligations to citizens? If the state does not provide the means or services to ensure social participation, integration or the acquisition and maintenance of skills, surely collective reciprocity is undermined. The *possibility* of economic participation must be created if the language of mutual responsibilities and obligations is to be respectable.

Advocates of 'fair workfare' link citizenship with labour obligations. According to Gutman and Thompson (1996, p. 293):

> In our society having a job is a necessary condition of what has been called social dignity – maintaining the respect of one's fellow citizens. (Having a job of course includes being a homemaker in a family where others have a job outside the home.) The point is not merely that having a job shows that you can take care of yourself; more important, it shows that you are carrying your share of the social burden. What your fellow citizens think of you in this sense should matter.

This justification of workfare raises substantial difficulties. Many people in society have social dignity without having a job, just as many who have a job lack any sense of social dignity. Put the sentence to a simple test. I am a sewage cleaner; you are a lawyer. Whether in my eyes or yours, in what way would my job give me social dignity? One could insert other jobs in place of sewage cleaning. Similarly, once you allow that work as 'homemaker' counts as a job, then there is no reason to exclude any activity that has use value for the individual. And why should someone be accepted as having a job if they were 'homemaking' when others from the household were in jobs outside the home, whereas they would not be counted as in a job if they were 'homemaking' if no other household members had jobs? The next sentence is also unclear. Someone may have a job that did not provide enough on which to live, and as already emphasised, it is unclear what is meant by carrying your share of the social burden. Does the amount of time spent working for wages matter, or the type of job?

It may seem unfair to dissect a particular text. But this is an attempt by two well-respected analysts to present a justification that goes beyond euphemisms and platitudes. Their text merely shows that the functional citizenship argument is paternalistic and suspect because the terms are arbitrary and hazy.

Workfare increases the stigmatisation of the poor. They are subject to pressures and scrutiny, as well as discretionary judgments and directions by officials who may or may not be trained to make such decisions fairly. Even if they were, the imposition of obligations should raise a question about the contractarian justice of the transaction. The person is in a vulnerable position, dependent on the goodwill of the caseworker. To talk about the relationship reflecting a 'new social contract', as commentators have described workfare, is to imply that it is a contract entered voluntarily and based on freedom. It is difficult to envisage how this dependent relationship strengthens functional citizenship. Workfare is paternalistic control, with many signs that policing of the behaviour of the poor is part of the process. For instance, in March 1995 New York's *Work Experience Programme* began with insistence that applicants for welfare benefits had to be finger-printed in order to satisfy tight tests for eligibility.

Such treatment humiliates and stigmatises, and would make most people fearful about applying. It is no use defenders of workfare saying that such official action is not part of workfare, since a mix of pressures, threats and sanctions is the essence of workfare. They must justify those pressures.

(iii) Combating Dependency?

Another claim is that workfare imposes a work test, which is the most effective test of need. This is based on a presumption that incentives do not work for the poor, a view supported by evidence that there were only marginal changes in labour supply in response to the income maintenance experiments of the 1960s. Thus, it was argued, those who do not wish to work or to take jobs on offer cannot need the income very much. From this reasoning, we soon arrive at controversial notions of 'deserving' and 'undeserving' poor. Debates in the USA on workfare and welfare reform in the 1980s and 1990s became embroiled in this dichotomy of dubious pedigree. A compromise proposal was to give those deemed to be unemployable, such as mothers with young children, a higher guaranteed income, and therefore less incentive to take paid employment because of the implicit high marginal tax rate (poverty trap), while those regarded as employable (e.g., husbands) should have a low, means-tested entitlement coupled with an obligation to work. Such distinctions between the employable and unemployable are also somewhat subjective.

The problem, according to workfare advocates, is that welfare recipients lose the will to work and sink into a state of dependency. Some go a step further, opposing 'new-style' workfare precisely on the grounds that it does not remove dependency. They support workfare as a threat, to ensure that welfare recipients seek and take jobs or training promptly. According to Lawrence Mead (1997,

p. 168), 'The dependent poor appear to react more strongly to *requirements* to work than incentives ...'

Critics are not impressed by the claim that the long-term unemployed or others outside the labour force who receive transfers are immersed in a 'dependency culture'. They see assertions about dependency as exaggerated. For example, an evaluation of the workfare scheme in Massachusetts found that a majority of long-term unemployed men put on workfare could have found employment without the 'work experience' imposed on them (Friedman et al., 1981). And studies (e.g., Goodwin, 1983) have shown that the poor want to work just as much as the non-poor.

One might argue that social security systems have eroded non-institutional forms of social solidarity and induced new forms of dependency (Delruelle-Vosswinkel, 1988). But workfare does nothing to recreate such non-institutional solidarity. By turning some parts of the population into workfare targets (those designated as employable and thus, implicitly, undeserving welfare recipients) and others into welfare recipients (those designated as unemployable), the false dichotomy between those expected to be productive citizens and those expected to be unproductive is intensified.

The dependency-combating argument put forward by workfare proponents is double-edged. Why stop at the poor? What about middle-class dependency, which is considerable? In many countries the more affluent strata are dependent on tax relief that allows them to contract enormous debts, such as mortgages. Indeed, many middle-income earners are dependent on fiscal welfare.

The anti-dependency lobby pushes for welfare to be converted from universalism to selectivity and from grants to loans, on the pattern of the UK's Social Fund, which gave the poor 'emergency' loans, not grants. The rationale is that this encourages the poor to manage their own budgets and obliges them to go out to work. This reasoning has accompanied an orientation towards workfare, especially since giving loans to those who cannot pay may be seen as a way of turning paupers into debtors as well, at which point workfare advocates can depict the work obligation as a way of repaying the financial obligation. This is a punitive approach, because it sees the poor as being where they are simply by their own actions.

The dichotomy of the deserving and undeserving has dogged social policy through the ages. As Alexis de Tocqueville recognised in his *Memoir on Pauperism*, it is practically impossible and inequitable to 'separate unmerited misfortune from an adversity produced by vice'. Workfare adherents have yet to demonstrate that de Tocqueville was wrong.

There is one further variant of the anti-dependency justification for workfare to be considered. One libertarian argument in favour of unconditional workfare is that the objective should be personal *independence*. According to this view, guaranteeing jobs for welfare recipients is unjustifiable, because that would create a new form of dependency and reinforce the culture of poverty. This is a nice twist to the conventional argument, challenging to paternalists of any persuasion.

(iv) Restoring the 'Work Ethic'?

One claim voiced strongly by workfare advocates is that it would inculcate or restore the 'work ethic'. Some go further, saying that the welfare system *should* cultivate labour discipline and that since other social institutions already exist to do that, such as churches and schools, there should be no objection to one or more institution doing so. In the UK, for instance, some economists have argued that, since general schooling has been advanced by compulsion, so should post-school vocational training, for all teenagers (Layard and Prais, 1990). Why stop there?

Opponents remain unimpressed, claiming that workfare is misguided because implicitly it blames the victim, in that it *assumes* that the target group lacks a 'work ethic' and needs to be compelled. Rather, the problem may be a poverty trap, with prospective earnings from jobs being less than welfare, which was the case in all US states (Tanner et al., 1995). Or it may be non-work barriers to taking a job. Many AFDC recipients had personal constraints, such as disability, drug or alcohol problems, housing difficulties, low skills, health limitations, disabled small children or elderly parents (Olson and Pavetti, 1996). In the USA, one-third of unemployed welfare recipients reported that lack of childcare was the reason for their non-employment (Maynard, 1995). About one in seven had health impediments preventing or impeding them from working (Zill et al., 1991). Or the problem may simply be a lack of employment opportunities, or a lack of facilities to unblock a barrier to taking employment. Or it may be that many would want or be able to work only so-called non-standard hours (Presser and Cox, 1997). There is ample evidence that the premise underlying workfare is dubious. Moreover, if workfare leads to a proliferation of artificial, 'unreal' jobs, it may weaken any work ethic if the poor and unemployed are forced to take them.

It is often not the case that those receiving state benefits are in the status of 'dependency' suggested by popular accounts, dependent on benefits and unable and unwilling to seek or take employment. In the USA, contrary to the powerful image of women living on AFDC benefits for years without employment, it seems that most recipients did not depend totally on AFDC and many cycled back and forth between employment and welfare (Spalter-Roth et al., 1995). The common problem has been that they take jobs that do not last long, or are forced to take inappropriate jobs, or cannot afford to remain in them, and thus end up returning to 'welfare'. In other words, it is not a cultural aversion to work *per se* that is the cause of the marginalisation, and thus a paternalistic or coercive policy would be misdirected.

As with reducing dependency, creating or restoring a work ethic through workfare smacks of social engineering. The apparatus and institutions set up to oversee workfare could be transformed easily into mechanisms of coercion. This is not to attribute such intentions to most workfare advocates; the motives of many should not be impugned just because a coercive intention is the motivation of a few. However, many observers have concluded that as workfare spread in the 1980s and 1990s, so compulsion gained primacy over the emphasis on incentives (Moffitt, 1986). Because workfare gives discretionary power to local bureaucrats, it must lead to subjective judgments being made at local 'workfare offices'. It depends ultimately on sanctions, and in practice the onus of proof of appropriate behaviour will be put on the unemployed or other needy individual, who may be inarticulate or unable to prove legitimate activity.

Essentially, workfare regulates individual and group behaviour and leads to directed labour. It therefore undermines the *right* to work, a point to which we shall return. At the very least, it is paternalistic. According to one review supportive of workfare,

> Often a state puts job-hunting welfare recipients into a job club, a sort of therapy group in which peers offer motivation and moral support. In San Diego, when a job club member tells the group she has found employment, the group leader, a social worker, rings a cowbell. (Williams, 1986, p. 80)

Less colourfully, paternalism has been revealed by the tendency of workfare proponents to condemn 'non-directive' welfare programmes on the grounds that they encourage beneficiaries to undertake training only for jobs they would like, which apparently results in them subsequently working fewer hours than before because the training prepares them for work that is 'beyond their reach' rather than for 'the more menial jobs actually available to them' (Mead, 1986, p. 65).

Such language should leave critics feeling uncomfortable. If nobody wants to do such menial jobs, then either the wage should be raised or the jobs should be automated, or ways should be found of doing without them. Conversely, if many workers want to do some types of attractive work, then the market wage of such jobs should be allowed to drop relative to that of menial jobs. In other words, one should not criticise the non-employed if they respond to market signals by choosing their own way to reintegrate. Mainstream norms are not necessarily universally valid. Workfare is a form of regulation that 'integrates' lower-class people in a way they may not like.

(v) Cost-reducing Social Policy?

One advantage claimed for workfare is that the labour obligation will reduce the cost of the welfare system by generating extra output and hence tax revenue. Directed work, it is also claimed, reduces caseload costs, including those arising from the administrative need to check that welfare benefit recipients are seeking, and are available for, paid employment.

Critics retort that the financial advantages of eliminating a few 'scroungers' from the benefit rolls is small compared with the social and economic cost to needy claimants, and that in practice where real, productive jobs are involved workfare participants tend to displace workers in regular employment, thereby leading to additional costs. Such displacement effects were observed, for example, in evaluations of the San Diego workfare experiments (Goldman et al., 1985).

The proponents' claim that workfare can reduce welfare expenditure is also dubious, because enforcement and other administrative costs may deter effective implementation (Casey, 1986). To be efficient, workfare requires costly institutional reform, because of a need to merge welfare and labour market agencies.[3] Workfare evaluations have rarely taken account of these, or of deadweight and displacement effects, so they have given an upward bias to the estimated benefit–cost ratios.

In the USA, in the 18 months after the welfare reform came into effect many people dropped off welfare rolls. The difficulty is to know what explains the drop, since it continued a longer-term decline. Between 1993 and 1997 the number dropped by nearly 3 million. In May 1997, the White House's Council of Economic Advisers attributed 40 per cent of the fall to economic growth and 31 per cent to policy changes, including earned income tax credit for low-income workers, increased child support collections and spending on daycare for children of welfare mothers (Council of Economic Advisers, 1997). But the Council Chairwoman, Janet Yellen, admitted that they did not know what had happened to those who had left welfare, adding, 'Are we pushing more people into poverty by revamping welfare programmes? We just don't know until there is more research.' Other studies have concluded that a large proportion have dropped off welfare and the labour force as well.

In the UK, the Government claimed that its pilot workfare scheme in 1996 resulted in a 20 per cent drop in the number of registered unemployed claiming benefits, twice as many as had found jobs. The Government interpreted the decline in claimants to benefit fraud, claiming that it 'flushed out of the system people who have been cheating'. But there was no check on whether people withdrew for that reason.

Although some economists have concluded that workfare is 'expensive', financial costs may be less than anticipated because fewer claim or gain entitlement to benefits. The change in direct costs should not be equated with social costs. Additional income insecurity among potential beneficiaries of welfare support may result in more need for financial support later.

(vi) Cutting the Black Economy?

Workfare, it is suggested, will diminish the black economy, because it makes it harder for welfare recipients who are actually working – but outside the taxable economy – to obtain benefits. To this, critics might respond that workfare cannot make much of a dent in the black economy, since most of those in it are also employed in other jobs. Various empirical studies have shown that those with regular jobs are more likely than the unemployed to have such informal work as well.

Perhaps workfare schemes reduce the extent of petty, undeclared informal work by the poor, but in the absence of convincing evidence to the contrary one can presume that the effect is of minor significance in the debate over workfare. It could be beneficial if the threat of obligations brought some part-time employment into the legal economy. But it could end some casual income earning by preventing people from continuing the work or discouraging them from persisting with what they know is illegal; the result might be that their income insecurity would be overwhelming. Often the reality is that the poor do casual jobs in the evenings, at weekends or when they find the time, whereas for family or other reasons they could not do paid jobs at 'standard' times or on conventional work schedules.

(vii) Restoring Equity in Welfare

According to supporters, workfare is more equitable than orthodox welfare. The reasoning starts from the premise that any individual's full income consists of both money and leisure time. With conventional welfare payments, recipients without time-using obligations effectively receive more than many low wage earners, whose lost 'free time' can be equated with forgone income. Related to this is the claim that it is unfair that, with conventional welfare, some workers are paid benefit for not doing unpleasant jobs when others are doing them for wages.

To critics, this smacks of sophistry. If it were accepted that the full income of welfare exceeds the monetary value because of hidden leisure, it would help justify an unconditional transfer, because it implies that the poverty and unemployment traps that exist with means-tested schemes are even worse than income comparisons suggest.

Workfare proponents have made much of the claim that it strengthens the family unit by stressing responsible social behaviour by employable adults, a theme given prominence during the passage of the US welfare reform. However, it is surely unfair to penalise a whole family or household by withholding benefit because one or other parent does not fulfil some behavioural condition for benefits on which all family members rely. And the surmise that 'learnfare' for teenagers subjects families to economic insecurity and stress is almost certainly true (Corbett et al., 1989). Rather than strengthen the nuclear family by imposing behavioural norms, workfare may erode it by increasing the internal tension. That is surely not equitable.

(viii) Legitimising Social Transfers?

An overtly political justification for workfare is the claim that the imposition of work on welfare recipients enhances political support for welfare programmes in general. It also demonstrates to others, including potential employers, that those 'on welfare' are really employable. However, rather than attract support, workfare may weaken public endorsement of welfare in general by stigmatising the poor and encouraging a perception of 'them-and-us'. It undermines a principle of citizenship, which is that everybody should be treated on an inclusive, equal basis.

By contrast with workfare, a transfer without a work-related obligation would separate the government's social responsibility for basic income security from the individual's personal responsibility for developing skills and a 'lifetime' sense of occupation, which in the coming era will consist increasingly of individual bundles of skills, interests and experience rather than predetermined, standardised packages.

Finally, workfare is unlikely to be effective because no group directly involved favours it. The participants try to avoid or resent being in it; the officials in the workfare agencies prefer to have willing clients and so are loath to force welfare clients to take menial jobs; the public authorities and firms are reluctant to employ welfare clients because they expect such workers, even if subsidised, to be unreliable, have high turnover and require close supervision; trade unions resent them as a threat to their employed members' jobs, pay and benefits; and other workers feel threatened by the presence of workfare placements because they fear being displaced by lower-paid substitutes or having overtime, working hours or promotion prospects reduced.

(ix) Reducing Poverty?

Workfare supporters also claim that it raises participants' longer-term income above what they would receive on welfare. Studies have shown that this may be true for the important group of single-parent families; one US study, by the Manpower Demonstration Research Corporation (1983), suggested that workfare participants' subsequent income was higher than that of those who remained on welfare. However, that study also indicated that the income gains were insufficient to lift the recipients out of poverty, that is, remove them from eligibility for welfare transfers. Other studies also showed that the income gain was small, that only short-run effects were measured, and that subsequent incomes of two-parent families were actually reduced by workfare (Friedlander et al., 1986; Friedlander and Gueron, 1990). Burtless (1997) concluded that it was unrealistic to expect that pushing welfare recipients into the type of job they could expect would lift them out of poverty.

There is also an indirect sequence of effects to be considered, since the jobs usually envisaged by workfare proponents have low productivity, status and pay – cleaning streets, sweeping leaves, being maids or waitresses, and so on. Most do not enhance the probability of employment in higher-strata activities and do little to reverse the structural tendency to marginalise a substantial proportion of the labour force. If the poor pushed into workfare slots see little chance of thereby joining the economic mainstream, the coercive element cannot lead to self-reliant individualism, let alone higher income in the longer term.

There are other reasons for doubting that workfare is an efficient means of reducing poverty. A large-scale workfare scheme introduces distortions into the lower end of the labour market. It will probably give overwhelming emphasis to maximising the 'placement rate', to the detriment of genuine skill development.

Cheap labour undermines better labour, leading – as observed even in Sweden – to substitution/displacement effects and a weakening of the bargaining position of lower-status, lower-income groups among the employed.

Another, easily overlooked effect is that workfare schemes in the USA have resulted in many non-employed women being placed in jobs with very low wages, without health benefits, sick leave or paid vacation. This was shown to be the case for three-quarters of those placed under the *Greater Avenues for Independence* (GAIN) scheme set up in California (Riccio et al., 1994). Similar figures were found for the New Chance scheme, and for schemes in New Jersey (Hershey and Pavetti, 1997).

There is growing evidence that the *wage displacement* effect of workfare may be stronger than the *employment displacement* effect. According to Bernstein (1997), placing welfare recipients in jobs, giving them a 'grant' below the going wage, appeared to lower the wages of the low-paid workforce by a substantial amount in 1996–97.

The overall effect of workfare on poverty depends on a series of outcomes that are unknown prior to the policy coming into operation. This is unlike social protection as usually perceived, whereby the vulnerable, near-poor and poor are given prior assurance of income *security*. The poverty effect of time limits and workfare obligations depend on the income received in the jobs, the costs of taking and remaining in jobs, the income mobility potential of those jobs and the effect on the poverty status of those in or potentially in jobs that are taken by workfare participants. Thus, the overall effect must take into consideration the impact not just on those on workfare but on low-income groups in general.

The effect on workfare participants themselves depends crucially on the costs of jobholding, and in the USA these have been shown to be a cause of many participants leaving jobs and returning to claim benefits (Hershey and Pavetti, 1997). The cost of childcare, transport, clothes, processed food and so on, quite apart from loss of other transfers or informal support from relatives, friends or non-governmental organisation, may easily make low-wage jobs an impoverishing experience.

For the poor and near-poor, taking a job may tip them from a subsistence equilibrium into financial crisis. They may take a low-paid job, losing entitlement to benefits, in the hope that high initial costs are an investment that will be worthwhile when the income rises in the longer term. In this frame of mind, they build up debts, only to find their hopes – perhaps induced by their social caseworker – are ill-founded, leaving them with unsustainable debts. At least one study (Edin, 1995) has found that many women who went from welfare to jobs ended up sinking into substantial debt. This form of poverty trap has received insufficient attention.

The ability of those relying on welfare support to find jobs at all is also questionable. Although it will take several years before full evaluation of the US welfare reform is possible – and by 1998, several multi-million-dollar research projects were underway – research based on workfare experiments, the profiles of the target population and official job projections are not encouraging. Not only is the wage displacement large but, as one careful study concluded, 'alarming numbers of low-income families may face sanctions or benefit cutoffs as a result of the time limits mandated by the 1996 welfare legislation' (Duncan et al., 1997).

In the USA, the notion of 'time limits' is meant to be a shock tactic, or what its advocates call 'tough love'. A concern is that many will not be able to meet the criteria, and will be made destitute. The rhetoric opens social policy to the awesome prospect of a credibility 'shoot out'. Suppose after two years, and more dramatically after five years, millions of citizens are unable to satisfy the workfare criteria and cease to be entitled to welfare benefits. There is a strong prospect that this will be the case. If the State then started to make exceptions to meet desperate cases, the policy's credibility and its fragile residual fairness would be undermined. If it did not give way, the consequences for the poor would be terrible.

In 1999, one could predict that this moral dimension would consume public debate in 2000. Other countries moving down the same road may benefit from lessons that will emerge from that debate. It will be accentuated because of the extraordinary fact that the workfare policy launched in mid-1996 was 'fund capped'. The welfare budget was declared in advance, involving a $56 billion cut up to 2002. But the number of claimants over that period could only be forecast contingently and was unknown. If the economy slowed, the number would rise, which would strain the diminished block grants. Some policymakers expressed fears about this, and one can predict that some states will operate a more restrictive regime as a result of the uncertainty. Again, this aspect of the conditionality opens up the prospect of politicising social policy beyond any economic or social rationale.

A similar sort of distributive twist had already arisen by 1997, in that as a result of concentrating on placing welfare recipients in jobs, in some states resources had been diverted from childcare for the working poor to pay for the placements, jeopardising the ability of the employed poor to stay in jobs (Waller, 1997). This outcome is likely when policy focuses on one group and when job placement is the primary concern.

Another potential source of impoverishment is the relationship between the statutory minimum wage and the level of welfare payments. In 1997, it was decided that workfare participants were covered by the *Fair Labour Standards Act* of 1938, entitling them to the minimum wage. This caused consternation. For relatively low-income states, such as Alabama, since the existing welfare payments were equal to less than half the minimum wage, the ruling meant that the cost of placing workfare participants in jobs would more than double. If the state could not meet the requirement to place welfare recipients in jobs, its block grant would be reduced. As of early 1998, the debate centred on what counted as the minimum wage. The outcome could be crucial for the effect of workfare on poverty in general.

In assessing the effect on poverty, what is most striking is that workfare was launched with no evidence that it would reduce poverty, and some evidence that it would make it much worse, in spite of rhetoric to the contrary.

(x) Reducing Unemployment?

A commonly stated rationale for 'welfare-to-work', workfare and 'active labour market policy' is that it would reduce not only unemployment but the NAIRU. Workfare has been depicted as reducing unemployment not only directly but by discouraging welfare claimants from registering as unemployed jobseekers and by encouraging employers to offer more low-wage jobs (The Employment Centre, 1987). Related to this is the argument that workfare is needed because most unemployment in affluent societies is 'voluntary', primarily because the poor do not like the type of jobs they are able to obtain and repeatedly quit in the hope of finding something better.

This argument does not stand close scrutiny, partly because the voluntary unemployment claim is based on dubious or unverified assumptions. In any case, to reduce unemployment by discouraging genuine claimants from registration is scarcely a legitimate policy. To do so merely intensifies the poverty of those not satisfying the conditions for support. This has, for example, been reported as the outcome of a policy change in the UK that made teenagers eligible for housing benefits only if they joined the government-funded *Youth Training Scheme*. Growing homelessness and other adverse social consequences have been attributed to that change.

A related claim is that workfare removes the 'unemployment trap', i.e., the fact that with most welfare systems unemployed people taking low-paying jobs face what are effectively very high marginal tax rates, losing access to benefits as their earned income rises. Some economists who favour workfare do so partly because they believe that marginal income tax rates *should* be higher at the lower end of the scale, on the grounds that the better-off should be given more incentive to work because of their higher productivity, whereas the lost output of the poor discouraged from working by very high marginal tax rates would not matter very much. On this reasoning, workfare is a way of avoiding the unemployment trap.

Not only is the differential tax rate argument dubious theoretically (the substitution effect may offset the income effect), but the rationale is inequitable. Leaving that aside, if removal of the unemployment trap were the objective, then an unconditional income transfer would surely be a preferable alternative.

Another criticism of workfare as a means of combating unemployment is that it may actually *raise* frictional unemployment. Almost by definition, workfare participation interrupts the unemployed's job search process, and may therefore increase labour market inefficiency. It is difficult to search for the type of work you want, or think you might be able to do, if you are having to participate in a workfare scheme at the same time. Indeed, MDRC evaluations of male AFDC-

UP (Unemployed Parents) participants in workfare programmes in the USA found that workfare delayed labour market re-entry. In Baltimore, for instance, there was a vibrant 'living wage' campaign in the 1990s, led by local churches and trade unions, with the objective of raising wages of the low paid. Campaign leaders claimed that raising the wages lowered labour turnover, because workers were enabled to afford to stay in their jobs. Workfare reversed this, thus threatening to raise frictional unemployment as well as income insecurity.

A more standard criticism of workfare and its welfare-to-work cousins is that it largely fails to reduce unemployment because of substantial *employment displacement effects*, or *substitution effects* (placing people in posts instead of others already in or previously in those jobs), as well as because of *deadweight effects* (placing people in jobs in which they would have been placed anyhow). Although these are often regarded as the most serious drawbacks of workfare, they are introduced at this stage to emphasise that they are not necessarily the major criticism, even though many advocates attempt to defuse this criticism almost to the exclusion of addressing others.

In any case, obliging the unemployed to take jobs could have the effect of displacing others in similar jobs, and numerous studies have suggested that the displacement could be so large that the net effects on employment and unemployment are modest. There is also evidence that the unemployed are often obliged to enter jobs that would have been created for them anyhow or perversely would not exist, and need not be done, were they not obliged to perform them.

An example of displacement hard to attribute directly to workfare is what happened to employment in New York's parks department. Having reduced direct employment by over 40 per cent, half by dismissals, over a three-year period, the department deployed 6,000 'Weps' (participants in the Work Experience Program, the workfare scheme) at lower cost. The fact that the lay-offs preceded the deployment of Weps made it possible to claim there was no displacement, yet surely this amounts to it.

In a tightening labour market, as in the USA during the period when workfare was extended, the employment displacement effect may not appear to be very significant, although it is unfair to those displaced and to those denied a proper waged job. However, when unemployment is higher, the issue of displacement should be regarded as a primary aspect of economic and social evaluation of workfare.

In 1998, under its *New Deal* welfare-to-work scheme, the UK Government was planning to oblige some unemployed youth aged 16 to 24 to work for six months in the 'voluntary sector'. This was ironic in that it seems to mean making some do jobs that others do voluntarily. The unemployed were to receive their benefits, if entitled, plus a small grant. The effect on unemployment would be modest if there were substantial displacement effects, and the adverse effects on the services could be considerable if reluctant or inexperienced unemployed created friction with volunteers working alongside them, leading to an erosion of the charity's reputation or capacities.

(xi) Moderating Wage Inflation?

Workfare, it is further claimed, puts downward pressure on wages and thus boosts employment indirectly. This should be seen in context. Proponents usually stipulate that those put on workfare should be paid only the equivalent of their welfare benefit or that plus a supplement to cover their costs of employment. Often they suggest that workfare should pay *less* than the lowest-level jobs. This has been the usual situation in the USA.

There is probably something in this claim. But besides raising problems of equity, surely using workfare explicitly to reduce wages at the lower end of the labour market distorts market mechanisms. As indicated earlier, workfare is a powerful means of lowering the wages of the low paid, and is thus a mechanism for achieving downward wage flexibility and intensifying the segmented character of the labour market, since it applies predominantly to the low-wage segment of employment.

(xii) Developing Skills?

Workfare-type programmes have been represented as a means of enhancing skills, whether through direct training or through the work experience involved, thus making participipients more employable and favouring the social reintegration of marginalised groups. The 'employability' theme was strongly asserted during public debates in the USA in the mid-1990s and in western Europe in 1997.

The main counter-claim is that workfare generates few skills, since – if linked to skill development at all – the type of jobs involved provide little more than 'orientation' or 'work preparation' training, rather than training for a genuine craft or occupation. Such training may boost the employment chances of some but marginalise others, perhaps by causing firms to substitute workers with 'formal' certification for those with informal but valuable skills. In any case, training schemes should surely *attract* workers by their intrinsic worth; the training should be perceived by potential trainees as improving their 'skill'. Participation in a workfare scheme may, on the contrary, actually reduce the participants' capacity or desire to undertake appropriate vocational training (Patino, 1986). Those obliged to take low-level, static jobs have less time and energy to pursue occupational education or training. Even at the lowest levels, unless there are incentives for firms and workers to make skill development part of the workfare scheme, the result is more likely to be deskilling. It seems that on-the-job training is relatively likely to yield reasonable economic returns. However, given the low level of education of many welfare recipients in the USA, off-the-job training would be required to enable most to take and to remain in employment (Taylor, 1997).

Workfare presumes that social integration can be achieved by doing a 'job', sometimes under the 'professional guidance' of some local official. One can think of many jobs that offer little prospect of doing any such thing. It also presumes an answer to an unclear question. It presumes that what needs to be reformed is people's behaviour rather than the institutions supposed to serve them. For example, one form of workfare – obliging teenagers to attend a school or training institution in return for welfare benefits – described as 'learnfare' in Wisconsin, is a classic case of a response to a problem that was not clearly identified. Perhaps teenagers do need discipline, though critics might feel uneasy about beating them into compliance with a social security stick. But are policymakers sure that is the real problem? Suppose schools are teaching subjects that are not relevant, or not appropriate to those expected to study them. Should a high drop-out rate be attributed to cultural background, to the teenagers' behavioural traits, or to the schools? The point is that subjective judgments about school attendance are not a reliable basis for deciding whether an individual *deserves* income support.

The possibility that workfare would have a *skill displacement* effect has received little attention. Those combining training with employment on their own initiative, or even with assistance from others, could be discouraged if there were an influx of others provided with comparable training, if the expected earnings from that type of job declined or if opportunities to use those skills appeared to worsen.

Workfare relates to another structural aspect of skill development, close to the spirit of this book. The thinking that has led governments in the direction of workfare is that it is justified because of welfare dependency and behavioural deficiencies on the part of the poor and unemployed. It focuses on the supply side, directly and indirectly lowering the reservation wage and distorting the dynamics of the labour market. The message is that the unemployed or other welfare recipient should alter his or her behaviour and attributes. The state may help, perhaps with a conditional grant or loan, perhaps with advice or job-seeking assistance. In this, the motives may be entirely benevolent. However, the policy alters the balance in the labour market in a way that lessens the pressure on firms and job designers to make jobs an avenue to occupation. There is less need to make jobs attractive and a source of skill development if applicants are driven to accept whatever is available through fear and insecurity.

10.4 CONCLUSIONS

In the 1980s, it was predicted that workfare and variants would be the reaction to growing labour market flexibility in the emerging era of market regulation (Standing, 1990). This has materialised, and the trend is likely to continue until the end of the century. Workfare is the ultimate policy of labour *control*.

Workfare has several drawbacks – it is judgmental, it is paternalistic, it erodes real freedom, it is socially divisive, and it may block forms of social and economic participation, such as voluntary community service, since workfare officials could claim that the person would not be searching for wage employment and would not be available for it at short notice, and therefore should not be classified as unemployed or receive benefits. The conditionality erects barriers to social participation and to community involvement and integration. Ironically, it could prevent people from participation, rather than induce it.

A message proclaimed by the repealers has been that industrialised societies cannot afford social protection, public pensions, public health care, public housing and so on. Hardly anybody has had the temerity to challenge this orthodoxy. The presumption or belief that extensive welfare cannot be afforded has been linked to globalisation, to the implied need for greater national competitiveness, and to the need to reduce public budget deficits (as in the case of targets set for monetary union under the Maastricht Treaty). But the rollback, or 'reorientation', of welfare has also been advocated as a desirable objective by libertarians, on grounds of social justice and as a pragmatic means of 'reducing welfare dependency'.

Workfare is a labourist and paternalistic response to the crisis of insecurity. There is room for disquiet. Workfare stigmatises the poor by associating certain activities with prior failure and by eroding the right to income security even further than recent labour market developments have done. It is coercive social policy. It is also a morally soft option. When the paternalistic family was seen as the social norm, women were expected to stay out of the labour force, so that labour conditionality was not regarded as reasonable. Now the norm is that women should be in wage jobs, so the paternalism dictates that women, even with young children and without a regular partner, should be obliged to take jobs. The application of norms to social policy is surely misguided, whichever norm is popular at the time.

Workfare represents a movement away from the insurance principle of social security without strengthening the *right* to work or income security. It is the outcome of the move away from universalism, and the drift to 'targeting' and selectivity, since means testing and work testing turn recipients of social protection into a category easily stigmatised by a majority in society. The drift to selectivity prepared the ground for workfare because politicians could play on the sentiment that the median worker or taxpayer is paying for the support and subsidised training and education of others.

Workfare also derives from a strange concept of mutual obligation – strange because it is not clear that 'mutual' or 'obligation' can be satisfactorily defined. In the more flexible society emerging in industrialised economies and elsewhere, *diversity* of behaviour should be facilitated, rather than curtailed by mechanisms designed to pressurise the poor to conform to some State-determined norm. Workfare neither addresses the structural features of labour markets that create and intensify marginalisation, nor enhances the prospects of more equitable outcomes. It is an unpromising road to take.

Part V

Shadow of the Future

It is from the champions of the impossible
rather than the slaves of the possible
that evolution draws its creative force.

Barbara Wootton

I ... pondered how men fight and lose the battle, and the thing that they fought for comes about in spite of their defeat, and when it comes turns out not to be what they meant, and other men have to fight for what they meant under another name.

William Morris, 1886

11 News from Somewhere: A Redistributive Agenda

11.1 THE NATURE OF THE CHALLENGE

We are coming to the end of the century of the labouring man. It began with calls echoing around the world for the *rights of labour* – the right to improved social status, dignity, security and autonomy. It was a call for freedom *from* labour. By mid-century, in the wake of the Depression and a world war, reformers were demanding the *right to labour*, seeking to ennoble the drudgery of being in a job and hinging everything on 'Full Employment', which was the full-time employment of men, supported by women intermittently in the labour force when needed. The century is ending with libertarians and many others advocating and introducing policies to strengthen the *duty to labour*, the state-enforced obligation to labour to obtain entitlement to be treated as a citizen and receive state benefits. In the process, governments are making it harder to survive without labour, without being in a job.

The twenty-first century will move away from the model of the labouring man, and it will move away from regarding labour as the centre and objective of human existence. It will strengthen the distinction between work and labour, and focus on the creativity, community, individuality and self-control that work can provide, and that labour cannot. To move away from the *labourist error* of the twentieth century successfully, reformers will have to take advantage of technological and economic changes to forge a new strategy for distributive justice.

The era of market regulation will not be 'the end of history'. Each era of flexibility and insecurity offers an opportunity to usher in a new scheme for distributive justice. The twentieth century has seen the rise and fall of a scheme that placed labour at the heart of the strategy for justice. Dominated by the image of industrial society, with laws and regulations to keep the balance between capital and labour, and with labour protection being the essence of social protection, in the end distributional conflicts could not be overcome by statutory regulations and the enhancement of labour security. For a while, the welfare state achieved great progress. However, no scheme fits all societies, and models devised in the twentieth century may not match the needs of the coming era.

Globalised labour markets are characterised by flexibility in which new forms of control and co-ordination are displacing Taylorist mechanisms. The outcomes include more insecurity, socio-economic fragmentation and detachment, a transformation of mechanisms of social protection, and a 'feminisation' of labour relations. The latter has been both negative and positive. It represents the spread of insecurity and flexibility. It also represents a recognition of multiple identities, because in many societies women have long been expected to combine different forms of work and labour, with little notion of 'career' outside the familial realm. The norm that guided thinking in the early and middle parts of the twentieth century assumed that men had *careers*, or increasingly *jobs*, while women had *roles* to fill (wife, mother, secondary worker, carer). As the century progressed, the gender dualism has crumbled – not by enough certainly – but so far all that has happened is that labour has become the norm, in a context of labour insecurity. An irony of the late twentieth century is that politicians (mostly male) have been devoting a large amount of effort to cajoling young mothers into jobs, into labour.

Traditionally, the multiple role of women has been presumed to undermine the capacity to organise their collective voice. Yet, perhaps because more men are facing the prospect of similar situations, in terms of the uncertainty and instability of their working lives, there may be a growing quest for alternative mechanisms for representation, redistribution and security based on this pattern of work and identity. A challenge is to recognise that the dilemma is not just the spread of insecurity and social fragmentation but the need to confront the belief that *labour* is the answer.

11.2 DISTRIBUTIVE JUSTICE: REPOSITIONING SECURITY

Modern society is largely determined by its labour market. To identify the qualities of a desirable and feasible labour market, one must ask a larger prior question: what is a Good Society? Nobody trying to come to grips with the conundrums of a Good Labour Market can legitimately skip the larger question.

A Good Society is a just society. There has been a rich debate since the early 1970s on distributive justice. All modern theories of justice begin with the premise that everyone should be treated as equal in some respect. Chapter 2 concluded that the Good Society should be one in which freedom, security and self-control should be part of the *equalisandum* (that which should be pursued as part of the bundle of social needs to be equalised as far as possible). This seems consistent with John Rawls' magisterial *Theory of Justice* and with extensions by Amartya Sen and others.

A common starting point is that justice requires the equalisation of advantages that are the consequence of circumstances and traits for which the individual could not be held responsible (Roemer, 1996, p. 8). There are several ways of expressing this. Thus Arnesan postulated that justice requires 'equality of opportunity for welfare', and Cohen put it as 'equality of access to advantage'. It is just as important to emphasise that justice requires equality of self-control and equality of basic security. A fear spreading around the world is that social progress was arrested in the late twentieth century, when flexibility came to mean insecurity, and when more people found themselves living in isolated space, without social responsibilities beyond themselves and their immediate family, and without the prospect of assistance from those around them. In the last few years of the century, individualism seemed to be a prescription for unbridled opportunism and the morality of the marketplace. This induces fragmented, unequal societies, in which legal controls, complex systems of auditing and detailed contracts are required to check *opportunism* and the lack of *trust*. Against a background of growing individualism, security and self-control are the prerequisites for a just society.

With Rawls' *Theory of Justice*, egalitarian theories moved beyond utilitarianism. He emphasised that justice depended on the provision of 'primary goods' and the Difference Principle, i.e., that a just society should maximise the bundle of *primary goods* available to the least well-off in society. These include basic liberties, such as freedom of association, freedom of movement and choice of occupation, and the social bases of self-respect. Again, although Rawls gave less attention to it, primary social goods should include *security* in which to pursue 'a rational plan of life'.

Amartya Sen (1980) extended Rawls' analysis by arguing that distributive justice requires equalisation of *capabilities*, not primary goods, where capabilities comprise opportunities and competencies. For Sen, the focus should be on the means for escaping morbidity, for being adequately nourished, achieving self-respect, participating in the community and being happy (Sen, 1993). Income *per se* should not be equalised because, for example, a disabled person would need more than someone else in order to achieve the same level of *functionings*. Recognising that slaves, housewives, the unemployed and the destitute tend to have 'cheap tastes', because of their deprivation, he concluded that justice should concentrate on improving individual *functionings*, rather than incomes (Sen, 1987, p. 11). He recognised a trade-off between distributive objectives, which left him open to the charge that he does not have a theory of justice (Roemer, 1996, p. 193). However, to include self-control and security as basic functionings would be consistent with Sen's work.

Dworkin (1981a, 1981b) rejected welfare equalisation as the appropriate principle of social justice, on the grounds that equalising the welfare of everybody would justify giving more to those with *expensive tastes*. He claimed that justice requires an equal distribution of a bundle of resources, but because resources include 'native talents' that are unequally endowed, he proposed that compensation be provided for inequalities in circumstances over which individuals are not responsible, but not for those due to their exercise of preferences. He thus integrated the notion of *'responsibility'* into egalitarianism, by allowing for types of inequality due to the exercise of preferences and actions for which individuals are responsible, and with which they identified at the time decisions were made.

Cohen (1992) added another caveat to Rawlsian justice theory by demonstrating that justice requires *fraternity* in which the talented are not purely self-regarding, and are prepared to compensate and support the less talented. This is significant, because if social groups become more *detached* from each other in terms of security and lifestyle, the sense of fraternity or community will be eroded, just as having some groups control the activity and advantages of others must do so.

While egalitarian theories of justice have wrestled with what it is that should be equalised, the era of market regulation ushered in libertarianism, which sat comfortably with the 'revolution' associated with the Chicago school of law and economics. The libertarian theory of justice was articulated by Robert Nozick in his influential *Anarchy, State and Utopia*, published in 1974. The central thesis of this profoundly inegalitarian theory is that justice is not concerned with outcomes but with *processes* by which individuals interact. For Nozick, there should be 'justice in acquisition' and 'justice in transfer', and these determine entitlements. As long as persons or firms acquire something legally, they are entitled to it, and nobody has any right to infringe their ownership. This allows monopolies, rejects redistributive taxation and state transfers, allows labour market discrimination and accepts the operation of labour controls, while asserting that any infringement on 'self-ownership' is an injustice.

Libertarianism gives overwhelming priority to liberty, but it gives *negative liberty* too much authority, that is, freedom from interference, preventing actions limiting freedom. Libertarianism neglects the need for an equal *opportunity* principle. By contrast, egalitarianism respects liberty as a constitutional principle, but limits it to allow for equal opportunity.

Libertarianism has been the most influential perspective on social and labour policy since the 1970s. It is based on the notion of 'self-ownership' and the doctrine of entitlements. Derived from Millian liberalism, self-ownership amounts to the view that everyone possesses (or should possess) full and exclusive rights of control and use of himself or herself, and his or her competencies and capacities (Cohen, 1995). *As such, nobody owes any service or product to anyone else unless he or she has contracted to supply it to someone.*

Libertarianism draws on a view expressed by John Locke justifying private appropriation from nature, subject to leaving 'enough and as good in common for others'. Critics have pointed out that there should be no presumption that natural resources were 'unowned' prior to private acquisition; one could presume that they were 'jointly owned' or 'communally owned'. Arneson (1991) has cited joint ownership, Cohen communal ownership. They have also criticised the principle of justice in acquisition, based on Rawls' argument that there is no right to income when that is due to *luck*, whether genetic or environmental.

Both egalitarians and libertarians have come to recognise that *responsibility* must figure in the theory of justice. But unlike libertarians, modern egalitarians have differentiated responsibility according to whether or not the individual could reasonably be said to have *control*. Roemer's scholarly review of theories of distributive justice concluded that there are philosophical difficulties to be resolved in treating responsibility. However, we may conclude that justice requires that everybody should be provided with basic security and a situation of self-control in which to form *preferences* responsibly and in which to take actions that are not induced by social situations in which they would not choose to find themselves. Without basic security and self-control, the demand for responsibility seems eminently unfair. *Real* freedom requires a rock of security – or it is the liberty of the outcast.

In this, there may be advance to be gained through Cohen's idea of *midfare*, which is supposed to be what one enjoys from one's *functionings* (capabilities) (Cohen, 1993). We might say that midfare – unlike welfare and workfare – requires that individuals be provided with the basic freedoms, including self-control and basic security, in which to act and decide with social responsibility. Sen's critique of Rawls for focusing on primary goods amounts to a plea to equalise midfare across persons. As such, justice depends on equalising *access to advantage*.

The conclusion to draw from this review of recent theories is that a just society, and by implication a good labour market, requires policies and institutions that enhance self-control and basic security. These objectives are compatible with both egalitarian and libertarian theories. Moreover, following the Difference Principle, distributive justice requires that policies should improve the position of the worst-off in society, which can only mean increasing their degree of self-control. A just society would be one in which – in Rawlsian terms – there would be *maximin security*, in which policies were regarded as just if and only if they minimised the difference between the degree of insecurity of the least advantaged and the remainder of society.

This leads to a reconsideration of the idea of security, and what sort of security we should desire for a Good Society. Subject to incentive and dynamic efficiency constraints, distributive justice depends on equalising economic security. Yet we have learned that some forms of security are neither wanted nor desirable. Security without rights is symbolic of state control. It fails. The state socialism model showed that. Rights without security is symbolic of market regulation and welfare residualism. It fails too. Security with rights is the desirable objective – balancing liberty and security. Before turning to this and what it implies, we should establish where we stand with respect to labour and to paternalism.

11.3 THE NEW PATERNALISM

Of the seven forms of labour security, those given primacy during the twentieth century, namely labour market and employment security, are *potentially* dispensable, because they are mainly instrumental, cannot be offered equally or fairly in a globalising economy and could be attained only at the cost of sacrifice of more valuable forms of security. Labour market security cannot be envisaged with current or foreseeable economic policies, in which a NAIRU is seen as a basic requirement, which means that governments deliberately maintain a pool of unemployed, whatever the rhetoric to the contrary. The feasible ways of lowering NAIRUs impinge on the liberty and security of vulnerable groups.

Employment security is merely a privilege for a small minority. Even in the dynamic US economy, the average life of *Fortune 500* companies (the leading firms) is only 40 years, so employment security for most workers entering firms is scarcely realistic. At best, only a minority could have strong employment security. And as chapter 6 concluded, there are other reasons for giving such security lower priority.

This does not mean that labour market and employment security are undesirable. The claim rather is that they should not be given top priority. To make progress, we must escape from the labourist bias. Only a romantic utopian would imagine the 'end of labour'. Yet labour is a means to an end, not to be idealised as an end in itself. Maximising the number of people in labour has been a fetish of the twentieth century. This can be done, usually at a cost, in terms of lower wages, less social protection, more stress, social illnesses and inequality. We need freedom from labour, so that we can pursue work in conditions where multiple forms of *activity* are valued as preserving community and fraternity. It is no coincidence that the most thriving work at the end of the century is that taking place outside the labour relationship, in voluntary service and community work, in which people are organised around their enthusiasms.

Labour should not be idealised for several reasons, among which are that for a growing number of people, the returns to labour are uncertain, and for many people obtaining income security through the labour market is not possible, because the social wage and jobs available are inadequate. Increasingly, in industrialised economies, and elsewhere, the main means of ensuring decent income security is to participate in the capital market. Yet everywhere the capital market participation rate (CMPR) is well below the labour force participation rate (LFPR). Social progress in the twenty-first century might be measured by both rates, with more emphasis given to the CMPR.

The *labourist prejudice* that the difference in income security between those on the margins, outside jobs, and those in employment *should* be large should be rejected. There should be no presumption of any sort. This prejudice has been asymmetrical in the twentieth century, not used to justify taking away from the rich who do not labour but used to justify reducing the income security of the poor. There *may* be reasons for *narrowing* the income differences between those in jobs and those outside them, but these are not relevant to the point that there should be no *presumption* that a large differential is desirable. Those in jobs and their representatives would be well-advised to reject the superficial appeal of that sentiment.

In his well-known analysis of citizenship, Marshall suggested that *civil rights* emerged in the eighteenth century, *political rights* in the nineteenth and *social rights* in the twentieth. Perhaps *economic rights* will emerge as the norm of decency in the twenty-first century. Those must include the *right to work*, and for this to be more than the duty to labour, that must allow for the right *not* to work. And the right to work must mean a right to choose what one perceives as rational activity, for only that can contribute to proper citizenship and occupational security. Jobs for their own sake are not consistent with this sense of rationality. And the right to a job that is chosen for you by somebody else against your wishes, however well meaning, is no right at all.

The crisis at the end of the century of labouring man is epitomised by the desire of reformers to find ways of maximising jobs and pushing more people into them. The conventional wisdom is that people need jobs, because that is good for them, and those who do not want jobs must be induced to want and accept jobs, because that leads to 'social inclusion'. This modern paternalism is found everywhere. However, while work is valuable if it contributes to human creativity and development, there is no reason to suppose that maximising labour is the best – or even feasible – means of facilitating the optimum amount or quality of work in society. Much of the most creative and useful work is not labour and could not be easily or sensibly turned into jobs. This is well-known, yet an extraordinary number of people find it impossible to integrate that insight into their proposals. They seek ways of multiplying the number of jobs and the pressure on the poor to slip into jobs. Jeremy Rifkin and others are wrong when they refer to the end of jobs. There are more of them than ever.

For the vulnerable and disadvantaged, the form of control that has come into ascendancy is what has been called by Mead (1997) and others the *new paternalism*. The state is expected to oblige the poor to behave in a certain way in their own interest and in society's interest. This applies to welfare policy, where reform has meant attempts to require adults to take a job, stay in school or take a specified training course if they wish to retain entitlement to state benefits. It has also been applied to the homeless, required to abide by rules set for them in return for shelter. The paternalism is the close supervision of the poor and dependent.

This is a reflection that market regulation, globalisation and flexibility have spread insecurity and inequality of income, wealth, status and control. High returns to capital and advanced technology associated with globalisation are the driving force for the inequalities. In this situation, we need a new vision of distributive justice.

We can begin by rejecting the neo-liberal claims that insecurity and substantial inequality are essential for economic growth, and somehow desirable. Behind this lies a woolly neo-Darwinian view of human beings endangered by security, captured in the use of such terms as 'dependency'. Society is made up of inter-dependency, yet what was regarded as social rights of citizenship in the middle of the century were by the end of it often regarded as illegitimate. The message conveyed by society's privileged that 'they' must not be 'dependent' is one of the ugly undertones of the era. The paternalistic approach is that obligations must be imposed as part of a crusade for social responsibility. The alternative is to have greater faith in personal freedom, and assert that rights induce responsibility – controls undermine those rights.

Some have tried to advance libertarianism by stating that pure self-interest cannot be acceptable because social responsibility would be merely a matter of 'free-floating conscience'. They have recognised that property rights alone would not generate a responsible society, because there would be no pressure to care for the rest of the community, for pollution, and so on. From this, they have argued that labour should be a citizenship *obligation*. Yet what constitutes acceptable work? Why should there be such an obligation? Would the obligation apply equally to all 'citizens' or only to those with no savings or rich relatives? As Ralf Dahrendorf has put it, work is a private relationship, whereas citizenship is a social one. If labour were made part of the citizenship contract, it would not have a voluntary character, and for many it would become forced labour.

Another labourist premise is that 'active' social and labour market policy must be directive in character, an instrument of regulation and control. Proponents of active labour market policy should be asked to demonstrate that any policy that they recommend is not *paternalistic*, with the onus of proof placed on them to demonstrate that the policy is not a device to control the behaviour of some groups in ways that would not apply to the majority or the privileged 'most free' groups in society.

The crisis of labour has many ramifications. Not only is there socio-economic fragmentation, bringing with it several forms of detachment, but there is fragmentation in the use of time and civic engagement (Putman, 1995, p. 664). Pushing the poor into demeaning jobs may tip them into an unsustainable crisis of time use, destroying their fragile hold on their lives. Labourist policy presumes the opposite, presuming that having a job *integrates* the person into society. Some jobs may help to integrate, some certainly do not. Consider a young woman with a small child who wishes to study to escape from the prospect of a series of 'McJobs' paying below the subsistence wage. If forced to take a job, she may be exposed to disadvantages that may create unsustainable pressures. She may lose her welfare benefits; she may have to spend less time looking after her child, who becomes prone to sickness and possibly longer-term disadvantage in learning. The woman's studying may become dilatory, her concentration powers diminished as a result of the triple time pressure. She may have to pay for childcare, and so on. Pushing such a person into a low-paying job is not an answer to a carefully defined problem. Of course, not all those without jobs are in this position. Nor should one imply that such time–income crises are relevant only to young women with children. A priori, however, the paternalistic response is potentially *dis*-integrating. That is all we need in order to reject it, although there are other reasons for doing so as well.

Work in occupation is a privilege, labour in a job is not. Labour can be a constraint on work, restricting the development, application and refinement of skills through a career. Habituation to labour of low complexity erodes intellectual flexibility and the capacity for self-direction and high-productivity work (Kohn and Schooler, 1978). Labour gives little scope for creative and regenerative contemplation. So-called *workaholism* should be called *labouraholism*, were it not such an ugly word. The addiction to job, and the stress it brings stem from turning work into labour. Although largely a sickness of middle-income and higher-income groups, this extends to the lower reaches of the labour market. Workfare and the paternalistic decision that everybody should labour must restrict the flexibility and creativity of those driven into labouring or fearful of being driven that way. To borrow from Beveridge's aphorism cited earlier, if people are driven through fear, insecurity and coercion, they will respond like cattle.

So, labour as such should not be idealised and paternalistic controls over those on the margins of the labour market should be regarded as a source of insecurity and a threat to liberty. Work is valuable, as well as essential for production and income generation. The issue is what sort of work and what sort of security should be promoted in place of paternalism and the jobholder society.

11.4 CITIZENSHIP AND OCCUPATIONAL SECURITY

The pivotal forms of security required for the Good Society of the twenty-first century are *citizenship security* and *occupational security*. Citizenship conveys the sense of belonging to community, the true sense of fraternity, on the basis of individual liberty, which implies autonomy with responsibility. Citizenship gives freedom, by strengthening a sense of identity and the necessary basis of self-control.

For citizens living in a work-based society, the source of distributive justice is the opportunity to pursue *occupation*. This involves the positive senses of skill and creativity, activity and self-control – the pride of craft. Occupation is never a finished process. One bundles competencies and 'functionings', learning, refining and extending the self through work, always allowing for leisure and contemplation. Since occupation is necessarily risk-taking activity, it accepts that some insecurity is tolerable, but is premised on basic security in the same way that Rawls and others have regarded fair opportunity as a necessary condition for distributive justice.

Occupational security requires *complexity* in work, sufficient freedom from supervision to realise responsibility, a sense of occupational *discipline*, and some freedom from routine, to permit creativity. It has been accepted since Durkheim's great work of 1893 that 'activity becomes richer and more intense as it becomes more specialised' (Durkheim, 1964, p. 404). Recalling the comments in chapter 1 on occupation, it is important to take account of what is valued in work and what is required to ensure occupational security. In this respect, social psychologists and others have shown how important *self-direction* and *self-control* are to human personality. As a group studying the process over many years concluded, 'The experience of occupational self direction has a profound effect on people's values, orientation, and cognitive functioning' (Kohn et al., 1990, p. 967).

Occupational security would create socially healthy communities. Those who can exercise self-control and self-direction in their occupation value these traits in other realms of life (Kohn and Schooler, 1983). They are less likely to exhibit traits termed the 'authoritarian personality', so chillingly associated with the mid-century madness of fascism. All forms of control undermine the sense of responsibility, and this applies to paternalism of any sort as well as to cruder forms.

Durkheim thought that modern life would depend on occupation, seeing the nation state and organisations as too large and distant to provide individuals with a sense of security and meaning. He rightly condemned dilettantism and spoke up for occupational depth. But since Durkheim we have learned that the technical division of labour can turn the specialist into the specialised. To prevent dilettantism or a life of *flexiworking* or detailed labour, individuals must have self-control and access to good opportunity. They must, in extremis, be able to refuse oppressive, exploitative, dehumanising labour. This requires both income security and representation security. History shows that without an *association* to represent it, an occupation withers under the pressures of other control systems. But it also requires the individual to have the freedom to opt out of collective control. Only if individuals have the 'Drop dead!' option will institutions remain representative, and only then will state and commercial bodies be constrained from opportunistic or paternalistic control behaviour.

Occupational security requires standards, regulation and forms of income protection appropriate to the occupation in question. Most types of work have scope for opportunism in terms of performance, and most have scope for skill broadening *or* dilution. Those in an occupation would wish to control job content and the mobility between jobs. Individualistic opportunism could harm those practising the work; there are externalities. So, security must include the preservation of standards, while allowing for diversity. It comes from facilitating creativity and ingenuity, while limiting fraudulent gimmickry, which could undermine the reputation, credibility and sustainability of the occupation. As a worker, the individual needs the collective, and the collective needs the individuality that establishes the occupation's legitimacy. This is why *voice regulation* of occupation, through associations or other representative bodies, should complement statutory regulation (licensing, standard-setting, etc.).

Occupational security is not the same as professionalism, which is a mechanism of privilege and control by exclusion. Professionalism does possess positive characteristics that should be part of occupational security, but it also *detaches*, in that its ideology is that only members of the profession possess the specialised knowledge to give it legitimacy, status and control. Unless occupations are open and subject to social regulation, they will be opportunistic and operate to command more than their fair share of society's income. Many observers would agree that this has been the case with lawyers, surgeons, accountants and several other professions.

Many economists have vociferously criticised unions for allegedly protecting 'insiders' at the expense of unemployed 'outsiders', but have been silent about middle-class professions that have jealously guarded the mysteries of their profession and the income accruing to them, notably by restrictive practices over recruitment, licensing, qualifications, and so on.

Professionalism is a feature of labour fragmentation. The sense of occupational security that one wishes to promote is one of societal integration, consistent with what Durkheim seems to have had in mind. Deskilling and occupational erosion through *job insecurity* have been features of Taylorism, bureaucratic enterprises and much of what is covered by external and functional flexibility. Professionalism, with its exclusive associations, symbols and presumed authority over clients, has been a defence against administrative control and a mechanism for economic advantage and rent seeking. By contrast, occupational security must apply to the lowliest workers as much as to those with mighty qualifications and the taboos of history behind their names.

With flexible production systems, the scope for occupational security will be enhanced. That does not mean that it will be realised. That will depend on the combination of appropriate forms of *collective* voice representation, coupled with *individual* opportunity. For that, basic income security and representation security will be essential – the real basis for reciprocity and societal solidarity. The representation will have to permeate the governance structures of occupations as well as companies and policy institutions. In the 1990s, a great deal of attention has been given to corporate governance and the characteristics of good firms. Remarkably little has been given to *occupational governance*. This will require more flexible forms of voice regulation than have characterised the twentieth century.

Occupational security could evolve only if there were mechanisms to reduce hierarchical administrative and managerial control and to prevent the opportunism and rent seeking inherent in occupational control in professions. There are examples of experimental structures that may point the way forward. Probably none have been unqualified successes, and to succeed they may require state intervention to overcome institutional weaknesses. The essence of the initiatives is that members – or in the currently popular jargon, *stakeholders* – construct an organisation in which complementary groups of workers *all* have a voice in the governance and structuring of the organisation, where intra-preneurship is encouraged, and where costs and benefits are shared. In this mould, there have been health collectives, community service collectives, non-governmental charity organisations and producer co-operatives. In these, there is some mutual control, to limit opportunism and to enable different groups to have access to information possessed by others in the firm, so as to give members the opportunity to rotate work tasks, if feasible or desired, and to share in control over the unit's work and development.

Lack of hierarchical control does create problems. Some observers have characterised them as *organised anarchy* (March and Olsen, 1976). There tends to be ambiguity over objectives, unstable membership, time-consuming decision-making, fuzzy evaluation and monitoring, and so on. The great question is whether these failings are inevitable, or whether the processes can be adapted to the more flexible work and production patterns that are emerging.

The good news is that there have been many cases of successful *democratic communities*, where a sense of occupation and self-control have been encouraged in an atmosphere of security. They have tended to be in niches and to be service-oriented. They have included law clinics, alternative schools, food co-operatives and community health centres. They are apparently difficult to maintain, and are subject to external pressures, such as bureaucratic requirements from state authorities and donor demands and obligations (Rothschild and Whitt, 1986). They are also subject to internal pressure to become more hierarchical. What seems essential for success is that the occupational basis of the organisation's existence must be preserved and enhanced (Jackall and Levin, 1984). Those who are skilful and occupationally good must be allowed to do what they are skilful and good at doing. 'De-professionalisation' must not be allowed to breed dilettantism or anti-intellectualism. Unless occupational skill is preserved and valued, the viability of the democratic enterprise will be undermined.

Occupational security will also require support for a more flexible lifetime system of career learning – not a whirl of short-term jobs and modules of employable skill, as captured by the image of the *flexiworker*, but a sense of progression, improving technical skill, status and craft control. One novel idea, proposed by Charles Handy (1998, p. 217) and to be applauded, is a 'university of the community', by which people could be apprenticed to a registered non-profit organisation, receiving a diploma at the end of a period of community work, which would licence them to do similar work elsewhere.

Occupational security is not a prescription for privilege for an elite or one applicable only to the educated or to those belonging to well-established professions. We all have occupations in ourselves. It is the bundle of enthusiasms, competencies and functionings that we develop. We will never have total freedom and opportunity to develop and apply those bundles. The goal should be to enable as many people as possible to pursue their own sense of occupation with security, and to enable them to benefit themselves and their communities without doing harm to others.

11.5 CITIZENSHIP WORK

Two trends in work are subversively eroding the labourist bias of the twentieth century – the legitimation of *care* and the spread of *voluntary work*. Distinctions between what counts as labour and what does not are breaking down, to the dismay of mostly male representatives of labouring man. Governments are recognising this by introducing payments for activities hitherto regarded as work but not labour.

Care work has become topical as the century of the labouring man comes to an end. This recalls the struggle in the early years of the twentieth century to enable women to undertake caring work, through 'breadwinner' or family wages, pensions for widows and single mothers, maternity leave and protection for women. That care regime made women dependent on husbands. If initial reforms mainly meant liberation from labour, in mid-century there was a two-track system, with family compensation, benefits paid to husbands and a professional care system, as part of the 'service state'. Care was an integral part of socio-economic security, in different ways in different welfares. In the era of market regulation, entitlement to care has been cut, in terms of social assistance for single mothers, maternity leave and residential and home care for the elderly (Jamieson, 1991a, b). But new forms of care have been legitimised, such as parental leave and subsidised privatised care.

Citizenship rights have omitted the need for care and the need to give care (Knijn and Kremer, 1997). Because it was domestic work, it was not recognised socially or economically. As more women have become regular labour force participants, loss of citizenship status while caring and being out of the labour force has become more transparently peculiar. To overcome the gender bias in systems of social protection, care must become a dimension of citizenship with rights equal to those received from employment.

Libertarians support the marketisation of care because purchased services widen individual choice and encourage efficient delivery. Others welcome the trends because they see them as empowering (Morris, 1993). One middle way is *vouchers*, which are attractive to governments as a means of formalising the grey labour market, thereby raising tax revenue. Although retaining a paternalistic danger to be overcome, one imagines a future in which each citizen has a voucher card, with so many points for care, so many for education, so many for basic health, so many for training, and so on.

Feminists see care as leading in two directions, towards what Nancy Fraser has called the Universal Breadwinner model, where state services are provided for day care for children so that women can go to jobs, or towards a Caregiver Parity model, legitimising and rewarding informal care work through caregiver allowances. One might say that the first is the labour line, the second the work line.

One strength of an approach that brings care work into the market economy, through allowances and so on, is that it boosts small-scale local activities and organisations, including charities and other voluntary NGOs, strengthening community and trust (Evers, 1994). The 'new volunteering' can be a means of social integration of both carers and recipients of care. The danger of most approaches taken so far is that they give insufficient attention to the issue of *control*. Three classic failings of labour must be overcome. The caregiver model could lead to carers being confined to private care roles, isolated from the public sphere. Ruth Lister (1994), in a brilliant flash, captured the problem by describing it as 'the modern variant of Wollstonecraft's dilemma'. If commodifying care merely strengthened the sexual division of labour, with women doing most of the care, it would be a form of inequality. The loneliness of the long-distance caregiver is an image of female dependency associated with social hierarchies of the worst kind. An individualised system could also lead to the *Taylorisation of care*, with individuals having to obtain licences to perform care of certain types, and restrictions based on demarcation and procedural rules.

This would prevent occupational security, and induce moral hazards. And it could intensify *self-exploitation*, in the Chayanovian sense, whereby the carer gives more time and effort than justified by the allowance because the 'gift' relationship dominates the 'market' relationship. Or it could intensify exploitation through the care recipient taking advantage of the other's labour. These dangers suggest that the care market could remain sexually and ethnically segregating.

The way to avoid these dangers must be through a mix of citizenship rights and strong voice regulation. Unless there are associations to give collective voice to carers *and* care recipients, the goal of *balanced reciprocity* could not be obtained. Intermediary associations have been springing up all over the world to fill these representation spaces, and are an exciting development. But they must give representation and other forms of security, notably work security. The dangers of stress and burn-out are extreme in care work.

There are three types of care relationship (Waerness, 1984). There are *personal services* given by a dependent person to someone in a position of financial, social or labour control. There is *caregiving work* given to those who are frail or otherwise dependent on help. And there is *spontaneous care*, where each person is equal in the eyes of the other and in their own eyes, and where there is balanced reciprocity. It is this that should be sought through policies and institutions.

In this regard, the much-used notion of *dependence* has been pernicious. Only a fool believes in full independence. In society, individuals are interdependent. The attack on 'dependency' has been a cry of the privileged throughout history. For the future, we need institutions that enhance self-control in a context of mutual dependency, which some call *fraternity* and others conviviality. The atomisation of consumer-based individualism is a pathological prescription, creating a wild west independence. When politicians and libertarians criticise 'dependency', they should be reminded that they too are dependent – we all are. We cannot work and develop occupation without others' support, and we cannot predict what support they might give, how indirect that might be, or even when we will need it. Recognition of these eternal verities is what defines the human community we call society. This is why the right to live as a human being with dignity – the right to self-respect – overrides the paternalistic reciprocity principle. What right or superior quality do I possess that I should deny you basic security in which to pursue *your* sense of occupation? This question should be addressed to paternalists and labourists everywhere.

The ways policymakers treat labour market services and care work will determine the character of society and work in the future. The issue of care raises one of the great dilemmas of the movement from a labour-based society to a work-based society. How can it be compensated in a way that does not merely provide income security while confining women, in most cases, to a lower-status, socially-excluding role? This is Ruth Lister's Wollstonecraft dilemma.

Part of this dilemma is how to pay for care. If payment were indirect, through tax credits or family-based benefits, it would be gender-segregating, and so not give citizenship rights, since it would be a family-unit entitlement, not an individual right. If care were provided directly by the state, paternalism and bureaucratic control of access, cost, inclusion and so on would come into play, with discretionary judgments all over the place. If a payment were given to the caregiver, that would strengthen individual rights, but it could produce moral hazards and monitoring problems. For instance, the carer could make the recipient dependent on the need for care, or not provide the care for which compensation is paid. The recipient would be unlikely to be in a position to 'voice regulate'. Finally, if a payment were made to the care recipient, analogous problems would arise. Often the person would not know what is required or even provided, perhaps being young, elderly or frail. So, each of the options – paying the carer, paying the cared-for, family-based benefits or tax credits, and direct public or private provision – raise distinct problems.

The trend towards cash payments represents a reduction in bureaucratic control and promotes 'welfare citizenship', by giving contractual rights (contractual justice) rather than merely procedural rights. Payment for care, although a commodification, represents legitimation of work that is not labour. The monetary payment allows more self-control in principle and reduces the drawbacks of the paternalism of social workers and professionals. It also erodes the distinction between the gift and the market economy. However, the trouble is that individuals are not equal in their bargaining position, or with respect to the information needed to make optimal decisions.

11.6 TOWARDS A STRATEGY FOR DISTRIBUTIVE JUSTICE

What would be a feasible strategy for distributive justice that placed work and occupation at the centre of society, appropriate for the flexible open economies that characterise the era of global capitalism? The sensible way forward is to erect a system based on three principles – basic income security (so that choices are made in real freedom), universal representation security (voice), and the Difference Principle (reforms are justifiable only if they improve the position of the worst-off). The objectives should be *equality of basic security* and *good opportunity*, coupled with *equal liberty for all*. If liberty comes from self-control and security, the strategy must satisfy those principles and promote *dynamic efficiency*.

Neither of the main twentieth-century models offered the prospect of all these conditions, and nor has the era of market regulation. A primary failing of state socialism was denial of liberty coupled with subordinated security, which stifled incentives and diversity. The failing of welfare state capitalism was less pronounced. It promoted liberty and security through citizenship rights and a welfare state underpinned by social protection that was never as universal as its advocates liked to believe. For a while, the norms on which it was based were *sufficiently* widespread to make the system functional and amenable to marginal extensions to cater for various other situations. That is no longer true. Above all, single-adult and single-person households have become much more common. For instance, in the Netherlands between 1975 and 1995 the number of one-person households more than doubled, and by the 1990s more than one-third of all households had only one person. Fukuyama (1997) has called this international phenomenon 'the great disruption', attributing it in part to the welfare system. The explanation is doubtful, the trend unmistakable.

Individualisation in society has accompanied individualisation in employment and more flexible, insecure labour markets. Means-tested, work-tested benefits and workfare erode liberty by regulating behaviour. Even if one dislikes the apparent sloth of one's neighbour, once policy goes down the road of directing and controlling the activity of the victims and the vulnerable, the liberty and opportunity of others will soon be threatened. Paternalism is never benign for long, since unless it carries an implicit threat of coercion, exercised from time to time, it loses credibility.

In developing an alternative strategy for distributive justice – to re-embed the economy in society and reduce insecurity – the following premises and stylised facts must be taken into account.

First, reforms must build on the recognition that the character of production and distribution is creating socio-economic *detachment*, materially and psychologically. Even to talk about *equality* is to invite disdain; even those who perceive themselves as 'progressive' feel uncomfortable about the word, in a way they would not have done in the post-1945 era. A reason – among others – is that most of those in positions of status, influence or leadership, or who anticipate being or who desire to be in such positions, feel more comfortable in being detached from the poor and disadvantaged in society than used to be the case. The tenuous solidarity between the 'middle' and 'working' classes, between 'them' and 'us', was partly an *emotional* one built on a sense of common history and social identity. Now 'we' see a fragmented, IT-driven, globalising society where more of the affluent could echo Napoleon's immortal quip, '*Je suis un parvenu*', living a trajectory that flashes by without roots or solid ties of reciprocity. The detaching character of relations of production in global capitalism undermines the sense of balanced reciprocity on which all societies have depended.

If social and economic progress are to be in step – if the economy is to be re-embedded in society – the socio-economic *distance* between groups, particularly between people as workers, must shrink. This would create the basis of solidarity, a coalition coalescing around a feasible redistributive agenda. The perception of distance has tended to preclude such a vision, and until such a coalition arises, fear will not change sides again to the extent that representatives of the privileged see egalitarian redistribution as desirable.

Second, the strategy must recognise that in a globalising, flexible economy, a growing number of jobs will not offer adequate earnings to provide a viable social income for the individual. Also, inequality is growing due to the rising returns to capital and the diminishing capacity of progressive taxation.

Third, statutory protective regulations are weakened in open flexible economies, as are traditional voice mechanisms. A system that lacks effective regulation cannot provide basic security and good opportunity. Distributive justice will depend on achieving a better balance between the forms of labour regulation (statutory, market and voice) and on reducing faith in *market regulation*, so that *statutory regulation* can more effectively establish basic standards of decency while there are adequate measures to promote *voice regulation*, which means mechanisms to enable *all* groups to put pressure on the powerful to redistribute gains of growth.

Fourth, privatisation of social policy will continue, making it likely that the selectivity will intensify insecurity and strengthen paternalistic social policy. In societies with flexible labour markets, income security cannot be provided by complex formulae and systems of entitlement based on intrusive work tests, means tests and the like. Simplicity, transparency, equity and efficiency must be the principles.

Fifth, the strategy must secure political and social legitimation. In the era of market regulation, the legitimacy of welfare state policies has been eroded, in part because an increasing proportion of the benefits has gone to the middle class, because the drift to selective, conditional schemes has revived the distinction between the 'deserving' and 'undeserving' poor, because selectivity reduces the constituency identifying with particular schemes, and because increased conditionality has resulted in stigmatisation and what might be called *distributive justice failure*, due to large numbers of those who should be entitled being excluded or not reached.

Sixth, the strategy must facilitate flexibility, and above all promote *lifestyle work flexibility*. In this regard, it should take account of the limitations of *statutory working-time reductions*, which in practice means primarily cutting hours in paid jobs. Ironically, this is proposed as a means of generating employment – reducing some people's as a means of increasing others'. There may be reasons for cutting hours, but since some would want to work longer for more income, the policy could lead to restrictions on long workweeks, leading to rigidities, coercion and even punitive taxes.

As a response to unemployment, working time reductions would have little effect in part because part-time working has spread already. The likelihood is that substantial cuts in working time would lead more of those in regular jobs to take additional part-time jobs. If those in regular jobs have, on average, more skills and contacts than the unemployed, cutting working time could actually increase the unequal distribution of paid employment. And if working hours were cut, whose hours would be targeted? It is hard to cut the working time of many professional and salaried workers, because they need to work intensively to stay in touch with technical and social developments. Labouring part time is not without costs in a system oriented to full-time participation. If it were the working time of manual workers that were cut – and this is the image – anything less than full wage compensation would worsen income inequality.

None of this means that cutting time spent in labour is undesirable. Liberation *from* labour remains a legitimate objective in so far as it is compatible with an increase in personal autonomy, or *self* control, and as long as it is accompanied by an improvement in income security. The challenge is to find ways of enabling people to adjust their working time flexibly according to their needs and workstyles, without endangering the survival or dynamic efficiency of firms in which they work.

Bearing these premises in mind, the principle that must underlie any feasible redistributive strategy is that it should enhance personal security and allow a social sharing of the proceeds of technological advance and capital, while promoting an ecologically and socially sustainable rate of economic growth based on adequate incentives to work, save and invest. In the following sections, three complementary policy *directions* are considered, which together offer a feasible strategy for distributive justice based on the principles and objectives stated earlier.

(i) The Right to Income Security: Citizenship Income

A decent provision for the poor is the true test of civilisation.
Dr Johnson

... the plan we are advocating amounts essentially to this: that a certain small income, sufficient for necessaries, should be secured to all, whether they work or not, and that a larger income – as much larger as might be warranted by the total amount of commodities produced – should be given to those who are willing to engage in some work which the community recognises as useful. On this basis we may build further.
Bertrand Russell, 1918

If one accepts that a Good Society must involve greater self-control, security and good opportunity to pursue occupation, then basic income security would be a necessary condition. The challenge is to find a feasible way of providing this for everybody in society. The idea that everybody should receive a basic citizenship income as a *right* has a long history. Some find it in Thomas More's *Utopia*. It certainly guided Thomas Paine in his *Rights of Man*. Since then it has attracted philosophers, prominent economists, religious thinkers, and others. It has also had its critics from across the spectrum. In the twentieth century, advocates owe much to Denis Milner, who elaborated a scheme during the First World War, and passed on ideas to economists such as James Meade and political scientists such as G.D.H. Cole (van Trier, 1996). Since the early 1980s, a considerable literature has grown up, which we will not try to summarise.[1] Supporters in recent times have included those from the political left and from the right.[2]

In a sense, all countries that ratify the United Nations' *Universal Declaration of Human Rights* are committed to the principle. Article 40 of the Declaration is clear:

> Everyone has the right to a standard of living adequate for the health and well-being of himself and his family, including food, clothing, housing and medical care and the necessary social services, and the right to security in the event of unemployment, sickness, disability, widowhood, old age or other lack of livelihood in circumstances beyond his control.

Others have found their own ethical justification. In the following, the basic proposal is stated, followed by a review of the standard objections and primary advantages. Before turning to the specifics, it is worth recalling Albert Hirschman's perceptive assessment of the reaction to every progressive idea (Hirschman, 1991). He observed that there are claims of *futility*, that is, that it would be ineffectual, *jeopardy*, that it would endanger other goals or accomplishments, and *perversity*, that is, it would have unintended consequences that would undermine the benefits. This sequence of objections has been the common reaction to proposals that everyone should be provided with a basic income, even among those who vehemently proclaim that poverty should be combated by all means possible.

The long-term objective should be to establish a *right* to a basic income for every individual, regardless of work status, marital status, age or other income. It would be given as an *individual right*. It would not require any past or present labour performance, nor would it be made conditional on any labour commitment. The thrust of the idea is to give income security that is not based on class or labouring status but on *citizenship*. It would give income security based not on judgmental decisions about 'deserving' and 'undeserving' behaviour or status, merely on the need for, and right to, basic security. However, it would be a modest security, so as to give incentives for work and for *sustainable risk-taking*.

Before considering the pros and cons, *two important caveats* should be emphasised. A citizenship income must not be understood as a panacea. It is only part of a redistributive strategy that would be consistent with globalisation and flexible product and labour markets. Without other components, it would be ineffectual. And one should think of *moving in the direction* of citizenship income security, not imagining that such a scheme could be introduced overnight. Only crises such as war or a depression facilitate such a radical shift. We should think of gentler ways forward.

Citizenship is the unifying principle of society, and for real citizenship ordinary people must be able to impose order on chaos, as the novelist Norberto Bobbio has put it, which requires that insecurity be limited. To strengthen citizenship is to help in the institutionalisation of tolerance. A citizenship income would be a means of strengthening the sense of citizenship. If social policy is a tool of democracy, as it should be, a citizenship income would help strengthen the democratic basis of society.

One moral justification, with a long and distinguished pedigree, is that we all have an equal right to the inheritance of social progress. Paine, with his *Agrarian Justice*, written in 1795, was one of the earliest proponents of a minimum income as a right of citizenship. This went forward into the welfare proposals in the *Rights of Man*. He argued that property is an acquired, not a natural, right. His religious argument was that the earth was jointly owned by all, given as a 'garden' rather than something to cultivate for a land-owning elite. For Paine, the fruits of property should be shared through entitling everyone to an adequate income.

At the time of Paine, a person doing hard work would have earned about 4 per cent of the average real earnings in the USA today, implying that about 96 per cent of the increase in earnings over the two centuries has been attributable to historical inheritance of technological development. Who has the right to the inherited contributions to technological knowledge? Take Bill Gates, with a fortune of $9 billion in 1995, about $20 billion in 1996, over $40 billion in 1997 and $50 billion by March 1998, and over $90 billion in early 1999. As someone put it, he made a pebble of a contribution to a Gibraltar of technology. Yet he put the touches to a long process which turned the product into a money-spinner, such that his income was multiplying to such an extent that by the late 1990s not only was he the richest person in the world but his income was growing almost exponentially.[3] Paine, and his followers, would have regarded it a matter of social justice that everybody should have shared in the fruits of technological progress, particularly as applied to the productivity of land. This is the *inheritance* justification of citizenship income.

Another moral justification is the claim, which has preoccupied some philosophers, that citizens have a right to *equal liberty* to pursue their life plans, as long as they do not harm others. Another argument, undeveloped so far, is that the objective of policy should be equalisation of *basic security* and *self-control*. Without those, there can be no equal *basic opportunity*, which Rawls and other philosophers have accepted as the basis of social justice.

Another attractive perspective is that it accords to a view of justice that behind a *veil of ignorance* and through deliberation ordinary people are likely to find reasonable. The methodological difficulty is finding a way of achieving those conditions. One important analysis achieved this (Frohlich and Oppenheimer, 1992). It set out to determine what principle of distributive justice people would support through a series of social laboratory experiments. It put groups of people together behind a *veil of ignorance* in that they were not informed of the task in advance, were told they would not know where they would be in the spectrum of income distribution, and were requested to decide collectively which principle of distributive justice they supported. They were given four options:

(1)   setting a floor constraint (an income below which citizens could not go);
(2)   the Rawlsian Difference Principle (maximising the lowest income);
(3)   maximising average income;
(4)   setting a range constraint (a range for individual incomes).

The experiments were carried out across Canada and the USA, and covered people with different backgrounds and values. Overall, 78 per cent chose the floor constraint. The authors concluded that the choices emerged from deliberation, discussion and the exercise of impartial reasoning induced by the experimental conditions. The floor constraint was the only principle that gained support as discussion proceeded. This leads to a point relevant to a later proposal. The institutional arrangement contributed to the strengthening of support for a principle of justice. In effect, the *voice mechanism* makes a difference to the *choice* of a principle of distributive justice. A sensible deduction is that if the institution represents a narrow interest, it would tend to opt for a competitive stance to secure more for its group, whereas a broader association that brought in the community's voices – of the street, of the fields and of the homes as well as of the factories and offices – would bind round the floor constraint principle *and* the Difference Principle, the latter being more relevant for structural *change*. Indeed, lack of support for the Difference Principle in the Frohlick–Oppenheimer study could be explained by this and the fact that the participants were asked to select *one* fundamental principle of justice.

Another finding was that once the veil of ignorance was removed, so that individuals were allowed to opt for whatever principle they wished once they could take account of the fact that they would not be direct beneficiaries of the floor constraint, a majority still opted for that principle. The authors concluded that 'the source of the stability seems to be far less individualistic; it seems rather to be the result of the emergence of the social acceptance and bonding engendered in the discussion and choice'.

In the light of these considerations, the position proposed here is that a basic citizenship income is justifiable on the basis of two principles, subject to three constraints. The first, well-known Equal Opportunity Principle is:

> EOP: Each person should have equal opportunity to pursue a conception of the good life.

The second might be called the Occupational Security Principle:

> OSP: Each individual should have an equally good opportunity to pursue his or her idea of occupation.

The three constraints are what might be called the Non-Harm Constraint, the Sustainability Constraint, and the Incentives Constraint:

> NHC: The rights under EOP and OSP are conditional on the activities not doing harm to the welfare or good opportunity of others.

> SC: The Citizenship Income giving OSP should not impair the sustainable living standards of the community.

> IC: The Citizenship Income should allow for adequate incentives to work, save and invest.

This summarises the rationale for a citizenship income. Criticisms can be split into moral, political and economic. The main moral objection is the claim that people should receive income only if they make a corresponding *contribution* to society, usually interpreted to mean paid labour. Some deny that a citizenship income would be socially just because it would deny the principle of reciprocity (see, e.g., White, 1997). A lazy person would receive income that would come from income generated by a person who 'works' and 'contributes' to society. Benefits should be matched by contributions. This they see as linked to the principle of opportunity, which should guide 'individual responsibility'. As Gutmann and Thompson (1996, p. 279) put it, '... To demand income but to refuse to work is to make a claim on one's fellow citizens that they may reasonably reject...'

Leaving aside the questionable words 'demand', 'refuse' and 'claim', consider this proposition dispassionately. Throughout history, society has allowed and legitimised non-reciprocity, and has functioned deliberately on the basis of non-reciprocity. The ancient Greeks had leisure and income and freedom for themselves, rather less for their slaves; feudal societies have rested on landlords and their kin receiving high incomes without conspicuous work from them; capitalism has always existed with a leisured elite, with vicarious consumption by relatives of the affluent (memorably evaluated by Thorsten Veblen), and with inherited wealth and the transfer of valuable gifts that have no relationship whatsoever to the individual 'contribution' of the recipient (except in cases connected with age, beauty or some such quality). Gutmann and Thompson, and others taking their position, condemn unconditional income for the poor but are silent on the wider ramifications of applying the supposed principle of reciprocity, particularly to those who inherit wealth or are provided with privileged access to elite schooling. Is there not something unseemly about preaching the reciprocity principle – telling the poor that to be entitled to poverty-level benefits they must meet objectionable obligations – when the top 1 per cent of the citizens are receiving more than the bottom 40 per cent put together, or when the 400 richest people in society have a net worth equal to the combined GNP of India, Bangladesh, Nepal and Sri Lanka, as has recently been the case in the USA?

If one were to apply the reciprocity principle consistently, one should be drawn to Paine's justification for an unconditional basic income – what might be called the *social inheritance principle*, that everybody should have an equal share of the economic surplus generated by past generations. This is associated with the argument of Herbert Spencer (1851) for a universal endowment derived from each person's right to a fair share of the natural resources (or land). That runs into other difficulties, to be considered shortly, but it is more distributively just than a policy of requiring the poor to labour in return for a modest benefit while not requiring others to do anything in return for receiving a much higher income.

Gutmann and Thompson's position is also unclear about what counts as 'work'. This was raised in connection with workfare. A person might believe that for the long-term pursuit of occupation and personal development, a part-time wage job coupled with home-based unpaid work and study, coupled with voluntary community work and caring for dependants, might be beneficial for a while. One suspects that such a course of action would be condemned by the labourist for not making a contribution, ruling out the person from entitlement to an income transfer from the state. If not, then one must accept that any line between what is deemed 'work' and what is not will be arbitrary. It is surely preferable to err on the side of liberty rather than on the side of paternalism.

What divides those who support a citizenship income and many of those who oppose it is the labourist bias. On the one side are those who, citing the reciprocity principle, argue that there should be entitlement to income security only based on social insurance (the rest is charity). This means that, except for the incapacitated, only labour counts, so that one only 'earns' entitlement if one pays taxes, in the past (pensions), recently (unemployment benefits, etc.) or in the near future (youth labour force entrants). Non-taxpaying work does not count. On the other side are those who believe that there are many forms of work besides paid labour, and that it is unjust to give income security only to those in jobs. Most of those doing labour could not survive without the unpaid work of carers, most of whom are women. The economic value of such work is enormous.[4] Yet social insurance rests on the premise that such work is worthless and undeserving of *income entitlement*. Not only housework is excluded from the labourist calculus. There is also the vast amount of social, political and community service work done in all societies.

A few words about the *timing* of reciprocity might also show the labourist bias. Implicitly, those who cite the 'reciprocity principle' have in mind that anybody wanting a state transfer should labour *now* in return for income *later*. Purely on their own terms, there should be nothing to stop the rule being reversed, so that people could receive income *now* for the promise of labour, or the stated intention to perform labour, *later*. If one accepts this reversibility rule as inherent to a fair principle of reciprocity, then one must deal with the nature of the underlying bargain. Since one cannot foresee all circumstances that might prevent desired behaviour from becoming actual behaviour, some labourists might reject the reversibility rule on grounds of uncertainty. Thus, the paternalism would show itself more openly.

A related argument against an unconditional basic income is the following:

> Citizens who decline to work are in effect refusing to participate in a scheme of fair social co-operation that is necessary to sustain any adequate policy of income support. Society's capacity to secure a basic income for needy citizens depends on economic productivity, and economic productivity depends in turn on citizens' willingness to work. (Gutman and Thompson, 1996, pp. 279–80)

All the familiar objections come to mind about the *type*, *timing* and *amount* of 'work'. But in addition, this presumes the existence of a 'scheme of fair co-operation'. If one accepts that most people are denied self-control, as chapter 2 argued, one might question the fairness of whatever 'scheme' is supposed to characterise society. If a growing proportion of the population, through no fault of their own, are exposed to unchosen insecurity, then fairness and social co-operation cannot be strong. In the *fragmentation* that flexible labour markets and open economies generate, co-operation is weaker than in the *solidaristic* society presumed at the height of welfare state capitalism or, in its more warped form, in state socialism. It is also more asymmetrical. While the poor are supposed to labour in dreary jobs, in return for modest, conditional, contingent protection, elites and others detached at the upper end of the income and status spectrum receive the protection that they need to live comfortably and to retain their income and wealth, even if some do not contribute to the 'economic productivity' of the country in which they reside. How could one mention reciprocity without tongue in cheek if vast subsidies were being given to corporations and affluent individuals to attract them to the country, and if taxes were being cut on higher-income groups and on capital on grounds of expediency, i.e., that if they were taxed more than the international norm they would move abroad?

In short, a basic income would in a small way compensate for the economic and technological requirements of an 'unfair scheme of economic co-operation'.

Gutmann and Thompson (1996, p. 280), adopting the image originally proposed by John Rawls, argue that if citizens 'choose to spend their life surfing at Malibu, they cannot reasonably expect their fellow citizens to support them'. Among the responses to this is that all who live affluently benefit from the work of previous generations, who have created the infrastructure and technology to enable them to live well, so that everybody should have the *opportunity* to live better through working and earning higher income. Those who receive a basic income might find it impossible to live the multi-dimensional existence of good opportunity for occupation if they chose to dissipate their youth in surfing or reading books. However, it is not demonstrably true that doing either of these apparently leisurely pursuits is more undeserving and exploitative than working in an office making tea for the boss or doing some other labour activity that would presumably count as 'contributing' to society.

Moreover, some of the great contributions to social, artistic and technological progress have come from individuals who have dissipated their youth or idled away a period of their life. This is not to justify this or any other lifestyle, merely to question the legitimacy of making any a priori judgment about what is or is not 'deserving'. It is to oppose the paternalistic twitch.

In discussing workfare, we had to confront the issue of 'obligations', and criticised the libertarian view that the poor had definable obligations. Defining the collective obligations of the state has exercised the minds of many social thinkers. One approach has been to suggest that we (the collective) are responsible for those who are *vulnerable* to our actions (Goodin, 1985). Given the increased technological and social integration of society, people in general have become more dependent on, and therefore vulnerable to, the actions of others. Dependence relations have become more abstract and distant, giving rise to 'secondary responsibilities', which can only be discharged by the welfare state. If we define vulnerability in terms of socio-economic *participation*, it leads to a familiar justification of the welfare state:

> If full participation in our societies is conditional upon a person's being a minimally independent agent, then morally we must not only serve the needs of those who are dependent upon us but also do what we can to render those persons independent ... [The welfare state] secures for them the sort of minimal independence that is required for them to participate in the other market and quasi-market sectors of their society. (Goodin, 1988, p. 183)

Not any more. The drift to selectivity and workfare precludes that. Indeed the reasoning is a good justification of moving towards basic income security. It justifies *protecting* the vulnerable and *preventing* vulnerability.

Another justice-based argument against the labourist fiction of reciprocity is that liberty and justice require opportunity for pursuit of *occupation*. If the economy does not provide enough good opportunities for that, it seems more reasonable to compensate those denied the opportunity rather than to penalise them. Unless one could be sure that there were an adequate number of good opportunities, some people must be excluded. Anybody objecting to that reasoning on the grounds that it is vague should be reminded of the extraordinary vagueness of the proponents of 'obligations' and 'reciprocity'.

There is another justification for maintaining the principle of *good* opportunity. Only then would there be adequate pressure for the bundle of characteristics of actual jobs to change towards opportunity for the pursuit of occupation. If a woman can refuse to labour for a very low wage in an onerous job in unsociable hours, such jobs will disappear or their character will be changed or the wages will rise until some workers find the characteristics attractive enough to take that type of job. Changing the characteristics of jobs into those compatible with the pursuit of occupation should be a social objective, instead of forcing people to take the most unattractive dead-end jobs because of penury.[5]

The *economic* objections to a citizenship income have been that it would be too costly and would undermine the labour market by reducing labour supply. The issue of cost can be answered in several ways. One could refer to priorities, and argue that if the egalitarian principle is accepted the policy should be given sufficiently high priority in the allocation of public resources. Another is to consider the feasibility of converting existing social transfers into a basic income, or a partial basic income with needs-based supplements, keeping tax rates constant. Calculations done in several European countries have shown that one could introduce a partial basic income instead of social assistance and insurance-based benefits without having to raise taxes (Parker, 1989). Such calculations are actually too onerous, since they ignore the potential of altering labour market behaviour favourably. If means testing and behavioural regulations were reduced, poverty traps, unemployment traps and mobility traps would be reduced, so more people would be encouraged to enter the legitimate economy, thereby generating more tax revenue, through social contributions and taxes. Further cost-saving would come from a reduced need to 'police' the poor, reducing the practice of checking to see if they 'deserve' income support, so reducing the public cost of a huge administrative service. These issues should be taken into account, as should the cost of the subsidies given to firms to create 'jobs' as a means of reducing state transfers.

An ingenious way of approaching the costing issue has been proposed by Philippe Van Parijs (1995, 1997), who has argued that the Equal Opportunity Principle implies that each person is entitled to an equal share of external wealth, which can be equated with an unconditional basic income. The external wealth for the tax base for financing a basic income consists of natural resources, private bequests and inheritances and 'jobs'. His argument for including 'jobs' is that they are assets, in that they are in short supply and determine chances of a good life. There will always be involuntary unemployment, because some of the unemployed would be prepared to work for less than the prevailing wage, which is above the market-clearing level, due to efficiency considerations and turnover costs that firms want to avoid. If there is involuntary unemployment, those in jobs receive an *employment rent*, which should be included in the tax base for financing a basic income. One might object to the 'jobs assets' perspective, in that many jobs are not chosen and are not compatible with occupation. Nevertheless, those who regard jobs as the source of welfare and midfare should accept that a tax on jobs (supposedly a privilege) to compensate those denied the privilege could help to pay for a citizenship income. If one accepts that jobs are assets, this reasoning has much to commend it.

Other costing exercises begin by postulating a suitable basic income and then estimating what income tax rate would be required to pay for it. Excellent research has been done in this vein in Ireland (Clark and Healy, 1997; Ward, 1994; O'Toole, 1995). This concluded that a realistic basic income could be financed if the average and marginal rate of income tax was 48 per cent. A former *Taoiseach* (Prime Minister), Garret FitzGerald, welcomed the findings and concluded that obstacles to change were political rather than fiscal (FitzGerald, 1997). In the UK, Meghnad Desai (1997), drawing on work by Holly Sutherland, has estimated that if a citizenship income were introduced instead of Job Seekers' Allowance (unemployment benefits), the State Pension, Income Support and Family Credit, leaving other state benefits unaltered, a basic income of £50 a week could be financed with a standard income tax rate of 35 per cent. Not only is it affordable at this rate, but it is moderately progressive, in that the primary beneficiaries would be those households in the bottom decile, with more moderate gains for those in the next three deciles, while the highest income decile would be the loser, albeit only moderately.

Two aspects not taken into account in such exercises mean that the costs are overstated. A citizenship income would save on administrative costs because it would simplify the complex schemes, make them more transparent and reduce the amount of intrusive enquiry. And it would reduce poverty and unemployment traps (to be discussed later), thereby inducing greater labour supply and encouraging those involved in the grey economy to enter the legal, tax-paying mainstream of society.

The cost issue is also related to the view that a citizenship income is an appropriate redistributive instrument for the era. In many countries, it could be linked to privatisation. Thus, although it might appear that a basic income for eastern Europe would be impossible because of the economic decline and stagnation, the scope for moving in that direction may exist because social expenditure is still a high share of GDP, and is still legitimised, and because there is a windfall gain to be realised by the state through 'privatisation', providing income that could be used in part to enable the state to honour a form of social compact.

One criticism is that it would conflict with a *minimum wage*. Indeed, some have vehemently opposed the idea because they claim it would lead to less pressure to secure an adequate minimum wage. But a basic income would strengthen pressures to raise wages at the lower end of the labour market, since it would help those exposed to low wages to resist with more strength. In any case, there is nothing to rule out having a minimum wage *and* a citizenship income. As for reducing the pressure for a minimum wage, in recent years there has been rather little pressure, to little effect.

A related argument concerns social insurance, since some commentators have depicted citizen's income as an *alternative* to social insurance. There is no reason for this to be the case, although social insurance *in practice* has not been providing protection to the poor and vulnerable. The counter-argument is that since a basic income would provide the poor with modest income security, it would strengthen their ability to bargain or hold out for more reasonable wages.

Another advantage is that it would enable some to take low-paying jobs that were low paying because the activity was low productivity or because the person had only limited capacity to be productive (perhaps due to age or disability). Wages should be a labour market issue, concerned with efficiency, incentives, demand and supply. The only way for wages to be adequately protected is through collective voice in the labour market coupled with sufficient income security to enable people to make choices. In any case, a citizenship income could allow for greater wage flexibility, if that were required to raise employment or for other reasons, and it was for that reason that just before he died the Nobel Laureate James Meade (1994) advocated a basic income coupled with wage flexibility to achieve Full Employment.

Another criticism is one raised by Lawrence Mead, which has had a pervasive influence in the 1990s. He decried US welfare programmes because they gave benefits without expecting much in return, which he claimed eroded the individual's will, inducing apathy and incompetence, which is why he favoured workfare. While his thesis has been criticised on empirical grounds, it suffers from theoretical shortcomings as well. There is no reason to *presume* that a transfer giving modest unconditional income would induce apathy and incompetence. Indeed, by giving people more self-confidence that comes from a sense of basic security it may do precisely the opposite.

Another criticism is that 'young people might be encouraged to opt for a basic income and to drop out of school prematurely and uncertificated' (Adriaansens and Dercksen, 1993, p. 201). However, rather than a drawback, this may be an advantage, since it would focus decision-making on the quality of schooling. It would encourage firms to make entry-level jobs more attractive, rather than dull and alienating as so many of the available jobs must be for potential drop-outs from schools. It is paternalistic to presume that people should be discouraged from dropping out of school rather than to make schooling more attractive, and to make it easier for the poor to attend and complete school.

Some supporters of basic income worry about the likelihood of it generating sufficient support to make it politically feasible. Among the concerns are the following. People are attached to social insurance; many would fear they would lose from a shift towards a basic income; 'loafers', the idle and 'surfers' should not be subsidised; tax rates would have to be too high; the change would be too radical to be feasible; and the civil service responsible for administering the existing tax-cum-welfare system would oppose the change because it would threaten its size and security.

Some of these arguments are variants of Hirschmann's predicted reactions to all progressive ideas. Some we have discussed already, and some are practical matters that would have to be resolved politically. The major obstacle is political – politicians and others are reluctant to dispense with the comforting rationalisation of social insurance, that it is a system for matching risks and benefits, and are reluctant to move away from the superficially appealing idea of 'targeting' through means testing. They will continue to resort to the slogan that nobody should receive something for nothing. Partial moves in the direction of a citizen's income are all that one could reasonably expect in the near future. This was recognised by early advocates of the French *Revenue Minimum d'Insertion* and by those making similar proposals in the Netherlands and elsewhere.[6]

One criticism is that it would be impractical to shift to a citizenship income because it would be too radical for people to accept. Some proponents argue that it would not be introduced at once, and could be introduced as a *partial basic income* or by gradually loosening the conditionality for income security. In some respects, tax and benefit reforms in the 1980s and 1990s, such as the US EITC and the UK's Family Credit, have been creating elements for such a system. In Alaska, they have launched such a scheme, with remarkable success. And in several industrialising economies, such as Brazil and Argentina, pilot schemes have been introduced that are seen by their advocates as steps towards an unconditional citizenship income.[7]

One bloc that, with exceptions, has traditionally opposed the idea is the trade union movement, as was apparent during the Kreisky Commission hearings in the 1980s. However, unions are changing, and the influx of more women and the growing concern for women's work patterns within unions have begun to change this attitude. For instance, unions in the Netherlands have taken a more constructive attitude to basic income in part because the independent Women's Federation, part of the Dutch Trade Unions (FNV), has been interested, as has the Food Workers' Union, which has openly supported the proposal.

Another worry, sometimes expressed by supporters of traditional unions, is that an unconditional income would sever the solidarity between the employed and those dependent on income transfers from the state (Coenen, 1993, p. 185). Associated with this is the view that the income differential between those in jobs and the unemployed *should* be large, so that labour receives a 'proper' reward. This is the reaction of those who wish to control workers and reflects a paternalism that is atavistic and inappropriate for the type of flexible economy that is emerging.

A common claim is that it would subsidise voluntary unemployment. This is argued from the 'left' and the 'right' (Elster, 1986). One response is that many work activities other than paid labour are socially valuable and should be legitimised in a civilised society. Another is that involvement in learning, training or recuperation, may be just as 'productive' in the longer term as paid labour, for the individual and the community. Above all, there is evidence that in industrialised economies, a majority of people *want* to work, and express the opinion that they would wish to continue to do so even if they had an assured income. In the British Social Attitude Surveys, for instance, about three of every four respondents responded positively to the question: if without having to work you had what you would regard as a reasonable income, do you think you would still prefer to have a paid job or wouldn't you bother?

Between 1984 and 1993, the proportion responding positively increased (Hedges, 1994). Some have interpreted this as supporting Full Employment while claiming that a basic income would undermine the desire to work. This is inconsistent. In fact, it suggests that a basic income would *not* undermine the desire to work.

The strongest argument in favour of moving towards a basic income is that it would provide a basis for free choice on activity mixes between productive and reproductive activities. If one is optimistic about human aspirations and behaviour, freedom of choice will lead to more skill acquisition and more creative and productive endeavour, rather than 'loafing'. Basic income security would lessen the tendency to ignore social costs or environmental considerations in the pursuit of employment. There would be less resistance to closure of obsolescent, polluting factories and machinery, often kept going solely to protect costly jobs. It would also make 'an ecological critique of industrialism more affordable' (Offe, 1993, p. 228).

To some, a basic income seems so radical that it is impractical to advocate it. However, in a piecemeal way fiscal and transfer policy has been moving in that direction, particularly with the US EITC and moves toward a negative income tax. The labourist intentions of tax credits or wage subsidies, and their limitations, make them questionable as liberating and redistributive instruments in an era of growing flexibility. However, they have established a fiscal basis for moving towards a citizenship income. Opposition will soften as it is realised that the elements for such a system are taking shape. Tax credits are a negative income tax; the spread of wage subsidies bolsters the low-paid. The main remaining condition is labour. Why should those who do low-productivity, low-status jobs receive a tax credit (payment) when those doing voluntary social work, caring and so on do not receive anything?

The main motivations for tax credits have been to induce people to shift from reliance on benefits, or to 'make work pay' for low-earning families, and to strengthen the family unit. That still leaves the benefits system dualistic in character, with measures for those out of employment and measures for those in employment. Moving towards a basic income would reduce this dualism.

A citizenship income might also reduce gender inequality. Under existing selective systems, women tend to receive less and have greater difficulty in obtaining entitlement to benefits. An individualised system of citizenship income would remove this inequitable form of gender inequality.

A basic income would strengthen the right to work, while weakening the obligation to labour. It could give substance to the notion to 'freely chosen' employment, and both recognise and encourage work-related activities that are socially and personally 'useful' without being conventional employment. Some advocates of a citizenship income, such as Tony Atkinson, recognise the difficulty of obtaining legitimacy by proposing a *participation income guarantee*, where in return for a basic income every adult should agree to participate in society.[8] This seems reasonable, although what is intended is suitably broad – paid employment, self-employment, education, training, caring for dependants, old-age or disability retirement and job-seeking unemployment. It would be difficult to define what constitutes social participation without being arbitrary and inequitable. By all means let us express the idea in terms of participation, since it opens up the debate on what constitutes work in flexible labour markets of the twenty-first century. It would make it easier to legitimise politically, as long as safeguards were biased towards liberty and security, rather than paternalism and social control. And the rule should apply to everybody, so that the poor and rich had an obligation to perform some community or voluntary work, not just the poor.

With or without a participation component, a basic income could limit the growth of the detached stratum, or 'underclass'. It would improve social integration by reducing the stigma associated with being 'out of employment'. It would also give income to those performing types of work other than those counted as labour. Millions of women (mostly) spend much of their lives as carers. Unpaid, they save the state and employers part of their labour costs, in providing a back-up part of social income. If the imputed cost were added to existing social expenditure, the net cost of a basic income would be further reduced.

A citizenship income would also reduce the state's directive role in regulating economic and social behaviour. It would be a blow against bureaucratic paternalism. It would facilitate personal experimentation with work, allowing people more security in which to take risks. It would also be a defensive measure against the 'welfare backlash'. The challenge is to find ways of mobilising an alliance of social and economic interests to support this move.

It would also put pressure on enterprises to improve work organisation, because by giving greater income security it would strengthen the position of those demanding better working conditions. It would tilt the balance in favour of better working conditions, since employers of low-paid labour would be encouraged to improve the attractiveness of jobs, as they would have to attract workers rather than rely on financial necessity.

One reason for favouring an individual citizenship income is the *individualisation* of economic and social relationships. The share of single-person households has grown almost everywhere. Most welfare state policies have been based on a nuclear family household. Because of social diversity, administration of social policy has become increasingly complex and discretionary. A couple receives less than two individuals, so that there is a moral hazard, giving a premium to those living separately or to those who can appear to be living separately. A household-based welfare system paradoxically encourages single parenting, which incurs extra social expenditure. For instance, in 1997 a single unemployed person in the UK received about £48 per week with an extra £30 for an 'adult dependent' (husband or wife). Thus the couple would have been better off by £18 if they had separated.

No other system offers the prospect of removing poverty in flexible labour markets. We have seen that social protection has drifted towards *selectivity*, more conditions for securing and maintaining entitlement, more conditions applied to the period after entitlement has been established, tighter definitions of categories 'at risk', a greater policing character in the application of conditions, greater onus of proof of entitlement placed on potential claimants, more intrusive policing of 'scroungers', more scope for discretionary judgments by local officials, more cost or barriers to appeal against disentitlement. If one accepts that these trends are what has been happening, one should ask whether the existing system is compatible with security, freedom or self-control. It is intrusive, paternalistic, directive and inegalitarian.

Reducing means-tested benefits could also check the growing 'illegality' of economic activity. If, as is the case for many people in the late-1990s, the poor can only avoid high tax rates by working in informal activities, and can retain entitlement to state benefits only through concealment of such activities, then the base of the welfare state will continue to shrink. A citizenship income would be consistent with flexible labour relations, where avoidance of the appearance of income earning is easier, tax evasion more likely, and so on. This is not a marginal issue. A report by the European Commission in 1998 estimated that undeclared jobs accounted for up to 16 per cent of the EU's GNP, and over 20 per cent in some countries. Overall, it may account for over 20 million 'jobs' or 15 per cent of EU 'employment' (Smith, 1998). The bureaucratic instinct is to condemn this as the 'black economy' and to try to prevent it.

A CI would reduce the poverty trap and unemployment trap. These have become more important in flexible labour markets, in the context of the drift to means-tested transfers, notably those based on the household as the tax-paying, benefit-receiving unit. As shown in the first part of Figure 11.1, means testing entails high marginal rates of tax on the income of the poor, which create poverty traps and encourage growth of the shadow economy.[9] The horizontal axis measures gross income before tax, the vertical axis measures income net of tax. Once a person enters the wage system, he loses heavily. So, if an unemployed worker relying on insurance-based, earnings-related benefits were to take a part-time job, loss of unemployment benefits and means-tested supplements could mean that he would face a 'tax' rate of up to 100 per cent or even higher, implying that he would be irrational to take such work. It is to overcome such circumstances that officials resort to the regulatory stick, through workfare, 'job refusal' tests for entitlement to benefits, or other measures.

However, two alternative options are available. The middle part of Figure 11.1 shows the negative income tax, due to Milton Friedman in 1962, which has guided the development of earned-income tax credits. Below the crossover, the 'tax unit' receives an income subsidy, which tapers as earned income rises until it starts to pay tax. This removes the worst of the poverty trap. However, it has the drawbacks of being household-family-based, being paid after the accounting has been done (so being received after the need has arisen) and only going to those in income-earning activity. A basic income would achieve the same result except that it would avoid those three drawbacks. This is shown in the third part of the diagram, in which everybody receives a basic gross income and is taxed proportionately on *all* earned income.

Even a partial basic income must have a liberating effect on labour market behaviour, encouraging mobility, more varied lifestyles, combinations of part-time jobs and own-account work, and periods of training interspersed with partial labour force participation. Whereas advocates of workfare and 'active' labour

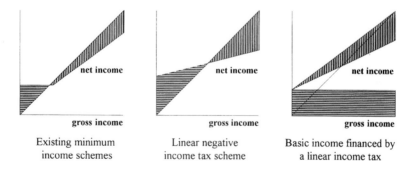

| Existing minimum income schemes | Linear negative income tax scheme | Basic income financed by a linear income tax |

Figure 11.1 Alternative income support schemes

A Citizenship Credit Card

Social protection is under strain. The desire to cut public spending and improve efficiency has led to targeting, selectivity, rationing of benefits, privatisation, multi-tierism, a shift in the incidence of contributions, user fees and a remonetisation of welfare. The administration of all this has been enormously expensive, with much churning of taxes and benefits, with form filling, a vast amount of paper work and auditing. Meanwhile, electronic technology has created the potential for an *integrated* system. Movement in this direction is accelerating, with the French *Carte Sante*, the German *Versichertenkarten*, and the US Federal Electronic Benefit Transfer Task Force, set up at the initiative of Vice-President Al Gore.

This could lead to a **citizenship welfare card**. Everybody would have individual needs-based entitlements to different social benefits and services on top of a basic amount for their self-determined basic living needs, which they could spend each month as and when they chose.

Something like this will happen before the twenty-first century is very old. Thoughts about the implications should start sooner. This shift to citizenship welfare will require **advisory voice mechanisms**, to represent the low-income and ill-informed groups so that they can make rational decisions. The basic credit must be allied to voice to produce just outcomes.

---

market policy speak of integration and obligations, and rely on directive regulations and sanctions against those who do not wish to accept the options offered them by kindly employment exchange officials, a citizenship income would rely on incentives and opportunities to strengthen socio-economic integration. Liberty would gain, paternalism would not.

A CI would help transform one outgrowth of the labourist society – the notion that life is split into three parts – school, work, and retirement – and that idleness by those over age 60 is a sensible norm, while idleness at any other age is deplorable (lazy, irresponsible, anti-social). Many older people want to work and are blocked or discouraged from doing so, whereas many younger people would like 'to parent' or to study or to idle for a while, but cannot do so for fear of stigmatisation.

One way of moving towards a CI would be through a system of *social drawing rights*. This would give all citizens a personalised account of entitlements. Individuals could build up their SDRs through participating in school (n points for each year attended, perhaps), community work, paid employment, care, voluntary service (overseas or in the local community), which would give them rights to income or leave from work (*sabbaticalisation*). This relates to Gosta Rehn's idea of a *time bank,* although it should also have points for disability, for childbearing, and so on (Rehn, 1977). It would be a form of saving for those earning income, and a form of social income for those not receiving a money income.

Except for paternalists, and those who believe that society requires inequality or who fear the poor having the freedom from labour controls, a citizenship income scheme should have appeal. At this stage, moves in the direction of that ideal should be favoured over moves away from it. Instead of hostility to such moves, more effort should be devoted to finding ways of making that feasible. Perhaps in the end it will be called one of the most basic rights of all.

(ii) Distributive Justice Through Economic Democracy

Another component of a redistributive strategy in flexible labour markets must be some form of capital and profit sharing, in the spirit of *economic democracy*. A premise is that income accruing to capital and to those making technological advance has been rising, while the income going to labour has been lagging. As noted in chapter 3, taxes on capital are becoming less effective and are being cut due to globalisation and other forces.[10] And there is a global trend towards 'flexible' pay systems based on individualised profit sharing, profit-related pay, performance-related pay and so on, which are widening earnings differentials. Ordinary workers and their families and communities are being left behind, as well as the unemployed, flexiworkers and lumpenised elements in society.

While the detached are left out of the growth process, *economic control* is being concentrated in the hands of a few institutions, and in some industries a few individuals. In some countries, private pension funds and a few other financial institutions own most enterprises. Pension funds and insurance companies own over 75 per cent of UK public companies (*Observer*, 25 January 1998). In some countries control is not so concentrated, but the global trend is to greater concentration. This has pushed firms to maximise dividends, and fuelled the stock markets in New York, London and elsewhere, generating huge portfolio capital flows. Unless capital dispersion occurs, pension funds and other financial institutions will continue to be the means of redistributing income from stakeholders within firms to outside shareholders.

The response to all this should be a search for a way to achieve at least the equivalent redistribution as in the era of welfare state capitalism, while not undermining investment incentives so as to maintain economic growth. Ideally, the appropriate policy would also stabilise global capital mobility, which means there would have to be a better balance between short-term profit maximisation and longer-term profitability and dynamic efficiency.

In the euphemism of the time, the most feasible option for reversing the divisive growth of inequality is to incorporate workers, unions and their communities into the economic mainstream as **stakeholders**, to enable them to share the surplus with those currently gaining from capital, while enabling all groups to have an effective voice in decisions on work, investment and distribution. This implies some form of profit sharing and corporate governance restructuring.

Experience and research around the world have shown that profit sharing can have beneficial economic effects (Estrin et al., 1994; Vaughan-Whitehead, 1992). It encourages longer-term investment, rather than the dispersion of profits to external principals, to shareholders not directly involved in production. It encourages training investment by firms. It boosts productivity; can improve employment, and can improve income distribution, although some profit-sharing schemes have been a method of facilitating wage flexibility and a method of pooling risks in firms with high wage flexibility. Many benefits could be gained, *if the design of the surplus sharing is appropriate*.

The majority view among economists on *employee ownership* has ebbed and flowed, with some contending that it undermines efficiency, others that after a while it reverts to standard hierarchical systems, others that it fosters dynamic efficiency and equity. Events have shaped the intellectual climate. For example, the success of the US United Airlines after its workforce assumed majority ownership in July 1994 gave confidence to those who believe that it could be a crucial mechanism in a redistributive strategy. From being a sick company, United Airlines outperformed its rivals over the next few years. Similarly, the spread of ESOPs (Employee Stock Ownership Plans) has enhanced the legitimacy of profit sharing, although these are really a deferred, defined-benefit contributory pension system. Nevertheless, in 1997, about ten million US workers in 10,000 firms were part owners of their firms through ESOPs (Mackin, 1997). There is evidence that they have encouraged functional flexibility, boosting dynamic efficiency. Some companies have even provided workers with stock in return for concessions on working practices. This might be a positive form of 'progression bargaining' or 'investment bargaining'. It gives a hint of the potential for diffusion of conventional control functions.

The key research findings are the following:

(1) Employee ownership coupled with participatory management has advantages over conventional shareholder ownership. In terms of employment and sales growth, the combination of participation and employee partial ownership seems to work better than one or other taken alone.

(2) To be a mechanism for redistribution, it must be some collective profit sharing, since individual profit sharing accentuates inequality. Profit sharing in which only top managers receive profit shares not only widens inequality, but induces managerial caution. Various studies have concluded that while it is good for top executives to have equity stakes in their company, they may grow excessively cautious if their stakes become too large.

(3) Minority employee-ownership, as with US ESOPs, is associated with increased stability for firms, making it less likely that firms will go bankrupt, or be taken over and be subject to asset stripping (Blair et al., 1998). A growing number of firms put blocks of shares in the hands of their employees as a way of

protecting themselves from hostile takeovers. Sizable shareholding by employees in their own companies is also associated with greater employment stability.

(4) Employee shareholding is not more likely than traditional capital–labour relations to induce shirking where labour input is complex.

(5) Claims that efficiency is reduced by stakeholder governance, where control rights are shared between workers and shareholders, are not proven (Hansmann, 1996). Indeed, there is evidence that it can raise dynamic efficiency. The criticism that employee ownership would induce shirking because of the difficulty of monitoring (known as the 1/n problem) is undermined by the tendency of surplus sharing to induce mutual monitoring by workers, who all stand to lose or gain by each other's efforts. Workers also have an interest in pressurising management to be efficient. Evidence suggests that governance mechanisms that break down hierarchical management, such as employee-involvement programmes in the USA, work better in raising productivity if combined with employee ownership or profit sharing (Blasi et al., 1996).

(6) Stakeholder ownership can promote efficiency by reducing what were called adjustment costs in chapter 4, by making management claims about crises more credible, thus making workers more amenable to compromises, and by making management claims that workers would share in the benefit of changes more credible. Minority employee ownership is conducive to efficiency, restructuring and equity (Henzler, 1992; Levine and D'Andrea Tyson, 1990; Acs and FitzRoy, 1994).

(7) Economic democracy would promote *skill reproduction security*, since it would imply that in a downturn for a firm there would be fewer layoffs and more income sharing, so that workers' investment in firm-specific skills would be protected, giving them more incentive to acquire those skills in the first place (Blair, 1995).

(8) Economic democracy would be more effective if statutory or other regulations overcame potential externalities. Unless *most* firms adopted principles of stakeholderism, the likelihood of free riding and opportunism would be high, so that, for instance, in a recession firms that cut short-term costs by laying off workers might gain competitive advantage over those that did not (Levine, 1995). This is where statutory regulations (perhaps fiscal) would promote dynamic efficiency and equity.

(9) To prevent profit-sharing or stakeholder firms from reverting to conventional firms dominated by external blockholder principals (banks, pension funds, etc.), there must be a mechanism for ensuring that all the stakeholders are involved in voice regulation over the allocation of economic surplus and the timing of its realisation.

As with citizenship income, the conditions for economic democracy are emerging in bits and pieces. 'Stakeholder capitalism' and individualised profit sharing, both of which have probably widened economic inequality, could evolve into collective forms of capital sharing. This is where the rapidly growing literature on corporative governance overlaps with consideration of new forms of labour regulation and social policy. Capital sharing must become broader than company-level profit sharing because disaggregated production and flexible labour markets mean that, with company-level profit sharing, those in high-technology, high-value-added, high-profit firms would accentuate their advantage and relative income security. Where a few high-tech, high-profit firms adopt profit sharing, the result could be greater inequality in society and within the workforce.[11] Similarly, flexiworkers, as well as the unemployed and detached, would be left out.

A redistributive strategy will require **communal profit sharing**, by which some of the profits of firms making profits would go into local social investment and 'social security' funds. This should combine incentives to investment and work with tangible forms of redistribution.

The surplus sharing system must embrace the intermittently employed flexiworkers and the community around the firm. Among the benefits would be that income inequalities between those inside and outside employment would be reduced, and social pressures would be placed on those not in employment to play the role of socially responsible citizens. Firms would benefit from an enlarged pool of skilled workers, given the increased training in the firm and the social pressure to make the training available for the community's benefit.

In this, as in so many spheres of social policy, the 1990s has been a period of experimentation. We can appreciate what is required, without being able to see the ideal system. This is why it is welcome that an international *Federation of Employed Shareholders* was established in early 1998. One of its primary tasks should be to monitor the numerous experimental *stakeholder* schemes, and the means by which worker shareholding can benefit communities, firms and workers. An example of communal profit sharing emerging from more traditional institutions is the initiative taken by the St Petersburg trade union federation. In 1993, it encouraged workers to invest their privatisation vouchers in an investment fund, which was used to invest in enterprises in the region to yield a return for ordinary people *and* to induce the firms to adopt practices that the unions wanted for the benefit of their members. This is a case of trying to combine redistribution with increased voice and representation.

One idea, associated with James Meade among others, is to have two types of shares in registered firms, one giving voting rights in control over the firm's decisions, one giving only income-earning rights. An alternative and perhaps more promising route would be to limit the controlling voice of certain types of shareholder to issues of concern to the interest that they represent. For example, to ensure the community were taken into account the local authority might have a bloc of shares, which could be used only for voting on spheres affecting community development and the local environment, not on allocative decisions within the enterprise. In this spirit, shares that represented specific stakeholders would have to be non-tradable, since one purpose would be to ensure continuing voice representation security of different interests.

Communal profit sharing would strengthen the sense of community and citizenship. The challenge is to give voice to groups that would check winner-takes-all mechanisms. High taxes do not work well in an open global economic system. Yet unless the inequalities are addressed, distributive justice is impossible. Sharing through democratic control over the identification, monitoring and allocation of economic surplus could ensure a balance between competing claims. But stakeholder democracy must incorporate the Difference Principle, so that checks would have to prevent powerful combinations. If control were concentrated in the hands of any particular type of shareholder, that interest might opt for short-term, high-return investment and distribute dividends as quickly as possible to a few shareholding institutions. This would have adverse consequences for others, including actual and potential workers in the firm and in the community. The challenge is to ensure that all stakeholder groups have a meaningful voice in the control process, and that sustainable investment coexist with sustainable redistribution to the vulnerable, insecure and surrounding community.

(iii) Socially Just Firms: The HDE and Stakeholderism

> *The only people who work this hard are people who want to. The only people who want to are people with enough freedom to do the things they want to do. Netscape is a company that consciously undermanages.*
>
> Netscape

> *Today's leaders understand that you have to give up control to get results.*
>
> R. Waterman, 1994

What should be the legitimate role of 'markets' in a Good Society? They perform the valuable functions of allocative efficiency and information generation. The less attractive features are that they generate unequal outcomes and are based on intrinsically unattractive motivations – greed, fear, insecurity, opportunism, withholding information and obtaining control over others, usually to take advantage of them. Markets are also not good at generating *dynamic efficiency*. They do not create the incentives to be co-operative and creative, and these are essential for successful firms, economies and societies.

Labour markets function in and around 'firms', whose practices help shape society, as well as the production and distribution system. If there is to be distributive justice, firms must be vehicles for it, and must create communities and be communities. They must become places of human development, which is different from places where people are treated as 'human resources', an ugly notion.

Good firms should move away from twentieth-century notions of control – whether Tayloristic, bureaucratic or paternalistic. The late century fad of 're-engineering', and the earlier notion of 'human relations' theory associated with the Hawthorne experiment, have continued in the tradition of administrative control, inducing people to behave in ways that managers want. A goal should be to break down distinctions between controllers and the controlled and to replace them with ideas of *partnership*, *citizenship* and *stakeholdership*. Yet if the firm of the future will replace the language of engineering, control and hierarchy with one of partnership and community, *all* groups in firms must have equal and meaningful voice. If unions have too much power, it might jeopardise the firm's efficiency and profitability. If outside shareholders have too much power, they might suck out dividends and turn the firm into a short-term profit-maximising shell. If managements have too much control, they will pay themselves too well, emphasise short-term profit and be opportunistic. If all the preceding have too much power, the outside community could suffer from environmental neglect, other externalities and loss of social income.

The literature on firms and management has been a growth industry in recent years. Debates have raged over the merits and demerits of 'shareholder value' and 'stakeholder value', 'loyalty' and 'trust', 'social responsibility' and much more. Rare is the management consultant who has not invented several buzz words. Basically it is about repositioning ideas of security, flexibility and dynamic efficiency in the context of a growing range of organisational and management-style *options*. It is because options are greater that policymakers should wish to identify and promote practices that are compatible with a combination of dynamic efficiency, profitability, extension of human capabilities and distributive justice. Of course, firms exist in local, national and international spaces and labour markets are broader than encompassed by the firm. Practices of a good firm must be complemented by policies and institutions to provide security and flexibility in the surrounding labour market.

Concern about institutional structures has been inadequately addressed by mainstream economics. Supply-side economics gives *institutional* concerns minimal attention, is hostile towards collective entities, and favours liberalisation and privatisation of economic and social policy. For it, firms exist for one purpose only. As a father of the orthodox approach, the Nobel Prize winner, Milton Friedman, put it, 'The social responsibility of business is to make a profit.'

In this reasoning, enterprise performance and adjustment to market forces would be assisted by the removal of regulations, i.e., statutory and institutional mechanisms, notably protective labour regulations, including minimum wages, employment protection, labour codes and unions. This adheres to the Chicago school of law and economics, in which the guiding principle is 'Pareto optimality', leading to the view that regulations are justified only if they promote economic growth and if some people gain while nobody loses. The perspective can be summarised as stating that firms should be freed from social responsibilities and should focus on maximising shareholder value. As the consultancy firm Price Waterhouse (1997) put it, 'The management of a business must have one prime focus: maximising the value of its equity.'

In contrast to the Chicago school, the following starts from the Rawlsian Difference Principle that, assuming an institutional framework providing for *equality of opportunity* and *equal liberty,* distributive justice improves only if a change in a practice improves the position of the 'worst off' or most vulnerable groups. A second principle guiding the analysis is: *the powerful need protecting from themselves.*

Less abstractly, an alternative to the orthodox perspective is one that looks to regulations, institutions and incentive-structures to encourage human development, while recognising that reasonably flexible markets are essential. Constructive thinking starts from the need to create conditions for competition 'regulated' to ensure that it is based on competition between strong partners who are simultaneously rivals and co-operative. Such competition must promote equity *and* dynamic efficiency, which is derived from having rivals that are strong. Managers may not *like* having strong, well-informed negotiators sitting opposite them, and vice versa. They may not *like* the prospect of having to sit opposite them again and again. But these conditions are the best because those involved are best placed to know when to compromise and when to press the other side to improve *their* efficiency and competence. By the same token, societies are dynamic to the extent that their organisations reflect internal pressures to be equitably efficient (Chandler, 1993, p. 310).

What is a Good Enterprise for the twenty-first Century?   The notion of 'good' conjures up images of socially decent, which may prompt scepticism from neo-liberals. Accordingly, it must be stated that a good enterprise must be compatible with dynamic efficiency and profitability, for without efficiency it will not be economically viable.

Defining a good firm is not easy. A sweatshop does not contribute to the human development of those required to work in it, and an economy of sweatshops would not do well on human development generally. Nor would working in polluting, dangerous, noisy, hierarchically-controlled factories. On this most would agree. Yet what *is* wanted is harder to determine than what is *not.*

To make progress, we might construct an *ideal type* of a firm that would contribute to distributive justice and promote occupational security. This section outlines what is called a **Human Development Enterprise (HDE),** that is, a type of firm with exemplary practices and mechanisms in terms of the following:

- skill reproduction security;
- social equity;
- work security (health and safety);
- economic equity (income security);
- democracy (representation security).

Human development involves all those dimensions. People need to develop and refine work skills. We need equitable treatment, in which discrimination based on non-changeable human characteristics is a denial of human rights. We need a fair distribution of the income generated by the efforts of workers, managers, employers and those working on their own account. And we need Voice in the work process, recognising that absence of democracy there is a denial of democracy in general.

Left out are other dimensions of stakeholder responsibility. A Good Firm is surely one that yields a reasonable return to shareholders and one that does not pollute or have other costly externalities. We will not discuss these issues here, although they should be integrated into the proposed approach.

In terms of a firm, one can identify *indicators* of each dimension and combine them to create an HDE *index* to rank firms by performance. This has been done and applied to firms in a series of national *Enterprise Labour Flexibility Surveys*. Although the indicators are only proxies, the objective is to define an approach, clarify practices to regard as exemplary, and then find ways of measuring them.

The context is a caveat to what follows, since it might be desirable to modify some criteria to fit the capacities of certain types of firm and economies at different levels of development. For instance, a good firm in Russia or South Africa is likely to be modest by the standards of one in Switzerland. However, the *principles* should be adaptable to all countries.

The idea is not novel, although it is an attempt to develop a particular approach. Besides the Malcolm Baldridge National Quality Award scheme in the USA, others have mooted similar ideas. An interesting report by the Royal Society for the Arts in 1995 referred glowingly to their proposed 'inclusive approach' to 'tomorrow's company'. The report cited the *Balanced Business Scorecard*, proposed by US scholars (Kaplan and Norton, 1992, 1993). And it mentioned the 'self-assessment models' developed by Baldridge and by the European Foundation for Quality Management (1992). But it stopped short of indexes, skirting issues such as the value of *adversarialism* in labour transactions, which is crucial.

To identify a firm oriented to human development, we need indicators that capture the essence of desirable practices, principles and outcomes. This means some subjectivity and pragmatism, in part due to absence of data or difficulty of obtaining measurable information on some issues.

Some methodological points should be borne in mind. In developing an HDE 'index', sets of 'indicators' of underlying phenomena are used. In putting indicators together for any particular area – such as the firm's orientation to skill formation – there are difficulties of 'weighting' variables. Although there are statistical techniques for dealing with these, there is virtue in transparency. *The more complex the way an index is constructed, the greater the suspicion that the data have been 'massaged'.* It is better to be able to interpret an index than to have to unravel it to make sense of it, even if we have to sacrifice a little in terms of 'scientific' accuracy. Although this could be modified, this is the justification for using an ordinal scale for the indexes.

Inclusion of any indicator is a matter of preference, and does not affect the essence of the approach. If policymakers chose to promote the HDE and did not believe that, say, economic democracy was desirable, the relevant indicators could be excluded. If environmental concerns were deemed desirable (as they are), relevant indicators could be included. Whatever they are, four types of indicator are needed:

(1) indicators of *revealed preference*, or *principles*, reflecting a commitment to desirable practices and outcomes;
(2) indicators of *institutional mechanisms*, or *processes*, by which desirable outcomes could be translated into actual outcomes;
(3) indicators of *outcomes*, to reflect whether or not preferences and mechanisms are working;
(4) indicators that are *sustainable*, not jeopardising the enterprise's long-term profitability and dynamism.

In this exploratory exercise, we construct a *hierarchy* of HDE indexes, built by adding sets of indicators of skill orientation, social equity, work security, economic equity and economic democracy, in that order (Figure 11.2).

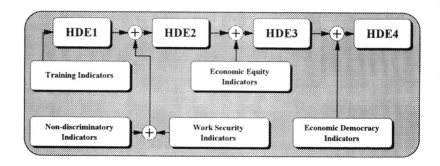

Figure 11.2 Hierarchy of Human Development Enterprise indexes

Starting with HDE1, a good enterprise should provide opportunities for skill acquisition, and promote a *voluntary learning environment*. Although there is much talk about making firms centres of learning, one must be careful about idealising training. The notion of *lifelong learning*, or continuous learning, is not unambiguously good, if it entails job insecurity. The thought of having to learn new competencies every few months could be unsettling and a source of discordant performance, deterring workers from trying to become excellent in particular skills. Emphasis must be on *opportunity* for learning, coupled with reasonable prospects of 'reward' from investment in training. And there must be a *voluntary* culture of learning, so that those opting not to train or acquire new skills are not penalised.

We consider as indicators of an orientation to skill formation three layers of training, namely:

(1) entry-level training for newly recruited workers,
(2) retraining to improve job performance or to transfer workers to other jobs with similar skills, and
(3) retraining for upgrading workers or promotion.

We should also take account of type of training. If a firm only gave informal, on-the-job training, that would deserve less weight than if 'class room' and structured training, including apprenticeship, were involved. Accordingly, for each level, a distinction is made between 'informal' and 'formal' training, with the latter being presumed to have greater value. Given economic and institutional realities, the difference between formal and informal may be exaggerated. Yet training with a quantifiable cost should be preferable to 'on-the-job-pick-it-up-as-you-go' training.

Finally, we include a variable measuring whether or not the firm pays for training, by funding an institute, paying training fees to an institute or giving stipends to workers who go on courses. With each variable having a value of 0 or 1, the HDE1 index is operationalised with a value of between 0 and 7, with zero meaning that the firm gave no training. The index implies that each level of training is given equal importance, and formal training is given twice as much significance as informal. For Russian factories, for example, in 1995 the modal value was 3, the mean 3.0, with only 2 per cent having a value of 7 and with 4.6 per cent having a value of zero.

Returning to Figure 11.2, the HDE1 is extended by incorporating *work security*, for which there are *input* mechanisms and *outcome* variables. For our purposes, a work security index is defined in terms of (1) whether the firm has a department or worker–employer committee responsible for safety and health at work, (2) whether the number of accidents in the workplace in the past year, expressed as a ratio to employment, was less than 50 per cent of the sectoral mean, and (3) whether the number of work days lost through illness or injury in the past year was less than 50 per cent of the sectoral mean. Of course, other indicators could be devised in the same spirit.

As for *social equity*, to be exemplary, an enterprise should act in ways that reduce or avoid labour segregation based on personal characteristics such as race, gender or disability. Although measuring discrimination is notoriously difficult, both employer *attitudes* and *outcomes* must be taken into account. For instance, a firm might have a 'preference' but not put it into effect, or might inadvertently discriminate by hiring on the basis of characteristics that had the effect of excluding certain groups.

Again, although more complexity could be incorporated, one can measure it in terms of non-discrimination in recruitment and training. In surveys conducted so far, although race has also been covered (notably in South Africa and Malaysia) indicators of non-discrimination were mainly related to gender. In recruitment, if management reported that there was no preference for men or women, this was regarded as a positive factor. It would be an inequity for men if we gave a positive value if management said they preferred women, as was sometimes the case.

A second indicator is commitment to provide training equally to men and women. Stated preferences are weak proxies. Accordingly, as well as stated preferences, we incorporate an outcome variable – the percentage of higher-level 'employee' jobs taken by women. If that was above 40 per cent, the firm was given a positive score in the index. This is not ideal, because the outcome could reflect differences in relative supply of men and women. However, it focuses on the better jobs and identifies performance in a key area of discrimination.

One could make the share sectorally specific, giving a positive score in the index if a firm had a high percentage of women in training relative to the average for all firms in the sector. But this is not as justifiable as it seems, since it allows for gender-based industrial segregation of employment. For instance, it would be inappropriate to give a positive score to an energy-sector firm in which 12 per cent of its higher-level 'employees' were women just because the industry's average was 10 per cent.

Where relevant, comparable indicators of preferences, training shares and employment shares for racial equity should be applied, as was done in the survey of firms in South Africa, where the existence of 'affirmative action' plans was also given a positive value. Another indicator of discrimination is whether the firm employed *workers with registered disabilities*. Coupled with the gender variables, this results in an index of non-discrimination, which could be extended to cover racial or other issues. Adding this to the work security and skill development indexes gives HDE2.

Next, a good firm must be Economically Equitable, which we define as minimising internal differences in earnings and benefits to the point where efficiency is not jeopardised, subject to a Rawlsian caveat – with priority given to improvement of the 'worst off' workers. Besides justice considerations, there are also efficiency reasons for favouring economic equity. Labour productivity depends on co-operation as well as individual effort. If there were wide differences between groups in a firm, the disadvantaged or those feeling inequitably treated would withhold 'tacit knowledge' and not commit themselves to the exchange of information that contributes to dynamic efficiency. Narrow pay differentials within firms are associated with cohesion, trust of management, productivity gains, and commitment to management goals (Levine, 1992; Cowherd and Levine, 1992). There is evidence that advanced companies in countries such as the USA have compressed wage differentials, which they have coupled with fewer job classifications and fewer controls; with smaller wage differentials, pay becomes a less focal issue in bargaining and in the firm's culture (Pfeffer, 1994). Thus, the equity of narrow wage differentials goes with efficiency benefits.

The Economic Equity Index was developed for several eastern European countries. Three factors were used, with greatest weight given to the first, since it relates to treatment of the 'worst off' in the firm. A phenomenon in Russian industry in the mid-1990s was the growth of groups paid *much* lower wages than anybody else. An economically equitable firm should have few if any workers paid a small fraction of the firm's average. So, if more than 5 per cent received the lowest wage the firm was given a low score on economic equity. A positive score was also given if the minimum payment was equal to or greater than 50 per cent of the average wage. In South Africa, measures of relative wages of whites and blacks were also used.

Another consideration is whether the average wage is equitable relative to that paid in other firms. To reflect technological and market factors, the proxy used is whether the firm's average wage was greater than the sectoral average. If so, a positive score was provided. As equity is also improved if the firm provides benefits and entitlements that represent security against personal contingencies and improve the workers' standard of living, an additional point was given if the firm provided workers with ten or more specified non-wage benefits.

Finally, a good firm should be *economically democratic*. Democracy based on the ritual election of politicians will fail if there is no democracy in the institutions of society, primarily within the production process. Economic equity and the maintenance of other good practices depend on mechanisms and processes of 'voice regulation'. And in the workplace, the 'stakeholders' bearing the greatest risk and uncertainty should be able to regulate decisions affecting labour practices. This is perhaps the greatest quandary for corporate governance. Can management be made more democratic and accountable while promoting dynamic efficiency for the benefit of all in the enterprise?

Democracy beyond casting votes is also about institutional safeguards, the most effective of which is the capacity of the vulnerable to exercise restraint on those in decision-making positions, giving substance to the Rawlsian 'maximin' principle. Democracy is also about attempts to ensure co-operation in the interest of all representative groups. Successful co-operation requires '*the shadow of the future*', that is, mechanisms to ensure that competitive interest groups know that they will have to deal with and co-operate with each other in the future.

In any firm, management has more scope for opportunism, through control of information, a limited circle of people and a capacity to take unilateral decisions. To limit opportunism by authorities, there must be reciprocal monitoring and a capacity to impose sanctions when abuses are detected. This is important for enterprise restructuring everywhere, for without mechanisms for voice regulation, the capacity of the vulnerable to influence the outcomes is minimal. It is also unlikely that the process would achieve dynamic efficiency if workers become sullen, 'excluded insiders'.

In short, we need an Economic Democracy Index. Once again, the indicators should depend in part on national contexts, although the principles should be the same. In the Russian case, cited merely for illustrative purposes, economic democracy was defined in terms of six indicators.

First, it was assumed that workers' Voice is strengthened by high unionisation. Having a mechanism to represent workers creates a basis for dynamic efficiency.

Shadow of the Future

Without a union, there would be no shadow of the future to concentrate the minds of managers and workers on developing decent and efficient labour practices. This does not mean that we presume unions always behave appropriately. However, a representative mechanism is a necessary condition for voice regulation.

In Russia, this was defined as being the case if more than 50 per cent of the workers belonged to a union, because of the traditionally (artificially) high level of unionisation. Elsewhere, it would also be appropriate to identify the *type* of union, since an industrial union should represent a broader group of workers than a craft union, and a union that had members who were potential workers as well as those actually in employment would be more likely to ensure that the concerns of those in the labour market were also taken into account.

Second, democratic potential is greater if the main union is independent, which in the Russian context meant that management should *not* be members. In 'Soviet' enterprises management belonged to the union and both managers and union representatives were subject to Party commands. Thus, non-membership by management is an indicator of independent Voice. Elsewhere, an alternative measure of union independence would be more appropriate. In East Asia, the relevant difference is whether the union is an industrial or company union. The form makes a substantial difference to wage level, wage differentials and training (Standing, 1992).

Third, there should be a bargaining mechanism. For this, a collective agreement between the union and firm is taken as a positive sign, even though in the mid-1990s, in Russian firms collective agreements were more formal than substantive.

Fourth, democracy is taken to be greater if workers own a large percentage of the firm's shares. The critical level for a positive value is taken to be 30 per cent. Elsewhere the appropriate percentage might be lower. In Russian industry, given the lack of work discipline and legacy of the Soviet era in which effort was low and monitoring ineffectual, worker ownership and governance should have *potential* benefits as a means of overcoming the incompleteness of labour contracts.

Ownership of a flow of income should be distinguished from ownership of property rights. In terms of corporate governance, minority share ownership turns workers into *outsider principals* – monitoring the performance of managers and providing a mechanism for replacing them. The objection to sole existence of *insider principals* is that a coalition between managers and workers could result in short-term concerns predominating over strategy. However, with worker share ownership, workers and managers become outsider agents as well, having an interest in the flow of income from shares as well as their earnings from work.

Fifth, it was taken as a positive element if top management were elected by the workers, not appointed by a Ministry or enterprise board. This to some extent is institutionalised in Germany in *co-determination*. But we use this solely for the circumstances of Russian enterprises in the 1990s, when other appointment mechanisms were more dubious. It recognises the value of accountability to stakeholders, limiting managerial opportunism and encouraging behaviour in favour of long-term profit maximisation and efficiency.

There has been a diversification in the means by which Russian managers have been appointed. Achieving a balance in managerial accountability to workers and to the firm is difficult, since commercial decisions might be jettisoned in favour of decisions that enjoyed short-term worker support. Appointment by workers could result in managerial conservatism and a reluctance to restructure. Yet if workers were broader stakeholders, 'short-termism' would be less likely, although this is a justification for appointments to be for sufficiently long to encourage managers to take decisions that combine concern for today's workers and the firm's future.

Sixth, economic democracy is taken to be greater if there is a profit-sharing pay system. Many trade unionists have opposed profit-sharing pay on the grounds that it intensifies workers' income insecurity. However, if one gives a positive value to the broadening of democratic decision-making, it is appropriate to balance that by valuing mechanisms that share the risks and benefits. If economic democracy is to be an integral part of a strategy for distributive justice, it should be encouraged at the firm level.

The resultant Economic Democracy Index has a value of between 0 and 6. By adding this to the HDE3, we obtain the **Human Development Enterprise Index**, HDE4. This has a maximum value of 24, and if the index identifies exemplary standards, there should be a tapering in the distribution of firms, with fewer as the scores rise, and no excessive bunching.

The technique and questionnaires for measuring HDE indexes are developed at greater length elsewhere. The point of the exercise is to suggest a way of turning abstract notions of socially good enterprise into a measurable concept. Neo-liberals may object that there is no point in converting commercial entities into social institutions, because they would go bankrupt. Therefore, it is encouraging that even in the Russian and Ukrainian cases, there was a positive correlation between the value of HDE and indicators of enterprise economic performance. In other words, performing well on worker security and development was compatible with profitability and efficiency. The causation might be from profitability to security, but the correlations at least point to compatibility, while the multiple-round nature of the survey showed that high HDE scores were associated with better economic performance subsequently.

This is consistent with other analyses in more propitious circumstances. In November 1996, Kleinwort Benson Investment Management launched a *Tomorrow's Company* investment fund and portfolio service, which was to lend to firms that maintain five good relationships – with investors, employees, customers, suppliers and the community. Kleinwort had estimated that companies that had done well on these five outperformed the national all-share index over a substantial period. Its managers believe that backward-looking financial measures such as return on assets or profitability do not capture the key issue, and that it is an accounting truism that the most profitable time in a firm's life is the period between the moment it stops investing and the moment when it goes bust. Essentially, the investment fund had concluded that broadening the role of companies was compatible with dynamic efficiency. Implicitly, they were also recognising that because of externalities, there would be no automatic tendency for socially responsible firms to predominate without inducements.

The HDE idea is consistent with several other proposals, such as the 'mutual gains' enterprise in the USA (Kochan and Osterman, 1994). It is also suited to an era of increasing emphasis on incentives to good practice rather than sanctions against bad. If 'labour standards' are obligatory and rigid, even those who support them will do so with reservation. Some will pay scant attention to the sins of others in case their own sins, real or imaginary, are exposed to scrutiny. By contrast, rewarding good practice and shining the light on exemplary cases would be in keeping with mature cultures.

The approach also corresponds to advanced management thinking, epitomised by top companies in the USA and elsewhere. Firms that put the interest of their workers first appear to perform better (Pfeffer, 1994). And firms that give relatively high priority to 'objectives beyond profit' over the long term tend to outperform those that focus more exclusively on profits (Centre for Tomorrow's Company, 1998). There are also positive externalities. Thus, economically democratic firms are likely to promote democratic behaviour *outside* them. There is evidence that skills learned inside firms improve participation in the wider community (Smith, 1985). One need not turn this into an ideological battleground. Rather one should seek ways of refining the approach to secure a consensus, and foster communities of Human Development, bearing in mind the 'network externalities' that would come from firms adopting good employment systems.

So far, we have applied the HDE concept to some inauspicious cases, although it seems suited to the ethics of South East Asian society or to the restructuring needs of South Africa. It would apply more easily in the USA or western Europe. In the USA, Robert Reich, the former Secretary of Labour, has proposed that firms failing in their 'responsibility' to maintain jobs should pay more tax. If that meant using sanctions rather than incentives, one could anticipate opposition and a lack of consensus on promoting good practices that way.

What constitutes an HDE could be decided by negotiation, legislation, or by a combination. The way it has been measured is merely illustrative. In East Asia, indicators were included to measure *employment security*, i.e., comprising an index to measure whether the firm gave workers employment protection as good as or better than the average. Firms relying on casual, temporary or contract labour to a substantial extent were regarded less favourably than those that gave most of their workers regular employment contracts. If one extended the idea to include elements of *labour market security*, one might give positive value if the firm gave relatively long notice in retrenchments and reasonable redundancy payments, and give value to firms that had 'social plans' ready to assist workers affected by structural adjustment or employment cuts.

One reason for emphasising incentives to good practice rather than sanctions against those who do not measure well is that more flexible production systems mean there are many inherently risky small firms on the technological frontier. They tend to have short dynamic lives. For instance, 'silicon valley' has thrived in part because small firms have risen and closed quickly, the economy's success being built on their high failure rate (Bahrani and Evans, 1995). Such 'flexible re-cycling' may be an integral part of the future production and labour market process, just as 'flexiworkers' and unattached 'proficians' (respectively with low-skill and high-skill competencies in varying work statuses) will be part of it. The HDE leaves out such phenomena. This is why it must be complemented by community-level voice mechanisms and *basic income security*.

This leads to a challenge for those wishing to promote something like the HDE. It depends on the existence of viable voice mechanisms. In most of the world, traditional unionism is on the wane, yet enterprise and economic democracy cannot be envisaged without strong representative organisations. There is a need to re-examine alternative forms of union, as long as ways can be found to overcome well-known drawbacks and as long as such unions can cross sectoral and occupational boundaries in securing members. In East Asia, where the HDE idea was first applied, a positive value was given if the union was an *independent* rather than an *enterprise union*. For both workers and firms, independent unions had advantages, although enterprise unions were better for workers than *no* union. The reason for concern about enterprise unions is that they tend to be co-opted, if not set up by management to pre-empt independent unions.

A similar ambivalence exists in the USA about 'employee involvement programmes'(EIP), which are an alternative to unions or a means of eroding worker interest in them. Yet enterprise unions and EIPs (or their equivalents) are spreading, while craft and industrial unions are shrinking. The old-style 'craft' was an ideal of a past age. Now, industrial unions are facing the fate of craft unions, and industrial solidarity is under pressure almost everywhere. Increasingly, loyalties cross craft and sectoral boundaries, and workers identify more with their local community – to the extent that they identify with anything.

For the HDE to be viable, worker representation of some sort is essential. The more representation is *autonomous*, the more meaningful the voice. Some US analysts have sought the ideal in *independent local unions* (ILU) (Jacoby and Verma, 1992). Those were established in the wake of the *Wagner Act*, which made it an unfair labour practice for an employer to dominate, interfere with, or provide financial assistance to a union. Difficulties with ILUs and unaffiliated unions include their financial *vulnerability*, and a tendency to suffer from the 'golden handcuffs' technique of management. Their appeal is that they are relatively democratic because their officials come from a smaller community. But they may have insufficient 'clout' to force themselves into boardrooms to shape corporate strategy. ILUs also fail a test of industrial unions, the desire to take wages and standards out of the sphere of 'competition' by standardising them in an industry or occupation. But industrial unions cannot do that either. With globalisation and labour market flexibility, they cannot set effective rules on labour practices.

We need to identify the voice mechanism offering the best prospect for democracy. The literature on socially responsible companies has neglected the tendency for 'good employers' to turn into 'paternalistic employers' and into more Orwellian creatures of 2004. Consider a widely-cited book on 'successful' US companies (Collins and Portas, 1995). *The Economist* (8 July 1995), without irony, summarised its main message:

> Successful companies put a huge amount of effort into turning new recruits into company men and women, sending them on in-house training courses (both McDonald's and Walt Disney have their own 'universities'), influencing the way they speak and dress,and encouraging them to spend time with other company people. Procter and Gamble, a consumer goods company, ruthlessly rejects applicants who do not conform to the 'company type'. Wal-Mart, a discount retailer, gets new recruits to raise their right hand and swear to smile at their customers, 'so, help me, Sam'. Until recently IBM expected its workers to wear white shirts. 'Nordies', as the employees of Nordstrom, a retail chain, happily call themselves, start every day with the collective chant: 'We want to do it for Nordstrom'.

This is not too attractive. It is a powerful argument for independent voice regulation, for economic democracy that can constrain the tendency to go from management to manipulation, from incentives to coercion.

In sum, while the HDE could be refined and adjusted to meet the specific conditions of different countries, it should be seen as an organising concept, which could be used to grade enterprises by explicit criteria that could be justified as desirable or otherwise. Since an objective is to encourage firms to develop exemplary practices, to promote such enterprises, a foundation or organisation might wish to launch a national **HDE Award** scheme, with annual competitions, award ceremonies and badges of recognition. It has been done for export, technology and safety performance. Why not for stakeholder performance?

A few countries could be selected, and a survey conducted to identify HDE performance criteria. Ideally, the survey should be a census. However, it need not be more than a representative sample survey. An objective should be to have a demonstration effect. If the process were legitimised, it could lead to support from leading companies, unions and government officials.

Once the data had been analysed, a conference of managements, government officials and trade unionists should be convened, and HDE Awards could be presented to, say, the top 5 per cent of firms. The personnel departments of the top ten companies might be presented with financial awards, if a suitable funder were prepared to sponsor the process, while exemplary enterprises would be awarded with an HDE plaque. The award-giving conference could be televised, and the publicity would surely be welcomed by the firms and have a demonstration effect on others.

Subsequently, other companies could apply for the Award or the survey could be extended to a new sample each year. Questions of renewal of the Award could then be addressed, just as other such schemes have developed continuity. The concept of an HDE could be used for framework legislation, and collective bargaining could push the firm closer to the desirable model.

The HDE should be seen as part of a network of policies to encourage socio-economic *inclusion* and to re-embed economic processes in society. Fiscal and incentive regulations could encourage this, and these should be tailored to promote distributive justice and dynamic efficiency. How much better than sanctioning the behaviour of the losers and the disaffected.

(iv) Reviving Representation Security and Voice Regulation

I'll Be There
    Pledge of *Jobs With Justice*, USA, 1997

Of the three modes of labour regulation – statutory, market and voice – voice regulation is the most compatible with flexible labour markets. The onus on voice regulation is that the institutions and processes must be sufficiently representative and responsive in order to promote distributive justice and dynamic efficiency.

In the end of the century of the labouring man, reformers have tried to strengthen links between wage labour and social entitlements, and dominant institutions have canvassed for those links to be made stronger. The unions spoke of the emancipation of labour, but what they have struggled for is more and better labour, not liberation from labour. The erosion of labour security has shown the limitations of that strategy. The position of unions – wanting better labour, but wanting labour – has made it difficult for them to respond to labour market flexibility and insecurity. Yet for social progress, those who have coalesced around unions must develop a strategy for emancipation from labour and for distributive justice.

The erosion of representation security provided by trade unions and neo-corporatist, tripartite structures prompts consideration of what type of *voice* institution could emerge for the more flexible labour markets. Some analysts argue that globalisation requires 'global solutions' and 'global identities'. This seems too abstract. What is required is what Benedict Anderson (1983) has called 'imagined communities', beyond notions of class or state. There is need for *institutional security*, which means that forms of collective bodies suitable for more flexible labour systems must evolve to replace old forms that cannot provide the individual forms of security that are needed or other aspects of distributive justice. For this, a *network* of citizenship associations is needed to give voice to *all* those faced by insecurity.

To be effective, voice regulation must be based on incorporating those on the margins of the labour market and on the margins of society. They too must be part of the *shadow of the future*. They must be given voice in the institutions of labour market regulation and social policy, and they must be taken into account in regulatory and redistributive decisions. Today's insiders must understand that in flexible systems tomorrow they may be outsiders. What this means, in short, is that in the emerging flexible economies, multi-partite structures must displace atavistic institutions better suited to the early days of industrial society.

Mancur Olsen (1996), among others, captured a crucial point in asserting that dynamically efficient societies require a series of social bargains, since for legitimacy a competitive market economy depends on social *co-operation*. Arthur Okun (1975) famously stated that there was an 'invisible handshake' in society alongside Adam Smith's 'invisible hand' in market transactions. Unfortunately, in the era of market regulation and globalisation, the imagery of handshakes is rather less credible than in the previous era, largely because of the social detachment and fragmentation.

Of all forms of *labour* security, the most crucial are representation and income security. The only feasible way of reversing the growing insecurity and fragmentation is that the declining *statutory* regulation, increasingly ineffectual and potentially counter-productive, must be supplemented by stronger *voice regulation*. Representation security implies that participants in the labour market must have a secure capacity to bargain and influence the character of employment, to have an adequately strong 'voice' to ensure that distributive justice is pursued. Without that, all other forms of labour security will be jeopardised.

With the welfare state presumption of a closed economy gone, and downward pressure on the social wage increasingly a global pressure, there has been an effort to revive the Keynesian idea of a *social clause* in international trade, as part of World Trade Organisation rules. One core labour standard would be freedom of association, the objective being to limit the degree of 'unfair competition'. Ruling elites in developing countries are opposed to any social clause, while some employer organisations are scarcely enthusiastic. The prospects of national unions resisting the pressure of beggar-my-neighbour competitiveness arguments are not promising. It is essential to convince representatives of employers everywhere of the *Polanyian imperative*, that it is in the interest of economic stability to establish an international framework of social decency, with scope for scrutinising those abusing their position. That is part of the process of re-embedding the economy in society.

In the broadening number of industrialised countries, there may be resistance to *regulation competitiveness*. The European Union has been trying to develop a minimum framework of good employment practices for adoption by member countries. The European Trade Union Institute has been pushing for consultative works councils and employee participation schemes for all companies, giving institutional impetus to resistance to use of differential regulations. And organisationally, some national unions are forging international links that cater for labour mobility. For instance, the UK's GMB has signed a membership agreement with IG Chemie in Germany to enable their respective members to enjoy union rights in each other's country.

These are signs of adaptation and new strategy. Nevertheless, in both industrialising and industrialised countries, the need is for greater *voice regulation* of labour market relations. Representation security must be the basis of any strategy for distributive justice, and the form should ideally foster dynamic efficiency and a trend towards economic equality. However, unions have limited experience of bargaining to enable workers to obtain capital, which in current circumstances should be a priority, and they have difficulty responding to flexible labour systems.

Traditional craft and industrial unions are inappropriate in flexible labour markets in which a growing proportion of workers have no long-term commitment to specific industries, crafts or large formal occupational groups. Craft unions have long been weak, and the shrinking industrial unions have been merging into big general unions. But this tendency will increase the alienation of unions from actual and potential members, who understandably equate bigness with bureaucracy and social distance. The one form to show resurgence in recent years is the *company union*, due to the fact that it has been the main form in South East Asia, notably in Japan, the Republic of Korea and Malaysia. It has been spread to Chile and Mexico, and is spreading in Europe as well. 'Company unions' rose to prominence in the USA in the 1920s, as a paternalistic ('welfare capitalism') alternative to the bitter struggle between anti-union employers and national unionism.[12] The New Deal temporarily resolved the conflict by ushering in the era of statutory regulation, through favouring 'tripartism' and welfare state policies. Since then, company unions have had a bad name in American industrial relations. Yet in the 1990s, in the wake of the AFL-CIO's institutional weakness, pro-union advocates have been reconsidering company unions. This was shown by the Dunlop Commission Report issued at the end of 1994.

In a survey carried out for the Commission, over half the workers had no workplace representation, and while 63 per cent said that they would like to have more influence in workplace decisions, *few workers wanted a union* – 48 per cent of blue-collar workers, against 38 per cent who did not want one (Freeman and Rogers, 1995). In manufacturing, 47 per cent said they would not vote to join a union. Yet most workers favoured a type of employee organisation to give them more influence in the workplace. This led the Commission to recommend that workplace non-union employee participation schemes should be legalised to cover production issues, product quality, safety, health, training and dispute resolution 'as long as they do not allow for the rebirth of company unions'.

There is debate on the relative effectiveness and labour market impact of industrial and enterprise unions. Evidence from Japan and South East Asia suggests that enterprise unions have less effect on wages than industrial unions but more successfully promote *employment security* for their members, while promoting the firm's employment. It is awkward for critics that economies with enterprise unions have been relatively dynamic, have promoted functional flexibility and have had favourable employment records. It also seems that enterprise unions do provide scope for voice regulation, at least at the workplace.

These interpretations should not be construed as a recommendation for enterprise unions. Their limitations are that they are likely to be little more than instruments of management, thus justifying pejorative epithets such as 'pet unions', and are likely to favour 'insiders' over 'outsiders' to a greater degree than industrial unions, encouraging current members' employment and income security by fostering the dualistic character of employment that has characterised Japanese enterprises. Even in Japan, enterprise unions have not had appeal to the growing number of flexiworkers.

So, internationally, the situation in the late 1990s is that industrial unions have declining appeal and effectiveness, while enterprise unions have been an instrument for promoting functional flexibility and employment security for core workers. The scope for representation security in flexible labour markets thus appears bleak. One can dimly see what is needed – institutions that can resist pressures of co-option, promote dynamic efficiency in production and have a redistributive effect beyond the confines of an individual firm. Are there any germs of hope?

Well, perhaps. We have been witnessing the emergence of numerous quasi-representative 'non-government organisations', in what one observer has called a 'global associational revolution' (Salamon, 1994). These constitute a transforming phenomenon, and increasingly more of them are taking on global form, with 'international' in their titles. Although they are often romanticised as 'organs of civil society' and 'social stakeholders', they do contain the potential for a radical role. In terms of flexible labour relations, what is needed is a movement that brings together bodies representing local groups of employed and those at the margin of the labour force to bargain over distributional, security and production issues.

What might be called *community unions* or *citizenship associations* could be the most effective way forward if a strategy for distributive justice is to be pursued. For this, traditional unions must recognise that their long-term representative capacity will depend on their appeal to flexiworkers and those on the labour force margins. Only if they organise workers of all types in local communities will they be able to put effective pressure on local networks of firms.[13] The agenda of community unions would differ from that of enterprise unions, giving higher priority to social income issues, including environmental protection and shared entitlement to social benefits by those in regular and non-regular forms of employment, and from industrial unions, in that they would give less emphasis to the money wage relative to other components of the social income. Community unions would offer a better prospect than other types of promoting democratically exemplary practices within firms, because they would comprise a wider coalition of workers. Such associations should develop a governance role in rapidly growing employment agencies, where they could limit the *potentially* adverse effects and strengthen the *potentially* beneficial effects of the flexible employment that they offer. In this respect it is moderately encouraging that in the USA there have been attempts (e.g., in Baltimore and New York) to organise the new workfare labour force, to try to limit substitution effects and secure equal wages and benefits for workfare placements.

In this vein, the *Jobs With Justice* (JWJ) movement in the USA has been fostering ties between trade unionists and community, senior citizen, student, consumer, environmental and religious organisations, creating a national network of workers' and social rights activists (Early and Cohen, 1997). Since its inception in 1987 it has grown on principles of reciprocity – everyone joining having to promise to participate in others' struggle for rights at least five times a year. The JWJ is based on local coalitions and is determined to remain an informal social movement, uniting interests of workers and those working for other interests. It may be a harbinger of citizenship associations.

There are several terms jostling for attention to describe the new forms of representation. One is *social movement unionism* (Waterman, 1993). Another is *associational unionism* (Heckscher, 1996). Perhaps preferable would be one that conveys links between worker interests and those of the local community, and that stresses the sense of citizenship solidarity. Whatever they are called, associations that combined the functions of representing people as workers, as consumers and as citizens could overcome a dilemma highlighted by Cole in 1920, when he commented, '... a person requires as many forms of representation as he has distinct organisable interests or points of view'.

The idea of multiple forms of representation, coupled with multiple forms of stakeholder in firms, relates to the *federal structure* outlined in chapter 2 and multi-tierism of social protection noted in chapter 8. The essence of federal structures is that power and control are dispersed across quasi-autonomous units, and the ability to control is reduced. The hollowing-out of enterprises and shrinking of 'head offices' erode their control and encourage partnership rather than hierarchy. The forms of representation will have to match the inherent flexibility of those developments.

Community unions would offer the best prospect for creating that most vital factor in redistributive justice – *the shadow of the future*. For effective representation, those facing each other over the bargaining tables must have the strong prospect of having to deal with each other for the foreseeable future.

Union-type organisations could also play a role as employment agencies, or as 'employee mutuals', independently or in combination with commercial firms, giving workers voice representation in what should be non-profit organisations. The mutuals could offer training courses, perhaps sub-contracted to specialist agencies, and could offer employment services to workers according to their aspirations and skills. This would be compatible with external labour flexibility and the inability of traditional unions to cover flexiworkers effectively.

Before the era of welfare state capitalism, unions in some industrial economies strengthened *job security* by controlling labour supply. Particularly in the USA, they controlled job content through apprenticeship schemes that they helped to design and regulate. As corporations became large, oriented to securing a *loyal* labour force, they took over many of these functions. Now, with firms outsourcing and downsizing, splintering and 're-engineering', those functions may pass to labour market institutions and agencies. Probably these will be private, commercial agencies. But it is an opportunity for representative associations to emerge, not just *lobbying* for statutory protective regulations but to try to *control* the labour supply and conditions of employment.

A pivotal role in flexible labour markets will be played by *intermediary agencies* linking firms as productive units with individual workers. Only if the voice of workers is part of the governance of such intermediaries will their interests be enhanced. There has been a change in attitude to 'middle management', with more scepticism about the need for middle-level controllers. To some extent, this is being replaced by external intermediary controllers, through government agencies with their conditionality and through employment agencies. Voice representation in both will be vital countervailing power.

Unions have also begun to participate in the privatisation of social policy and develop as commercial entities in competition with private firms. As aspiring service agencies, some have started to provide free life insurance, legal services, car insurance, discount travel, discount car hire, credit cards and household insurance. In the Netherlands the major trade union federation has been issuing plastic Traveller's Aid and Shopper's Advantage cards. In the USA, similar practices have been spreading (Tasini, 1995). Unions are almost becoming individualistic insurance-oriented mechanisms for selective protection *and* promoting consumption. This may attract and retain members, but it must remain peripheral to the objective of being a powerful voice for promoting occupational security and distributive justice. The voice of workers and those on the margins of labour must be incorporated in the design and delivery of social protection – or re-incorporated in some countries. This could be a feature of new pension systems; in the UK, the Government has indicated that unions might have a role in the proposed second-tier 'stakeholder pension'. Such avenues might strengthen the workers' voice, as long as the voices of all groups are incorporated, including those on the margins of society.

Presuming that in most societies, for some time selective systems of social protection will continue to be provided by complex formula and systems of entitlement based on intrusive work tests, means tests and the like, community-level associations could give voice to those dependent on the good will of government officials or their private agents. These could dispense aid and advice, just as trade unions traditionally did. However, there is another role citizenship associations could – and, one predicts, will – play. The character of representative associations shapes how people formulate and adhere to principles of distributive justice. If those bring together people from 'many walks of life' and allow all strata to be heard, deliberative democracy will generate support for universal basic social and economic rights. A lesson from the distributive justice experiments mentioned earlier was that group deliberation strengthened support for the floor constraint. And surely, in communal associations notions of deserving and undeserving would soon yield to the perception of the basic similarity of the human condition.

Voice and the New Controllers

The desired character of the voice mechanism can be appreciated by considering the main labour market trends. In the era of market regulation, the employment function is becoming more indirect, with intermediaries being labour controllers. Governments are trying to cut back their direct provision, are integrating social and labour market policies and are privatising the delivery of social services. Although these trends are at an early stage in many countries, in some they are firmly established. In the USA, large companies have emerged to take over the functions of determining who receives state transfers, delivering them and integrating welfare beneficiaries into jobs.

Integrating welfare and employment policy would increase the paternalistic character and control function of both. This is what is happening, so that the labour market is changing from employer–worker to employer–agency–worker, where the agency may be a public service or private employment agency. There may be one intermediary or several. Whose interests do they serve? If the caseworker acts as mediator with employers, landlords and others to facilitate work or retention of a job by the welfare recipient, then the person becomes dependent on the skill and attitude of the case manager. The intermediary is a new form of labour market intervention, and is subject to all the usual principal–agent dilemmas. Whose interests does the intermediary represent?

A case is *America Works*, a commercial agency that places welfare participants in jobs and gives supporting services. It may be a valuable firm. It is partial controller, partial representative of the participant. The locus of trust and loyalty shifts to the agency–worker relationship. The agency is supposed to be a jobseeking service, a job retention service, a social worker, job training adviser, and perhaps something else as well. It is also a commercial operation, and as such understandably would want to place workers in any job and put pressure on its 'placements' to remain in jobs even if they did not like them and wished to leave. There is a structural conflict of interest. Only organisations representing jobseekers and workers in jobs could resolve this.

The privatisation of employment services will accelerate the evolution of an emerging 'profession' that might be called the 'employment agent'.[14] This involves a heady mixture of social psychology, social policy with knowledge of benefit systems, social work, training, community health, counselling, para-legal service and personnel practice. It is not clear whose interests such a profession represents.

There are commercial and political pressures to emphasise their role as paternalistic controller, as part of the workfare agenda, making them primarily agents to maximise job placement rates. There is the countervailing public service function, to provide a service to clients. But the clients most likely to influence employment agent behaviour will be potential employers, particularly if firms pay for most or all of the services. To complicate the incentive structure further, government authorities may push them to maximise placement and job retention rates, and offer subsidies and grants to encourage that. The unemployed and workers cannot compete with those inducements. In such circumstances, employment agents will be assimilated into the labour control system, even though many taking up the profession will be intent on providing a neutral public service and have impeccably balanced objectives. The market pressures are just too unbalanced. To counter this, public authorities should regulate the governance of employment services and ensure voice regulation by those who use them. Only then could the paternalistic tendency and opportunistic treatment of vulnerable clients be combated.

11.7 CONCLUDING REFLECTIONS: DISTRIBUTIVE JUSTICE AND THE LABOUR MARKET

A just system must generate its own support.
John Rawls

Let us conclude by returning to where we began. The labour market can be regarded as a means of assisting in the allocative process of the means of production and as a means of realising human development, through facilitating 'work' as creative and social activity. What is encompassed by the labour market is not just the means of raising income in order to consume goods, services and to afford leisure. In assessing a labour market, one should also be concerned with notions of social justice. Is a labour market in which 30 per cent of those in employment are subject to rigid controls or are highly exploited better or worse than one in which 40 per cent are in such circumstances? Is a labour market with 5 per cent unemployment better or worse than one with 10 per cent? If we feel we can answer that the former is better in both cases, what is the reason for reaching that intuitively appealing conclusion? And beyond such normative judgments, what should we regard as the socially just characteristics of a Good Labour Market?

The Good Society and the Good Labour Market will be those that ensure that everybody has sufficient security to enable them to have a decent human existence and pursue their sense of occupation. Distributive justice is about the distribution of security just as much as about the distribution of income and the balance of control and freedom. The great failing of the two dominant development models of the twentieth century was the primacy given to labour market security.

The dominant model of the 1980s and 1990s has been largely devoid of visions of distributive justice. We need to focus on what the State should or could do. This was the subject of the World Bank's 1997 *World Development Report*, which was oriented to promoting institutions for a market economy. It would have been expecting too much to expect to find a vision of a Good Society emphasising redistribution, income security, freedom and occupational opportunity. But the state can create institutions and a regulatory framework that tilt society in that direction. One way would be through strengthening means of providing the 'community benefit' part of social income and the elements of civil society that can provide them, in ways that avoid the dangers of being subsumed by the state and becoming opportunistic expressions of interest groups competing for 'sound bites', access to philanthropic gestures and the like.

In terms of work, the growth areas of the late twentieth century have been care and voluntary and paid work in non-governmental service organisations, usually non-profit, welfare-oriented groups. Much of this is work, not labour. The fetish with labour has resulted in the denigration or undervaluation of this work. Societal health in the twenty-first century will depend on how community work blends with other forms of economic activity. Much of it will remain non-contractual, with little or no pay. Its spread and extraordinary dynamism testify to the fact that it is not just the prospect of a wage that makes a person work. But it will flourish only if it becomes socialised work, as part of the mainstream of society. Pushing people into full-time wage labour, or taking away entitlements if they do not seek or remain in it, is not the way to legitimise this work or to encourage the flexibility of working that new technologies and work arrangements enable us to envisage. It will do that only if the state adopts a *passively* supportive relationship to such activity.

With the emerging patterns of activity and institutions of a new civil society, the need to dethrone jobs and labour will become urgent and clear. Consider this forecast by Lester Thurow in 1997, culled from others who had reached similar conclusions:

> The era of lifelong company jobs with regular promotions and annual wage increases is over. It is your responsibility to manage your own lifetime career. But you won't have a lifetime career. No one can manage his or her own career without a road map, and economic road maps cannot be drawn unless there are career ladders across companies. And they simply don't exist. In Europe, the Middle Ages saw vast numbers of masterless labourers wandering back and forth across the countryside. Walled cities and towns were the answer. The Japanese talk about the chaos of having samurai without masters. Our future is the

masterless American labourer, wandering from employer to employer, unable to build a career.

There is some appeal in these predictions. Yet they presume that one needs 'masters' and are suffused with a deterministic pessimism. A tendency towards 'careerlessness' may exist, although having a career has always been the privilege of an elite. There never was an era of 'lifelong jobs' for the vast majority of the American population any more than there was such an era anywhere else. The fatalism that careerlessness is the future is unjustified. The challenge is to find the means of ensuring that a growing proportion of the population do have the opportunity, capacity and desire to build their own career, without needing or wanting 'masters'.

If attention is given to occupational security rather than labour market or employment security, we will focus on different aspects of work. For instance, companies could improve their performance and advance occupational security by reducing controls within the workplace. The company 3M operates a '15% rule' under which employees can spend that amount of work time on their own pet projects. This would appear to deprive shareholders of profits. But it leads to many innovations, and helps dynamic efficiency.

Occupational security will grow when social, economic and institutional policies create an environment in which a growing proportion of the population in any country and any community are able, if they choose, to pursue their own sense of occupation. Mechanisms that delink income security from labour will help, as will mechanisms for redistributing income that is increasingly going to capital.

A universalistic welfare state in an economy with a flexible, fragmenting labour market will have to move away from a labour-conditional form of universalism if it is to achieve the principles of distributive justice espoused earlier. The *floor constraint* would have to be a citizenship allowance, delinked from the performance of wage labour, and the Difference Principle would have to be pursued by capital sharing. These should not be approached in terms of the old ideological split, although the privileged have always opposed any diminution of privilege and usually find it emotionally wrenching to assume a position of the veil of ignorance.

We must restore the status of leisure and contemplative activity. Both should figure as part of what Amartya Sen called 'functionings'. There has been occasion to cite aphorisms of Bertrand Russell several times during this book. We may reflect on two more in this context, written in 1935:

> The idea that the poor should have leisure has always been shocking to the rich. The wise use of leisure ... is a product of civilisation and education. A man who has worked long hours all his life will be bored if he becomes suddenly idle.

While agreeing with these sentiments, they prompt another that would probably not have occurred to Russell's generation, at least not to the same extent as it should at the end of the twentieth century. This is that over-labour is ecologically unbalanced and unsustainable. Energy and time are consumed intensively leaving little attention to reproductive pursuits, whether personal, social or ecological. Intensified pursuit of individual economic gain leaves no space for attention to the finer points of nature, only for the central, larger elements. The finer points include what Russell called *idleness* and Arendt and Aristotle called *contemplation*. With existing institutions, a powerful coalition of interests favour economic growth. Each generation of economists has produced its sages who deplore the unbridled pursuit of growth. Yet, unless the maldistribution of income, economic power and security are addressed, those voices will continue to be heard with little more than a benevolent smile.

The Good Society of the twenty-first century will be one based on the promotion of the right of occupation, or *occupational security*, where increasing numbers of people will be able to combine competencies to create their own occupation, with varying work statuses, and moving in and out of economic activity. In one sense, this will be an extension of individuality, with a growth in the realm of autonomy. In another, the individuality will only flourish if there is a sense of collective security, a sense of community to which the individual belongs. There is a real danger that without a collective anchor, individual flexibility could mean for many a careerless sort of nomadic existence, as suggested by the socio-economic fragmentation that seems to have characterised the era of market regulation. Individual security without collective security is inconceivable. The character and strength of representative organisations and the networking that they facilitate will be crucial to both personal security and the development of the right to occupation.

The pursuit of occupational security requires fresh thinking about the institutional structures to make that feasible and desirable. Traditional notions of household, firm and state, and class, are not appropriate. We must recreate the imagined community and the sense of socio-economic solidarity. What is needed is a structure of firms, associations and public agencies that generate and thrive on *communal individualism*. For this, we must be sceptical about all forms of control, except self-control. Control does not engender loyalty; it obtains obedience, for a while and at a cost. Use of controls reflects a lack of trust and loyalty. If *loyalty* is important, between workers and managers, between citizens, and between those who do wage labour and those who do other forms of work – and it is important for dynamic efficiency and distributive justice – then promoting self-control must be essential. This can only come from ceding control over others and from providing all with basic security and good opportunity. Provide the poor with *assistance, community* and *services*, not controls. Overcoming the oppressive controls exercised by village elders, powerful landlords, commercial middlemen and sundry others is the beginning of freedom. But so too is overcoming the administrative controls exercised in hierarchical firms and the paternalistic controls exercised by bureaucrats who push workfare from the safety of their middle-class affluence and from detachment from the regulatory process applied to the losers of the flexible labour market.

Besides democratic citizenship associations, citizenship income and communal profit sharing, other institutional changes are needed to redress the social fragmentation associated with flexible labour markets and globalisation. However, economic democracy within the production process is essential if political and social democracy are to be meaningful and sustainable. An era of democratic regulation favouring distributive justice may seem a distant prospect at the end of the millennium, yet critics must stop looking back in anger and despair. We must stop being traumatised by the era of market regulation. Every such era has bred a new set of progressive possibilities. That is where history and economics come together. Nemesis is not far when the era's victors think we are at the end of history. The forward march is usually resumed when the losers remember their history and find their voice.

Notes

1 OF WORK, LABOUR AND EMPLOYMENT

1. Similar points were argued by the present writer in a paper prepared for Bruno Kreisky's Commission on European Employment in 1986, in which Dahrendorf and myself had a 'minority' view, the majority favouring a Keynesian approach. For the final report, see Kreisky, 1989.
2. As one document produced in the light of the 1988 revision of International Standard Classification of Occupations (ISCO) put it, 'An occupational classification is a tool for presenting information about the types of work which are performed in the jobs found in an establishment, an industry or a country and for organising this information systematically.' Hoffmann, 1995, p. 1.
3. *Classification of Occupations and Directory of Occupational Titles* (London, Her Majesty's Stationery Office, 1972), Vol.1. Emphasis added.

2 STATUS, CONTROL AND REGULATION

1. Of course, there have been alternatives. For one emphasising 'fairness', see Solow, 1990.

3 THE PURSUIT OF FLEXIBILITY

1. One analysis identified dimensions of what was called 'job insecurity', namely uncertainty about the continuity of the relationship between employer and employee, limited capacity for control over employment, existence of surveillance of working conditions, lack of legal and social protection, and low wages. All are aspects of security, but most are unconcerned with our notion of 'job security'. Meulders, Plasman and Plasman, 1994, p. 234.
2. Arguably, ILO Conventions and Recommendations set the seal of approval for this presumption of social progress. This was a *raison d'être* of the International Labour Organisation, set up in 1919 in the aftermath of the October Revolution for humanitarian and political reasons and to encourage states to provide workers with a growing range of entitlements, to dissuade them from radical thoughts and actions.
3. *Nouvel Observateur*, 15–21 February, 1996, p. 53.
4. The protests of 1968 scared the middle class into acceding the moral case for diversity of behaviour and attitudes. However, the prevailing institutions and forms of social protection were suited to a social norm. Introducing changes to allow for diversity put more strain on the system, undermining the legitimacy of both diversity and the system.
5. Speech to World Bank meeting, Hong Kong, September 1997.
6. There is an analogy with philosophy of science. Following Thomas Kuhn, once a *paradigm* is established, with ways of thinking dictated by its premises, the succeeding period is dominated by puzzle solving that does not question the paradigm itself. Only when a new paradigm emerges into legitimacy do the questions change. This happened with the shift from Keynesianism in the 1970s, leaving defenders of the old verities to whistle ineffectually in the wind.

7. In the European Union, there have been recent cuts, notably in Sweden and in the UK. *The Economist*, Special Supplement on The World Economy, 20 September 1997, p. 8.
8. Numerous examples could be given. Two will suffice. In the 1980s, after years of complaints by employers about job control by printers, British newspaper proprietors were able to introduce new technology and dismiss striking workers. Similarly, in the car industry the collapse of confidence in employment stability led to union acceptance of new work practices, managerial control over job structures and work organisation, and the overthrow of 'shop-steward power'. Managerial control became more direct, no longer transmitted through union representatives.

4 THE RENEWED GROWTH OF LABOUR FLEXIBILITY

1. Decentralisation might be reversed for extraneous reasons, or because of pressure by workers or others. In 1997, an international lobby opposed to child labour successfully pressured major sportswear companies to reverse their use of contract labour in Asian countries. In a factory, firms could prevent workers passing on the work to children.
2. Manning, 1992; Shalev, 1988. The evolution of benefits in Russian enterprises was covered in a multiple-round labour flexibility survey. Standing, 1996a, 1996b.
3. Note that an economic system might lack micro-level flexibility but have macro-level flexibility, because assurance of welfare might induce unions and workers to moderate wage demands or accept real wage cuts in recessions.
4. An anecdotal example: in Malaysia, during a labour flexibility survey, we visited a furniture 'factory', in what was a large house, where about 30 workers were working in various rooms. When asked how many workers he employed, the owner said two. The others were 'sub-contractors'. Indirect labour costs were minimal.
5. *Financial Times*, 23 October 1997. The largest temporary employment agencies in Europe were the Swiss–French company Adecco, Manpower and Randstad.
6. The firm disliked the term 'teleworking' because of its association with 'freelancing'. *Financial Times*, 10 September 1997.
7. This complicates interpretation of data on part-time working, since it may be classified as 'voluntary' in labour force surveys, when it is *force majeure*.
8. John Chait, cited in the *International Herald Tribune*, 2 September 1997.
9. *Financial Times*, 25 October 1996. It was contentious because of last-minute removal of graphs purporting to show the need for more flexibility.

5 THE CRUMBLING OF LABOUR MARKET SECURITY

1. The natural rate supposedly is above the NAIRU, because of the convexity of the Phillips' curve.

6 INSECURITY IN EMPLOYMENT

1. It was puzzling that the OECD (1997a, p. 149) did not find a significant inverse relationship between notice time required and workers' perceived employment security, and found no cross-country relationship between extent of temporary employment and perceived employment insecurity. Since the existence of notice is part of the definition

of employment security, as is non-casual employment, this prompts reservations about the data and consideration of intervening variables.

2. For a study based on a survey of over 3,000 companies in Malaysia, see Standing, 1991.

3. The OECD (1997a, p. 140) stated that 'average tenure did not change between 1985 and 1995 in nine of the ten countries'. But according to their data, tenure fell from 8.3 to 7.8 years in the UK and from 11.5 to 9.1 in Spain. It rose from 9.8 to 10.8 years in Germany and also rose in Australia, Canada, Finland, France, Japan and the Netherlands. The fall in the USA was minimal.

4. The OECD (1997, p. 144) contended that retention rates for the less educated had fallen. However, according to the data they cited, between 1985 and 1995, the rate rose strongly in Australia and slightly in Japan. It fell strongly in Germany.

5. The questionnaire used by the CPS Job Displacement Survey was changed, with a three-year reference period rather than five and changes in the wording of the screening question. There has been a vagueness about whether the person had left a *job* or employment with a particular firm. The distinction between 'voluntary' quits and 'involuntary' job loss is also fuzzy.

6. A friend in an African country told me recently that he had 'been visited by the informal sector', meaning that his house had been burgled. The romanticising of 'the informal sector' has been a feature of labour market and development economics.

7. *Independent*, 31 August 1991. Japan has not ratified any ILO Convention on working time or paid leave.

8. The survey was of 7,400 men and women in London. Known as the Whitehall Study, the findings were published in *The Lancet* (London), July 1997.

9. Chairman, Investor, with directorships and ownership of firms in many countries, employing two million workers.

10. W. Pfaff, 'Job security is disappearing around the world', *International Herald Tribune*, 8 July 1996.

11. For more extended analysis of issues raised in this section, see Standing, July 1997.

7   INCOME INSECURITY IN EMPLOYMENT AND UNEMPLOYMENT

1. That the latest statistics are years out of date indicates the low priority given to tackling poverty and inequality. Unemployment data are produced every month, and relate to the previous month.

2. A deduction is that appropriate policies would be more training and education. Some also conclude that 'rules of trade' should be modified to include labour standards. See, for a review of economists' views, 'Differences in incomes in US suggest trade pacts do hurt unskilled workers', *International Herald Tribune*, 3 November 1997.

3. US Department of Labor, cited in *International Herald Tribune*, 6 March 1996, p. 6.

4. Availability-for-work tests were tightened in the mid-1980s through 'Restart' interviews. Only one-third of those suspended from entitlement were subsequently disentitled on review. So, the majority were wrongly barred for some months.

5. Since UI benefits became taxable, the tax-induced disincentive to claim would have grown stronger since that study.

6. Scarpetta used an average of statutory replacement rates for different durations of unemployment, family situations and earnings. This ignores the probability of entitlement. Some countries may have a high probability of entitlement and a low replacement rate, others a low probability of entitlement and a low replacement rate; in some the unemployed may be concentrated in groups with high replacement rates, in others in groups with low replacement rates, and so on.

7. The probability of being passively unemployed should be inversely related to probability of entitlement to benefits. The index could omit this *probability of claiming* ratio.

8 SOCIAL PROTECTION, FRAGMENTATION AND DETACHMENT

1. This was the estimate of Julien Le Grand, cited in *The Economist*, 20 September 1997, p. 25.
2. Assar Lindbeck, the Swedish economist, produced a series of papers that represented the most intelligent work in this vein. There was even talk about a 'golden rule' for the percentage share of GNP to be spent on social policies.
3. Invalidity benefit has been a function of the degree of incapacity for employment and has been based on a basic rate, close to the gross minimum wage. Thus, it has fallen relative to other incomes, reflecting the decline in the statutory minimum wage.
4. It has also been a remarkably expensive business, with millions of dollars spent on preparation of international reports, pension reform plans and private consultancies.
5. The Russian authorities produced a series of plans, attracted by variants of a funded pillar scheme. The 1997 version envisaged a three-tier system, with a basic social assistance pension, a second tier of a 'labour pension' (dependent on 25 years employment for men and 20 years for women), and a savings account scheme that would gradually become the major pillar, by 2010.
6. This paragraph draws on work by Clare Ungerson. I would also like to thank Mary Daly and Ilona Ostner, who have been working on care issues in Germany and elsewhere.
7. Many people over several decades made contributions to the development of the personal computer. Bill Gates came at the end of the chain. While he made a technical contribution, did he receive his marginal product? In 1999, he was easily the richest individual in the world.
8. The UK Labour Party was fairly typical in thinking that the objective (as expressed in Clause IV of its Constitution) was to obtain for workers 'the full fruits of their labour', which literally would mean that those on the margins of the labour market and of society would be excluded from any income.

9 MINIMUM WAGES, SUBSIDIES AND TAX CREDITS

1. Those who believe high unemployment has become mainly a problem of long-term unemployment, and that if the long-term unemployed were assisted into jobs it would assist the Phillips curve trade-off, should recall the statistical relationship in chapter 5 showing that the long-term unemployment share of unemployment has not increased.
2. Although he had other criticisms, and advocated closing the EITC, Phelps (1997, p. 89) commented, 'According to any standard economic analysis, the tax credit program operates to *reduce* the wage of low-wage workers before the tax credit is taken into account ... For those workers not qualifying for the tax credit, therefore, the effect must be a *reduction* in their wage before and after taxes.'

10 THE ROAD TO WORKFARE

1. On waivers, see 'State efforts to reform welfare', Appendix to 'The future of children', *Welfare to Work*, Vol. 7, No. 1, Spring 1997, pp. 138–44; Savner and Greenberg, 1995.

2. Among early schemes regarded as relatively successful was the Massachusetts Work Experience Programme (MASSWEP), which unlike most was directed at unemployed men. It did not require compulsory work, whereas schemes in states such as West Virginia and North Carolina put emphasis on compulsion. Gueron, 1986.
3. An alternative approach, also costly in public expenditure terms, has been followed in some workfare-type schemes in the USA, where local welfare agencies responsible for them have contracted out work-related activities. That raises questions of public accountability and quality control.

11 NEWS FROM SOMEWHERE: A REDISTRIBUTIVE AGENDA

1. In 1986, the Basic Income European Network (BIEN) was formed, with academics and policy specialists from across Europe. By the late 1990s, it had membership from across the world. BIEN has produced a quarterly newsletter summarising ongoing research, publications, meetings and policy reforms connected with citizenship income.
2. For liberal rationales, see Brittan and Webb, 1990; Parker, 1989.
3. There are other examples. In September 1997, Ted Turner, founder of CNN, announced he was donating $1 billion to good causes, stating that this was his income from the past nine months.
4. The UNDP's *Human Development Report 1995* guesstimated that globally women's housework was worth $17 billion. In the UK, based on a time-use survey, the Office for National Statistics estimated that housework would have cost the equivalent of $550 billion had it been paid at market wages, nearly as much as the workforce received from wage labour. Women did about 60 per cent of the unpaid work. *Financial Times*, 2 October 1997.
5. It is part of the paternalistic twitch to claim that there is 'structural unemployment' that must be rectified by overcoming the 'lack of skills', through more 'training'. How often do politicians, bureaucrats and economists say that the jobs must be changed to suit workers' skills and aspirations?
6. Significantly, only a few weeks before the RMI was sprung on a surprised French public during a Presidential election, government advisers and officials were sceptical that such a move was feasible.
7. For instance, on a pilot basis in 44 cities in Brazil, mothers of young children have been given a basic income on the condition that they send their children to school. That helped to legitimise the scheme. The income has had the triple advantage of combating poverty, improving the independence of poor women, and combating child labour. I am grateful for discussions with Eduardo Suplicy, Senator for Sao Paulo, a leading reformer in this direction.
8. This was also the position of Andre Gorz (1992). He subsequently came to support an unconditional basic income (Gorz, 1997).
9. Some economists believe that it is better to lower marginal tax rates for higher-income earners and raise them for low-income recipients because if that reduces the labour supply of the latter, this does not matter much because they have low social productivity. This view is unedifying.
10. Recall that while the share of national income going to profits has risen, the share of tax revenue coming from capital has declined, and while the share of national income going to labour has declined, the share of tax revenue coming from labour has risen.
11. Thus, profit-sharing pay in Volvo helped undermine the Swedish model, since it eroded the solidaristic wage system that was a vital part of its redistributive strategy (Standing, 1988, chapter 6).

12. A leading proponent was John D. Rockefeller, who presented the company as a sphere of harmony. In fact, it was an attempt to escape from the violent labour relations in the early years of the century.
13. The notion of community means more and less than a geographical location. A community for organisational and distributional purposes may be defined as an association of persons having common or compatible interests, which may be in part geographical, in part an association of people facing a similar set of insecurities.
14. The equivalent to a *real estate agent* or *estate agent*. As befits a 'profession', there have been claims that only those licensed to do so should be allowed to do this job.

Bibliography

Acs, Z., FitzRoy, F. 'A constitution for privatising large Eastern enterprises', *Economics of Transition*, Vol. 2, No.1, 1994, pp. 83–94.

Adriaansens, H., Dercksen, W. 'Labour force participation, citizenship and a sustainable welfare state in the Netherlands', in H. Coenen and P. Leisink (eds), *Work and Citizenship in the New Europe* (Aldershot, Edward Elgar, 1993), pp. 191–204.

ALF-CIO *The Changing Situations of Workers and their Unions: A Report by the ALF-CIO Committee on the Evolution of Work* (Washington DC AFL-CIO, February 1985).

AFL-CIO *Workers' Compensation and Unemployment Insurance under State Laws* (Washington, DC, AFL-CIO, Publication 36, 1989).

AFL-CIO *Unions and Changing Technology* (Washington, DC, AFL-CIO Department of Economic Research, 1993).

Anderson, B. *Imagined Communities: Reflections on the Origin and Spread of Nationalism* (London, Verso, 1983).

Anker, R. *Gender and Jobs: A Global Analysis* (Geneva, ILO, 1998).

Antonelli, C. 'The emergence of the network firm', in C. Antonelli (ed.), *New Information Technology and Industrial Change: The Italian Case* (London, Kluwer Academic, 1988), pp. 13–32.

Aoki, M. *Information, Incentives and Bargaining in the Japanese Economy* (Cambridge, Cambridge University Press, 1988).

Appelbaum, E., Gregory, J. 'Union responses to contingent work. Are win-win outcomes possible?', in K. Cristensen and M. Murphree (eds), *Flexible Workstyles: A Look at Contingent Labor* (Washington DC, US Department of Labor's Women's Bureau, 1988), pp. 69–82.

Appelbaum, E., Schettkat, R. 'Employment and productivity in industrialised countries', *International Labour Review*, Vol.134, No. 4–5, 1995, pp. 605–23.

Arendt, H. *The Human Condition* (Chicago, University of Chicago Press, 1957).

Arneson, R. 'Lockean self-ownership. Towards a demolition', *Political Studies*, Vol. 39, 1991, pp. 36–54.

Asad, T. 'Equality in nomadic social systems', *Critique of Anthropology*, Spring 1978, Vol. 3, No. 11, pp. 57–65.

Ashton, D.N. 'The transition from school to work', *Sociological Review*, Vol. 1, No. 1, 1973, pp. 107–25.

Atkinson, A.B. 'Seeking to explain the distribution of income', in J. Hills (ed.), *New Inequalities. The Changing Distribution of Income and Wealth in the United Kingdom* (Cambridge, Cambridge University Press, 1996), pp. 19–48.

Atkinson, A.B., Hills, J. 'Social Security in developed countries. Are there lessons for developing countries?', in E. Ahmad, J. Drize, J. Hills and A. Sen (eds), *Social Security in Developing Countries* (Oxford, Clarendon Press, 1991), pp. 81–111.

Atkinson, A.B., Micklewright, J. *Turning the screw. Benefits for the unemployed 1979–88* (London, Economic and Social Research Council, Research Report, 1988).

Atkinson, A.B., Micklewright, J. 'Unemployment compensation and labour market transitions. A critical review', *Journal of Economic Literature*, Vol. XXIX, No. 4, December 1991, pp. 1679–727.

Atkinson, J. *Flexibility, Uncertainty and Manpower Management* (London, Institute of Manpower Studies Report, No. 89, 1985).

Atkinson, J. 'Flexibility and fragmentation? The United Kingdom labour market in the eighties', *Labour and Society*, Vol. 14, No. 4, October 1989, pp. 363–407.

Baddeley, M., Martin, R., Tyler, P. *European Regional Unemployment Disparities: Convergence or Persistence?* (Cambridge, University of Cambridge, Department of Land Economy, 1997).

Bahrani, H., Evans, S. 'Flexible re-cycling and high-technology entrepreneurship', *California Management Review*, No. 37, Part 3, June 1995, pp. 62–89.

Balisacan, A.M. 'Comment on political economy of alleviating poverty' by T. Besley, *Annual World Bank Conference on Development Economics 1996* (Washington, DC, The World Bank, 1997), pp. 135–8.

Bardhan, P., Rudra, A. 'Types of labour attachment in agriculture. Results of a survey in West Bengal', *Economical and Political Weekly*, Vol. XV, No. 35, August 30 1980, pp. 1477–84.

Baron, J.N., Dobbins, F.R., Jennings, P.D. 'War and Peace. The evolution of modern personnel administration in US industry', *American Journal of Sociology*, Vol. 92, 1986, pp. 350–83.

Bay, C. 'Self-respect as a human right. Thoughts on the dialectics of wants and needs in the struggle for human community', *Human Rights Quarterly*, Vol. 4, No. 1, Winter 1982, pp. 53–75.

Bellmann, L., Dull, H., Kuhl, J., Lahner, M., Lehmann, U. *Patterns of Enterprise Flexibility in Germany. Results of the IAB Establishment Panel 1993–1995* (Nuremberg, Institute for Employment Research of the Federal Employment Institute, 1996).

Belous, R.S. *The Contingent Economy. The Growth of Temporary, Part-Time and Sub-contracted Workforce* (Washington, DC, National Planning Association, 1989).

Benabou, R. *Inequality and Growth* (Cambridge, MA, National Bureau of Economic Research, Macroeconomics Annual 1996).

Berg, P., Applebaum, E., Bailey, T., Kalleberg, A. 'Performance effects of modular production in the apparel industry', *Industrial Relations*, Vol. 35, No. 3, July 1996, pp. 356–73.

Berman, E., Bound, J., Griliches, Z. 'Changes in the demand for skilled labor within US manufacturing. Evidence from the annual survey of manufactures', *Quarterly Journal of Economics*, Vol. 107, 1992, pp. 35–78.

Bernstein, J. *Welfare Reform and the Low-wage Labour Market. Employment, Wages and Wage Policies* (Washington, DC, Economic Policy Institute, November 1997).

Bertola, G. 'Job security, employment and wages', *European Economic Review*, No. 34, 1990, pp. 851–86.

Besley, T. 'Political economy of alleviating poverty. Theory and institutions', *Annual World Bank Conference on Development Economics 1996* (Washington, DC, The World Bank, 1997), pp. 117–34.

Beveridge, W.H. *Full Employment in a Free Society* (London, George Allen and Unwin, 1944).

Bishop, J., Haveman, R. 'Selective employment subsidies. Can Okun's law be repealed?', *American Economic Review*, Vol. 69, May 1979, pp. 124–30.

Bishop, J., Montgomery, M. 'Does the targeted jobs tax credit create jobs at participating firms?', *Industrial Relations*, Vol. 32, Fall 1993, pp. 289–306.

Blackburn, R.M., Mann, M. *The Working Class in the Labour Market* (Basingstoke, Macmillan, 1979).

Blair, M. *Ownership and Control: Rethinking Corporate Governance for the Twenty-First Century* (Washington, DC, The Brookings Institution, 1995).

Blair, M., Kruse, D., Blasi, J. 'Is employee ownership an unstable form? or a stabilising force?' (Washington, DC, The Brookings Institution, 1998, mimeo.).

Blank, R.M. 'Are part-time jobs bad jobs?', in G. Burtless (ed.), *A Future of Lousy Jobs?* (Washington, DC, The Brookings Institution, 1990), pp. 123–64.

Blasi, J., Conte, M., Kruse, D. 'Employee ownership and corporate performance among public corporations', *Industrial and Labor Relations Review*, Vol. 50, No. 1, October 1996, pp. 60–79.

Boeri, T. 'Enforcement of employment security regulations, on-the-job search and employment duration' (University of Bucconi, 1997, mimeo.).

Boisjoly, J., Duncan, J.G., Smeeding, T. 'Have highly-skilled workers fallen from grace? The shifting burdens of involuntary job losses from 1968–1992' (North-Western University, 1994, mimeo.).

Boltho, A., Glyn, A. 'Can macroeconomic policies raise employment?', *International Labour Review*, Vol. 134, Nos 4–5, 1995, pp. 451–70.

Booth, C: 'Occupations of the people of the United Kingdom 1801–81', *Journal of the Royal Statistical Society*, June 1886, Vol. XLIX.

Borjas, G.J., Ramey, V.A. 'Foreign competition, market power and wage inequality. Theory and evidence' (Cambridge, MA, National Bureau of Economic Research, Working Paper No. 4556, 1993).

Boserup, E. *Women's Role in Economic Development* (New York, St Martin's Press, 1970).

Bound, J., Johnson, G. 'Changes in the structure of wages in the 1980s. An evaluation of alternative explanations', *American Economic Review*, Vol. 82, June 1992, pp. 371–92.

Bowles, S. 'Markets as social institutions' (University of Massachusetts at Amherst, Department of Economics, 1998, mimeo.).

Bowles, S., Gintis, H. *Schooling in Capitalist America* (New York, Basic Books, 1975).

Boyer, R. *The Search for Labour Market Flexibility* (Oxford, Clarendon Press, 1988).

Boyer, R. 'The eighties. The search for alternatives to Fordism', in B. Jessop, H. Kastendiek, K. Nielsen and O.K. Pedersen (eds), *The Politics of Flexibility* (Aldershot, Edward Elgar, 1991), pp. 106–32.

Bradshaw, J., et al. *The Employment of Lone Parents. A Comparison of Policy in 20 Countries* (York, Family Policy Studies Centre, 1996).

Braverman, H. *Labor and Monopoly Capital. The Degradation of Work in the 20th Century* (New York, Monthly Review Press, 1974).

Bregger, J.E. 'Labour force data from the CPS to undergo revision in January 1983', *Monthly Labor Review*, November 1982, pp. 3–6.

Breman, J. 'Seasonal migration and co-operative capitalism. The crushing cane and of labour by the sugar factories of Bardoli, South Gujarat', *Journal of Peasant Studies*, Vol. 6, No. 1, 1978, pp. 41–70.

Brewster, C., Hegewisch, A., Mayne, L. 'Flexible working practices. The controversy and the evidence', in C. Brewster and A Hegewisch (eds), *Policy and Practice in European Human Resource Management* (London and New York, The Price Waterhouse Cranfield Survey, 1994), pp. 168–93.

Brittan, S., Webb, S. *Beyond the Welfare State. An Examination of Basic Incomes in a Market Economy* (Aberdeen, Aberdeen University Press, 1990).

Bronowski, J. *The Ascent of Man* (London, BBC Books, 1973).

Brown, G. *Sabotage* (Nottingham, Spokesman Books, 1977).

Brown, R. 'Work histories, career strategies and the class structure', in A. Giddens and G. Mackenzie (eds), *Social Class and the Division of Labour: Essays in Honour of Ilya Neustadt* (Cambridge, Cambridge University Press, 1982), pp. 119–36.

Brown, W., Deakin, S., Ryan, P. 'The effect of British industrial relations legislation 1979–97', *National Institute Economic Review*, July 1997.

Buechtemann, C.F. 'The socio-economics of individual working time reduction. Empirical evidence for the Federal Republic of Germany', in J.B. Agassi and S. Heycock (eds), *The Redesign of Working Time. Promise or Threat?* (Berlin, Sigma, 1989), pp. 178–206.

Burchardt, T., Hills, J. *Private Welfare Insurance and Social Security* (York, York Publishing Services, 1997).

Burchell, B. 'The effects of labour market position, job insecurity and unemployment on psychological health', in D. Gallie, C. Marsh and C. Vogler (eds), *Social Change and the Experience of Unemployment* (Oxford and New York, Oxford University Press, 1993), pp. 188–212.

Burda, M., Sachs, J. *Labour Markets and Employment in West Germany* (Cambridge, MA, NBER, 1987).

Bureau of National Affairs. 'The changing workplace: New directions in staffing and scheduling' (Washington, DC; 1986, mimeo.).

Burgess, R., Stern, N. 'Social security in developing countries. What, why, who, and how?', in E. Ahmed, J. Drize, J. Hills and A. Sen (eds), *Social Security in Developing Countries* (Oxford, Clarendon, 1991), pp. 41–80.

Burgess, S. 'The reallocation of employment and the role of employment protection legislation' (London School of Economics, Centre for Economic Performance Discussion Paper No.193, 1994).

Buroway, M. *Manufacturing Consent* (Chicago, University of Chicago Press, 1979).

Burtless, G.T. 'Are targeted wage subsidies harmful? Evidence from a wage voucher experiment', *Industrial and Labor Relations Review*, Vol. 39, October 1985, pp. 105–14.

Burtless, G.T. 'Welfare recipients' job skills and employment prospects', *Welfare to Work*, Vol. 7, No. 1, Spring 1997, pp. 39–51.

Byres, T.J. (ed.): 'Sharecropping and sharecroppers', Special Issue, *The Journal of Peasant Studies*, January–April 1983, Vol. 10, Nos 2 and 3, pp. 7–40.

Byrne, D., Jacobs, J. 'Disqualified from benefit. The operation of benefit penalties', *Low Pay Pamphlet, No. 49* (London, Low Pay Unit, 1988).

Card, D., Kramarz, F., Lemieux, T. 'Changes in the relative structure of wages and employment. A comparison of the US, Canada and France' (National Bureau of Economic Research Working Paper, No. 5487, Cambridge, MA, 1996).

Card, D., Krueger, A. *Myth and Measurement. The New Economies of the Minimum Wage* (Princeton, New Jersey, Princeton University Press, 1995).

Card, D., Robins, P.K. 'Do financial incentives encourage welfare recipients to work? Evidence from the randomized evaluation of the self-sufficient project' (*National Bureau of Economic Research Working Paper* No. 5701, Cambridge, MA, 1996).

Casey, B. 'Back to the poor law? The emergence of "workfare" in Britain, Germany and the USA', *Policy Studies*, Vol.7, No.1, July 1986, pp. 52–64.

Casey, B., Metcalf, H., Milward, N. *Employers' Use of Flexible Labour* (London, Policy Studies Institute, 1997).

Castles, F.G., Mitchell, D. 'Identifying welfare state regimes. The links between politics, instruments and outcomes', *Governance: An International Journal of Policy and Administration*, Vol. 5, No. 1, 1992, pp. 1–26.

Centre for Tomorrow's Company. *The Inclusive Approach and Business Success. The Research Evidence* (London, CTC, 1998).

Chandler, A.D. 'Organisational capabilities and industrial restructuring. A historical analysis', *Journal of Comparative Economics*, Vol.17, No. 2, 1993, pp. 309–37.

Chikanova, L., Smirnov, P. 'The Disabled Workers in Russia', paper prepared for ILO-CEET (Budapest, July 1993, mimeo.)

Child, J. 'New technology and development in management organisation', *Omega*, Vol.12, No. 3, 1984.

Chote, R. 'A fashion for independence', *Financial Times*, 9 June 1997.

Christian, L.P., Vakasquez, M. 'Unemployment insurance. Theoretical approaches and empirical evidence', *International Social Security Review*, Vol. 49, No.1, 1994, pp. 37–54.

Cichon, M. 'The European Welfare states at the crossroads. Are there better ways to cut the cake?', Issues in Social Protection, Discussion Paper 3, ILO, February 1997.

Clark, C.M.A., Healy, J. *Pathways to a Basic Income* (Dublin, Report for the Justice Commission of the Conference on Religious of Ireland (CORI), April, 1997).

Clark, P.B., Laxton, D. 'Phillips Curves, Phillips Lines and the unemployment costs of overheating' (Washington, DC, International Monetary Fund, Working Paper WP/97/17, February 1997).

Clarke, S. (ed.). *Labour Relations in Transition: Wages, Employment and Industrial Conflict in Russia* (Cheltenham, Edward Elgar, 1996).

Coenen, H., 'The concept of work in the trade unions. Towards a debate on economic rights', in H. Coenen and P. Leisink (eds), *Work and Citizenship in the New Europe* (Aldershot, Edward Elgar, 1993), pp. 173–87.

Coenen H., Leisink, P. (eds) *Work and Citizenship in the New Europe* (Aldershot, Edward Elgar, 1993).

Cohen, G.A. 'Incentives, inequality and community', in G.B. Peterson (ed.), *The Tanner Lectures on Human Values* (Salt Lake City, University of Utah Press, 1992).

Cohen, G.A. 'Equality of what? On welfare, goods and capabilities', in M. Nussbaum and A. Sen (eds), *The Quality of Life* (Oxford, Clarendon Press, 1993), pp. 9–29.

Cohen, G.A. *Self-Ownership, Freedom and Equality* (Cambridge, Cambridge University Press and Editions de la Maison des Sciences de l'Homme, 1995).

Colclough, C. (ed.). *Public Sector Pay and Adjustment: Lessons from Five Countries* (London, Routledge, 1998).

Cole, G.D.H. *Guild Socialism Restated* (London, Leonard Parsons, 1920).

Collins, J.C., Portas, J.I. *Built to Last – Successful Habits of Visionary Companies* (New York, Century, 1995).

Committee for Economic Development: *American Workers and Economic Change* (New York, 5 July 1996).

Commons, J.R. *Institutional Economics* (New York, Macmillan, 1934).

Conference Board, The *Implementing the New Employment Compact* (New York, Human Resource Executive Review, The Conference Board, 1997).

Connock, S. 'Workforce flexibility: Juggling time and task', *Personnel Management*, October 1985.

Cooper, C.L., Liukkanen, P., Cartwright, S. *Stress Prevention in the Workplace. Assessing the Costs and Benefits to Organisations* (Dublin, European Foundation for the Improvement of Living and Working Conditions, 1996).

Copeland, L. 'Valuing diversity, Part 1. Making the most of cultural difference at the workplace', *Personnel*, June, 1988a, pp. 53–60.

Copeland, L. 'Valuing diversity, Part 2. Pioneers and champions of change', *Personnel*, July 1988b, pp. 44–9.

Corbett, T., Deloya, J., Manning, W., Uhr, L. 'Learnfare: The Wisconsin experience', *Focus* (University of Wisconsin-Madison, Institute for Research on Poverty), Vol. 12, No. 2, Fall–Winter, 1989, pp. 1–10.

Cornfield, D.B. 'Labour union responses to technological change: past, present and future', *Perspectives on Work*, Vol.1, No.1, 1997, pp. 35–8.

Corson, W., Nicholson, W. 'Unemployment insurance, income maintenance and re-employment trade-offs in a competitive world economy', *The Secretary's Seminars on*

Unemployment Insurance (Washington, DC, Department of Labor, Occasional Paper 89–1, 1989).

Council of Economic Advisers *Explaining the Decline in Welfare Receipt, 1993–1996* (Washington, DC, US Government Printing Office, Technical Report, 1997).

Cowherd, D.M., Levine, D. 'Product quality and pay equity between lower-level employees and top management. An investigation of distributive justice theory', *Administrative Science Quarterly*, Vol. 37, No. 2, 1992, pp. 302–20.

Cox, D., Jiminez, E. *The Connection between Social Security: Private Transfers in Peru* (Washington, DC, The World Bank, Public Economics Division, 1989).

Crouch, C., Traxler, T. (eds) *Organized Industrial Relations in Europe. What future?* (Aldershot, Avebury, 1995).

Cusan, A. and Motivans, A. 'Education in transition. Trends in finance, access and quality', paper prepared for Fifth UNICEF Monitoring Report, UNICEF-International Child Development Centre, Florence, January 1998.

Dahrendorf, R. *The Modern Social Conflict. An Essay on the Politics of Liberty* (New York, Weidenfeld and Nicolson, 1988).

Dallago, B. *The Irregular Economy* (Aldershot, Dartmouth, 1990).

Daly, M. 'Welfare states under pressure. Cash benefits in European welfare states over the past ten years', *Journal of European Social Policy*, Vol. 7, No. 2, May 1997, pp. 129–46.

Deane, P., Cole, W.A. *British Economic Growth 1888–1959. Trends and Structure* (Cambridge, Cambridge University Press, 1967).

Debelle, M., Fischer, G. *Goals and Outlines and Constraints Facing Monetary Policymakers* (Boston, Federal Reserve Bank of Boston, 1994).

Delruelle-Vosswinkel, N. 'The socio-cultural factors of new poverty', paper presented at the Seminar on New Poverty in the European Community, Brussels, Université Libre de Bruxelles, 28–29 April, 1988.

de Neubourg, C. *Unemployment and Labour Market Flexibility: The Netherlands* (Geneva, ILO, 1990).

Derber, C.(ed.): *Professionals as Workers. Mental Labour in Advanced Capitalism* (Boston, G.K. Hall, 1982).

Desai, M. 'A basic income proposal' (London, London School of Economics, June 1997, mimeo.).

Deshpande, S., Standing, G., Deshpande, L. *Labour Flexibility in a Third World Metropolis* (New Delhi, Commonwealth Publishers, 1998).

de Tocqueville, A. *Discours sur le droit au travail*, (Paris, Librairie L. Curmer, 1848) pp. 7–9.

de Tocqueville, A. 'Memoir on pauperism', in S. Drescher (ed.), *Tocqueville and Beaumont on Social Reform* (New York, Harper and Row, 1968).

Deyo, F.C. 'State and labor. Modes of political exclusion in East Asian development', in F.C. Deyo (ed.), *The Political Economy of the New Asian Industrialism* (Ithaca, New York, Cornell University Press, 1987), pp. 182–202.

Dickens, R. 'Wage mobility in Great Britain', *Employment Audit* (London), Spring 1997.

Dickert, S., Hauser, S., Scholz, J. 'The earned income tax credit transfer programs. A study of labour market and program participation', in J. Poterba (ed.), *Tax Policy and the Economy* (Cambridge, MA, Massachusetts Institute of Technology Press, 1995).

Diebold, F.X., Neumark, D., Polsky, D. 'Job stability in the United States', *Journal of Labor Economics*, Vol. 15, No. 2, 1997, pp. 206–33.

Dobb, M.H. *Studies in the Development of Capitalism* (London, Routledge and Kegan Paul, 1946).

Doeringer, P., Christensen, K., Flynn, P.M., Hall, D.T., Katz, H.C., Keefe, J.H., Ruhm, C.J., Sum, A.M., Useem, M. *Turbulence in the American Workplace* (New York and Oxford, Oxford University Press, 1991).

Duncan, G.J., Harris, K.M., Boisjoly, J. 'Time limits and welfare reform. New estimates of the number and characteristics of affected families' (North-Western University, 1997, mimeo.).

Dunning, J.H. *The Globalisation of Business* (London, Routledge, 1993).

Durkheim, E. *The Division of Labour in Society* (New York, The Free Press, 1964 edition).

Dworkin, R. 'What is equality? Part I: Equality of welfare', *Philosophy and Public Affairs*, Vol. 10, 1981b, pp. 185–246.

Dworkin, R. 'What is equality? Part 2: Equality of resources', *Philosophy and Public Affairs*, Vol. 10, 1981a, pp. 283–345.

Early, S., Cohen, L. 'Jobs with Justice. Mobilising labor-community coalitions', *Working USA*, November–December 1997, pp. 49–57.

Economic Council of Canada: *Good Jobs, Bad Jobs: Employment in the Service Economy* (Ottawa, Economic Council of Canada, 1990).

Edin, K.J. 'The myths of dependence and self-sufficiency. Women, welfare and low-wage work', *Focus*, Fall/Winter 1995, No. 2, pp. 1–9.

Edwards, R. *Contested Terrain* (New York, Basic Books Incorporated, 1979).

Edwards, S. 'Terms of trade, tariffs and labour market adjustment in developing countries', *The World Bank Economic Review*, Vol. 2, No. 2, 1988, pp. 165–85.

Egger, P., Poschen, P. (eds) *Contract Labour: Looking at Issues – Nine Country Cases* (Geneva, ILO, 1997).

Eisner, R. *The Misunderstood Economy. What Counts and How to Count it* (Boston, MA, Harvard Business School Press, 1995).

Eissa, N., Leibman, J. 'Labour supply response to the earned income tax credit', *Quarterly Journal of Economics*, May 1996, Vol. CXI, Issue 2, pp. 605–37.

Elson, D., Pearson, R. 'The subordination of women and the internationalisation of factory production and of marriage and the market', in K. Young, C. Wolkowitz and O.R. McCullagh (eds), *Of Marriage and the Market. Women's Subordination in International Perspective*, (London, CSE Books, 1981).

Elster, J. *Ulysses and the Sirens in Rationality and Irrationality* (Cambridge, Cambridge University Press, 1979).

Elster, J. 'Comment on Van der Veen and Van Parijs', *Theory and Society*, Jrg.15, 1986, pp. 709–21.

Employment Centre, The *Would Workfare Work?* (Buckingham, University of Buckingham, 1987).

Engbersen, G. 'Modern poverty and second-class citizenship', in H. Coenen and P. Leisink (eds), *Work and Citizenship in the New Europe* (Aldershot, Edward Elgar,1993), pp. 35–48.

EPOC Research Group: *Direct Employee Participation in Europe* (Dublin, Foundation for the Improvement of Living and Working Conditions, 1997).

Equal Opportunities Commission, *Code of Practice* (London, HM Stationery Office, 1985).

Esping-Andersen, G. *The Three Worlds of Welfare Capitalism* (Cambridge, Polity Press, 1990).

Esping-Anderson, G. 'Hybrid or unique? The Japanese welfare state between Europe and America', *Journal of European Social Policy*, Vol. 7, No. 3, August 1997, pp. 179–89.

Estrin, S., Perotin, V., Wilson, N. 'Profit-sharing revisited: Miracle cure or mirage?' (Paris OECD, 1994).

Ettighoffer, D. *Enterprise Virtuelle: ou les Nouveaux Modes de Travail* (Paris, Odile Jacob, 1992).

412   *Global Labour Flexibility*

European Commission *Social Protection in the Member States of the European Union* (Luxembourg, Office for Official Publications of the European Communities, 1994a).

European Commission *White Paper: Growth, Competitiveness, Employment. The Challenges and Ways Forward into the 21st Century* (Brussels, EC Directorate General V, June 1994b).

European Commission *Performance of the European Union Labour Market. Results of an Ad Hoc Labour Market Survey covering Employers and Employees* (Brussels, European Economy Reports and Studies No. 3, 1995).

European Commission *1997 Annual Economic Report: Growth, Employment and Convergence on the Road to the EMU* (Brussels, COM(97)27, European Commission, February 1997).

European Commission *Green Paper: Partnership for a New Organisation of Work* (Brussels, Com (97) 128, April 1997).

European Foundation for Quality Management. 'Total quality management', *The European Model for Self Appraisal: Guidelines for Identifying and Addressing Total Quality Issues* (Brussels, European Foundation for Quality Management, 1992).

European Industrial Relations Review No. 182, March 1989, pp. 11–16.

European Industrial Relations Review No. 258, July 1995, pp. 16–18.

European Industrial Relations Review No. 263, December 1995, p. 13.

Eurostat *Work Organisation and Working Hours 1983–92* (Luxembourg, Eurostat, 1995).

Eurostat *Labour Force Survey: Results 1995* (Luxembourg, Eurostat, 1996).

Evers, A. 'Payments for care. A small but significant part of a wider debate', in A. Evers, M. Pijl and C. Ungerson (eds), *Payments for Care. A Comparative Overview* (Aldershot, Avebury, 1994), pp. 27–8.

Farber, H.S. 'The changing face of job loss in the United States, 1981–1993' (Princeton University, Industrial Relations Section, Working Paper No. 360, 1996).

Farber, H.S. 'The changing face of job loss in the US, 1981–95', *Brookings Papers on Economic Activity: Microeconomics* (Washington, DC, The Brookings Institution, 1997), pp. 55–128.

Farber, H.S. 'Has the rate of job loss increased over time?', paper presented at the Annual General Meeting of the Industrial Relations Research Association, Chicago, January 1998.

Feldstein, M. 'Would social security raise economic welfare?' (Cambridge, MA, National Bureau of Economic Research, Working Paper No. 5281, 1996).

Feldstein, M., Samwick, A. 'The transition path in privatising social security' (Cambridge, MA, National Bureau of Economic Research, Working Paper No. 5761, 1996).

Felstead, A., Jewson, N. 'Working at home. Estimates from the 1991 Census', *Employment Gazette*, March 1995.

Field, F. *Losing Out. The Emergence of Britain's Underclass* (Oxford, Blackwell, 1989).

Finance and Development: 'Wage dispersion and growth in the United States', *Finance and Development*, June 1995, pp. 16–20.

Fisher, S. 'Real balances, The exchange rate and indexation. Real variables in disinflation' (Cambridge, MA, National Bureau of Economic Research Working Paper No. 1497, 1984).

FitzGerald, G. 'Basic income system has merit for Ireland', *Irish Times*, 12 April 1997.

Foucault, M. 'Disciplinary power and subjection', in S. Lukes (ed.), *Power* (New York, New York University Press, 1986).

Frank, R.H., Cook, P.J. *The Winner-Take-All Society* (New York, Free Press, 1995).

Franzmeyer, F., Lindlar, L., Trabold, H. *Does Internationalisation Constrain National Employment and Social Policies?* (Berlin and The Hague, Ministry of Social Affairs, Government of the Netherlands, November 1996).

Fraser, N. 'After the family wage. Gender equality and the welfare state', *Political Theory*, Vol. 22, No. 4, 1993, pp. 591–618.

Freeman, C. *Technology Policy and Economic Performance: Lessons from Japan* (London, Francis Pinter, 1987).

Freeman, R., Kleiner, M.M. 'From piece rates to time rates: Surviving global competition', paper presented at the Industrial Relations Research Association Meeting, Chicago, January 3, 1998.

Freeman, R., Medoff, J. *What Do Unions Do?* (New York, Basic Books, 1984).

Freeman, R., Rodgers, J. *Worker Representation and Participation in the US* (Princeton, Princeton Survey Research Associates, 1995).

Friedlander, B., Goldman, B., Gueron, J., Long, D. 'Initial findings from the demonstration of State work/welfare initiatives', *American Economic Review*, Vol. 76, No. 2, May 1986, pp. 224–9.

Friedlander, B., Gueron, J. *Are High Cost Services Less Effective than Low Cost Services?* (New York, Manpower Demonstration Research Corp., 1990).

Friedman, B., Davenport, B., Evans, R., Hahn, A., Hausman, L., Paprirno, C. *An Evaluation of the Massachusetts Work Experience Program* (Washington, DC, US Department of Health and Human Services, 1981).

Friedman, G. *The Anatomy of Work* (London, Heineman, 1961).

Friedman, M. *Capitalism and Freedom* (Chicago, University of Chicago Press, 1962).

Friedman, M. 'The social responsibility of business is to increase its profit', *New York Times Magazine*, 13 September 1970, pp. 32–3.

Frohlich, N., Oppenheimer, J.A. *Choosing Justice. An Experimental Approach to Ethical Theory* (Berkeley, University of California Press, 1992).

Fukuyama, F. *The End of Order* (London, The Social Market Foundation, September 1997).

Gallie, D., White, M., Chang, Y., Tomlinson, M. *Restructuring the Employment Relationship* (Oxford, Oxford University Press, 1998).

Gillespie, A., Li, F. 'Teleworking, work organisations and the workplace', in R. Mansell (ed.), *Management of Information and Communication Technologies* (London, ASLIB, 1994), pp. 261–72.

Gillespie, A., Richardson, R., Cornford, J. *Review of Telework in Britain. Implications for Public Policy* (Newcastle upon Tyne, Centre for Urban and Regional Development Studies, February 1995).

Glenndenning, C., McLaughlin, E. *Paying for Care: Lessons from Europe* (London, Social Security Advisory Committee Research Paper No. 5, HMSO, 1993).

Glennerster, H., Evans, M. 'Beveridge and his assumptive worlds. The incompatibilities of a flawed design', in J.Hills et al. (eds), *Beveridge and Social Security* (Oxford, Clarendon Press, 1994).

Goldman, B. et al. *Findings from the San Diego Job Search and Work Experience Demonstration* (New York, Manpower Demonstration Research Corporation, 1985).

Gonzalez, P. 'Indicators of the relative performance of women in the labour market' (University of Cambridge, 1995, mimeo.).

Goodin, R. *Protecting the Vulnerable. A Re-Analysis of our Social Responsibilities* (Chicago, Chicago University Press, 1985).

Goodin, R. *Reasons for Welfare* (Princeton, Princeton University Press, 1988).

Goodin, R., LeGrand, J.(eds) *Not Only the Poor: The Middle Classes and the Welfare State* (London, Allen and Unwin, 1987).

Goodman, R., Peng, I. 'The east Asian welfare states', in G. Esping-Andersen (ed.), *Welfare States in Transition* (London, Sage, 1996), pp. 192–224.

Goodwin, L. *Causes and Cures of Welfare. New Evidence on the Social Psychology of the Poor* (Lexington, MA, D.C. Health, 1983).

Gorz, A. *Farewell to the Working Class. An Essay on Post-Industrial Socialism* (London, Pluto Press, 1983).

Gorz, A. 'L' allocation universelle: version de droite et version de gauche', *Revue Nouvelle*, No. 81, 1985, pp. 419–28.

Gorz, A. 'On the difference between society and community, and why basic income cannot by itself confere full membership of either', in P.Van Parijs (ed.), *Arguing for Basic Income* (London, Verso, 1992), pp. 178–84.

Gorz, A. *Miseres du present, richesse du possible* (Paris, Galille, 1997).

Gough, I., Bradshaw, J., Ditch, J., Earkley, T., Whiteford, P. 'Social assistance in the OECD countries', *Journal of European Social Policy*, Vol.7, No.1, February 1997, pp. 17–44.

Gramsci, A. 'Americanism and Fordism', in Q. Hoare and G.N. Smith (eds), *Selections from the Prison Notebooks of Antonio Gramsci* (London, Lawrence and Wishart, 1971).

Granovetter, M. 'Economic action and social structure. The problem of embeddedness', *American Journal of Sociology*, Vol. 91, No. 3, November 1985, pp. 481–510.

Gray, J. 'When the dream turns into a nightmare', *Financial Times*, 23 March 1998.

Gregg, P., Wadsworth, J. 'A short history of labour turnover, job tenure and job security', *Oxford Review of Economic Policy*, Spring 1995, pp. 73–90.

Gregg, P., Wadsworth, J. 'Mind the gap please. The changing nature of entry jobs in Britain' (London School of Economics, Centre for Economic Performance, Discussion Paper No. 303, 1996).

Greif, A. 'Cultural beliefs and the organisation of society. A historical and theoretical reflection on collectivist and individualistic societies', *Journal of Political Economy*, Vol. 102, No. 5, 1994, pp. 912–50.

Greif, A. 'Contracting, enforcing and efficiency. Economics beyond the law', presented at the Annual World Bank Conference on Developmental Economics 1996 (Washington, DC, The World Bank, 1997).

Grimshaw, D., Rubery, J. 'Workforce heterogeneity and unemployment benefits. The need for policy reassessment in the European Union', *Journal of European Social Policy*, Vol. 7, No. 4, November 1997, pp. 291–318.

Gueron, J.M. 'Work for people on welfare', *Public Welfare*, Vol. 44, No. 1, 1986, pp. 7–12.

Gutmann, A., Thompson, D. *Democracy and Disagreement* (Cambridge, MA, Harvard University Press, 1996).

Habermas, J. *Legitimation Crisis* (London, Heineman, 1976).

Hakim, C. 'Workforce restructuring in Europe in the 1980's', *International Journal of Comparative Labor Law and Industrial Relations*, Vol. 5, No. 4, 1990, pp. 220–40.

Handy, C. *The Hungry Spirit* (New York, Broadway Books, 1998).

Hansmann, H. *The Ownership of Enterprise* (Cambridge, Harvard University Press, 1996).

Haveman, R. 'Reducing poverty while increasing employment. A primer alternative strategies and a blueprint', *OECD Economic Studies*, No. 26, 1996/1, pp. 8–42.

Hawkins, R., Webb, J., Corry, D. 'Sense of well-being. The process of forming a well-being index raises many issues', *New Economy*, Vol. 3, Issue 1, Spring 1996.

Hayek, F. *The Road to Serfdom* (London, Routledge and Kegan Paul, 1944).

Heckscher, C. *The New Unionism: Employee Involvement in Changing Corporation* (Ithaca and London, Cornell Press, 1996 edition).

Hedges, B. 'Work in a changing climate', *British Social Attitudes* (London, Social and Community Planning Research, 11th Report, 1994).

Held, D. 'Between state and civil society', in G. Andrews (ed.), *Citizenship* (London, Lawrence and Wishart, 1991), pp. 19–25.

Henzler, H.A. 'The new era of Eurocapitalism', *Harvard Business Review*, July–August, 1992, pp. 57–63.

Hershey, A.M., Pavetti, L.A. 'Turning job finders into job keepers', *Welfare to Work*, Vol. 7, No. 1, Spring 1997, pp. 74–86.

Heycock, S. 'New technology in the coal industry and its affects upon patterns of work organisation', in J.B. Agassi and S. Heycock (eds), *The Redesign of Working Time: Promise or Threat?* (Berlin, Edition Sigma, 1989), pp. 84–95.

Heycock, S. 'With every pair of hands you get a free brain', in H. Coenen and P. Leisink (eds), *Work and Citizenship in the New Europe* (Aldershot, Edward Elgar, 1993), pp. 150–1.

Hirschman, A. *The Rhetoric of Reaction: Perversity, Futility, Jeopardy* (Cambridge, MA, Harvard University Press, 1991).

Hirst, P., Thompson, G. *Globalisation in Question* (London, Polity Press, 1996).

HMSO. *Classification of Occupations and Directory of Occupational Titles* (London, Her Majesty's Stationary Office, 1972), Vol.1.

Hobson, B. 'No exit, no voice: A comparative analysis of women's dependency and the welfare state', *Acta Sociologica*, Vol. 33, No. 3, 1990, pp. 235–50.

Hochschild, A.R. *The Time Bound* (New York, Metropolitan Books, H. Holt and Co., 1997).

Hodgson, G. *Economics and Institutions. A Manifesto for a Modern Institutional Economics* (Oxford, Polity Press, 1988).

Hoffmann, E., Elias, P., Embury, B., Thomas, R. 'What kind of work do you do?: Data collection and processing strategies when measuring "occupation" for statistical surveys and administrative records' (STAT Working Paper, No. 95–1, ILO, Bureau of Statistics, 1995).

Huws, U. *Teleworking in Britain* (London, Employment Department, Research Series No.18, October 1993).

Huws, U. *Follow-up to the White Paper: Teleworking* (Brussels, European Commission, DGV Employment Task Force, September 1994).

Huws, U. 'Teleworking. An overview of the research' (London, report prepared for the Government, 1996, mimeo.).

Illich, I. *The Right to Useful Unemployment* (London, Marion Boyars Ltd, 1978).

Illich, I. *Towards a History of Needs* (New York, Bantam Books, 1980).

Illingsworth, M.M. 'Virtual managers', *Information Week*, 13 June, 1994.

ILO, *Constitution of the ILO, Annex: Declaration Concerning the Aims and Purposes of the ILO* (Geneva, ILO, 1982).

ILO International Labour Conference, 69th Session, 1983, 'Resolution concerning employment', adopted June 21, 1983, *Record of Proceedings* (Geneva, ILO, 1983).

ILO *Social and Labour Bulletin* ILO No.1, March 1985.

ILO *ISCO-88: International Standard Classification of Occupations* (Geneva, ILO, 1988).

ILO 'Telework', *Conditions of Work Digest*. Vol. 9, No. 1. (Geneva, ILO, 1990).

ILO *World Employment Report 1995* (Geneva, ILO, 1995a).

ILO *Report to the Director General: Fifth European Regional Conference, Warsaw, September 1995* (Geneva, ILO, 1995b).

ILO *World Employment Report 1997* (Geneva, ILO, 1997a).

ILO *World Labour Report 1997* (Geneva, ILO, 1997b).

ILO 'Minimum wage fixing in the Netherlands' (Geneva, ILO, Labour Law and Labour Relations Briefing note No.7, July 1997).

ILO 'Minimum wage fixing in Portugal' (Geneva, ILO, Labour Law and Labour Relations Briefing note No. 8, August 1997).

IMF *World Economic Outlook* (Washington, DC, International Monetary Fund, April 1997).

IMF *World Economic Outlook* (Washington, DC, International Monetary Fund, September 1997).

Inoue, S., Suzuki, F. 'The high road to development: Japan and the stakeholder agenda', in D. Foden and P. Morris (eds), *The Search for Equity* (London, Lawrence and Wishart, 1998), pp. 51–8.

INSEE *Nomenclature des Professions et Categories Socioprofessionelles* (Paris, INSEE, 1982).

International Survey Research: *Employee Satisfaction: Tracking European Trends* (London, ISR, 1995).

Jackall, R., Levin, H.M. (eds) *Worker Co-operatives in America* (Berkeley, University of California Press, 1984).

Jackman, R., Layard, R. 'A wage tax, worker subsidy policy for reducing the natural rate of unemployment', in W. Beckerman (ed.), *Wage Rigidity* (Baltimore, Johns Hopkins University Press, 1986), pp. 153–69.

Jacoby, S.M. 'Current prospects for employee representation in the US. Old wine in new bottles?', *Journal of Labor Research*, Vol. XVL, No. 3, Summer 1995, p. 388.

Jacoby, S.M. 'What the founders thought. Excerpts from industrial relations research of the post-war period', *Perspectives on Work*, Vol.1, No.1, 1997, pp. 6–9.

Jacoby, S.M., Verma, A. 'Enterprise unions in the United States', *Industrial Relations*, Vol. 31, No. 1, Winter 1992, pp. 137–58.

Jamieson, A. 'Community care for older people. Policies in Britain, West Germany and Denmark', in G. Room (ed.), *Towards a European Welfare State* (Bristol, SAUS, 1991a) pp. 107–26.

Jamieson, A. *Home Care for Older People in Europe: A Comparison of Politics and Practices* (Oxford, Oxford University Press, 1991b).

Jaques, E. *Equitable Payment* (London, Heineman, 1961).

Jefferys, S. 'European industrial relations and welfare states', *European Journal of Industrial Relations*, Vol. 1, No. 3, November 1995, pp. 317–40.

Joekes, S. 'The influence of international trade expansion on women's work', paper prepared for the ILO, Project on Equality for Women in Employment (Geneva, ILO, June 1993).

Kamata, S. *Japan in the Passing Lane* (London, Allen and Unwin, 1983).

Kantor, R.M. *When Giants Learn to Dance* (New York, Simon and Schuster, 1989).

Kaplan, R.S., Norton, D.P. 'The Balanced Scorecard – Measures that drive performance', *Harvard Business Review*, January–February 1992, pp. 71–9.

Kaplan, R.S., Norton, D.P. 'Putting the balanced scorecard to work', *Harvard Business Review*, September–October 1993, pp. 134–47.

Katz, L. *The Undeserving Poor: From the War on Poverty to the War on Welfare* (New York, Pantheon Books, 1989).

Katz, L. 'Wage subsidies for the disadvantaged' (Harvard University and NBER, July 1996, mimeo.).

Katz, L., Krueger, A. 'The effect of the minimum wage on the fast food industry', *Industrial and Labour Relations Review*, Vol. 46, No. 1, October 1992, pp. 6–21.

Keen, P.G.W. *Shaping the Future: Business Design through Information Technology* (Cambridge, MA, Harvard Business School Press, 1991).

Kerr, C. 'The balkanisation of labour markets', in G.W Bakke (ed.), *Labour Mobility and Economic Opportunity* (New York, Wiley and Sons, 1954).

Kleiman, C. 'Changing jobs at the drop of a hat', *Washington Post*, 5 May 1990.

Kletzer, L.C. 'Increasing foreign competition and job insecurity. Are they related?' paper presented at the Industrial Relations Research Association Meeting, Chicago, 3 January 1998.

Knight, J. 'Labour market policies and outcomes in post-Independence Zimbabwe. Lessons for Southern Africa', paper presented at 16th Arne Ryde Symposium, University of Lund, 22–24 August 1996a.

Knight, J. 'Labour market policies and outcomes in Zimbabwe' (University of Oxford, Centre for the Study of African Economies, August 1996b, mimeo.).

Knijn, T., Kremer, M. 'Gender and the caring dimension of welfare states. Towards inclusive citizenship', *Social Politics: International Studies in Gender, State and Society*, Vol. 4, No. 3, Fall 1997, pp. 328–61.

Kochan, T.A., Osterman, P. *The Mutual Gains Enterprise. Forging a Winning Partnership Among Labour, Management and Government* (Boston, MA, Harvard Business School Press, 1994).

Kohn, M.L., Naoi, A; Schoenbach, C., Schooler, C., Slomocyznski, K.M. 'Position in the class structure land psychological functioning in the United States, Japan and Poland', *American Journal of Sociology*, Vol. 95, No. 4, January 1990, pp. 964–1008.

Kohn, M.L., Schooler, C. 'The effects of the substantive complexity of the job on intellectual flexibility. A longitudinal perspective', *American Journal of Sociology*, Vol. 84, 1978, pp. 24–52.

Kohn, M.L., Schooler, C. *Work and Personality: An Inquiry into the Impact of Social Stratification* (Norwood, Ablex Publishing Corporation, 1983).

Kolberg, J.E., Uusitalo, H. 'The interface between the economy and the welfare state: A sociological account', in Z. Ferge and J. Kolberg (eds), *Social Policy in a Changing Europe* (Frankfurt and New York, European Centre for Social Welfare Policy and Research, 1992), pp. 77–94.

Korte, W.B., Robinson, S., and Steinle, W.J. (eds) *Telework: Present Situation and Future Development of a New Form of Work Organisation* (Amsterdam, North Holland, 1988).

Kosters, D.C. *When Corporations Rule the World* (San Francisco, Brett-Koehler, 1995).

Koutsogeorgopoulou, V. 'The impact of minimum wages on industrial wages and employment in Greece', *International Journal of Manpower*, Vol.15, No. 2/3, 1994, pp. 86–99.

Kreisky Commission. *A Programme for Full Employment in the 1990s* (Oxford, Pergamon Press, 1989).

Krugman, P. 'Growing world trade: Causes and consequences', *Brookings Papers on Economic Activity*, No.1, 1995 (Washington, DC, Brookings Institutions, 1995), pp. 327–77.

Kuttner, R. *Everything for Sale* (New York, Knopf, 1997).

Lal, D. *The Real Aspects of Stabilisation and Structural Adjustment Policies: Analytic and Political Economy* (Washington, DC, The World Bank, 1985).

Larson, M.S. *The Rise of Professionalism* (Berkeley, University of California Press, 1977).

Lawrence, R.Z. 'Trade and wages. The past and the future', paper presented to Centre for Social Theory and Comparative History, University of California at Los Angeles, 22 April 1996.

Layard, R., Jackman, R., Nickell, S. *Unemployment: Macroeconomics Performance and the Labour Market* (Oxford, Oxford University Press, 1991).

Layard, R., Prais, S. 'Employment training. Time to think about compulsion', *Financial Times*, 15 March 1990, p. 15.

Lazear, E.P. 'Job security provisions and unemployment', *Quarterly Journal of Economics*, Vol. 105, 1990, pp. 699–726.

Lazear, E.P. 'Performance pay and productivity' (Cambridge, MA, National Bureau of Economic Research, Working Paper No. 5672, July 1996).

Leamer, E.E. 'US wages, technological change and "globalisation"' paper presented to Annual Colloquium Series, Center for Social Theory and Comparative History, University of California at Los Angeles, 1996, mimeo.

Lee, E. 'Is full employment still desirable and feasible?', *Economic and Industrial Democracy*, Vol. 18, No. 1, February 1997, pp. 35–54.

Leibfried, S. 'Towards a European welfare state? On integrating poverty regimes into the European Community', in C. Jones (ed.), *New Perspectives on the Welfare State* (London, Routledge, 1993) pp. 133–56.

Leibfritz, W., Roseveare, D., van den Noord, P. 'Fiscal policy, government debt and economic performance', *OECD Economics Department Working Paper, No.144* (Paris, OECD, 1994).

Leisink, P., Beukema, L. 'Participation and autonomy at work. A segmented privilege', in L. Coenen and P. Leisink (eds), *Work and Citizenship in the New Europe* (Aldershot, Edward Elgar, 1993).

Lerman, R.I. 'A comparison of employer and worker wage subsidies', in R.H. Havenman and J.L. Palmer (eds), *Jobs for Disadvantaged Workers. The Economics of Employment Subsidies*, (Washington, DC, The Brookings Institution, 1982), pp. 159–86.

Levine, D. 'Public policy implications of worker participation', *Economic and Industrial Democracy*, Vol. 13, 1992, pp. 183–206.

Levine, D. *Re-Inventing the Workplace* (Washington, DC, Brookings Institution, 1995).

Levine, D.L., D'Andrea Tyson, L. 'Participation, productivity and the firms environment', in A. Blinder (ed.), *Paying for Productivity* (Washington, DC, Brookings Institution, 1990).

Lewin, D., Peterson, R. *The Modern Grievance Procedure in the United States* (New York, Quorum Books, 1988).

Lewis, J. 'Gender and the development of gender regimes', *Journal of European Social Policy*, Vol. 2, No. 3, 1992, pp. 159–73.

L'Hebdo: 'Le fin de l'absenteeisme', *L'Hebdo*, 8–19 February, 1998, pp. 10–17.

Lie, M. *Is Remote Work the Way to 'The Good Life' for Women as Well as Men?* (Trondheim, Norway, Institute for Industrial Research, 1985).

Liff, S. *Managing Diversity: New Opportunities for Women?* (University of Warwick, Warwick Papers in Industrial Relations, No. 57, January 1996).

Lim, L.Y.V. 'Social welfare in Singapore', in K.S. Sandhu and P. Wheatley (eds), *Singapore: The Management Success*, (Singapore, Oxford University Press, 1989).

Linder, M., Nygaard, I. *Void Where Prohibited: Rest Breaks and the Right to Urinate on Company Time* (Cornell, ILR Press, 1998).

Linder, S.B. *The Harried Leisure Class* (New York, Columbia University Press, 1970).

Lipsett, B., Ressor, M. *Flexible Work Arrangements* (Ottawa, Human Resources Development Canada, 1997).

Lipsky, M. *Street-level Bureaucracy: Dilemmas of the Individual in Public Services* (New York, Basic Books, 1980).

Lister, R. 'Dilemmas in engendered citizenship', paper presented at Crossing Borders Conference, University of Stockholm, May 1994.

Littler, C.R. *The Development of the Labour Process in Capitalist Societies* (London, Heineman, 1982).

Loop, van der, T. *Industrial Dynamics and Fragmented Labour Markets: Construction Firms and Labourers in India* (New Dehli, Sage Publications, 1996).

Lopez, R.A., Riveros, L.A. *Expenditure and Wage Policies in a Segmented Labour Market: A Theoretical Analysis* (Washington, DC, The World Bank, March 1989).

MacErlean, N. 'Workers unite – with your bosses', *Observer*, 5 April 1998, Work, p. 1.

Mackin, C. 'Employment ownership and industrial relations', *Perspectives on Work*, Vol. 1, No. 1, 1997.

Maier, T., Edelmann, C., Hirning S. *Flexispace/Mobility of Work. A Problem Study on the Future of Spatially Flexible Forms of Work* (Dublin, European Foundation for the Improvement of Living and Working conditions, Working paper, No. 29, 1995).

Manning, N. 'Social policy in the Soviet Union and its successors', in B. Deacon, N. Castle-Kanerova, N. Manning and F. Millard (eds), *The New Eastern Europe: Social Policy Past, Present and Future* (London, Sage, 1992), pp. 31–66.

Manpower Demonstration Research Corp. *Workfare. The Impact of the Reagan Programme on Employment and Training* (New York, MDRC, 1983).

Mansell, R. *The New Telecommunications. A Political Economy of Network Organisations* (London, Sage, 1994a).

Manufacturing Institute, The *Improving the Condition of the American Worker* (Washington, DC, The US National Association of Manufacturers, 1996).

March, J., Olsen, J. *Ambiguity and Choice in Organisations* (Bergen, Universitetsforlaget, 1976).

Marglin, S. 'What do bosses do?', *Review of Radical Political Economy*, Vol. 6, No. 2, Summer 1974, pp. 60–112.

Mars, G. *Cheats at Work. An Anthropology of Workplace Crime* (Boston, Allen and Unwin, 1982).

Marshall, T.H. *Citizenship and Social Class* (Cambridge, Cambridge University Press, 1950).

Marshall, T.H. *Class, Citizenship and Social Development* (Westwood, Connecticut, Greenwood Press, 1973).

Marsland, D. 'The roots and consequences of paternalistic paternalism: Beveridge and his influence', *Social Policy and Administration*, Vol. 26, No. 2, 1992, pp. 144–50.

Martin, J. 'Measures of replacement rates for the purpose of international comparisons. A note', *OECD Economic Studies*, No. 26, 1996/1, pp. 99–116.

Marx, K. *Capital* (Harmondsworth, Penguin, 1976).

Mathematica Policy Research Inc. *An Examination of Declining UI Claims during the 1980s* (Princeton, MRP, September 1988).

Mayer, J. 'The concept of the right to work in international standards and the legislation of ILO member States', *International Labour Review*, Vol. 124, No. 2, March–April 1985, pp. 225–42.

Maynard, R.A. 'Subsidised employment and non-labour market alternatives for welfare recipients', in D.S. Nightingale and R.H. Haveman (eds), *The Work Alternative. Welfare Reform and Realities of the Job Market*, (Washington, DC, Urban Institute Press, 1995), pp. 109–36.

Mayntz, R. 'Legitimacy and the directive capacity of the political system', in L.N. Lindberg, R, Alford, C. Crouch and C. Offe (eds), *Stress and Contradiction in Modern Capitalism* (Lexington, MA, Lexington Books, 1975), pp. 261–74.

McFate, K., Lawson, R., Wilson, W.J. (eds): *Poverty, Inequality and the Future of Social Policy: Western States in the New World Order* (New York, Russell Sage Foundation, 1995).

Mead, L. *Beyond Entitlement. The Social Obligations of Citizenship* (New York, Free Press, 1986).

Mead, L. *The New Politics of Poverty: The Non-Working Poor in America* (New York, Basic Books, 1992).

Mead, L. (ed.) *The New Paternalism. Supervisory Approaches to Poverty* (Washington, DC, Brookings Books, 1997).

Meade, J. *Full Employment is Possible* (London, Institute for Fiscal Studies, 1994).

Melgar, A., Guinovart, B. *Sistema de salario minimo en Uruguay* (Geneva, ILO, mimeo., 1997, 1997).

Mendell, M. 'Karl Polanyi and feasible socialism', in K. Polanyi-Levitt (ed.), *The Life and the Work of Karl Polanyi* (Montreal, Black Rose Books, 1990), pp. 66–77.

Meszaros, I. *Marx's Theory of Alienation* (London, Merlin, 1970).

Meulders, D. *Women and the Five Essen Priorities* (Brussels, Universite Libre de Bruxelles, February 1996).

Meulders, D.:, Plasman, O., Plasman, R. *Atypical Employment in the European Community* (Aldershot, Dartmouth, 1994).

Meulders, D., Plasman, R., Vander Stricht, V. *Position of Women on the Labour Market in the European Community* (Aldershot, Dartmouth Publishing, 1993).

Midgley, J. *Social Security, Inequality and the Third World* (Chichester, John Wiley and Sons, 1984).

Mishan, E.J. *The Costs of Economic Growth* (London, Staples Press, 1967).

Moffitt, R. 'Work incentives in the AFDC system. An analysis of the 1981 reforms', *American Economic Review*, Vol. 76, No. 2, May 1986, pp. 219–23.

Monod, T. (ed.) *Pastoralism in Tropical Africa* (London, Oxford University Press, 1975).

Moore, B. *Injustice: The Social Bases of Obedience and Revolt* (Basingstoke, Macmillan, 1978).

Moore, D. 'Tackling sources of stress in high-risk groups', *ILO World of Work* (Geneva, No.18, 1996).

Morris, J. *Independent Lives? Community Care and Disabled People* (Basingstoke, Macmillan, 1993).

Morris, W. *News from Nowhere*, in *Three Works by William Morris* (London, Lawrence and Wishart, 1977), pp. 179–401.

Mortensen, D. 'Reducing supply-side disincentives to job creation', *Reducing Unemployment: Current Issues and Policy Option* (Kansas City, Federal Reserve Bank, 1994).

Mosley, H., Kruppe, T. 'Short-time work in structural adjustment: European experience', *European Journal of Industrial Relations* Vol. 2, No. 2, 1996, pp. 131–51.

Murray, C. *Losing Ground: American Social Policy 1950–1980* (New York, Basic Books, 1984).

Murray, C. *What it Means to be a Libertarian* (New York, Broadway, 1997).

Myrdal, G. *Challenge to Affluence* (London, Victor Gollanz, 1964).

Nash, M. *Primitive and Peasant Economic Systems* (San Francisco, Chandler Publishing Co., 1966).

National Displaced Homeworkers Network (NDHN) *Unionisation: A Way Out of Low-Wage Work* (Washington, DC, NDHN, 1991).

National Labour Institute and Gandhi Peace Foundation *National Survey of the Incidents of Bonded Labour* (New Delhi, St Paul's Press, 1979).

Nelson, K. 'Labour demand, labour supply and the suburbanisation of low-wage office work', in A.J. Scott and M. Storper (eds), *Production Work and Territory. The Geographical Anatomy of Industrial Capital* (Boston, Allen and Unwin, 1986), pp. 149–71.

Nerb, G. 'Employment problems: Views of businessmen and the workforce – Results of an employee and employer survey on labour market issues in the member states', *European Economy*, Vol. 27, 1986, pp. 5–110.

Neumark, D., Polsky, D., Hansen, D. 'Has job stability declined yet? New evidence for the 1990s' paper presented at the Industrial Relations Research Association meeting, Chicago, January 1998.

Nichols, A., Zekhauser, R. 'Targeting transfers through restrictions on recipients', *American Economic Review*, Vol. 72, 1982, pp. 372–7.

Nickel, J.W. 'Is there a human right to employment?', *Philosophical Forum*, No.10, 1978–79.

Nickell, S. 'The Collapse in the Demand for the Unskilled: What can be Done?' paper presented at Conference on Demand-Side Strategies and Low-Wage Labour markets, Russell Sage Foundation, New York, June 1995.

Nozick, R. *Anarchy, State and Utopia* (New York, Basic Books, 1974).

OECD *The OECD Observer No.127*, March 1984.

OECD *Flexibility in the Labour Market* (Paris, OECD, 1986).

OECD *Employment Outlook 1992* (Paris, OECD,1992).

OECD *Employment Outlook 1993* (Paris, OECD, 1993).

OECD *The Jobs Study* (Paris, OECD, 1994a).

OECD *The OECD Jobs Study: Evidence and Explanations*, Vol.1, (Paris, OECD, 1994b).

OECD *National Income Accounts* (Paris, OECD, 1994c).

OECD *The OECD Observer No.192*, Feb.-March, 1995a.

OECD *Employment Outlook 1995* (Paris, OECD, 1995b).

OECD *Employment Outlook 1996* (Paris, OECD, 1996).

OECD *Income Distribution and Poverty in Selected Countries* (Paris, OECD, 1997a).

OECD *Employment Outlook, 1997* (Paris, OECD, 1997b).

OECD 'Labour market policies. New challenges – policies for low paid workers and unskilled job seekers' (Paris, OECD, 1997c, mimeo.).

Offe, C. *Contradictions of the Welfare State* (London, Hutchinson, 1984).

Offe, C. 'The politics of social policy in East European transitions. Antecedents, agents and agenda of reform', *Social Research*, Vol. 60, No. 4, Winter 1993.

Offe, C. 'A non-productivist design for social policies', in H. Coenen and P. Leisink (eds), *Work and Citizenship in the New Europe* (Aldershot, Edward Elgar, 1993).

Office of the Government Plenipotentiary for Social Security Reform *Security Through Diversity. Reform of the Pension System in Poland* (Warsaw, June 1997).

Ogborn, K. 'Workfare to America. An initial guide to the debate', *Social Security Review Background/Discussion Paper No. 6* (Canberra, Department of Social Security, 1986).

Okun, A.M. *Equality and Efficiency: The Big Trade-off* (Washington, DC, Brookings Institution, 1975).

Ollman, B. *Alienation* (New York, Cambridge University Press, 1976).

Olsen, M. 'Big bills left on the sidewalk. Why some nations are rich and others are poor', *Journal of Economic Perspectives*, Vol. 10, No. 2, Spring 1996, pp. 3–24.

Olson, K., Pavetti, L. *Personal and Family Challenges to the Successful Transition from Welfare to Work* (Washington, DC, The Urban Institute, May 1996).

Osterman, P. 'Work/family programs and the employment relationship', *Administrative Science Quarterly*, Vol. 40, December 1995, pp. 681–700.

O'Toole, F. 'The costings of a basic income scheme', in CORI, *An Adequate Income Guarantee for All: Desirability, Viability and Impact* (Dublin, CORI, 1995).

Overbye, E. 'Mainstream pattern, deviant cases. The New Zealand and Danish pension systems in an international context', *Journal of European Social Policy*, Vol. 7, No. 2, 1997, pp. 101–17.

Pagoda Associates. *Managing the Mobile Workforce* (London, Pagoda Associates, 1997).

Palme, J. *Pension Rights in Welfare Capitalism. The Development of Old-Age Pensions in 18 OECD Countries* (Stockholm, Swedish Institute of Social Research, 1990).

Palmer, J.L. *Creating Jobs: Public Employment Programmes and Wage Subsidies* (Washington, DC, Brookings Institution, 1978).

Palpacuer, F., Parisotto, A. 'Global production and local jobs. Issues for discussion', paper presented at an international workshop organised by the International Institute for Labour Studies, Geneva, March 9–10, 1998.

Parker, H. *Instead of the Dole* (London, Routledge, 1989).

Patino, D. 'Finding work for the poor in Arizona', *Public Welfare*, Vol. 44, No. 1, 1986, pp. 16–17.

Pearse, A. *The Latin American Peasant* (London, Frank Cass, 1975).

Pearson, R., Mitter, S. 'Employment and working conditions of low-skilled information processing workers in less developed countries', *International Labour Review*, Vol. 132, No. 1, April 1993, pp. 53–69.

Peillon, M. 'A qualitative comparative analysis of welfare legitimacy', *Journal of European Social Policy*, Vol. 6, No. 3, 1996, pp. 175–90.

Persson, T., Tabellini, G. *Is Inequality Harmful for Growth? Theory and Evidence*, (Cambridge, MA, National Bureau of Economic Research, 1991).

Pfeffer, J. 'Administrative regulations and licensing: Social problems or solution?' *Social Problems*, Vol. 21, 1974, pp. 468–79.

Pfeffer, J. *Competitive Advantage Through People* (Cambridge, MA, Harvard Business School Press, 1994).

Phelps, E.S. 'Wage subsidy programmes. Alternative designs,' in G. de la Dehesa and D. Snower (eds), *Unemployment Policy: Government Options for the Labour Market* (London, Centre for Economic Policy, 1996), pp. 206–44.

Phelps, E.S. *Rewarding Work: How to Restore Participation and Self-Support to Free Enterprise* (Cambridge, MA, Harvard University Press, 1997).

Phelps-Brown, H. 'The counter-revolution of our time', *Industrial Relations*, Vol. 29, No. 1, Winter 1990, pp. 1–14.

Piore, M., Sabel, C. *The Second Industrial Divide* (New York, Basic Books, 1984).

Polanyi, K. *The Great Transformation: Origins of Our Time* (New York, Rinehart, 1944).

Polsky, D. 'Changes in the consequences of job separations in the US economy' (University of Pennsylvania, 1996, mimeo.).

Pope John Paul II: *Centesimus Annus* (Rome, The Vatican, May 1991).

Posthuma, A. *The Internationalisation of Clerical Work. A Study of Offshore Office Work in the Caribbean* (Brighton, University of Sussex, SPRU Occasional Paper No. 24, 1995).

Potucek, M. *Quo vadis: Social policy in Czechoslovakia* (Prague, Charles University, Department of Sociology and Social Policy, 1992).

Power, M. *The Audit Society* (Oxford, Oxford University Press, 1997).

Pratt, J.H., Davies, J.A. *Measurement and Evaluation of the Populations of Family-Owned and Home-Based Businesses* (Dallas,Texas, J.H. Pratt, 1985).

Presser, H.B., Cox, A.G. 'The work schedules of low-educated American women and welfare reform', *Monthly Labor Review*, April 1997, pp. 25–33.

Price, R. 'The decline and fall of the status divide', in K.Sissons (ed.), *Personnel Management in Britain* (Oxford, Blackwell, 1993), pp. 3–50.

Price-Waterhouse. *In Search of Shareholder Value* (London, Pitman, 1997).

Putman, R.D. *Making Democracy Work: Civic Traditions in Modern Italy* (Princeton, Princeton University Press, 1993).

Putman, R.D. 'Tuning in, tuning out. The strange disappearance of social capital in America', *Political Science and Politics*, Vol. 28, No. 4, 1995.

Rajan, A., van Eupen, P., Jaspers, A. 'Britain's flexible labour market. What next?'(London, Department for Education and Employment Research Study No. 50, 1997).

Ramos, L. 'Minimum wage in Brazil' (Geneva, ILO, 1997).

Ramsamy, T. 'Criteria used to determine minimum wages in Mauritius' (Geneva, ILO, 1997, mimeo.).

Rawls, J. *The Theory of Justice* (Cambridge, Cambridge University Press, 1973).

Rehn, G. 'Towards a society of free choice', in J.J. Wiatr and R. Rose (eds), *Comparing Public Policies* (Wroclaw, Ossolineum, 1977), pp. 121–57.

Rejda, G.E. *Social Insurance and Economic Security* (Englewood Cliffs, NJ, Prentice Hall, 1994).

Revenga, A.L. 'Exporting jobs? The impact of import competition on employment and wages in US manufacturing', *Quarterly Journal of Economics*, Vol. 107, No. 1, 1992, pp. 255–84.

Riccio, J., Friedlander, D., Freedman, S. *GAIN: Benefits, costs and the three-year impact of a welfare-to-work program* (New York, Manpower Development Research Corporation, September 1994).

Rodrick, D. *Has Globalisation Gone Too Far?* (Cambridge, MA, Harvard University Press, 1997).

Roemer, J. *Theories of Distributive Justice* (Cambridge, MA, Harvard University Press, 1996).

Rosen, S. *The Economics of Superstars* (Chicago, Department of Economics and Graduate School of Business, University of Chicago, 1981).

Rosenberg, S. 'From segmentation to flexibility', *Labour and Society*, Vol. 14, No. 4, October 1989, pp. 363–407.

Rothman, R.A. 'Deprofessionalization: The case of the law in America', *Work and Occupations* Vol.11, 1984, pp. 183–206.

Rothschild, J., Whitt, A.A. *The Cooperative Workplace: Potentials and Dilemmas of Organisational Democracy and Participation* (Cambridge, Cambridge University Press, 1986).

Royal Society for the Encouragement of Arts, Manufacturers and Commerce, *Tomorrow's Company* (London, RSA, 1995).

Rubery, J., Grimshaw, D. 'Workforce heterogeneity and unemployment benefits. The need for policy reassessment in the European Union', *Journal of European Social Policy*, Vol. 7, No. 4, November 1997, pp. 291–315.

Rubery, J., Smith, M., Fagan, C. *Changing Patterns of Work and Working Time in the European Union and the Impact on Gender Divisions* (Report for the Equal Opportunities Unit, European Commission Directorate General V, V/6203/95-EN, April 1995).

Ruskin, J. *The Two Paths* (New York, Wiley, 1865).

Ruskin, J. *The Stones of Venice* (New York, Brian Taylor and Co., 1894).

Russell, B. *In Praise of Idleness* (London, Unwin Books, 1960 edition).

Russell, B. *Roads to Freedom* (London, Unwin Books, 1966, first published in 1918).

Saeger, S.S. *Trade and De-industrialisation: Myth and Reality in the OECD* (Cambridge, MA, Department of Economics, Harvard University, 1995).

Sahlins, M. *Stone Age Economics* (London, Tavistock Press, 1974).

Sainsbury, D. 'Dual welfare and sex segregation of access to social benefits. Income maintenance policies in the UK, the US, the Netherlands and Sweden', *Journal of Social Policy*, Vol. 22, No. 1, 1993, pp. 69–98.

Sainsbury, D. (ed.). *Gender Welfare States* (London, Sage, 1994).

Saint-Paul, G. 'Exclusion and Fiscal Conservatism' (London, Centre for Economic Policy, Research Paper No. 998, 1996).

Salamon, L.M. 'The rise of the non-profit sector', *Foreign Affairs*, Vol. 73, No. 4, July–August 1994, pp. 2–16.

Salonen, T. *Margins of Welfare. A Study of Modern Functions of Social Assistance* (Lund, Hallestad Press, 1993).

Salter, W.E.G. *Productivity and Technical Change* (Cambridge, Cambridge University Press, 1960).

Samuelson, P. 'Wages and interest. A modern dissection of Marxian economic models', *American Economic Review*, Vol. 47, No. 6, 1957, pp. 884–912.

Samuelson, R.J. 'Temps: The new workforce', *Washington Post*, 12 July 1989, p. A23.

Sarel, M. 'How macroeconomic factors affect income distribution. The cross country evidence', *IMF Working Paper* (Washington, DC, IMF WP/97/152, November 1997).

Savner, S., Greenberg, M. *The CLASP Guide to Welfare Waivers: 1992–1995* (Washington, DC, Centre for Law and Social Policy, May 1995).

Scarpetta, S. 'Assessing the role of labour market policies and institutional settings on unemployment: A cross-country study', *OECD Economic Studies*, No. 26, 1996/1, pp. 43–98.

Schacht, R. 'Economic alienation. With and without tears', in R.F. Geyer and D. Schweitzer (eds), *Alienation: Problems of Meaning, Theory and Method* (London, Routledge and Kegan Paul, 1981), pp. 36–67.

Schmid, G., Reissert, B. 'Unemployment compensation and labour market transitions', in G. Schmid, J. O'Reilly and K. Schomann (eds), *International Handbook of Labour Market Policy and Evaluation* (Cheltenham, Edward Elgar, 1996), pp. 235–76.

Schor, J. *The Overworked American* (New York, Basic Books, 1991).

Scoville, J.G. 'A theory of jobs and training', *Industrial Relations*, Vol. 9, No. 1, October 1969, pp. 36–53.

Secretary's Commission on Achieving Necessary Skills: *What Work Requires of Schools* (Washington, DC, US Department of Labor, 1991).

Sen, A. 'Equality of what?', in S. McMurrin (ed.), *The Tanner Lectures on Human Values* (Salt Lake City, University of Utah Press, 1980), Vol. 1.

Sen, A. *The Standard of Living* (Cambridge, Cambridge University Press, 1987).

Sen, A. 'Capability and well-being', in M. Nussbaum and A. Sen (eds), *The Quality of Life* (Oxford, Clarendon Press, 1993), pp. 30–53.

Shadur, M. *Labour Relations in a Developing Country. A Case Study on Zimbabwe* (Aldershot, Avebury, 1994).

Shalev, M. 'The political economy of employment-based social protection' paper presented at ISA workshop on Comparative Research in Social Policy, Stockholm, August 25–28, 1988.

Shanin, T. 'The nature and logic of the peasant economy', *The Journal of Peasant Studies*, October 1973, Vol. 1, No. 1, pp. 63–80.

Shapiro, C., Stiglitz, J. 'Equilibrium unemployment as a worker discipline device', *American Economic Review*, Vol. 72, No. 3, 1984, pp. 433–44.

Shapiro, I., Nichols, M. *Unemployed and Uninsured* (Washington, DC, Centre on Budget and Policy Priorities, March 1991).

Siegel, R.L. *Employment and Human Rights. The International Dimension* (Philadelphia, PA, University of Pennsylvania Press, 1994).

Simon, H.A. 'A formal theory of the employment relationship', *Econometrica*, July 1951, pp. 293–305.

Simpson, R.L. 'Social control of occupations and work', *Annual Review of Sociology*, Vol. 11, 1985, pp. 415–36.

Singh, A. 'Institutional requirements for full employment in advanced economies', *International Labour Review*, Vol. 134, No. 4–5, 1995, pp. 471–95.

Slichter, S.H. 'The current labour policies of American industries', *Quarterly Journal of Economics*, , Vol. XLII, No. 3, May 1929, pp. 393–435.

Smith, M. 'EU moves against black economy', *Financial Times*, 8 April 1998.

Smith, P. (ed.): *The Key Note Guide to Teleworking* (London, Key Note, 1995).

Smith, S. 'Political behaviour as an economic externality. Econometric evidence on the spillover of participation in US firms to participation in community affairs', *Advances in the Economic Analysis of Participatory and Labour-managed Firms*, No. 1, 1985, pp. 123–36.

Smith, S. 'On the economic rationale for co-determination law', *The Journal of Economic Behaviour and Organisation*, Vol. 16, 1991, pp. 261–81.

Soares, A. 'The hard life of the unskilled workers in new technologies: Data-entry clerks in Brazil', in H.J. Bullinger (ed.), *Human Aspects of Computing* (Amsterdam, Elsevier Science Publishers, 1991).

Solow, R. *The Labour Market as a Social Institution* (Cambridge, Basil Blackwell, 1990).

Spalter-Roth, R., Burr, B., Hartmann, H., Shaw, L.B. *Welfare that Works. The Working Lives of AFDC Recipients* (Washington, DC, Institute for Woman's Policy Research, 1995).

Spencer, B. 'Reactions to a flexible labour market', in R. Jowell, J. Curtice, A. Park, L. Brook and K. Thomson (eds), *British Social Attitudes. The 13th Report* (Dartmouth, Aldershot, 1996).

Spencer, H. Social Statistics (London, Jonathan Chapman, 1851).

Standing, G. *Labour Force Participation and Development* (Geneva, ILO, 1978 and 1981).

Standing, G. 'Migration and modes of exploitation: Social origins of immobility and mobility', *Journal of Peasant Studies*, Vol. 8, No. 2, 1981, pp. 173–211.

Standing, G. (ed.) *Labour Circulation and the Labour Process* (London, Croom Helm, 1985).

Standing, G. 'Meshing labour flexibility with security: An answer to British unemployment?', *International Labour Review*, Vol. 125, No. 1, January–February, 1986, pp. 87–106.

Standing, G. *Unemployment and Labour Market Flexibility Sweden* (Geneva, ILO, 1988).

Standing, G. 'Global feminisation through flexible labour', *World Development*, Vol. 17, No. 7, 1989a, pp. 1077–95.

Standing, G. 'European unemployment, insecurity and flexibility. A social dividend solution', *Labour Market Analysis Working Paper*, No.23 (Geneva, ILO, 1989b).

Standing, G. 'The road to workfare: Alternative to welfare or threat to occupation?', *International Labour Review*, Vol. 129, No. 6, 1990, pp. 677–91.

Standing, G. 'Structural adjustment and labour market policies. Towards social adjustment?', in G. Standing and V. Tokman (eds), *Towards Social Adjustment Labour Market Issues in Structural Adjustment* (Geneva, ILO, 1991a), pp. 5–52.

Standing, G. *Labour Market Flexibility in an Industrialising Economy* (Geneva, ILO, 1991b).

Standing, G. 'Do unions accelerate or impede structural adjustment?', *Cambridge Journal of Economics*, Vol. 16, No. 3, 1992, pp. 327–54.

Standing, G. 'Why is measured unemployment in Russia so low? The net with many holes', *Journal of European Social Policy*, Vol. 4, No. 1, February 1994, pp. 35–49.

Standing, G. *Russian Unemployment and Enterprise Restructuring: Reviving Dead Souls* (Basingstoke, Macmillan, 1996a).

Standing, G. *The 'Shake Out' in Russian Factories. The RLFS Fifth Round, 1995* (Geneva, ILO, 1996b).

Standing, G. 'Labour market governance in Eastern Europe', *European Journal of Industrial Relations*, Vol. 3, No. 2, July 1997, pp. 133–59.

Standing, G. 'The folly of social safety nets. Why basic income is needed in Eastern Europe', *Social Research*, Vol. 64, No. 4, Winter 1997, pp. 1339–79.

Standing, G. 'Societal impoverishment. The challenge for Russian social policy', *Journal of European Social Policy*, Vol. 8, No. 1, February 1998, pp. 23–42.

Standing, G., Sender, J., Weeks, J. *Restructuring the Labour Market. The South African Challenge* (Geneva, ILO, 1996).

Standing, G., Vaughan-Whitehead, D. (eds) *From Protection to Destitution? The Minimum Wage in Central and Eastern Europe* (Budapest, European University Press, 1995).

Standing, G., Zsoldos, L. *Labour Market Crisis in Ukrainian Industry. The 1995 ULFS* (Geneva, ILO, 1995).

Steiger, T.L., Form, W. 'The labour process in construction. Control without bureaucratic and technological means', *Work and Occupations*, Vol. 18, 1991, pp. 251–70.

Streefkerk, H. *Industrial Transition in Rural India Artisans, Traders and Tribals in South Gujarat* (Bombay, Popular Prakashan, 1985).

Summers, L. 'Some simple economics of mandated benefits', *American Economic Review Proceedings*, Vol. 79, No. 2, May 1989, pp. 177–83.

Suzuki, H. 'Minimum wage fixing in Japan' (Geneva, ILO, 1995, mimeo).

Szalkowski, A., Olbrycht, J. *Social Functions of the Post-Socialist State* (Cracow, Academy of Sciences, Seminar Papers No.10, 1992).

Takahashi, Y. 'The labour market and lifetime employment in Japan', *Economic and Industrial Democracy*, Vol. 18, No. 1, February 1997, pp. 55–66.

Tanner, M., Moore, S., Hartman, D. 'The work vs welfare trade-off. An analysis of the total level of welfare by State', *Policy Analysis* (Washington, DC, Cato Institute No. 240, 19 September 1995).

Tanzi, V. *Taxation in an Integrating World* (Washington, DC, Brookings Institution, 1995).

Tapiola, K. 'Trade union development in the CEEC's', *Transfer*, Vol. 1, No. 3, 1995, pp. 360–77.

Tasini, J. *The Edifice Complex Rebuilding the American Labor Movement to Face the Global Economy* (New York, Labour Research Association, 1995).

Taylor, F.W. *The Principles of Scientific Management* (New York, Harper and Row, 1967; first published in 1911).

Taylor, J.C. *Learning at Work in a Work-based Welfare System Opportunities and Obstacles* (Boston, MA, Jobs for the Future, April 1997).

TELDET *Pan-European Telework Surveys, 1994* (TELDET, November 1994).

Thompson, E.P. *The Making of the English Working Class* (Harmondsworth, Penguin, 1963).

Titmuss, R.M. *Essays on the Welfare State* (London, Allen and Unwin, 1963).

Titmuss, R.M. *Social Policy: An Introduction* (London, Allen and Unwin, 1974).

Tomaney, J., Winterton, J. 'The transformation of work? Technical change and work relations in the British coal mining industry', in paper presented at the 12th World Congress of Sociology, Madrid, 1990.

Touraine, A. 'An historical theory of the evolution of industrial skills' in L.F. Davis and J.C. Taylor (eds), *Design of Jobs* (Harmondsworth, Penguin, 1972), pp. 56–62.

Training Agency *Training in Britain* (London, HM Stationery Office, 1989).

Treiman, D.J; Cain, P.S. 'The Dictionary of Occupational Titles as a source of occupational data', *American Sociological Review*, Vol. 46, No. 3, June 1981, pp. 253–78.

Trice, H.M. *Occupational Subcultures in the Workplace* (Ithaca, New York, ILR Press, 1993).

Turner, H.A. *Trade Union Growth, Structure and Policy* (London, Allen and Unwin, 1962).

UK Government. *Statistics in Social Trends 1997* (London, HM Stationery Office, January 1997).

Ulmann, S. 'Le travail sur appel sera-t-il le nouvel esclavage de l'an 2000?', *Tribune de Geneve*, 27 June, 1997, p. 11.

UN Economic and Social Council *Studies on Special Techniques for Enumerating Nomads in African Censuses and Surveys* (New York, United Nations, 1977).

UN Economic Commission for Europe *Economic Survey of Europe in 1996–97* (Geneva, ECA, 1997).

UNCTAD *Incentives and Foreign Direct Investment* (Geneva, UNCTAD, 1995a).

UNCTAD *Trade and Development Report* (Geneva and New York, UNCTAD, 1995b).

UNDP *The Human Development Report 1995* (New York, UNDP, 1995).

UNDP *The Shrinking State: Governance and Sustainable Human Development* (New York, UNDP, 1997).

UNESC *Studies on Special Techniques for Enumerating Nomads in African Censuses and Surveys* (New York, United Nations, 1977).

Ungerson, C. 'Social politics and the commodification of care', *Social Politics*, Vol. 4, No. 3, Fall 1997, pp. 362–81.

Upchurch, M. 'Social Partnerships, the market and trade-union involvement in training: Britain and Germany compared', *Journal of European Social Policy*, Vol. 7, No. 3, 1997, pp. 191–208.

US General Accounting Office: *Workers at Risk Increased Numbers in Contingent Employment Lack Insurance, Other Benefits* Report to the Chairman, Subcommittee on

Employment and Housing, Committee on Government Operations, House of Representatives (Washington, DC, US Government Printing Office, March 1991).

van der Veen, R. 'Citizenship and the modern welfare state. Social integration, competence and the reciprocity of rights and duties in social policy', in H. Coenen and P. Leisink (eds), *Work and Citizenship in the New Europe* (Aldershot, Edward Elgar, 1993).

Van Maanen, J., Bailey, S.R. 'Occupational communities. Control of the organisations', in B.M. Shaw and L. Cummings (eds), *Research in Organisational Behaviour* (Greenwich, Conn., JAI Press, 1994) pp. 287–365.

van Oorschot, W. 'Non take-up of social security benefits in Europe', *Journal of European Social Policy*, Vol. 1, No. 1, 1991, pp. 15–30.

Van Parijs, P. *Real Freedom for All: What (if anything) can Justify Capitalism?* (Oxford, Clarendon Press, 1995).

Van Parijs, P. 'Reciprocity and the justification of an unconditional basic income. Reply to Stewart White', *Political Studies*, Vol. XVL, 1997, pp. 327–30.

van Trier, W. 'Every man a King!' (Antwerp, 1996, mimeo.).

Vaughan-Whitehead, D. *Interessement, Participation, Actionnariat: Impacts economiques dans l'entreprise* (Paris, Economica, 1992).

Vericik, J. 'Incomes in Central Europe: Distributions, patterns and perceptions', *Journal of European Social Policy*, Vol. 6, No. 2, 1996, pp. 101–22.

Villeval, M.C. 'Labour market restructuring and deprivation processes', paper presented at the 1990 EALE Conference, University of Lund, September 20–23, 1990.

Vinocur, J. '"Secret" wealth undermines the social model', *International Herald Tribune*, 16 October 1997, p. 7.

Visser, J. 'Continuity and change in Dutch industrial relations', in G. Baglioni and C. Crouch (eds), *European Industrial Relations* (London, Sage, 1991), pp. 199–242.

Vittas, D. *Swiss-Chilanpore: The Way Forward for Pension Reform?* (Washington, DC, The World Bank Working Paper Series 1093, 1993).

Waerness, K. 'Caring as women's work in the welfare state', in H. Holter (ed.), *Patriarchy in a Welfare Society (Oslo, Universitetsforlaget, 1984)*, pp. 67–87.

Waller, M. *Welfare-to-Work and Child Care: A survey of the Ten Big States* (Washington, DC, Progressive Policy Institute, July 1997).

Ward, S. *A Basic Income System for Ireland, Towards an Adequate Income for All* (Dublin, CORI, 1994).

Waterman, P. 'Social movement unionism. A new model for a new world order', *Review*, Vol. 16, No. 3, Summer 1993, pp. 245–78.

Waterman, R. *The Frontiers of Excellence. Learning from Companies that Put People First* (London, Nicholas Brealey Publishing, 1994), published in the USA under title *What America Does Right* (New York, Norton, 1994).

Weeks, J. 'Economic integration in Latin America: Impact on labour' (Geneva, ILO, 1998, mimeo.).

Weir, M., Orloff, A., Skocpol, T. 'The future of social policy in the United States', in M. Weir, A. Orloff and T. Skocpol (eds), *The Politics of Social Policy in the United States* (Princeton, Princeton University Press, 1988).

Weisskopf, T., Bowles, S., Gordon, D. *Beyond the Wasteland* (New York, Doubleday, 1983).

Welfare to Work. 'State efforts to reform welfare. The future of children', *Welfare to Work*, Vol. 7, No. 1, Spring 1997, pp. 138–44.

West, J.M. 'South Korea's entry into the International Labour Organisation. Perspectives on corporatist labour law during a late industrial revolution', *Stanford Journal of International Law*, Vol. 23, Issue 2, 1987, pp. 477–546.

White, S. 'Liberal equality, exploitation and the case for an unconditional basic income', *Political Studies*, Vol. XLV, 1997, pp. 312–26.

Wilensky, H.L. 'The professionalism of everyone', *American Journal of Sociology*, Vol. 70, 1964, pp. 137–58.

Wilkinson, R. *Unhealthy Societies. The Afflictions of Inequality* (New York, Routledge, 1996).

Williams, M.J. 'Is workfare the answer?', *Fortune Magazine* (New York), 27 October 1986, p. 80.

Williams, R. *Keywords* (London, Basic Books, 1976).

Williamson, O., Ouchi, W. 'The markets and hierarchies and visible hands perspectives', in A. Van de Ven and W. Joyce (eds), *Perspectives on Organisational Design and Behaviour* (New York, Wiley, 1981), pp. 347–70.

Williamson, O.E. 'Hierarchical control and optimum firm size', *Journal of Political Economy* Vol. 75, April 1967, pp. 123–38.

Williamson, O.E. *Markets and Hierarchies: Analysis and Antitrust Implications* (New York, Free Press, 1975).

Williamson, O.E. *The Economic Institutions of Capitalism* (New York and London, The Free Press, 1985).

Wilson, W.J. *The Truly Disadvantaged: The Inner City, the Underclass and Public Policy* (Chicago and London, University of Chicago Press, 1987).

Windmuller J.P., Albeda, W., Albage, L.G., Blanpain, R. *Collective Bargaining in Industrialised Market Economies: A Reappraisal* (Geneva, ILO, 1987).

Wolf, M. 'To fund or not to fund', *Financial Times*, 4 March 1997.

Won, K.J. 'Minimum wage in Korea' (Geneva, ILO, 1997, mimeo.).

Wood, A. 'North–South trade and female labour in manufacturing. An asymmetry', *Journal of Development Studies*, Vol. 27, No. 2, January, 1991, pp. 168–89.

Wood, A. *North–South Trade, Employment and Inequality: Changing Fortunes in a Skill-Driven World* (Oxford, Clarendon Press, 1994).

Wootton, B. *In a World I Never Made* (London, Allen and Unwin, 1967).

World Bank. *Averting the Old Age Crisis: Politics to Protect the Old and Promote Growth* (Oxford, Oxford University Press, 1994).

World Bank *Global Economic Prospects and the Developing Countries* (Washington, DC, The World Bank, 1995a).

World Bank *World Development Report 1995. Workers in an Integrating World* (New York, Oxford University Press, 1995b).

World Health Organisation *The Submerged Economy and Health*. Summary of Study Group on Unemployment and the Submerged Economy, Barcelona, June 19–21, 1989, Copenhagen, WHO, 1990.

World Health Organisation *Health for All* (Geneva, WHO, 1996).

Wright Mills, C. *White Collar* (New York, Oxford University Press, 1956).

You, J. 'Labour standards and economic development: South Korean experience' in paper presented to Symposium on Labour Standards and Development, Washington, DC, December 1988.

Zill, N., Moore, K., Stief, T. *Welfare Mothers as Potential Employees. A Statistical Profile based on National Survey Data* (Washington, DC, Child Trends, 1991).

Index

Index compiled by Auriol Griffith-Jones